IF FOUND, please notify and arrange return to owner. This te[x]
the owner's career and/or exam preparation.

Name: ______________________

Address: ______________________

City, State, ZIP: ______________________

Telephone: (____) ____________ Email: ______________________

All orders must be prepaid. Shipping and handling charges will be added to all orders. Library and company orders may be purchased on account. Add applicable sales tax to shipments within Florida. All payments must be in U.S. funds and payable on a U.S. bank. Please write or call for prices and availability of all foreign country shipments. Orders will usually be shipped the day your request is received. Allow 10 days for delivery in the United States. Please contact us if you do not receive your shipment within 2 weeks.

Gleim Publications, Inc., guarantees the immediate refund of all resalable texts, unopened and un-downloaded Test Prep Software, and unopened and un-downloaded audios returned within 30 days. Accounting and Academic Test Prep online courses may be canceled within 30 days if no more than the first study unit or lesson has been accessed. In addition, Online CPE courses may be canceled within 30 days if the outline has not yet been accessed. Accounting Exam Rehearsals and Practice Exams may be canceled within 30 days of purchase if they have not been started. Aviation online courses may be canceled within 30 days if no more than two study units have been accessed. This policy applies only to products that are purchased directly from Gleim Publications, Inc. No refunds will be provided on opened or downloaded Test Prep Software or audios, partial returns of package sets, or shipping and handling charges. Any freight charges incurred for returned or refused packages will be the purchaser's responsibility. Returns of books purchased from bookstores and other resellers should be made to the respective bookstore or reseller.

REVIEWERS AND CONTRIBUTORS

Garrett W. Gleim, B.S., CPA (not in public practice), received a Bachelor of Science degree from The Wharton School at the University of Pennsylvania. Mr. Gleim coordinated the production staff, reviewed the manuscript, and provided production assistance throughout the project.

D. Scott Lawton, B.S., is a graduate of Brigham Young University–Idaho and Utah Valley University, and he has passed the EA exam. Mr. Lawton participated in the technical editing of the manuscript.

Lawrence Lipp, J.D., CPA (registered), is a graduate from the Levin College of Law and the Fisher School of Accounting at the University of Florida. Mr. Lipp provided substantial editorial assistance throughout the project.

A PERSONAL THANKS

This manual would not have been possible without the extraordinary effort and dedication of Jacob Brunny, Julie Cutlip, Eileen Nickl, Teresa Soard, Joanne Strong, Candace Van Doren, and Jennifer Vann, who typed the entire manuscript and all revisions, and drafted and laid out the diagrams and illustrations in this book.

The author also appreciates the production and editorial assistance of Melissa Del Valle, Chris Hawley, Katie Larson, Cary Marcous, Shane Rapp, Drew Sheppard, and Martha Willis.

The author also appreciates the critical reading assistance of Ellen Buhl, Reed Daines, Stephanie Garrison, Daniela Guanipa, Alyssa Hagerty, and Jerry Mathis.

Finally, we appreciate the encouragement, support, and tolerance of our families throughout this project.

2013 EDITION

EA REVIEW

PART 1

INDIVIDUALS

by

Irvin N. Gleim, Ph.D., CPA, CIA, CMA, CFM, RTRP

and

James R. Hasselback, Ph.D.

ABOUT THE AUTHORS

Irvin N. Gleim is Professor Emeritus in the Fisher School of Accounting at the University of Florida and is a member of the American Accounting Association, Academy of Legal Studies in Business, American Institute of Certified Public Accountants, Association of Government Accountants, Florida Institute of Certified Public Accountants, The Institute of Internal Auditors, and the Institute of Management Accountants. He has had articles published in the *Journal of Accountancy*, *The Accounting Review*, and *The American Business Law Journal* and is author/coauthor of numerous accounting and aviation books and CPE courses.

James R. Hasselback is the Mary Ball Washington Eminent Scholar at the University of West Florida. A member of the American Accounting Association and the American Taxation Association, he has published over 160 papers in professional and academic journals, including *The Accounting Review*, *The Tax Adviser*, *Financial Management*, *Journal of Real Estate Taxation*, and the *American Business Law Journal*. Dr. Hasselback has presented papers at many national and regional professional meetings and has served as chairman at tax sessions of professional conferences. He regularly presents continuing education seminars for certified public accountants. In addition, he has been coauthor and technical editor of a two-volume introductory taxation series published by CCH, Inc., for the past 30 years and has served as technical editor of several publications by CCH and Harper-Collins. Dr. Hasselback has compiled 35 editions of the *Accounting Faculty Directory*.

Gleim Publications, Inc.
P.O. Box 12848
University Station
Gainesville, Florida 32604
(800) 87-GLEIM or (800) 874-5346
(352) 375-0772
Fax: (352) 375-6940
Internet: www.gleim.com
Email: admin@gleim.com

For updates to this 2013 edition of ***EA Review: Part 1, Individuals***

Go To: www.gleim.com/updates

Or: Email update@gleim.com with **EA 1 2013-1** in the subject line. You will receive our current update as a reply.

Updates are available until the next edition is published.

ISSN: 1523-6722

ISBN: 978-1-58194-317-7 *EA 1: Individuals*
ISBN: 978-1-58194-328-3 *EA 2: Businesses*
ISBN: 978-1-58194-330-6 *EA 3: Representation, Practices, and Procedures*
ISBN: 978-1-58194-341-2 *EA Review: A System for Success*

ACKNOWLEDGMENTS

The authors appreciate and thank the Internal Revenue Service and Prometric for their cooperation. Questions have been used from the 1978-2005 Special Enrollment Examinations.

TABLE OF CONTENTS

DETAILED TABLE OF CONTENTS

PREFACE

The purpose of this book is to help **you** prepare to pass Part 1, Individuals, of the IRS Special Enrollment Exam, which we refer to as the EA (enrolled agent) exam. Our overriding consideration is to provide an inexpensive, effective, and easy-to-use study program. This book

1. Explains how to optimize your grade by focusing on Part 1 of the EA exam.
2. Defines the subject matter tested on Part 1 of the EA exam.
3. Outlines all of the subject matter tested on Part 1 in 13 easy-to-use-and-complete study units, reflecting 2012 tax law (which is what will be tested on the 2013 EA exam).
4. Presents multiple-choice questions from past EA examinations to prepare you for questions in future EA exams. Our answer explanations are presented to the immediate right of each question for your convenience. Use a piece of paper to cover our answer explanations as you study the questions.
5. Suggests exam-taking and question-answering techniques to help you maximize your exam score.

The outline format, the spacing, and the question-and-answer formats in this book are designed to facilitate readability, learning, understanding, and success on the EA exam. Our most successful candidates use the Gleim EA Review System*, which includes books, Test Prep Online, Audio Review, Gleim Online, Exam Rehearsals, and access to a Personal Counselor. Students who prefer to study in a group setting may attend Gleim Professor-Led Reviews, which combine the Gleim Review System with the coordination and feedback of a professor. (Check our website for live courses we recommend.) This review book and all Gleim EA Review materials are compatible with other EA review materials and courses that are based on Prometric's Exam Content Outlines.

To maximize the efficiency and effectiveness of your EA review program, augment your studying with *EA Review: A System for Success*. This booklet has been carefully written and organized to provide important information to assist you in passing the EA examination.

Thank you for your interest in our materials. We deeply appreciate the thousands of letters and suggestions we have received from CIA, CMA, CPA, RTRP, and EA candidates and accounting students and faculty during the past 5 decades.

If you use the Gleim materials, we want YOUR feedback immediately after the exam and as soon as you have received your grades. The EA exam is NONDISCLOSED, and you must maintain the confidentiality and agree not to divulge the nature or content of any EA question or answer under any circumstances. We ask only for information about our materials, i.e., the topics that need to be added, expanded, etc.

Please go to www.gleim.com/feedbackEA1 to share your suggestions on how we can improve this edition.

Good Luck on the Exam,

Irvin N. Gleim
James R. Hasselback

February 2013

*Visit www.gleim.com or call (800) 874-5346 to order.

PREPARING FOR AND TAKING THE IRS ENROLLED AGENT EXAMINATION

FOLLOW THESE STEPS TO PASS THE EXAM

1. Read this **Introduction** to familiarize yourself with the content and structure of Part 1 of the EA exam. In the following pages, you will find
   a. An **overview of Part 1** and what it generally tests, including
      1) Prometric's exam content breakdown by section for Part 1, cross-referenced with the Gleim study units/subunits that contain each topic
   b. A detailed plan with **steps to obtain your EA certification**, including
      1) The order in which you should apply, register, schedule your exam, and buy your study materials
      2) How to organize your study schedule to make the most out of each resource in the Gleim EA Review System (i.e., books, Test Prep Online, Audio Review, Gleim Online, Exam Rehearsals, etc.)
   c. Tactics for your **actual test day**, including
      1) Time budgeting, so you complete all questions with time to review
      2) Question-answering techniques to obtain every point you can
      3) An explanation of how to be in control of your EA exam
2. Scan the Gleim ***EA Review: A System for Success*** booklet and note where to revisit later in your studying process to obtain a deeper understanding of the EA exam.
   a. ***EA Review: A System for Success*** has six study units:

      Study Unit 1: The EA Examination: An Overview and Preparation Introduction
      Study Unit 2: EA Exam Content Outlines
      Study Unit 3: Content Preparation, Test Administration, and Performance Grading
      Study Unit 4: Multiple-Choice Questions
      Study Unit 5: Preparing to Pass the EA Exam
      Study Unit 6: How to Take the EA Exam

   b. If you feel that you need even more details on the test-taking experience, access Prometric's **Free Tutorial/Sample Test** at www.prometric.com/demos/irs/index.htm.
      1) This tutorial is most useful to candidates who have little or no experience with computerized exams and have anxiety about performing well in unfamiliar circumstances.

3. BEFORE you begin studying, take a **Diagnostic Quiz** at www.gleim.com/EADQ or use our **Gleim Diagnostic Quiz App** for iPhone, iPod Touch, or Android.
   a. The Diagnostic Quiz includes a representative sample of 40 multiple-choice questions and will determine your weakest areas in Part 1.
   b. When you are finished, one of our **Personal Counselors** will consult with you to better focus your review on any areas in which you have less confidence.
4. Follow the steps outlined on page 8, "How to Study a Study Unit Using the Gleim EA Review System." This is the **study plan** that our most successful candidates adhere to. Study until you have reached your **desired proficiency level** (e.g., 75%) for each study unit.
   a. As you proceed, be sure to check any **Updates** that may have been released.
      1) Gleim Online and Test Prep Online are updated automatically.
      2) Book updates can be viewed at www.gleim.com/updates/, or you can have them emailed to you. See the information box on page iv for details.
   b. **Review the *EA Review: A System for Success* booklet** and become completely comfortable with what will be expected from you on test day.
5. Shortly before your test date, take an **Exam Rehearsal** (complimentary with the EA Review System!) at www.gleim.com/eaexamrehearsal.
   a. This timed and scored exam emulates the actual EA exam and tests you not only on the content you have studied, but also on the question-answering and time-management techniques you have learned throughout the Gleim study process.
   b. When you have completed the exam, study your results to discover where you should **focus your review during the final days before your exam.**
6. **Take and PASS** Part 1 of the EA exam!
   a. When you have completed the exam, please go to www.gleim.com/feedbackEA1 to give us your **suggestions, comments, and corrections**. We want to know how well we prepared you for your testing experience.

OVERVIEW OF EA EXAMINATION

The total exam is 10.5 hours of testing (12 hours total seat time to include tutorials and surveys). It covers **federal taxation; tax accounting; and the use of tax return forms for individuals, partnerships, corporations, trusts, estates, and gifts**. It also covers **ethical considerations and procedural requirements.**

The **exam consists of three parts, with 3.5 hours for each part** (4 hours total seat time to include tutorial and survey). The questions on the examination are directed toward the tasks that enrolled agents must perform to complete and file forms and tax returns and to represent taxpayers before the Internal Revenue Service. Each part of the examination consists of **100 multiple-choice questions** and covers the following tax topics:

Part 1 - Individuals
Part 2 - Businesses
Part 3 - Representation, Practices, and Procedures

Based on the experience of our customers who have taken all three parts of the exam, Gleim recommends that candidates sit for Parts 1 and 2 before taking Part 3. Feedback indicates that Part 3 candidates may be given questions related to topics covered in Parts 1 and 2.

EXAM CONTENT OUTLINES WITH GLEIM CROSS-REFERENCES

This section contains the Part 1 Exam Content Outlines. The outlines are subdivided into sections, and each section has one or more topics, which are further divided into specific items. According to the IRS's *Candidate Information Bulletin* (available at www.prometric.com/irs), not every topic in the outlines will appear on the exam, and the list of topics may not be all-inclusive. However, the outlines are meant to reflect the knowledge needed for tasks performed by EAs.

Next to each topic, we have provided a cross-reference to the most relevant Gleim study unit(s)/ subunit(s).

Section 1: Preliminary Work and Taxpayer Data (15 items)

a. **Preliminary Work to Prepare Tax Returns**

1) Use of prior years' returns for comparison (e.g., reviewing prior Individual Form 1040 returns) – 1.1
2) Accuracy of prior year's return (e.g., review of prior year's return for compliance, accuracy, and completeness) – 1.1
3) Taxpayer biographical information (e.g., date of birth, age, marital status, dependents) – 1.1
4) Immigration status and/or citizenship (e.g., citizen, visas, green cards, resident alien, or non-resident alien) – 1.1
5) Taxpayer filing status (e.g., single, MFJ, MFS, widow, HOH) – 1.2
6) Sources of all income (e.g., interest, wages, business, sales of property, dividends, interest, rental income) – 2.1
7) Sources of applicable adjustments to gross income (e.g., retirement plans, HSAs, alimony, health insurance, moving expenses, self-employment tax) – 4.1
8) Sources of applicable deductions (e.g., itemized, standard) – 1.3, 3-5
9) Sources of applicable credits (e.g., education, file tax, retirement, energy, child care) – 6.1
10) Tax payments (e.g., withholding, estimated payments, earned income tax credit) – 6
11) Determine if individual and/or business entity involved (e.g., methods of determination) – 1.1
12) Items that will affect future returns (e.g., carryover, operating losses, NOL, Schedule D, 8801) – 1.1
13) All required taxes filed (e.g., employment, gift, estimated) – 1.1
14) Special filing requirements (e.g., gifts, foreign income, presidentially declared disaster areas) – 1.1

b. **Tax Returns for Individuals, Taxpayer Data**

1) Filing requirements for tax returns and extensions (e.g., dates) – 1.3
2) Personal exemptions including dependents – 1.4
3) Taxation of unearned income of certain minor children (Kiddie tax) – 1.5
4) Special requirements for Form 1040-NR – 1.3

Section 2: Income and Assets (25 items)

a. **Income**

1) Taxability of wages, salaries, and other earnings (e.g., earned income) – 2.1
2) Interest income (e.g., taxable and non-taxable) – 2.2
3) Dividends and other distributions from mutual funds, corporations, and other entities (e.g., qualified dividends) – 2.3
4) Rental income and expenses (e.g., vacation homes, NFP rentals, calculation of depreciation) – 2.4
5) Gambling income and allowable deductions (e.g., W-2G, documentation) – 2.1
6) Tax treatment of forgiveness of debt (e.g., 1099C) – 2.1
7) Tax treatment of a U.S. citizen/resident with foreign earned income (e.g., individual tax treaties, Form 2555) – 2.1
8) Other income (e.g., scholarships, fellowships, Social Security benefits, barter income, independent contractor income, hobby income, alimony, non-taxable combat pay, earned income vs. non-earned income) – 2.1
9) Constructive receipt of income (e.g., cash vs. accrual) – 2.1

b. **Retirement Income**

1) Basis in a traditional IRA (Form 8606) – 11.2
2) Comparison of traditional IRA and Roth IRA – 11.4
3) Distributions from qualified plans (e.g., pre-tax, after-tax) – 11.1
4) Excess contributions and tax treatment (e.g., penalties, 1099R) – 11.3
5) Prohibited transactions and tax effects relating to IRAs – 11.2
6) IRA conversions and recharacterizations (Form 8606) – 11.2, 11.4
7) Excess accumulations and required minimum distributions – 11.3
8) Loans from IRC section 401(k) plans and other qualified plans – 11.3

c. **Property, Real and Personal**

1) Capital gains and losses (e.g., netting effect, short-term, long-term) – 8.3
2) Basis of assets (e.g., purchased, gifted, or inherited) – 7
3) Basis of stock after stock splits and/or stock dividends (e.g., research, schedules, brokerage records, options) – 7.5
4) Sale of property (e.g., documentation) – 9, 10
5) Sale of a personal residence (e.g., Sec 121 exclusions) – 10.1
6) Installment sales (e.g., related parties, original cost, date of acquisition, possible recalculations, and recharacterization) – 9.3

d. **Adjustments to Income**

1) Adjustments to income (e.g., retirement contributions, student loan interest, alimony) – 2, 11
2) Self-employment tax – 6.2

Section 3: Deductions and Credits (25 items)

a. **Retirement Deductions (relating to IRAs)**

1) Contribution limits and deductibility of contributions – 11
2) Earned compensation – 11.1
3) Modified adjusted gross income – 11.4

b. **Itemized Deductions**

1) Medical and dental expenses (e.g., subject to AGI limitation) – 5.1
2) Deductibility of various types of taxes (e.g., sales, real estate, state, and local) – 5.2
3) Interest expense (e.g., mortgage interest, investment interest, tracing rules, points) – 5.3
4) Charitable contributions (e.g., cash, non-cash, 50% vs. 30%, documentation required) – 5.4
5) Nonbusiness casualty and theft losses (e.g., Form 4864) – 5.5
6) Nonbusiness bad debts (e.g., documentation required) – 3.1
7) Miscellaneous itemized deductions (e.g., subject or not subject to 2%) – 5.6, 5.7
8) Employee travel, transportation, and entertainment expenses (e.g., business purpose) – 5.6
9) Employee education expenses – 5.6
10) AGI limitations on itemized deductions – 5.6
11) Allowed itemized deductions for Form 1040-NR – 1.6

c. **Credits**

1) Child and dependent care credit – 6.1
2) Child tax credit – 6.1
3) Education credits – 6.1
4) Foreign tax credit – 6.1
5) Earned income tax credit (EIC) – 6.1

Section 4: Taxation and Advice (20 items)

a. **Taxation**

1) Alternative minimum tax – 6.2
2) Credit for prior year minimum tax – 6.2
3) Premature distribution(s) from retirement plans – 11.3
4) Household employees (e.g., Schedule H) – 6.2
5) Estimated tax – 6.3
6) Injured spouse (e.g., applicable rules) – 1.2
7) Conditions for filing a claim for refund (e.g., amended returns, Form 911, documentation) – 6.3

b. **Minimization of Taxes Paid**

1) Adjustments, deductions, and credits – 3-6
2) Retirement plans – 11
3) Earned income credit (e.g., eligibility, preparer documentation) – 6.1
4) Education credits and tuition deduction – 6.1
5) Adoption credits (e.g., carryovers, limitations, disabled child) – 6.1
6) Use of capital gain rates versus ordinary income rates (e.g., character of transaction) – 8.3

c. **Advising the Individual Taxpayer**

1) Reporting obligations for individuals (e.g., sale of home) – 10.1
2) Property sales (e.g., real and personal, such as homes, stocks, businesses, Internet sales) – 9
3) Education planning (e.g., Hope [American Opportunity] credit, lifetime learning credit, IRC Section 529 plans) – 6.1, 12.2
4) Estate planning (e.g., gift versus inheritance, trusts, family partnerships, charitable giving, LTC) – 13
5) Retirement planning (e.g., annuities, IRAs, employer plans, early retirement rules, required minimum distribution, beneficiary ownership) – 11
6) Marriage and divorce (e.g., pre- and post-nuptial agreements, divorce settlement, common-law, or community property) – 2.1, 4.5

Section 5: Specialized Returns for Individuals (15 items)

a. **Estate Tax**

1) Gross estate – 13.1
2) Taxable estate: calculations and payments – 13.2, 13.3
3) Unified credit – 13.2
4) Jointly-held property – 13.1
5) Life insurance and taxable estate – 13.1
6) Marital deduction and other marital issues – 13.2
7) IRAs and retirement plans – 11.2
8) Filing requirements – 13.3

b. **Gift Tax**

1) Gift-splitting – 12.3
2) Annual exclusion – 12.2
3) Unified credit – 12.2
4) Effect on estate tax (e.g., generation-skipping tax) – 13.4
5) Filing requirements – 12.1

EA's NONDISCLOSURE AGREEMENT

The EA exam is nondisclosed. The following is taken verbatim from the IRS's *Candidate Information Bulletin* dated October 2012. It is reproduced here to remind all EA candidates about the IRS's strict policy of nondisclosure, which Gleim consistently supports and upholds.

> *This exam is confidential and proprietary. It is made available to you, the examinee, solely for the purpose of assessing your proficiency level in the skill area referenced in the title of this exam. You are expressly prohibited from disclosing, publishing, reproducing, or transmitting this exam, in whole or in part, in any form or by any means, verbal or written, electronic or mechanical, for any purpose, without the prior express written permission of the IRS.*

You can use the past releases of EA questions as good indicators of what may be on your exam. The IRS released numerous nearly identical questions on certain topics. You should pay close attention to these questions and expect to see similar ones on your exam. The Gleim EA materials emphasize knowing exactly what will be expected of you during the EA exam and preparing you for what is required. To maintain our competitive edge, we ask you and other EAs and EA candidates for feedback and suggestions on how to improve our materials, with emphasis on topics to be strengthened and/or added. Please go to www.gleim.com/feedbackEA1 to provide us with your comments and suggestions.

DATES OF THE EXAMINATION/TAX LAW COVERED

The 2013 examination test window will begin May 1, 2013, and examinations will be offered continuously through February 28, 2014.

Each testing year's EA exam (up through February of the following year) covers the tax law in effect the previous December 31. For example, the May 1, 2013–February 28, 2014, testing window will test tax law in effect December 31, 2012.

EXAM COSTS

There are three fees you must pay to take the EA exam.

1. PTIN Application Fee - $64.25 (or PTIN Renewal Fee - $63.00)
2. Exam Scheduling Fee - $105.00 per part
3. Enrollment to Practice before the IRS Application Fee - $30.00

IRS STUDY MATERIAL

In studying for the examination, candidates may wish to refer to the Internal Revenue Code, Circular 230 (reproduced in Appendix A of *EA Review: Part 3*), IRS publications, and IRS tax forms and accompanying instructions, which can be found at www.irs.gov/Forms-&-Pubs or ordered from the IRS as a DVD for $30. You may order the IRS Tax Products DVD (Publication 1796) by calling 877-233-6767. There is an additional $6 handling fee if ordered by phone, fax, or mail. To avoid the handling fee, order online at www.ntis.gov/products/irsdvd.aspx. Use these IRS publications as references to the Gleim EA Review System.

STEPS TO BECOME AN EA

1. Become knowledgeable about the exam, and decide which part you will take first.
2. Purchase the **Gleim EA Review System** to thoroughly prepare for the EA exam. Commit to our systematic preparation for the exam as described in our review materials, including *EA Review: A System for Success.*
3. Communicate with your Personal Counselor to design a study plan that meets your needs. Call (800) 874-5346 or email EA@gleim.com.
4. Apply and register to take the exam as far in advance as possible. To simplify this process, use www.irs.gov/ptin and www.prometric.com/irs. See www.gleim.com/accounting/ea/steps for detailed instructions.
5. Schedule your test with Prometric (online, or by calling the national 800 number or your local Prometric testing site). You have a window of 1 year from registration to schedule, but Gleim recommends you schedule immediately.
6. Work systematically through each study unit in the Gleim EA Review System.

7. Create an unlimited number of Practice Exams in the Gleim EA Test Prep Online, which contains thousands of questions, all updated to the appropriate tax law. Listen to EA Audio Review as a supplement.
8. Sit for and PASS the EA exam while you are in control. Gleim Guarantees Success!
9. Enjoy your career and pursue multiple certifications (CIA, CMA, CPA, etc.), recommend Gleim to others who are also taking these exams, and stay up-to-date on your Continuing Education requirements with Gleim CE.

More specifically, you should focus on the following **system for success** on the EA exam:

1. **Understand the exam, including its purpose, coverage, preparation, format, administration, grading, and pass rates.**
   a. The better you understand the examination process from beginning to end, the better you will perform.
   b. Study the Gleim *EA Review: A System for Success*. Be sure you have a copy of this useful booklet (also available at www.gleim.com/sfs/).
2. **Learn and understand the subject matter tested.** The IRS's Exam Content Outlines for Part 1 are the basis for the study outlines that are presented in each of the 13 study units that make up this book.* You will also learn and understand the material tested on the EA exam by answering numerous multiple-choice questions from past EA exams. Multiple-choice questions with the answer explanations to the immediate right of each question are a major component of each study unit.
3. **Practice answering past exam questions to perfect your question-answering techniques.** Answering past exam questions helps you understand the standards to which you will be held. This motivates you to learn and understand while studying (rather than reading) the outlines in each of the 13 study units.
   a. Question-answering techniques are suggested for multiple-choice questions in Study Unit 4 of *EA Review: A System for Success*.
   b. Our **EA Test Prep Online** contains thousands of additional multiple-choice questions that are not offered in our books. Additionally, EA Test Prep Online has many useful features, including documentation of your performance and the ability to simulate the exam environment and create as many Practice Exams as you want.
   c. Our **EA Gleim Online** is a powerful Internet-based program that allows EA candidates to learn in an interactive environment and provides feedback to candidates to encourage learning. It includes multiple-choice questions in Prometric's format. Each EA Gleim Online candidate has access to a Personal Counselor, who helps organize study plans that work with busy schedules.
   d. Additionally, candidates can access Prometric's free tutorial/sample test at www.prometric.com/demos/irs/index.htm.
4. **Plan and practice exam execution.** Anticipate the exam environment and prepare yourself with a plan: When to arrive? How to dress? What exam supplies to bring? How many questions and what format? Order of answering questions? How much time to spend on each question? See Study Unit 6 in *EA Review: A System for Success*.
   a. Expect the unexpected and adjust! Remember, your sole objective when taking an examination is to maximize your score. You must outperform your peers, and being as comfortable and relaxed as possible gives you an advantage!
5. **Be in control.** Develop confidence and ensure success with a controlled preparation program followed by confident execution during the examination.

---

*Please fill out our online feedback form (www.gleim.com/feedbackEA1) IMMEDIATELY after you take the EA exam so we can adapt to changes in the exam. Our approach has been approved by the IRS.

PRELIMINARY TESTING: THE GLEIM EA DIAGNOSTIC QUIZ

The Gleim EA Diagnostic Quiz provides a representative sample of 40 multiple-choice questions for Part 1 to identify your preliminary strengths and any weaknesses before you start preparing in earnest for this part of the EA exam. It also provides you with the actual exam experience, i.e., what you will encounter when you take the EA exam at Prometric.

When you have completed the quiz, one of our Personal Counselors will consult with you to better focus your review on any areas in which you have less confidence. After your consultation, you will be able to access a Review Session, where you can study answer explanations for the correct and incorrect answer choices of the questions you answered incorrectly.

For smart phone users, there is also a Gleim Diagnostic Quiz App for iPhone, iPod Touch, and Android. See our website (www.gleim.com/ea) for more information.

HOW TO STUDY A STUDY UNIT USING THE GLEIM EA REVIEW SYSTEM

To ensure that you are using your time effectively, we recommend that you follow the steps listed below when using all of the EA Review System materials together (books, Test Prep Online, Audio Review, and Gleim Online):

1. (30 minutes, plus 10 minutes for review) In the EA Gleim Online course, complete Multiple-Choice Quiz #1 in 30 minutes. It is expected that your scores will be lower on the first quiz than on subsequent quizzes.
    a. Immediately following the quiz, you will be prompted to review the questions you marked and/or answered incorrectly. For each question, analyze and understand why you were unsure or answered it incorrectly. This step is an essential learning activity.
2. (30 minutes) Use the online audiovisual presentation for an overview of the study unit. EA Audio Review can be substituted for audiovisual presentations and can be used while driving to work, exercising, etc.
3. (45 minutes) Complete the 30-question True/False quiz. It is interactive and most effective if used prior to studying the Knowledge Transfer Outline.
4. (60 minutes) Study the Knowledge Transfer Outline, particularly the troublesome areas identified from the multiple-choice questions in the Gleim Online course. The Knowledge Transfer Outlines can be studied either online or from the books.
5. (30 minutes, plus 10 minutes for review) Complete Multiple-Choice Quiz #2 in the Gleim Online course.
    a. Immediately following the quiz, you will be prompted to review the questions you marked and/or answered incorrectly. For each question, analyze and understand why you were unsure or answered it incorrectly. This step is an essential learning activity.
6. (60 minutes) Complete two 20-question Practice Exams in the EA Test Prep Online. Review as needed.

When following these steps, you will complete all 13 study units in about 60 hours. Then spend 10-20 hours taking customized Practice Exams in the EA Test Prep Online until you approach your desired proficiency level, e.g., 75%+. Use Study Sessions as needed to get immediate feedback on questions in your problem areas.

EA FINAL REVIEW

Final review is the culmination of all your studies and topics and should occur one week prior to when you sit for your exam. All study units in Gleim Online should be completed by this time.

Step 1: Take the EA Exam Rehearsal at the beginning of your final review stage. The Exam Rehearsal is 3.5 hours (210 minutes) long and contains 100 multiple-choice questions, just like the EA exam. This will help you identify any weak areas for more practice. Discuss your results with your Personal Counselor for additional guidance.

Step 2: Work in Gleim EA Test Prep Online, focusing on your weak areas identified from your Exam Rehearsal. Also, be sure to focus on all the material as a whole to refresh yourself with topics you learned at the beginning of your studies. View your performance chart to make sure you are scoring 75% or higher.

EA GLEIM ONLINE

EA Gleim Online is a versatile, interactive, self-study review program delivered via the Internet. It is divided into three courses (one for each part of the EA exam).

Each course is broken down into individual, manageable study units. Completion time per study unit will be about 4.5 hours. Each study unit in the course contains an audiovisual presentation, 30 true/false study questions, a Knowledge Transfer Outline, and two 20-question multiple-choice quizzes.

EA Gleim Online provides you with access to a Personal Counselor, a real person who will provide support to ensure your competitive edge. EA Gleim Online is a great way to get confidence as you prepare with Gleim. This confidence will continue during and after the exam.

STUDYING WITH GLEIM BOOKS AND TEST PREP ONLINE

Twenty-question Practice Exams in the **EA Test Prep Online** will help you focus on your weaker areas. Make it a game: How much can you improve?

Our EA Test Prep Online Practice Exams force you to commit to your answer choice before looking at answer explanations; thus, you are preparing under true exam conditions. It also keeps track of your time and performance history for each study unit, which is available in either a table or graphical format.

If you are using only the book and Test Prep Online to prepare, follow our suggested steps listed below and on the next page. DO NOT omit the step in which you diagnose the reasons for answering questions incorrectly; i.e., learn from your mistakes while studying so you avoid making similar mistakes on the EA exam.

1. Create and complete a 20-question diagnostic Practice Exam before studying any other information.
2. Study the Knowledge Transfer Outline for the corresponding study unit in your Gleim book.
   a. Place special emphasis on the weaker areas that you identified with the initial exam in Step 1.
3. Take two or three 20-question Practice Exams after you have studied the Knowledge Transfer Outline.
4. Immediately following each exam, you will be prompted to review the questions you marked and/or answered incorrectly. For each question, analyze and understand why you were unsure or answered it incorrectly. This step is an essential learning activity.

5. Continue this process until you approach a predetermined proficiency level, e.g., 75%+. Use Study Sessions as needed to get immediate feedback on questions in your problem areas.
6. Modify this process to suit your individual learning process.
   a. Learning from questions you answer incorrectly is very important. Each question you answer incorrectly is an **opportunity** to avoid missing actual test questions on your EA exam. Thus, you should carefully study the answer explanations provided so you understand why you chose the incorrect answer. This study technique is clearly the difference between passing and failing for most EA candidates.
   b. Reasons for missing questions include
      1) Misreading the requirement (stem)
      2) Not understanding what is required
      3) Making a math error
      4) Applying the wrong rule or concept
      5) Being distracted by one or more of the answers
      6) Incorrectly eliminating answers from consideration
      7) Not having any knowledge of the topic tested
      8) Employing bad intuition when guessing
   c. It is also important to verify that you answered correctly for the right reasons. Otherwise, if the material is tested on the EA exam in a different manner, you may not answer it correctly.
   d. It is imperative that you complete your predetermined number of study units per week (see Study Unit 5, Subunit 4, in *EA Review: A System for Success* for more information on study schedules) so you can review your progress and realize how attainable a comprehensive EA review program is when using the Gleim EA Review System. Remember to meet or beat your schedule to give yourself confidence.

GLEIM AUDIO REVIEWS

Gleim **EA Audio Reviews** provide an average of 30 minutes of quality review for each study unit. Each review provides an overview of the Knowledge Transfer Outline for each study unit in the *EA Review* book. The purpose is to get candidates "started" so they can relate to the questions they will answer before reading the study outlines in each study unit.

The audios get to the point, as does the entire **Gleim System for Success**. We are working to get you through the EA exam with minimum time, cost, and frustration. You can listen to sample audio reviews on our website at www.gleim.com/accounting/demos.

TIME-BUDGETING AND QUESTION-ANSWERING TECHNIQUES FOR THE EXAM

The following suggestions are to assist you in maximizing your score on multiple-choice questions. Remember, knowing how to take the exam and how to answer individual questions is as important as studying/reviewing the subject matter tested on the exam.

1. **Budget your time.** We make this point with emphasis. Just as you would fill up your gas tank prior to reaching empty, so too should you finish your exam before time expires.
   a. You will have 3 hours and 30 minutes (210 minutes) to answer 100 multiple-choice questions.
   b. As you work through the individual multiple-choice items, monitor your time. Your goal is to answer all of the items and achieve the maximum score possible.
   c. If you allocate 1.5 - 2 minutes per question, you will require 150 - 200 minutes to finish all questions, leaving 10 - 60 minutes to review your answers and "marked" questions (see item 2.b. on the next page). Spending 2 minutes should be reserved for only the most difficult questions. You should complete 10 questions every 15 - 20 minutes. If you pace yourself during the exam, you will have adequate time.

d. On your Prometric computer screen, the time remaining (starting with 03:30:00) appears in the top right corner of the screen.

2. **Answer the items in consecutive order.**

   a. Do **not** agonize over any one item. Stay within your time budget.

   b. Note any items you are unsure of by clicking the "mark" button and return to them later if time allows. Plan on going back to all marked questions.

   c. Never leave a question unanswered. Make your best guess in the time allowed. Your score is based on the number of correct responses. You will not be penalized for guessing incorrectly.

3. **For each multiple-choice question,**

   a. **Try to ignore the answer choices at first.** Do not allow the answer choices to affect your reading of the question.

      1) If four answer choices are presented, three of them are incorrect. These incorrect answers are called **distractors** for good reason. Often, distractors are written to appear correct at first glance until further analysis.

      2) In computational items, distractors are carefully calculated such that they are the result of making common mistakes. Be careful, and double-check your computations if time permits.

   b. **Read the question** carefully to determine the precise requirement.

      1) Focusing on what is required enables you to ignore extraneous information and to proceed directly to determining the correct answer.

         a) Be especially careful to note when the requirement is an **exception**; e.g., "Which of the following is **not** includible in gross income?"

   c. **Determine the correct answer** before looking at the answer choices.

      1) However, some multiple-choice items are structured so that the answer cannot be determined from the stem alone. See the stem in b.1)a) above.

   d. **Now, read the answer choices carefully.**

      1) Even if the first answer appears to be the correct choice, do not skip the remaining answer choices. Questions often ask for the "best" of the choices provided. Thus, each choice requires your consideration.

      2) Treat each answer choice as a true/false question as you analyze it.

   e. **Click on the best answer.**

      1) If you are uncertain, guess intelligently (see item 5. below). Improve on your 25% chance of getting the correct answer with blind guessing.

      2) For many of the multiple-choice questions, two answer choices can be eliminated with minimal effort, thereby increasing your educated guess to a 50-50 proposition.

4. After you have answered all 100 questions, return to the questions that you marked. Then, verify that all questions have been answered.

5. **If you don't know the answer,**

   a. Again, guess; but make it an educated guess, which means selecting the best possible answer. First, rule out answers that you feel are obviously incorrect. Second, speculate on the IRS's purpose and/or the rationale behind the question. Third, select the best answer or guess between equally appealing answers. Your first guess is usually the most intuitive. If you cannot make an educated guess, read the stem and each answer, and pick the best or most intuitive answer. It's just a guess!

   b. Make sure you accomplish this step within your predetermined time budget.

IF YOU HAVE QUESTIONS FOR GLEIM

Content-specific questions about our materials will be answered most rapidly if they are sent to us via email to accounting@gleim.com. Our team of accounting experts will give your correspondence thorough consideration and a prompt response.

Questions regarding the information in this Introduction (study suggestions, studying plans, exam specifics) should be emailed to personalcounselor@gleim.com.

Questions concerning orders, prices, shipments, or payments should be sent via email to customerservice@gleim.com and will be promptly handled by our competent and courteous customer service staff.

For technical support, you may use our automated technical support service at www.gleim.com/support, email us at support@gleim.com, or call us at (800) 874-5346.

HOW TO BE IN CONTROL

Remember, you must be in control to be successful during exam preparation and execution. Perhaps more importantly, control can also contribute greatly to your personal and other professional goals. Control is a process whereby you

1. Develop expectations, standards, budgets, and plans.
2. Undertake activity, production, study, and learning.
3. Measure the activity, production, output, and knowledge.
4. Compare actual activity with expected and budgeted activity.
5. Modify the activity to better achieve the desired outcome.
6. Revise expectations and standards in light of actual experience.
7. Continue the process.

Exercising control will ultimately develop the confidence you need to outperform most other EA candidates and PASS the EA exam! Obtain our ***EA Review: A System for Success*** booklet for a more detailed discussion of control and other exam tactics.

The Gleim Team wishes you luck on your exam!

STUDY UNIT ONE
FILING REQUIREMENTS

(13 pages of outline)

To determine the proper tax liability, the taxpayer must claim the appropriate filing status, elect the available exemption(s) and/or deductions, and comply with the necessary filing requirements.

1.1 PRELIMINARY WORK TO PREPARE TAX RETURNS

Prior Year Return

1. Use of prior year's returns for comparison helps prevent gross mathematical errors and identify significant changes.
   a. If the comparison shows that there were no significant changes, then the current year return should result in similar amounts and tax liability/refund.
   b. Comparison of prior years' returns helps to identify applicable items that are not common to all individuals (retirement pay, sale of principal residence, itemized deductions, applicable taxes, etc.).
2. The accuracy of the prior year's return affects the accuracy of the current year's return in areas in which the prior year is relied upon (state taxes paid/refund). It also increases efficiency in completing the current return.

Biographical Information

3. Taxpayer biographical information (e.g., date of birth, age, marital status, dependents) is used to verify the identity of the taxpayer and related dependents.
   a. The age of an individual determines if (s)he qualifies for additional deductions (65 and over), retirement distributions, dependency, etc.
   b. Married filing jointly status often increases beneficial dollar limits for deductions, exemptions, and credits.

Nationality

4. Immigration Status and/or Citizenship (e.g., citizen, resident alien, or nonresident alien)
   a. If a taxpayer is an alien (not a U.S. citizen), (s)he is considered a nonresident alien unless either the green card test or the substantial presence test for the calendar year is met.
   b. Even if a taxpayer does not meet either of these tests, (s)he may be able to choose to be treated as a U.S. resident for part of the year (dual-status aliens). This usually occurs in the year of arrival in or departure from the United States.

Individual/Business

5. Determine if an individual and/or a business entity is involved.
   a. A personal, living, or family expense is not deductible unless the Code specifically provides otherwise. Nondeductible expenses include
      1) Rent and insurance premiums paid for the taxpayer's own dwelling;
      2) Life insurance premiums paid by the insured;
      3) Upkeep of an automobile;
      4) Personal interest; and
      5) Payments for food, clothing, or domestic help.

Items Affecting Future Returns

6. Certain items from the prior-year return may be needed to complete the current-year return (state income tax refund, AMT for credit, gain/loss carryover, charitable gift carryover, etc.).

All Required Taxes Filed

7. Income tax, withholding (estimated tax), FICA (self-employment tax) and FUTA, AMT, estate tax, gift tax, GST tax.

Special Filing Requirements

8. Foreign income. For purposes of determining whether a taxpayer must file a return, gross income includes any income that can be excluded as foreign earned income or as a foreign housing amount.
9. If a taxpayer is a U.S. citizen or resident alien, the rules for filing income, estate, and gift tax returns and for paying estimated tax are generally the same whether the taxpayer is in the United States or abroad.
   a. A taxpayer's income, filing status, and age generally determine whether a taxpayer's income tax return must be filed.

Stop and review! You have completed the outline for this subunit. Study questions 1 and 2 on page 25.

1.2 FILING STATUS

The amount of the standard deduction, personal exemptions, and applicable tax rates vary with filing status.

1. **Married Filing a Joint Return**
   a. Two individuals are treated as legally married (Publication 504) for the entire tax year if, on the last day of the tax year, they are
      1) Legally married and cohabiting as husband and wife
      2) Legally married and living apart, but not separated pursuant to a valid divorce decree or separate maintenance agreement
      3) Separated under a valid divorce decree that is not yet final

      NOTE: If a spouse dies, status for each spouse is determined when the spouse dies, unless the surviving spouse remarries before the end of the tax year (in which case the decedent files married filing separate).
   b. A joint return is not allowed if one spouse was a nonresident alien (NRA) at any time during the tax year, unless the U.S. citizen and the NRA spouse so elect and agree to be taxed on their worldwide income.
   c. If one spouse files separately, so must the other.

d. Once a joint return has been filed for the year and the time for filing the return of either spouse has expired, the spouses may not amend the return to file separate returns.

e. Married individuals who file separate returns may later file a joint (amended) return. Payment of the entire joint tax liability is not required at the time the amended return is filed.

f. If an individual obtains a marriage annulment (no valid marriage ever existed), the individuals must file amended returns claiming a filing status of single or head of household, whichever applies.

   1) All prior tax years not closed by the statute of limitations must be amended.

g. A joint return is signed by both spouses. Generally, the spouses are jointly and severally liable for the tax due and any interest and penalties.

   1) One spouse may be relieved of joint and several liability under the "innocent spouse" provisions in very limited circumstances.

h. Married individuals who file a joint return account for their items of income, deduction, and credit in the aggregate.

   1) A joint return is allowed when spouses use different accounting methods.
   2) Spouses with different tax years may not file a joint return.

i. **Injured Spouse**

   1) When a joint return is filed and only one spouse owes a past-due amount, the other spouse can be considered an injured spouse.

      a) An injured spouse can get a refund for his/her share of the joint overpayment that would otherwise be used to pay the past-due amount.

   2) To be considered an injured spouse, the taxpayer must

      a) File a joint return,
      b) Have reported income (such as wages, interest, etc.),
      c) Have made and reported tax payments (such as federal income tax withheld from wages or estimated tax payments) or claimed the Earned Income Credit or other refundable credit, and
      d) Not be required to pay a past-due amount.

   3) File Form 8379.

j. **Innocent Spouse Relief**

   1) Generally, both spouses are responsible for paying the full amount of tax, interest, and penalties due on a joint return. However, if qualified for innocent spouse relief, a taxpayer may be relieved of part or all of the joint liability.
   2) Qualifying events include (a) an understatement of tax because the spouse omitted income or claimed false deductions or credits, and the innocent taxpayer was not aware of the understatement; (b) an understatement of tax, and the innocent taxpayer is divorced or otherwise no longer living with the spouse; or (c) given all the facts and circumstances, it is not fair to hold the innocent taxpayer liable for the tax.
   3) Related types of relief include separation of liability relief, equitable relief, and relief from liability arising from community property law.

Married Filing Separate Returns

2. Each spouse accounts separately for items of income, deduction, and credit. A spouse who uses his/her own funds to pay expenses of jointly owned property is entitled to any deduction attributable to the payments.

Qualifying Widow(er)

3. This status is available for 2 years following the year of death of the husband or wife and may be elected if
   a. The surviving spouse did not remarry during the tax year.
   b. The surviving spouse qualified (with the deceased spouse) for married filing joint return status for the tax year of the death of the spouse.
   c. The surviving spouse maintained a household for the taxable year. Household maintenance means the spouse furnishes more than 50% of the costs to maintain the household for the tax year.
      1) The household must be the principal place of abode of a dependent of the surviving spouse. The spouse must be entitled to claim a dependency exemption amount for the dependent.
      2) The dependent must be a son/daughter, a stepson/stepdaughter, or an adopted child. This does not include a foster child.
   d. A spouse who survives can file a joint return in the tax year of the death of the spouse.
      1) (S)he is also entitled to the full personal exemption amount for the deceased spouse.
      2) The surviving spouse must not have remarried prior to the end of the year.

Head of Household

4. An individual qualifies for head of household status if (s)he satisfies conditions with respect to filing status, marital status, and household maintenance.
   a. Filing status. The individual may not file as a surviving spouse.
   b. Marital status. A married person does not qualify for head of household status unless the conditions in d. (on the next page) are satisfied. An individual is not treated as married for head of household status if the spouse is a nonresident alien at any time during the tax year.

Household Maintenance

   c. An individual must maintain a household that is the principal place of abode for a qualifying individual.
      1) To maintain a household for federal filing status purposes, an individual must furnish more than 50% of the costs of maintaining the household during the tax year.

Qualifying Expenditures	Nonqualifying Costs
Property tax	Clothing
Mortgage interest	Education
Rent	Medical treatment
Utilities	Life insurance
Upkeep	Transportation
Repair	Vacations
Property insurance	Services by the taxpayer
Food consumed on premises	Services by the dependent

Qualifying Person and Time

      2) The taxpayer must maintain a household that constitutes the principal place of abode for more than half of the taxable year for at least one qualified individual who is
         a) A qualifying child or
         b) A qualifying relative. (See Subunit 1.4 for definitions.)

3) Note that there are two special rules concerning a qualifying person.

a) First, the taxpayer with a dependent parent qualifies even if the parent does not live with the taxpayer.

b) Second, if a qualifying child lives with the taxpayer, the qualifying child need not be the taxpayer's dependent.

Otherwise, the IRS maintains that the qualifying individual must occupy the same household (except for temporary absences).

d. A married individual who lives with a dependent apart from the spouse will be considered unmarried and qualify for head of household status if, for the tax year,

1) (S)he files separately;
2) (S)he pays more than 50% toward maintaining the household;
3) For the last 6 months, the spouse is not a member of the household;
4) The household is the principal home of the individual's child, stepchild, qualified foster child, or adopted child for more than half the year; and
5) The individual can claim a dependency exemption for the child.

Single

5. An individual must file as an unmarried individual if (s)he neither is married nor qualifies for surviving spouse or head of household status.

The Standard Deduction

6. Taxable income is adjusted gross income (AGI) minus the deduction for personal exemptions and either itemized deductions or the standard deduction.

a. The taxpayer itemizes deductions if the total allowable itemized deductions, after all limits have been applied, is greater than the standard deduction. Otherwise, (s)he claims the standard deduction. A person must elect to itemize, or no itemized deductions will be allowed.

1) Election is made by filing Schedule A of Form 1040.
2) Election in any other taxable year is not relevant.
3) Election may be changed by filing an amended return (Form 1040X).
4) A person who itemizes may not file either Form 1040EZ or Form 1040A.

Ineligible

b. The following persons are not allowed the standard deduction:

1) Persons who itemize deductions
2) Nonresident alien individuals
3) Individuals who file a "short period" return
4) A married individual who files a separate return and whose spouse itemizes
5) Partnerships, estates, and trusts

c. The standard deduction is the sum of the basic standard deduction and the additional standard deduction.

Basic Standard Deduction

d. The basic standard deduction amount depends on filing status and dependency status on another's return. Refer to the table on the following page.

1) The basic standard deduction amount of a child under age 19 or a student under age 24 who can be claimed as a dependent on another individual's income tax return is limited to the greater of either

a) $950 or

b) Earned income for the year plus $300 up to the otherwise applicable standard deduction.

2) Earned income does not include either dividends or capital gains from the sale of stock.

Additional Standard Deduction

e. Additional standard deduction amounts, indexed for inflation, appear in the table below.

1) An individual who has attained the age of 65 or is blind is entitled to the amount.

a) "Blind" in this context means no better than 20/200 vision in the better eye even with corrective lenses.

2) An individual who has both reached age 65 and is blind is entitled to twice the amount.

3) The individual is entitled to the amount if (s)he attains age 65 before the end of the tax year.

a) Even if (s)he dies before the end of the year

b) But not if (s)he dies before attaining age 65, even if (s)he would have otherwise reached age 65 before year's end

4) A person who becomes blind on or before the last day of the taxable year is entitled to the amount.

5) Once qualified, the standard deduction is allowed in full.

a) It is not prorated if a person dies during a tax year.

STANDARD DEDUCTION AMOUNTS	2012	
Filing Status	Basic	Additional
Married Filing Jointly	$11,900	$1,150
Qualifying Widow(er)	11,900	1,150
Head of Household	8,700	1,450
Single (other than above)	5,950	1,450
Married Filing Separately	5,950	1,150

Stop and review! You have completed the outline for this subunit. Study questions 3 through 11 beginning on page 26.

1.3 FILING REQUIREMENTS

An individual must file a federal income tax return if gross income is above a threshold, net earnings from self-employment is $400 or more, or (s)he is a dependent with more gross income than the standard deduction or with unearned income over $950.

Gross Income Threshold

1. The gross income threshold amount generally is the sum of the standard deduction (excluding any amount for being blind) and personal exemption amounts (excluding dependency exemptions).

a. The EA exam has not required candidates to memorize the gross income thresholds; however, they are presented below for your information.

b. Filing requirements: 2012 gross income thresholds

Filing Status	Standard Deduction	Personal Exemption	Total	Exception to General Rule
Married Filing Jointly	$11,900	$7,600	$19,500	
Qualifying Widow(er)	11,900	3,800	15,700	
Head of Household	8,700	3,800	12,500	
Single	5,950	3,800	9,750	
Married Filing Separately				$3,800

NOTE: Except for married filing separately, the filing requirement limitations are increased for taxpayers by the additional standard deductions for being over 65.

c. Married individuals filing separately are not allowed to include the standard deduction in the threshold computation because if one taxpayer itemizes his/her deductions, the other is required to itemize.

d. Each individual who is over age 65 is entitled to an additional standard deduction when calculating the gross income threshold.

Additional Standard Deduction	
Married Filing Jointly Qualifying Widow(er) Married Filing Separately	$1,150
Head of Household Single	$1,450

e. Any personal residence disposition gain that was excluded and any foreign earned income that was excluded must be added back to gross income for purposes of this filing requirement.

f. Special conditions may also require filing, e.g., liability for a special tax, such as AMT or receipt of wages from a church.

g. Even if not required, an individual should file to obtain a refund and possibly to establish a record and trigger running of statutes of limitation.

Due Date

2. The income tax return must be filed (postmarked) not later than the 15th day of the fourth month following the close of the tax year. This is April 15 for calendar-year taxpayers. If the 15th day is a Saturday, a Sunday, or a legal holiday, the due date is the next day that is not a Saturday, a Sunday, or a legal holiday.

   a. An automatic extension of 6 months is provided for an individual who files Form 4868 or uses a credit card to make the required tax payment on or before the initial due date.

   b. A U.S. citizen or resident who is on military or naval duty outside the U.S. (or Puerto Rico) on April 15 is given an automatic 2-month extension without the necessity of filing Form 4868.

      1) Filing of Form 4868 during the 2 months will allow another 4-month extension.

   c. The due date for a decedent's final return is the date on which the return would have been due if death had not occurred.

   d. A Form 1040NR nonresident alien's tax return (when not subject to wage withholding) must be filed by the 15th day of the sixth month after the close of the tax year (unless extended).

      1) A nonresident alien must file his/her tax return on the 15th day of the fourth month after the close of the tax year (unless extended) if his/her wages are subject to withholding.

Liability Payment

3. Tax liability must be paid when the return must be filed. Automatic extension for filing the return does not extend time for payment.

   a. Interest will be charged from the original due date.

   b. A penalty of 5% per month up to 25% of unpaid liability is assessed for failure to file a return.

   c. In general, a failure to pay penalty is imposed from the due date for taxes (other than the estimated taxes) shown on the return.

      1) The penalty is .5% per month of the tax not paid, up to 25%.
      2) A failure to pay penalty may offset a failure to file penalty.

3) When an extension to file is timely requested, a failure to pay penalty may be avoided by paying an estimate of unpaid tax in conjunction with the extension request.

a) The payment may not be less than 90% of the actual tax liability due, and the balance must be paid when the return is filed.

b) Exceptions and adjustments to these rules do apply in unique situations.

Record Keeping

4. Books of account or records sufficient to establish the amount of gross income, deductions, credit, or other matters required to be shown in any tax or information return must be kept.

   a. Records must be maintained as long as the contents may be material in administration of any internal revenue law.

   b. Employers are required to keep records on employment taxes until at least 4 years after the due date of the return or payment of the tax.

5. If an individual is required to report employment taxes or give tax statements to employees, (s)he must have an employer identification number (EIN).

   a. The EIN is a nine-digit number the IRS issues to identify the tax accounts of employers.

6. Penalties are applied when an employer fails to make a required deposit of taxes on time.

   a. The penalties do not apply if any failure to make a proper and timely deposit was due to reasonable cause and not to willful neglect.

   b. For amounts not properly or timely deposited, the penalty rates are

      1) 2% for deposits made 1 to 5 days late
      2) 5% for deposits made 6 to 15 days late
      3) 10% for deposits made 16 or more days late

Form 1040EZ

7. Taxpayers may be eligible to file Form 1040EZ. The only credit allowed on the return is the Earned Income Credit.

Stop and review! You have completed the outline for this subunit. Study questions 12 through 20 beginning on page 29.

1.4 PERSONAL EXEMPTIONS

An individual's deduction for personal exemptions is the sum of a personal exemption amount for the individual, a spouse, and each qualified dependent. The amount is $3,800 for 2012. Thus, an individual who files an income tax return is allowed a personal exemption amount for him/herself, for his/her spouse, and for any other dependent who satisfies the dependent status tests discussed in this subunit.

Personal Exemptions for the Spouse

1. A taxpayer filing as married filing separately may deduct an exemption for the spouse if the spouse has no gross income and is not a dependent of another taxpayer.

   a. If divorced or legally separated, no exemption is allowed.

   b. If a spouse dies in the current year, an exemption is allowed as long as the spouse would have qualified for an exemption on the date of death and the surviving spouse does not remarry during that year.

Dependent Status

2. To qualify as a dependent, the individual must be a qualifying child or a qualifying relative.

Qualifying Child

a. To be a qualifying child, four tests must be met:

1) Relationship – The child must be the taxpayer's son, daughter, stepson, stepdaughter, brother, sister, stepbrother, stepsister, or any descendant of any such relative. Adopted individuals and eligible foster children meet the relationship test.
2) Age – The child must be under the age of 19 or a full-time student under the age of 24.
3) Principal Residence – The child must have the same principal place of abode as the taxpayer for more than half of the year.
4) Not Self-Supporting – The child must not have provided over half of his/her own support.

Qualifying Relative

b. To be a qualifying relative, the following tests [1) – 4)] must be met:

1) Relationship or residence. An individual must satisfy either a relationship or a residence requirement to qualify as a dependent.
   a) Residence. The residence requirement is satisfied for any individual who merely resides with a potential claimant (of a dependency exemption amount) for the entire tax year.
   b) Relationship. The relationship requirement is satisfied by existence of an extended (by blood) or immediate (by blood, adoption, or marriage) relationship. The relationship need be present to only one of the two married persons who file a joint return. Any relationship established by marriage is not treated as ended by divorce or by death.
      i) Extended relationships: grandparents and ancestors; grandchildren and descendants; uncles/aunts; nephews/nieces
      ii) Immediate relationships
         - Parent: natural, adoptive, stepparent; father/mother-in-law
         - Child: natural, adoptive, stepchild; son/daughter-in-law; foster child
         - Sibling: full or half brother/sister; adoptive brother/sister; stepbrother/sister; brother/sister-in-law
2) Gross income of the individual (to be claimed as a dependent) must be less than the amount of the dependency exemption ($3,800 for 2012).
   a) Gross income for the gross income dependency test is all income that is received, but not exempt from tax.
      i) Any expenses from rental property do not reduce rental income.
      ii) Gross income from a business is the total net sales minus the cost of goods sold, plus any miscellaneous income from the business.
      iii) Gross income includes all unemployment compensation.

3) Support. The person who may claim an individual as a dependent must provide more than 50% of the (economic) support of the individual for the year.

   a) Support includes welfare benefits, Social Security benefits, and any support provided by the exemption claimant, the dependent, and any other person.

   b) Only amounts provided during the calendar year qualify as support. However, amounts paid in arrears (i.e., payment for child support for a previous year) are not considered as support for the current year.

   c) Support includes money and items, or amounts spent on items, such as

      i) Food, clothing, shelter, utilities
      ii) Medical and dental care and insurance
      iii) Education
      iv) Child care, vacations, etc.

   d) Excluded. Certain items (or amounts spent on them) have not been treated as support, e.g., scholarship received by a dependent, taxes, life insurance premiums.

      i) The purchase of capital items (e.g., furniture, appliances, and cars) cannot be included in total support if they are purchased for personal and family reasons and benefit the entire household.

   e) The amount of an item of support provided in a form other than cash is usually its cost, if purchased, or FMV, if otherwise obtained.

   f) Support received as a single amount is prorated among more than one possible dependent, e.g., three children.

   g) A divorced or separated individual need not meet the support test if (s)he and the (ex-)spouse meet (or have met) the following conditions:

      i) Provided more than 50% of the support
      ii) Had (between them) custody for more than 50% of the year
      iii) Lived apart for the last half of the year
      iv) Did not have a multiple support agreement in effect

      NOTE: The parent having custody for more than 50% of the year is entitled to the exemption, but the exemption amount may be allocated to the noncustodial parent if there is an agreement signed by both parents and attached to the noncustodial parent's return.

   h) Multiple support agreement (Form 2120). One person of a group that together provides more than 50% of the support of an individual may, pursuant to agreement, be allowed the dependency exemption amount.

      i) The person must be otherwise eligible to claim the exemption and must provide more than 10% of the support.
      ii) No other person may provide more than 50% of the support.
      iii) Each other person in the group who provided more than 10% of the support must sign a written consent filed with the return of the taxpayer who claims the exemption.

4) The individual must not be a qualifying child of the taxpayer or any other taxpayer.

   a) A child being adopted is eligible to be claimed as a dependent by the adopting parents if an identifying number for the child is obtained. Initially, an adoption taxpayer identification number (ATIN) is assigned.

   b) Both a dependent who dies before the end of the calendar year and a child born during the year may be claimed as dependents.

Qualifying as a Dependent

c. There are special rules that apply to individuals qualifying as a dependent:

1) Dependent taxpayer test. If an individual meets the requirements to be classified as a dependent on another person's tax return, the individual (dependent) is not entitled to the deduction for personal exemptions for him/herself.

a) The individual will be treated as having no dependents for the tax year.

2) Filing status (occasionally referred to as the joint return test). An individual does not qualify as a dependent on another's return if the individual is married and files a joint return.

a) However, such an individual can qualify as a dependent if (s)he files a joint return solely to claim a refund of withheld tax without regard to the citizenship test.

EXAMPLE

Mr. and Mrs. Kind provided more than half the support for their married daughter and son-in-law who lived with the Kinds all year. Neither the daughter nor the son-in-law is required to file a 2012 tax return. They do so only to get a refund of withheld taxes. The Kinds may claim the daughter and the son-in-law as dependents on their 2012 joint return.

3) Citizenship or resident. To qualify as a dependent, an individual must be, for any part of the year, a U.S. citizen, resident, or national, or a Canadian or Mexican resident.

4) Taxpayer identification number. The taxpayer must provide the correct taxpayer identification number (TIN) of a dependent on the income tax return.

Stop and review! You have completed the outline for this subunit. Study questions 21 through 34 beginning on page 32.

1.5 RETURNS OF DEPENDENTS

1. An individual qualifying as a dependent on another taxpayer's return is not eligible to claim a personal exemption on his/her own return.

2. The standard deduction for a dependent with unearned income is limited to the greater of $950 or the amount of earned income plus $300.

Kiddie Tax

3. Net unearned income (NUI) of a dependent under 19 (under 24 for full-time students) at the close of the tax year is taxed to the dependent at the parent's marginal rate.

a. Net unearned income is unearned income minus the sum of

1) $950 (first $950 clause) and

2) The greater of (a) $950 of the standard deduction or $950 of itemized deductions or (b) the amount of allowable deductions that are directly connected with the production of unearned income.

b. A dependent is allowed at least $1,900 reduction in unearned income.

c. This rule does not apply to an 18-year-old dependent (under 24 for full-time students) if the dependent has earned income that exceeds one-half of the dependent's support.

4. The tax on a dependent is the greater of

TI -- dependent	$X,XXX		TI -- dependent	$X,XXX
Times: rate	.XX	OR	Less: NUI	(XX)
Total tax	$X,XXX		Total (1)	$X,XXX
			TI -- parent	$X,XXX
			Plus: NUI	XX
				$X,XXX
			Times: rate (parent)	.XX
			Total (2)	$X,XXX
			(1)	$X,XXX
			(2)	X,XXX
				$X,XXX
			Less: tax on parent's TI	(X,XXX)
			Total tax	$X,XXX

5. If more than one child has NUI, the parents' total NUI must be proportioned among the children to determine the amount taxed to each child.

Stop and review! You have completed the outline for this subunit. Study questions 35 and 36 on page 36.

1.6 NONRESIDENT AND DUAL-STATUS ALIENS

1. A taxpayer is considered a dual-status alien if the taxpayer was both a nonresident and resident alien during the year.
2. Generally, a taxpayer is considered a resident alien if either the green card test or the substantial presence test is met. Even if the taxpayer does not meet either of these tests, (s)he may be able to choose to be treated as a U.S. resident for part of the year.

Green Card Test

3. A taxpayer is a resident for tax purposes if (s)he was a lawful permanent resident (immigrant) of the United States at any time during the year.

Substantial Presence Test

4. A taxpayer is considered a U.S. resident if (s)he was physically present in the United States for at least
   a. 31 days during 2012 and
   b. 183 days during 2012, 2011, and 2010, counting all days of physical presence in 2012 but only 1/3 the number of days of presence in 2011 and only 1/6 the number of days in 2010.
5. A nonresident alien may file a joint return if (s)he is married to a U.S. citizen or resident at the end of the year.
   a. If the couple files a joint return, both spouses are treated as U.S. residents for the entire tax year.
6. If a taxpayer chooses to be treated as a U.S. resident, both spouses are taxed on worldwide income.
7. A taxpayer is considered unmarried for head of household purposes if the taxpayer's spouse was a nonresident alien at any time during the year and the taxpayer does not choose to treat his/her nonresident spouse as a resident alien.
   a. A taxpayer's spouse is not a qualifying person for head of household purposes.
   b. A taxpayer must have another qualifying person and meet the other tests to be eligible to file as a head of household.

8. Even if a taxpayer is considered unmarried for head of household purposes because the taxpayer is married to a nonresident alien, the taxpayer is still considered married for purposes of the Earned Income Credit.
   a. A taxpayer is not entitled to the credit unless a joint return is filed and other qualifications are met.
9. Nonresident aliens can deduct certain itemized deductions if income is received that is effectively connected with U.S. trade or business.
   a. These deductions include state and local income taxes, charitable contributions to U.S. organizations, casualty and theft losses, and miscellaneous deductions.
10. If a taxpayer is a nonresident alien who is married to a U.S. citizen or resident at the end of the year and chooses to be treated as a U.S. resident, (s)he can take the standard deduction.
11. A nonresident alien is not eligible for the credit for the elderly and the education credits unless (s)he elects to be treated as a U.S. resident.
12. There is no requirement to file a return for nonresident aliens who earn wages effectively connected with a U.S. trade or business that are less than the amount of one personal exemption.
13. Most types of U.S. source income received by a foreign taxpayer are subject to a tax rate of 30%.
14. A scholarship, fellowship, grant, etc., received by a nonresident alien for activities conducted outside the U.S. is treated as foreign source income (Publication 515).

Stop and review! You have completed the outline for this subunit. Study questions 37 through 39 on page 37.

QUESTIONS

1.1 Preliminary Work to Prepare Tax Returns

1. When preparing a current-year tax return, which of the following benefits are derived from the use of the previous year's return?

I. Prevents gross mathematical errors
II. Identifies significant changes
III. Increases efficiency

A. I and II only.

B. I and III only.

C. II and III only.

D. I, II, and III.

Answer (D) is correct.
REQUIRED: The benefits of having the previous year's return available when preparing the return of the current year.
DISCUSSION: Use of the prior-year return helps to prevent gross mathematical errors or identify significant changes. The accuracy of the prior-year return increases efficiency in completing the current-year return. These are just a few of the benefits of obtaining a copy of the previous year's return (Publication 17).

2. Which taxpayer information is necessary to have before preparing a tax return?

A. Immigration status.

B. Age of an individual.

C. Marital status.

D. All of the information is needed.

Answer (D) is correct.
REQUIRED: The information that is necessary to have before preparing a tax return.
DISCUSSION: Taxpayer biographical information (e.g., date of birth, age, marital status, dependents, etc.) is used to verify the identity of the taxpayer and related dependents. The age of an individual determines if (s)he qualifies for additional deductions (65 and over), retirement distributions, dependency, etc. MFJ status often increases beneficial dollar limits for deductions, exemptions, and credits. If a taxpayer is an alien (not a U.S. citizen), (s)he is considered a nonresident alien, unless either the green card test or the substantial presence test for the calendar year is met.
Answer (A) is incorrect. The individual's age and marital status are also needed. Answer (B) is incorrect. The individual's immigration status and marital status are also needed. Answer (C) is incorrect. The individual's immigration status and age are also needed.

1.2 Filing Status

3. John and Linda Smith are a childless married couple who lived apart for all of the current year. On December 31 of the current year, they were legally separated under a decree of separate maintenance. Based on the facts, which of the following is the only filing-status choice available to them for the current year?

A. Married filing joint return.

B. Married filing separate return.

C. Head of household.

D. Single.

Answer (D) is correct.

REQUIRED: The proper filing status for the taxpayer.

DISCUSSION: The determination of whether an individual is married is made as of the close of the taxable year, so John and Linda are both single for the current year (Publication 17).

Answer (A) is incorrect. They are unmarried at year end. Answer (B) is incorrect. They are unmarried at year end. Answer (C) is incorrect. They are not maintaining a home as a principal place of abode for a child or other dependent.

4. Lisa was married with two dependent children in 2012. Her husband died in April, and she did not remarry before the end of 2012. Which filing status should Lisa use for her tax return in 2012?

A. Single.

B. Married Filing Jointly.

C. Head of Household.

D. Qualifying Widow(er) with Dependent Child.

Answer (B) is correct.

REQUIRED: The filing status for a widow(er) whose spouse dies during the year.

DISCUSSION: Two individuals are treated as legally married (Publication 504) for the entire tax year if, on the last day of the tax year, they are

1. Legally married and cohabiting as husband and wife
2. Legally married and living apart, but not separated pursuant to a valid divorce decree or separate maintenance agreement
3. Separated under a valid divorce decree that is not yet final

If a spouse dies, status is determined when the spouse dies unless the surviving spouse remarries before the end of the tax year (Publication 17).

Answer (A) is incorrect. Lisa is permitted to file as married filing a joint return. Her marital status is determined at the date of her husband's death, provided she has not remarried. Answer (C) is incorrect. Head of household filing status is only available to married persons if certain criteria are met. Moreover, married filing jointly provides a more favorable tax return than head of household. Answer (D) is incorrect. The qualifying widow(er) with dependent child status is available for 2 years following the death of the spouse.

5. Which of the following is not a requirement that must be met in determining whether a taxpayer is considered unmarried for head of household filing-status purposes?

A. An individual must file a separate return.

B. An individual must pay more than one-half the cost of keeping up a home for the tax year.

C. An individual's home must be, for the entire year, the main home of his/her child, stepchild, or adopted child whom (s)he or the noncustodial parent can properly claim as a dependent.

D. An individual's spouse must not have lived in their home for the last 6 months of the tax year.

Answer (C) is correct.

REQUIRED: The item that is not a requirement in determining if a taxpayer is unmarried for head of household filing-status purposes.

DISCUSSION: In determining if a taxpayer qualifies for head of household filing status, the taxpayer is considered unmarried if the following requirements are met:

1. The taxpayer filed a separate return.
2. The taxpayer paid more than half the cost of keeping up the home for the tax year.
3. The taxpayer's spouse did not live in the home during the last 6 months of the tax year.
4. The home was, for more than half the year, the main home of the taxpayer's child, stepchild, or adopted child whom the taxpayer or the noncustodial parent can properly claim as a dependent.

Therefore, this answer is correct because the requirement is that the home be the main home of the child, stepchild, or adopted child for more than half the year, not the entire year [Publication 17 and Sec. 2(b)].

6. Which of the following is not a requirement you must meet to claim head of household filing status?

A. Your spouse did not live in your home during the last 6 months of the tax year.

B. You paid more than half of the cost of keeping up your home for the entire year.

C. Your home was the main home of your foster child for the entire year.

D. You are unmarried or considered unmarried on the last day of the year.

Answer (C) is correct.

REQUIRED: The item that is not a requirement in determining if a taxpayer is unmarried for head of household filing-status purposes.

DISCUSSION: In determining if a taxpayer qualifies for head of household filing status, the taxpayer is considered unmarried if the following requirements are met:

1. The taxpayer filed a separate return.
2. The taxpayer paid more than half the cost of keeping up the home for the tax year.
3. The taxpayer's spouse did not live in the home during the last 6 months of the tax year.
4. The home was, for more than half the year, the main home of the taxpayer's child, stepchild, or eligible foster child whom the taxpayer or the noncustodial parent can properly claim as a dependent.
5. The taxpayer must be able to claim an exemption for the child.

The requirement is that the home be the main home of the child, stepchild, or eligible foster child for more than half the year [Publication 17 and Sec. 2(b)].

Answer (A) is incorrect. This is a requirement you must meet to qualify for head of household filing status. Answer (B) is incorrect. This is a requirement you must meet to qualify for head of household filing status. Answer (D) is incorrect. You must be unmarried or considered unmarried [according to Sec. 2(b)].

7. For 2012, Jane is unmarried and paid more than half the cost of keeping up her home. All of the following dependents would qualify Jane to file as head of household except

A. Jane's grandson, who lived with her but was absent from her home for 9 months in 2012 while attending boarding school.

B. Jane's father, whom she can claim as a dependent and whose main home for 2012 was a home for the elderly for which Jane paid more than one-half the cost.

C. Jane's married son, who could properly be claimed as a dependent on his father's return only.

D. Jane's sister, whom Jane can claim as a dependent and who lived with Jane until she died in May 2012.

Answer (C) is correct.

REQUIRED: The person who does not qualify as the taxpayer's dependent for head of household filing-status purposes.

DISCUSSION: A taxpayer qualifies for head of household filing status if (s)he is not married at the close of the tax year, is not a surviving spouse, and maintains a household that is also the principal place of abode for more than half of the year for any one of certain qualifying individuals.

A married son, stepson, daughter, or stepdaughter is a qualifying individual only if the taxpayer is entitled to the dependency exemption or the taxpayer by written declaration allows the noncustodial parent the dependency deduction.

Jane must have been able to claim the married son as a dependent in order to qualify as head of household.

Answer (A) is incorrect. Time spent at school is deemed temporary and does not apply to the 6-month test. Answer (B) is incorrect. A taxpayer can maintain a separate household for a parent, such as a rest home, and still qualify as a head of household. Answer (D) is incorrect. Brothers and sisters are qualifying relatives for head of household status.

8. Phil is unmarried in 2012. His dependent daughter, Susan, lived with him all year. Property taxes of $2,500 and mortgage interest of $5,000 on the home where he and Susan live are divided equally with his ex-wife. Phil paid the utilities of $200 per month. What amount may Phil use as the costs of keeping up a home to qualify for head of household filing status?

A. $6,150

B. $4,950

C. $3,750

D. $9,900

Answer (A) is correct.

REQUIRED: The qualifying expenditures for determining head of household filing status.

DISCUSSION: An individual must maintain a household that is the principal place of abode for a qualifying individual. To maintain a household for federal filing status purposes, an individual must furnish more than 50% of the costs of maintaining the household during the tax year. Qualifying expenditures include property tax, mortgage interest, rent, utilities, upkeep, repair, property insurance, and the food consumed on the premises (Publication 17).

Phil pays 50% of the property taxes and mortgage interest, as well as 100% of the utilities. Since all of these are qualified expenditures, he may deduct the portion of these costs in which he paid. Thus, the amount that Phil may use as the costs of keeping up a home to qualify for head of household filing status is $6,150 [($5,000 × 50%) + ($2,500 × 50%) + ($200 × 12 months)].

Answer (B) is incorrect. This amount only includes 50% of the utilities paid, when Phil paid 100% of the utilities for the year. Answer (C) is incorrect. This amount does not include the utilities that were paid by Phil during the year. Answer (D) is incorrect. Phil only paid 50% of the property taxes and mortgage interest. Thus, he can only include the portion of the costs that he actually paid.

9. Joe is 37 years old. His wife died during the tax year, and he has not remarried. His deceased wife had no income. He has two minor children living with him. Joe paid all of the costs for keeping up his home for the tax year, and he has paid for all of the support of his wife and these children. The filing status with the lowest tax rate for which Joe qualifies is

A. Qualifying widower with dependent child.

B. Married filing separately.

C. Head of household.

D. Married filing jointly.

Answer (D) is correct.

REQUIRED: The filing status with the lowest rate for the taxpayer.

DISCUSSION: Publication 501 states, "If your spouse died during the year, you are considered married for the whole year for filing status purposes. If you did not remarry before the end of the tax year, you can file a joint return for yourself and your deceased spouse. For the next 2 years, you may be entitled to the special benefits described later under *Qualifying Widow(er) With Dependent Child*." (See also Publication 17.)

Answer (A) is incorrect. Qualifying widower with dependent child, or surviving spouse, status is only available for 2 years following the year of death of spouse. Answer (B) is incorrect. Joe qualifies for married filing jointly status in the year of his wife's death. Answer (C) is incorrect. Joe qualifies for married filing jointly status in the year of his wife's death.

10. Which dependent relative does not have to live in the same household as the taxpayer claiming head of household filing status?

A. Daughter.

B. Mother.

C. Uncle.

D. Sister or brother.

Answer (B) is correct.

REQUIRED: The relative who does not have to live in the same household as the taxpayer claiming head of household filing status.

DISCUSSION: Sec. 2(b) provides head of household status for an unmarried taxpayer who maintains a household that constitutes the principal place of abode of the taxpayer's father or mother, but only if the taxpayer is entitled to a dependency exemption for the parent. The taxpayer is considered as maintaining a household only if (s)he furnishes over half of the cost of maintaining it. In the case of anyone other than the taxpayer's father or mother, such person(s) must actually occupy the taxpayer's own household for the taxpayer to be considered a head of household (Publication 17).

11. Ms. N, who is married, wants to file as a single person for the current year. Which of the following will prevent her from filing as a single person?

A. Her spouse lived in her home for the final 6 months of the current year.

B. She and her husband did not commingle funds for support purposes.

C. She paid more than half the cost of keeping up her home for the tax year.

D. Her home was, for more than 6 months of the year, the principal home of her son, whom she can claim as a dependent.

Answer (A) is correct.

REQUIRED: The item that will prevent the taxpayer from filing as a single person.

DISCUSSION: The determination of whether an individual is married is made as of the close of the taxable year. A taxpayer's filing status is single if the taxpayer is unmarried or is separated from his/her spouse by a divorce or separate maintenance decree and does not qualify for another filing status. As Ms. N is married, the fact that her spouse lived in her home for the final 6 months of the tax year will prevent her from filing as a single person (Publication 17).

Answer (B) is incorrect. The fact that she and her husband did not commingle funds for support purposes will not prevent her from filing as a single person. Answer (C) is incorrect. Although this is a requirement that must be met in order to file as a head of household, it would not prevent Ms. N from filing as a single taxpayer. Note, however, that, if all the requirements are met, it would be advantageous for the taxpayer to file as a head of household because lower tax rates apply than for a taxpayer filing as a single person or a married person filing a separate return. Answer (D) is incorrect. Although this is a requirement that must be met in order to file as a head of household, it would not prevent Ms. N from filing as a single taxpayer. Note, however, that, if all the requirements are met, it would be advantageous for the taxpayer to file as a head of household because lower tax rates apply than for a taxpayer filing as a single person or a married person filing a separate return.

1.3 Filing Requirements

12. Mr. Todd, who is 43 years old, has lived apart from his wife since May 2012. For 2012, his two children, whom he can claim as dependents, lived with him the entire year, and he paid the entire cost of maintaining the household. Assuming that Mr. Todd cannot qualify to file a joint return for 2012, he must, nevertheless, file a return if his gross income is at least

A. $3,800

B. $8,700

C. $9,750

D. $12,500

Answer (D) is correct.

REQUIRED: The minimum amount of gross income a taxpayer must earn to be required to file a return.

DISCUSSION: Generally, a taxpayer must file a tax return if the taxpayer's gross income equals or exceeds the sum of his/her personal exemption and standard deduction [Sec. 6012(a)]. Sec. 151 allows a $3,800 personal exemption for each taxpayer in 2012. Standard deductions in 2012 are $11,900 for married filing jointly, $8,700 for heads of household, and $5,950 for single individuals (Publication 501). A taxpayer who has two children and files as a head of household must file a return if his/her gross income equals or exceeds $12,500 ($8,700 + $3,800).

Answer (A) is incorrect. The amount of $3,800 is only the personal exemption. Answer (B) is incorrect. The amount of $8,700 is only the standard deduction for heads of household. Answer (C) is incorrect. The amount of $9,750 is the personal exemption plus the standard deduction for single individuals.

13. Ms. Maple, a single woman age 65, retired in 2012. Prior to her retirement, she received a $3,000 bonus plus $1,950 in wages. After her retirement, she received $9,000 in Social Security benefits. Which of the following is true?

A. Ms. Maple does not have to file a 2012 income tax return.

B. Ms. Maple has to file a 2012 income tax return.

C. Ms. Maple has to file a 2012 income tax return but may exclude the $3,000.

D. Ms. Maple has to file a 2012 income tax return but may exclude the $9,000 in Social Security benefits from income.

Answer (A) is correct.

REQUIRED: The true statement concerning filing an income tax return.

DISCUSSION: In general, a taxpayer does not have to file a return if his/her gross income is less than the sum of his/her personal exemption and the standard deduction [Publication 501 and Sec. 6012(a)]. For single individuals who are 65 or over, the standard deduction increases by $1,450. Therefore, the filing threshold will be $11,200 ($7,400 standard deduction + $3,800 personal exemption). Because the Social Security benefits are not included in income when applying this threshold, Ms. Maple does not have to file a return.

14. In which of the following situations is no return required to be filed for 2012?

A. Single, filing status single, under age 65, gross income $15,000.

B. Married, joint filing status, both spouses under age 65, gross income $25,000.

C. Single, filing status single, age 70, gross income $11,000.

D. Married, separate filing status, age 65, gross income $10,000.

Answer (C) is correct.

REQUIRED: The situation not requiring a return to be filed.

DISCUSSION: Generally, a taxpayer must file a tax return if the taxpayer's gross income equals or exceeds the sum of his/her personal exemption and standard deduction [Sec. 6012(a)]. Sec. 151 allows a $3,800 personal exemption in 2012. Standard deductions in 2012 are $11,900 for married filing jointly, $5,950 for married filing separately, $8,700 for heads of households, and $5,950 for single individuals. For single individuals or heads of household who are over 65, the standard deduction increases by $1,450. Married taxpayers filing separately must file a return when their gross income equals or exceeds their personal exemption amount ($3,800). They are not allowed to use the standard deduction amount. (See Publication 501.) The threshold for a single individual over age 65 is $11,200 ($5,950 + $3,800 + $1,450).

Answer (A) is incorrect. Gross income exceeds $9,750 ($5,950 + $3,800). Answer (B) is incorrect. Gross income exceeds $19,500 ($11,900 + $7,600). Answer (D) is incorrect. Gross income exceeds the $3,800 personal exemption (married filing separately is an exception to the general rule).

15. Which of the following statements is true regarding the filing of a Form 4868, *Application for Automatic Extension of Time to File U.S. Individual Income Tax Return*, for your 2012 tax return?

A. Interest is not assessed on any income tax due if a Form 4868 is filed.

B. Form 4868 provides the taxpayer with an automatic additional 8-month extension to file.

C. Even though you file Form 4868, you will owe interest and may be charged a late payment penalty on the amount you owe if you do not pay the tax due by the regular due date.

D. A U.S. citizen who is out of the country on April 15 will be allowed an additional 12 months to file as long as "Out of the Country" is written across the top of Form 4868.

Answer (C) is correct.

REQUIRED: The true statement regarding filing Form 4868.

DISCUSSION: An automatic extension of 6 months is provided for an individual who files Form 4868 or uses a credit card to make a required tax payment on or before the initial due date. The tax liability, however, must be paid when the return must be filed. Automatic extension for filing the return does not extend time for payment. Interest will be charged from the original due date, and penalties may accrue (Publication 17).

Answer (A) is incorrect. Interest will accrue from the original due date. Answer (B) is incorrect. Form 4868 provides a 6-month extension, not an 8-month extension. Answer (D) is incorrect. No such exception applies. Form 4868 provides for a 6-month extension. A longer extension is only available for those serving in military or naval duty outside of the U.S.

16. John Stith, whose father died June 15, 2012, is the executor of his father's estate. John is required to file a final income tax return for his father. When is this return due if he does not file for an extension (ignoring Saturdays, Sundays, and holidays)?

A. October 15, 2012.

B. March 15, 2013.

C. April 15, 2013.

D. June 15, 2013.

Answer (C) is correct.

REQUIRED: The due date for a decedent's final return.

DISCUSSION: The final return of a decedent is due by the date on which the return would have been due had death not occurred. Thus, the final return is generally due by April 15 (Publication 17).

17. During 2012, Hanya was a nonresident alien engaged in a business in the United States. All of her income was from self-employment. Hanya is a calendar-year taxpayer. When is Hanya's income tax return due if she does not apply for an extension of time to file (ignoring weekends and holidays)?

A. April 15, 2013.

B. June 15, 2013.

C. August 15, 2013.

D. October 15, 2013.

Answer (B) is correct.

REQUIRED: The due date for a nonresident alien's income tax return.

DISCUSSION: A nonresident alien not subject to wage withholding generally may file a return as late as the 15th day of the sixth month after the close of the tax year (Publication 17).

Answer (A) is incorrect. April 15 is the due date for nonresident aliens who are subject to withholding. Answer (C) is incorrect. Hanya did not apply for an extension of time to file. Answer (D) is incorrect. Hanya did not apply for an extension of time to file.

18. Which of the following is true regarding the filing of Form 4868, *Application for Automatic Extension of Time to File a U.S. Individual Income Tax Return*?

A. Filing Form 4868 provides an automatic 2-month extension of time to file and pay income tax.

B. Any U.S. citizen who is out of the country on April 15, 2013, is allowed an automatic 6-month extension of time to file his/her 2012 return and pay any federal income tax due.

C. Interest is charged on tax not paid by the due date of the return even if an extension is obtained.

D. Electronic filing cannot be used to get an extension of time to file.

Answer (C) is correct.

REQUIRED: The true statement regarding Form 4868, *Application for Automatic Extension of Time to File a U.S. Individual Income Tax Return.*

DISCUSSION: An automatic extension of 6 months is provided for an individual who files Form 4868 or uses a credit card to make the required tax payment on or before the initial due date. Tax liability must be paid on the original due date of the tax return. Automatic extension for filing the return does not extend time for payment. Interest will be charged from the original due date. If the required payment is made by the regular due date for the return, the return can be filed anytime before the 6-month extension period ends.

Answer (A) is incorrect. Filing Form 4868 provides a 6-month extension of time to file the individual tax return, but it does not provide an extension of time for the payment of tax due. Answer (B) is incorrect. A U.S. citizen or resident who is on military or naval duty outside the U.S. on April 15 is only given a 2-month extension for time to file. Answer (D) is incorrect. An extension request using Form 4868 may be filed electronically.

19. Mr. and Mrs. X plan to file a joint return for 2012. Neither is over 65 or blind, nor do they have any dependents. What is the amount of gross income required before they must file a return?

A. $11,900

B. $20,650

C. $15,700

D. $19,500

Answer (D) is correct.

REQUIRED: The minimum amount of gross income for which a joint return must be filed when there are no dependents.

DISCUSSION: In general, a return must be filed if a taxpayer's gross income equals or exceeds the sum of the personal exemption to which (s)he is entitled plus the standard deduction amount applicable to the taxpayer's filing status [Publication 501 and Sec. 6012(a)(1)]. Sec. 151 allows a $3,800 exemption for each taxpayer in 2012. For a joint return, the standard deduction is $11,900 in 2012, and no additional standard deductions are allowed for taxpayers who are not over age 65 or blind. The couple must file a return if their gross income equals or exceeds $19,500 ($11,900 + $3,800 + $3,800).

Answer (A) is incorrect. Personal exemptions are included in the gross income limit. Answer (B) is incorrect. There is no additional standard deduction. Answer (C) is incorrect. Both taxpayer personal exemptions are included in the gross income limit.

20. All of the following concerning extension of time to file are correct except

A. An automatic 6-month extension can be requested by filing Form 4868.

B. If the required payment is made by credit card by the regular due date for the return, the return can be filed any time before the 6-month extension period ends.

C. Requesting an automatic 6-month extension before the regular due date for the return postpones the requirement to make payment of any tax due.

D. A U.S. citizen or resident who is on military or naval duty outside the U.S. (or Puerto Rico) on April 15 is given an automatic 2-month extension without the necessity of filing Form 4868.

Answer (C) is correct.

REQUIRED: The incorrect statement regarding the extension of time to file.

DISCUSSION: An individual who is required to file an income tax return is allowed an automatic 6-month extension of time to file the return by filing Form 4868. However, no extension of time is allowed for payment of the tax due. A taxpayer desiring an extension of time to file his/her tax return and avoid the failure to pay penalty must file Form 4868, accompanied by the payment of tax estimated to be owed for the year and not yet paid, by the normal due date of the tax return (Publication 17).

Answer (A) is incorrect. An automatic extension is available by either filing Form 4868 or using a credit card to make the required tax payment by the due date of the return. The taxpayer may file the return any time before the 6-month extension period ends. Answer (B) is incorrect. It is a correct statement concerning extension of time to file. Answer (D) is incorrect. It is a true statement concerning citizens or residents outside the U.S. or Puerto Rico who are on military or naval duty. Additionally, filing Form 4868 during the 2 months will allow another 4-month extension.

1.4 Personal Exemptions

21. Jill and John, married filing jointly, have provided more than 50% of the support for two minor children and Jill's mother. The children each had interest income of less than $700. Jill's mother received a taxable pension of $2,500, dividends of $1,500 and interest of $1,000. How many exemptions can the taxpayers claim, including themselves, on their 2012 tax return?

A. 3

B. 5

C. 4

D. 2

Answer (C) is correct.

REQUIRED: The correct number of exemptions.

DISCUSSION: Jill and John each receive an exemption and receive one exemption for each dependent they claim. The children meet the definition of "qualifying child." There are five requirements that a qualifying relative must meet to be classified as a dependent of the taxpayer.

1. The taxpayer must provide more than 50% of the dependent's support.
2. The dependent must earn less than the exemption or be the taxpayer's child that meets one of the following requirements:
   a. Is under age 19
   b. Is under age 24 and full-time student
3. The dependent must be related to or reside with the taxpayer.
4. If the dependent is married, (s)he must not file a joint return.
5. The dependent must be a U.S. citizen, national, resident, or must reside in Canada or Mexico. (See Publication 17.)

Answer (A) is incorrect. Three exemptions include three dependents, but neither of the taxpayers. Jill's mother should not be included because she earned more than the $3,800 exemption amount. Answer (B) is incorrect. Five exemptions includes all the members of the household. Jill's mother should not be included because she earned more than the $3,800 exemption amount. Answer (D) is incorrect. It does not include any exemptions for dependents, and both of the children qualify as dependents.

22. In meeting the "gross income" test for claiming his father as a dependent, a taxpayer had to consider the income received by his father. This income included gross rents of $4,000 (expenses were $2,000), mutual fund municipal bond interest of $1,200, corporate bond interest of $1,000, dividends of $1,400, wages of $2,000, and Social Security of $4,000. What is the father's gross income for dependency test purposes?

A. $2,000

B. $8,400

C. $9,600

D. $11,600

Answer (B) is correct.

REQUIRED: The gross income amount that is included in calculations for the "gross income" test for claiming a dependent.

DISCUSSION: Gross income used for the test of dependency is defined in Sec. 61 and Publication 501. It is all income except that specifically excluded in the code. Some of the exclusions are listed in Sec. 101-139. A few examples of income that are excluded from gross income are nontaxable scholarships, tax-exempt bond interest, and nontaxable Social Security benefits.

Answer (A) is incorrect. This amount only includes wages. It excludes gross income from rent, corporate bond interest, and dividends, which should also be included. Answer (C) is incorrect. This amount also includes tax-exempt bond interest, which should not be included. Answer (D) is incorrect. It includes the tax-exempt bond interest, Social Security benefits, and expenses from the rent income. The former two are not part of gross income. The latter is a part of adjusted gross income deductions.

23. John and Joanne are the sole support of the following individuals, all U.S. citizens, none of whom lives with them. None of these individuals files a joint return or has any gross income.

Jennie, John's mother
Julie, Joanne's stepmother
Jonathan, father of John's first wife

How many exemptions for dependents may John and Joanne claim on their joint return?

A. 3

B. 2

C. 1

D. 0

Answer (A) is correct.

REQUIRED: The number of exemptions to which the taxpayer is entitled.

DISCUSSION: To qualify for the dependency exemption, the taxpayer must provide over 50% of the support of a U.S. citizen who meets certain relationship tests stated in Sec. 152(a). Sec. 152 allows dependency exemptions for fathers, mothers, stepfathers, and stepmothers. Relationships established by marriage are not ended by death or divorce (Publication 501). Thus, each of the individuals listed qualifies under the relationship test of Sec. 152.

24. In meeting the gross income test for claiming his father as a dependent, Doug considered the income received by his father. This income included gross rents of $4,000 (expenses were $2,000), municipal bond interest of $1,200, dividends of $1,400, and Social Security of $4,000. What is Doug's father's gross income for dependency test purposes?

A. $3,400

B. $5,400

C. $9,400

D. $8,600

Answer (B) is correct.

REQUIRED: The income included in the computation of gross income for the purposes of meeting the gross income dependency test.

DISCUSSION: Gross income defined for the purposes of the gross income dependency test is all income that is received, but is not exempt from tax. In addition, any expenses from rental property should not be deducted for the purposes of this computation. Any tax-exempt income, such as Social Security, is not included in gross income for this purpose (Publication 501). Doug should only consider the gross rents and the dividends in the computation of gross income from his father for the purposes of the gross income for dependency test. Thus, the total income of Doug's father is $5,400 ($4,000 + $1,400).

Answer (A) is incorrect. Expenses from the rental income should not be deducted for the purposes of the gross income for dependency test. Answer (C) is incorrect. Social Security is considered tax-exempt income and should not be included in gross income for dependency test purposes. Answer (D) is incorrect. Municipal bond interest and Social Security are considered tax-exempt income and should not be included in gross income for dependency test purposes. In addition, the expenses from rental activity should not be deducted from the gross rents.

25. Luis and Rosa, citizens of Costa Rica, moved in 2010 to the United States, where they both lived and worked. In 2012, they provided the total support for their four young children (all under the age of 10). Two children lived with Luis and Rosa in the U.S., one child lived with his aunt in Mexico, and one child lived with her grandmother in Costa Rica. None of the children earned any income. All of the children were citizens of Costa Rica. The child in Mexico was a resident of Mexico, and the child in Costa Rica was a resident of Costa Rica. How many total exemptions (personal exemptions plus exemptions for dependents) may Luis and Rosa claim on their 2012 joint income tax return?

A. 2

B. 4

C. 5

D. 6

Answer (C) is correct.

REQUIRED: The total number of exemptions that may be claimed.

DISCUSSION: In order to qualify as a dependent, an individual must be a citizen, national, or resident of the United States or a resident of Canada or Mexico at some time during the calendar year in which the tax year of the taxpayer begins (Publication 501). Therefore, Luis and Rosa may claim themselves, the two children living in the United States, and the child living in Mexico as dependents for a total of five exemptions.

Answer (A) is incorrect. The two children living in the U.S. and the child living in Mexico qualify as dependents. Answer (B) is incorrect. The child living in Mexico qualifies as a dependent. Answer (D) is incorrect. The child living in Costa Rica does not qualify as a dependent.

26. All of the following are true except

A. A brother-in-law must live with the taxpayer the entire year to be claimed as a dependent even if the other tests are met.

B. A son, age 21, was a full-time student who earned $3,900 from his part-time job. The money was used to buy a car. Even though he earned $3,900, his parents can claim him as a dependent if the other exemption tests were met.

C. For each person claimed as a dependent, the Social Security number, adoption taxpayer identification number, or individual taxpayer identification number must be listed.

D. If a married person files a separate return, (s)he can take an exemption for his/her spouse if the spouse had no gross income and was not the dependent of another taxpayer.

Answer (A) is correct.

REQUIRED: The false statement regarding the relationship requirement.

DISCUSSION: The relationship requirement is satisfied by existence of an extended (by blood) or immediate (by blood, adoption, or marriage) relationship. The relationship need be present to only one of the two married persons who file a joint return. Any relationship established by marriage is not treated as ended by divorce or by death. An individual must satisfy either a relationship or a residence requirement but does not have to satisfy both (Publication 501).

Answer (B) is incorrect. Gross income of the individual (to be claimed as a dependent) must be less than the amount of the dependency exemption ($3,800 for 2012). However, this test does not apply to a child of the claimant who is either under 19 years of age or a student under 24 years of age. Answer (C) is incorrect. For each person claimed as a dependent, the Social Security number, adoption taxpayer identification number, or individual taxpayer identification number must be listed. Answer (D) is incorrect. If a married person files a separate return, (s)he can take an exemption for his/her spouse if the spouse had no gross income and was not the dependent of another taxpayer.

27. Sec. 152 of the Code contains two sets of tests, "qualifying child" and "qualifying relative," either of which may be applied to determine whether an individual has dependency status and may therefore be claimed as an exemption by a taxpayer. Which of the following is not a test under both classifications?

A. Citizenship or residency test.

B. Principal place of abode test.

C. Joint return test.

D. Gross income test.

Answer (D) is correct.

REQUIRED: The test that is not a criterion for determining dependency.

DISCUSSION: The four tests under the "qualifying child" classification are (1) relationship, (2) age, (3) principal place of abode, and (4) support. The four tests under the "qualifying relative" classification are (1) relationship, (2) gross income, (3) support, and (4) dependency. Both the qualifying child and qualifying relative tests require that the dependent not file a joint return, meet the citizenship or resident requirement, and provide his/her taxpayer identification number. The gross income test only applies to the qualifying relative (Publication 501).

Answer (A) is incorrect. The citizenship/residency test is in both lists. Answer (B) is incorrect. Principal place of abode is one of the tests for qualifying child. Answer (C) is incorrect. The joint return test is required of both.

28. Holly and Harp Oaks were divorced in 2011. The divorce decree was silent regarding the exemption for their 12-year-old daughter, June, in 2012. Holly has legal custody of her daughter and did not sign a statement releasing the exemption. Holly earned $8,000, and Harp earned $80,000. June had a paper route and earned $4,000. June lived with Harp 4 months of the year and with Holly 8 months. Who may claim the exemption for June in 2012?

A. June may, since she had gross income over $3,800 and files her own return.

B. Since June lived with both Holly and Harp during the year, they both may claim her as an exemption.

C. Holly may, since she has legal custody and physical custody for more than half the year.

D. Harp may, since he earned more than Holly and therefore is presumed to have provided more than 50% of June's support.

Answer (C) is correct.

REQUIRED: The taxpayer who may claim the personal exemption on the child of divorced parents.

DISCUSSION: A divorced or separated individual need not meet the support test if (s)he and the (ex-)spouse met the following conditions:

1. Provided more than 50% of the support
2. Had (between them) custody for more than 50% of the year
3. Lived apart for the last half of the year
4. Did not have a multiple support agreement in effect

The parent having custody for more than 50% of the year is entitled to the exemption. But the exemption amount may be allocated to the noncustodial parent if there is an agreement signed by both parents and attached to the noncustodial parent's return. Since there was no agreement or statement that would allow Harp to claim the personal exemption and Holly has custody for the majority of the year, Holly may claim the personal exemption for June (Publication 501).

Answer (A) is incorrect. Since June is under 19, she qualifies as a dependent of her parents regardless of her income. Answer (B) is incorrect. Only one personal exemption may be claimed per individual, thus only one parent may claim the exemption for June. Answer (D) is incorrect. Without an agreement giving Harp the right to claim the personal exemption for his daughter, he may not do so because he did not have custody of her for the majority of the year.

29. Under Pete's divorce decree, he must pay $500 a month to Laura, his former spouse, for the support of their two children. In 2011, he paid $5,500 instead of the $6,000 he was required to pay. In 2012, he paid $6,000 child support for 2012 and $500 towards child support he neglected to pay in 2011. For purposes of determining whether Pete may claim his children as dependents, which of the following statements accurately represents the amount of support attributable to each year?

A. $5,500 for 2011; $6,500 for 2012.

B. $6,000 for 2011; $6,000 for 2012.

C. $5,500 for 2011; $6,000 for 2012.

D. $5,500 for 2011; $6,000 for 2012; $500 for 2010.

Answer (C) is correct.

REQUIRED: The amount Pete can claim as support to pass the dependency support test.

DISCUSSION: A taxpayer must furnish one-half of the total support provided during the calendar year before claiming an exemption for a dependent under the qualifying relative rules. Amounts received as arrearages in payment for support of a child for a previous year are not considered contributions in the current year in determining whether the husband furnished more than half of the support for the taxable year. There are three exceptions to the rule about claiming the exemption: first, when there is a multiple support agreement; second, when a parent releases his/her right to the dependency exemption with Form 8332; and finally, when the exception applies to certain pre-1985 divorce decrees (Publication 501).

Authors' Note: The amount Pete pays each year is irrelevant if the children are qualifying children of the former spouse and he has Form 8332 signed by his former spouse.

Answer (A) is incorrect. Pete cannot include prior-period child support payments to determine the amount of dependency support. Answer (B) is incorrect. Pete did not provide $6,000 of support in the prior year. Answer (D) is incorrect. Pete cannot include prior-period child support payments to determine the amount of dependency support.

30. Mrs. Brown had taxable income of $600, Social Security benefits of $1,800, and tax-exempt interest of $200. She used all of these amounts for her own support. Her son paid the rest of her support. Which of the following amounts of support paid by her son would meet the support test to allow him to claim Mrs. Brown as a dependent?

A. $900

B. $1,800

C. $2,100

D. $2,700

Answer (D) is correct.

REQUIRED: The amount of support required to claim someone as a dependent.

DISCUSSION: A dependent under the qualifying relative rules is defined in Sec. 152(a), which requires the taxpayer to provide over one-half of the support of the individual. Mrs. Brown's son must give her more than $2,600 ($600 + $1,800 + $200) of support in order to satisfy this requirement (Publication 501).

31. With regard to claiming a dependent, all of the following statements are true except

A. A person does not meet the member-of-the-household test if at any time during the tax year the relationship between the taxpayer and that person violates local law.

B. A person who died during the year, but was a member of your household until death, will meet the member-of-the-household test.

C. To meet the citizenship test, a person must be a U.S. citizen or resident, or a resident of Canada or Mexico.

D. In calculating a person's total support, do not include tax-exempt income used to support that person.

Answer (D) is correct.

REQUIRED: The statement regarding dependents that is false.

DISCUSSION: A taxpayer must furnish more than one-half of the total support provided during the calendar year before claiming an exemption for a dependent. The support may come from taxable income, tax-exempt receipts, or loans (Publication 501).

Answer (A) is incorrect. The relationship test is failed if the relationship is in violation of local law. Answer (B) is incorrect. A full exemption is allowed in the year of death. Answer (C) is incorrect. Residents of Canada and Mexico qualify as dependents regardless of their citizenships.

32. All of the following are included in calculating the total support of a dependent except

A. Child care even if the taxpayer is claiming the credit for the expense.

B. Amounts veterans receive under the GI bill for tuition and allowances while in school.

C. Medical insurance benefits, including basic and supplementary Medicare benefits received.

D. Tax-exempt income, savings, or borrowed money used to support a person.

Answer (C) is correct.

REQUIRED: The item not taken into account in determining total support of a dependent.

DISCUSSION: A taxpayer must provide over one-half of the support for a person to be considered a dependent [Sec. 152(a)]. The term support includes food, shelter, clothing, medical and dental care, education, and other items contributing to the individual's maintenance and livelihood [Reg. 1.152-1(a)(2)]. Although medical care is an item of support, medical insurance benefits are not included. Medical insurance premiums are included (Publication 501).

Answer (A) is incorrect. Child care contributes to the maintenance and livelihood of the individual and is considered support. Answer (B) is incorrect. Education contributes to the maintenance and livelihood of the individual and is considered support. Answer (D) is incorrect. All funds used to support a person, whether tax exempt, borrowed, or from savings, contribute to the maintenance and livelihood of the individual and are considered support.

33. In the current year, Sam Dunn provided more than half the support for his wife, his father's brother, and his cousin. Sam's wife was the only relative who was a member of Sam's household. None of the relatives had any income, nor did any of them file an individual or a joint return. All of these relatives are U.S. citizens. Which of these relatives should be claimed as a dependent or dependents on Sam's current-year joint return?

A. Only his wife.

B. Only his father's brother.

C. Only his cousin.

D. His wife, his father's brother, and his cousin.

Answer (B) is correct.

REQUIRED: The relative(s) who could be claimed as a dependent on the taxpayer's return.

DISCUSSION: Sec. 152(a) lists those relatives who may be claimed as dependents if they receive over half of their support from the taxpayer. The taxpayer's uncle is included in this list, so Sam's father's brother may be claimed by him as a dependent (Publication 501).

Answer (A) is incorrect. Sam's wife is entitled to her own personal exemption and is not classified as a dependent. Answer (C) is incorrect. Sec. 152(a) does not include cousins in its list of relatives, and Sam's cousin was not a member of the household. Answer (D) is incorrect. Sam's wife is entitled to her own personal exemption and is not classified as a dependent. Also, Sec. 152(a) does not include cousins in its list of relatives, and Sam's cousin was not a member of the household.

34. Paula filed a separate return and paid more than half the cost of keeping up her home. Her spouse did not live in her home during the last 6 months of the tax year. Which one of the following dependents would qualify Paula to file as head of household?

A. Paula's son, who lived with her but was absent from her home for 9 months during the year while attending boarding school.

B. Paula's uncle, whom she can claim as a dependent and whose main home during the current year was a home for the elderly for which Paula paid more than one-half the cost.

C. Paula's married son, who could properly be claimed as a dependent on his father's return only.

D. Paula's sister, whom Paula can claim as a dependent and who lived with Paula until she died in May.

Answer (A) is correct.

REQUIRED: The person who qualifies as the taxpayer's dependent for head of household filing status purposes.

DISCUSSION: In determining if a married taxpayer is considered unmarried and thus qualifies for head of household filing status, the taxpayer's home must be, for more than half the year, the main home of the taxpayer's child, stepchild, or adopted child whom the taxpayer can properly claim as a dependent. However, the taxpayer can still meet this test if the taxpayer cannot claim the exemption only because the noncustodial parent is allowed to claim the exemption. Time spent at school is deemed temporary and does not apply to the 6-month test (Publication 501).

Answer (B) is incorrect. The special rule regarding a qualifying person states that a taxpayer with a dependent parent (not uncle) qualifies even if the parent does not live with the taxpayer. Answer (C) is incorrect. Paula cannot claim her son as a dependent; she cannot qualify as a head of household. Answer (D) is incorrect. Paula's sister is not a child, stepchild, or adopted child.

1.5 Returns of Dependents

35. When will a minor's income be taxed at his/her parent's rate?

A. When a child has any income and is under age 18.

B. When a child has net unearned income regardless of his/her age.

C. When a child has unearned income and is under age 18.

D. When a child has net unearned income and is under age 18 with at least one living parent.

Answer (D) is correct.

REQUIRED: The circumstances that require a minor's parent's rates to be used to tax a minor's income.

DISCUSSION: Sec. 1(g) provides in general that unearned income of certain minor children will be taxed to the child at the top rate of the parents. For this purpose, a minor is any child under 18 years of age at the end of the tax year, or 18 (under 24 and a full-time student) and not having earned income in excess of one-half of his/her support and has at least one living parent. The provision applies to net unearned income, which is specially defined (Publication 17).

Answer (A) is incorrect. The child must have net unearned income. Answer (B) is incorrect. Income is taxed at the parent's rate only if the child

1. Is under 18 or
2. Is 18 or a full-time student under 24 and does not have earned income in excess of one-half of his/her support.

Answer (C) is incorrect. The child must have net unearned income, not just unearned income.

36. Marcy, age 12, earned $400 from babysitting during 2012. Her parents claim her as a dependent. She also had interest and dividends of $2,500 during the year. She did not itemize deductions. What is her net unearned income for 2012?

A. $2,900

B. $2,500

C. $1,550

D. $600

Answer (D) is correct.

REQUIRED: The amount of a child's net unearned income.

DISCUSSION: Net unearned income is defined in Sec. 1(g)(4) as unearned income less the sum of (1) $950, plus (2) the greater of $950 or, if the child itemizes, the amount of allowable deductions directly connected with the production of the unearned income. However, unearned income may not exceed the child's taxable income (Publication 929). Marcy's unearned income consists of $2,500 of interest and dividends. Her net unearned income is $600 [$2,500 – ($950 + $950)].

Answer (A) is incorrect. This amount is earned income plus interest and dividends, which are unearned income items. Answer (B) is incorrect. This amount is unearned income, not net unearned income. Answer (C) is incorrect. An additional $950 should be subtracted to obtain net unearned income.

1.6 Nonresident and Dual-Status Aliens

37. Jean Blanc, a citizen and resident of Canada, is a professional hockey player with a U.S. hockey club. Under Jean's contract, he received $68,500 for 165 days of play during the current year. Of the 165 days, 132 days were spent performing services in the United States and 33 playing hockey in Canada. What is the amount to be included in Jean's gross income on his Form 1040NR?

A. $0

B. $34,250

C. $54,800

D. $68,500

Answer (C) is correct.

REQUIRED: The U.S gross income of a nonresident alien who performs services in the U.S. for part of the year.

DISCUSSION: A nonresident alien must include in U.S. gross income that income from U.S. sources effectively connected with the conduct of a trade or business in the United States (Sec. 871). Under Sec. 864, the performance of personal services in the U.S. constitutes a trade or business in the United States. If income is derived therefrom, it is considered to be from a U.S. source (Publication 17). According to the IRS and the courts, services of a professional hockey player are allocable to U.S. and non-U.S. time periods during the preseason training camp, the regular season, and post-season playoffs, but not the off-season. Therefore, Jean must include the portion of his income that is attributable to the performance of personal services in the U.S., i.e., 80% (132 ÷ 165 days). Eighty percent of $68,500 is $54,800, which must be reported as U.S. income.

38. Mr. H is a foreign student studying for a degree in the United States. There is no income tax treaty between his country and the United States. During the 9 months of the school year, Mr. H is employed part-time by a corporation incorporated in his home country doing business in the United States. During summer vacation, Mr. H returns home, where he is employed by the same company. Which of the following statements is true regarding U.S. taxes?

A. All income is taxable on a U.S. tax return.

B. All income is excludable and filing a U.S. tax return is not required.

C. Only income earned for services in the United States is taxable.

D. All income is taxable on a U.S. tax return and credit is allowed for foreign taxes paid on his summer income.

Answer (C) is correct.

REQUIRED: The U.S. taxation of compensation earned both in the U.S. and abroad by a foreign student in the United States.

DISCUSSION: Under Sec. 871, income from U.S. sources effectively connected with a U.S. trade or business must be included in a nonresident alien's U.S. gross income. The performance of personal services in the United States constitutes a trade or business in the United States (Publication 17 and Sec. 864). Therefore, the income earned by Mr. H while employed part-time in the United States is taxable.

Answer (A) is incorrect. A nonresident alien has no U.S. income when the personal services income is earned outside the United States and is not connected with the conduct of a U.S. trade or business. Answer (B) is incorrect. The income earned in the United States is taxable. Answer (D) is incorrect. A nonresident alien has no U.S. income when the personal services income is earned outside the United States and is not connected with the conduct of a U.S. trade or business.

39. A nonresident alien received a $50,000 scholarship from a U.S. corporation to go to a gymnastic camp in the individual's resident country, which has a 20% flat tax. How much U.S. tax must be paid on the scholarship?

A. $0

B. $15,000

C. $10,000

D. $6,650

Answer (A) is correct.

REQUIRED: The tax on a scholarship given to a nonresidential alien.

DISCUSSION: A scholarship, fellowship, grant, etc. received by a nonresident alien for activities conducted outside of the U.S. is treated as foreign source income (see Publication 515). Because the scholarship will not be treated as U.S. source income, there is no U.S. tax.

Answer (B) is incorrect. A 30% rate could apply if it were U.S. source income. Answer (C) is incorrect. The 20% tax is what the foreign country might assess. Answer (D) is incorrect. FICA tax is applied against U.S. source income at a rate of 13.3%, not against foreign source income to a foreigner.

Visit the GLEIM® website for free updates,

which are available until the next edition is published.

gleim.com/updates

STUDY UNIT TWO
GROSS INCOME

(21 pages of outline)

The following formula is an overview of the steps to compute federal income tax liability for individual taxpayers. This study unit presents items that are included in gross income (GI), income items that are excluded from gross income, and income items for which the Internal Revenue Code provides a partial exclusion from gross income.

Individual Income Tax

FORMULA

GROSS INCOME
– Sec. 62 Deductions (above the line)
= **ADJUSTED GROSS INCOME**
– Greater of Itemized Deductions or Standard Deduction
– Personal Exemptions
= **TAXABLE INCOME**
× Tax Rate
= **GROSS TAX Liability**
– Credits
= **NET TAX Liability or Refund Receivable**

2.1 GROSS INCOME

The IRC (Internal Revenue Code) defines gross income as all income from whatever source derived except as otherwise provided.

1. Section 61(a) enumerates types of income that constitute gross income. The list is not exhaustive.
   a. Compensation for services, including fees, commissions, and fringe benefits
   b. Gross income derived from business
   c. Gains derived from dealings in property
   d. Interest
   e. Rents
   f. Royalties
   g. Dividends
   h. Alimony and separate maintenance payments
   i. Annuities
   j. Income from life insurance and endowment contracts
   k. Pensions
   l. Income from discharge of indebtedness
   m. Distributive share of partnership gross income
   n. Income in respect of a decedent (income earned but not received before death)
   o. Income from an interest in an estate or trust

2. Other types of income also constitute gross income unless a statute specifically excludes them.
   a. This specifically includes income derived from all sources regardless of whether the taxpayer receives a Form W-2 or Form 1099.
3. Items are included in income based on the method of accounting used by the taxpayer.
   a. The cash method of accounting includes income when constructively received.
   b. The accrual method of accounting reports income when
      1) All events have occurred fixing the right to receive the income.
      2) The amount can be determined with reasonable accuracy.
   c. The accrual method of accounting is required when there are inventories.
   d. The hybrid method allows a business to use the cash method for the portion of the business that is not required to be on the accrual method.
   e. Income is reported when it can be estimated with reasonable accuracy. Adjustments are made in a later year for any differences between the actual amount and the previously reported amounts.

Constructive Receipt

4. Income, although not actually in a taxpayer's possession, is constructively received in the taxable year during which it is credited to his/her account, set apart for him/her, or otherwise made available so that (s)he may draw upon it at any time, or so that (s)he could have drawn upon it during the taxable year if notice of intention to withdraw had been given (Reg. 1.451-2).
   a. A check received in the mail is considered to be income on that date, whether or not it is cashed.
   b. To determine receipt of income from securities trades, the trade date, rather than the settlement date, should be used.
   c. However, income is not constructively received if the taxpayer's control of its receipt is subject to substantial limitations or restrictions.

Claim-of-Right Doctrine

5. A taxpayer receiving income under a claim of right and without restrictions on its use or disposition is taxed on that income in the year received even though the right to retain the income is not yet fixed or the taxpayer may later be required to return it.

Compensation for Services

6. All compensation for personal services is gross income. The form of payment is irrelevant.
   a. If services are paid for in property, its fair market value at the time of receipt is gross income.
   b. The amount included in income becomes the basis in the property.
   c. If services were performed for a price agreed on beforehand, the price will be accepted as the FMV of the property only if there is no evidence to the contrary.
   d. Gross income of an employee includes any amount paid by an employer for a liability (including taxes) or expense of the employee.
   e. Income from self-employment is included in gross income. The director of a corporation is considered self-employed, and all fees are included in gross income.
   f. Reported and unreported compensation (e.g., tips) is gross income.
      1) Food service employers required to allocate tip income use 8% of food and drink sales to determine the allocable amount.

`(Food/drink sales × 8%) - All employee's reported tips = Amount to be allocated`

Prepaid Income

7. Generally, prepaid income is taxable in the year received whether the taxpayer is on the cash or accrual method of accounting.
   a. Prepayments for merchandise inventory are not income until the merchandise is shipped.

Bartering

8. Bartered services or goods are included in GI at the fair market value of the item(s) received in exchange for the services.

Assignment of Income

9. Gross income includes income attributable to a person even though the income is received by other persons. This doctrine imposes the tax on income on those who earn it, produce the right to receive it, enjoy the benefit of it when paid, or control property that is its source.

EXAMPLE

Swift, a life insurance salesperson, directs his employer to pay his commissions to his daughter. The commissions paid to Swift's daughter are gross income to Swift.

   a. The doctrine applies to income earned by personal services or derived from property.

EXAMPLE

Taxpayer makes a gift of interest earned on securities to her 20-year-old daughter who attends college. The interest is gross income to Taxpayer.

   b. Assignment of an income-producing asset is effective to shift the gross income to the assignee.

EXAMPLE

Taxpayer gives the underlying securities to her 20-year-old daughter. Interest earned after the transfer is gross income to the daughter.

   c. Effective assignment requires that the transfer of property be complete and bona fide, with no control retained over either the property or the income it produces, and that the transfer take place before the income is actually earned.

Alimony

10. Alimony and separate maintenance payments are included in the gross income of the recipient (payee) and are deducted from the gross income of the payor.
   a. A payment is considered to be alimony (even if paid to a third party, e.g., home mortgage) when it is
      1) Paid in cash
      2) Paid pursuant to a written divorce or separation instrument
      3) Not designated as other than alimony
      4) Terminated at death of recipient
      5) Not paid to a member of the same household
      6) Not paid to a spouse with whom the taxpayer is filing a joint return

Child Support

b. Child support payments are an exclusion from the gross income of the recipient and are not deductible by the payor. These payments are not alimony.

1) If the divorce or separation instrument specifies payments of both alimony and child support, and only partial payments are made, then the partial payments are considered to be child support until this obligation is fully paid, and any excess is then treated as alimony.

2) If the payment amount is to be reduced based on a contingency relating to a child (e.g., attaining a certain age, marrying), the amount of the reduction will be treated as child support.

Property Settlement

c. Property settlements, which are simply a division of property, are not treated as alimony.

1) Property transferred to a spouse or former spouse incident to a divorce is treated as a transfer by gift, which is specifically excluded from gross income.

a) "Incident to a divorce" means a transfer of property within 1 year after the date the marriage ceases or a transfer of property related to the cessation of the marriage.

b) This exclusion does not apply if the spouse or former spouse is a nonresident alien.

Alimony Recapture

d. Current tax law includes a recapture provision, which is intended to prevent large property settlements from being treated as alimony. Recapture occurs if payments significantly decrease in the second or third year after a divorce. The following steps show how to calculate the final amount of recapture:

1) Second-year alimony recapture is equal to

$$\text{2nd-year alimony} - (\$15{,}000 + \text{3rd-year alimony})$$

2) First-year alimony recapture is equal to

$$\text{1st-year alimony} - \left[\frac{(\text{2nd-year alimony} - \text{2nd-year recapture}) + \text{3rd-year alimony}}{2} + \$15{,}000\right]$$

3) Both the first-year and second-year recapture amounts are included in the payor's gross income and deducted from the payee's gross income in Year 3.

EXAMPLE

After Lisa divorced Jed in Year 1, she paid him $60,000 of alimony in Year 1, $40,000 in Year 2, and $10,000 in Year 3. Excess alimony in Year 2 was $15,000 [$40,000 – ($15,000 + $10,000)]. Excess alimony in Year 1 was $60,000 – [($40,000 – $15,000 + $10,000) ÷ 2 + $15,000], or $27,500. In Year 3, Lisa must include in gross income the total of Year 1 and Year 2 excess alimony, or $42,500. Jed is also allowed a deduction of the same amount.

Annuity Contracts

11. The portion of amounts received under an annuity contract for which a statute does not provide an exclusion is gross income. Taxpayers are permitted to recover the cost of the annuity (the price paid) tax-free.

401(k) Plans

12. Employer contributions generally are not included in the income of the participant.

Income from Life Insurance and Endowment Contracts

13. Proceeds received due to the death of the insured are generally excluded from gross income.
    a. Interest paid on the proceeds of a policy that is paid out over time is gross income to the beneficiary.
    b. The amount excluded from gross income of an applicable policy holder with respect to an employer-owned life insurance contract is not to exceed the premiums and other amounts paid by the policyholder for the life insurance policy.
        1) The income inclusion applies to all contracts issued after August 17, 2006.
        2) The income inclusion rule does not apply to a member of the insured's family, to any individual who is the designated beneficiary of the insured under the contract (other than an applicable policy holder), to a trust established for the benefit of the insured family or a designated beneficiary, or to the estate of the insured.

Debt Discharge

14. Discharge of indebtedness can result in gross income.
    a. Gross income includes the cancelation of indebtedness when a debt is canceled in whole or in part for consideration.
        1) If a creditor cancels a debt (Form 1099C) in consideration for services performed by the debtor, the debtor must recognize income in the amount of the debt as compensation for his/her services.
        2) Income from discharge of indebtedness is reported on the same form as for any other income (i.e., Schedule C for a sole proprietor).
    b. Generally, a corporation has gross income from discharge of indebtedness when it satisfies a debt by transferring its own corporate stock to the creditor.
        1) The amount of gross income is the amount by which the principal of the debt exceeds the value of the transferred stock, plus the value of any other property transferred.
    c. If a creditor gratuitously cancels a debt, the amount forgiven is treated as a gift (the IRC generally provides for exclusion of gifts from gross income).
    d. Exception. Gross income does not include discharges that
        1) Occur in bankruptcy, except the stock for debt transfer as described in item b. above.
        2) Occur when the debtor is insolvent, but not in bankruptcy.
            a) The amount excluded is the smaller of the debt canceled or the amount of insolvency, based on the excess of liabilities over the FMV of assets on the date of debt cancelation.
        3) Are related to qualified farm indebtedness.
        4) Are a discharge of qualified real property business indebtedness.
        5) Are related to principal residence indebtedness. The basis of the residence is reduced by the excluded income where the taxpayer retains the residence.

e. When a taxpayer excludes discharge of indebtedness under d.1), 2), or 3) on the previous page, the taxpayer must reduce his/her tax attributes in the following order:

1) NOLs
2) General business credit
3) Minimum tax credit
4) Capital loss carryovers
5) Basis reductions

NOTE: The taxpayer may first elect to decrease the basis of depreciable property.

f. The Mortgage Forgiveness Debt Relief Act permanently excludes discharges of up to $2 million ($1 million if married filing separately) of indebtedness, which is secured by a principal residence and which is incurred in the acquisition, construction, or substantial improvement of the principal residence.

1) This exclusion applies to discharge of debt occurring after 2006.
2) The amount excluded from gross income reduces the basis of the residence, but not below zero, and only when the taxpayer retains the residence.
3) Principal residence has the same meaning as when used in Section 121.
4) The exclusion does not apply if the discharge is due to any reason not directly related to a decline in the home's value or the taxpayer's financial condition.

Student Loan Forgiveness

g. Federal, state, and/or local government student loan indebtedness may be discharged if the former student engages in certain employment, e.g., in a specified location, for a specified period, for a specified employer.

1) Such income from discharge of indebtedness is excluded from gross income.

Nonbusiness Debt

h. When a canceled debt is a nonbusiness debt (e.g., discount for early payment of a mortgage loan), it is to be reported as other income on line 21 of Form 1040.

Social Security Benefits

15. Social Security benefits are generally not taxable unless additional income is received. The gross income inclusion is dependent upon the relation of provisional income (PI) to the base amount (BA) and the adjusted base amount (ABA).

a. PI = Adjusted GI (AGI) + Tax-exempt interest/excluded foreign income + 50% of Social Security benefits.

b. Base amount (BA) means $32,000 if married filing jointly (MFJ); $0 if married filing separately and having lived with spouse at any time during the tax year (MFSLT); or $25,000 for all others.

c. Adjusted base amount (ABA) is the BA plus $12,000 if MFJ, $0 if MFSLT, or $9,000 for all others.

d. If PI < BA, there is no inclusion. If PI falls between BA and ABA, up to 50% of Social Security benefits will be included. If PI > ABA, up to 85% of Social Security benefits will be included.

EXAMPLE

Mr. and Mrs. Slom, both over 65 and filing jointly, received $20,000 in Social Security benefits. Additionally, they reported $30,000 of taxable interest, $15,000 of tax-exempt interest, $18,000 in dividends, and a taxable pension of $16,000. Therefore, their AGI excluding Social Security benefits is $64,000 ($30,000 taxable interest + $18,000 dividends + $16,000 taxable pension payments).

- Provisional income is $89,000 [$64,000 AGI + $15,000 tax-exempt interest + 50% of SS benefits ($10,000)].
- The adjusted base amount is $44,000.
- GI will include $17,000 (85% of SS benefits) since this amount is less than 85% of the excess of PI over the ABA plus the lesser of 50% of the incremental BA ($6,000) or 50% of SS benefits.
- Calculation of included Social Security benefits:

1)	AGI, excluding SS benefits		$64,000
2)	+ Tax-exempt interest/excluded foreign income	+	15,000
3)	= Modified AGI	=	$79,000
4)	+ 50% of SS benefits	+	10,000
5)	= Provisional income (PI)	=	$89,000
6)	– BA ($32,000, $25,000, or $0)	–	32,000
7)	= Excess PI (If < $0, then $0 inclusion)	=	$57,000
8)	– Incremental base amount ($12,000, $9,000, or $0)	–	12,000
9)	= Excess PI	=	$45,000
10)	Smaller of amount in line 7 or 8		12,000
11)	50% of line 10		6,000
12)	Smaller of amount in line 4 or 11		6,000
13)	Multiply line 9 by 85%		38,250
14)	Add lines 12 and 13		44,250
15)	SS benefits × 85%		17,000
16)	Taxable benefits = Smaller of amount in line 14 or 15		17,000

Illegal Activities

16. Income from illegal activities is gross income.

Scholarships

17. Amounts received by an individual as scholarships or fellowships are excluded from gross income to the extent that the individual is a candidate for a degree from a qualified educational institution and the amounts are used for required tuition or fees, books, supplies, or equipment (not personal expenses, such as room and board).
    a. Gross income includes any amount received, e.g., as tuition reduction, in exchange for the performance of services, such as teaching or research.
    b. Generally, a reduction in undergraduate tuition for an employee of a qualified educational organization does not constitute gross income.
    c. Subsistence payments administered by Veteran Affairs are excluded from gross income.

Prizes and Awards

18. If the prize or award is in a form other than money, the amount of gross income is the FMV of the property. The honoree may avoid inclusion by rejecting the prize or award. Some prizes and awards are excludable.
    a. Certain employee achievement awards may qualify for exclusion from the employee's gross income as a de minimis fringe benefit.
        1) An award recipient may exclude the FMV of the prize or award from his/her gross income if
            a) The amount received is in recognition of religious, scientific, charitable, or similar meritorious achievement;
            b) The recipient is selected without action on his/her part;
            c) The receipt of the award is not conditioned on substantial future services; and
            d) The amount is paid by the organization making the award to a tax-exempt organization (including a governmental unit) designated by the recipient.
        2) A prize or award may qualify for exclusion as a scholarship.
        3) Employee achievement awards may qualify for exclusion from the recipient employee's GI if they are awarded as part of a meaningful presentation for safety achievement or length of service and
            a) The awards do not exceed $400 (cost to employer) for all nonqualified plan awards or
            b) The awards do not exceed $1,600 (cost to employer) for all qualified plan awards.
        4) Awards in excess of limitations:
            a) If the employer exceeds the cost limitations for the award and loses a portion of the deduction, the employee's exclusion from income is only preserved in part. In this case, the employee must include in his/her gross income the greater of
                i) An amount equal to the portion of the cost to the employer of the award that was not allowable as a deduction to the employer (as opposed to the excess of the fair market value of the award) or
                ii) The amount by which the fair market value of the award exceeds the maximum dollar amount allowable as a deduction to the employer.

EXAMPLE

Assume that an award cost the employer $500.00, rather than $400.00, and its fair market value is $475.00. In this case, the employer's deduction is limited to $400.00, and the amount includible by the employee in his or her income is $100.00, i.e., the greater of

- The difference between the item's cost and the deduction limitation ($100.00) or
- The amount by which the item's fair market value exceeds the deduction limitation ($75.00).

If the fair market value was $600.00, the amount includible in the employee's income would be $200.

The remaining portion of the fair market value of the award, $375 ($475 – $100), is not included in the employee's gross income.

        5) A qualified plan award is an employee achievement award provided under an established written program that does not discriminate in favor of highly compensated employees.

Unemployment Benefits

19. Unemployment benefits received under a federal or state program, as well as company-financed supplemental plans, are gross income.
    a. Strike benefits received from a union are also included in income.

Compensation for Injury or Sickness

20. Gross income does not include benefits specified that might be received in the form of disability pay, health or accident insurance proceeds, workers' compensation awards, or other "damages" for personal physical injury or physical sickness.
    a. Specifically excluded from gross income are amounts received
        1) Under workers' compensation acts as compensation for personal injuries or sickness
        2) Under an accident and health insurance policy purchased by the taxpayer even if the benefits are a substitute for lost income
        3) By employees as reimbursement for medical care and payments for permanent injury or loss of bodily function under an employer-financed accident or health plan
        4) As a pension, annuity, or similar allowance for personal injuries or sickness resulting from active service in the armed forces of any country
    b. The following are excluded from gross income regardless of whether the damages are received by lawsuits or agreements or as lump sums or periodic payments:
        1) Damages received for personal physical injury or physical sickness
        2) Payments received for emotional distress if an injury has its origin in a physical injury or physical sickness
    c. Compensation for slander of personal, professional, or business reputation is included in gross income.
    d. An in- or out-of-court settlement for lost profits in a business or court-awarded damages is included in gross income.
    e. Punitive damages received are included in gross income, even if in connection with a physical injury or physical sickness.
        1) An amount for both actual and punitive damages must be allocated.
    f. Wrongful death damages can be excluded to the extent they were received on account of a personal injury or sickness.
    g. Damages received solely for emotional distress are included in gross income. These damages include amounts received for claims, such as employment or age discrimination.
    h. Interest earned on an award for personal injuries is included in gross income.

Recovery of Medical Deductions

i. If the taxpayer incurred medical expenses in Year 1, deducted these expenses on his/her Year 1 tax return, and received reimbursement for the same medical expenses in Year 2, the reimbursement is included in gross income on the Year 2 return to the extent of the previous deduction.

Accident and Health Plans

21. Benefits received by an employee under an accident and health plan under which the employer paid the premiums or contributed to an independent fund are excluded from gross income of the employee.
    a. The benefits must be either
        1) Payments made due to permanent injury or loss of bodily functions or
        2) Reimbursement paid to the employee for medical expenses of the employee, spouse, or dependents.
            a) Any reimbursement in excess of medical expenses is included in income.
    b. The plan must not discriminate in favor of highly compensated executives, shareholders, or officers.
    c. Any excess reimbursement over the actual cost of medical expenses may be excluded only to the extent the taxpayer contributed to the plan.

Disability Policies

22. Proceeds from disability insurance policies are tax-free if paid for by the employee.
    a. If the employer contributed to the coverage (employer contributions are excluded), then the amount received must be prorated into taxable and nontaxable amounts.
    b. Payments made from a qualified trust on behalf of a self-employed person are considered employer contributions.
    c. For example, if the employer pays 75% of the insurance premiums of a disability policy, 75% of the proceeds are includible in income.

Employer-Provided Life Insurance

23. Proceeds of a life insurance policy for which the employer paid the premiums are excluded from the employee's gross income. Certain premiums paid by the employer are, however, included in the employee's gross income.
    a. The cost of group term life insurance up to a coverage amount of $50,000 is excluded from the employee's gross income.
        1) The amount included is the premiums representing excess coverage (over $50,000) less any amounts paid by the employee on the insurance policy.

Long-Term Care Coverage

24. Contributions by an employer to an employee's long-term care coverage are nontaxable employee benefits.

Pensions

25. Pensions are most often paid in the form of an annuity. Therefore, the rules for pensions are similar to the rules for annuities. Employees are able to recover their cost tax-free.
    a. The investment in the contract is the amount contributed by the employee in after-tax dollars.
    b. Amounts withdrawn early are treated as a recovery of the employee's contributions (excluded from gross income) and of the employer's contributions (included in gross income).
        1) After all contributions are withdrawn, additional withdrawals are included in gross income.
    c. Persons retired on disability before they reach minimum retirement age must report their taxable disability payments as wages (see Publication 575).

Death Benefits

26. All death benefits received by the beneficiaries or the estate of an employee from, or on behalf of, an employer are included in gross income.
    a. This is for employer-paid death benefits, not to be confused with the death benefits of a life insurance plan provided by an employer.

Rental Value of Parsonage

27. Ministers may exclude from gross income the rental value of a home or a rental allowance to the extent the allowance is used to provide a home, even if deductions are taken for home expenses paid with the allowance. The exclusion is the smaller of
    a. The actual expenditures of the minister for the home,
    b. The amount designated with the employer as a rental allowance, or
    c. The fair rental value of the housing, plus the cost of utilities.

    The parsonage allowance is subject to self-employment taxes. A minister should include any offerings given directly to him/her for church-related functions (e.g., marriages).

Combat Zone Compensation

28. Military officers may exclude compensation up to an amount equal to the highest rate of basic pay at the highest pay grade that enlisted personnel may receive (plus any hostile fire/imminent danger pay).
    a. The exclusion applies only to compensation received while serving in a combat zone or while hospitalized as a result of wounds, disease, or injury incurred in a combat zone.
    b. Military personnel below officer level (i.e., enlisted) are allowed the same exclusion without the cap.

Gifts or Inheritance

29. The IRC provides for exclusion from the gross income of the recipient the value of property acquired by gift or inheritance. A gift is a transfer for less than full or adequate consideration that results from the detached and disinterested generosity of the transferor.
    a. Gift transfers include inter vivos (between the living) gifts and gifts by bequest (of personal property by a will), devise (of real property by a will), and inheritance (under state intestacy law).
    b. Voluntary transfers from employer to employee are presumed to be compensation, not gifts.

Treasure Trove

30. Treasure trove is gross income for the tax year in which it is undisputedly in the taxpayer's possession.

EXAMPLE

Rich purchased an old piano for $500 15 years ago. In the current year, Rich finds $10,000 hidden in the piano. Rich must report the $10,000 as gross income in the current year.

Gambling

31. All gambling winnings are gross income and may require reporting by payor on Form W-2G.
    a. Gambling losses, e.g., nonwinning lottery tickets, are deductible only to the extent of winnings and only as a miscellaneous itemized deduction not subject to the 2% reduction.
    b. Gambling losses over winnings for the taxable year cannot be used as a carryover or carryback to reduce gambling income from other years.

Recovery of Tax Benefit Item

32. The tax benefit rule includes, in gross income, items received for which the taxpayer received a tax benefit in a prior year.

EXAMPLE

Taxpayer writes off bad debt 5 years ago. In the current year, the debtor pays Taxpayer the principal of the debt written off, which must be included in gross income since the deduction 5 years ago reduced the tax liability.

a. Sec. 111 provides for exclusion of amounts recovered during the tax year that were deducted in a prior year to the extent the amount did not reduce income tax.

EXAMPLE

Taxpayer pays $2,000 state income tax and itemizes deductions. Subsequent refunds must be included. However, if Taxpayer used the standard deduction, the refund would not be included.

Reimbursements for Moving Expenses

33. Qualified reimbursements are excluded from gross income. If the reimbursement is not for qualified moving expenses, it is included in gross income.

Adoption Assistance Programs

34. Qualified adoption expenses paid to a third party or reimbursed to an employee by an employer under a written adoption assistance program are excludable from the employee's gross income.

a. An adoption assistance program is a written plan that

1) Benefits employees who qualify under rules set up by the employer that do not favor highly compensated employees or their dependents,
2) Does not pay more than 5% of its payments each year to shareholders or owners of more than 5% of the stock,
3) Provides for adequate notice to employees of their eligibility, and
4) Requires employees to provide reasonable substantiation of qualified expenses that are to be paid or reimbursed.

Adoption Exclusion

b. The maximum exclusion for 2012 is $12,650.

1) The phase-out range for upper income taxpayers is $189,710 to $229,710 for 2012.
2) Adoption expenses must be reduced by an amount used in determining the adoption credit.

c. For a child who is a U.S. citizen or resident, the exclusion is taken in the year the payments were made whether or not the adoption became final.

1) For the adoption of a foreign child, the exclusion cannot be taken until the adoption becomes final.

d. The excluded amount is not subject to income tax withholding. However, the payments are subject to Social Security, Medicare, and federal unemployment taxes.

e. An eligible child must be under 18 years of age or must be physically or mentally incapable of self care.

f. Qualified adoption expenses are reasonable and necessary adoption expenses, including adoption fees, court costs, attorney fees, and other directly related expenses.

1) Expenses that are not eligible for the adoption exclusion include

a) Costs associated with a surrogate parenting arrangement,

b) Expenses incurred in violation of state or federal law, and

c) Expenses incurred in connection with the adoption of a child of the taxpayer's spouse.

Reimbursement for Living Expenses

35. Insurance payments received by a taxpayer whose residence is damaged or destroyed and who must temporarily occupy another residence are excluded. This includes taxpayers with an undamaged residence who are required not to occupy the home due to a disaster.

a. The exclusion is limited to the excess of actual living expenses over normal living expenses.

Reimbursed Employee Expenses

36. If reimbursements equal expenses and the employee makes an accounting of expenses to the employer, the reimbursements are excluded from the employee's gross income, and the employee may not deduct the expenses (accountable plan).

a. This rule also applies if reimbursements exceeding expenses are returned to the employer and the employee substantiates the expenses.

b. If excess reimbursements are not returned or if the employee does not substantiate them, the reimbursements are included in the employee's gross income, and all the expenses are deducted from AGI below-the-line deductions.

1) These expenses are an itemized deduction subject to the 2% floor (nonaccountable plan) on Schedule A.

Employee Housing

37. Employee housing at an academic health center is excluded from income if the rent paid by the employee exceeds 5% of the fair market value of the housing.

Fringe Benefits

38. An employee's gross income does not include the cost of any fringe benefit supplied or paid for by the employer that qualifies as a(n)

No-additional-cost service
Qualified employee discount
Working condition fringe
De minimis fringe
Qualified transportation fringe
Qualified moving expense reimbursement
Employer-provided educational assistance

No-Additional-Cost Service

a. The value of a no-additional-cost fringe benefit provided to employees, their spouses, or their dependent children by employers is excluded from gross income.

1) A no-additional-cost fringe is a service or product that the employer offers for sale to customers in the ordinary course of business in which the employee performs substantial services.

a) The employer must not incur any substantial additional costs in providing the service to the employee.

b) An example is free telephone service to a phone company employee.

2) The fringe benefits must be available to employees on a nondiscriminatory basis; e.g., benefits available only to executives are included in their gross income.

Employee Discount

b. Certain employee discounts on the selling price of qualified property or services of their employer are excluded from gross income. "Qualified property or services" are offered in the ordinary course of business in which the employee is performing services and are purchased by the employee for his/her own use.

1) The employee discount may not exceed

a) The gross profit percentage in normal offers by the employer to customers or

b) 20% of the price offered to customers in the case of qualified services.

2) The discounts must be available to employees on a nondiscriminatory basis.

Working Condition Fringe

c. The FMV of property or services provided to an employee by an employer as a working condition fringe benefit is excludable by the employee to the extent the employer can deduct the costs as an ordinary and necessary business expense.

1) Property or services provided to an employee qualify as a working condition fringe benefit only if

a) The employee's use of the property or services relates to the employer's trade or business,

b) The employee would have been entitled to a business expense deduction if the property or services that were provided by the employer had been purchased by the employee, and

c) The employee maintains the required records, if any, with respect to the business use of the property or services provided by the employer.

2) The maximum value of employer-provided vehicles first made available to employees for personal use in 2012 for which the cents-per-mile valuation may be used is $15,900.

EXAMPLE

Top Corp. provides a car to its sales manager. She drove the car 10,000 total miles during the tax year: 7,500 miles for Top Corp. and 2,500 miles for personal use. The rental value of the use was $2,000. The total amount includible in her gross income for the tax year is $500 ($2,000 × 25% personal use).

De Minimis Fringe

d. The value of property or services provided to an employee is excludable as a de minimis fringe benefit if the value is so minimal that accounting for it would be unreasonable or impracticable.

1) The following are examples of de minimis fringes:
   a) Occasional use of company copy machines
   b) Typing of personal letters by a company secretary
   c) Occasional company parties or picnics
   d) Tickets to entertainment events, if only distributed occasionally
   e) Occasional taxi fare or meal money due to overtime work
   f) Coffee and doughnuts
   g) Traditional noncash holiday gifts with a small FMV
   h) Tokens, vouchers, and reimbursements to cover the costs of commuting by public transit as long as the amount of reimbursement provided by the employer does not exceed $240 a month for any month (2012)
2) An eating facility for employees is treated as a de minimis fringe benefit if
   a) It is located on or near the business premises of the employer and
   b) The revenue derived from the facility normally equals or exceeds its direct operating costs.

   NOTE: The excess value of the meals over the fees charged to employees is excluded from employees' income.
3) The value of an on-premises athletic facility provided by an employer is generally excluded from gross income of employees.

Transportation Fringe

e. Qualified transportation fringe benefits. Up to $240 per month (2012) may be excluded for the value of employer-provided transit passes and transportation in an employer-provided "commuter highway vehicle" (must seat six adults with 80% of mileage used for employee commuting when the vehicle is at least 1/2 full) between the employee's residence and place of employment.

1) Additionally, up to a $240-per-month exclusion (2012) is available for employer-provided parking (except residential).
   a) Employers may offer the cash equivalent of the parking benefit without the loss of the $240 employee exclusion for employee-provided parking.
   b) If an employee chooses the cash option, cash amounts received are included in gross income.
2) Employees may use both of these exclusions (i.e., qualified parking at a subway terminal).

Moving Expense Fringe

f. Qualified moving expense reimbursements are excludable amounts received from an employer that would be deductible if paid by the individual.

Employer-Provided Educational Assistance

g. Up to $5,250 may be excluded by the employee for employer-provided educational assistance.

1) This rule does not apply to graduate teaching or research assistants who receive tuition reduction under Sec. 117(d).

2) Excludable assistance payments may not include tools or supplies that the employee retains after the course or the cost of meals, lodging, or transportation.

NOTE: Any cash benefit or its equivalent (e.g., use of a credit card or gift certificate) cannot be excluded as a de minimis fringe benefit under any circumstances. Season tickets to sporting events, commuting use of an employer-provided car more than once a month, or membership to a private country club or athletic facility are never excludable as de minimis fringe benefits.

Foreign-Earned Income Exclusion

39. U.S. citizens and qualifying resident aliens may exclude up to $95,100 of foreign-earned income and a statutory housing cost allowance from gross income.

a. To qualify for exclusion, the taxpayer must have foreign-earned income, a tax home in a foreign country, and be one of the following:

1) A U.S. citizen who is a bona fide resident of a foreign country or countries for an uninterrupted period that includes an entire tax year,

2) A U.S. resident alien who is a citizen or national of a country with which the United States has an income tax treaty in effect and who is a bona fide resident of a foreign country or countries for an uninterrupted period that includes an entire tax year, or

3) A U.S. citizen or a U.S. resident alien who is physically present in a foreign country or countries for at least 330 full days during any period of 12 consecutive months.

b. The $95,100 limitation must be prorated if the taxpayer is not present in (or a resident of) the foreign country for the entire year (Form 2555).

c. This exclusion is in lieu of the foreign tax credit.

d. Deductions attributed to the foreign-earned income (which is excluded) are disallowed.

Foreign Housing Allowance

40. The inflation-adjusted standard cost-allowance for 2012 is $28,530 ($95,100 × 30%) for those locations not on the IRS's list of high-cost locations. Foreign housing allowances are broken into three categories:

a. The first $15,216 ($95,100 × 16%) of any foreign housing reimbursement is includible in income;

b. The next portion of any reimbursement up to the greater of $28,530 or the amount listed for the city on the IRS's list of high-cost locations is excludable from income; and

c. Any reimbursements exceeding the amount in b. is includible in income.

Rebate

41. A rebate to the purchaser is treated as a reduction of the purchase price. It is not included in gross income.

Stop and review! You have completed the outline for this subunit. Study questions 1 through 23 beginning on page 60.

2.2 INTEREST INCOME

1. Interest is value received or accrued for the use of money.
   a. Interest is reported under the doctrine of "constructive receipt" when the taxpayer's account is credited with the interest.
   b. Accrued interest on a deposit that may not be withdrawn at the close of an individual's tax year because of an institution's actual or threatened bankruptcy or insolvency is not includible until the year in which such interest is withdrawable.
   c. All interest is gross income for tax purposes unless an exclusion applies.
   d. Examples of taxable interest include
      1) A merchandise premium, e.g., a toaster given to a depositor for opening an interest-bearing account
         a) Under Rev. Proc. 2000-30, a non-cash de minimis gift is tax-free if it does not have a value of more than $10 for a deposit of less than $5,000 or $20 for a deposit of $5,000 or more.
      2) Imputed interest on a below-market term loan

Imputed Interest

2. Loans at below-market interest rates may be the economic equivalent of a receipt of income in the amount of forgone interest. Thus, interest is imputed on below-market loans.

Below-Market Loan

3. Below-market loans (BMLs) are categorized as demand loans or term loans.
   a. Demand loans are payable in full on demand or have indefinite maturity dates. A term loan is any loan other than a demand loan.
   b. A below-market demand loan is a loan on which interest is payable at a rate lower than the applicable federal rate. The excess of the interest that would have been payable in that year under the applicable federal rate over the actual interest payable is treated as imputed interest.
      1) The imputed interest is deemed transferred by the borrower to the lender on the last day of each year. It may be deductible by the borrower. The imputed interest is then deemed to be retransferred to the borrower by the lender. It could be either a gift, compensation (employment relationship), or a dividend (corporation/shareholder relationship) to the borrower.
   c. A below-market term loan is a loan in which the amount lent exceeds the present value of all payments due under the loan.
      1) Gift term loans. The lender is treated as transferring the excess of the amount of the loan over the present value of all principal and interest payments due under the loan, at one time, when the loan is first made. The retransfer, however, is computed at the end of each year.
      2) Non-gift term loans are treated as original issue discount. Thus, the lender has interest income over the course of the loan, and the borrower has interest expense.
   d. The imputed interest rules apply to any below-market loan that is a
      1) Gift loan
      2) Loan between a corporation and a shareholder
      3) Compensation-related loan between an employer and an employee or between an independent contractor and a person for whom the independent contractor provides services
      4) Loan that has tax avoidance as one of its principal purposes

BML Exceptions

e. No interest is imputed for any day on which the total loans between borrower and lender are below certain amounts.

1) If the BML (gift loan) between individuals is $10,000 or less, then there is no interest imputation unless the loan was made to acquire income-producing assets.

a) In the case of gift loans between individuals, if the total debt is less than $100,000, the amount deemed as transferred is limited to the borrower's net investment income, and such net investment income is treated as $0 unless it exceeds $1,000. This exception allows family gift loans without penalizing the lender.

2) If the BML between a corporation and its shareholder is $10,000 or less, there is no interest imputation unless the loan's principal purpose was tax avoidance.

3) Certain loans without a significant tax effect are excluded from the BML rules.

Original Issue Discount (OID)

4. OID is the excess, if any, of the stated redemption price at maturity over the issue price and is included in income based on the effective interest rate method of amortization.

a. If there is OID of at least $10 for the calendar year and the term of the obligation exceeds 1 year, the interest income must be reported on Form 1099-OID.

EXAMPLE

Cathy purchases a 20-year 7% bond at original issue for $10,000. The stated redemption price is $12,400, and interest is paid annually. The ratable monthly portion of OID is $10. Assume that the effective rate of interest is 10%. During the first year held, interest income is $1,000 ($10,000 × 10%) and interest received is $868 ($12,400 × 7%). The difference of $132 ($1,000 – $868) is included in income under the effective interest rate method. This amount increases the investor's book value from $10,000 to $10,132. The second year's interest is $1,013.20, and the discount amortization is $145.20.

Redemption of U.S. Savings Bonds to Pay Educational Expenses

5. If a taxpayer pays qualified higher education expenses during the year, all or a part of the interest received on redemption of a Series EE, or I, U.S. Savings Bond may be excluded.

a. To qualify,

1) The bond must have been issued to the taxpayer after December 31, 1989, at a discount.

2) The taxpayer, the taxpayer's spouse, or a dependent incurs tuition and fees to attend an eligible educational institution.

3) The taxpayer's modified adjusted gross income must not exceed a certain limit. The exclusion is phased out when certain levels of modified adjusted gross income are reached.

a) The phaseout is inflation-adjusted each year. The reference point for the inflation adjustment is 1989.

b) The exclusion is reduced when AGI exceeds a threshold of $72,850 ($109,250 if a joint return) for tax years beginning in 2012. The amount at which the benefit is completely phased out is $87,850 ($139,250 if a joint return) for tax years beginning in 2012.

4) The purchaser of the bonds must be the sole owner of the bonds (or joint owner with his/her spouse).

5) The issue date of the bonds must follow the 24th birthday(s) of the owner(s).

6) Married taxpayers must file a joint return.

b. If the qualified expenses are less than total amount of principal and interest redeemed, the interest is multiplied by the exclusion rate to determine the amount excludable. The exclusion rate is qualified expenses divided by the total of principal and interest.

Interest on State and Local Government Obligations

6. Payments to a holder of a debt obligation incurred by a state or local governmental entity (e.g., municipal or "muni" bonds) are generally exempt from federal income tax.
   a. Exclusion of interest received is allowable even if the obligation is not evidenced by a bond, is in the form of an installment purchase agreement, or is an ordinary commercial debt.
   b. These obligations must be in registered form.
   c. The exclusion applies to obligations of states, the District of Columbia, U.S. possessions, and political subdivisions of each of them.
   d. The interest on private activity bonds, which are not qualified bonds, and arbitrage bonds is not excluded from gross income.
      1) Private activity bonds are bonds of which more than 10% of the proceeds are to be used in a private business and more than 10% of the principal or interest is secured or will be paid by private business property, or more than 5% or $5,000,000 of the proceeds are to be used for private loans.
      2) Interest on qualified private activity bonds can still be excluded if the bond is for residential rental housing developments or public facilities (such as airports or waste removal), or for a qualified mortgage or VA bond, qualified small issue bond, qualified student loan bond, qualified redevelopment bond, or qualified exempt organization bond.
   e. Interest on state, local, and federal tax refunds is includible in income.
   f. Tax-exempt interest is still reported on the taxpayer's federal income tax return.

Stop and review! You have completed the outline for this subunit. Study questions 24 through 29 beginning on page 67.

2.3 INCOME FROM SECURITIES

Dividends

1. Amounts received as dividends are ordinary gross income.
   a. **Qualified dividends** are dividends from domestic corporations or a qualified foreign corporation and are taxed at a 15% rate (0% for taxpayers in the 10% or 15% tax brackets). The dividends must be held for more than 60 days (90 days for preferred stock).
   b. A dividend for purposes of taxable income is, generally, any distribution of money or other property made by a corporation to its shareholders, with respect to their stock, out of earnings and profits.
   c. Any distribution in excess of earnings and profits (both current and accumulated) is considered a recovery of capital and is therefore not taxable.
   d. Distributions in excess of E&P reduce basis.
   e. Once basis is reduced to zero, any additional distributions are capital gain and are taxed as such.
   f. Dividends paid or credited by a credit union or savings and loan are not qualified dividends.

Mutual Funds

2. Mutual fund distributions depend upon the character of the income source.
   a. Distributions or dividends from a fund investing in tax-exempt securities will be tax-exempt interest.
   b. Capital gain distributions are treated as long term regardless of the actual period the mutual fund investment is held.
   c. If the capital gain remains undistributed, the taxpayer still must report the amount as gross income (i.e., as if the capital gain were actually received).
   d. For 2012, the tax rates for long-term capital gains are 15% (0% for taxpayers in the 10% or 15% tax bracket), 25%, and 28%.
   e. Mutual funds and REITs may retain their long-term capital gains and pay tax on them instead of distributing them.
      1) A taxpayer must treat his/her portion of these long-term capital gains as a distribution even though the taxpayer did not actually receive a distribution.

Dividend Reinvestment Plans

3. A dividend reinvestment plan allows a taxpayer to use his/her dividends to buy more shares of stock in the corporation instead of receiving the dividends in cash.
   a. The basis of stock received as a result of a dividend reinvestment plan is fair market value, even if purchased at a discounted price.
   b. A member of a dividend reinvestment plan that lets the member buy more stock at a price equal to its fair market value must report the dividends as income.
   c. A member of a dividend reinvestment plan that lets the member buy more stock at a price of less than fair market value must report as income the fair market value of the additional stock on the dividend payment date.
   d. If the dividend reinvestment plan allows members to invest more cash to buy shares of stock at a price of less than fair market value, the member must report as income the difference between the cash the member invests and the fair market value of the stock purchased. Fair market value of the stock is determined on the dividend payment date.
   e. Any service charge subtracted from the cash dividends before the dividends are used to buy additional stock is considered dividend income.
   f. Reinvested dividends are taxable in the year paid.
   g. Reinvested dividends are added to the basis of the stock or mutual fund.
   h. Reinvested dividends are treated as ordinary dividends.

Stock Dividends

4. Generally, a shareholder does not include in gross income the value of a stock dividend (or right to acquire stock) declared on its own shares unless one of five exceptions applies:
   a. If any shareholder can elect to receive cash or other property, none of the stock dividends are excluded (shareholders may, however, receive cash for fractional shares, which is included in gross income).
   b. Some shareholders receive cash or other property, and other shareholders receive stock, which increases their proportionate interest in earnings.
   c. Some common stock shareholders receive preferred stock, while other common stock shareholders receive common stock.
   d. The distribution is of preferred stock (but a distribution of preferred stock merely to adjust conversion ratios as a result of a stock split or dividend is excluded).
   e. If a shareholder receives common stock and cash, for a fractional portion of stock, only the cash received for the fractional portion is included in gross income.

Stop and review! You have completed the outline for this subunit. Study questions 30 through 34 beginning on page 69.

2.4 ROYALTIES AND RENTAL INCOME

Royalties

1. Royalties are payments to an owner from people who use a right belonging to that owner. Royalties constitute ordinary gross income and are not a return of capital.

Rental Income

2. Rent is income from an investment, not from the operation of a business.
   a. A bonus received by a landlord for granting a lease is included in gross income.
   b. A lessee's refundable deposit intended to secure performance under the lease is not income to the lessor.
   c. Value received by a landlord to cancel or modify a lease is gross income.
      1) Amounts received by a lessee to cancel a lease, however, are treated as amounts realized on disposition of an asset/property (a capital gain).
   d. An amount paid by a lessee to maintain the property in lieu of rent, e.g., for property tax, is gross income to the lessor.
      1) The lessor may be entitled to a deduction for all or part of the amount.
   e. The FMV of lessee improvements made to the property in lieu of rent is also gross income to the lessor.
      1) The FMV of the lessee improvements are also allowable as a deduction in the computation of income from the rental activity.
   f. The value of lessee improvements that are not made in lieu of rent is excluded from the lessor's gross income.
   g. Prepaid rent is income when received whether the lessor uses the cash or accrual method of accounting.
   h. Rental income from a residence is included in gross income unless the residence is rented out for less than 15 days a year.
      1) If rental income is excluded from gross income, the corresponding rental deductions are also disallowed.
   i. Rental income received by an individual where no significant services are provided should be reported along with any respective rental expenses on Schedule E (Form 1040).
      1) If significant services are provided, the rental income and expenses should be reported on Schedule C (Form 1040).
   j. Income and expenses from business should be reported on Schedule C, *Profit or Loss from Business*.

Stop and review! You have completed the outline for this subunit. Study questions 35 through 40 beginning on page 71.

QUESTIONS

2.1 Gross Income

1. Jean is a U.S. citizen living and working in France for all of 2012. She received wages of $150,000, dividends of $10,000, and alimony of $20,000 in 2012. She decides to use the foreign earned income exclusion available to her and file Form 2555. What is the amount of Jean's foreign earned income before any limitations are applied?

A. $0

B. $95,100

C. $150,000

D. $180,000

Answer (C) is correct.

REQUIRED: The amount of foreign earned income before any limitations.

DISCUSSION: Earned income is income that is received from a job for payment of services performed as a self-employed individual or as an employee of a business. Income that is otherwise received due to investments or alimony is not considered earned. Thus, Jean's foreign earned income is only the amount of income that she earned through wages of $150,000 (Publication 54).

Answer (A) is incorrect. Jean's wages of $150,000 are considered foreign earned income. Answer (B) is incorrect. Jean's wages of $150,000 are considered foreign earned income. Answer (D) is incorrect. The dividends and the alimony received are not earned income; thus, they are not included in the computation for foreign earned income.

2. Ruby Diaz is a commissioned salesperson. She is a cash-method taxpayer. At the end of the current year, her earnings for the year were $75,000. During the year, she also received $10,000 in advances on future commissions and repaid $8,000. How much income should Ruby report for the current year?

A. $77,000

B. $75,000

C. $87,000

D. $85,000

Answer (A) is correct.

REQUIRED: The income reported for a cash-basis taxpayer.

DISCUSSION: Both cash- and accrual-basis taxpayers must include amounts in gross income upon actual or constructive receipt if the taxpayer has an unrestricted claim to such amounts under Reg. 1.61-8(b). All commissions received should be included in the current year's gross income. The $8,000 repaid reduces gross income [Publication 17 and IRC Reg. 1.61-8(b)]. Ruby should report $77,000 ($75,000 + $10,000 – $8,000).

Answer (B) is incorrect. Ruby must include the amount of advances on future commissions that she did not repay as income on her current year return. Answer (C) is incorrect. The amount of advanced future commissions is not included in income to the extent that it has been repaid. Answer (D) is incorrect. The $8,000 repaid reduces gross income.

3. All of the following are considered "constructive receipt" of income except

A. Lori was informed her check for services rendered was available, but she did not pick it up.

B. Pierre earned income that was received by his agent but was not received by Pierre.

C. Jacque bought a 9-month certificate of deposit in November of the current year. It earned $200 interest in the current year. She can withdraw the principal and interest in the current year if she pays a penalty of one month's interest ($100).

D. A payment on a sale of real property was placed in escrow pending settlement, at which time title would be conveyed.

Answer (D) is correct.

REQUIRED: The occurrence that is not considered "constructive receipt" of income.

DISCUSSION: Income, although not actually in a taxpayer's possession, is constructively received in the taxable year during which it is credited to his/her account, set apart for him/her, or otherwise made available so that (s)he may draw upon it at any time or so that (s)he could have drawn upon it during the taxable year if notice of intention to withdraw had been given (Reg. 1.451-2). However, income is not constructively received if the taxpayer's control of its receipt is subject to substantial limitations or restrictions (Publication 538). Since the taxpayer's control of the receipt of the funds in the escrow account is substantially limited until the transaction has closed, the taxpayer has not constructively received the income until the closing of the transaction in the following year.

Answer (A) is incorrect. The check for services rendered was made available to the taxpayer during the current year. Answer (B) is incorrect. The receipt of income by the taxpayer's agent makes it available to the taxpayer; therefore, it is constructively received. Answer (C) is incorrect. The funds are available regardless of whether a penalty would be imposed.

4. In return for $5,000, Simon canceled Mike's debt of $15,000. The cancelation was not a gift but is part of Mike's bankruptcy. Which of the following statements is true?

A. Simon has $5,000 of taxable income.

B. Mike has $10,000 of taxable income.

C. Mike has $15,000 of taxable income.

D. Neither Simon nor Mike has any taxable income from this transaction.

Answer (D) is correct.

REQUIRED: The true statement of income recognized from a cancelation of a debt.

DISCUSSION: Under Sec. 61(a)(12), gross income includes income from the discharge of indebtedness unless it is excluded under Sec. 108. The cancelation is excluded since the debt was canceled due to a bankruptcy action. If the debtor were neither insolvent nor bankrupt, he would have included $10,000, the amount of the obligation that was canceled ($15,000 – $5,000), in gross income (Publication 17).

Answer (A) is incorrect. The repayment of an outstanding loan is not income to the lender. Answer (B) is incorrect. A discharge of indebtedness is not included in gross income when the discharge occurs in bankruptcy. Answer (C) is incorrect. A discharge of indebtedness is not included in gross income when the discharge occurs in bankruptcy.

5. Kelley's employer gave her stock in the current year for services performed with the condition that she would have to return the stock unless she completed 3 years of service. At the time of the transfer, her employer's basis in the stock was $6,000, and its fair market value was $8,000. Kelley did not make the Sec. 83(b) election. How much should she include in her income for the current year, and what would be her basis in the stock?

A. Income of $8,000; basis of $8,000.

B. Income of $6,000; basis of $6,000.

C. Income of $8,000; basis of $3,000.

D. Kelley would not report any income or have any basis in the stock until she has completed 3 years of service.

Answer (D) is correct.

REQUIRED: The basis in stock received as compensation but subject to a substantial limitation on alienability.

DISCUSSION: Under the claim-of-right doctrine, a taxpayer receiving income under a claim of right and without restrictions on its use or disposition is taxed on that income in the year received even though the right to retain the income is not yet fixed or the taxpayer may later be required to return it (Publication 538). In this case, however, there is a substantial limitation on the stock's use and/or disposition because Kelley must return the stock if she does not complete 3 years of service. Therefore, Kelley will not report any income or have any basis in the stock until she has completed 3 years of service.

6. Ms. Miller set up a computer system for Mr. Town's business. In return, Mr. Town gave Ms. Miller a storage facility. Ms. Miller plans to use this facility for business purposes and plans to depreciate it. The fair market value of Ms. Miller's services and the storage facility was $50,000. Mr. Town's basis in the storage facility was $30,000. How should Ms. Miller treat the transaction, and what is her depreciable basis for the property?

A. Ms. Miller should include the $50,000 in income and use $30,000 as the depreciable basis for the storage facility she received.

B. Mr. Town should include the $30,000 in his income and use the $50,000 as the depreciable basis for the storage facility.

C. Ms. Miller should include $30,000 in income and $50,000 as the depreciable basis for the storage facility.

D. Ms. Miller should include $50,000 in income and use $50,000 as the basis for the storage facility.

Answer (D) is correct.

REQUIRED: The income and basis for property received in exchange for a service performed.

DISCUSSION: All compensation for personal services is gross income. The form of payment is irrelevant. If services are paid for in property, its fair market value at the time of receipt is gross income. The amount included in income becomes the basis in the property. Since the building's FMV at the time of the exchange is $50,000, the amount of income recognized and Ms. Miller's basis in the property is equal to $50,000 (Publication 17).

Answer (A) is incorrect. The depreciable basis in the property is also equal to $50,000. Answer (B) is incorrect. Mr. Town is giving the building to Ms. Miller in payment for her services and should only recognize the gain on the sale of the building of $20,000. Also, he will not be able to depreciate the building because it belongs to Ms. Miller. Answer (C) is incorrect. Ms. Miller must include the FMV of the building received ($50,000) in income.

7. When Joe's financial institution offered a substantial discount of $5,000 for early payment of his home mortgage, he borrowed from a family member to take advantage of this offer. How should Joe treat this discount transaction?

A. No actions or reporting required.

B. Report $5,000 on line 21, Other Income, on Form 1040.

C. Reduce his home mortgage interest deduction by $5,000.

D. Report $5,000 original issue discount as interest income.

Answer (B) is correct.

REQUIRED: The appropriate treatment of a discount on a home mortgage.

DISCUSSION: According to Publication 17, if a financial institution offers a discount for the early payment of a mortgage loan, the amount of the discount is canceled debt. When the canceled debt is a nonbusiness debt, it is to be reported as other income on line 21 of Form 1040.

Answer (A) is incorrect. When a discount is offered for the early payment of a mortgage loan by a financial institution, it is treated as a canceled debt. Canceled debt must be reported as income. Answer (C) is incorrect. A canceled debt has no effect on the amount of interest deduction to be taken. Answer (D) is incorrect. Canceled debt has no effect on the amount of original issue discount interest income to be reported.

8. Gene Wingo had the following potentially taxable transactions in the current year. How much, if any, should be included on his current-year return?

- $200 credited to his savings account on December 31 of the current year. He did not withdraw any money from the account during the entire year.
- $2,000 withheld from his paycheck by his employer to satisfy a garnishment by his doctor.
- $1,000 discount given by his bank when he paid off his home mortgage 5 years early.
- $500 check received December 31 of the current year from an individual for one of Gene's original drawings. Gene did not cash or deposit the check until the next year.

A. $1,700

B. $2,700

C. $3,700

D. $3,200

Answer (C) is correct.

REQUIRED: The amount includible in gross income.

DISCUSSION: Gross income includes compensation for services ($2,000 + $500), interest ($200), and income from discharge of indebtedness ($1,000), among other items. Gene should include all $3,700 in gross income on his current year return (Publication 17).

Answer (A) is incorrect. The $2,000 withheld from his paycheck is still attributable to him as compensation for services, even though Gene does not receive the income and it is used to pay his doctor. Answer (B) is incorrect. Gross income includes the cancelation of indebtedness when a debt is canceled in whole or part for consideration. If a creditor cancels a debt in consideration for services performed by the debtor, the debtor must recognize income in the amount of the debt as compensation for his/her services. Answer (D) is incorrect. The $500 check is received on December 31 of the current year; thus, it is in Gene's possession. The income is realized even though he does not cash or deposit the check until the next year.

9. Mr. and Mrs. McGriff are both over 65 years of age and are filing a joint return. Their income for 2012 consisted of the following:

Taxable interest	$ 3,600
Social Security payments	30,000
Tax-exempt interest	1,200
Taxable pension	24,000

How much of the Social Security benefits is taxable?

A. $5,300

B. $5,900

C. $11,800

D. $15,000

Answer (B) is correct.

REQUIRED: The amount of Social Security benefits included in gross income.

DISCUSSION: Under Sec. 86, if the sum of the "modified" adjusted gross income plus one-half of Social Security benefits exceeds $32,000 on a joint return but does not exceed $44,000, part of the Social Security benefits will be included in gross income. Modified adjusted gross income equals adjusted gross income plus tax-exempt interest [Sec. 86(b)(2)]. The includible portion of Social Security benefits is the lesser of one-half of the Social Security benefits or one-half of the excess as noted above (Publication 17). Mr. and Mrs. McGriff would include $5,900, since it is less than one-half of the Social Security benefits ($30,000 × .5 = $15,000).

Modified AGI ($3,600 + $1,200 + $24,000)	$28,800
One-half of Social Security benefits	15,000
Less $32,000 base amount	(32,000)
	$11,800
50% of excess or	$ 5,900
50% of Social Security ($30,000 × 50%)	$15,000

Answer (A) is incorrect. Tax-exempt interest is included in determining modified adjusted gross income. Answer (C) is incorrect. Only 50% of the excess is includible. Answer (D) is incorrect. The includible portion of benefits is the lesser of one-half of the Social Security benefits or one-half of the excess.

10. If your Social Security benefits are considered taxable, the maximum percent of net benefits received that can be included in income is

A. 0%

B. 50%

C. 85%

D. 100%

Answer (C) is correct.

REQUIRED: The maximum percentage of Social Security benefits includible in gross income.

DISCUSSION: The taxable portion of Social Security benefits will depend upon the amount of provisional income in relation to the base amount and the adjusted base amount. If provisional income exceeds the adjusted base amount, up to 85% of Social Security benefits may be taxable (Publication 17).

11. Gordon, age 70, is retired and works part-time as a security guard earning $8,000. He received $5,000 interest from a savings account and $2,500 interest from tax-exempt municipal bonds. His Social Security benefits were $12,000 and his taxable pension was $6,000. To determine if any of his Social Security is taxable, Gordon should compare how much of his income to the $25,000 base amount?

A. $27,500

B. $21,500

C. $19,000

D. $25,000

Answer (A) is correct.

REQUIRED: The amount of taxable Social Security income.

DISCUSSION: Under Sec. 86, if the sum of the "modified" adjusted gross income plus one-half of Social Security benefits exceeds $25,000 on a single return but does not exceed $34,000, part of the Social Security benefits will be included in gross income. Modified adjusted gross income equals adjusted gross income plus tax-exempt interest (modified AGI = $8,000 + $6,000 + $5,000 + $2,500 = $21,500). The sum of the taxpayer's modified AGI of $21,500 and one-half of their $12,000 in Social Security is equal to $27,500, which should then be compared to the $25,000 minimum (Publication 17).

Answer (B) is incorrect. The taxpayer's $6,000 pension should be included in modified AGI. Answer (C) is incorrect. The $2,500 in tax-exempt interest and $6,000 in pension income should be included in modified AGI. Answer (D) is incorrect. The $2,500 in tax exempt interest should be included in modified AGI.

12. Mr. Hines received a $6,200 grant from a local university for the fall of the current year. Mr. Hines was a candidate for a degree and was required to be a research assistant, for which services he received payment under the grant. The $6,200 grant provided the following:

Tuition	$3,600
Books and supplies	500
Pay for services as research assistant	2,100

Mr. Hines spent the entire $6,200 on tuition, books, and supplies. What amount must Mr. Hines include in his income for the current year?

A. $2,100

B. $2,600

C. $3,600

D. $6,200

Answer (A) is correct.

REQUIRED: The amount required to be included in income.

DISCUSSION: Although Sec. 117 excludes from gross income amounts received as qualified scholarships and tuition reduction to be used for tuition and related expenses, this exclusion does not apply to amounts representing payments for teaching, research, or other services performed by the student that are required as a condition for receiving the qualified scholarship or tuition reduction (Publication 17).

Answer (B) is incorrect. Books and supplies qualify as a Sec. 117 exclusion. Answer (C) is incorrect. Tuition qualifies as a Sec. 117 exclusion. Answer (D) is incorrect. Only payments for services are included in gross income.

13. During the current year, Mr. French received state unemployment benefits of $2,500 and $700 of supplemental unemployment benefits from a company-financed fund. The union paid Mr. French an additional $2,000 as strike benefits. What amount must Mr. French include in income for the current year?

A. $2,500

B. $3,200

C. $4,500

D. $5,200

Answer (D) is correct.

REQUIRED: The amount of the items listed that must be included in gross income.

DISCUSSION: Gross income is defined under Sec. 61 as all income from whatever source derived that is not specifically excluded. Unemployment benefits received under a federal or state program are gross income [Sec. 85(a)].

Reg. 1.85-1(b)1(i) provides that amounts paid pursuant to private nongovernmental unemployment compensation plans are includible in income without regard to Sec. 85. Thus, the $700 from the company-financed fund and the $2,000 from the union must also be included in gross income (Publication 17).

Answer (A) is incorrect. The $700 from the company-financed fund and the $2,000 from the union also must be included in gross income. Answer (B) is incorrect. The $2,000 from the union must be included in gross income. Answer (C) is incorrect. The $700 from the company-financed fund must be included in gross income.

14. Unemployment compensation generally includes any amount received under an unemployment compensation law of the United States or of a state. Which of the following statements is false?

A. Benefits received from a company-financed fund, to which you did not contribute, are taxable wages.

B. Benefits paid to you as an unemployed member of a union out of regular union dues are not included in your gross income.

C. You may be liable for estimated taxes if you receive unemployment compensation.

D. Payments you receive from your employer during periods of unemployment, under a union agreement that guarantees you full pay during the year, are taxable as wages.

Answer (B) is correct.

REQUIRED: The false statement about unemployment compensation.

DISCUSSION: Gross income means all income from whatever source derived unless specifically excluded (Sec. 61). This is an intentionally broad and all-encompassing definition. Unemployment compensation is included in gross income under Sec. 85.

Reg. 1.85(b)1(i) provides that amounts paid pursuant to private nongovernmental unemployment compensation are includible without regard to Sec. 85. Thus, any payments made from any employer or from a union are taxable wages (Publication 17).

Answer (A) is incorrect. Payments made from a company-financed fund to which you did not contribute are included as wages. Answer (C) is incorrect. Unemployment compensation is included in gross income and is taxable. Answer (D) is incorrect. Payments from guaranteed annual wage plans constitute taxable income in the year received.

15. On February 10 of the current year, Rose was in an automobile accident while she was going to work. The doctor advised her to stay home for 6 months because of her injuries. On February 25 of the current year, she filed a lawsuit. On July 20 of the current year, Rose returned to work. On December 15 of the current year, the lawsuit was settled and Rose received the following amounts:

Compensation for lost wages	$25,000
Personal injury damages awarded (none of which was for punitive damages)	40,000

How much of the settlement must Rose include in ordinary income on her current-year tax return?

A. $0

B. $25,000

C. $40,000

D. $65,000

Answer (A) is correct.

REQUIRED: The amount of gross income from the payments received as a result of the injury.

DISCUSSION: In 1996, Sec. 104(a)(2) was amended to exclude from gross income damages received on account of personal physical injury or physical sickness only. The House Committee Report for the 1996 changes states, "If an action has its origin in a physical injury or physical sickness, then all damages (other than punitive) that flow therefrom are treated as payments received on account of physical injury or physical sickness..." Therefore, Rose's compensation for lost wages is excluded from gross income (Publication 17).

Answer (B) is incorrect. Compensation for lost wages is excluded from gross income. Answer (C) is incorrect. Personal injury damages are excluded from gross income by Sec. 104(a). Answer (D) is incorrect. Damages received on account of personal physical injury or physical sickness are excluded from gross income.

16. Which of the following does not have to be included in gross income?

A. Unemployment compensation.

B. Damages from personal injury suit involving back injuries.

C. Prize from church raffle.

D. Free tour from travel agency for organizing a group of tourists.

Answer (B) is correct.

REQUIRED: The item that does not have to be included in gross income.

DISCUSSION: Gross income means all income from whatever source derived unless specifically excluded (Sec. 61). This is an intentionally broad and all-encompassing definition. Sec. 104(a)(2) includes punitive damages in gross income, even in connection with a physical injury or physical sickness. However, Sec. 104(a)(2) excludes nonpunitive damages awarded for personal injuries involving physical injury or physical sickness (Publication 17).

Answer (A) is incorrect. Unemployment compensation is included in gross income under Sec. 85. Answer (C) is incorrect. A prize received in a raffle (whether from a church or any other organization) is included in gross income under Sec. 74. Answer (D) is incorrect. The fair market value of a free tour is the receipt of an economic benefit, which is included in gross income as compensation since no provision excludes it.

17. At their annual budget meeting, the Downtown Church voted to set the salary package for their pastor as follows:

Basic salary	$30,000
Housing allowance (at fair rental value)	$10,000
Maximum reimbursement for travel (reports must be filed with receipts attached)	$ 5,000

How much of the salary package is includible in the pastor's taxable income?

A. $30,000

B. $35,000

C. $40,000

D. $45,000

Answer (A) is correct.

REQUIRED: The amount includible in a pastor's gross income.

DISCUSSION: Under Sec. 61, salaries and fees for personal services are always included in gross income. A pastor should include in his/her salary the offerings given directly to him/her for marriages, baptisms, funerals, etc., and the other outside earnings donated by him/her to the organization in his/her gross income. Reg. 1.107-1 excludes from gross income the rental value of a home, or a rental allowance to the extent it is used to rent or provide a home, furnished to a pastor as a part of his/her compensation. Reimbursements are not included in the pastor's taxable income. (See Publication 517.)

Answer (B) is incorrect. The reimbursement for travel is not taxable income. Answer (C) is incorrect. The housing allowance is not taxable income. Answer (D) is incorrect. The reimbursement for travel and the housing allowance are not taxable income.

18. Pastor Green received an annual salary of $20,000 as a full-time minister in 2012. The church also paid him $1,000 designated as a housing allowance to pay for his utilities. His church owns a parsonage that has a fair rental value of $6,000 in which he lives rent free. Neither the rental allowance nor the rental value of the parsonage is included in his W-2. All amounts are considered provided for services he renders as a licensed pastor. He is not exempt from self employment tax. Compute the amount of Pastor Green's income that is subject to income tax on his 2012 return.

A. $19,000

B. $20,000

C. $27,000

D. $26,000

Answer (B) is correct.

REQUIRED: The income included in gross income for a minister who lives in a parsonage for free and receives a rental allowance.

DISCUSSION: Ministers may exclude from gross income the rental value of a home or a rental allowance to the extent the allowance is used to provide a home, even if deductions are taken for home expenses paid with the allowance. However, a minister should include any offerings given directly to him/her for church-related functions (Publication 517). Accordingly, Pastor Green may exclude the rental value ($6,000) of the parsonage in which he lives and the $1,000 rental allowance given to him by the church. He should claim $20,000 of income on his income tax return for 2012.

Answer (A) is incorrect. The amount of $19,000 assumes that the $1,000 was included in the $20,000, when it was not. Answer (C) is incorrect. Pastor Green may exclude the rental value ($6,000) of the parsonage in which he lives and the $1,000 rental allowance given to him by the church. Answer (D) is incorrect. Pastor Green may exclude the rental value of the parsonage ($6,000) from his income.

19. An ordained minister cannot exclude the following from gross income:

A. Rental allowance.

B. Fees for marriages, baptisms, and funerals.

C. Fair rental value of parsonage.

D. Actual cost to provide a home.

Answer (B) is correct.

REQUIRED: The income an ordained minister cannot exclude.

DISCUSSION: Under Sec. 61, salaries and fees for personal services are always included in gross income. A minister should include his/her salary; the offerings given directly to him/her for marriages, baptisms, funerals, etc.; and the other outside earnings donated by him/her to the organization in his/her gross income. Reg. 1.107-1 excludes from gross income the rental value of a home, or a rental allowance to the extent it is used to rent or provide a home, furnished to a minister as a part of his/her compensation. A minister is entitled to deduct mortgage interest and real property taxes paid on a personal residence even if the amounts are derived from an allowance that is excluded from gross income (Publication 517).

Answer (A) is incorrect. Rental allowance is specifically excluded under Reg. 1.107-1 from the gross income of an ordained minister. Answer (C) is incorrect. Fair rental value of parsonage is specifically excluded under Reg. 1.107-1 from the gross income of an ordained minister. Answer (D) is incorrect. The actual cost to provide a home is specifically excluded under Reg. 1.107-1 from the gross income of an ordained minister.

20. Generally, which of the following should be included in gross income?

A. Life insurance proceeds.

B. Child support payments.

C. Cash rebate from a dealer when a car is purchased.

D. Reimbursements from your employer of a moving expense you properly deducted on last year's tax return.

Answer (D) is correct.

REQUIRED: The item that must be included in gross income.

DISCUSSION: Sec. 82 specifically provides that, except as provided in Sec. 132(a)(6), gross income includes amounts received as reimbursement of moving expenses that are attributable to employment. Under Sec. 132(a)(6), the reimbursement is excluded if the expense would be deductible under Sec. 217 if paid by the employee. It may not be excluded, however, if the expense was actually deducted on the individual's return for any prior tax year. (See Publication 521.)

Answer (A) is incorrect. Life insurance proceeds are specifically excluded under Sec. 101(a). Answer (B) is incorrect. Sec. 71(c) excludes payments for the support of children. Answer (C) is incorrect. A rebate on a new automobile is merely a reduction of the purchase price of the automobile, not income.

21. During the current year, Dave, a member of the clergy, received a salary of $14,000 and a house with a fair rental value of $6,000 as pay for his duties as an ordained minister. Dave also was employed part-time as a limousine driver receiving a salary of $3,000, tips of $1,000, and a Christmas bonus of $200. Dave became disabled in November and received $2,800 as a disability pension. He made no contributions to the pension. What amount must Dave include in gross income on his current-year tax return?

A. $18,200

B. $21,000

C. $26,800

D. $27,000

Answer (B) is correct.

REQUIRED: The amount that an ordained minister must include in gross income.

DISCUSSION: Under Sec. 61, salaries and fees for personal services are always included in gross income. A minister should include his/her salary; the offerings given directly to him/her for marriages, baptisms, and funerals; tips; cash bonuses; and pension benefits, when no personal contributions were made to the pension fund. Reg. 1.107-1 excludes from gross income the rental value of a home, including utilities, furnished to a minister as a part of his/her compensation (Publication 517). Dave must include

Salary	$14,000
Outside earnings	3,000
Tips	1,000
Bonus	200
Pension	2,800
Total	$21,000

Answer (A) is incorrect. The disability pension should be included in gross income. Answer (C) is incorrect. The fair rental value of a house is not included in gross income, but bonuses are included. Answer (D) is incorrect. The fair rental value of a house is not included in gross income.

22. Mr. and Mrs. Garden filed a joint return for 2012. Mr. Garden received $8,000 in Social Security benefits and Mrs. Garden received $4,000. Their income also included $10,000 taxable pension income and interest income of $2,000. What part of their Social Security benefits will be taxable for 2012? (The base amount for married filing jointly is $32,000 for 2012.)

A. $0

B. $6,000

C. $24,000

D. $12,000

Answer (A) is correct.

REQUIRED: The amount of Social Security benefits that are taxable in 2012.

DISCUSSION: Social Security benefits are generally not taxable unless additional income is received. The gross income inclusion is dependent on the relation of provisional income (PI) to the base amount (BA) and the adjusted base amount (ABA). If PI < BA, there is no inclusion. If PI falls between BA and ABA, up to 50% of Social Security benefits will be included. If PI > ABA, up to 85% of Social Security benefits will be included (Publication 17). The Gardens' provisional income is calculated below.

AGI, excluding Social Security benefits	$12,000
+ 50% of Social Security benefits	6,000
= Provisional Income	$18,000

Since the Gardens' provisional income is less than their base amount of $32,000, none of their social security benefits will be taxed.

Answer (B) is incorrect. The amount of $6,000 is the portion of the Social Security benefits that must be added to the Gardens' AGI to determine provisional income. Answer (C) is incorrect. The amount of $24,000 is the total amount of income the Gardens received for 2012, not the Social Security benefits that must be included in gross income. Answer (D) is incorrect. None of the Social Security benefits are taxable.

23. How much income should Devin, who uses the cash method of accounting, report on his Year 1 return from the following transactions?

- $300 was garnished from his wages to pay his debts
- $500 (gross) paycheck received December 28, Year 1, but not cashed until January 2, Year 2
- $900 (gross) wages paid directly to his mother at his request

A. $1,200

B. $1,700

C. $1,400

D. $800

Answer (B) is correct.

REQUIRED: The amount includible in gross income.

DISCUSSION: A taxpayer using the cash basis method of accounting should include income when it is constructively received. Income, although not actually in a taxpayer's possession, is constructively received in the taxable year during which it is credited to his/her account, set apart for him/her, or otherwise made available without restriction (Reg. 1.451-2 and Publication 538).

Answer (A) is incorrect. The $500 check was constructively received and should be included in income. Answer (C) is incorrect. The $300 in garnished wages were constructively received by the taxpayer. Answer (D) is incorrect. The $900 in wages paid to the taxpayer's mother were constructively received by the taxpayer.

2.2 Interest Income

24. Janice dropped off her annual records for preparation of her tax return. Determine the amount of taxable interest to be reported on Janice's return.

- $1,000 interest earned on her 19-year-old son's savings account (he had no other income and did not file a tax return)
- $50 interest income reported on Form 1099-OID
- $200 interest earned on a certificate of deposit (your client borrowed the entire $3,000 to purchase this CD)
- $30 value of a calculator that was a gift from the bank for opening a savings account
- $6,000 received on a prior year installment sale, of which $4,000 is interest and $2,000 is principal

A. $4,250

B. $7,280

C. $5,250

D. $4,280

Answer (D) is correct.

REQUIRED: The amount of interest includible in gross income.

DISCUSSION: The $50 of interest income reported on Form 1099-OID is included, since it does not qualify as de minimis. The interest from the CD is also included in taxable interest. The value of the calculator is not a gift but is consideration (interest) for opening a savings account. The $4,000 interest from the installment sale is also included. Also, only parents of a child under 18 can elect to include the child's dividend and interest income on their own return [Sec. 1(g)(7) and Publication 17].

Answer (A) is incorrect. The value of the calculator is considered consideration (interest) furnished for the opening of a savings account. Answer (B) is incorrect. The principal from the installment sale and the $1,000 interest in the child's savings account are not includible as interest on the parents' return. Answer (C) is incorrect. The $1,000 interest in the child's savings account is not included and the value of the calculator is considered consideration (interest) furnished for the opening of a savings account.

25. Ms. Guy's books and records reflect the following for 2012:

Salary	$57,000
Interest on money market account (credited to her account in 2012, withdrawn in 2013)	1,865
Deposit from the pending sale of her rental property	4,000
Interest on savings account (credited to her account in 2011, withdrawn in 2012)	200

What is the amount Ms. Guy should include in her gross income for 2012?

A. $45,865

B. $58,865

C. $62,865

D. $63,065

Answer (B) is correct.

REQUIRED: The amount recorded in gross income for the current year.

DISCUSSION: Ms. Guy's gross income will include the $57,000 of salary as compensation for services. Interest on money market accounts earned in the current year but not withdrawn is still taxed in the current year under the doctrine of constructive receipt. Therefore, the $1,865 from interest credited in 2012 should be included in gross income, but the $200 credited in 2011 should not be included in gross income. The $4,000 deposit from the pending sale of rental property is not included because the income has not constructively been received; there are still substantial limitations on the control of the receipt (Publications 17 and 538 and IRC Sec. 61).

Answer (A) is incorrect. Gross income includes salary and interest credited during the current year. Answer (C) is incorrect. The deposit from the pending sale is not constructively received. Answer (D) is incorrect. Neither the deposit from a pending sale nor interest earned in a prior year is included in current-year income.

26. Maria had municipal bond interest of $6,000, certificate of deposit interest of $4,000, reinvested corporate bond interest of $2,000, mutual fund municipal bond interest of $7,000, and savings account interest of $1,000. What is Maria's taxable interest?

A. $3,000

B. $7,000

C. $20,000

D. $16,000

Answer (B) is correct.

REQUIRED: The amount of interest income included in Maria's taxable income.

DISCUSSION: All interest is included as income unless excluded by the tax code. Municipal bond interest and mutual fund municipal bond interest may be excluded from income (Publication 17).

Maria's taxable interest is:

Certificate of deposit interest	$4,000
Reinvested corporate interest	2,000
Savings account interest	1,000
Total taxable interest	$7,000

Answer (A) is incorrect. The certificate of deposit interest is also included in income. Answer (C) is incorrect. The municipal bond interest and the mutual fund municipal bond fund are excludable from income. Answer (D) is incorrect. The municipal bond interest and the mutual fund municipal bond fund are excludable from income. In addition, the certificate of deposit interest should be included in income.

27. Mr. and Mrs. Apple received the following income during 2012:

- $200 in interest credited to their bank account but not withdrawn or used by them during the year
- $2,000 in interest received as a beneficiary in a trust established by Mr. Apple's father and included on Schedule K-1 from the trust
- $100 in interest on a bond issued by the State of Georgia
- $1,000 bond interest, City of Atlanta municipal bond

How much taxable interest income must Mr. and Mrs. Apple report on their 2012 tax return?

A. $3,300

B. $0

C. $2,200

D. $1,300

Answer (C) is correct.

REQUIRED: The interest that is taxable and must be reported on the 2012 tax return.

DISCUSSION: Interest is the value received or accrued for the use of money. Interest is reported under the doctrine of "constructive receipt" when the taxpayer's account is credited with the interest. Accrued interest on a deposit that may not be withdrawn at the close of an individual's tax year because of an institution's actual or threatened bankruptcy or insolvency is not includible until the year in which such interest is withdrawable. All interest is gross income for tax purposes unless an exclusion applies. Payments to a holder of a debt obligation incurred by a state or local governmental entity (e.g., municipal or "muni" bonds) are generally exempt from federal income tax (Publications 17 and 538). Accordingly, Mr. and Mrs. Apple should report $2,200 ($2,000 + $200) on their 2012 income tax return, because all interest is taxable income unless an exclusion applies and there is an exclusion for the interest earned on state and local bonds.

Answer (A) is incorrect. The interest earned on the state and local bonds are excluded from income on the 2012 tax return. Answer (B) is incorrect. The interest that is in their bank account and the interest received from the trust are taxable. Answer (D) is incorrect. The $1,000 is interest received from a local bond and is excluded from income. In addition, the $2,000 of interest received from the trust should be included in income on the 2012 tax return.

28. All of the following are taxable interest income except

A. Interest on a federal tax refund.

B. Interest on an IRA before its withdrawal.

C. Interest on GI insurance dividends.

D. Interest on U.S. Treasury bills.

Answer (B) is correct.

REQUIRED: The type of interest income that is excluded from gross income.

DISCUSSION: Interest income is included in gross income under Sec. 61 unless specifically excluded in another section. Sec. 408 provides in most cases that individual retirement accounts (IRAs) are taxed to the owner only on distribution (Publication 17).

Answer (A) is incorrect. There is no exclusion for interest on U.S. government obligations derived from tax refunds. Answer (C) is incorrect. There is no exclusion for interest on U.S. government obligations derived from GI insurance. Answer (D) is incorrect. There is no exclusion for interest on U.S. government obligations derived from Treasury bills.

29. In December of the current year, Mr. Stone cashed qualified Series EE U.S. Savings Bonds, which he had purchased in January 2003. The proceeds were used for his son's college education. All of the following statements are true concerning the exclusion of the interest received except

A. He cannot file as married filing separate.

B. Eligible expenses include room and board.

C. If the proceeds are more than the expenses, he will be able to exclude only part of the interest.

D. Before he figures his interest exclusion, he must reduce his qualified higher educational expenses by certain benefits.

Answer (B) is correct.

REQUIRED: The exclusion rules concerning U.S. savings bond income used for higher education.

DISCUSSION: An individual who redeems any qualified U.S. savings bonds in a year in which qualified higher education expenses are paid may exclude from income amounts received under such redemption, provided certain requirements are met (Sec. 135). Qualified higher education expenses include tuition and fees required for enrollment at an eligible educational institution. Room and board are not classified as qualified higher education expenses, and interest used to cover these expenses may not be excluded (Publication 17).

Answer (A) is incorrect. The exclusion is not available to married individuals who file separate returns. Answer (C) is incorrect. Only part of interest may be excluded if the proceeds are more than the expenses. Answer (D) is incorrect. He must reduce his qualified higher educational expenses by certain benefits before he figures his interest exclusion.

2.3 Income from Securities

30. Emily bought 50 shares of stock in Year 1 for $500. In Year 2, she received a return of capital of $100. She received an additional return of capital of $50 in Year 3. What must Emily report as long-term capital gain on her tax return for Year 3?

A. $150

B. $50

C. $100

D. $0

Answer (D) is correct.

REQUIRED: The character of return of capital distributions.

DISCUSSION: A return of capital is a tax-free distribution that is not made out of a corporation's earnings and profits that reduces a stock's basis by the amount of the distribution. It is not taxed until the stock's basis has been fully recovered (Publication 17).

Answer (A) is incorrect. The amount of $150 is the basis reduction and is not taxed until the basis is recovered. Answer (B) is incorrect. The amount of $50 is the basis reduction for Year 3. Answer (C) is incorrect. The amount of $100 is the basis reduction for Year 2.

31. In the current year, Sam received the following corporate distributions:

- $1,500 dividend on stock held in a public corporation that offers a dividend reinvestment plan that lets him choose to use the dividend to buy (through an agent) more stock in the corporation at a price equal to its fair market value instead of receiving the dividends in cash. Sam chose to take part in the plan.
- $2,500 dividend on stock held in a public corporation that offers a dividend reinvestment plan that lets him choose to use the dividend to buy (through an agent) more stock in the corporation at a price less than its fair market value. The fair market value of shares Sam purchased through the plan on the dividend payment date in the current year was $3,000.
- $2,000 return of capital distribution reported on Form 1099-DIV.

Based on the above information, how much ordinary dividend income must Sam report on his current-year return?

A. $4,000

B. $4,500

C. $6,000

D. $6,500

Answer (B) is correct.

REQUIRED: The amount of dividend income under a dividend reinvestment plan.

DISCUSSION: Dividends are gross income [Sec. 61(a)(7)]. A shareholder who, under a dividend reinvestment plan, elects to receive shares of greater value than his/her cash dividend would otherwise receive a taxable distribution under Sec. 301(a) to the extent of the value of the shares (Rev. Rul. 78-375). The Sec. 301(A) distribution is generally a taxable dividend to the extent of the corporation's earnings and profits (Publication 17). Sam's gain is $4,500 ($3,000 + $1,500) because the gain must equal the FMV of the shares purchased. The return of capital distribution is a tax-free distribution that reduces a stock's basis by the amount of the distribution.

Answer (A) is incorrect. The FMV of the shares purchased is used to determine the gain. Answer (C) is incorrect. The FMV of the shares purchased is used to determine the gain and the return of capital distribution is tax-free. Answer (D) is incorrect. The return of capital distribution is tax-free.

32. Joe has owned shares in a company that has a dividend reinvestment plan since 2000. The plan allows him to invest more cash to buy additional shares of stock at a price less than fair market value. In the current year, Joe took advantage of that option and purchased 100 additional shares for $30 each. On the dividend payment date, the fair market value of the shares he purchased was $32 per share. Based on this information, Joe must report

A. $0. No income must be reported until the shares are sold.

B. $200 as ordinary income, based on the difference between the amount Joe paid and the fair market value of the shares.

C. $200 of short-term capital gain income, based on the fact that Joe could not have taken advantage of the option to buy the shares at the discounted price if he had not taken part in the dividend reinvestment plan.

D. $200 of long-term capital gain income, based on the fact that Joe has owned shares in the company for more than 12 months.

Answer (B) is correct.

REQUIRED: The amount and character of income under a dividend reinvestment plan.

DISCUSSION: Dividends are gross income [Sec. 61(a)(7)]. A shareholder who, under a dividend reinvestment plan, elects to receive shares of greater value than his/her cash dividend would otherwise be, receives taxable income based on the difference between the amount (s)he paid and the fair market value of the shares (Publication 17). Joe will report $200 ordinary income [100 × ($32 – $30)].

Answer (A) is incorrect. Income must be recognized when shares are received that have a greater value than the cash dividend. Answer (C) is incorrect. The distribution is a form of dividends, and dividends are included in ordinary income. Answer (D) is incorrect. The distribution is a form of dividends, and dividends are included in ordinary income.

33. Ms. X, a cash-method taxpayer, received notice from her mutual fund that it has realized a long-term capital gain on her behalf in the amount of $2,500. It also advised her that it has paid a tax of $500 on this gain. The mutual fund indicated that it will not distribute the net amount but will credit the amount to her account. All of the following statements are true except

A. X must report a long-term capital gain of $2,500.

B. X is allowed a $500 credit for the tax since it is considered paid by X.

C. X is allowed to increase her basis in the stock by $2,000.

D. X does not report a long-term capital gain because nothing was paid to her.

Answer (D) is correct.

REQUIRED: The false statement concerning an undistributed long-term capital gain in a mutual fund.

DISCUSSION: A mutual fund is a regulated investment company, the taxation of which is determined by Sec. 852. Shareholders are taxed on dividends paid by the mutual fund. If part or all of the dividend is designated as a capital gain dividend, it must be treated as such by the shareholders. Undistributed capital gains also must be included in income by shareholders, but they are allowed a credit for their proportionate share of any tax on the capital gain paid by the mutual fund (Publication 17).

Answer (A) is incorrect. X must include the undistributed capital gain in income. Answer (B) is incorrect. X is allowed a credit for her share of the tax paid by the mutual fund on the capital gain. Answer (C) is incorrect. X does increase her basis by the difference between the amount of such includible gains and the tax deemed paid by X [Sec. 852(b)(3)(D)(iii)].

34. John and Mary, a married couple, have a wide variety of investments and are cash-basis taxpayers. Because their self-employment earnings are considerable, they reinvested the following: $4,000 of mutual fund dividends and $5,000 of certificate of deposit interest. They also earned dividends on corporate stock of $12,000 that they received and spent. Interest of $2,000 that had accrued on a loan to a friend was not paid until the following year. What is the amount of interest and dividends currently taxable to them?

A. $21,000

B. $14,000

C. $16,000

D. $23,000

Answer (A) is correct.

REQUIRED: The amount of interest and dividends currently taxable.

DISCUSSION: Mutual fund dividends, certificate of deposit interest, and corporate stock dividends are all taxable in the current year. All dividends and interest, even those that have been reinvested, are taxable, unless a specific provision in the tax code exempts the tax. (See Pub. 550.) None of the income earned qualifies for a tax exemption. The interest is not taxable until it is received because John and Mary are cash-basis taxpayers.

Answer (B) is incorrect. The amount of $14,000 includes the accrued interest, which is not taxable until it is received by a cash-basis taxpayer. In addition, it excludes both of the reinvested incomes from the mutual fund dividends and the certificate of deposit interest. Answer (C) is incorrect. The amount of $16,000 excludes the taxable interest from the certificate of deposit. Answer (D) is incorrect. The amount of $23,000 includes the accrued interest, which is not taxable until it is received by a cash-basis taxpayer.

2.4 Royalties and Rental Income

35. Which of the following is not rental income in the year received?

A. Security deposit, equal to 1 month's rent, to be refunded at the end of the lease if the building passes inspection.

B. Payment to cancel the remaining lease.

C. Repairs paid by the tenant in lieu of rent.

D. January 2013 rent received December 2012.

Answer (A) is correct.

REQUIRED: The correct treatment regarding income from rental property.

DISCUSSION: Rental income is any payment received for the use of occupation of property. When a payment is made to cancel a lease, the amount paid is rental income. If property or services are offered in lieu of rent, the FMV of the property or services is regarded as rent. Advance rent is treated as rental income for the period in which it is received. Security deposits held to ensure tenants live up to the terms of the lease are not treated as rental income (Publication 17).

Answer (B) is incorrect. When a payment is made to cancel a lease, the amount paid is rental income. Answer (C) is incorrect. If property or services are offered in lieu of rent, the FMV of the property or services is regarded as rent. Answer (D) is incorrect. Advance rent is treated as rental income for the period in which it is received.

36. Troy, a cash-basis taxpayer, owns an office building. His records reflect the following for 2012:

On March 1, 2012, office B was leased for 12 months. A $900 security deposit was received, which will be used as the last month's rent.

On September 30, 2012, the tenant in office A paid Troy $3,600 to cancel the lease expiring on March 31, 2013.

The lease of the tenant in office C expired on December 31, 2012, and the tenant left improvements valued at $1,400. The improvements were not in lieu of any required rent.

Considering just these three amounts, what amount must Troy include in rental income on his income tax return for 2012?

A. $5,900

B. $5,000

C. $4,500

D. $1,800

Answer (C) is correct.

REQUIRED: The amount of rental income given security deposits, leasehold improvements, and a cancelation payment.

DISCUSSION: Rental income includes the $900 security deposit and the $3,600 lease cancelation payment. The security deposit must be included because it was intended as rent, and the cancelation payment was in lieu of rent, so it also must be included. The $1,400 of leasehold improvements are excluded from income since they were not in lieu of rent (Publication 17 and IRC Sec. 109).

Answer (A) is incorrect. The leasehold improvements are not included in gross income. Answer (B) is incorrect. The security deposit is included in gross income and the improvements are not. Answer (D) is incorrect. Both the security deposit and the lease cancelation payment should be included in rental income.

37. Ms. Oak rented a small house to Mr. Acorn for $500 a month for all of the current year. The house was in serious need of rehabilitation. Mr. Acorn, an electrician, approached Ms. Oak with a proposal that he would rewire the house in lieu of payment of his January through April rent (4 months). Ms. Oak accepted Mr. Acorn's offer, and Mr. Acorn completed his work in July. In August, Ms. Oak notified Mr. Acorn that she would be out of town for 3 months starting at the beginning of September, and she asked him to "look after things." While she was away, he paid $200 to have the furnace repaired. When she returned at the end of November, he paid her $1,300 (3 months' rent for September, October, and November less the $200 he had paid for the furnace). Mr. Acorn timely paid his rent on the first of each month for May, June, July, August, and December. What amount should Ms. Oak include in her current-year gross rental income?

A. $4,000

B. $4,200

C. $6,000

D. $6,200

Answer (C) is correct.

REQUIRED: The amount of rental income to be recognized.

DISCUSSION: In general, improvements made by a lessee on the lessor's property are excluded from income under Sec. 109 unless they are in lieu of rent. In this case, Mr. Acorn rewired the house in lieu of 4 months' rent. The $2,000 ($500 × 4) of improvements must be included in income. If a lessee pays any of the expenses of his/her lessor, such payments are additional rental income to the lessor [Reg. 1.61-8(c)]. Since the expenses are in effect treated as if paid by the lessee to the lessor and then paid by the lessor to a third party, the lessor may deduct them (Publication 17). Therefore, Ms. Oak must include all 12 months of rent in income, for a total of $6,000.

Answer (A) is incorrect. The improvements were made in lieu of rent and are indirect rent. Answer (B) is incorrect. The improvements were made in lieu of rent and are included. Answer (D) is incorrect. The expenses may be deducted from income so that they are not taxed twice.

38. Mr. Cypress owned a small three-unit apartment building in Detroit, Michigan. The rent on each apartment was $1,000 per month. During 2012, he received the following payments:

Apt. A - Timely rent payments for 12 months

Apt. B - The apartment was vacant in January and February. On 3/1/12, a new tenant entered into a 1-year lease from 3/1/12 through 2/28/13. The tenant paid first and last month's rent and a security deposit of $1,500. The security deposit is to be returned at the end of the lease if the tenant lives up to the terms of the lease. The tenant timely paid the rent for the next 9 months (April through December) on the first of each month.

Apt. C - In December, after timely paying the rent for 12 months of the year, the tenant came to Mr. Cypress and told him that he had been transferred to a new job location in Tennessee. He asked to be released from his 2-year lease obligation, which was scheduled to expire on June 30, 2013. Mr. Cypress agreed to accept 3 months' rent to cancel the lease. The tenant paid Mr. Cypress $3,000 to cancel the lease in December.

Assuming Mr. Cypress is a cash-basis taxpayer, what amount should Mr. Cypress include in his 2012 gross income from the apartment building?

A. $35,000

B. $35,500

C. $38,000

D. $39,500

Answer (C) is correct.

REQUIRED: The landlord's rental income from various types of payments.

DISCUSSION: Both cash- and accrual-basis taxpayers must include amounts in gross income upon actual or constructive receipt if the taxpayer has an unrestricted claim to such amounts under Reg. 1.61-8(b). Thus, all the rent payments should be included in the current year's gross rental income. Security deposits are income only if the lessor becomes entitled to the funds because of the lessee's violation of the terms of the lease. Therefore, Mr. Cypress does not have an unrestricted claim to the security deposit. The cancelation payment is in lieu of rent, so it must be included in income like rent. Mr. Cypress should recognize $12,000 from Apt. A ($1,000 rent × 12 months) plus $11,000 from Apt. B ($10,000 for rent + $1,000 last month's rent) plus $15,000 from Apt. C ($12,000 rent + $3,000 cancelation payment), for a total of $38,000 (Publication 17).

Answer (A) is incorrect. The lease cancelation payment must be included in income. Answer (B) is incorrect. The gross income includes only all the rent paid in the current period plus the lease cancelation payment. Answer (D) is incorrect. The security deposit is not included in income if it is not intended as rent.

39. In the current year, Jerry signed a 5-year lease to rent space to the MacBee restaurant. That year, MacBee paid Jerry $24,000 for the first year's rent and $24,000 for the last year's rent. Jerry reports his income using the accrual method of accounting. How much of the $48,000 is included in Jerry's current-year income?

A. $24,000

B. $120,000

C. $48,000

D. $0

Answer (C) is correct.

REQUIRED: The amount includible in gross income.

DISCUSSION: Both cash- and accrual-basis taxpayers must include amounts in gross income upon actual or constructive receipt if the taxpayer has an unrestricted claim to such amounts under Reg. 1.61-8(b) (Publication 17). Since Jerry has an unrestricted claim to the $24,000 of rent paid in advance, it would be included in his rental income.

Answer (A) is incorrect. Jerry must recognize the last year's payment because he has an unrestricted claim to it. Answer (B) is incorrect. Jerry only has actually or constructively received $48,000. Answer (D) is incorrect. Income must be recognized when rent is received.

40. The Becks own and operate an assisted-living facility. They provide maid service and meals in a common dining room. Where should they report the income and expenses from this activity?

A. Other Income on Form 1040 and expenses as itemized deductions on Schedule A.

B. Income and expenses on Schedule E, *Supplemental Income and Loss.*

C. Income and expenses on Schedule C, *Profit or Loss from Business.*

D. Short-term capital gain on Schedule D.

Answer (C) is correct.

REQUIRED: The schedule on which to report income and expenses from business.

DISCUSSION: Income and expenses from a non-passive activity, other than farming activities, are reported on Schedule C, *Profit or Loss from Business* (Publication 17).

Answer (A) is incorrect. The income and expenses are reported on Schedule C. Answer (B) is incorrect. This is an active trade or business that requires reporting on Schedule C. Answer (D) is incorrect. This is an activity trade or business. Thus, the income and expenses should be reported on Schedule C.

STUDY UNIT THREE
BUSINESS DEDUCTIONS

(12 pages of outline)

Gross income is reduced by deductions to compute taxable income. No amount can be deducted from gross income unless allowed by the Internal Revenue Code (IRC). **Above-the-line deductions** are deducted from gross income to arrive at adjusted gross income (AGI). Several deductions and credits are limited by reference to AGI. **Below-the-line deductions** are deducted from AGI to arrive at taxable income.

Employee business expenses are generally deductible, but their tax treatment depends on the employer's reimbursements. If reimbursements equal expenses and the employee makes an accounting of expenses to the employer, the reimbursements are excluded from the employee's gross income, and the employee may not deduct the expenses (accountable plan).

1. This rule also applies if reimbursements exceeding expenses are returned to the employer and the employee substantiates the expenses.
2. If excess reimbursements are not returned or if the employee does not substantiate them, the reimbursements are included in the employee's gross income, and all the expenses are deducted from AGI (below-the-line deductions). These expenses are an itemized deduction subject to the 2% floor (nonaccountable plan).
   a. The employee reports these expenses on Form 2106, *Employee Business Expenses.*
3. Reimbursements for transportation not exceeding $.555/mile for 2012 are considered adequately substantiated by a record of time, place, and business purpose.
4. The employer decides which plan to use, and this determines the employee's tax consequences.

3.1 BUSINESS EXPENSES

1. A deduction from gross income is allowed for all ordinary and necessary expenses paid or incurred during a tax year in carrying on a trade or business.
   a. A sole proprietor claims these deductions on Schedule C.

Trade/Business and Expenses Defined

2. A trade or business is a regular and continuous activity that is entered into with the expectation of making a profit.
   a. "Regular" means the taxpayer devotes a substantial amount of business time to the activity.
3. An activity that is not engaged in for a profit is a hobby (personal).
   a. An activity that results in a profit in any 3 of 5 consecutive tax years (2 out of 7 for the breeding and racing of horses) is presumed not to be a hobby.
   b. Deductions for hobby expenses are discussed in Study Unit 5.

4. An expense must be **both** ordinary and necessary to be deductible.
   a. "Ordinary" implies that the expense normally occurs or is likely to occur in connection with businesses similar to the one operated by the taxpayer claiming the deduction.
      1) The expenditures need not occur frequently.
   b. "Necessary" implies that an expenditure must be appropriate and helpful in developing or maintaining the trade or business.
   c. Implicit in the "ordinary and necessary" requirement is the requirement that the expenditures be reasonable. For example, if the compensation paid to a shareholder exceeds that ordinarily paid for similar services (reasonable compensation), the excessive payment may constitute a nondeductible dividend.

Expense Treatment

5. **Allocation**
   a. Only the portion of an expenditure that is attributable to business activity is deductible.
   b. A reasonable method of allocation may be used. It must clearly reflect income.
6. **Compensation**
   a. Cash and the FMV of property paid to an employee are deductible by the employer.
7. **Rent**
   a. Advance rental payments may be deducted by the lessee only during the tax periods to which the payments apply.
   b. Even a cash-method taxpayer must amortize prepaid rent expense over the period to which it applies.

Travel

8. While away from home overnight on business, travel expenses are deductible. Travel expenses include transportation, lodging, and meal expenses in an employment-related context.
   a. No deduction is allowed for
      1) Travel that is primarily personal in nature
      2) The travel expenses of the taxpayer's spouse unless
         a) There is a bona fide business purpose for the spouse's presence,
         b) The spouse is an employee, and
         c) The expenses would be otherwise deductible.
      3) Commuting between home and work
      4) Attending investment meetings
      5) Travel as a form of education
   b. **Substantiation**
      1) A taxpayer must substantiate the amount, time, place, and business purpose of expenses paid or incurred in traveling away from home.
   c. There are four exceptions to the commuting expense deduction disallowance.
      1) The costs of going between one business location and another business location are generally deductible (Rev. Rul. 55-109, 1955-1 CB 261).
      2) The costs of going between the taxpayer's residence and a temporary work location outside the metropolitan area where the taxpayer lives and normally works are generally deductible (Rev. Rul. 94-47, 1994-2 CB 18).
         a) A work location is considered temporary if it is expected to last less than 1 year even if it ultimately lasts more than 1 year.

b) A work location is considered indefinite if it is expected to last more than 1 year even if it ultimately lasts less than 1 year.

c) A work location that is expected to be temporary but that becomes indefinite is considered to be indefinite from the point at which the employment time becomes indefinite.

3) If the taxpayer has one or more regular work locations away from his/her residence, (s)he may deduct commuting expenses incurred in going between the residence and a temporary work location in the same trade or business, regardless of the distance.

4) If a taxpayer's residence is the taxpayer's principal place of business within the meaning of Section 280A(c)(1)(A), the taxpayer may deduct commuting expenses incurred in going between the residence and another work location in the same trade or business, regardless of whether the work location is regular or temporary and regardless of the distance.

Transportation while Traveling

d. Actual expenses for automobile use are deductible (e.g., services, repairs, gasoline, depreciation, insurance, and licenses).

1) Alternatively, the taxpayer may deduct the standard mileage rate ($.555/mile for 2012), plus parking fees, tolls, etc.

2) If a taxpayer switches from using the standard mileage rate to actual expenses, the depreciation deduction must be computed using the straight-line method.

e. To determine a taxpayer's principal place of business for purposes of travel expenses, the location of an individual's tax home must be determined. When a taxpayer has multiple places of business, the IRS determines the principal place of business using a three-pronged test:

1) The total time spent at each place of business
2) The degree of business activity at each place of business
3) The relative income earned at each place of business

Foreign Travel

f. Traveling expenses of a taxpayer who travels outside of the United States away from home must be allocated between time spent on the trip for business and time spent for pleasure.

EXAMPLE

Scott's foreign trip is for more than a week, and he spends most of his time as a personal vacation. However, he spends some time at a business-related conference.

Only the expenses related to the conference, including lodging and local travel, etc., may be deducted.

1) No allocation is required when

a) The trip is for no more than 1 week, and

b) A personal vacation is not the major consideration or the personal time spent on the trip is less than 25% of the total time away from home.

2) A deduction for travel expenses will be denied to the extent that they are not allocable to the taxpayer's business when

a) The trip is longer than 1 week or

b) 25% or more of the time away from home is spent for personal reasons.

Conventions

g. Convention Travel Expenses

1) Deductible

a) Travel expenses for attending a convention related to the taxpayer's business, even when the taxpayer is an employee

i) The fact that an employee uses vacation or leave time or that attendance at the convention is voluntary will not necessarily negate the deduction.

2) Not deductible

a) Expenses for a convention or meeting in connection with investments, financial planning, or other income-producing property

3) Limited deduction

a) Expenses for conventions on U.S. cruise ships.

b) The deduction is limited to $2,000 with respect to all cruises beginning in any calendar year.

c) It applies only if

i) All ports of such cruise ship are located in the U.S. or in U.S. possessions,

ii) The taxpayer establishes that the convention is directly related to the active conduct of his/her trade or business, and

iii) The taxpayer includes certain specified information in the return on which the deduction is claimed.

Transportation Expenses

9. Transportation expenses for employees include taxi fares, automobile expenses, tolls and parking fees, and airfare.

a. These expenses are treated as travel expenses if the employee is away from home overnight. Otherwise, they are transportation expenses.

b. Commuting costs are nondeductible.

1) An employee who uses an automobile to transport tools to work will be allowed a deduction for transportation expenses only if additional costs are incurred, such as renting a trailer. A deduction is allowed only for the additional costs incurred to transport the tools to work.

c. Actual automobile expenses may be used for the deduction, or the taxpayer may use the standard mileage rate.

1) The standard mileage rate is $.555/mile for 2012, plus parking fees and tolls. This rate applies to vehicles that are owned or leased.

a) This standard mileage rate cannot be used when the taxpayer owns or leases five or more cars (i.e., a fleet) that are used for business at the same time.

b) As of 2011, this rate also can be used for cars used for hire (e.g., taxicabs).

2) Actual expenses must be allocated between business use and personal use of the automobile. A deduction is allowed only for the business use.

a) Actual automobile expenses include the following: gas and oil, lubrication and washing, repairs, garage and parking fees, insurance, tires and supplies, tolls, interest expense, leasing fees, licenses, and depreciation. Remember, depreciation is only taken on the business portion of the automobile; therefore, all depreciation is deductible.

3) The deduction is reported on Schedule A and is subject to the 2%-of-AGI limitation.

d. The following illustration summarizes the rules for transportation expense deductions:

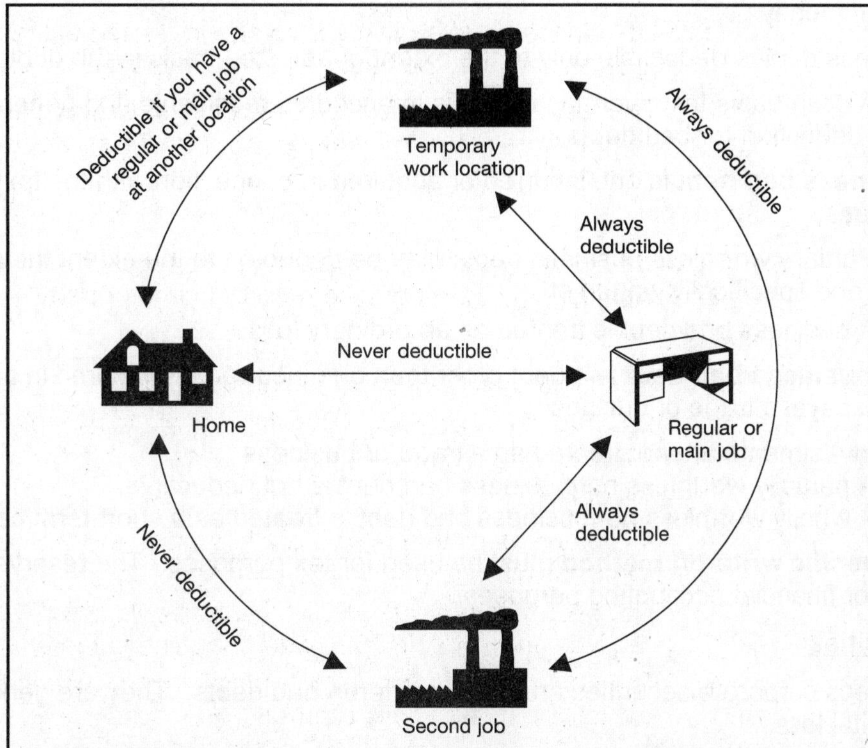

Home: The place where you reside. Transportation expenses between your home and your main or regular place of work are personal commuting expenses.

Regular or main job: Your principal place of business. If you have more than one job, you must determine which one is your regular or main job. Consider the time you spend at each, the activity you have at each, and the income you earn at each.

Temporary work location: A place where your work assignment is realistically expected to last (and does in fact last) 1 year or less. Unless you have a regular place of business, you can only deduct your transportation expenses to a temporary work location <u>outside</u> your metropolitan area.

Second job: If you regularly work at two or more places in one day, whether or not for the same employer, you cannot deduct your transportation costs between your home and a second job on a day off from your main job.

10. The following factors are used to determine a taxpayer's tax home:

    a. The taxpayer performs part of his/her business in the area surrounding his/her main home and uses that home for lodging while doing business in the area.

    b. The taxpayer has living expenses at his/her main home that are duplicated because his/her business requires him/her to be away from that home.

    c. The taxpayer has not abandoned the area in which both his/her traditional place of lodging and his/her main home are located, members of his/her family live at his/her main home, or (s)he often uses that home for lodging.

<u>Insurance Expense</u>

11. Trade or business insurance expense paid or incurred during the tax year is deductible.

    a. A cash-method taxpayer may not deduct a premium before it is paid.

    b. Prepaid insurance must be apportioned over the period of coverage.

    c. Self-employed persons may deduct from gross income 100% of amounts paid for health insurance premiums.

Bad Debts

12. A bad-debt deduction is allowed only for a bona fide debt arising from a debtor-creditor relationship based upon a valid and enforceable obligation to pay a fixed or determinable sum of money.
13. Worthless debt is deductible only to the extent of adjusted basis in the debt.
    a. A cash-basis taxpayer has no basis in accounts receivable and generally has no deduction for bad debts.
14. A **business bad debt** is one incurred or acquired in connection with the taxpayer's trade or business.
    a. Partially worthless business debts may be deducted to the extent they are worthless and specifically written off.
    b. A business bad debt is treated as an ordinary loss.
15. A **nonbusiness bad debt** is a debt other than one incurred or acquired in connection with the taxpayer's trade or business.
    a. Investments are not treated as a trade or business.
    b. A partially worthless nonbusiness bad debt is not deductible.
    c. A wholly worthless nonbusiness bad debt is treated as a short-term capital loss.
16. The **specific write-off method** must be used for tax purposes. The reserve method is used only for financial accounting purposes.

Worthless Securities

17. Worthless corporate securities are not considered bad debts. They are generally treated as a capital loss.
18. The **loss on deposits** can occur when a bank, credit union, or other financial institution becomes bankrupt or insolvent.
    a. The individual may treat the nonbusiness account loss as a personal casualty loss in the year in which the loss can be reasonably estimated.
    b. Alternatively, the individual can elect to treat the loss as a nonbusiness ordinary loss arising from a transaction entered into for profit.
    c. If no election is made, the default classification for the nonbusiness bad debt is a short-term capital loss subject to a $3,000 annual limit.

Business Gifts

19. Expenditures for business gifts are deductible. They must be ordinary and necessary.
    a. Deduction for business gift expenditure is disallowed unless the taxpayer substantiates, by adequate records, the following:
        1) Amount (cost) of the gift,
        2) Date of the gift,
        3) Description of the gift,
        4) Business purpose of the gift, and
        5) Business relation of the recipient to the taxpayer.
    b. Deduction is limited to $25 per recipient per year for excludable items.
        1) The $25 limit does not apply to incidental items costing (the giver) not more than $4 each.
        2) A husband and wife are treated as one taxpayer, even if they file separate returns and have independent business relationships with the recipient.

Employee Achievement Awards

20. Up to $400 of the cost of employee achievement awards is deductible by an employer for all nonqualified plan awards.
    a. An employee achievement award is tangible personal property awarded as part of a meaningful presentation for safety achievement or length of service.
21. Deduction of qualified plan awards is limited to $1,600 per year.
    a. A qualified plan award is an employee achievement award provided under an established written program that does not discriminate in favor of highly compensated employees.
        1) If the average cost of all employee achievement awards is greater than $400, it is not a qualified plan award.

Depreciation

22. Deduction is permitted for obsolescence or wear and tear of property used in a trade or business.

Start-Up Costs

23. Taxpayers can deduct up to $5,000 of start-up costs and $5,000 of organizational expenditures in the taxable year in which the business begins.
    a. Examples of start-up costs include the costs of investigating the creation or acquisition of an active trade or business, to prepare to enter into the trade or business, to secure suppliers and customers, and to obtain certain supplies and equipment (noncapital).
    b. For 2012, any start-up costs or organizational expenditures in excess of the $5,000 limit are capitalized and amortized proportionally over a 15-year period beginning with the month in which the active trade or business begins.
        1) These amounts are reduced, but not below zero, by the cumulative cost of the start-up costs or organizational expenditures that exceed $50,000.
    c. A taxpayer is deemed to have made the election; therefore, a taxpayer is not required to attach a separate statement to the return.

Reforestation Cost

24. Amounts paid or incurred for reforestation may be expensed in the current year up to $10,000. Any remaining balance is to be amortized over a period of 7 years.

Vacant Land

25. Interest and taxes on vacant land are deductible.

Demolition

26. If a structure is demolished, demolition costs, undepreciated (remaining) basis, and losses sustained are not deductible. They are allocated to the land.

Abandoned Assets

27. A loss is deductible in the year the assets are actually abandoned with no claim for reimbursement.
    a. The loss equals the adjusted basis in the abandoned property.

COGS

28. Cost of goods sold (COGS) is not a "business deduction." It reduces gross income.

`Sales - COGS = Gross income`

Medical Reimbursement Plans

29. The cost of such a plan for employees is deductible by the employer.

Political Contributions

30. Contributions to a political party or candidate and, generally, lobbying expenses are not deductible.

> **EXAMPLE**
>
> Craft Store pays for advertising in the program for a political party's convention. Proceeds are used for the party's activities. The expense is a political contribution, which is not deductible.

   a. However, expense in connection with appearances before and communications with any **local** council or similar governing body with respect to legislation of direct interest to the taxpayer is deductible.
   b. Up to $2,000 of direct cost of such activity at the state or federal level is deductible.
      1) Also, if total direct costs exceed $2,000, then this de minimis exception is entirely unavailable.

Debt of Another

31. Payment of a debt of another party is generally not ordinary for a trade or business and thus is not deductible.
   a. A legal obligation or definite business requirement renders the payment deductible, e.g., if required by suppliers to stay in business.

Intangibles

32. The cost of intangibles must generally be capitalized.
   a. Amortization is allowed if the intangible has a determinable useful life, e.g., a covenant not to compete or if a code section specifically so provides.

Tax-Exempt Income

33. An expenditure related to producing tax-exempt income is not deductible, e.g., interest on a loan used to purchase tax-exempt bonds.

Public Policy

34. A trade or business expenditure that is ordinary, necessary, and reasonable may be nondeductible if allowing the deduction would frustrate public policy.
   a. Examples are
      1) Fines and penalties paid to the government for violation of the law
      2) Illegal bribes and kickbacks
      3) Two-thirds of damages for violation of federal antitrust law
      4) Expenses of dealers in illegal drugs
         a) However, adjustment to gross receipts is permitted for the cost of merchandise.

Impairment-Related Expenses

35. Expenses of a handicapped individual for attendant care services at his/her place of employment and/or other expenses connected to his/her place of employment necessary for the individual to work are deductible expenses. The expenses are itemized deductions (other miscellaneous deductions), which are not subject to the 2% floor.

Miscellaneous Expenses

36. Miscellaneous ordinary and necessary business expenses are deductible.
   a. Examples include costs of office supplies, advertising, professional fees, and bank fees.

Withdrawal Penalties

37. Penalties on the early withdrawal of interest income are deductible as above-the-line deductions.

Business Use of Home

38. Expenses incurred for the use of a person's home for business purposes are deductible only if strict requirements are met.
    a. The portion of the home must be used exclusively and regularly as
        1) The principal place of business for any trade or business of the taxpayer;
        2) A place of business that is used by patients, clients, or customers in the normal course of the taxpayer's trade or business; or
        3) A separate structure that is not attached to the dwelling unit that is used in the taxpayer's trade or business.
    b. If the taxpayer is an employee, the business use of the home must also be for the convenience of the employer.
    c. The exclusive-use test is strictly applied. Any personal use of the business portion of the home by anyone results in complete disallowance of the deductions. There are two exceptions to the exclusive-use test:
        1) Retail/wholesale. A retailer or wholesaler whose **sole** location of his/her business is his/her home need not meet the exclusive-use test.
            a) The ordinary and necessary business expenses allocable to an identifiable space used regularly for inventory or product sample storage by a taxpayer in the active pursuit of his/her trade or business are deductible.
        2) Day care. If the business portion of a home is used to offer qualifying day care, the exclusive-use test need not be met.
    d. If the taxpayer has more than one business location, the primary factor in determining whether a home office is a taxpayer's principal place of business is the relative importance of the activities performed at each business location.
        1) If the primary location cannot be determined by the relative importance test, then the amount of time spent at each location will be used.
    e. A home office qualifies as a "principal place of business" if used by the taxpayer to conduct administrative or management activities of the taxpayer's trade or business and there is no other fixed location where the taxpayer conducts such activities.
    f. Deduction for business use is limited to
        1) Gross income derived from the use, minus
        2) Deductions allocable to the home, allowed regardless of business or personal use, e.g., interest or taxes, minus
        3) Deductions allocable to the trade or business for which the home office is used that are not home office expenses, e.g., employee compensation.
    g. Any currently disallowed amount is deductible in succeeding years, subject to the same limitations.

EXAMPLE

Tammy has $32,000 of gross income from a business activity conducted in a home office. She may deduct $10,000 of mortgage interest and property taxes allocable to the home office as personal expenses. Tammy has $6,000 of home office expenses other than depreciation, $3,500 in depreciation, and $15,000 of business deductions that are not home office expenses. Only $1,000 [$32,000 – ($10,000 + $15,000 + $6,000)] of the depreciation is deductible as home office expenses.

Stop and review! You have completed the outline for this subunit. Study questions 1 through 23 beginning on page 84.

3.2 ENTERTAINMENT AND MEALS

Limit

1. The amount deductible for meal and entertainment expense is 50% of the actual expense.
   a. The limit also applies to the taxpayer's own meals.
   b. Related expenses, such as taxes, tips, and parking fees, but not transportation to and from a business meal, are also subject to the 50% limit.
   c. The IRS has denied deductions for any meal or entertainment expense over $75 for which the claimant did not provide substantiating evidence: documented dates, amounts, location, purpose, and business relationship.
   d. For employees subject to Department of Transportation hours-of-service rules, the deductible meals percentage is 80% after 2007.

Related/Associated Expenses

2. The expense must be directly related to or associated with the active conduct of a trade or business. The predominant purpose must be the furthering of the trade or business of the taxpayer incurring the expense.
   a. "Directly related" means that business is actually conducted during the entertainment period.
   b. "Associated with" means that the entertainment must occur directly before or after a business discussion.

Entertainment Defined

3. Entertainment includes recreation, e.g., entertaining guests at a nightclub, sporting event, or theater, or by vacations, trips, etc., and furnishing a hotel suite, an automobile, food and beverages, or the like to a customer or a member of the customer's family.
   a. Club dues for social gatherings are not deductible. Dues paid to professional clubs (e.g., Kiwanis) are deductible if they are paid for business reasons and the principal purpose of membership is professional and not for entertainment.
   b. The allowable deduction for the cost of a ticket for any entertainment activity is generally limited to the face value of the ticket.
      1) Tickets for certain sports events that are primarily organized to benefit a tax-exempt charitable organization are not subject to the face value limitation.
   c. In addition, the cost of a luxury box or skybox may be limited if it is leased out for more than one event.
      1) When the luxury box is leased out for multiple events, the cost of the luxury box is limited to the cost of nonluxury box seat tickets multiplied by the number of seats in the luxury box.
      2) The deductible portion of the luxury box is further limited to the 50% meal and entertainment threshold.

Attendance

4. Meal expenses are not deductible if neither the taxpayer nor an employee of the taxpayer is present at the meal.

Ownership of Facility

5. Expenses in connection with the use of an entertainment facility that the taxpayer owns are not deductible as a business expense.
   a. Any property that a taxpayer rents, owns, or uses for entertainment purposes is considered to be an entertainment facility.
   b. Swimming pools, cars, hotel suites, and yachts are all examples of entertainment facilities.

Stop and review! You have completed the outline for this subunit. Study questions 24 through 30 beginning on page 91.

3.3 RENTAL PROPERTY EXPENSES

1. Expenses related to the production of rental income are generally deductible to arrive at adjusted gross income.
   a. Rental property expenditures may be deducted by depreciation. Generally, a Section 179 deduction is not allowed for rental property. The exceptions to this disallowance include leasehold improvement property (not residential), restaurant property, and retail improvement property.
2. Special rules limit deductions on the rental of a residence or a vacation home.

Minimum Rental Use

   a. The property must be rented for more than 14 days during the year for deductions to be allowable.

Minimum Personal Use

   b. The vacation-home rules apply when the taxpayer uses the residence for personal purposes for the greater of (1) more than 14 days or (2) more than 10% of the number of days for which the residence is rented.
      1) When the residence is rented for less than 15 days, the rental income does not need to be reported. Any corresponding rental expenses cannot be deducted.
3. A residence is deemed to have been used by the taxpayer for personal purposes if the home is used by
   a. The taxpayer for personal purposes, by any other person who owns an interest in the rental property, or by the relatives of either
      1) However, if the taxpayer rented or tried to rent the property for 12 or more consecutive months, the days during which (s)he used the property as a main home do not count as personal days.
   b. Any individual under a reciprocal arrangement, whether or not rent is charged
   c. Any individual unless a fair rental is charged
4. If the taxpayer spends substantially full-time repairing or maintaining the rental property, such time does not count toward the personal-use test.

Vacation Home Rules

5. If the property passes the minimum rental-use test but fails the minimum personal-use test, the property is considered a vacation home, and rental deductions may not exceed gross income derived from rental activities.
   a. When deductions are limited to gross income, the order of deductions is
      1) The allocable portion of expenses deductible regardless of rental income (e.g., mortgage interest and property taxes)
      2) Deductions that do not affect basis (e.g., ordinary repairs and maintenance)
      3) Deductions that affect basis (e.g., depreciation)
   b. Expenses must be allocated between the personal use and the rental use based on the number of days of use of each.

6. If the property passes both the minimum rental-use test and the minimum personal-use test, then all deductions may be taken and a loss may occur, subject to the passive loss limits.

Minimum Use Tests		
	Rental Use	Personal Use
Pass	> 14 days	≤ 14 days or < 10%
Fail	≤ 14 days	greater of > 14 days or > 10%

7. Expense deductions for not-for-profit (NFP) rentals are limited to income from such rentals. Neither loss nor carryforward is allowed for NFP expenses in excess of NFP income.

Stop and review! You have completed the outline for this subunit. Study questions 31 through 41 beginning on page 93.

QUESTIONS

3.1 Business Expenses

1. With respect to an employer's reimbursement of employee business expenses, which of the following statements is not a requirement of an accountable plan?

A. The expenses incurred by the employee must have a business purpose.

B. The reimbursement of meal and entertainment expenditures is limited to 50% of the amount incurred.

C. The employee must provide an accounting to the employer within a reasonable period of time.

D. The employee must return any excess reimbursement or allowance to the employer within a reasonable period of time.

Answer (B) is correct.

REQUIRED: The false statement regarding an employer's reimbursement of employee business expenses.

DISCUSSION: The reimbursement of meal and entertainment expenditures is not limited except by their total amount. The employer can reimburse 100% of allowable meal and entertainment expenses; however, the employer can deduct only 50% of the allowable meal and entertainment expenses on his/her tax return. Further, since the plan is an accountable one, the employer will not recognize the reimbursements as taxable wages, and the employee will not recognize the deductions on his/her return (Publication 463).

2. During 2012, Ted drives his car 5,000 miles to visit clients, 10,000 miles to get to his office, and 500 miles to attend business-related seminars. He also spent $300 for airfare to another business seminar and $200 for parking at his office. Using 55.5 cents per mile, what is his deductible transportation expense?

A. $300

B. $3,105

C. $3,553

D. $8,903

Answer (B) is correct.

REQUIRED: The deduction for transportation expense.

DISCUSSION: Commuting expenses between a taxpayer's residence and a business location within the area of the taxpayer's home are generally not deductible. In addition, the cost of parking at a taxpayer's place of work is not deductible. However, transportation between home and a temporary work location in the same trade or business may be deducted. Thus, the travel expenses to visit clients and the business-related seminars are all deductible (Publication 463).

Mileage	$3,053	(5,500 miles × $.555/mile)
Airfare	300	
Deductible travel costs	$3,353	

Answer (A) is incorrect. This amount excludes the deduction for the mileage traveled to clients and the business-related seminars. Answer (C) is incorrect. The fee paid for parking at the office is not a deductible travel expense. Answer (D) is incorrect. The 10,000 miles of travel to the office is not deductible.

3. In order to qualify as an accountable plan for reimbursement of travel expenses, the employer plan must satisfy all of the following except

A. The expenses have a business connection.

B. The employee must make an adequate and timely accounting to the employer.

C. The employer must pay a per diem for meals.

D. The employee must timely return any excess reimbursements.

Answer (C) is correct.

REQUIRED: The statement that is not required to satisfy requirements as an accountable plan for reimbursement of travel expenses.

DISCUSSION: For a reimbursement plan to qualify as an accountable plan, all three of the following conditions must be met:

1. There must be a business connection to the expenses.
2. The employee must verify or be reported to have verified the expenses.
3. The employee must return any amounts that exceed the verified expenses.

Per diem allowances for meals is a substitute plan for an accountable plan in which the company deducts a "reasonable amount" for the cost of travel expenses (See Publication 463).

Answer (A) is incorrect. It is a requirement that the expenses have a business connection for an accountable reimbursement plan. Answer (B) is incorrect. It is a requirement that the employee make adequate and timely accounting to the employer for an accountable reimbursement plan. Answer (D) is incorrect. It is a requirement that the employee timely return any excess reimbursements for an accountable reimbursement plan.

4. Jack received $3,000 in educational assistance benefits from his employer during 2012 to reimburse him for the cost of course tuition and fees for him to earn a degree. The benefits were paid under an accountable plan and were not included in Jack's W-2. He has a modified adjusted gross income of $20,000, and he files single. A list of Jack's 2012 expenses follows. What is Jack's deductible tuition and fee expense?

- $500 for a bowling class not required for his degree
- $2,000 for accounting courses required for his degree
- $1,000 for room and board
- $500 for textbooks
- $500 for lab fees for courses required for his degree

A. $0

B. $4,500

C. $4,000

D. $3,000

Answer (A) is correct.

REQUIRED: The expenses that are deductible under an accountable plan.

DISCUSSION: Educational expenses are generally deductible. However, if a taxpayer receives reimbursements from his/her employer, the tax treatment depends on the employer's reimbursements. If reimbursements equal expenses and the employee makes an accounting of the expenses to the employer, the reimbursements are excluded from the employee's gross income, and the employee may not deduct the expenses. This is referred to as an accountable plan (Publication 463). Since Jack is accounting for his educational expenses to his employer under an accountable plan, he cannot deduct any educational expenses.

Answer (B) is incorrect. The tuition for the bowling class and the expenses for the room and board are not deductible for tax purposes. Furthermore, Jack cannot deduct any tuition and fees that are required for his degree because his employer has already reimbursed him for these expenses under an accountable plan. Answer (C) is incorrect. Room and board are never deductible for tax purposes, and Jack cannot deduct any tuition and fees that are required for his degree because his employer has already reimbursed him for these expenses under an accountable plan. Answer (D) is incorrect. Jack cannot deduct any tuition and fees that are required for his degree because his employer has already reimbursed him for these expenses under an accountable plan.

5. Which of the following is not a deductible transportation expense?

A. Cost of round-trip transportation between an individual's home and a temporary training site in the same city.

B. Cost of round-trip transportation between an individual's home and office if the employee is conducting business on his/her car phone.

C. Cost of round-trip transportation between an individual's qualifying office in the home and his/her client's place of business.

D. Cost of round-trip transportation between an individual's office and his/her client's place of business.

Answer (B) is correct.

REQUIRED: The situation in which transportation costs are not deductible.

DISCUSSION: An employee is permitted a deduction for transportation expenses paid in connection with services performed as an employee. The use of a vehicle to report to and return home each evening from a temporary or minor assignment beyond the general area of one's regular place of work would qualify as a deductible transportation expense. The transportation expense deduction also includes the cost of any travel by a taxpayer having a regular place of business between home and temporary work stations regardless of the distances. If the taxpayer's home serves as his/her place of business, travel between his/her home and a client will not be considered personal. However, a taxpayer may not deduct the costs of commuting to and from work as a transportation expense. It is irrelevant if the taxpayer uses a phone for business during that travel (Publication 463).

6. In which situation would local transportation expenses not be deductible?

A. From the regular or main job to the second job.

B. From the regular or main job to a temporary work location.

C. From the second job to a temporary work location.

D. From home (residence) to the second job on your day off from your main job.

Answer (D) is correct.

REQUIRED: The situation in which local transportation expenses are not deductible.

DISCUSSION: An employee is permitted a deduction for transportation expenses paid in connection with services performed as an employee. However, a taxpayer may not deduct the costs of commuting to and from work as a transportation expense (Publication 463).

7. In Year 1, Laura lent Pat $2,000. At that time, Pat signed an enforceable note agreeing to repay the $2,000. The loan was not made in the course of Laura's business. The loan had not been repaid in Year 3 when Pat died insolvent. For Year 3, Laura should report the nonpayment of the loan as a(n)

A. Short-term capital loss.

B. Long-term capital loss.

C. Ordinary loss.

D. Miscellaneous itemized deduction.

Answer (A) is correct.

REQUIRED: The treatment of a debt extinguished by the death of the debtor.

DISCUSSION: A loss from a business debt is an ordinary loss, while a loss from a nonbusiness debt is treated as a short-term capital loss. A nonbusiness bad debt is a debt other than one incurred or acquired in connection with the trade or business of the taxpayer. Therefore, when Pat died in Year 3, Laura cannot be assumed to have forgiven the loan, and the amount is not considered a gift. A short-term capital loss results (Publication 550).

8. All of the following may be deducted by a taxpayer as a transportation expense except

A. Getting from one workplace to another in the course of your business or profession.

B. Commuting expenses if you work during the commuting trip using your telephone to make business calls or have business associates ride with you to and from work and you have a business discussion in the car.

C. Visiting clients or customers after going to your office.

D. Going to a business meeting away from your regular workplace.

Answer (B) is correct.

REQUIRED: The transportation expenses that are deductible.

DISCUSSION: A taxpayer's costs of commuting between the taxpayer's residence and the taxpayer's place of business or employment generally are nondeductible personal expenses. However, the costs of going between one business location and another business location are generally deductible. A taxpayer may deduct daily transportation expenses incurred in going between the taxpayer's residence and a temporary work location outside the metropolitan area where the taxpayer lives and normally works. Making business calls or meeting with associates while commuting between a residence and place of business does not permit the transportation expenses to be deducted. (See Publication 463.)

9. Kenneth's employer gives him $500 a month ($6,000 for the year) for his business expenses. Kenneth does not have to provide any proof of his expenses to his employer, and he can keep any funds that he does not spend. His actual expenses for the year were $1,000 for lodging, $600 for meals while away from home, and $2,000 for entertainment. What reporting is required of Kenneth's employer, and what reporting is required of Kenneth?

A. Employer adds $6,000 to wages reported on Kenneth's Form W-2; Kenneth reports $3,600 as a miscellaneous itemized deduction on Schedule A.

B. Employer adds $6,000 to wages reported on Kenneth's Form W-2; Kenneth reports $3,600 on Form 2106, *Employee Business Expenses*.

C. Employer does not include any amount in Kenneth's Form W-2; Kenneth reports $2,400 as "Other Income" on the front of his return.

D. Employer adds $2,400 to wages reported on Kenneth's Form W-2; Kenneth takes no deductions on Form 2106 or Schedule A.

Answer (B) is correct.

REQUIRED: The employee and employer reporting requirements for amounts paid under a nonaccountable business expense plan.

DISCUSSION: Amounts paid under a nonaccountable plan are included in the employee's gross income, reported on Form W-2. Form 2106, *Employee Business Expenses*, is then used to report the expenses paid by Kenneth. (See Publication 463.)

NOTE: 100% of meals is reported on Form 2106, but then 50% of meals is calculated on Form 2106 and carried over to Form 1040 Schedule A as an itemized deduction.

Answer (A) is incorrect. The $3,600 is reported on Form 2106. Answer (C) is incorrect. Under a nonaccountable plan, all of the amounts received are included in gross income and then Form 2106 is filed to claim a deduction for the business expenses. Answer (D) is incorrect. Under a nonaccountable plan, all of the amounts received are included in gross income and then Form 2106 is filed to claim a deduction for the business expenses.

10. Lisa travels to various locations during her work week. Using the following data, determine the number of miles she may claim as transportation expenses for this period:

- Monday – 40 miles, round trip, from home to her full-time job
- Tuesday – 20 miles from home to her full-time job, then 10 miles from her full-time job to her part-time job, then 30 miles to her home
- Wednesday – 60 miles, round trip, from her home to her part-time job; she did not work at her full-time job

A. 160 miles.

B. 40 miles.

C. 60 miles.

D. 10 miles.

Answer (D) is correct.

REQUIRED: The amount of miles that can be claimed as a transportation expense.

DISCUSSION: A taxpayer's cost of commuting between the taxpayer's residence and the taxpayer's place of business or employment are generally nondeductible personal expenses. However, the costs of going between one business location and another business location are generally deductible (Publication 463). The only miles that may be deducted as a transportation expense are the miles between Lisa's two places of business, which is 10 miles.

Answer (A) is incorrect. Only the miles that were traveled between Lisa's two places of business are deductible, not the travel from her home to a place of business. Answer (B) is incorrect. The 40 miles round trip are not deductible since they are from Lisa's home to her place of business, while the 10 miles between her two places of business are deductible. Answer (C) is incorrect. The 60 miles round trip are not deductible since they are from Lisa's home to her place of business, while the 10 miles between her two places of business are deductible.

11. Cindy is a salesperson employed by a window manufacturing company, and she travels to various locations to sell her products. She drives 12,000 miles a year. She adequately accounts to her employer for her business expenses. Her employer reimburses her $3,960 for the mileage driven at 33 cents per mile. Based on the standard mileage rate of 55.5 cents per mile, her expense was $6,660. Cindy is entitled to deduct on Schedule A, *Itemized Deductions*, transportation expenses of

A. $0 since Cindy was reimbursed by her employer.

B. $2,700 as excess expense over the reimbursed expense.

C. $3,960 since she was reimbursed for that amount.

D. $6,660 since she can claim the standard mileage rate.

Answer (B) is correct.

REQUIRED: The amount of the deduction when the taxpayer is partially reimbursed for expenses incurred.

DISCUSSION: Actual automobile expenses may be used for the deduction, or the taxpayer may use the standard mileage rate. If the taxpayer is reimbursed for some of the expenses, the taxpayer may only deduct the portion of expenses that are not reimbursed (Publication 463). Using the standard mileage rate, Cindy's expense was $6,660 (12,000 × $.555). Her reimbursement was $3,960 (12,000 × $.33). Thus, her deductible expense is $2,700 ($6,660 – $3,960).

Answer (A) is incorrect. Cindy was not fully reimbursed by her employer. Answer (C) is incorrect. Cindy may only deduct the portion she was not reimbursed for. Answer (D) is incorrect. She cannot deduct the entire amount of her expenses unless she received no reimbursement for those expenses. She can only deduct the expenses she was not reimbursed for.

12. Samuel, a civil engineer, drives his own vehicle to various locations to inspect bridges for safety standard requirements. His employer reimburses Samuel $400 each month for various business expenses and does not expect Samuel to provide proof of his expenses. His employer included this $4,800 reimbursement in Samuel's 2012 W-2 as part of his wages. In 2012, Samuel incurred $3,000 in transportation expense, $1,000 in parking and tolls expense, $1,800 in car repairs expense, and $600 for expenses while attending a professional association convention. Assume Samuel uses the vehicle for business purposes only and that he maintains adequate documentation to support all of his above expenditures. What amount is Samuel entitled to deduct on his Schedule A, *Itemized Deductions*?

A. $6,400 of expenses, subject to the 2% of adjusted gross income limitation.

B. $1,600, the difference between his expenditures and what he was reimbursed.

C. $0, since his employer follows nonaccountable plan.

D. $4,800, since his employer follows nonaccountable plan.

Answer (A) is correct.

REQUIRED: The deduction of vehicle expenses under a nonaccountable plan.

DISCUSSION: Vehicle travel expenses are deductible on Schedule A, subject to a 2%-of-AGI limitation. Actual expenses must be allocated between business use and personal use of the automobile. A deduction is allowed only for the business use. Since the vehicle is used solely for business use, Samuel will not have to proportion expenses. Actual automobile expenses include the following: gas and oil, lubrication and washing, repairs, garage and parking, insurance, tires and supplies, tolls, interest expense, and depreciation. Samuel should deduct the total of the expenses, $6,400 ($3,000 transportation expense + $1,000 parking and tolls + $1,800 car repairs expense + $600 expenses incurred while attending a professional association convention), on his Schedule A, subject to the 2%-of-AGI limitation. (See Publication 463.)

Answer (B) is incorrect. The amount of itemized deductions for vehicle expenses does not equal deductible expenses less any reimbursement. Answer (C) is incorrect. Samuel can deduct the expenses under a nonaccountable plan. Answer (D) is incorrect. The amount of itemized deductions for vehicle expenses does not necessarily equal the amount of reimbursement. The amount of expenses could be more or less.

13. Sydney is an outside salesman with a sales territory covering several states. His employer's main office is in Milwaukee, but Sydney does not go there for business reasons. Sydney's work assignments are temporary, and he has no way of knowing the locations of his future assignments. He often stays with a sister in Cleveland or a brother in Chicago over some weekends during the year, but he does not work in those areas. He does not pay his sister or brother for the use of the rooms. Which location is considered Sydney's tax home?

A. Milwaukee.

B. Chicago.

C. Cleveland.

D. Sydney does not have a tax home.

Answer (D) is correct.

REQUIRED: The determination of a tax home.

DISCUSSION: Sydney does not have a tax home. Sydney is an itinerant since he has no established residence (Publication 463).

14. In determining which place of business constitutes an individual's tax home, all of the following factors are taken into account except

A. Total time spent at each place of business.

B. The degree of business activity at each place of business.

C. The relative income earned at each place of business.

D. The amount of expenses incurred at each place of business.

Answer (D) is correct.

REQUIRED: The determination of an individual's home for tax purposes.

DISCUSSION: The IRS maintains that the tax home for an individual is the location of the principal place of business for the purpose of travel expenses. When the taxpayer has two places of business, the IRS determines the principal place of business using a test based on three factors: (1) the total time spent at each place of business, (2) the degree of business activity at each place of business, and (3) the relative income earned at each place of business (Publication 463).

15. Sam uses his personal vehicle to make business deliveries. He submits the number of miles he drives to his employer and is reimbursed an amount per mile that exceeds the federal rate. Sam's actual expenses are more than the federal rate. His employer includes the amount up to the federal rate in box 12 of Form W-2 where it is not taxable to Sam. The excess allowance is included in box 1 of the Form W-2 as wages. How should Sam report or claim this mileage?

A. File Form 2106 to deduct the excess expenses.

B. Repay the excess to his employer.

C. He cannot claim any of the expenses since his employer reimbursed him for all expenses.

D. If he files Form 2106 he need not reduce his mileage expense by his reimbursed amount.

Answer (A) is correct.

REQUIRED: The method of reporting business expenses that may be claimed by an employee when the employer accounts for business expenses under an unaccountable plan.

DISCUSSION: If excess reimbursements are not returned, or if the employee does not substantiate them, the reimbursements are included in the employee's gross income, and all the expenses are deducted from AGI. These expenses are a miscellaneous itemized deduction subject to the 2% floor (nonaccountable plan). The employee reports these expenses on Form 2106, *Employee Business Expenses*. Since Sam has actual business expenses in excess of the standard rate and his reimbursement was included in his income, he will want to deduct any excess expenses on Form 2106 (Publication 463).

Answer (B) is incorrect. Sam has actual expenses in excess of the standard rate; thus, he needs only deduct the expenses in excess of the standard rate. Answer (C) is incorrect. When the taxpayer's employer uses an unaccountable plan, the reimbursement is included in income and the expenses may be deducted by the taxpayer as a miscellaneous deduction. Answer (D) is incorrect. Only the expenses that are greater than the standard rate should be reported on Form 2106.

16. Which of the following is a false statement concerning use of the standard mileage rate in computing deductible transportation expenses?

A. You may use up to four cars at a time in the business.

B. You must own or lease the vehicle.

C. You may use the vehicle for hire, such as a taxi.

D. You must use the vehicle over 50% of the time for business.

Answer (D) is correct.

REQUIRED: The item not required when using the standard mileage rate.

DISCUSSION: The standard mileage rate is allowed under the tax code. Instead of deductions for actual costs, depreciation, etc., the standard mileage rate is deductible for business miles driven. There is no required percentage of business use of the vehicle. The standard mileage rate can be used for any occasional business use of a vehicle. The standard mileage rate is adjusted (to the extent warranted) by the IRS (Publication 463).

17. Which of the following is true regarding a nonbusiness bad debt?

A. It is deductible as a short-term capital loss.

B. It is not deductible.

C. It is deductible only if you itemize.

D. It is deductible as a long-term capital loss.

Answer (A) is correct.

REQUIRED: The true statement regarding a nonbusiness bad debt.

DISCUSSION: A nonbusiness bad debt is a debt other than one incurred or acquired in connection with the taxpayer's trade or business. A shareholder loan to protect his/her investment in the corporation is not treated as a business loan. A partially worthless nonbusiness bad debt is not deductible. A wholly worthless nonbusiness bad debt is treated as a short-term capital loss. This question assumes that the nonbusiness bad debt is wholly worthless. As such, it is deductible as a short-term capital loss (Publication 550).

Answer (B) is incorrect. Only a partially worthless nonbusiness bad debt is not deductible. Answer (C) is incorrect. Capital losses are deductible whether you itemize or not. Answer (D) is incorrect. Nonbusiness bad debt is only deductible as a short-term capital loss.

18. Patsy lent money to Scarlett in Year 1. Scarlett signed a loan agreement and made the agreed-upon monthly payments until May of Year 3, when she stopped making payments. Patsy called Scarlett and wrote her a letter requesting payment but received no response. Then Patsy read in the newspaper that Scarlett had filed for bankruptcy with no assets. Patsy can take a deduction for a bad debt

A. Only on her timely filed Year 3 return.

B. By amending her Year 3 return within 3 years.

C. By amending her Year 1 return.

D. On her timely filed Year 3 return or by amending her Year 3 return within 7 years.

Answer (D) is correct.

REQUIRED: The action required to take a deduction for a bad debt.

DISCUSSION: A nonbusiness bad debt is defined as any debt other than one acquired in connection with the taxpayer's trade or business. Bad debts must be deducted in the year they become worthless (Publication 550). Furthermore, the statute of limitations to take a deduction for bad debts and worthless securities is 7 years.

Answer (A) is incorrect. Year 3 is not the only year in which the bad debt may be deducted. Answer (B) is incorrect. The statute of limitations for bad debts and worthless securities is 7 years. Answer (C) is incorrect. The bad debt did not occur until Year 3. Thus, Patsy may not amend her Year 1 return for the bad debt.

19. David and Carmen were divorced in 2009. Under the final divorce decree, David was ordered to pay Carmen $800 a month for the support of their two children, who remained in the custody of Carmen. Over the next 2 years, David was very inconsistent in making child support payments to Carmen. In 2011, he missed three payments. In 2012, he made up one of the 2011 payments and missed five more payments. Assuming Carmen is a cash-basis taxpayer, what amount of nonbusiness bad debt may she claim in 2011 and 2012?

A. $2,400 in 2011 and $4,000 in 2012.

B. $1,600 in 2011 and $4,000 in 2012.

C. $2,400 in 2011 and $3,200 in 2012.

D. None in either year.

Answer (D) is correct.

REQUIRED: The amount of nonbusiness bad debt that can be claimed.

DISCUSSION: A nonbusiness bad debt is any debt other than a debt that is created or acquired in the course of a trade or business of the taxpayer. Nonbusiness debt cannot be a bad debt for tax purposes unless it becomes completely worthless. Unpaid child support and alimony cannot be deducted as bad debt. The taxpayer has no basis in the obligation (Publication 550).

20. A loss on deposits can occur when a bank, credit union, or other financial institution becomes insolvent or bankrupt. If you incur such a loss, you may be able to deduct it as any one of the following except

A. Short-term capital loss.

B. Long-term capital loss.

C. Casualty loss.

D. Ordinary loss.

Answer (B) is correct.

REQUIRED: The unavailable treatment of a loss of deposit from a bankrupt or insolvent financial institution.

DISCUSSION: The tax code provides that a taxpayer incurring a loss on deposits in a bankrupt or insolvent financial institution may choose to treat the loss as an ordinary loss or a casualty loss rather than as a nonbusiness bad debt (short-term capital loss). This treatment is allowed provided that the taxpayer is not at least a 1% owner or officer of the financial institution or related to that owner or officer (Publication 550). The casualty loss alternative is subject to the $100 floor and 10%-of-AGI limitations. The taxpayer, however, is unable to treat the loss as a long-term capital loss.

21. Elsie, a cash-basis taxpayer, had the following nonbusiness bad debts for the current year:

Loan to sister-in-law to buy gifts, forgiven	$ 250
Loan to neighbor made in 2007, evidenced by note	1,500
Loan to son to pay college tuition	1,200
Back rent due from tenants for 3 months	600

What is the amount Elsie may claim as nonbusiness bad debts for the current year?

A. $600

B. $1,450

C. $1,500

D. $2,100

Answer (C) is correct.

REQUIRED: The amount claimed as nonbusiness bad debts.

DISCUSSION: A bad-debt deduction may be taken only for a bona fide debt arising from a valid debtor-creditor relationship based upon a valid and enforceable obligation to pay a fixed or determinable sum of money. Loans to family members are usually considered to be gifts unless the taxpayer can prove that a debtor-creditor relationship and a bona fide debt existed. Here, the loan to the sister-in-law was forgiven and there is no evidence supporting a bona fide debt to the sister-in-law or the son. Therefore, the loans to the sister-in-law and son do not qualify as bona fide debts. The back rent due likewise does not qualify because Elsie is a cash-basis taxpayer and does not accrue the rent owed. The loan to the neighbor, however, does constitute a nonbusiness bad debt since it was evidenced by a note. (See Publication 550.)

Answer (A) is incorrect. The back rent does not qualify as a nonbusiness bad debt. Answer (B) is incorrect. The loans to the sister-in-law and son do not qualify as nonbusiness bad debts. Answer (D) is incorrect. The back rent does not qualify, but the loan to the neighbor does.

22. During the year, Susan received $4,800 as interest income and also paid an early withdrawal penalty of $1,200 on a certificate of deposit she had at a local bank. Which of the following is the correct way for Susan to report these items on her tax return?

A. Include $3,600 interest in gross income.

B. Include $4,800 interest in gross income.

C. Include $4,800 interest in gross income and deduct $1,200 as an itemized deduction.

D. Include $4,800 interest in gross income and deduct $1,200 as an adjustment to income.

Answer (D) is correct.

REQUIRED: The way to report interest earned and the penalty for its early withdrawal.

DISCUSSION: Interest income earned must be reported in full. The $4,800 of interest must be included in gross income. The $1,200 penalty is a deduction for adjusted gross income (Publication 550).

Answer (A) is incorrect. Penalties are not netted against interest income. Answer (B) is incorrect. The penalty is deductible as an above-the-line deduction. Answer (C) is incorrect. The penalty is deductible as an above-the-line deduction.

23. Ernest, a self-employed watchmaker, traveled to Germany in September of 2012. During his 5-day stay in Germany, he attended a 10-hour watchmaking seminar in the city of Berlin on a Monday and took a 12-hour tour of a watch manufacturing facility in Dresden on a Wednesday. The rest of the time Ernest spent hiking and touring the countryside. Ernest incurred the following costs for this trip:

- Round-trip airfare of $500
- Lodging of $1,000
- Meals of $300
- Seminar and tour registration fees of $200

In 2012, what is the amount that Ernest can deduct for travel, meals, and entertainment for this trip?

A. $2,000

B. $1,160

C. $200

D. $0

Answer (B) is correct.

REQUIRED: The amount of deductible foreign travel expenses when personal reasons account for less than 25% of the time away from home.

DISCUSSION: Generally, traveling expenses of a taxpayer who travels outside of the United States away from home must be allocated between time spent on the trip for business and time spent for pleasure. When a trip is for no more than 1 week and a personal vacation was not the major consideration, no allocation is required. Primarily for vacation/personal reasons means business activities were brief. Business activities relatively equal to a full business day are considered entirely for business. Ernest will be able to deduct the entire cost of the airfare, 2/5 of the lodging, a portion of the meals, and all of the seminar and registration fees (Publication 463). The total deduction equals $1,160 [$500 + ($1,000 × 2/5) + ($300 × 1/2 × 2/5) + $200]. If the time spent at the seminar and tour were only 2 hours and 4 hours (significantly less than a full day for each), respectively, then the travel would be considered "primarily for personal reasons" and only the seminar and tour registrations for $200 would be deductible.

3.2 Entertainment and Meals

24. Generally, which of the following expenses paid by Kathy, a salesperson, are deductible as entertainment expenses?

A. Chamber of Commerce dues.

B. Cover charges and cost of meals for taking a client to a nightclub.

C. Country club dues where she entertains clients.

D. Weekly meals with business associates at local restaurants (they take turns paying).

Answer (B) is correct.

REQUIRED: The expense that is deductible as an entertainment expense.

DISCUSSION: According to Publication 463, an entertainment, amusement, or recreation cost must meet one of the following criteria to be considered a deductible entertainment expense:

1. Directly related to active conduct of trade or business
2. Associated with such business if expense occurs right before or right after a substantial and bona fide business discussion

Answer (A) is incorrect. No entertainment expense deduction is permitted for Chamber of Commerce dues. Answer (C) is incorrect. No business deduction is permitted for country club dues. Answer (D) is incorrect. An entertainment-related meal is not deductible unless the taxpayer can establish that the meal was directly related to the active conduct of the trade or business. The Tax Court has held that frequency of their lunches together and the reciprocal nature of their meal arrangement belied the existence of a business purpose for the meal.

25. James works in sales and does not receive any reimbursement for his entertainment expenses from his employer. In May, he had the following expenses:

- $500 for use of a yacht for a day's fishing with two clients
- $50 lunch with a client with whom he discusses a new product line
- $200 for dues to the country club where he plays golf with a client who provides James with 40% of his commissions
- $50 for a cheese package given to one of his clients on the client's birthday

Before the consideration of any limitations, what is the total of his deductible expenses for May?

A. $75

B. $100

C. $800

D. $600

Answer (B) is correct.

REQUIRED: The deductible entertainment expenses.

DISCUSSION: The entertainment expense must be directly related or associated with the active conduct of a trade or business. The predominant purpose must be the furthering of the trade or business of the taxpayer incurring the expense. "Directly related" means that business is actually conducted during the entertainment period. "Associated with" means that the entertainment must occur directly before or after a business discussion. Entertainment includes recreation; however, club dues for social gatherings are not deductible (Publication 463). James is able to deduct $50 for the lunch with a client, during which he discussed a new product line, and $50 for a cheese package as a birthday present. This results in total deductible entertainment expenses of $100 before any limitations. However, entertainment expenses are only 50% deductible, and business gifts are limited to $25.

Answer (A) is incorrect. The amount deductible for entertainment expenses is $100. Answer (C) is incorrect. The $500 for the yacht and the $200 in dues for the country club are not deductible as entertainment expenses. Answer (D) is incorrect. The $500 for the yacht is not deductible as an entertainment expense.

26. With regard to meal and entertainment expenses, all of the following statements are true except

A. Club dues are not allowed as a deduction.

B. An entertainment expense must meet one of the two tests: the "directly related" test or the "associated with" test.

C. The deductible limit on business meals and entertainment expenses is 50%.

D. The allowable deduction for the cost of a Super Bowl ticket is limited to twice the face value of the ticket.

Answer (D) is correct.

REQUIRED: The false statement concerning meal and entertainment expenses.

DISCUSSION: The allowable deduction for the cost of a ticket for any entertainment activity or facility is limited to the face value of the ticket. This limitation, however, does not apply to tickets for certain sports events that are organized for the primary purpose of benefiting a tax-exempt charitable organization (Publication 463).

Answer (A) is incorrect. A deduction generally is not allowed for any expense paid or incurred with respect to an entertainment, recreation, or amusement facility. Answer (B) is incorrect. Both types of expenses are allowed. Answer (C) is incorrect. Since 1994, the deductible limit on business meals and entertainment expenses has been 50%.

27. Bethany and Michael (wife and husband) are itemizing their Schedule A expenses on their 2012 return. Michael traveled to Japan for his employer but was not reimbursed. His meal expenses totaled $500. How much can Michael deduct for meals prior to the 2% limitation?

A. $250

B. $500

C. $150

D. $0

Answer (A) is correct.

REQUIRED: The amount of meal expenses deductible if not reimbursed by employer.

DISCUSSION: The amount deductible for meal and entertainment expense is 50% of the actual expense. The limit also applies to the taxpayer's own meals. The expense must be directly related or associated with the active conduct of a trade or business. The predominant purpose must be the furthering of the trade or business of the taxpayer incurring the expense (Publication 463). Thus, Michael can deduct $250, 50% of the meal expenses incurred.

Answer (B) is incorrect. Michael is only allowed a deduction of $250. Answer (C) is incorrect. The percentage of the meals deductible is 50%, not 30%. Answer (D) is incorrect. The meal expense is directly related to the taxpayer's trade or business.

28. Thom is sole proprietor of a small company. He recently negotiated a substantial sale. Following the signing of the contract, Thom took the clients to dinner at a cost of $150. What is Thom's deductible entertainment expense on his Schedule C for the current year?

A. $112.50

B. $0

C. $150

D. $75

Answer (D) is correct.

REQUIRED: The amount and character of deductible entertainment expense.

DISCUSSION: Business meals and entertainment expenses, if properly substantiated and related or associated with a business purpose, are deductible subject to a 50% limitation (Publication 463). This expense meets the associated test. The associated test states that expenses qualify if entertainment is associated with trade or business and directly precedes or follows substantial business discussion.

Answer (A) is incorrect. Qualifying business meals and entertainment expenses are deductible. However, they are subject to a 50% limitation. Answer (B) is incorrect. This dinner qualifies and the deduction is permitted to 50% of cost of meal. Answer (C) is incorrect. Qualifying business meals and entertainment expenses are deductible. However, they are subject to a 50% limitation.

29. Sam owns a plumbing supply business that he reports as a sole proprietorship. Sam spends a great deal of time and money entertaining clients. A lot of Sam's business is conducted in restaurants and on the golf course. In 2012, Sam incurred the following expenses:

- $2,000 in meal expenditures for client business dinners
- $300 in babysitting fees during client business dinners
- $1,000 in golf club membership dues
- $200 in golf equipment

In 2012, what is the amount that Sam can deduct for business entertainment expense?

A. $3,000

B. $2,000

C. $1,500

D. $1,000

Answer (D) is correct.

REQUIRED: The deductible portion of entertainment and meals.

DISCUSSION: The amount deductible for meal and entertainment expenses is 50% of the actual expense. The limit also applies to the taxpayer's own meals. Club dues for social gatherings are not deductible. The expense must be for a bona fide business reason and not purely for entertainment purposes. Sam may deduct 1/2 of the expenses paid for meals (Publication 463). Thus, Sam may deduct $1,000 ($2,000 × 1/2).

Answer (A) is incorrect. Sam cannot include the golf membership as a deductible expense because it is considered a social gathering. Also, Sam is only allowed 1/2 of the actual meal expenditures as a deduction. Answer (B) is incorrect. Sam is only allowed 1/2 of the actual meal expenditures as a deduction. Answer (C) is incorrect. Sam cannot include the babysitting fees or expenditure for the golf equipment. Both of these expenditures are personal in nature.

30. During the year, Sally Sales purchased tickets to three theater performances and two sporting events. She purchased two tickets for each event for a total of 10 tickets. Sally gave these tickets away to legitimate business customers and has records to prove it. Sally did not go with these customers to the event or performance. Sally can claim

A. The tickets as a business gift expense.

B. The tickets as business entertainment expense.

C. The tickets as either a business gift expense or as a business entertainment expense, whichever is to her advantage.

D. No deduction at all since she did not attend the event with her customers.

Answer (C) is correct.

REQUIRED: The appropriate treatment of tickets to an entertainment event.

DISCUSSION: Sally may either claim the tickets as a business gift or deduct them as a business entertainment expense. Entertainment at which the taxpayer is not present is generally considered not to meet the "directly related" test. However, this presumption is rebuttable with proof. Nevertheless, the expenses may meet the "associated with the active conduct of the business" standard. If Sally chooses to treat the tickets as a business gift, her deduction is limited to $25 per individual donee for each year. In addition, for both alternatives, certain other requirements, such as adequate records, must also be maintained. (See Publication 463.)

Answer (A) is incorrect. Sally may claim a deduction for either a business gift expense or a business entertainment expense. Answer (B) is incorrect. Sally may claim a deduction for either a business gift expense or a business entertainment expense. Answer (D) is incorrect. She is not required to attend.

3.3 Rental Property Expenses

31. Which of the following is not considered a day of personal use of a dwelling unit for determining if it is used as a home?

A. A day on which the dwelling unit is rented to a relative at a fair rental price.

B. A day on which a related person uses the dwelling unit as her main dwelling and pays fair rental value.

C. A day on which an unrelated person uses the dwelling unit as her main dwelling and pays less than fair rental value.

D. A day on which an unrelated co-owner uses the dwelling unit for personal purposes.

Answer (B) is correct.

REQUIRED: The rental not considered a personal-use day.

DISCUSSION: If the taxpayer rents the home at a fair rental value to any person (including a relative) for use as that person's main dwelling, such use by that person is not considered personal use by the taxpayer (Publication 527).

32. During the year, Dan had the following expenses for his rental house:

1. Replaced a screen in the storm door
2. Replaced the heating system
3. Sowed grass seed in some bare spots on the lawn
4. Built a detached two-car garage
5. Installed a new dishwasher
6. Bought a welcome mat for the front stoop

Which of these items must be depreciated rather than deducted as an expense on his Schedule E?

A. 1, 3, 4, and 5.

B. 2, 4, 5, and 6.

C. 2, 4, and 5.

D. 3, 4, and 6.

Answer (C) is correct.

REQUIRED: The items that must be depreciated on Schedule E.

DISCUSSION: The heating system, two-car garage, and new dishwasher must be depreciated instead of expensed because they add value to the rental home and must be capitalized. The replacement of a screen, sowing of grass seed, and the acquisition of a welcome mat for the front step are routine expenses (Publication 527).

Answer (A) is incorrect. Items 1 and 3 are expenses, and item 2 should be included as a depreciable item. Answer (B) is incorrect. Item 6 is not a depreciable item, and it should be expensed. Answer (D) is incorrect. Item 3 should not be included as depreciable, but as an expense. Item 2 should be included as a depreciable item.

33. Paul owns a second home at the lake. During the year, he spent 3 weeks (21 days) at the lake home, rented it to his daughter for three 3-day weekends for a total of $220, and rented it to friends for 10 weeks (70 days) at fair rental value of $300 per week. His expenses for the year include

Depreciation	$2,000
Insurance	100
Mortgage interest	1,000
Real estate taxes	2,000
Utilities	1,000

What amount may he deduct for expenses on his Schedule E, *Rental Income*?

A. $2,100

B. $3,000

C. $3,220

D. $4,620

Answer (B) is correct.

REQUIRED: The amount of deductible expenses that can be reported on Schedule E, *Rental Income*.

DISCUSSION: This is an example of an IRS question that has more than one correct answer. Expect to see a handful of vague questions on your exam.

When a taxpayer rents real property that (s)he also uses for personal property, then all or part of mortgage interest, real estate taxes, casualty losses, or other rental expenses not related to the taxpayer's use of the unit as a home may be deducted by the taxpayer if (s)he does not occupy the property for more than the greater of 14 days or 10% of the total days it was rented to others at a fair rental price. However, if the taxpayer does not meet this requirement, (s)he may only deduct the expenses that are in proportion to the period the residence was rented. If there is still income in excess of the deductions previously listed, other expenses, including depreciation, may be deducted up to the amount of the remaining income. (See Publication 527.)

	70 days	Rental use
21 + 9 =	30 days	Personal use (use by family qualifies as personal use if they do not pay fair market value)
	100 days	Total use

Proportion of rental use: 70/100 = .70 × 100 = 70%

Proportion of expenses to be allocated to rental expenses:

Mortgage interest	$1,000	×	70%	=	$ 700
Real estate taxes	$2,000	×	70%	=	1,400
Insurance	$ 100	×	70%	=	70
					$2,170

Other expenses:

Depreciation	$2,000	×	70%	=	$1,400
Utilities	$1,000	×	70%	=	700
					$2,100

These expenses may be deducted up to the total amount of income.

Note on Schedule E, *Rental Income*:

- If it is interpreted as only the rent received from the qualified rental use, then $3,000 ($300/week × 10 weeks) is the total income from rent. Thus, $2,170 plus $830 of other expenses may be deducted.
- If it is interpreted as all rent received by the taxpayer for all persons who rented (either by discount or FMV), then $3,220 [($300/week × 10 weeks) + $220] is the total income from rent. Thus, $2,170 plus $1,050 of other expenses may be deducted.
- Based upon the facts, it can be argued that both $3,000 and $3,220 are plausible answers.

Answer (A) is incorrect. A portion of the mortgage interest, real estate taxes, and insurance will be deductible expenses.

Answer (C) is incorrect. The $220 of rent received by Paul's daughter is not considered qualified rental use. Answer (D) is incorrect. The expenses are limited to income.

34. Kathy rented out her summer home for 80 days and used it personally for 20 days. She paid $1,000 for repairs and $2,000 for utilities. Rental income was $8,000. What was Kathy's net rental income?

A. $0

B. $5,000

C. $5,600

D. $8,000

Answer (C) is correct.

REQUIRED: The amount of rental income from the summer home that is both rented and used for personal purposes.

DISCUSSION: If the taxpayer uses rental property for personal purposes more than the greater of (1) more than 14 days or (2) more than 10% of the number of days the property is rented, the property is considered a vacation home. Expenses of vacation homes are limited to gross income. Expenses must be allocated between the personal use and the rental use based on the number of days of use of each (Publication 527). Kathy's rental income is $5,600 [$8,000 – ($2,000 + $1,000) × 80%].

Answer (A) is incorrect. Kathy rented out the home for more than 14 days. Therefore, she must include the income derived from the rental property. Answer (B) is incorrect. Twenty percent of the expenses are personal in nature and thus are not deductible. Answer (D) is incorrect. Kathy is allowed a deduction for the nonpersonal expenses incurred relating to the rental property.

35. John offers his beach cottage for rent from June through August 31 (92 days). His family uses the cottage during the last 2 weeks in May (15 days). He was unable to find a renter for the first week in August (7 days). The person who rented the cottage for July allowed him to use it over a weekend (2 days) without any reduction in, or refund of, rent. The cottage was not used at all before May 16 or after August 31. Total income received was $11,000. Total expenses were $4,000. What percentage of the expenses for the cottage can John deduct as rental expenses?

A. 25%

B. 83%

C. 85%

D. 100%

Answer (C) is correct.

REQUIRED: The percentage of expenses deductible as rental expense.

DISCUSSION: When a taxpayer has a vacation home, the expenses must be allocated between personal use and rental use (Publication 527). There was a total of 100 days of usage during the year (15 days in May, 92 days from June through August 31, less 7 days unrented in August). Total days of rental were 85 days (92 days from June through August 31, less the 7 days unrented in August). The proportion of rental use is 85% (85 days of rental divided by the 100 days of total usage). The taxpayer had personal usage for the 15 days in May. The 2-day period of personal use in the cottage while it was rented at fair market value does not count as personal use.

Answer (A) is incorrect. There was a total of 100 days of usage during the year, of which 15 were personal use. The expenses must be allocated between personal use and rental use. Answer (B) is incorrect. The 2-day period of personal use in the cottage when it was rented at fair market value does not count as personal use. Answer (D) is incorrect. The expenses must be allocated between personal use and business use.

36. Mr. and Mrs. Bradshaw own a vacation home at the lake. They are trying to determine their days of personal use for the current year. Which of the following would be considered personal-use days?

A. Mr. and Mrs. Bradshaw, their daughter, and grandchildren spent 7 days in May at the vacation home. Mr. Bradshaw spent substantially all of his time painting the interior. Mrs. Bradshaw and the others spent all of their time on recreation.

B. Mr. and Mrs. Bradshaw rented the house for 4 days in September to Mrs. Bradshaw's nephew, Jacob. Jacob paid fair rental price.

C. Mr. and Mrs. Bradshaw rented a mountain cabin from Lucia for 4 days in October. Lucia rented their lake house for 4 days also. They each paid a fair rental price.

D. The Bradshaw's son, Seth, rented the lake house for 30 days in December. He does not have an interest in the property, and he used it as his main home. Seth paid fair rental price.

Answer (C) is correct.

REQUIRED: The determination of days of personal use.

DISCUSSION: A vacation home is deemed to have been used by Mr. and Mrs. Bradshaw if, for any part of the day, the home is used by any individual under a reciprocal arrangement, whether or not a rental price is charged (Publication 527).

Answer (A) is incorrect. Days spent working on rental property do not constitute personal days. Answer (B) is incorrect. A nephew is not considered a related taxpayer under the tax code. Family members include brothers, sisters, spouse, ancestors, and lineal descendants. Answer (D) is incorrect. Personal use does not include rental use at fair market value for use as that person's main dwelling.

37. Peter owned a cottage on the lake that he bought in Year 1. In Year 2, he rented the cottage for 10 days to a stranger and used the cottage for 20 days for his own personal use. The cottage was not used the rest of the year. Peter had rental income of $1,000, and he paid $600 for repairs. How should he report these activities on his Year 2 return?

A. $1,000 income, $600 expense.

B. $333 income, $200 expense.

C. $0 income, $0 expense.

D. $667 income, $400 expense.

Answer (C) is correct.

REQUIRED: The amount to be reported as income and expense from rental activity.

DISCUSSION: When a residence is rented for less than 15 days, the rental income does not need to be reported as income. However, any corresponding rental expenses cannot be deducted (Publication 527).

38. Sid and Rudy co-own a lakeside cabin that they rent to vacationers whenever possible. The cabin was not used as a main home by anyone until October 1 of the current year. During the current year, the following occurred:

1. Rudy used the cabin for a 3-week (21-day) vacation.
2. Sid's brother, Chester, rented the cabin for 2 months (61 days) at less than fair rental price.
3. Prior to October 1, Sid and Rudy spent a total of 26 days at the cabin working substantially full time repairing and maintaining the cabin.
4. Starting October 1 and continuing for the balance of the year (92 days), Sid and Rudy rented the cabin to Sid's son, Martin, who used the cabin as his main home and paid a fair rental price.

What is the number of personal-use days that Sid will use in dividing his current-year expenses between rental-use and personal-use days?

A. 61 days.

B. 82 days.

C. 174 days.

D. 200 days.

Answer (B) is correct.

REQUIRED: The number of personal-use days used for allocating rental expenses.

DISCUSSION: A vacation home is deemed to have been used by the taxpayer for personal purposes if, for any part of the day, the home is used by

1. The taxpayer, any other person who owns an interest in the home, or the relatives of either
2. Any individual who uses the home under a reciprocal agreement whether or not rent is charged
3. Any individual who uses the home unless a fair rental is charged

An exception exists when a relative rents the home at a fair rental value for use as a principal residence. Sid's personal days include the 21 days Rudy spent at the cabin and the 61 days Chester rented the cabin at less than the fair rental (Publication 527).

Answer (A) is incorrect. Any use by a co-owner is considered a personal day for all owners. Answer (C) is incorrect. Martin paid the fair rental price and used the cabin as his principal residence. Answer (D) is incorrect. Days spent working on a rental property do not constitute personal days.

39. Tammy owns a house at the beach, which she rented out from May 1 through October 31 of the current year. During April of the current year, she spent 10 days there on vacation. In November, she spent 5 days at Dionne's mountain home and paid Dionne fair rental value. Dionne also paid Tammy a fair rental price for using her beach house for 9 days in December of the current year. Also, during November, Tammy's grandson stayed at the beach house for 3 days without any charge. How many days would the beach house be considered to have been used for personal purposes when applying the rules to vacation homes and dwellings?

A. 0

B. 10

C. 13

D. 22

Answer (D) is correct.

REQUIRED: The number of days used for personal purposes when applying the rules to vacation homes.

DISCUSSION: The tax code restricts the deductions with respect to a dwelling unit used by the taxpayer as a residence. A taxpayer is deemed to use a dwelling unit as a residence if (s)he uses it for personal purposes for a number of days that exceeds the greater of 14 days or 10% of the number of days during the year for which the unit is rented at a fair rental. The home is deemed to be used by the taxpayer for personal purposes if, for any part of the day, the home is used by any individual under a reciprocal arrangement, whether or not rent is charged. Similarly, the home is considered to be used for personal purposes when a relative stays at the home unless it is considered a main dwelling and a fair rental is charged (Publication 527).

40. For purposes of the rules that apply to vacation homes and other dwelling units, consider the following information; then compute Kim's allowable depreciation for the current year.

Days rented in the current year	120
Personal-use days	25
Gross rents received in the current year	$2,000
Expenses for the current year allocated to rental use:	
Interest and taxes	$1,000
Repairs	500
Depreciation	8,000

A. $0

B. $500

C. $6,400

D. $8,000

Answer (B) is correct.

REQUIRED: The allowable depreciation for a vacation home.

DISCUSSION: The tax code restricts the deductions with respect to a dwelling unit used by the taxpayer as a residence. A taxpayer is deemed to use a dwelling unit as a residence if (s)he uses it for personal purposes for a number of days that exceeds the greater of 14 days or 10% of the number of days during the year for which the unit is rented at a fair rental. Since Kim rented the house for 120 days, she was allowed to use it for personal purposes for only 14 days without treating it as a residence. Therefore, Kim's house is treated as her residence. When a dwelling unit is used by the taxpayer as a residence, the tax code disallows a deduction for expenses exceeding gross income derived from rents, reduced by deductions allowable (e.g., taxes and interest), whether or not the unit was used for rental purposes. Under the tax code, the order of deductions is (1) the allocable portion of expenses deductible regardless of rental activity, (2) deductions not affecting basis, and (3) those that do affect basis.

Gross rent	$2,000
Interest and taxes	(1,000)
Repairs	(500)
Depreciation	(500)
Income	$ 0

41. Jerry, a general contractor by trade, is a tenant of Montgomery Apartments. In exchange for 4 months' rent ($900/month), Jerry provided the following items and services for Paul, the owner of the apartments:

Paint and miscellaneous supplies for the apartments	$ 700
Labor for painting and miscellaneous repairs	1,000
Labor and supplies for paving the apartment parking area	1,900

How should Paul treat this transaction on his current-year Schedule E?

A. Rental income of $3,600 and rental expenses of $3,600.

B. No rental income or rental expenses to be reflected on the Schedule E because the net effect is zero.

C. Rental income of $3,600 and depreciation computed on the capital expenditures of $3,600.

D. Rental income of $3,600, rental expenses of $1,700, and depreciation computed on the capital expenditures of $1,900.

Answer (D) is correct.

REQUIRED: The correct treatment of rental income and expenses.

DISCUSSION: As a general rule, if a lessee pays any of the expenses of his/her lessor, such payments are additional rental income to the lessor. Since the expenses are in effect treated as if paid by the lessee to the lessor and then paid by the lessor to a third party, the lessor may deduct them. The $1,700 cost of painting and miscellaneous repairs is for routine maintenance costs and can be deducted as rental expenses. The $1,900 cost of paving the parking area should be capitalized and properly depreciated (Publication 527).

Answer (A) is incorrect. The $1,900 cost of paving is a capital expenditure. Answer (B) is incorrect. Income must be recognized when received; then the expenses can be properly deducted. Answer (C) is incorrect. The $1,700 cost of painting and repairs can be deducted as rental expenses.

STUDY UNIT FOUR
ABOVE-THE-LINE DEDUCTIONS AND LOSSES

(11 pages of outline)

Deductions to compute taxable income are heavily tested on the EA exam. The business expense deductions explained in this study unit are also tested in the corporate context. You should focus on classifying each deduction as an above-the-line or itemized deduction and be able to apply each deduction limit without hesitation. Gross income is reduced by deductions to compute taxable income. No amount can be deducted from gross income unless allowed by the Internal Revenue Code (IRC). Above-the-line deductions are deducted from gross income to arrive at adjusted gross income (AGI). Several deductions and credits are limited by reference to AGI. Below-the-line deductions are deducted from AGI to arrive at taxable income. Above-the-line deductions are also referred to as deductions to arrive at AGI and as deductions for AGI.

4.1 EDUCATOR EXPENSES

1. In 2012, primary and secondary school educators may claim an above-the-line deduction for up to $250 annually in unreimbursed expenses paid or incurred for books and supplies used in the classroom. Each taxpayer (educator) on a joint return may deduct up to $250.
   a. Books, supplies, computer equipment (including related software and services) and other equipment, and supplementary materials used in the classroom qualify for the deduction.
   b. An eligible educator is an individual who, for at least 900 hours during a school year, is a kindergarten through grade 12 teacher, instructor, counselor, principal, or aide.
   c. The term "school" is defined as one that provides elementary or secondary education, as determined under state law.

Stop and review! You have completed the outline for this subunit. Study questions 1 and 2 on page 109.

4.2 HEALTH SAVINGS ACCOUNT

1. A Health Savings Account is a tax-exempt trust or custodial account that you set up with a U.S. financial institution in which you can save money exclusively for future medical expenses. This account must be used in conjunction with a high-deductible health plan.
   a. The amount that may be contributed to a taxpayer's Health Savings Account depends on the nature of his/her coverage and his/her age.
      1) For self-only coverage, the taxpayer or his/her employer can contribute up to $3,100 ($4,100 for taxpayers aged 55-64).
      2) For family coverage, the taxpayer or his/her employer can contribute up to $6,250 ($7,250 for taxpayers aged 55-64).
      3) Contributions are not allowed for taxpayers aged 65 and over.

b. The taxpayer is no longer required to have the insurance for the whole year to contribute the full amount.

c. Contributions to a Health Savings Account for 2012 include contributions made until April 15, 2013.

Stop and review! You have completed the outline for this subunit. Study questions 3 and 4 on page 110.

4.3 MOVING EXPENSES

Deduction for the reasonable expenses of relocating in connection with the commencement of work is allowed.

1. Moving expenses are deductible to arrive at AGI to the extent the expenses are not reimbursed or paid for by the taxpayer's employer.
   a. Qualified moving expenses reimbursed by an employer are excluded from the employee's gross income as a qualified fringe benefit to the extent that the expenses are deductible.
   b. To the extent reimbursement is excluded from gross income, only the qualified expenses in excess of the reimbursement are deductible to arrive at AGI.
2. An individual qualifies for the moving expense deduction if
   a. The individual's new principal place of work is at least 50 miles farther from the former residence than was the former principal place of work.
      1) If the individual did not have a former principal place of work, the new principal place of work must be at least 50 miles from the taxpayer's former residence.
      2) Measurement is by the shortest possible commonly traveled route.
   b. The individual is employed full time in the new location during at least 39 weeks in the 12-month period immediately following the move.
   c. (S)he is a self-employed individual who
      1) Meets the above 39-week requirement and
      2) Is employed full time during at least 78 weeks of the 24-month period immediately following the move.
3. Moving expenses may be deducted in the year in which they were incurred even if the 39- or 78-week employment requirement has not yet been satisfied.
   a. If the time requirements are subsequently not met, an amended return must be filed or the amount of the deduction must be reported as gross income in the following year.

<u>Direct Expense</u>

4. The expenses of actually moving a taxpayer and his/her household goods and personal effects, and for travel (including lodging) from the former residence to the new residence, are deductible to arrive at AGI.
   a. In 2012, a mileage rate of $.23 can be used instead of actual expenses for driving one's own automobile.
   b. The cost of meals en route is not deductible as a direct moving expense.
   c. Expenses of an individual other than the taxpayer are deductible only if the individual had the old residence, and now has the new residence, as his/her principal place of abode and is a member of the taxpayer's household.

<u>Indirect Moving Expenses</u>

5. Indirect moving expenses, including a house-hunting trip; temporary living expenses; and expenses related to the sale, purchase, or lease of a residence, are not deductible.

Stop and review! You have completed the outline for this subunit. Study questions 5 through 9 beginning on page 110.

4.4 SELF-EMPLOYMENT DEDUCTIONS

1. **Self-Employment Tax**
   a. A self-employed person is allowed a deduction for the employer's portion of the FICA taxes paid to arrive at his/her AGI. Generally, the deduction for the employer's share is equal to 50% of the self-employment tax. However, for 2012 the deduction equals 57.51% of the self-employment tax or
      1) 6.2% of the first $110,100 of net self-employment income (see b.), plus
      2) 1.45% of net self-employment income (no cap).
   b. Net self-employment income is total net self-employed profits multiplied by 92.35%.
2. **Self-Employed SEP, SIMPLE, and Qualified Plans**
   a. A self-employed individual can deduct specified amounts paid on his/her behalf to a qualified retirement or profit-sharing plan, such as a SEP or SIMPLE plan.
   b. The most common self-employed retirement plan used is a SEP (Keogh) plan.
      1) The maximum annual deduction is limited to the lesser of 25% of the self-employed earnings or $50,000 (indexed for inflation).
      2) The annual contribution limit is the lesser of 100% of the earned income derived from the trade or business or $50,000.
      3) Self-employed earnings are reduced by the deductible part of self-employment taxes.
      4) Contributions to the plan are subtracted from net earnings to calculate self-employed earnings, creating a circular computation. For convenience, a standard rate of 20% is used to calculate the allowed deduction.

EXAMPLE

Alice has business income of net self-employed earnings of $125,000 before the deductible part of self-employment taxes of $25,000. The maximum annual deduction is calculated as follows:

($125,000 – $25,000) × 20% = $20,000

   c. Another option for a self-employed taxpayer is a Savings Incentive Match Plan for Employees (SIMPLE).
      1) Self-employed taxpayers may make both employer contributions and elective employee contributions.
      2) Employee contributions are considered deferred compensation and are limited to $11,500 in 2012.
      3) An employer match of up to 3% of self-employed earnings may be deducted as an above-the-line deduction.
3. **Self-Employed Health Insurance Deduction**
   a. Self-employed individuals can deduct 100% of payments made for health insurance coverage for the individual, his/her spouse, and dependents.
   b. The deduction is limited to the taxpayer's earned income derived from the business for which the insurance plan was established.

Stop and review! You have completed the outline for this subunit. Study questions 10 and 11 on page 112.

4.5 ALIMONY

Alimony and separate maintenance payments are gross income to the recipient and deductible by the payor (Publication 504).

Qualified Payments

1. Requirements for Qualified Alimony Payments
   a. Payment is made in cash or equivalent.
   b. Payment is received by or on behalf of a spouse under a divorce or separation agreement.
      1) Payments made to a third party on behalf of a spouse at the written request of the payee spouse will qualify as alimony.
         a) Common examples of payments made on behalf of the payee spouse include mortgage payments, rent, medical costs, and education.
   c. Payee spouse and payor spouse must not be members of the same household at the time of payments.
   d. The payor spouse is not liable for any payments after the death of the payee spouse.
   e. The spouses must not file joint returns with each other.

Jointly Owned Home

2. If the divorce or separation instrument states that the taxpayer must pay expenses for a home owned by the taxpayer and his/her spouse or former spouse, some of the payments may be alimony.

Mortgage Payments

   a. If required to pay all the mortgage payments (principal and interest) on a jointly owned home, and the payments otherwise qualify as alimony, a taxpayer can deduct one-half of the total payments as alimony.
      1) If deductions are itemized and the home is a qualified home, a taxpayer can claim half of the interest in figuring deductible interest.
   b. The spouse must report one-half of the payments as alimony received.
      1) If the spouse itemizes deductions and the home is a qualified home, (s)he can claim one-half of the interest on the mortgage in figuring deductible interest.

Taxes and Insurance

   c. If required to pay all the real estate taxes or insurance on a home held as tenants in common, a taxpayer can deduct one-half of these payments as alimony.
      1) The spouse must report one-half of these payments as alimony received.
      2) If a taxpayer and his/her spouse itemize deductions, each can claim one-half of the real estate taxes and none of the home insurance.
   d. If the home is held as tenants by the entirety or joint tenants, none of the payments for taxes or insurance are alimony.
      1) If a taxpayer itemizes deductions, (s)he can claim all of the real estate taxes and none of the home insurance.

Child Support

3. Child support payments and any part of an alimony payment designated as child support are not deductible.
   a. If any amount of an alimony payment is to be reduced based on a contingency relating to a child, such as the attainment of a certain age or graduation, the amount of the specified reduction is treated as child support.

b. If the divorce or separation instrument specifies payments of both alimony and child support, and only partial payments are made, then the partial payments are considered to be child support until this obligation is fully paid.

1) Any excess is treated as alimony.

Alimony Recapture

4. Current tax law includes a recapture provision, which is intended to prevent large property settlements from being treated as alimony. Recapture occurs if payments significantly decrease in the second or third year after a divorce. The following steps show how to calculate the final amount of recapture:

a. Second-year alimony recapture is equal to

$$\text{2nd-year alimony} - (\$15{,}000 + \text{3rd-year alimony})$$

b. First-year alimony recapture is equal to

$$\text{1st-year alimony} - \left[\frac{(\text{2nd-year alimony} - \text{2nd-year recapture}) + \text{3rd-year alimony}}{2} + \$15{,}000\right]$$

c. Both the first-year and second-year recapture amounts are included in the payor's gross income and deducted from the payee's gross income in Year 3.

EXAMPLE

After Lisa divorced Jed in Year 1, she paid him $60,000 of alimony in Year 1, $40,000 in Year 2, and $10,000 in Year 3. Excess alimony in Year 2 was $15,000 [$40,000 – ($15,000 + $10,000)]. Excess alimony in Year 1 was $60,000 – [($40,000 – $15,000 + $10,000) ÷ 2 + $15,000], or $27,500. In Year 3, Lisa must include in gross income the total of Year 1 and Year 2 excess alimony, or $42,500. Jed is also allowed a deduction of the same amount.

Stop and review! You have completed the outline for this subunit. Study questions 12 through 17 beginning on page 112.

4.6 RETIREMENT SAVINGS (IRA) CONTRIBUTIONS

Subject to certain qualifying rules and limitations, an individual who is not an active participant in an employer-maintained retirement plan may make contributions to an IRA that are fully deductible, up to the lesser of $5,000 or 100% of his/her includible compensation. Contributions must be made by the due date of the return, without regard to extensions, to qualify for return year.

1. Compensation includes alimony and earned income but not pensions, annuities, or other deferred compensation distributions.

2. An additional $5,000 may be contributed to the IRA for the taxpayer's nonworking spouse if a joint return is filed.

   a. The combined IRA contributions by both spouses may not exceed their combined compensation for the year.

Phaseout

3. If the taxpayer is an active participant in an employer-sponsored retirement plan and has modified AGI of over $92,000 in 2012 ($58,000 in 2012 for single taxpayers), the IRA deduction is proportionately reduced over a phaseout range.

   a. An individual is not labeled an active plan participant due to the status of that individual's spouse.

   b. If an individual's spouse is an active plan participant, that individual's deductible contribution will be phased out when modified AGI is between $173,000 and $183,000.

4. If an individual has reached age 50 before the close of the tax year, the regular contribution limit is increased by $1,000 for tax year 2012.
5. Excessive contributions (over the deductible amount) may be subject to a 6% excise tax. The distribution of excess contribution is reported on Form 1099-R in box 2a and coded in box 7.
6. The owner of an IRA must begin receiving distributions by April 1 of the calendar year following the calendar year in which the employee attains age 70 1/2 (or the calendar year in which the employee retires, if later, for active participants in an employer-sponsored plan).

10% Penalty

7. IRA distributions made before age 59 1/2 for a reason other than death or disability are subject to taxation as well as a 10% penalty tax.
   a. Distributions used to pay medical expenses in excess of 7.5% of AGI are not subject to the 10% penalty tax.
   b. A penalty-free distribution up to $10,000 may be used for qualified first-time homebuyer expenses.
   c. Distributions used to pay for "qualified higher education expenses" for the individual or his/her lineal relatives are not subject to the 10% penalty tax.

Stop and review! You have completed the outline for this subunit. Study question 18 on page 114.

4.7 HIGHER EDUCATION DEDUCTIONS

1. **Student Loan Interest Deduction**
   a. Taxpayers may deduct $2,500 of interest paid on qualified educational loans in 2012.
   b. The deduction is subject to income limits.
   c. The phaseout range begins when MAGI, without regard to this deduction, exceeds $60,000 ($125,000 for joint filers) and ends at $75,000 ($155,000 for joint filers).
   d. The amount of reduction in the deduction for a single filer can be calculated as follows:

$$\$2,500 \times \frac{AGI - \$60,000}{\$15,000}$$

   e. Qualified expenses include
      1) Room and board
      2) Tuition and fees
      3) Books, supplies, and equipment
      4) Other necessary expenses (e.g., transportation)

      NOTE: This list of qualified expenses is specific for educational interest expense deduction. Other educational deductions/credits are not as liberal (i.e., do not allow for inclusion of room and board).
2. **Tuition and Fees Deduction**
   a. An above-the-line deduction is allowed for qualified higher education expenses for calendar years 2002 through 2013.
      1) For 2012, the deduction is limited to $4,000 and is available in full to taxpayers whose adjusted gross income does not exceed $65,000 ($130,000 for joint filers).
      2) For 2012, taxpayers whose adjusted gross income falls between $65,000 and $80,000 ($130,000 and $160,000 for joint filers) may deduct $2,000.
      3) Married individuals filing a separate return are not eligible for the qualified higher education expense deduction.

4) Expenses eligible for the deduction include tuition and related fees (room and board are specifically excluded) required for the enrollment or attendance of the taxpayer, the taxpayer's spouse, or any dependent for whom the taxpayer is entitled to deduct a dependency exemption. Student activity fees and expenses for course-related books, supplies, and equipment are included in qualified education expenses only if the fees and expenses must be paid to the institution as a condition of enrollment or attendance.

Stop and review! You have completed the outline for this subunit. Study questions 19 through 24 beginning on page 115.

4.8 OTHER ABOVE-THE-LINE DEDUCTIONS

1. Performing artists qualify to deduct employee business expenses as an adjustment to gross income rather than as a miscellaneous itemized deduction if all of the following requirements are met:
   a. Performing-arts services were performed as an employee for at least two employers,
   b. At least $200 was received from each of any two of these employers,
   c. Related performing-arts business expenses are more than 10% of total gross income from the services, and
   d. AGI is not more than $16,000 before deducting these expenses.

   NOTE: Married persons not living apart at all times during the year must file a joint return and figure the requirements of a., b., and c. separately.
2. **Penalty on Early Withdrawal of Savings**
   a. Deduction is allowable for an early withdrawal of funds from certificates of deposit or other time savings accounts.
   b. The deduction is taken in the year the penalty is incurred.
3. **Domestic Production Activities**
   a. Generally, up to 9% of income derived from qualified production activities within the U.S. may be deducted.
4. **Archer MSAs** (previously called Medical Savings Accounts) allow individuals who are self-employed or employed by a small employer and who are covered by a high-deductible health insurance plan to make tax-deductible contributions to an Archer MSA and use those funds accumulated to pay medical expenses. The deduction for an Archer MSA is not included with other medical expenses and is not subject to the 7.5% limitation.
   a. Earnings generated by the plan and distributions from an Archer MSA used to pay medical expenses are nontaxable.
   b. Distributions not used for medical expenses are taxable and subject to a 15% penalty tax, unless made after age 65 or upon death or disability.
   c. Contributions to an Archer MSA are subject to an annual limitation, which is a percentage of the deductible of the required high-deductible health plan.
   d. The Archer MSA program is limited to 750,000 people.
   e. An Archer MSA can be rolled into a Health Savings Account tax-free.
5. Jury duty pay returned to an employer is deductible by the employee from gross income.
6. Expenses from the nonbusiness rental of personal property are deductible from gross income, but only up to the amount of income received.

Stop and review! You have completed the outline for this subunit. Study questions 25 through 29 beginning on page 116.

4.9 LOSS LIMITATIONS

1. A taxpayer's loss is limited by three different rules.
   a. The loss is limited
      1) To the amount of the taxpayer's basis in the activity,
      2) By the at-risk rules, and
      3) By the passive activity rules.
   b. The deductible loss becomes the smallest amount of the three limitations.

At-Risk Rules

2. The amount of a loss allowable as a deduction is limited to the amount a person has at risk in the activity from which the loss arose.
   a. A loss is any excess of deductions over gross income attributable to the same activity.
   b. The rules apply to individuals, partners in partnerships, members in limited liability companies, shareholders of S corporations, trusts, estates, and closely held C corporations.
      1) Personal holding companies, foreign personal holding companies, and personal service corporations are not subject to at-risk rules.
   c. The at-risk rules are applied separately to each trade or business or income-producing activity.
   d. A person's amount at risk in an activity is determined at the close of the tax year.
      1) A person's initial at-risk amount includes money contributed, the adjusted basis (AB) of property contributed, and borrowed amounts.
      2) Recourse debt requirements include the following:
         a) A person's at-risk amount includes amounts borrowed only to the extent that, for the debt, the person has either personal liability or property pledged as security (no more than the FMV when pledged minus prior or superior claims is included).
         b) The at-risk amount does not include debt if one of the following applies:
            i) Property pledged as security is used in the activity.
            ii) Insurance, guarantees, stop-loss agreements, or similar arrangements provide protection from personal liability.
            iii) A person with an interest in the activity or one related to him/her extended the credit.
      3) Nonrecourse debt is generally excluded from the amount at risk.
         a) The amount at risk in the activity of holding real property includes qualified nonrecourse financing (QNRF).
         b) In qualified nonrecourse financing, the taxpayer is not personally liable, but the financing is
            i) Used in an activity of holding real estate;
            ii) Secured by the real property;
            iii) Not convertible to an ownership interest; and
            iv) Either obtained from an unrelated third party, obtained from a related party but on commercially reasonable terms, or guaranteed by a governmental entity.

4) Adjustments to an at-risk amount are made for events that vary the investors' economic risk of loss.

   a) Add contributions of money and property (its AB), recourse debt increases, QNRF increases, and income from the activity.

   b) Subtract distributions (e.g., from a partnership), liability reductions (recourse or QNRF), and tax deductions allowable (at year end).

      i) If the amount at risk decreases below zero, previously allowed losses must be recaptured as income.

5) Disallowed losses are carried forward.

6) If the amount at risk decreases below zero, previously allowed losses must be recaptured as income.

7) If a deduction would reduce basis in property and part or all of the deduction is disallowed by the at-risk rules, the basis is reduced anyway.

Passive Activity Loss (PAL) Limitation Rules

3. The amount of a loss attributable to a person's passive activities is allowable as a deduction or credit only against, and to the extent of, gross income or tax attributable to those passive activities (in the aggregate).

   a. The excess is deductible or creditable in a future year, subject to the same limits.

4. The passive activity rules apply to individuals, estates, trusts, personal service corporations, and closely held corporations.

   a. Although passive activity rules do not apply to grantor trusts, partnerships, and S corporations directly, they do apply to the owners of these entities.

5. A passive activity is either rental activity or a trade or business in which the person does not materially participate.

   a. A taxpayer materially participates in an activity during a tax year if (s)he satisfies one of the following tests:

      1) Participates more than 500 hours
      2) Participation constitutes substantially all of the participation in the activity
      3) Participates for more than 100 hours and exceeds the participation of any other individual
      4) Materially participated in the activity for any 5 years of the 10 years preceding the year in question
      5) Materially participated in a personal service activity for any 3 years preceding the year in question
      6) Participates in the activity on a regular, continuous, and substantial basis

6. Passive activity rules do not apply to

   a. Active income/loss/credit
   b. Portfolio income/loss/credit
   c. Casualty and theft losses, vacation home rental, qualified home mortgage interest, business use of home, or a working interest in an oil or gas well held through an entity that does not limit the person's liability

7. Rental Real Estate

   a. All rental activity is passive.
   b. However, a person who actively participates in rental real estate activity is entitled to deduct up to $25,000 of losses from the passive activity from other than passive income.

c. This exception to the general PAL limitation rule applies to a person who
   1) Actively participates in the activity,
   2) Owns 10% or more of the activity (by value) for the entire year, and
   3) Has MAGI of less than $150,000 [phaseout begins at $100,000; see d.1) below].
d. Up to $25,000 of a tax year loss from rental real estate activities in excess of passive activity gross income is deductible against portfolio or active income.
   1) The $25,000 limit is reduced by 50% of the person's MAGI [i.e., AGI without regard to PALs, Social Security benefits, and qualified retirement contributions (e.g., IRAs)] over $100,000.
   2) Excess rental real estate PALs are suspended. They are treated as other PALs carried over.
e. Active participation is a less stringent requirement than material participation.
   1) It is met with participation in management decisions or arranging for others to provide services (such as repairs).
   2) There will not be active participation if at any time during the period there is ownership of less than 10% of the interest in the property (including the spouse's interest).
f. Real property trades or businesses rules include the following:
   1) The passive activity loss rules do not apply to certain taxpayers who are involved in real property trades or businesses.
   2) An individual may avoid passive activity loss limitation treatment on a rental real estate activity if two requirements are met:
      a) More than 50% of the individual's personal services performed during the year are performed in the real property trades or businesses in which the individual materially participates.
      b) The individual performs more than 750 hours of service in the real property trades or businesses in which the individual materially participates.
   3) This provision also applies to a closely held C corporation if 50% of gross receipts for the tax year are from real property trades or businesses in which the corporation materially participated.
   4) Any deduction allowed under this rule is not taken into consideration in determining the taxpayer's AGI for purposes of the phaseout of the $25,000 deduction.
   5) If 50% or less of the personal services performed are in real property trades or businesses, the individual will be subject to the passive activity limitation rules.
g. Suspension of loss is allowed.
   1) A PAL not allowable in the current tax year is carried forward indefinitely and treated as a deduction in subsequent tax years.
h. PALs continue to be treated as PALs even after the activity ceases to be passive in a subsequent tax year, except that it may also be deducted against income from that activity.
i. Disposition of a passive activity is subject to the following rules:
   1) Suspended (and current-year) losses from a passive activity become deductible in full in the year the taxpayer completely disposes of all interest in the passive activity.
   2) The loss is deductible first against net income or gain from the taxpayer's other passive activities. The remainder of the loss, if any, is then treated as nonpassive.

Wash Sales

8. Losses from wash sales are not deductible.
   a. A wash sale occurs when a taxpayer sells or trades an asset at a loss and, within 30 days before or after the sale, the taxpayer does one of the following:
      1) Purchases a substantially identical asset,
      2) Acquires a substantially identical asset in a fully taxable trade, or
      3) Acquires a contract or option to buy a substantially identical asset.
   b. The unrecognized loss is added to the basis of the asset that caused the wash sale.
   c. The holding periods of the original asset and the substantially identical asset are added together.

Stop and review! You have completed the outline for this subunit. Study questions 30 through 39 beginning on page 117.

QUESTIONS

4.1 Educator Expenses

1. During 2012, Caitlin served as a kindergarten aide for 1,000 hours. She incurred $350 in expenses for books and supplies used in the classroom and was not reimbursed by the school. What amount is Caitlin entitled to as the educator's expense deduction on her 2012 income tax return?

A. $175

B. $250

C. $350

D. $0

Answer (B) is correct.

REQUIRED: The amount that may be deducted as the educator's expense deduction.

DISCUSSION: Primary and secondary school educators may claim an above-the-line deduction for up to $250 annually in unreimbursed expenses paid or incurred for books and supplies used in the classroom. An eligible educator is an individual who, for at least 900 hours during a school year, is a kindergarten through grade 12 teacher, instructor, counselor, principal, or aide (Publication 553). Therefore, Caitlin may deduct $250 as an educator's expense.

Answer (A) is incorrect. The deduction is not limited to 50% of Caitlin's unreimbursed expenses. Answer (C) is incorrect. The maximum deduction allowed for education expenses is $250. Answer (D) is incorrect. Caitlin qualifies for a $250 deduction.

2. Julie and Frank were married on March 10, 2012. Both are full-time third-grade teachers, and together they incurred $350 in unreimbursed expenses for books and supplies used in the classroom and were not reimbursed by the school. What amount are they entitled to deduct as an education expense on their 2012 joint income tax return?

A. $175

B. $250

C. $350

D. $500

Answer (C) is correct.

REQUIRED: Allowable education deduction for classroom expenses.

DISCUSSION: Through 2012, primary and secondary school educators may claim a $250 deduction for AGI annually in unreimbursed expenses paid or incurred for books and supplies used in the classroom. For MFJ taxpayers, the deduction limit is doubled ($500). The deduction may not exceed actual expenses of $350.

Answer (A) is incorrect. The allowable deduction for MFJ taxpayers doubles that of other filers but may not exceed the actual expense amount. Answer (B) is incorrect. The limit for non-MFJ taxpayers is $250. Answer (D) is incorrect. Even though the general limit for MFJ taxpayers is $500, no deduction in excess of actual expenses is allowed.

4.2 Health Savings Account

3. Chris, age 35, contributes the following amounts to his self-only Health Savings Account:

- $500 on April 30, 2012
- $300 on September 15, 2012
- $750 on December 31, 2012
- $1,000 on February 5, 2013
- $1,500 on April 30, 2013

What amounts are considered contributions to the Health Savings Account for 2012?

A. $1,550

B. $2,550

C. $3,100

D. $4,050

Answer (B) is correct.

REQUIRED: The contributions to the Health Savings Account for 2012.

DISCUSSION: For self-only coverage, the taxpayer or his/her employer can contribute up to the amount of the annual health plan deductible, but not more than $3,100 (for taxpayers under 55). Contributions to a Health Savings Account for 2012 may be made until April 15, 2013 (Publication 969). Therefore, the contributions for 2012 equal $2,550 ($500 + $300 + $750 + $1,000).

Answer (A) is incorrect. The contribution on February 5, 2012, should be included. Answer (C) is incorrect. The maximum amount Chris can contribute for 2012 is $3,100, but the qualifying 2012 contributions only equal $2,550. Answer (D) is incorrect. The $1,500 contribution was made after April 15, 2013, and should not be included as a 2012 contribution.

4. James (33) and his wife Erica (31) established a Health Savings Account (in conjunction with a high-deductible heath plan) on February 1, 2012. The annual health plan deductible is $10,000. What is the maximum amount that can be contributed to the Health Savings Account?

A. $7,150

B. $5,638

C. $6,250

D. $10,000

Answer (C) is correct.

REQUIRED: The maximum amount that can be contributed to a Health Savings Account.

DISCUSSION: For family coverage, the taxpayer or his/her employer can contribute up to the amount of the annual health plan deductible, but not more than $6,250 for 2012. Under the last-month rule, a taxpayer is eligible for the entire year if the taxpayer is eligible on the first day of the last month of the year (Publication 969).

Answer (A) is incorrect. The maximum amount that can be contributed for family coverage for taxpayers who have reached age 55 is $7,250. Answer (B) is incorrect. The contribution is not reduced by one-twelfth. Answer (D) is incorrect. James and Erica can contribute up to the amount of the annual health plan deductible, but not more than $6,250.

4.3 Moving Expenses

5. Susan met all the requirements to deduct moving expenses when she moved from Arizona to Nevada this year. Which of the following are deductible as moving expenses?

A. Expenses of selling the old house.

B. Lease of a residence.

C. Expenses of buying a new home.

D. Traveling to her new home.

Answer (D) is correct.

REQUIRED: The item that is a deductible moving expense.

DISCUSSION: The definition of moving expenses under Sec. 217(b) includes only reasonable expenses of moving household goods and personal effects and for travel (including lodging) from the former residence to the new residence [Sec. 217(b)(1)]. Indirect moving expenses, including househunting trips, meals during the move, and temporary living expenses, are not deductible (Publication 521).

Answer (A) is incorrect. The expenses of selling a home are considered in the capital gain/loss calculation. Answer (B) is incorrect. The lease expense of a residence is not a deductible moving expense. Answer (C) is incorrect. The expenses of buying a home are considered in the capital gain/loss calculation.

6. Which of the following statements about moving expenses is true?

A. Temporary living expenses and expenses of getting or breaking a lease are deductible moving expenses.

B. Pre-move househunting expenses and meal expenses are deductible moving expenses.

C. Moving household goods and travel expenses (including lodging but not meals) to the new home are deductible moving expenses.

D. Mortgage payoff penalties and refitting carpets and draperies are deductible moving expenses.

Answer (C) is correct.

REQUIRED: The true statement about moving expenses.

DISCUSSION: The definition of moving expenses under Sec. 217(b) includes only reasonable expenses of moving household goods and personal effects and of travel (including lodging) from the former residence to the new residence (Publication 521).

7. Pat had the following moving expenses:

- Cost of packing and crating and transporting her household goods $1,200;
- Lodging for travel between her old home and her new home $550;
- Meals during the trip $150;
- $250 to break the lease on her old home.

Pat moved to start a new job and met the distance and time tests. What are the total moving expenses that can be deducted from total income to arrive at adjusted gross income?

A. $2,150

B. $1,900

C. $1,750

D. $2,000

Answer (C) is correct.

REQUIRED: The total moving expenses that can be deducted from total income to arrive at AGI.

DISCUSSION: Sec. 217(a) allows the deduction for moving expenses paid or incurred in connection with the commencement of work by a taxpayer in a new place of work. The expenses of actually moving a taxpayer and household goods and the traveling (including lodging) are deductible for AGI. Since December 31, 1993, indirect moving expenses, including a househunting trip; temporary living expenses; and qualified expenses related to the sale, purchase, or lease of a residence, have no longer been deductible. Therefore, the $250 to break the lease on her old home is not deductible. In addition, meals during the move are no longer deductible (Publication 521).

Allowable moving expenses:	
Packing, crating, and transporting household goods	$1,200
Lodging	550
Moving expense deduction	$1,750

Answer (A) is incorrect. The $150 for meals during the trip and $250 to break the lease on her old home are not deductible. Answer (B) is incorrect. The $150 for meals during the trip is not deductible. Answer (D) is incorrect. The $250 fee to break the lease on Pat's old home is not deductible as a moving expense.

8. Elana met all the requirements to deduct moving expenses when she moved from California to Maryland in the current year. Which of the following expenses that she incurred is not deductible?

A. Reasonable shipping cost for her cat.

B. Home improvements to help sell her home in California.

C. Storage costs incurred while her furniture was in transit from California to Maryland.

D. The cost of an oil change for her car while driving from California to Maryland during her move.

Answer (B) is correct.

REQUIRED: The item not considered a deductible moving expense.

DISCUSSION: The definition of moving expenses under Sec. 217(b) includes only reasonable expenses of moving household goods and personal effects and of travel (including lodging) from the former residence to the new residence [Sec. 217(b)(1)]. Improvements to enhance the salability of an old residence do not qualify as moving expenses (Publication 521).

9. Marco and Leigh Ann Green (husband and wife) moved from New Jersey to Florida on May 1, 2012, at Marco's request. Leigh Ann immediately found a job as a part-time substitute teacher but only worked 23 weeks during the year. Marco, a self-employed solar heating unit salesman, could not continue in the same line of work after the move. In Florida, he held one full-time job for 13 weeks, then another full-time job for 10 more weeks during 2012. Marco expects that he will start a new full-time job as an employee of a landscaping company in January of 2013. Can Marco and Leigh Ann claim a deduction for moving expenses on their 2012 jointly filed return?

A. They cannot, since Marco did not meet the 39-week test in 2012.

B. They can, since Leigh Ann worked 23 weeks and Marco worked 16 weeks for a total of 39 weeks.

C. They can, since Marco expects to meet the 39-week test in 2013.

D. They cannot, since both Leigh Ann and Marco have to meet the 39-week test individually.

Answer (C) is correct.

REQUIRED: Taxpayers' ability to deduct moving expenses.

DISCUSSION: A taxpayer may deduct moving expenses provided that the expenses are not reimbursed by the employer, the individual's new principal place of work is at least 50 miles farther from the former residence than was the former principal place of work, and the taxpayer is employed full-time in the new location during at least 39 weeks in the 12-month period following the move (or a self-employed individual meets the 39-week requirement and is employed full-time during at least 78 weeks of the 24-month period immediately following the move) (Publication 521). Thus, Marco expects to meet the 39-week test in 2013 before May 1, with 23 weeks in 2012 and 16 weeks in 2013.

Answer (A) is incorrect. The taxpayer has a 12-month period following the move to meet the 39-week test. Answer (B) is incorrect. The sum of the periods worked is not allowed for married taxpayers. Answer (D) is incorrect. Only one of the taxpayers must meet the 39-week test.

4.4 Self-Employment Deductions

10. Bernie is a self-employed accountant in 2012. He reported net income of $54,150 on his Schedule C for 2012. During the year, Bernie paid the following: $5,200 in child support, $5,000 in alimony, $6,000 in medical insurance premiums, self-employment tax of $6,651, and $2,000 to his IRA plan. What amounts are deductible in arriving at adjusted gross income?

A. $22,025

B. $20,025

C. $16,825

D. $24,851

Answer (C) is correct.

REQUIRED: Deductible amounts in calculating AGI.

DISCUSSION: Bernie is permitted to deduct certain expenses paid during the year from gross income. Alimony is deductible by the payor and income to the recipient. Medical insurance premiums are 100% deductible by self-employed individuals. Also, Bernie is permitted to deduct the employer's portion of self-employment taxes paid ($3,825), calculated as $6,651 × 57.51%. Bernie is allowed a deduction for his IRA contribution (Publication 17). Therefore, the total deductions to calculate AGI are $16,825 ($5,000 + $6,000 + $3,825 + $2,000).

Answer (A) is incorrect. Child support is not deductible. Answer (B) is incorrect. Child support is not deductible, and the IRA is deductible. Also, only a portion of self-employment taxes is deductible. Answer (D) is incorrect. Child support payments are not deductible. Also, only a portion of self-employment taxes is deductible.

11. For 2011 and 2012, Malcom and Julie, husband and wife, paid health insurance premiums of $3,000 each year ($1,500 for each person). Malcom was self-employed, and his net profit was $70,000 in 2011 and $80,000 in 2012. Julie was unemployed in 2011 then took a job in January 2012. She had the option to join a subsidized health plan for the family with her employer but declined. Since this expense is not deductible on Schedule C, what amount can they deduct elsewhere as a business expense on their 2011 and 2012 joint tax returns?

A. 2011: $0; 2012: $0.

B. 2011: $0; 2012: $3,000.

C. 2011: $3,000; 2012: $0.

D. 2011: $3,000; 2012: $3,000.

Answer (C) is correct.

REQUIRED: The amount of deduction available to self-employed persons.

DISCUSSION: Self-employed persons may deduct from gross incomes 100% of amounts paid during 2012 for health insurance for themselves, their spouses, and their dependents and 100% of amounts paid during 2011. The couple cannot take a deduction for 2012 since Julie was eligible for an employer health plan even though she declined to participate (Publication 17).

Answer (A) is incorrect. The expense for 2011 may be deducted. Answer (B) is incorrect. The expense may be deducted in 2011, and nothing is deductible in 2012. Answer (D) is incorrect. The full payment is deductible in 2011, and nothing is deductible in 2012.

4.5 Alimony

12. Starting in 2012, Mr. West must pay his former spouse $20,000 annually under a divorce decree in the following amounts:

- $1,000 a month for mortgage payments (including principal and interest) on a jointly-owned home
- $250 a month for tuition fees paid to a private school until their son attains the age of 18 or leaves the school prior to age 18
- $5,000-a-year cash payment to the former Mrs. West
- In addition to the above amounts, the former Mrs. West also received in 2012 a lump-sum amount of $150,000 from the sale of their other marital assets

Assume the parties did not file a joint return and were not members of the same household. Also, assume that there were no written statements between the parties as to how the amounts should be treated. What is the amount of Mr. West's 2012 alimony deductions?

A. $20,000

B. $155,000

C. $17,000

D. $11,000

Answer (D) is correct.

REQUIRED: Determining the amount of deductible alimony payments.

DISCUSSION: Alimony and separate maintenance payments are gross income to the recipient and deductible by the payor. Child support payments and any part of an alimony payment designated as child support are not deductible. If any amount of an alimony payment is to be reduced based on a contingency relating to a child, such as the attainment of a certain age or graduation, the amount of the specified reduction is treated as child support (Publication 17). Mr. West may deduct half of the payments on the jointly-owned home and the $5,000-per-year cash payment to Mrs. West. His total deduction and her inclusion equal $11,000 ($5,000 + $6,000).

Answer (A) is incorrect. Child support equals $2,000, and $6,000 is not considered alimony because Mr. West jointly owns the home. Answer (B) is incorrect. The lump-sum payment is not considered alimony. Rather, it is a property distribution. Answer (C) is incorrect. Only half of the mortgage payments are considered alimony.

13. Which of the following items may be considered alimony?

A. Noncash property settlement.

B. Payments you made under a written separation agreement for the mortgage and real estate taxes on a home you owned by yourself and in which your former spouse lived rent-free.

C. Payments made to a third party on behalf of the former spouse for the former spouse's medical expenses.

D. Payments made for the 3-month period after the death of the recipient spouse.

Answer (C) is correct.

REQUIRED: The item that may be considered alimony.

DISCUSSION: Payments of cash to a third party made at the written request of the payee spouse will qualify as alimony. Payments are often made on behalf of the payee spouse, such as payments for mortgages, rent, medical costs, or education (Publication 17).

Answer (A) is incorrect. Noncash property settlements are specifically excluded from qualifying as alimony. Answer (B) is incorrect. The mortgage payments, but not the real estate taxes paid, will qualify as alimony. Answer (D) is incorrect. Alimony payments must cease at the death of the recipient.

14. All of the following are requirements for a payment to be alimony (under instruments executed after 1984), except

A. Payments can be in cash or property.

B. Payments cannot be a transfer of services.

C. Payments are required by a divorce or separation instrument.

D. Payments are not required after death of the recipient spouse.

Answer (A) is correct.

REQUIRED: The item that is not a requirement for a payment to be alimony.

DISCUSSION: Sec. 215 allows a deduction for alimony or separate maintenance payments (Sec. 71). Sec. 71(b) defines alimony as any payment in cash if (1) it is received under a divorce or separation instrument, (2) the instrument does not designate the payment as not includible in gross income, (3) the payee spouse and payor spouse are not members of the same household at the time the payment is made, and (4) there is no liability to make such payment for any period after the death of the payee spouse. Thus, if the payments are in services or property and not cash, they cannot be considered alimony [Publication 17 and IRC Sec. 215, Sec. 71(b)].

15. Which of the following is not a payment deductible as alimony?

A. Payments for life insurance premiums required by the divorce decree.

B. Payments for medical expenses of your spouse under the terms of the divorce decree.

C. Half of the mortgage payment on a home jointly owned with your ex-spouse when required by the divorce decree.

D. Payments for child support required by the divorce decree.

Answer (D) is correct.

REQUIRED: The payments that qualify as alimony.

DISCUSSION: Alimony and separate maintenance payments are gross income to the recipient and deductible by the payor. The following are the requirements for qualified alimony payments.

1. The payment must be made in cash or equivalent.
2. Payment must be received on behalf of a spouse under a divorce or separation agreement.
3. Payee spouse and payor spouse must not be members of the same household at the time of payments.
4. The payor spouse is not liable for any payments after the death of the payee spouse.
5. The spouses must not file joint returns with each other.

In addition, child support payments and any part of an alimony payment designated as child support are not deductible. Since child support payments are not deductible to the payor, these payments are not considered alimony (Publication 17).

Answer (A) is incorrect. Payments for life insurance premiums required by a divorce decree is a payment that must be received on behalf of a spouse under a divorce decree or separation agreement, so it qualifies as alimony. Answer (B) is incorrect. Payments for medical expenses of your spouse under the terms of a divorce decree is a payment that must be received on behalf of a spouse under a divorce decree or separation agreement, so it qualifies as alimony. Answer (C) is incorrect. Half of the mortgage payment on a home jointly owned with your ex-spouse when required by a divorce decree is a payment that must be received on behalf of a spouse under a divorce decree or separation agreement, so it qualifies as alimony.

16. Each of the following would be one of the requirements for a payment to be alimony under instruments executed after 1984 except

A. Payments are not made to and from spouses in the same household at the date of payment.

B. Payments are from spouses filing a joint return.

C. Payments are not designated in the instrument as not alimony.

D. Payments are cash equivalents.

Answer (B) is correct.

REQUIRED: The item that is not a requirement for a payment to be alimony.

DISCUSSION: Sec. 215 allows a deduction for alimony or separate maintenance payments (Sec. 71). Sec. 71(b) defines alimony as any payment in cash if (1) it is received under a divorce or separation instrument, (2) the instrument does not designate the payment as not includible in gross income, (3) the payee spouse and payor spouse are not members of the same household at the time the payment is made, and (4) there is no liability to make such payment for any period after the death of the payee spouse. However, the spouses cannot be filing a joint tax return when the payments are made (Publication 17).

17. Todd and Susan divorced on September 1, 2012. As part of the divorce decree, beginning in September, Todd was to make payments of $2,000 a month for the balance of the year to Susan's doctor for recent medical expenses, child support payments of $500 per month, and $1,500 a month for the mortgage payment on a jointly owned home. Susan and the children will continue to live in the home. What is the amount that Todd can deduct as alimony for 2012?

A. $16,000

B. $11,000

C. $4,200

D. $9,600

Answer (B) is correct.

REQUIRED: The amount that can be deducted as alimony.

DISCUSSION: Sec. 215 allows a deduction for alimony or separate maintenance payments (Sec. 71). Sec. 71(b) defines alimony as any payment in cash if (1) it is received under a divorce or separation instrument, (2) the instrument does not designate the payment as not includible in gross income, (3) the payee spouse and payor spouse are not members of the same household at the time the payment is made, and (4) there is no liability to make such payment for any period after the death of the payee spouse. The mortgage payment attributable to Todd's ownership, or $3,000 ($750 × 4), is deductible as alimony. The payment for medical expenses are deductible as well. Therefore, the total alimony deduction is $11,000. Child support payments are not deductible (Publication 17).

Answer (A) is incorrect. Under Sec. 71(c), child support is not deductible. Todd can only deduct $750 (his portion) of the mortgage payment per month. Answer (C) is incorrect. The mortgage payment attributable to Todd's ownership and the payment for medical expenses are the expenses deductible as alimony. Answer (D) is incorrect. The mortgage payment attributable to Todd's ownership and the payment for medical expenses are the expenses deductible as alimony.

4.6 Retirement Savings (IRA) Contributions

18. Mrs. Domino made deductible contributions to traditional individual retirement accounts for several years. Mrs. Domino decides to withdraw $10,000 from one of her accounts in 2012. Mrs. Domino is 61 years old. How does this transaction affect Mrs. Domino's tax return for 2012?

A. Mrs. Domino must report the entire amount of $10,000.

B. Mrs. Domino does not have to report anything because she is older than 59 1/2 years.

C. Mrs. Domino does not have to report any amount because this was not withdrawn from a Roth IRA.

D. Mrs. Domino must report all of the distribution received but can elect to use the 10-year option.

Answer (A) is correct.

REQUIRED: Inclusion of IRA distributions after 59 1/2 years of age.

DISCUSSION: Traditional IRA contributions are made before-tax. Distributions made from a Traditional IRA before the age of 59 1/2 years are subject to federal income tax and a 10% penalty tax. Distributions from a Traditional IRA after the age of 59 1/2 years are subject to federal income tax only and must be reported. Mrs. Domino must report the distribution from her Traditional IRA (Publication 17).

Answer (B) is incorrect. This distribution is from a traditional IRA. Had this distribution been from a Roth IRA, Mrs. Domino would not declare the distribution from the IRA. Distributions from a traditional IRA must be reported. Answer (C) is incorrect. This withdrawal is from a traditional IRA, not a Roth IRA. Answer (D) is incorrect. Mrs. Domino must report the distribution in the year received. The 10-year option is not available on IRA deductions.

4.7 Higher Education Deductions

19. In 2012, Rusty paid $5,000 of interest on a qualified education loan. Rusty is not claimed as a dependent by another taxpayer. What is the maximum deduction available to him for the education loan interest?

A. $0

B. $2,000

C. $2,500

D. $5,000

Answer (C) is correct.

REQUIRED: The maximum amount of interest from education loans that may be allowed as a for-AGI deduction in 2012.

DISCUSSION: Individuals are allowed to deduct interest paid during the tax year on any qualified education loan. The maximum amount that may be deducted is $2,500.

Answer (A) is incorrect. Qualified education loan interest is allowed as a for-AGI deduction. Answer (B) is incorrect. The maximum deduction available is $2,500. Answer (D) is incorrect. The amount available as a deduction is limited to $2,500.

20. Rebecca graduated from college in 2011. She refinanced her qualified education loans in 2012 with another loan. She is not claimed as a dependent by another taxpayer. What is the maximum deduction available to her for the $3,000 paid for education loan interest in 2012?

A. $0

B. $1,500

C. $2,500

D. $3,000

Answer (C) is correct.

REQUIRED: The maximum for-AGI deduction available to an individual who refinances qualified education loan interest.

DISCUSSION: Individuals are allowed to deduct interest paid during the tax year on any qualified education loan. The maximum deduction for 2012 is $2,500. A qualified education loan also encompasses debt used to refinance the qualified education loan. Note, however, that if a homeowner obtains a home equity loan to refinance the qualified education debt, the homeowner may not utilize both the mortgage interest deduction and the education loan interest deduction (Publication 17).

21. Kathy paid $8,000 of interest on qualified education loans in 2012. Kathy is not claimed as a dependent by another taxpayer. Since she graduated from medical school 7 years ago, she has faithfully paid the minimum interest due each month. What is the maximum deduction available to her for education loan interest in 2012?

A. $0

B. $500

C. $2,500

D. $8,000

Answer (C) is correct.

REQUIRED: The amount of qualified education loan interest available for a deduction to arrive at AGI.

DISCUSSION: Individuals are allowed to deduct interest paid during the tax year on any qualified education loan. The maximum amount that may be deducted is $2,500 in 2012 (Publication 17).

22. Mr. Jones had a student loan for qualified higher education expenses on which interest was due. The loan payments were required from July 1, 2005, until December 31, 2012. The interest payments were $1,200 per year. How much may he deduct in arriving at adjusted gross income in 2012?

A. $0

B. $600

C. $1,200

D. $2,500

Answer (C) is correct.

REQUIRED: The interest expense a taxpayer may deduct in arriving at AGI.

DISCUSSION: Individuals are allowed to deduct interest paid during the tax year on any qualified education loan in 2012. The maximum amount that may be deducted is $2,500 in 2012. However, the deduction for Mr. Jones is limited to the amount paid (Publication 17).

Answer (A) is incorrect. Mr. Jones may deduct the interest paid on the school loans. Answer (B) is incorrect. The deduction for interest on a qualified education loan is not limited to the interest paid on the loan during the first 60 months in which interest payments are required. Answer (D) is incorrect. Mr. Jones is limited to the interest paid.

23. Without regard to AGI limitations, how much of Henderson's $10,000 tuition payment to Ouachita State University may be deducted for AGI in 2012?

A. $2,000

B. $2,500

C. $4,000

D. $10,000

Answer (C) is correct.

REQUIRED: Allowable tuition deduction for AGI.

DISCUSSION: Taxpayers may take an above-the-line deduction for qualified tuition and related expenses. In 2012, the deduction is limited to $4,000.

Answer (A) is incorrect. The maximum allowable Lifetime Learning Credit is $2,000. Answer (B) is incorrect. The maximum deductible amount of interest paid on a qualified education loan is $2,500. Answer (D) is incorrect. The deduction for AGI is limited.

24. Laurie is a sophomore in the University of Nebraska's degree program in dentistry. In 2012, Laurie paid $3,000 in tuition, $500 for books required to be purchased through the school, and $250 for required rented dental equipment. Laurie also paid room and board of $3,500. What is the total qualifying deductible educational expense for Laurie in 2012?

A. $3,500

B. $3,750

C. $7,250

D. $3,000

Answer (B) is correct.

REQUIRED: The total qualifying education expenses.

DISCUSSION: Qualifying education expenses include tuition and fees, books, and equipment required for classes. Room and board are specifically excluded. Thus, Laurie has $3,750 ($3,000 + $500 + $250) of qualifying education expenses.

Authors' Note: The 2005 exam did not include "required" in the question stem. Gleim added "required" for clarification; however, you should be prepared for the wording used on past exams.

Answer (A) is incorrect. Laurie can include the $250 paid for the rental equipment. Answer (C) is incorrect. Laurie cannot include the $3,500 paid for room and board. Answer (D) is incorrect. Laurie can include the $500 for books and $250 for rented dental equipment.

4.8 Other Above-the-Line Deductions

25. Consider the following expenditures and determine the total amount that would be deducted as adjustments to income in arriving at adjusted gross income (assuming no income limitations and including appropriate amounts in Gross Income as required) on Form 1040, *Individual Income Tax Return*:

- $1,000 interest paid on student loan
- $2,000 paid to a deductible IRA plan
- $100 jury duty pay given to the employer
- $500 expenses from the nonbusiness rental of personal property ($500 income received)

A. $3,600

B. $2,600

C. $3,100

D. $1,100

Answer (A) is correct.

REQUIRED: The amount of adjusted gross income deductions to be taken.

DISCUSSION: The $1,000 interest paid on a student loan is an allowed deduction in arriving at adjusted gross income (AGI) because individuals are allowed to deduct up to $2,500 of student loan interest as an adjustment to income (Publication 970). Employee contributions to an IRA are deductible on line 32 of Form 1040. Jury duty pay must be included in income, but if jury duty pay must be given to an employer because the employer continues to pay salary while the individual is serving on the jury, the amount of jury duty pay turned over to the employer can be deducted as an adjustment to gross income. The expenses from the nonbusiness rental of personal property are deductible as adjustments to gross income, but only up to the amount of income received. (See Publication 525.) Thus, the total deduction to be taken in arriving at AGI is $3,600 ($1,000 interest + $2,000 IRA contribution + $100 jury duty pay + $500 expenses from rental).

Answer (B) is incorrect. Excluding the $1,000 student loan interest results in $2,600. Taxpayers are allowed to deduct up to $2,500 of student loan interest as an adjustment to income. Answer (C) is incorrect. Excluding the $500 rental expense results in $3,100. The expenses from the nonbusiness rental of personal property are deductible as adjustments to gross income, but only up to the amount of income received. (See Publication 525.) Answer (D) is incorrect. Excluding the $2,000 paid to an IRA retirement plan and the $500 expenses from the nonbusiness rental of personal property results in $1,100. The expenses from the nonbusiness rental of personal property are deductible as adjustments to gross income, but only up to the amount of income received. (See Publication 525.)

26. Which one of the following is not an adjustment to total income in arriving at adjusted gross income?

A. Interest paid on student loans.

B. Portion of health insurance of self-employed persons.

C. Certain contributions to a medical savings account.

D. Contributions to a Roth IRA.

Answer (D) is correct.

REQUIRED: The item that is not an adjustment to total income in arriving at AGI.

DISCUSSION: Sec. 408A(c)(1) disallows any deduction for contributions made to a Roth IRA (Publication 17).

Answer (A) is incorrect. Interest paid on student loans is an allowed deduction in arriving at adjusted gross income under Sec. 62. Answer (B) is incorrect. A portion of health insurance of self-employed persons is an allowed deduction in arriving at adjusted gross income under Sec. 62. Answer (C) is incorrect. Certain contributions to a medical savings account are allowed as a deduction in arriving at adjusted gross income under Sec. 62.

27. Employer contributions to an Archer MSA are

A. Not included in the income of the employee and not included on the employee's W-2.

B. Not included in the income of the employee unless made through a cafeteria plan and included on the employee's W-2.

C. Included in income.

D. None of the answers are correct.

Answer (B) is correct.

REQUIRED: The treatment of employer contributions to an Archer MSA.

DISCUSSION: Archer MSAs (formerly called Medical Savings Accounts) are like IRAs created to defray unreimbursed medical expenses. Contributions to the account by an individual are deductible from adjusted gross income, and contributions made by the employer are excluded from income (unless made through a cafeteria plan). Employee contributions must be reported on the employee's W-2. Earnings of the fund are not included in taxable income for the current year (Publication 17).

28. When funds from an Archer MSA are distributed for qualified medical expenses, these funds are

A. Generally included in the income of the taxpayer.

B. Allocated between contributions made by the employer and the employee, and only the amount attributed to the contributions of the employee are included in income of the taxpayer.

C. Generally excluded from the income of the taxpayer.

D. Always included in the income of the taxpayer.

Answer (C) is correct.

REQUIRED: The proper treatment of distributions from an Archer MSA.

DISCUSSION: Distributions for qualified medical expenses incurred for the benefit of the individual, a spouse, or dependents are generally excluded from income. Qualified medical expenses usually are unreimbursed expenses that would be eligible for the medical expenses deduction (Publication 17).

29. Who is eligible for an Archer MSA in 2012?

A. All individuals who elected coverage in a high-deductible health plan.

B. A maximum of 750,000 individuals who have elected coverage in a high-deductible health plan and are only self-employed.

C. All individuals who elected coverage in a high-deductible health plan and are only employed by a small employer with no more than 50 workers when the Archer MSA is established.

D. A maximum of only 750,000 individuals who have elected coverage in a high-deductible health plan and are either self-employed or employed by a small employer with no more than 50 workers when the Archer MSA is established (Publication 969).

Answer (D) is correct.

REQUIRED: The individual who is eligible for an Archer MSA.

DISCUSSION: The Health Insurance Act of 1996 limited the availability of MSAs during the pilot period (1997-2000) to 750,000 individuals who buy a high-deductible health insurance plan and are either self-employed or employed by a small employer. The law defines a small employer as one with no more than 50 workers. The Archer MSA Program is still limited to 750,000 people (Publication 969).

4.9 Loss Limitations

30. Alex started his own welding business this year. He paid $8,000 for a truck, contributed $15,000 cash and paid $20,000 for tools for the business. His bank loaned $50,000 to buy a building for the business. The building secures the loan. What is Alex's at-risk amount for this activity?

A. $53,000

B. $43,000

C. $93,000

D. $103,000

Answer (B) is correct.

REQUIRED: The amount that is at-risk for an activity.

DISCUSSION: Sec. 465 generally limits losses from an activity for each year to the amount the taxpayer has at-risk in the activity at year end. A taxpayer is generally considered at-risk for money and the adjusted basis of property contributed to the activity and amounts borrowed for use in the activity. However, if amounts borrowed for use in the activity are secured by property used in the activity, those amounts are not considered at-risk. The at-risk amounts result only from amounts the taxpayer is personally liable for (Publication 925).

Answer (A) is incorrect. Money and the adjusted basis of property contributed to the activity are considered at-risk amounts. Answer (C) is incorrect. The building is not used in the activity of holding real estate. Answer (D) is incorrect. Money and the adjusted basis of property contributed to the activity are considered at-risk amounts.

31. Under the rules governing the existence of a passive activity, which of the following would not constitute material participation in a trade or business activity for a tax year?

A. You participated in the activity for more than 500 hours.

B. You participated in the activity for more than 100 hours during the tax year, and you participated at least as much as any other individual for the year.

C. You participated in the activity for less than 100 hours, but you participated on a regular, continuous, and substantial basis.

D. You participated in the activity for less than 50 hours, but you materially participated in the activity for 5 of the 10 preceding years.

Answer (C) is correct.

REQUIRED: The item that does not constitute material participation.

DISCUSSION: Generally, to be considered as materially participating in an activity during a tax year, an individual must satisfy any one of the following tests: (1) (S)he participates more than 500 hours; (2) his/her participation constitutes substantially all of the participation in the activity; (3) (s)he participates for more than 100 hours, and this participation is not less than the participation of any other individual; (4) the activity is a "significant participation activity," and his/her participation in all such activities exceeds 500 hours; (5) (s)he materially participated in the activity for any 5 years of the 10 years that preceded the year in question; (6) the activity is a "personal service activity," and (s)he materially participated in the activity for any 3 years preceding the tax year in question; or (7) (s)he satisfies a facts and circumstances test that requires him/her to show that (s)he participated on a regular, continuous, and substantial basis [Temporary Reg. Sec. 1.469-5T(a)]. The regulations state, however, that, if an individual participates in an activity for less than 100 hours, (s)he will be precluded from applying the facts and circumstances test. Thus, it does not matter that the participation was on a regular, continuous, and substantial basis since it amounted to less than 100 hours (Publication 925).

32. Which of the following would be considered passive activity income?

A. Alaska Permanent Funds dividends.

B. State, local, and foreign income tax refunds.

C. Personal service income.

D. None of the answers are correct.

Answer (D) is correct.

REQUIRED: Income classified as passive activity income.

DISCUSSION: There are two kinds of passive activities: (1) trade or business activities in which the taxpayer does not materially participate and (2) rental activities, unless the taxpayer is a real estate professional (Publication 925).

Answer (A) is incorrect. Alaska Permanent Funds dividends are reported as "other income" on Form 1040. Answer (B) is incorrect. Tax refunds are not a kind of passive activity income. Answer (C) is incorrect. Personal service income is earned by performing personal services in fields such as law and architecture and is classified as active income.

33. Bill took out a $100,000 non-recourse loan and bought an apartment building. The building is not security for the loan. Bill spent $25,000 of his own money on repairs before he rented the apartment building to the public. Bill is single, works full-time, and earns $80,000 per year. Bill's loss from the rental real estate activity, in which he actively participates, is $30,000. He has no passive income. For what amount is Bill at-risk, and how much of Bill's passive loss from his rental activity is deductible?

	At-Risk	Passive Loss
A.	$100,000	$25,000
B.	$25,000	$25,000
C.	$125,000	$30,000
D.	$125,000	$25,000

Answer (B) is correct.

REQUIRED: The amount at risk and the passive loss deductible from a taxpayer's rental activity.

DISCUSSION: IRS Publication 925 states that a taxpayer is not considered at risk for his/her share of any nonrecourse loan used to finance an activity or to acquire property used in the activity unless the loan is secured by property not used in the activity. Bill took out a nonrecourse loan, and the building is not security for the loan. Since Bill is deemed to actively participate in the rental real estate activity and Bill's adjusted gross income is less than $100,000, he is allowed to deduct $25,000 against other income.

Answer (A) is incorrect. The loan is a nonrecourse loan. Answer (C) is incorrect. The loan is a nonrecourse loan, and Bill is limited to $25,000 of his passive loss. Answer (D) is incorrect. The loan is a nonrecourse loan.

Authors' Note: Based on the information given, the answer is probably $25,000 at-risk and $25,000 passive loss. You are at-risk for qualified nonrecourse financing secured by real property used in the holding of real property. Since this problem stated that the building was not security for the loan (who would lend in that manner?) and no other real property was mentioned as security, we have to consider this loan to be non-risk.

34. Heathcliff and Gertrude file a joint income tax return for the current year. During the current year, Heathcliff received wages of $120,000 and taxable Social Security benefits of $5,000. Gertrude actively participated in a rental real estate activity in which she had a $30,000 loss. They had no other income during the current year. How much of the rental loss may they deduct on their current-year income tax return?

A. $0

B. $12,500

C. $15,000

D. $25,000

Answer (C) is correct.

REQUIRED: The amount a taxpayer may deduct for losses from active participation in rental real estate activities when adjusted gross income is in excess of $100,000.

DISCUSSION: The $25,000 allowance of losses from active participation in rental real estate activities against nonpassive income is reduced by 50% of the amount by which adjusted gross income (determined without regard to Social Security benefits, IRA contributions, and passive losses) exceeds $100,000 [Sec. 469(i)(3)]. Heathcliff and Gertrude's adjusted gross income exceeds $100,000 by $20,000. Therefore, the $25,000 allowance is reduced by $10,000 ($20,000 × 50%). This leaves $15,000 of losses that can be deducted (Publication 925).

Answer (A) is incorrect. The taxpayer is allowed to deduct a portion of the loss. Answer (B) is incorrect. The amount of the allowance is $12,500 including half of the Social Security payment, which should not be included. Answer (D) is incorrect. The $25,000 allowance must be reduced because income exceeds the $100,000 threshold.

35. During the current year, Amanda, who is single, received $110,000 in salary and realized a $30,000 loss from her rental real estate activities in which she actively participates. She contributed $2,000 to an IRA. What is the amount that Amanda may claim as loss from her current-year real estate activities?

A. $20,000

B. $21,000

C. $25,000

D. $30,000

Answer (A) is correct.

REQUIRED: The amount a taxpayer may deduct for losses from active participation in rental real estate activities when adjusted gross income is in excess of $100,000.

DISCUSSION: The $25,000 allowance of losses from active participation in rental real estate activities against nonpassive income is reduced by 50% of the amount by which adjusted gross income (determined without regard to Social Security benefits, IRA contributions, and passive losses) exceeds $100,000. Amanda's adjusted gross income exceeds $100,000 by $10,000 [Sec. 469(i)(3)]. Therefore, the $25,000 allowance is reduced by $5,000 ($10,000 × 50%). This leaves $20,000 of losses that can be deducted (Publication 925).

Answer (B) is incorrect. The $25,000 allowance is not reduced by $4,000. Answer (C) is incorrect. The $25,000 allowance must be reduced because income exceeds the $100,000 threshold. Answer (D) is incorrect. The entire loss is not deductible.

36. Larry purchased 100 shares of ABC stock on May 31, Year 1, for $100 per share. On October 28, Year 1, he sold the 100 shares for $90 per share. On November 22, Year 1, his wife, Vickie, purchased 100 shares of ABC stock for $80 per share. Vickie held the stock until September 30, Year 2. On that date, she sold the stock for $110 per share. They filed married filing separately on all returns.

A. Larry has a short-term loss of $1,000 on his Year 1 tax return.

B. Vickie has short-term gain of $3,000 on her Year 2 tax return.

C. Vickie will have a short-term gain of $3,000 on her Year 2 tax return, and Larry takes the short-term loss of $1,000 on his Year 1 tax return.

D. Vickie will have a long-term gain of $2,000 on her Year 2 tax return and Larry will not have any capital loss on his Year 1 tax return.

Answer (D) is correct.

REQUIRED: The amount of gain or loss on a wash sale.

DISCUSSION: Publication 550 states, "You cannot deduct losses from sales or trades of stock or securities in a wash sale. A wash sale occurs when you sell or trade stock or securities at a loss and within 30 days before or after the sale you:

1. Buy substantially identical stock or securities,
2. Acquire substantially identical stock or securities in a fully taxable trade, or
3. Acquire a contract or option to buy substantially identical stock or securities.

If you sell stock and your spouse or a corporation you control buys substantially identical stock, you also have a wash sale." Larry's unrecognized loss can be used to reduce Vickie's gain [$11,000 selling price – ($8,000 purchase price + $1,000 Larry's unrecognized loss) = $2,000 recognized gain]. The holding periods are added together, creating a long-term capital gain.

Answer (A) is incorrect. Larry cannot deduct losses from sales of securities in a wash sale. Answer (B) is incorrect. The holding periods of Larry and Vickie's stocks are added together, creating a long-term capital gain. The amount of Vickie's $3,000 gain is reduced by Larry's $1,000 short-term capital loss. Answer (C) is incorrect. Larry cannot deduct losses from sales of securities in a wash sale. The holding periods of Larry and Vickie's stocks are added together, creating a long-term capital gain. The amount of Vickie's $3,000 gain is reduced by Larry's $1,000 short-term capital loss.

37. In the current year, Heidi, a self-employed individual, had net profits from her Schedule C business of $125,000. Besides her Schedule C deductions, Heidi took an $8,831 deduction for her Social Security taxes, and her deduction for self-employed health insurance was $650. Heidi also realized a $30,000 loss from her rental real estate activity in which she actively participated. What is Heidi's deductible rental real estate loss for the current year?

A. $12,500

B. $12,825

C. $12,175

D. $25,000

Answer (B) is correct.

REQUIRED: The amount a taxpayer may deduct for losses from active participation in rental real estate activities when adjusted gross income is in excess of $100,000.

DISCUSSION: The $25,000 allowance of losses from active participation in rental real estate activities against nonpassive income is reduced by 50% of the amount by which adjusted gross income (determined without regard to Social Security benefits, IRA contributions, and passive losses) exceeds $100,000 [Sec. 469(i)(3)]. The health insurance, however, must be subtracted from her net profits, for a total of $124,350 ($125,000 – $650). Heidi's adjusted gross income exceeds $100,000 by $24,350. Therefore, the $25,000 allowance is reduced by $12,175 ($24,350 × 50%). This leaves $12,825 of losses that can be deducted (Publication 925).

Answer (A) is incorrect. The health insurance must be subtracted from net profits before calculating the limitation. Answer (C) is incorrect. The health insurance must be subtracted, not added, from net profits. Answer (D) is incorrect. The $25,000 must be reduced because profits exceed the $100,000 threshold.

38. Barry is a lawyer. He owns 10 apartment buildings that are managed by his brother's real estate business. At the end of the year, the apartment buildings resulted in a $40,000 loss. Barry earned $80,000 in wages. His wife, Claire, earned $20,000 from her part-time job. Their other income included $5,000 in dividends from their mutual funds. They had no other income. How much of the rental loss can Barry use assuming Barry actively participates in the apartment buildings?

A. $0

B. $25,000

C. $40,000

D. $22,500

Answer (D) is correct.

REQUIRED: The amount of rent allowable as a loss.

DISCUSSION: Any rental activity is a passive activity, whether or not the taxpayer participates in the activity. An individual who actively participates in rental real estate activity may use up to $25,000 of net losses from rental real estate activity to offset other income. The $25,000 is reduced by 50% of the amount by which AGI (determined without regard to Social Security, IRA contributions, and passive losses) exceeds $100,000. Barry has AGI of $105,000 ($80,000 + $20,000 + $5,000). Accordingly, his allowable $25,000 deduction will be reduced by $2,500 [($105,000 – $100,000) × 50%] and is therefore $22,500. If Barry does not actively participate, he is not allowed a deduction (Publication 925).

Answer (A) is incorrect. Barry may use a portion of the rental loss. Answer (B) is incorrect. Barry's loss must be reduced by 50% of the excess of his AGI over $100,000. Answer (C) is incorrect. Barry may not deduct the entire loss.

39. Tom Brown, who is single, owns a rental apartment building property. This is the only rental property that Tom owns. He actively participates in this rental activity as he collects the rents and performs ordinary and necessary repairs. In 2012, Tom had a loss of $30,000 on this rental activity and had no reportable passive income. His adjusted gross income, without regard to this rental loss, is $60,000. How much of the rental loss may Tom deduct on his 2012 return?

A. $30,000

B. $25,000

C. $0

D. $6,000

Answer (B) is correct.

REQUIRED: Deductibility of passive activity losses when the taxpayer actively participates.

DISCUSSION: All rental activity is passive. A person who actively participates in rental real estate activity is entitled to deduct up to $25,000 of losses from the passive activity from other-than-passive income, provided that the individual's income does not exceed $100,000. Single individuals and married individuals filing jointly can qualify for the $25,000 amount. Married individuals who live together for the entire year and file separately cannot qualify. Thus, Tom may deduct $25,000 of the loss (Publication 925).

Answer (A) is incorrect. Tom is not allowed to deduct the entire amount of the loss. Tom may carry over the remaining $5,000. Answer (C) is incorrect. Tom can deduct $25,000 of the passive activity losses in the current tax year. Answer (D) is incorrect. There is no 10%-of-AGI limitation on the amount of losses that may be deducted.

STUDY UNIT FIVE
ITEMIZED DEDUCTIONS

(14 pages of outline)

Below-the-line deductions are all the deductions that may be subtracted from AGI to arrive at taxable income. Each below-the-line deduction is either an itemized or standard deduction or a personal exemption.

```
Taxable income = Adjusted gross income - Greater of allowable itemized deductions on
        Schedule A or the standard deduction - Personal exemptions
```

5.1 MEDICAL EXPENSES

7.5% of AGI

Amounts paid for qualified medical expenses that exceed 7.5% of AGI may be deducted.

1. To qualify for a deduction, an expense must be paid during the taxable year for the taxpayer, the taxpayer's spouse, or a dependent and must not be compensated for by insurance or otherwise during the taxable year.
   a. The deduction is allowed for a person who was either a spouse or a dependent at the time medical services were rendered or at the time the expenses were actually paid.
      1) Medical expenses charged on a credit card are deductible in the year the medical expenses were incurred, not when the credit card bill is paid.
      2) To qualify as a dependent, the person (dependent)
         a) Must have over half of his/her support for the year paid for by the taxpayer;
         b) Must fall within a family relationship (including adopted children); and
         c) Must be a citizen, national, or resident of the U.S., Canada, or Mexico during a portion of the tax year.
   b. However, the individual need not satisfy the gross income test or the joint return test, and a child of divorced parents is treated as a dependent of both parents.
2. Deductible medical expenses are amounts paid for
   a. Diagnosis, cure, mitigation, treatment or prevention of disease, or for the purpose of affecting any structure or function of the body
   b. Transportation primarily for and essential to medical care
   c. Medical insurance
   d. Qualified long-term care premiums and services
   e. Smoking cessation programs and prescribed drugs designed to alleviate nicotine withdrawal
   f. Eyeglasses used for medical purposes

Professional Services

3. Deductible medical expenses include amounts paid to physicians, surgeons, dentists, chiropractors, osteopaths, chiropodists, podiatrists, psychiatrists, psychologists, etc., solely in their professional capacity.

Activity or Treatment

4. A medical expense deduction is not allowed for amounts paid for any activity or treatment designed merely to improve an individual's general health or sense of wellness, even if recommended by a physician.
   a. Examples include participation in a health club or a weight-loss institute.
      1) Such expenses may be deductible if the services are prescribed by a physician who provides a written statement that they are necessary to alleviate a physical or mental defect or illness.

Institutional Care

5. The cost of in-patient hospital care (including meals and lodging) is deductible as a medical expense.
   a. If the principal reason an individual is in an institution other than a hospital (a special school for the handicapped, a rest home, etc.) is the need for and availability of the medical care furnished by the institution, the full costs of meals, lodging, and other services necessary for furnishing the medical care are all deductible.

Prescription

6. Only **medicines and drugs** that require a prescription (except for insulin) are qualified medical expenses.

Capital Expenditures

7. The following are considered deductible medical expenses:
   a. Eyeglasses
   b. A guide dog
   c. Wheelchairs, crutches, or artificial limbs
   d. Special beds
   e. Air conditioning
   f. Dehumidifying equipment
8. Expenditures for new building construction or for permanent improvements to existing structures primarily for medical care may be deductible in part as a medical expense.
   a. The excess of the cost of a permanent improvement over the increase in value of the property is a deductible medical expense.
      1) Although the cost of the capital asset is not deductible, the cost of operating and maintaining the asset may be deductible when the asset is operated primarily for medical care.
   b. Construction of handicap entrance/exit ramps, installation of elevators, widening of doorways, or lowering of kitchen cabinets or equipment may each qualify.

EXAMPLE

Billy had bypass heart surgery in February 2012. At the advice of his doctor, he had an elevator installed in his home so that he would not have to climb stairs. The costs associated with this capital improvement are as follows:

Cost of elevator installed June 30, 2012	$5,000
Increase in value of home due to elevator	2,500
Maintenance and repair of elevator, September 30, 2012	500

The taxpayer may deduct the cost of the elevator installed (less any increase in FMV) plus any maintenance, repair, and operating expenses. Thus, the total allowable deduction is

Cost of Elevator Installed	$5,000
Less: Increase in FMV	(2,500)
Deductible Capital Expenditure	$2,500
Plus: Maintenance and Repair	500
Total Allowable Medical Expenses	$3,000

The maintenance and repair expenses might have qualified as medical expenses regardless of whether the elevator expenditure was deductible.

Travel

9. Amounts paid for transportation essential to (and primarily for) medical care are deductible.
   a. This includes the transportation cost of traveling to a warm climate on a doctor's order to alleviate a specific chronic ailment.
10. The taxpayer may choose between actual expenditures (e.g., taxis, airfare) or $.23 per mile for 2012 (plus the cost of tolls and parking).
11. Expenditures for lodging are deductible up to $50 per night per individual.
12. The cost of meals is not deductible.

Insurance

13. Premiums paid for medical insurance that provides for reimbursement of medical care expenses are deductible.
    a. Premiums paid on a policy that merely pays the insured a specified amount per week, etc., are not deductible.

Medicare

14. The basic cost of Medicare insurance (Medicare Part A) is not deductible unless voluntarily paid by the taxpayer for coverage.
    a. The extra cost of Medicare (Medicare Part B) is deductible.

Payment after Death

15. If a decedent's own medical expenses are paid by his/her estate within 1 year beginning on the day after the decedent's death, the expenses may be deducted on the decedent's tax return for the year incurred.
    a. Alternatively, the estate can deduct medical expenses as a claim against the estate for federal estate tax purposes.

Adopted Child

16. The amount paid by an adopting parent for medical expenses rendered directly to a child before his/her placement in the adopting parent's home constitute a medical expense, provided that
    a. The child qualifies as a dependent of the adopting parent at the time that the medical services are rendered or at the time the fees therefore are paid,
    b. The adopting parent can clearly substantiate that any deduction claimed is directly attributable to the medical care of the child, and
    c. The medical expenses are paid by the adopting parent or his/her agent for the medical care of the particular child.
        1) Reimbursement for expenses incurred and paid by someone other than the taxpayer prior to adoption negotiations are not considered deductible medical expenses.

Stop and review! You have completed the outline for this subunit. Study questions 1 through 8 beginning on page 134.

5.2 TAXES

A taxpayer who itemizes deductions is permitted to deduct the full amount of certain taxes that are paid and incurred during the taxable year.

Real Property

1. State, local, and foreign real property taxes are deductible by the person upon whom they are imposed (i.e., the owner) in the year in which they were paid or accrued.
    a. If real property is bought or sold during the year, the real property tax is apportioned between the buyer and the seller on the basis of the number of days each one held the property during the real property tax year.
        1) The purchaser is presumed to own the property on the date of sale.
    b. Taxes paid to a financial institution and held in escrow are deductible when the financial institution pays the funds over to the taxing body.
    c. Service charges for police and fire protection may be deductible if the funds are paid into a general revenue fund.
    d. Special assessments for local improvements increase the basis of the property and are not deductible.

Ad Valorem/Personal Property

2. Ad valorem and personal property taxes are deductible but only if the tax is
    a. Actually imposed,
    b. Imposed on an annual basis, and
    c. Substantially in proportion to the value of the property.
        1) For example, registration or licensing of vehicles is deductible if the tax is based on the value of the vehicle.

Income Taxes

3. State income taxes are deductible.
4. Foreign income taxes paid are deductible, unless the Foreign Tax Credit is claimed.

5. Individual taxpayers may claim an itemized deduction for general state and local sales taxes in lieu of state income tax.
    a. Taxpayers can deduct either actual sales tax amounts or a predetermined amount from an IRS table.

Nondeductible Taxes

6. The following taxes are not deductible:
   a. Federal taxes on income, estates, gifts, inheritances, legacies, and successions.
      1) A deduction may be available on the estate tax return for income taxes paid on account of a decedent.
   b. State taxes on cigarettes and tobacco, alcoholic beverages, gasoline, registration, estates, gifts, inheritances, legacies, and successions.
   c. Licensing fees of highway motor vehicles (if based on the weight instead of the value of the vehicle).
   d. Sales tax on business property. It is added to the basis of the acquired property.

Stop and review! You have completed the outline for this subunit. Study questions 9 through 12 beginning on page 137.

5.3 INTEREST EXPENSE

Personal Interest

1. The general rule is that no personal interest may be deducted.
2. Personal interest includes interest on credit card debt, revolving charge accounts and lines of credit, car loans, medical fees, and premiums, etc. Personal interest also includes any interest on underpaid tax liabilities.
3. Personal interest does not include
   a. Interest on trade or business debt
   b. Investment interest
   c. Passive activity interest
   d. Qualified residence interest
   e. Student loan interest

Investment Interest

4. The IRC allows the deduction of a limited amount of investment interest as an itemized deduction.
5. Investment interest is interest paid or incurred (on debt) to purchase or carry property held for investment.
   a. Generally, investment interest includes the following:
      1) Interest allocable to portfolio income under the PAL rules
         a) Passive activity interest is includible with passive activities and deductible within the passive loss rules.
      2) Any interest derived from an activity involving a trade or business in which the taxpayer does not materially participate and which is not treated as a passive activity under the PAL rules
      3) Any deductible amount in connection with personal property used in a short sale
   b. Investment interest does **not** include qualified residence interest or passive activity interest.
   c. Limit.
      1) Investment interest may be deducted only to the extent of net investment income.
         a) Net investment income is any excess of investment income over investment expense(s).

2) Investment income is

a) Nontrade or nonbusiness income from

i) Interest

ii) Dividends (not subject to the capital gains tax)

iii) Rents, royalties, and other gross income from property held for investment

b) Net gain on the disposition of property held for investment

i) A taxpayer may elect to treat all or a portion of long-term capital gains and qualified dividends as investment income.

c) Income treated as gross portfolio income under the PAL rules

d) Income from interests in activities that involve a trade or business in which the taxpayer does not materially participate, if the activity is not treated as passive activity under the PAL rules

3) Investment income does not include income from a rental real estate activity in which the taxpayer materially participates.

d. Disallowed investment interest is carried forward indefinitely. It is deductible to the extent of investment income in subsequent tax years.

Residence Interest

6. Qualified residence interest (see Publication 530) is deductible on no more than $1 million of acquisition indebtedness ($500,000 if married, filing separately) and $100,000 of home equity indebtedness (aggregate amount) ($50,000 if married, filing separately).

a. Qualified residence interest is interest paid or accrued during the tax year on acquisition or home equity indebtedness that is secured by a qualified residence (Form 1098).

1) Ministers and military personnel can deduct mortgage interest on their homes even when they receive a parsonage or military allowance that is excludable from gross income.

b. A qualified residence is the principal residence of the taxpayer and any one other residence owned by the taxpayer and used for personal purposes for the greater of 14 days or 10% of the number of days during the year in which it is rented.

c. A taxpayer who has more than two residences may select, each year, the residences used to determine the amount of qualified residence interest.

d. Acquisition indebtedness is debt incurred in acquiring, constructing, or substantially improving a qualified residence. The debt must be secured by such residence.

1) Any debt that is refinanced is treated as acquisition debt to the extent that it does not exceed the principal amount of acquisition debt immediately before refinancing.

e. Home equity indebtedness is all debt other than acquisition debt that is secured by the qualified residence.

1) Home equity indebtedness cannot exceed the fair market value of the residence (reduced by any acquisition debt).

Maximum home equity indebtedness = Property FMV − Acquisition indebtedness

2) Interest on home equity indebtedness is deductible even if the proceeds are used for personal expenditures.

3) Taxpayers cannot deduct home mortgage interest on equity debt if the proceeds of the mortgage are used to buy securities that produce tax-free income.

4) Up to $100,000 of acquisition indebtedness in excess of $1 million can be classified as home equity indebtedness.

Points Paid

f. Points paid by the borrower with respect to a home mortgage are prepaid interest, which is typically deductible over the term of the loan.

1) Amounts paid as points may be deducted in the year paid if

a) The loan is used to buy or improve a taxpayer's principal home and is secured by that home,

b) The settlement statement clearly designates the points or loan origination fees,

c) The points are computed as a percentage of the principal loan amount,

d) Payment of points is an established business practice in the area where the loan is made, and

e) The points paid do not exceed points generally charged in the area.

g. Points paid by the seller are selling expenses that reduce the amount realized on the sale.

1) The purchaser can elect to deduct points on the acquisition indebtedness of a principal residence by reducing the basis by the amount of the points.

Mortgage Insurance Premiums

7. Qualified mortgage insurance premiums are deductible as interest expense for 2007-2013 (Form 1098).

a. Applies only to policies issued during 2007-2013.

b. The insurance must be on acquisition indebtedness.

c. The deduction phases out for adjusted gross incomes exceeding $100,000 ($50,000 for married filing separately). The deduction is completely phased out for adjusted gross incomes exceeding $110,000 ($55,000 for married filing separately).

Stop and review! You have completed the outline for this subunit. Study questions 13 through 17 beginning on page 138.

5.4 CHARITABLE CONTRIBUTIONS

1. Charitable contributions are deductible only if they are made to qualified organizations.

2. Donations can be made in the form of cash or noncash property.

3. All rights and interest to the donation must be transferred to the qualified organization.

4. Generally, a deduction is allowed in the year the contribution is paid, including amounts changed to a bank credit card.

Qualified Organizations

5. Qualified organizations can be either public charities or private foundations.

a. Generally, a public charity is one that derives more than one-third of its support from its members and the general public.

b. Qualified organizations include

1) Corporations, trusts, community chests, funds, or foundations, created or organized in the U.S. and operated exclusively for religious, charitable, scientific, literary, or educational purposes, or for the prevention of cruelty to children or animals.

2) Posts or organizations of war veterans.

3) Domestic fraternal societies, orders, or associations only if the contribution is to be used exclusively for religious, charitable, scientific, literary, or educational purposes, or for the prevention of cruelty to children or animals.

Receipt

6. Donations must meet the following requirements:
   a. Clothing and household items donated must be in good or better condition.
      1) The exception to this rule is that a single item donation in less than good condition but still a $500 value or more is deductible with a qualified appraisal.
   b. Cash or cash equivalent donations require a bank record, or receipt, letter, etc., from the donee organization regardless of the amount. The receipt, etc., must
      1) Be written;
      2) State the name of the organization;
      3) Include the date and amount of the donation;
      4) State whether the qualified organization gave the donor any goods or services as a result of the contribution; and
      5) Be obtained on or before the earlier of
         a) The date the tax return is filed for the year of contribution or
         b) The date, including extensions, for filing the return.
   c. Donations of $250 or more require substantiation by a contemporaneous written receipt from the organization (the bank record alone is insufficient).

Property

7. If a donation is in the form of property, the amount of the donation depends upon the type of property and the type of organization that receives the property.
   a. Capital gain property is property on which a long-term capital gain would be recognized if it were sold on the date of the contribution.
   b. Ordinary income property is property on which ordinary income or short-term capital gain would be recognized if it were sold on the date of the contribution.
   c. For donation amounts, see the chart on page 130.
   d. If the donee organization disposes of the donated property (valued at $500 or more) within 3 years of acquisition, the donee organization must file Form 8282 within 125 days and provide a copy to the donor.

Limitations

8. There are basically two types of charitable organizations: those classified as 50% limit organizations and all others that are classified as **non**-50% limit organizations.

50% Limit Organizations

   a. The 50% limit organizations, which encompass the majority of qualified charitable organizations, are generally public organizations (although some private forms are acceptable) as follows (see IRS Pub. 526 for a complete, detailed list):
      1) Churches
      2) Educational organizations
      3) Hospitals and certain medical research organizations
      4) Organizations that are operated only to receive, hold, invest, and administer property and to make expenditures to or for the benefit of state and municipal colleges and universities
      5) The United States or any state, the District of Columbia, a U.S. possession (including Puerto Rico), a political subdivision of a state or U.S. possession, or a Native American tribal government
      6) Private operating foundations

7) Private nonoperating foundations that make qualifying distributions of 100% of contributions within 2 1/2 months following the year they receive the contribution

Non-50% Limit Organizations

b. Non-50% limit organizations encompass all other qualified charities that are not designated as 50% limit organizations.

1) They are primarily composed of other private organizations.
2) Charitable contribution deductions are subject to limitations.

a) The overall limitation on charitable deductions is 50% of AGI (applicable to the total of all charitable contributions during the year), but certain contributions may be individually limited to 30% or 20% of AGI, depending on the type of contribution given (see below).
b) Any donations that exceed this limitation can be carried forward and deducted in the next 5 tax years.

c. Further limitations

Regular 30% Limitation

1) This 30% limit applies to gifts to all qualified charitable organizations other than 50% limit organizations. (However, if capital gain property is donated, it may be subject to the 20% limitations discussed below.) See the chart on the next page.

Special 30% Limitation for Capital Gain Property

2) A special 30% limitation applies to gifts of capital gain property given to 50% limit organizations, but is only applicable if the donor elects **not** to reduce the fair market value of the donated property by the amount that would have been long-term capital gain if he had sold the property. If the reduction is elected, then only the 50% limitation applies. See the chart on the next page.

20% Limitation

3) This limitation applies to capital gain property donated to non-50% limit charities. The limit is actually the lesser of 20% of AGI or 30% of AGI minus capital gain contributions to public charities.
4) In accounting for the different limitations, all donations subject to the 50% limit are considered before the donations subject to the 30% limit.
5) In carrying over excess contributions to subsequent tax years, the excess must be carried over to the appropriate limitation categories. If a contribution in the 30% category is in excess of the limit, the excess is carried over and subject to the 30% limitation in the next year.

Services

9. The value of services provided to a charitable organization is not deductible.

a. However, out-of-pocket, unreimbursed expenses (e.g., uniforms or equipment) incurred in rendering the service are deductible.
b. Travel expenses incurred while performing the services away from home for the charitable organization are deductible if no significant element of personal pleasure, recreation, or vacation exists.

1) Individuals who qualify for the charitable deduction for the use of an automobile may use the statutory standard mileage rate of $.14 per mile (plus parking fees and tolls) or actual expenses incurred.

a) Depreciation and insurance are not deductible expenses.

Form of Property	Amount of Donation	Limitation
50% Limit Organizations (Mainly Public)		
Cash	Cash amount	50% AGI
Capital Gain Property	FMV (elect not to reduce FMV by potential long-term capital gain)	30% AGI (special limit)
• Tangible personal property unrelated to donee's purpose	Lower of FMV or AB	50% AGI
• Election to reduce property to adjusted basis	Lower of FMV or AB	50% AGI
Ordinary Income Property	Lower of FMV or AB	50% AGI
Services	Unreimbursed expenses	50% AGI
Non-50% Limit Organizations (Mainly Private)		
Cash	Cash amount	30% AGI (regular limit)
Capital Gain Property	Lower of FMV or AB	Lesser of 20% AGI or excess of 30% AGI over contributions to public charities
Ordinary Income Property	Lower of FMV or AB	30% AGI (regular limit)
Services	Unreimbursed expenses	30% AGI (regular limit)

Tickets

10. The value of a ticket to a charitable event is a deductible contribution to the extent the purchase price exceeds the FMV of the admission or privilege associated with the event.

Carryover

11. Generally, individuals may carry forward excess donations for 5 years.

Stop and review! You have completed the outline for this subunit. Study questions 18 through 25 beginning on page 140.

5.5 CASUALTY LOSSES

Taxpayers who itemize may deduct a limited amount for casualty losses to nonbusiness property that arise from theft, fire, storm, shipwreck, or other casualty.

Limitation

1. Only the amount of each loss over $100 is deductible. Only the aggregate amount of all losses over $100 each in excess of 10% of AGI is deductible.
   a. If the loss was covered by insurance, timely filing of an insurance claim is prerequisite to deduction.
      1) The portion of the loss usually not covered by insurance (i.e., a deductible) is not subject to this rule.
   b. The amount of a loss is the lesser of the decrease in FMV of the property due to the casualty or the property's adjusted basis minus any insurance reimbursements.
   c. Regardless of the 10% test, casualty losses are deductible against casualty gains.
2. If the net amount of all personal casualty gains and losses after applying the $100 limit (but before the 10%-of-AGI threshold) is positive, each gain or loss is treated as a capital gain or loss. If the net amount is negative, the excess over 10% of AGI is deductible as an itemized deduction.

3. Cost of appraising a casualty loss is treated as a cost to determine tax liability (a miscellaneous itemized deduction subject to the 2%-of-AGI exclusion).
4. The cost of insuring a personal asset is a nondeductible personal expense.

Federally Declared Disaster Areas

5. A taxpayer is subject to special rules if (s)he sustains a loss in a federally declared disaster area.
   a. Disaster loss treatment is available when a personal residence is rendered unsafe due to the disaster in the area and is ordered to be relocated or demolished by the state or local government.
   b. A disaster loss deduction is computed the same as a casualty loss.
   c. The taxpayer has the option of deducting the loss on
      1) The return for the year in which the loss actually occurred or
      2) The preceding year's return (by filing an amended return).
         a) Revocation of the election may be made before expiration of time for filing the return for the year of loss.
6. The loss is calculated on Form 4684, *Casualties and Thefts*, and carried over to Schedule A, *Itemized Deductions*.
7. Although net operating losses (NOL) are typically associated with businesses and not individuals, items such as personal casualty losses may create an individual NOL (see Publication 536).

Stop and review! You have completed the outline for this subunit. Study questions 26 through 29 beginning on page 143.

5.6 ITEMIZED DEDUCTIONS SUBJECT TO THE 2% AGI LIMITATION

1. Certain itemized deductions are subject to a 2% adjusted gross income limit.
2. Only that portion of the aggregate amount of these itemized deductions that exceeds the threshold amount of 2% of AGI may be deducted from AGI.
3. The disallowed portion is not carried over to other years.
4. The three fundamental categories of the 2% itemized deductions are employee expenses, tax determination expenses, and other expenses.

Employee Expenditures

5. Employee expenditures not reimbursed by the employer are itemized deductions.
6. These expenses are deductible because services as an employee are considered trade or business.
7. The following are examples of deductible employee expenditures:

Employee Travel Away from Home

   a. Travel expenses include transportation, lodging, and meal expenses incurred in an employment-related context.
   b. To qualify for a deduction, the taxpayer must be away from his tax home overnight, and the purpose of the trip must be connected with the taxpayer's business.
   c. Only 50% of meals are deductible. If employee meal expenses are reimbursed by the employer, the employer's deduction is limited to 50% of the expenses.

Employee Transportation Expenses

d. Transportation expenses include taxi fares, automobile expenses, tolls and parking fees, and airfare.

e. These expenses are treated as travel expenses if the employee is away from home overnight. Otherwise, they are transportation expenses.

   1) Commuting costs are nondeductible.
   2) Actual automobile expenses may be used for the deduction, or the taxpayer may use the standard mileage rate.
      a) The standard mileage rate is $.555/mile for 2012, plus parking fees and tolls.
      b) Actual expenses must be allocated between business use and personal use of the automobile. A deduction is allowed only for the business use.

f. Outside salesperson expenses.

Employee Entertainment Expenses

g. Entertainment expenses are subject to the 50% limitation and are deductible only if they are directly related to or associated with the taxpayer's employment.

h. Employee home office expenses.

i. Employee uniforms (provided they are not usable away from work).

j. Union dues and initiation fees.

k. Professional dues and memberships.

l. Subscriptions to business journals.

m. Job-seeking expenses (in the same business).

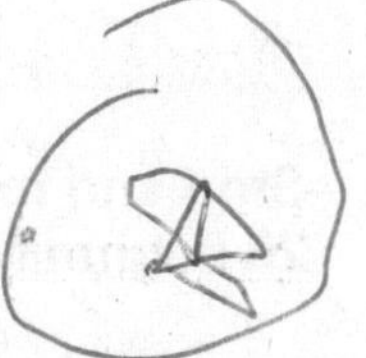

Education Expenses

n. Education expenses.

   1) Examples of deductible expenses include amounts paid for correspondence courses, travel, supplies, books, research and typing expenses related to the educational program, and tuition. They may be deductible only if incurred to maintain or improve skills that are required in the taxpayer's current employment context or if incurred to meet legal requirements or employer requirements.

o. In contrast, the expense of education to enter a trade, business, or profession or to meet the minimum education requirements is not deductible, even if state law requires the education.

   1) Travel as a form of education is not deductible (i.e., the travel itself is the educational purpose).
   2) Educational expenses that are personal or constitute an inseparable aggregate of personal and capital expenditures are not deductible.
   3) Veterans and other students may not deduct education expenses to the extent the amounts expended are allocable to the tax-exempt income.

p. There are two types of plans available: accountable plans and nonaccountable plans.

   1) **Nonaccountable plan.** If excess reimbursements are not returned or if the employee does not substantiate them, the reimbursements are included in the employee's gross income, and all the expenses are deducted from AGI subject to the 2%-of-AGI floor.

2) **Accountable plan.** If reimbursements equal expenses and the employee makes an accounting of expenses to the employer, the reimbursements are excluded from the employee's gross income, and the employee may not deduct the expenses. Employees in an accountable plan must meet the following rules:
   a) They must have paid or incurred deductible expenses while performing services as employees.
   b) They must adequately account for these expenses within a reasonable period of time.
   c) They must return any excess reimbursement or allowance within a reasonable period of time.

Tax Determination

8. Tax determination expenses include the following:
   a. Return preparation: manuals, legal and accounting advice, preprinted forms or tax packages, but not time preparing one's own return
   b. Representation in proceedings with the IRS
   c. Accountant and attorney fees to obtain a letter ruling
   d. Appraisal fees relating to the resolution of tax issues
   e. Contesting tax liability of another (if the tax liability is also personal to the taxpayer)

Other Expenses

9. Other expenses include the following:

Investment

   a. Investment expenses, including
      1) Safe-deposit box rental fees
      2) Subscriptions to investment journals
      3) Investment counsel fees

Hobby Expenses

   b. A hobby is an activity for which profit is not a primary motive.
      1) Some hobbies, however, do generate income.
      2) An activity is presumed not to be a hobby if profits result in any 3 of 5 consecutive tax years (in the case of breeding, training, showing, or racing horses, substitute 2 of 7 consecutive tax years).
      3) Hobby expenses may be deducted, but only to the extent of the hobby's income.
      4) If expenses exceed the income of a hobby, the expenses must be deducted in the following order:
         a) Expenses that are deductible even if not incurred in a trade, business, or investment activity (e.g., taxes, interest)
         b) Expenses that do not reduce the tax basis of any of the hobby's assets (e.g., utilities)
         c) Expenses that reduce the tax basis of the hobby's assets (e.g., depreciation)
      5) The amount of expenses that do not exceed the hobby's gross income are deductions from AGI. Item a) above includes first-tier itemized deductions. Items b) and c) above are miscellaneous itemized deductions subject to the 2%-of-AGI floor.
      6) The excess hobby expenses are not carried over to other years.

Legal Fees

c. Legal fees related to the collection of alimony payments.

1) Sec. 212 provides for a deduction for expenses incurred for the production and collection of income.

2) Legal fees incurred related to the collection of alimony are deductible subject to the 2%-of-AGI limitation.

Stop and review! You have completed the outline for this subunit. Study questions 30 through 37 beginning on page 145.

5.7 MISCELLANEOUS ITEMIZED DEDUCTIONS NOT SUBJECT TO THE 2% AGI LIMITATION AND OVERALL LIMITATION

Miscellaneous Itemized Deductions Not Subject to the 2% Limit

1. The following expenses are deductible as miscellaneous itemized deductions (not subject to the 2% limit) and are reported on line 28, Schedule A (Form 1040):

   a. Amortizable premium on taxable bonds
   b. Casualty and theft losses from income-producing property
   c. Federal estate tax on income in respect of a decedent
   d. Gambling losses up to the amount of gambling winnings
   e. Impairment-related work expenses of persons with disabilities
   f. Repayments of more than $3,000 under a claim of right
   g. Unrecovered investment in a pension

Overall Limitation on Itemized Deductions (Pease Rule)

2. In 2009, an individual whose AGI exceeded $166,800 ($83,400 if married filing separately) reduced the aggregate of itemized deductions by the lesser of 80% of otherwise allowable itemized deductions or 3% of the excess.

   a. However, this limitation was phased out 100% for 2010 through 2012. It will apply again in 2013 for MFS and qualifying widow(er) filers with at least $300,000 of AGI ($275,000 HH, $250,000 single, $150,000 MFS).

Stop and review! You have completed the outline for this subunit. Study questions 38 through 41 beginning on page 148.

QUESTIONS

5.1 Medical Expenses

1. To qualify for a medical expense deduction as your dependent, a person must be your dependent either at the time the medical services were provided or at the time you paid the expenses. A person generally qualifies as your dependent for purposes of the medical expense deduction if

A. The person would qualify as a dependent except for the amount of gross income.

B. The person was a foreign student staying briefly at your home.

C. The person is your sibling's unmarried adult child.

D. The person is the unrelated caregiver for your elderly parents.

Answer (A) is correct.

REQUIRED: The person who qualifies as a dependent for the purpose of a medical expense deduction.

DISCUSSION: For the purpose of a medical deduction, a person qualifies as a "dependent" if (s)he meets the requirements in Sec. 152 except for the following two criteria:

1. The amount of the individual's gross income is not considered [Reg. Sec. 1.213-1(a)(3)].
2. A child with divorced parents is treated as a dependent by both parents [Sec. 213(d)(5)].

(See Publication 502.)

Answer (B) is incorrect. A foreign student staying briefly at your home does not meet the citizenship requirement.
Answer (C) is incorrect. Your sibling's unmarried adult child generally will not meet the support requirement of dependency.
Answer (D) is incorrect. The unrelated caregiver of your elderly parents does not meet the relationship requirement of dependency.

2. Mr. Cedar broke his hip and must now use a wheelchair. He modified his home to accommodate the wheelchair. He had his home appraised for refinancing just before the improvements to his home. The value of his home was $200,000. After he made the modifications and improvements listed below, the value was $202,000. Mr. Cedar incurred the following expenses during the year. Without consideration of adjusted gross income limitations, compute the amount Mr. Cedar may claim on his 2012 tax return as a medical expense:

- $3,000 to construct a ramp in the entrance of his home to accommodate his wheelchair
- $4,000 for installation of a lift to transport the wheelchair from the first to the second floor of his house
- $1,000 for adding handrails around his tub
- $200 to repair his chimney

A. $8,200

B. $6,200

C. $6,000

D. $8,000

Answer (C) is correct.

REQUIRED: The expenditures that can be deducted as a medical expense.

DISCUSSION: Expenditures for new building construction or for permanent improvements to existing structures primarily for medical care may be deductible in part as a medical expense. The excess of the cost of a permanent improvement over the increase in value of the property is a deductible medical expense. Construction of handicapped entrance/exit ramps, installation of elevators, widening of doorways, or lowering of kitchen cabinets or equipment may each qualify. Mr. Cedar's total expenses to make his house more handicapped-accessible is $8,000. However, this must be reduced by the increase in value of his home of $2,000 ($202,000 – $200,000). Thus, Mr. Cedar may deduct $6,000 for medical expenses. (See Publication 502.)

Answer (A) is incorrect. The expenditures must be reduced by the increase in the value of Mr. Cedar's home, and the repair to his chimney is not deductible. Answer (B) is incorrect. The repair to Mr. Cedar's chimney is not deductible. Answer (D) is incorrect. The expenditures must be reduced by the increase in the value of Mr. Cedar's home.

3. During 2012, Mr. and Mrs. Duhon paid the following expenses for their son, Joel:

Medical insurance premiums	$1,500
Contact lenses	210
Household help recommended by a doctor	2,200

For 2012, Joel had gross income of $9,850. Because Joel had gross income of $9,850, the Duhons did not claim him as a dependent. How much of Joel's medical expenses can Mr. and Mrs. Duhon include with their deductible medical expenses?

A. $3,910

B. $1,710

C. $1,500

D. $0

Answer (B) is correct.

REQUIRED: The amount of medical expenses deductible for an individual whose income exceeds the dependent threshold amount.

DISCUSSION: An individual is entitled to an itemized deduction for expenses paid during the tax year for the medical care of the individual, the individual's spouse, or a dependent to the extent that such expenses exceed 7.5% of adjusted gross income. For purposes of this deduction, "dependent" is defined in Publication 502. The household help does not qualify as a medical expense. Therefore, $1,710 qualifies as deductible medical expenses. Even though Joel is not a dependent, the parents may claim the amount of qualified medical expenses.

Answer (A) is incorrect. The household help recommended by a doctor is not a deductible medical expense. Answer (C) is incorrect. The contact lenses are also deductible. Answer (D) is incorrect. Joel is not a dependent, but only due to his gross income; therefore, the qualified medical expenses may be deducted by the parents.

4. Mr. Green must use a wheelchair. Upon advice from his doctor, in 2012, he installed an elevator and widened the front entrance of his house, incurring $10,000 and $3,000 in respective costs. Mr. Green had purchased his house for $146,000. An appraisal showed the fair market value of Mr. Green's house immediately after these modifications at $154,000. Also in 2012, Mr. Green decided to join a health club primarily to improve business contacts and for recreational purposes. He paid a $1,250 annual membership fee to make use of this facility.

Compute Mr. Green's currently deductible medical expenses.

A. $14,250

B. $5,000

C. $13,000

D. $6,250

Answer (B) is correct.

REQUIRED: The amounts paid for qualified medical expenses that may be deducted.

DISCUSSION: Expenditures for new building construction or for permanent improvements to existing structures primarily for medical care may be deductible in part as a medical expense. The excess of the cost of a permanent improvement over the increase in value of the property is a deductible medical expense (Publication 502). Mr. Green incurred $13,000 in costs to make improvements to his house. The increase in value of his home was $8,000 ($154,000 – $146,000). Thus, Mr. Green may deduct $5,000 ($13,000 – $8,000).

Answer (A) is incorrect. Mr. Green must reduce the amount of the expenditures by the increase in value of the home. Also, Mr. Green cannot deduct the cost of the health club because it is a personal expense, not a medical expense. Answer (C) is incorrect. Mr. Green must reduce the amount of the expenditures by the the increase in value of the home. Answer (D) is incorrect. Mr. Green cannot deduct the cost of the health club because it is a personal expense, not a medical expense.

5. Josef had to have the following improvements made to his home because he was handicapped:

Cost of ramps 1/2/12	$ 300
Increase in value of home due to ramps	0
Cost of decorative lattice work over ramp area 1/2/12	100
Increase in value of home due to lattice work	50
Cost of chair lift on stairs 1/2/12	2,500
Increase in value of home due to chair lift	1,500
Cost of repairing ramps 12/1/12	50
Cost of repairing chair lift 12/1/12	200

None of the expenses were covered by insurance. How much would qualify as a deductible medical expense in 2012 (before any limitations)?

A. $1,430

B. $1,550

C. $2,800

D. $3,050

Answer (B) is correct.

REQUIRED: The amount of deductible medical expenses before any limitation.

DISCUSSION: Home-related capital expenditures incurred by a physically handicapped individual are deductible. An example of such an expenditure is an elevator needed for someone with a heart condition. However, the amount of any increase in value of the existing property cannot be deducted. Once a capital expense qualifies as a medical expense, amounts paid for the operation and upkeep also qualify as medical expenses. This is true even if the original capital expenditure was not entirely deductible (because it may have increased the fair market value of the residence). Therefore, the cost of the ramps ($300), the cost of the chair lift not attributed to an increase in the value of the property ($2,500 – $1,500 = $1,000), the cost of repairing the ramps ($50), and the cost of repairing the chair lift ($200) are deductible. These expenses total $1,550. The cost of the decorative work is not deductible (Publication 502).

Answer (A) is incorrect. The costs of expenditures not attributed to an increase in value and repairs are deductible. Answer (C) is incorrect. The costs of expenditures not attributed to an increase in value and repairs are deductible. Answer (D) is incorrect. The cost of the chair lift must be reduced by the increase in value of the home.

6. John has a heart ailment. On his doctor's advice, he installed an elevator in his home so that he would not have to climb stairs. The cost of the elevator was $7,000. An appraisal shows that the elevator increased the value of his home by $5,000. John can claim a medical deduction of

A. $2,000

B. $5,000

C. $7,000

D. None of the answers are correct.

Answer (A) is correct.

REQUIRED: The medical deduction a physically handicapped taxpayer may claim when the expense increases the value of the taxpayer's home.

DISCUSSION: Home-related capital expenditures incurred by a physically handicapped individual are deductible. An example of such an expenditure is an elevator needed for someone with a heart condition. However, the amount of any increase in value of the existing property cannot be deducted. Once a capital expense qualifies as a medical expense, amounts paid for the operation and upkeep also qualify as medical expenses. This is true even if the original capital expenditure was not entirely deductible (because it may have increased the fair market value of the residence). Therefore, $2,000 of the cost of the elevator is deductible as a medical expense ($7,000 cost – $5,000 increase in value of home). The maintenance and repair expense of the elevator is deductible, even though a portion of the cost of the elevator was not (Publication 502).

Answer (B) is incorrect. The amount by which the home increased in value is not deductible. Answer (C) is incorrect. The entire cost of the elevator is not deductible. Answer (D) is incorrect. John does qualify for a medical deduction.

7. Chris flew to Chicago for surgery. He incurred the following costs in connection with the trip:

Round-trip airfare	$ 350
Lodging ($100/night × 2 nights)	200
Restaurant meals	80
Hospital and surgeon	5,000

What is Chris's medical expense?

A. $5,490

B. $5,630

C. $5,000

D. $5,450

Answer (D) is correct.

REQUIRED: The medical expense deduction.

DISCUSSION: Medical expenses include amounts paid for the diagnosis, cure, mitigation, treatment, or prevention of disease or for the purpose of affecting any structure or function of the body; transportation cost of a trip primarily for and essential to medical care; qualified long-term care service; and medical insurance. A medical expense deduction is allowed for lodging, but not meals, while away from home on a trip primarily for and essential to medical care. This lodging deduction is limited to amounts that are not lavish or extravagant and cannot exceed $50 per night for each individual. The deduction may also be claimed for a person who must accompany the individual seeking medical care (Publication 17).

Answer (A) is incorrect. The round-trip airfare and lodging, but not meals, may be claimed as medical expenses. Answer (B) is incorrect. A limited amount of lodging, but none of the meals, may be claimed as a medical expense. Answer (C) is incorrect. The round-trip airfare and lodging may be claimed as medical expenses, but not meals.

8. Which of the following is deductible as medical insurance?

A. Medical portion of auto insurance policy that provides coverage for all persons injured in or by the taxpayer's car.

B. Insurance policy that pays you $50 a day if you are unable to work due to illness or injury.

C. Medicare Part B.

D. None of the answers are correct.

Answer (C) is correct.

REQUIRED: The item deductible as medical insurance.

DISCUSSION: To qualify for a deduction, a medical expense must be paid during the taxable year for the taxpayer, the taxpayer's spouse, or a dependent and must not be compensated for by insurance or otherwise during the taxable year. The basic cost of Medicare insurance (Medicare Part A) is not deductible unless voluntarily paid by the taxpayer for coverage. However, the extra cost of Medicare (Medicare Part B) is deductible (Publication 17).

Answer (A) is incorrect. If an insurance contract covers both medical care and nonmedical care, none of the insurance premium is deductible unless the amount of the premium allocable to medical care insurance is separately stated. Answer (B) is incorrect. Premiums paid on a policy that merely pays the insured a specified amount per day are not deductible. Answer (D) is incorrect. Medicare Part B is deductible as medical insurance.

5.2 Taxes

9. Taxes deductible as an itemized deduction include all of the following except

A. Real estate taxes based on the assessed value of the property and charged uniformly against all property.

B. State and local income taxes.

C. Taxes that the taxpayer paid on property owned by his/her parents or children.

D. Personal property taxes based on the value of the personal property.

Answer (C) is correct.

REQUIRED: The tax that is not deductible as an itemized deduction.

DISCUSSION: Publication 17 lists the taxes that are deductible from adjusted gross income; state and local income taxes withheld, real estate taxes paid, and personal property taxes are deductible as itemized deductions. However, taxes paid on another person's property are not deductible because the tax liability is the liability of the other person.

Answer (A) is incorrect. Under Sec. 164(a), real estate taxes based on the assessed value of the property and charged uniformly against all property is a tax that is deductible as an itemized deduction. Answer (B) is incorrect. Under Sec. 164(a), state and local income taxes are taxes that are deductible as an itemized deduction. Answer (D) is incorrect. Under Sec. 164(a), personal property tax based on the value of the personal property is a tax that is deductible as an itemized deduction.

10. Lonnie and Judy Landers bought a home July 1, 2012. Real estate taxes are assessed in their state on April 1, 2012, for property owned in 2011. The 2011 tax is due October 1, 2012. When the Landers bought the house they agreed to pay all taxes due after the date of purchase. Taxes of $1,200 for 2011 were due October 1, 2012, and the Landers paid this amount on October 1, 2012. In 2013, the Landers received a property tax bill for $1,500 for 2012. Payment is due October 1, 2013. What amount can the Landers deduct on their 2012 return as real property tax?

A. $1,200

B. $600

C. $750

D. $0

Answer (D) is correct.

REQUIRED: The amount deductible as real property tax.

DISCUSSION:. Real property taxes are generally deductible only by the person against whom the tax is imposed in the year in which they were paid or accrued. Since no tax paid in 2012 was imposed on the Landers ($1,200 imposed on the sellers for 2011), the Landers have a $0 deduction on their 2012 return. Sec. 164(d) requires real estate taxes to be apportioned between the buyer and the seller based on the number of days in the real property tax year that the property was held by each (Publication 17). Since the Landers paid $1,200 for 2011 taxes, they are capitalized as an additional cost of the property. For 2012 taxes, the total tax of $1,500 is apportioned based on the amount of time each party held the property for the year. Thus, the Landers are deemed to own the property for 50% of the year (183 days ÷ 365 days) and are permitted to deduct $750 ($1,500 × 50%) in 2013.

Answer (A) is incorrect. The $1,200 of taxes for 2011 is capitalized and added to the cost of the property. Answer (B) is incorrect. This amount is half of the 2011 taxes. Answer (C) is incorrect. This amount is the deduction for 2013.

11. In the current year, Maria paid the following taxes:

Special assessment to provide local benefits	$2,500
Real estate taxes paid on her vacation home	1,250
Sales taxes paid when she purchased a new auto	900
Personal property taxes paid to her local government	350

What amount is allowable as an itemized deduction for the current year?

A. $1,250

B. $2,500

C. $3,750

D. $5,000

Answer (B) is correct.

REQUIRED: The amount of taxes allowable as an itemized deduction.

DISCUSSION: Publication 17 and Sec. 164(a) list the taxes that are deductible from adjusted gross income. The state and local general sales tax (in lieu of state and local income taxes), the real estate taxes paid on her vacation home, and the personal property taxes are deductible as itemized deductions.

Answer (A) is incorrect. The real estate taxes paid on the vacation home are also deductible. Answer (C) is incorrect. The special assessment is not deductible, but the real estate taxes paid on the vacation home are deductible. Answer (D) is incorrect. The special assessment to provide local benefits is not deductible.

12. During the current year, Ms. Gonzales paid $2,000 for real estate taxes on property she rents to others and $3,425 real estate taxes on her residence. In addition, she paid gift taxes of $650 and $1,250 for state income taxes to New Jersey. What amount can Ms. Gonzales deduct as an itemized deduction on her tax return for the current year?

A. $4,675

B. $5,325

C. $6,675

D. $7,325

Answer (A) is correct.

REQUIRED: The amount that may be deducted as an itemized deduction.

DISCUSSION: Sec. 164(a) lists the taxes that are deductible from adjusted gross income. The real estate taxes on the personal residence and the state income taxes are deductible as itemized deductions. The real estate taxes on the rental property may be deductible, but not as an itemized deduction. Gift taxes are not deductible (Publication 17).

Answer (B) is incorrect. Gift taxes are not deductible. Answer (C) is incorrect. The real estate taxes on the rental property are not deductible as an itemized deduction. Answer (D) is incorrect. The real estate taxes on the rental property and the gift taxes are not deductible as itemized deductions.

5.3 Interest Expense

13. Keith and Margaret had adjusted gross income of $100,000. They had real estate taxes of $4,000, mortgage interest of $12,000, home equity loan interest of $6,000, automobile loan interest of $3,000, second home mortgage interest of $4,000, and credit card interest of $2,000. The total allowable interest deduction is

A. $31,000

B. $24,000

C. $22,000

D. $18,000

Answer (C) is correct.

REQUIRED: The total interest deduction allowed.

DISCUSSION: Qualified residence interest is interest paid or accrued during the tax year on acquisition or home equity indebtedness that is secured by a qualified residence. The general rule is that no personal interest may be deducted. Personal interest includes interest on credit card debt, revolving charge accounts, lines of credit, car loans, medical fees, and premiums. The real estate taxes are deductible but are not included in the total allowable interest deduction. (See Publication 17.)

Answer (A) is incorrect. This amount includes the car loan interest, credit card interest, and real estate taxes. Answer (B) is incorrect. This amount includes the credit card interest. Answer (D) is incorrect. This amount does not include the second home mortgage interest.

14. Which of the following would disqualify points from being fully deductible in the year paid?

A. The points were computed as a percentage of the amount of the mortgage.

B. The loan proceeds were used to purchase a second home.

C. The payment of points is common in your area.

D. The points are clearly stated on the settlement statement.

Answer (B) is correct.

REQUIRED: The situation that would disqualify points from being fully deductible in the year paid.

DISCUSSION: Points paid by the borrower with respect to a home mortgage are prepaid interest, which is typically deductible over the term of the loan. The amount paid as points for a home may only be deducted in the year paid if the points are paid on acquisition indebtedness and the home is the taxpayer's principal place of residence. (See Publication 17.)

Answer (A) is incorrect. The points were computed as a percentage of the amount of the mortgage would not disqualify points from being fully deductible in the year paid. Answer (C) is incorrect. The payment of points is common in your area would not disqualify points from being fully deductible in the year paid. Answer (D) is incorrect. The points are clearly stated on the settlement statement would not disqualify points from being fully deductible in the year paid.

15. Matt paid interest in 2012 as follows:

- $100 on his personal credit card
- $200 on funds borrowed in order to purchase $6,000 in tax-exempt securities
- $500 interest on his personal car loan since he does not use his car for business
- $10,000 on his home mortgage

What is the amount of Matt's deductible interest in 2012?

A. $17,400

B. $10,600

C. $10,000

D. $10,800

Answer (C) is correct.

REQUIRED: The amount of interest that is deductible.

DISCUSSION: The general rule is that no personal interest may be deducted. Personal interest includes interest on credit card debt, revolving charge accounts and lines of credit, car loans, medical fees, and premiums, etc. Personal interest also includes any interest on underpaid tax liabilities. Personal interest does not include interest on trade or business debt, investment interest, passive activity interest, qualified residence interest, or student loan interest. In addition, no expenses may be deducted on tax-exempt securities, including interest on a loan to purchase the securities (Publication 17). The only interest that Matt can deduct in 2012 is the $10,000 from his home mortgage.

Answer (A) is incorrect. The interest on the personal credit card, the funds to purchase securities, and the personal car loan are not deductible. In addition, the purchase price of the securities is not deductible. Answer (B) is incorrect. The interest on the personal car loan and the personal credit card are not deductible. Answer (D) is incorrect. The interest on the personal credit card, the funds to purchase securities, and the personal car loan are not deductible.

16. Johnny has been divorced for 4 years. He failed to make his alimony and support payments. The court ordered him to pay $1,500 as interest on the back alimony and support payments. He paid interest of $1,000 on a car loan, $2,500 on his outstanding credit card balance, $6,000 on a home equity loan and $10,000 on his mortgage. Other interest payments amounted to $2,500 on various appliance loan payments. How much is Johnny's deductible interest?

A. $18,500

B. $16,000

C. $23,500

D. $17,500

Answer (B) is correct.

REQUIRED: The amount of interest deductible.

DISCUSSION: Qualified residence interest is interest paid or accrued during the tax year on acquisition or home equity indebtedness that is secured by a qualified residence. The general rule is that no personal interest may be deducted. Personal interest includes interest on credit card debt, revolving charge accounts and lines of credit, car loans, medical fees, and premiums, etc. Publication 17 states, "You cannot deduct fines and penalties for violations of law, regardless of their nature."

Answer (A) is incorrect. This amount includes the $2,500 on appliance loan interest. Answer (C) is incorrect. This amount includes the car loan, credit card, and appliance loan interest, as well as court-ordered interest on back alimony and support payments. Answer (D) is incorrect. This amount includes the court-ordered interest on back alimony and support payments.

17. George had the following income and expenses:

- Interest and dividend income of $8,000
- Gross wages of $100,000
- Margin interest of $10,000
- Mortgage interest of $6,000
- Interest on a mobile home used as a second home, $3,000
- Credit card interest of $2,000

How much interest can George deduct on Schedule A?

A. $21,000

B. $18,000

C. $17,000

D. $19,000

Answer (C) is correct.

REQUIRED: The amount of interest that may be deductible on Schedule A.

DISCUSSION: A taxpayer generally can deduct interest paid or accrued during the tax year as long as the interest pertains to a debt of the taxpayer and results from a debtor-creditor relationship. [See Publication 17 and Sec.163(a).] Limitations and exclusions from interest deductions are listed below.

- Investment indebtedness interest. The deduction is limited to net investment income (margin interest). [See Sec. 163(d).]
- Life insurance. Interest on loans to pay life insurance premiums on certain contracts are not deductible.
- Personal interest. Personal interest (which includes credit card interest) is not deductible. [See Sec. 163(h).]
- Prepaid interest. Cash-basis taxpayers must generally capitalize prepaid interest and deduct it as it accrues. [See Sec. 461(g).]
- Loan to purchase and carry tax-exempt securities. Expenses (including interest) on tax-exempt securities is generally denied. [See Sec. 265(a).]
- Related taxpayers. Accrual-basis taxpayers can only deduct interest paid when interest is owed to related cash-basis taxpayers. [See Sec. 267(a).]

Thus, $8,000 of the margin interest is deductible (since it is limited to the interest and dividend income), in addition to the mortgage interest of $6,000 and the interest on the mobile home (since neither of these are excluded from deductibility).

Answer (A) is incorrect. This amount includes the $2,000 excess of margin interest over interest and dividend income and it includes the credit card interest. Credit card interest is not deductible because it is classified as personal interest.

Answer (B) is incorrect. This amount excludes the $3,000 of interest on the mobile home, but it includes the credit card interest. Credit card interest is not deductible because it is classified as personal interest. In addition, it includes the $2,000 excess of margin interest over interest and dividend income.

Answer (D) is incorrect. This amount includes the $2,000 excess of interest paid on the margin account over the interest and dividend income.

5.4 Charitable Contributions

18. The acknowledgment an individual needs from any charitable organization to claim a deduction for any cash contribution of $250 or more in a single donation must include which of the following?

A. The reason for the contribution.

B. The returned check showing the donation amount.

C. A description of past contributions and any plans for future contributions.

D. A contemporaneous written receipt.

Answer (D) is correct.

REQUIRED: The item that is required in an acknowledgment from a donee.

DISCUSSION: Generally, charitable contributions of $250 or more made on or after January 1, 1994, must be substantiated by a contemporaneous written acknowledgment from the donee organization. The acknowledgment must include the amount of cash contributed along with a description and good-faith estimate of the value of any goods or services (other than goods or services with insubstantial value) received for the contributions (Publication 17).

19. Mr. Hardwood has an adjusted gross income of $50,000. In 2012, he donated capital gain property valued at $25,000 to his church and did not choose to reduce the fair market value of the property by the amount that would have been long-term capital gain if he had sold it. His basis in the property was $20,000. In addition, he made the following contributions:

- $500 to upgrade the city public park
- $1,000 to the Hill City Chamber of Commerce
- $5,000 to a charitable organization in Germany

Compute Mr. Hardwood's deduction for charitable contributions in the current year (without regard to any carryover or carryback amounts).

A. $25,000

B. $31,500

C. $16,500

D. $15,500

Answer (D) is correct.

REQUIRED: The contributions that are deductible as a charitable contribution.

DISCUSSION: Charitable contributions are deductible only if they are made to qualified organizations. Donations can be made in the form of cash or noncash property. Qualified organizations include corporations, trusts, community chests, funds, or foundations, created or organized in the U.S. and organized and operated exclusively for religious, charitable, scientific, literary, or educational purposes or for the prevention of cruelty to children or animals. The amount that Hardwood may deduct for the capital gain property donated to the church is $15,000 ($50,000 × 30% special limitation). Hardwood also may deduct the $500 upgrade to the city public park. The donation to the charitable organization in Germany is not deductible, since donations to foreign organizations generally are not considered to be charitable contributions as defined in Sec. 170(c). The total charitable contribution deduction is equal to $15,500 ($15,000 + $500). (See Publication 17.)

Answer (A) is incorrect. The capital gain property that was donated to the church is limited to 30% of AGI. In addition, the upgrade to the park is also deductible. Answer (B) is incorrect. The capital gain property that was donated to the church is limited to 30% of AGI and the contribution to the Chamber of Commerce is not deductible. In addition, the upgrade to the park is also deductible. Answer (C) is incorrect. The contribution to the Chamber of Commerce is not deductible.

20. During the current year, John donated $100 to the United Way, $200 to Veterans of Foreign Wars, and $300 to his neighbor whose home was destroyed by a tornado. How much is John's deduction for charitable contributions?

A. $300

B. $400

C. $500

D. $600

Answer (A) is correct.

REQUIRED: The amount of the charitable contribution deduction.

DISCUSSION: Charitable contributions are deductible only if they are made to qualified organizations. Qualified organizations can be either public charities or private foundations. (Generally, a public charity is one that derives more than one-third of its support from its members and the general public.) Donations can be made in the form of cash or noncash property. However, any amounts donated to individuals are not allowed as a deduction (Publication 17).

Answer (B) is incorrect. The amount donated to his neighbor cannot be deducted since the neighbor is an individual. Answer (C) is incorrect. The $100 donated to the United Way is deductible as a donation made to a qualified organization, while his $300 donation to his neighbor is disallowed as a donation to an individual. Answer (D) is incorrect. The amount donated to his neighbor cannot be deducted since the neighbor is an individual.

21. Mr. Young's records for the year reflect the following information:

- Paid $7,500 to a church of which $4,500 was contributed to the church and $3,000 was paid to enroll his child in the school.
- Paid $100 to the local bank.
- Paid $1,000 cash to qualified public charitable organizations.
- Donated stock having a fair market value of $1,800 to a qualified charitable organization. He purchased the stock 5 months earlier for $1,000.

Mr. Young's adjusted gross income (AGI) for the year was $25,000. What is the amount of his charitable contribution deduction?

A. $6,500

B. $6,600

C. $7,500

D. $10,600

Answer (A) is correct.

REQUIRED: The amount of the charitable contribution deduction.

DISCUSSION: Taxpayers may deduct as a charitable contribution the excess of what they gave over the probable fair market value of what they received. Accordingly, Mr. Young may deduct the $4,500, out of $7,500, contributed to the church. The contribution to the bank is not deductible; the entity does not qualify as a charitable organization under Sec. 170. The cash contributions to the qualified public charitable organizations, however, are deductible in full. Since the stock was not held long term, it is considered ordinary income property. The amount of a charitable contribution of ordinary income property is the fair market value of the property reduced by the amount of gain that would not have been long-term capital gain if the property had been sold by the taxpayer at its fair market value [Sec. 170(e)(1)(4)]. Therefore, only the basis of the stock ($1,000) is considered in the charitable contribution deduction. The total amount of these deductions is $6,500, an amount below the 50%-of-AGI limit (Publication 17).

Answer (B) is incorrect. The bank contribution is not deductible. Answer (C) is incorrect. Only the basis of the stock is deductible. Answer (D) is incorrect. All of the contributions are not deductible.

22. Raul and Monika (husband and wife) are both lawyers, and they contribute money to various organizations each year. They file a joint return and their adjusted gross income for 2012 is $100,000. They contributed to the following organizations in 2012:

- $5,000 to Alta Sierra country club
- $10,000 to prevent cruelty to animals
- $2,000 to state bar association (This state bar association is not a political subdivision of the state, serves both public and private purposes, and the funds used are unrestricted and can be for private purposes.)
- $12,000 to cancer research foundation
- Donated clothing to Salvation Army (Raul purchased the items for $1,000, but the fair market value of the same items at a thrift store is equal to $50.)

How much can Raul and Monika deduct as charitable contributions for 2012?

A. $29,050
B. $25,000
C. $22,050
D. $24,000

Answer (C) is correct.

REQUIRED: The deductibility of charitable contributions.

DISCUSSION: Charitable contributions are deductible only if they are made to qualified organizations. Donations can be made in the form of cash or noncash property. The organizations may be both public and private but should be organized and operated exclusively for religious, charitable, scientific, literary, or educational purposes, or for the prevention of cruelty to children or animals. Charitable deductions also are subject to various AGI limitations (Publication 17). Raul and Monika may deduct $22,050 ($10,000 + $12,000 + $50) of their charitable contributions.

Answer (A) is incorrect. The contributions to the country club and the state bar association are not deductible. The country club and state bar association do not qualify under the criteria established for determining a charitable organization. Answer (B) is incorrect. The $2,000 contribution to the state bar is nondeductible. Also, the contribution to the Salvation Army is the FMV at the time of contribution, not the basis in the property. Answer (D) is incorrect. The state bar association contribution is nondeductible.

23. For the year, Mrs. Lynn had adjusted gross income of $30,000. During the year, she contributed $9,000 to her church, $10,000 to qualified public charities, and a painting she has owned for 8 years with a fair market value of $16,000 and a $4,000 adjusted basis to her city's library. What is the amount of Mrs. Lynn's charitable contributions deduction for the year?

A. $15,000
B. $19,000
C. $23,000
D. $35,000

Answer (A) is correct.

REQUIRED: The taxpayer's allowable charitable contribution deduction.

DISCUSSION: Mrs. Lynn's charitable deduction limitation is $15,000 (50% of her adjusted gross income). All of her contributions qualify under Sec. 170; thus, the amount of her contribution is $35,000. However, the amount of her allowable charitable contribution deduction for the year is limited to $15,000. The excess $20,000 [($16,000 – $9,000 painting 30% limitation) + $13,000 balance for 50% limit property] can be carried forward and deducted in the 5 succeeding tax years [Sec. 170(d)]. The amount of the contribution of the painting is its $16,000 FMV. The fair market value is not reduced by what would have been long-term capital gain had Mrs. Lynn sold it because it is presumed that the property is used in connection with the library's tax-exempt purpose. Even though no reduction occurs, the 30% limitation on contributions of capital gain property is applicable. (See Publication 17.)

Answer (B) is incorrect. The deduction is limited to 50% of her adjusted gross income for the cash donations and 30% of her adjusted gross income for the painting donation. Answer (C) is incorrect. The deduction is limited to 50% of her adjusted gross income for the cash donations and 30% of her adjusted gross income for the painting donation. Answer (D) is incorrect. This amount is the total contributions made during the year.

24. Brian kept the following information to be used in filing his 2012 tax return:

- Brian paid $100 to his church to go to a dinner-dance. The dinner and entertainment provided normally would have cost $50.
- Brian used his car to take a tax-exempt youth group on a caving trip. Brian was the only troop leader who attended and was in charge for the entire trip. He drove his car 500 miles and elected to use the standard rate for mileage. He also determined his time of 10 hours for the trip to be worth $10 per hour.
- Brian contributed $1,000 each to his church and the local chamber of commerce.

What is the amount that Brian can claim as a charitable contribution in 2012?

A. $1,478

B. $1,428

C. $1,220

D. $1,120

Answer (D) is correct.

REQUIRED: The amount that can be claimed as a charitable contribution.

DISCUSSION: Brian may deduct as a charitable contribution the excess of what he gave ($100) to the church over the probable fair market value ($50) of the dinner and entertainment he received. The 500 miles driven in the personal auto was directly related to the services performed for the tax-exempt youth group. Therefore, for the current tax year, the amount of that contribution will be $70 (500 miles × $.14 per mile). Brian is not able to deduct the value of his time contributed to the youth group. Finally, the contribution to the church of $1,000 is deductible, but the contribution to the chamber of commerce is not. A contribution is deductible only if made to an organization described in Sec. 170(c). Hence, the total amount that may be claimed as a charitable contribution is $1,120. (See Publication 17.)

Answer (A) is incorrect. The dinner-dance must be reduced, the mileage rate is not $.555, and the value of his services is not deductible. Answer (B) is incorrect. The mileage rate is not $.555, and the value of his services is not deductible. Answer (C) is incorrect. The value of his services is not deductible.

25. In 2012, Janice volunteered at her local art museum where she conducted art-education seminars. She was required to wear a blazer that the museum provided, but she paid the dry cleaning costs of $200 for the year. The blazer was not suitable for everyday use. Her travel to and from the museum was 1,000 miles for the year. She estimates the value of the time she contributed during the year at $2,000 ($20/hr × 100 hours). Her Schedule A deduction for charitable contributions is which of the following?

A. $2,340

B. $2,140

C. $140

D. $340

Answer (D) is correct.

REQUIRED: The amount of the charitable contribution deduction.

DISCUSSION: The tax code allows for a deduction for expenses and payments made to, or on behalf of, a charitable organization. However, the value of services rendered to an institution is not deductible as contributions. Deductions are allowed for transportation and other travel expenses incurred in the performance of services away from home on behalf of a charitable organization. Individuals who qualify for a deduction for the use of an automobile may use the statutory standard mileage rate of $.14 per mile. Also, out-of-pocket expenses are included if they involve items that can be used solely for the purpose of volunteer work (Publication 17). Therefore, Janice may deduct $340 of her expenses as a charitable contribution [($200 + (1,000 miles × $.14)].

Answer (A) is incorrect. The value of the services is not allowable as a charitable deduction. Answer (B) is incorrect. The value of the services is not allowable as a charitable deduction. However, the cleaning and purchase of clothing that can only be used for purposes of the charity can be deducted. Answer (C) is incorrect. The cleaning and purchase of clothing that can only be used for purposes of the charity can be deducted.

5.5 Casualty Losses

26. Frank and Melody's home was completely destroyed by fire. They had no insurance. On which of the following forms would they report their loss?

A. Form 4684, *Casualties and Thefts*, and Form 1040, *U.S. Individual Income Tax Return*, as an adjustment to gross income.

B. Schedule A, *Itemized Deductions*, only.

C. Form 4684, *Casualties and Thefts*, and Schedule A, *Itemized Deductions*.

D. Form 4684, *Casualties and Thefts*, only.

Answer (C) is correct.

REQUIRED: The forms on which a casualties loss is reported.

DISCUSSION: Form 4684, Section A – *Personal Use Property*, lists and calculates the amount of the loss. The amount of the loss is then added to Schedule A, *Itemized Deductions* (Publication 547).

Answer (A) is incorrect. Personal casualty losses are deductible as an itemized deduction. Answer (B) is incorrect. Schedule A is used in reporting Frank and Melody's casualty loss. Answer (D) is incorrect. Form 4684 is used in reporting Frank and Melody's casualty loss.

27. Alberta and Archie (wife and husband) had water damage in their home during 2012, which ruined the furniture in their basement. The following items were completely destroyed and not salvageable.

Damaged items	Fair market value just prior to damage	Original item cost
Antique bed frame	$5,000	$4,000
Pool table	$8,000	$10,000
Large-screen TV	$700	$2,500

Their homeowner's insurance policy had a $10,000 deductible for the personal property, which was deducted from their insurance reimbursement of $12,700. Their adjusted gross income for 2012 was $30,000. What is the amount of casualty loss that Alberta and Archie can claim on their joint return for 2012?

A. $10,600

B. $3,400

C. $6,900

D. $0

Answer (C) is correct.

REQUIRED: The amount of casualty loss that can be claimed.

DISCUSSION: The loss is the lesser of the decrease in FMV of the property due to the casualty or the property's adjusted basis. The loss is reduced by any amount recovered by insurance and a $100 floor to any nonbusiness loss. The $100 floor applies only once to a married filing joint return. The loss is also subject to a floor equal to 10% of the AGI. The casualty loss can therefore be calculated as follows: $12,700 loss – $2,700 insurance reimbursement – $100 floor – ($30,000 AGI × 10%) = $6,900. The $12,700 loss is calculated as follows: $4,000 from the antique bed frame (decrease in FMV > original cost); $8,000 from the pool table (original cost > decrease in FMV); $700 from the large-screen TV (original cost > decrease in FMV).

Answer (A) is incorrect. It uses the FMV just prior to damage as the basis and fails to reduce the loss by the amount recovered by insurance. Answer (B) is incorrect. It uses the FMV just prior to damage as the basis and reduces the loss by the $10,000 deductible and only 1% of the AGI, ignoring the floor. Answer (D) is incorrect. It fails to account for the deductible.

28. On March 28, 2013, Rita sustained a loss to her personal property due to an earthquake. The property was in an area declared by the President of the United States to be eligible for federal disaster assistance. Based on the following facts, what is the maximum amount of Rita's casualty loss that can be deducted on her 2012 tax return, due April 15, 2013?

Fair market value before the earthquake	$23,000
Fair market value after the earthquake	6,300
Cost basis	30,000
Disaster relief funds received to replace lost property	2,300
Adjusted gross income for 2012	27,000

A. $30,000

B. $16,700

C. $14,400

D. $11,600

Answer (D) is correct.

REQUIRED: The total casualty loss deduction for the year.

DISCUSSION: A federally declared disaster area loss is computed the same way as a casualty loss. Sec. 165(i) provides that a taxpayer who has suffered a disaster loss that is allowable as a deduction under Sec. 165(a) may, if the disaster is in an area that warrants assistance from the federal government under the Disaster Relief and Emergency Assistance Act, elect to deduct such loss for the taxable year immediately preceding the taxable year in which the disaster occurred. Sec. 165(h) allows a casualty deduction for nonbusiness casualty losses to the extent that each uninsured loss exceeds $100 and the aggregate of all such losses during the year exceeds 10% of AGI. The amount of a loss is the lesser of the decrease in the fair market value of the property resulting from the casualty or the property's adjusted basis. If any reimbursements result in casualty gains, the gains are netted against casualty losses before computing the casualty loss deduction (Publication 547).

Lesser of adjusted basis [$30,000 or decrease in FMV ($16,700)]	$16,700
Less: Disaster relief funds	(2,300)
$100 per occurrence	(100)
10% of AGI	(2,700)
Deductible casualty loss	$11,600

Answer (A) is incorrect. This amount is the cost basis of the property. Answer (B) is incorrect. This amount is the decrease in FMV (i.e., initial loss before adjustment for relief funds and floor amount). Answer (C) is incorrect. This amount does not include the limitations of $100 per occurrence and 10% of AGI floor.

29. In 2012, the U.S. President declared a federal disaster due to flooding in Minnesota. Lisa lives in that area and lost her home in the flood. What choice does she have regarding when she can claim the loss on her tax return?

A. It must be claimed in 2011 if the return has not been filed by the date of the loss.

B. It must be claimed in 2012 if the loss is greater than the modified adjusted gross income.

C. It may be claimed in 2013 if an election is filed with the 2012 return.

D. It may be claimed in 2011 or 2012.

Answer (D) is correct.

REQUIRED: The correct tax return to claim a loss from a federal disaster.

DISCUSSION: If a taxpayer has a casualty loss from a disaster that occurred in a federally declared disaster area, (s)he can choose to deduct that loss on the current year's tax return or (s)he may amend the return for the tax year immediately preceding the tax year in which the disaster occurred (Publication 547).

5.6 Itemized Deductions Subject to the 2% AGI Limitation

30. Karen is an accountant for XYZ Company. She had met the minimum educational requirements of her employer. However, XYZ changed the minimum requirements, and Karen was required to take a computer course to keep her job. The course cost $1,000, and XYZ reimbursed Karen $600 toward the cost of the course under an accountable plan. How much education expense can Karen deduct in 2012?

A. $0

B. $400

C. $600

D. $1,000

Answer (B) is correct.

REQUIRED: The deductibility of education expenses required to retain a job.

DISCUSSION: In general, expenditures made by an individual for education are deductible as ordinary and necessary business expenses so long as the minimum educational requirements have been met, the education is not for the purpose of qualifying for a new trade or business, and the education is necessary to maintain or improve skills in the established trade or business. The amount that is deductible, however, is reduced by any proceeds reimbursed by an employer (Publication 17). Thus, Karen may deduct $400 ($1,000 – $600). Education expenses required to retain a job or salary are deductible.

Answer (A) is incorrect. Karen qualifies for a deduction. Answer (C) is incorrect. The amount reimbursed by Karen's employer is not deductible. Answer (D) is incorrect. The deduction is reduced by the amount reimbursed by Karen's employer.

31. During the year, Ron paid $85 to have his tax return prepared. He also paid a lawyer $215 to prepare his will. At work, he paid union dues of $650, bought safety boots for $200, and contributed $75 to collections for sick coworkers. What is Ron's deduction on his Schedule A before the 2% limitation?

A. $935

B. $1,010

C. $1,150

D. $1,225

Answer (A) is correct.

REQUIRED: The itemized deduction on Schedule A, before the 2% limitation.

DISCUSSION: Itemized expenses on Schedule A include unreimbursed employee expenses, tax preparation fees, and other expenses. Some examples of employee expenses are uniforms, protective clothing, physical examinations, dues to professional organizations, and subscriptions to professional journals. Other expenses include certain legal and accounting fees, clerical help and office rent, and custodial fees (Publication 17). The deductions included are

Preparation of tax return	$ 85
Union dues	650
Safety boots	200
Total deduction before 2%-of-AGI floor	$935

Answer (B) is incorrect. This amount includes $75 for collections for sick coworkers, which is not a qualified organization. This does not qualify for a deduction. Answer (C) is incorrect. This amount includes the legal fees for the preparation of the will. Legal fees incurred in defending or perfecting title to property, in the acquisition or disposition of property, or in developing or improving property are not deductible. Answer (D) is incorrect. This amount includes both the collection for sick coworkers and the legal fees for the preparation of a will. The $75 is not deductible because it was not made to a qualified organization. Legal fees incurred in defending or perfecting title to property, in the acquisition or disposition of property, or in developing or improving property are not deductible.

32. Mr. and Mrs. Thurman's adjusted gross income for the current year was $60,000. During the current year, they incurred and paid the following expenses:

Subscriptions to investment journals	$ 300
Tax return preparation fee	100
Safe-deposit box rental fees	1,500
Voluntary unemployment benefit fund contribution	3,000
Fees and licenses on their personal cars	800
Dividend reinvestment plan service charge	300

Assuming they itemize, how much can Mr. and Mrs. Thurman claim as miscellaneous deductible expenses?

A. $1,000

B. $2,200

C. $4,000

D. $5,200

Answer (A) is correct.

REQUIRED: The deductible amount of various expenses.

DISCUSSION: Dividend reinvestment plan charges, tax preparation fees, subscriptions to investment journals, and safe-deposit box rental fees are second-tier itemized deductions. However, they are deductible only to the extent that they exceed 2% of AGI (Publication 17).

First-tier deductions		$ 0
Second-tier deductions		
Subscriptions to investment journals	$ 300	
Tax return preparation fee	100	
Safe-deposit box rental fees	1,500	
Dividend reinvestment plan service charge	300	
	$2,200	
Less 2% of AGI	(1,200)	1,000
Total deductible expenses		$1,000

Answer (B) is incorrect. The expenses are deductible only to the extent they exceed 2% of AGI. Answer (C) is incorrect. Voluntary unemployment benefit fund contributions are not second-tier itemized deductions. Answer (D) is incorrect. Voluntary unemployment benefit fund contributions are not second-tier itemized deductions.

33. Which of the following is not deductible as an educational expense?

A. Mr. Bard was employed as a patent chemist on the condition that he get a law degree at his own expense. He enrolled in evening law school. When he graduated from law school, he was promoted to patent attorney with a substantial increase in salary.

B. Ms. Roland owns an accounting practice and took several courses in taxation and accounting.

C. Mrs. Paine, a salesperson, was required by her employer to take a public speaking course at her own expense as a condition to retain her position.

D. Ms. Lane, an elementary school teacher, took additional courses to qualify her to teach mathematics in high school.

Answer (A) is correct.

REQUIRED: The expense that is not a deductible educational expense.

DISCUSSION: Expenditures made by an individual for education include amounts spent on correspondence courses, travel and transportation costs, supplies and books, and tuition. They are deductible as second-tier itemized deductions if the education maintains or improves skills required of the individual in his/her employment or other trade or business, or if it meets the express requirements of the individual's employer or the requirements of applicable law or regulations imposed as a condition to the retention by the individual of an established employment relationship, status, or rate of compensation. Personal education expenses are not deductible if they qualify the taxpayer for a new trade or business (Publication 17).

Answer (B) is incorrect. The expenses are used to maintain or improve Ms. Roland's accounting skills. Answer (C) is incorrect. The expenses meet the express requirements of the employer. Answer (D) is incorrect. The courses improve the skills of the school teacher.

34. Each month, Betsy's employer gives her $600 for her business expenses. Sometimes Betsy spends more than the $600. Once a year, she negotiates the amount of expense money with her employer, but she is not required to submit any proof of how she spends the $600 per month. How should Betsy report her expenses on her return?

A. No reporting required.

B. Deduct all of her expenses on Schedule C, *Profit or Loss From Business.*

C. Deduct all of her expenses on Form 2106, *Employee Business Expenses.*

D. Deduct her expenses in excess of $600 per month on Form 2106.

Answer (C) is correct.

REQUIRED: The reporting of business expenses under a nonaccountable plan.

DISCUSSION: For a nonaccountable plan, the employer includes the reimbursements in taxable wages and the employee may claim any business expenses substantiated as miscellaneous itemized deductions. (See Publication 463.)

Answer (A) is incorrect. Business expenses are reported on Form 2106. Answer (B) is incorrect. Business expenses are reported on Form 2106. Answer (D) is incorrect. All business expenses that are substantiated may be deducted for a nonaccountable plan.

35. To meet your employer's reimbursement or allowance arrangement accountable plan, which of the following are the requirements of his accountable plan?

A. Your expenses must have a business connection.

B. You must adequately account to your employer for these expenses within a reasonable period of time.

C. You must return any excess reimbursement or allowance within a reasonable period of time.

D. All of the answers are correct.

Answer (D) is correct.

REQUIRED: The requirements to meet an employer's reimbursement or allowance arrangement accountable plan.

DISCUSSION: Publication 535 states, "To be an accountable plan, your reimbursement or allowance arrangement must require your employees to meet all the following rules.

1. They must have paid or incurred deductible expenses while performing services as your employees.
2. They must adequately account to you for these expenses within a reasonable period of time.
3. They must return any excess reimbursement or allowance within a reasonable period of time."

36. Robin, an employee, had the following unreimbursed employee expenses during the current year:

- $100 professional license renewal
- $75 subscription to professional journal
- $500 business liability insurance

Her adjusted gross income was $40,000. What net amount can Robin deduct?

A. $675

B. $0

C. $575

D. $175

Answer (B) is correct.

REQUIRED: The amount to be deducted for unreimbursed employee expenses.

DISCUSSION: Licenses and regulatory fees, subscriptions to professional journals and trade magazines, and malpractice (liability) insurance premiums all qualify as unreimbursed employee expenses. Unreimbursed employee expenses are reported as miscellaneous itemized deductions on Schedule A (Form 1040). Miscellaneous itemized deductions are limited to include only the amount exceeding 2% of adjusted gross income. Thus, Robin is able to deduct any amount over $800 ($40,000 × 2%). However, her itemized deductions total $675, so none can be deducted. (See Publication 17.)

Answer (A) is incorrect. Qualifying unreimbursed employee expenses are reported as miscellaneous itemized deductions on Schedule A (Form 1040). Miscellaneous itemized deductions are limited to include only the amount exceeding 2% of adjusted gross income. For Robin, this amount is $800. Answer (C) is incorrect. All expenses are qualified unreimbursed employee expenses but fall below the 2%-of-AGI exclusion. Answer (D) is incorrect. All expenses are qualified unreimbursed employee expenses but fall below the 2%-of-AGI exclusion.

37. Which of the following items is not tax deductible as an education-related expense?

A. Certain transportation and travel costs.

B. The dollar value of vacation time or annual leave you take to attend a class.

C. Tuition, books, supplies, lab fees, and similar items.

D. Costs of research and typing when writing a paper as part of an educational program.

Answer (B) is correct.

REQUIRED: The item not tax deductible as an education-related expense.

DISCUSSION: Education expenses may be deductible only if incurred to maintain or improve skills that are required in the taxpayer's current employment context, or if incurred to meet legal requirements or employer requirements. Examples include correspondence courses, travel, supplies, books, research and typing expenses, and tuition. Not included is the dollar value of vacation time or annual leave you take to attend class (Publication 17).

Answer (A) is incorrect. Certain transportation and travel costs are deductible. Answer (C) is incorrect. Tuition, books, supplies, lab fees, and similar items are tax deductible. Answer (D) is incorrect. The cost of research and typing when writing a paper as part of an educational program is deductible.

5.7 Miscellaneous Itemized Deductions Not Subject to the 2% AGI Limitation and Overall Limitation

38. Paula won $5,000 in the lottery in 2012. She also won $200 playing bingo at her lodge hall. She is not a professional gambler. She kept meticulous records of the $6,550 she spent on gambling expenses. How much may she deduct on her Schedule A as a miscellaneous deduction not subject to the 2% limitation?

A. $0

B. $200

C. $5,200

D. $6,550

Answer (C) is correct.

REQUIRED: The amount of gambling expenses that may be deducted by a nonprofessional gambler on Schedule A as a miscellaneous deduction before the 2%-of-AGI limitation.

DISCUSSION: Gambling losses may be deducted, but only to the extent of gambling winnings. In order to deduct these expenses, they must be listed next to line 28 on Schedule A (Publication 17). The type and amount of each expense must be listed (a statement showing these expenses may be attached if there is not enough room). Paula had $5,200 in winnings ($5,000 + $200), thus $5,200 of the $6,550 of meticulously kept expenses may be deducted.

Answer (A) is incorrect. Gambling losses may be deducted to the extent of gambling income if good records of the expenses are kept. Answer (B) is incorrect. Gambling losses may be deducted to the extent of gambling income. Paula's total gambling income is $5,200 ($5,000 in lottery winnings plus $200 in bingo winnings). Answer (D) is incorrect. Gambling losses are only deductible to the extent of gambling income.

39. Which of the following are miscellaneous itemized deductions subject to the 2% adjusted gross income limitation?

A. Federal estate tax on income in respect of a decedent.

B. Gambling losses up to the amount of gambling winnings.

C. Casualty and theft losses from income-producing property.

D. Safety deposit box expenses.

Answer (D) is correct.

REQUIRED: The expenses that are miscellaneous itemized deductions that are not subject to the 2%-of-AGI limitation.

DISCUSSION: According to Publication 17, the following expenses are deductible as miscellaneous itemized deductions (not subject to the 2% limit) and are reported on line 28, Schedule A (Form 1040):

1) Amortizable premium on taxable bonds
2) Casualty and theft losses from income-producing property
3) Federal estate tax on income in respect of a decedent
4) Gambling losses up to the amount of gambling winnings
5) Impairment-related work expenses of persons with disabilities
6) Repayment of more than $3,000 under a claim of right
7) Unrecovered investment in a pension

Safety deposit box expenses are second-tier miscellaneous itemized deductions and are subject to the 2% adjusted gross income limitation.

Answer (A) is incorrect. Federal estate tax on income in respect of a decedent is a miscellaneous itemized deduction not subject to the 2%-of-AGI limit. Answer (B) is incorrect. Gambling losses up to the amount of gambling winnings are a miscellaneous itemized deduction not subject to the 2%-of-AGI limit. Answer (C) is incorrect. Casualty and theft losses from income-producing property are a miscellaneous itemized deduction not subject to the 2%-of-AGI limit.

40. Which of the following is not subject to the 2% adjusted gross income limitation on miscellaneous deductions on Schedule A?

A. Home office expense.

B. Federal estate taxes on income in respect of a decedent.

C. Trade association dues.

D. Job hunting expenses.

Answer (B) is correct.

REQUIRED: The item not subject to the 2% AGI limitation on miscellaneous deductions on Schedule A.

DISCUSSION: The three fundamental categories of miscellaneous itemized deductions are investment expenses, tax determination expenses, and employee expenses. The following are examples of deductible employee expenditures:

1) Employee travel away from home (including meals and lodging)
2) Employee transportation expenses
3) Outside salesperson expenses
4) Employee entertainment expenses
5) Employee home office expenses
6) Employee uniforms (provided they are not usable away from work)
7) Union dues
8) Professional dues and memberships
9) Subscriptions to business journals
10) Job-seeking expenses (in the same business)
11) Education expenses

Publication 17 specifically lists federal estate tax on income in respect of a decedent as an expense not subject to the 2% limit.

41. All of the following miscellaneous expenses are subject to the 2%-of-adjusted-gross-income limitation except

A. Gambling losses up to the amount of gambling winnings.

B. Fees paid to a broker to collect taxable bond interest or dividends on shares of stock.

C. Repayment of $3,000 of ordinary income that had been included in taxable income in an earlier year.

D. Damages paid to a former employer for breach of employment contract, when the damages are attributable to pay received from that employer.

Answer (A) is correct.

REQUIRED: The miscellaneous deduction not subject to the 2%-of-AGI floor.

DISCUSSION: Gambling losses are deductible to the extent of gambling winnings (Reg. 1.165-10). They are a loss deduction for adjusted gross income if gambling is a trade or business, but in most cases they are a first-tier itemized deduction (not subject to the 2%-of-AGI floor). [See Publication 17 and Sec. 67(b)(3).]

Answer (B) is incorrect. Fees paid to a broker to collect taxable bond interest or dividends on shares of stock are second-tier deductions subject to the 2% limitation. Answer (C) is incorrect. Repayment of $3,000 of ordinary income that had been included in taxable income in an earlier year is a second-tier deduction subject to the 2% limitation. Answer (D) is incorrect. Damages paid to a former employer for breach of employment contract, when the damages are attributable to pay received from that employer, is a second-tier deduction subject to the 2% limitation.

STUDY UNIT SIX
TAX CREDITS, OTHER TAXES, AND PAYMENTS

(16 pages of outline)

Tax credits are used to achieve policy objectives, such as encouraging energy conservation or providing tax relief to low-income taxpayers. A $1 credit reduces gross tax liability by $1. The first subunit discusses the various nonrefundable and refundable tax credits available. Most credits are nonrefundable, meaning that once the tax liability reaches zero, no more credits can be taken to produce refunds. Nonrefundable personal credits include

- Foreign Tax Credit
- Child and Dependent Care Credit
- Lifetime Learning Credit
- Retirement Savings Contribution Credit
- Child Tax Credit
- Nonbusiness Energy Property Credit
- Credit for the Elderly or Disabled
- Adoption Credit
- Residential Mortgage Interest Credit

Refundable credits are treated as payments and can result in refunds for the taxpayer. Refundable credits include

- American Opportunity Credit
- Additional Child Tax Credit
- Minimum Tax Credit
- Earned Income Credit

The next subunit discusses the other taxes a taxpayer may be subject to. These taxes include the alternative minimum tax and self-employment taxes. In the last subunit, we discuss payment requirements, claims for refunds, and the statute of limitations.

6.1 TAX CREDITS

Foreign Tax Credit (FTC)

1. A taxpayer may elect either a credit or a deduction for taxes paid to other countries or U.S. possessions.
   a. Generally, the FTC is applied against gross tax liability after nonrefundable personal credits and before all other credits.
   b. The FTC, as modified, may offset AMT liability.
      1) The FTC is not creditable against the accumulated earnings tax (AET) or the personal holding company (PHC) tax.
   c. **Pass-through entities** apportion the foreign taxes among the partners, shareholders (of an S corporation), or beneficiaries (of an estate).
      1) The taxpayers then elect and compute a credit or deduction on their personal returns.

d. For a **non-U.S. person**, the FTC is allowed only for foreign taxes paid on income effectively connected with conduct of a trade or business in the U.S. and against U.S. tax on the effectively connected income.

   1) Nonresident aliens and foreign corporations are included under this provision.

e. **Qualified foreign taxes (QFTs)** include foreign taxes on income, war profits, and excess profits.

   1) QFTs must be analogous to the U.S. income tax.

      a) They must be based on a form of net annual income, including gains.
      b) Concepts such as realization should be incorporated into the tax structure.

   2) Foreign taxes paid on foreign earned income or housing costs excluded as excessive may neither be credited nor deducted.

   3) Deemed QFT. A domestic corporation that owns at least 10% (voting) of a foreign corporation is deemed to have paid the foreign taxes paid by the foreign corporation on income that it distributed to the domestic corporation as a dividend.

f. **FTC limit.** The maximum amount of tax that may be credited is computed using the following formula:

$$FTC = U.S.\ income\ tax^{1} \times \frac{Foreign\ source\ taxable\ income^{2}}{Worldwide\ taxable\ income}$$

[1] Before the FTC
[2] Not more than worldwide TI

   1) The limit must be applied separately to nonbusiness interest income and all other income.

   2) The amount used for TI in the numerator and denominator is regular TI with adjustments. For example, an individual must add back personal exemptions.

g. The FTC is claimed on Form 1116, *Foreign Tax Credit*, unless the taxpayer meets all of the following conditions and elects to claim the credit on Form 1040, line 47:

   1) The taxpayer is an individual,
   2) The only foreign source income for the year is passive income that is reported on a payee statement, and
   3) The QFTs for the year do not exceed $300 ($600 for a joint return).

h. **Carryover.** Foreign tax paid in excess of the FTC limit may be carried back 1 year and forward 10, in chronological order. The carryover is treated as foreign tax paid subject to the FTC limit.

   1) The carryover may not be applied in any year when a deduction for foreign taxes is taken (in lieu of the FTC).

i. A credit (or deduction) cannot be taken for foreign income taxes paid on income that is excluded from U.S. tax under the foreign earned income exclusion.

j. A choice must be made to take either a credit or a deduction for all qualified foreign taxes.

Child and Dependent Care Credit

2. The Child and Dependent Care Credit is nonrefundable.

   a. A taxpayer is eligible for this credit only if b. and c. below and on the next page are satisfied.

   b. **Employment.** Child and dependent care expenses are incurred to enable the taxpayer to be gainfully employed.

      1) The expenses may be incurred when the claimant is employed or actively seeking employment.

c. **Household cost.** The taxpayer provides more than half the cost of maintaining a household for a dependent under age 13 or a physically or mentally incapacitated spouse or dependent.

1) Qualifying Expenses

a) Household services, such as baby-sitting, housekeeping, and nursery.

b) Outside services, such as day care. The outside expenses apply only if the qualified individual spends more than 8 hours a day in the taxpayer's home.

c) The cost of sending a child to school if the child is in a grade below kindergarten.

d) Payments to a relative for the care of a qualifying individual.

i) These payments do not qualify for the credit if the taxpayer claims a dependent exemption for the relative or if the relative is the taxpayer's child and is under age 19.

2) The cost of transporting a qualifying person from the home to the care location and back is a nonqualified expense.

3) Total child and dependent care expenses cannot exceed the taxpayer's earned income. For married taxpayers, the income for this limitation is the smaller income of the two.

a) If one of the spouses is a full-time student at an educational institution or is unable to care for himself/herself, (s)he is considered to have earned $250 per month if there is one qualifying individual and $500 per month if there are two or more qualifying individuals.

4) Child and dependent care expenses are limited to $3,000 for one qualifying individual and $6,000 for two or more individuals, less excludable employer dependent-care assistance program payments.

5) The credit is equal to 35% of the child and dependent care expenses.

a) This rate is reduced by 1% (but not below 20%) for each $2,000 (or part thereof) by which AGI exceeds $15,000.

b) Taxpayers with AGI over $43,000 will have a credit of 20% (Form 2441).

d. Taxpayers must provide each dependent's **taxpayer identification number** in order to claim the credit, as well as the identifying number of the service provider.

Education Credits

3. Two tax credits may be elected by low- and middle-income individuals for education expenses incurred by students pursuing college or graduate degrees or vocational training.

a. The American Opportunity Credit is partially refundable, and the Lifetime Learning Credit is nonrefundable.

b. **American Opportunity Credit (AOC).** The AOC provides a maximum nonrefundable tax credit of $2,500 per student for each of the first 4 years of post-secondary education.

1) The $2,500 per year is the sum of 100% of the first $2,000 of qualified expenses and 25% of the next $2,000 of qualified expenses.

2) The credit applies to the first 4 years of higher education received by the taxpayer, the taxpayer's spouse, and/or the taxpayer's dependents.

3) The credit applies to tuition and tuition-related fees, books, and other required course materials.

4) The credit cannot be claimed if
   a) An exclusion for an education IRA or a state tuition program is claimed for the same expenses.
   b) The student has been convicted of a federal or state felony offense consisting of the possession or distribution of a controlled substance.
   c) The student is not taking at least one-half of the normal full-time workload for at least one academic period that begins during the calendar year in which the credit is claimed.
5) The credit phases out for AGI between $80,000 and $90,000 for singles and between $160,000 and $180,000 on a joint return. Married taxpayers must file a joint return.
6) Up to 40% of the credit is refundable during 2012.

c. **Lifetime Learning.** The Lifetime Learning Credit provides a credit of 20% of qualified tuition expenses paid by the taxpayer for any year the AOC is not claimed.
   1) The maximum credit allowed per year is $2,000.
   2) This is based on 20% of up to $10,000 of qualified tuition and fees paid for the taxpayer, the taxpayer's spouse, and/or the taxpayer's dependents.
   3) The credit is figured on a per-taxpayer basis.
   4) It applies to any number of years of higher education.
   5) Eligible expenses for this credit include tuition and fees required for enrollment.
   6) The Lifetime Learning Credit phases out for AGI between $52,000 and $62,000 for singles and between $104,000 and $124,000 on a joint return.

d. The credits may not be used for room and board, activity fees, athletic fees, insurance expense, or transportation.
   1) The credits are not allowed if a similar above-the-line education deduction was taken.

Retirement Savings Contribution Credit

4. The Retirement Savings Contribution Credit is nonrefundable.
   a. Unlike most other tax topics allowing a credit or deduction, this credit is in addition to the exclusion or deduction from GI for qualified contributions.
      1) In general, a taxpayer may claim a credit for an eligible contribution to an eligible retirement plan.
      2) The AGI limit is $28,750 ($57,500 MFJ, $43,125 HH) in 2012.
      3) The maximum credit is 50% of up to $2,000 contribution (i.e., $1,000).

Child Tax Credit

5. The Child Tax Credit is nonrefundable; however, the "Additional" Child Tax Credit is refundable.
   a. Taxpayers who have qualifying children are entitled to a credit of $1,000 per child.
      1) **Qualifying child** is defined as a child, descendant, stepchild, eligible foster child, sibling, or descendant of siblings
         a) Who is a U.S. citizen,
         b) For whom the taxpayer claims a dependency exemption, and
         c) Who is less than 17 years old as of the close of the tax year.
      2) The credit is allowed only for tax years consisting of 12 months.

3) The credit is phased out when AGI reaches $75,000 for single filers ($110,000 for married filing jointly, $55,000 filing separately).
   a) The credit is reduced by $50 for each $1,000 that the taxpayer's AGI exceeds the threshold.

b. Through 2017, the credit is refundable up to 15% of earned income in excess of $3,000.
   1) The refund is capped at the per child amount.
   2) This portion of the credit is referred to as the "Additional" Child Tax Credit and is calculated on Form 8812.

Nonbusiness Energy Property Credit

6. The Nonbusiness Energy Property Credit is nonrefundable.
   a. A tax credit of up to $500 is available to individuals for nonbusiness energy property, such as residential exterior doors and windows, insulation, heat pumps, furnaces, central air conditioners, and water heaters.
      1) The credit is 10% of qualified costs.
      2) There is a lifetime limit of $500.
      3) The improvements must be installed in the taxpayer's principal residence in the United States.
      4) The basis of the residence must be reduced by the amount of the credit allowed.

Credit for the Elderly or Disabled

7. The Credit for the Elderly or Disabled is nonrefundable.
   a. An individual may be eligible for this credit if (s)he was age 65 before the close of the tax year or retired before the close of the tax year due to a total and permanent disability.
   b. The credit is equal to 15% times an initial base amount, which is $5,000 ($7,500 for married filing joint return with both spouses age 65 or older, $3,750 MFS), and limited to disability income if under age 65. This initial base amount is reduced by the following:
      1) Tax-exempt Social Security benefits,
      2) Pension or annuity benefits excluded from gross income, and
      3) One-half the excess of AGI over $7,500 ($10,000 for married filing jointly, $5,000 MFS).
   c. A married person filing separately who lives with the spouse at any time during the year may not claim the credit.

Adoption Credit

8. A nonrefundable Adoption Credit is allowed for qualified adoption expenses.
   a. An eligible child must be under 18 years of age or must be physically or mentally incapable of self-care.
   b. Qualified adoption expenses are reasonable and necessary adoption expenses, including adoption fees, court costs, attorney fees, and other directly related expenses.
      1) Expenses that are not eligible for the Adoption Credit include
         a) Costs associated with a surrogate parenting arrangement,
         b) Expenses incurred in violation of state or federal law,
         c) Expenses incurred in connection with the adoption of a child of the taxpayer's spouse, and
         d) Infant care supplies.

c. The maximum credit is $12,650 per child, including a special-needs domestic adoption.

1) The amount of the credit allowable for any tax year is phased out for taxpayers with MAGI in excess of $189,710 and is fully eliminated when MAGI reaches $229,710.

$$\text{Credit} = \$12{,}650 \times \left[1 - \left(\frac{\text{MAGI} - \$189{,}710}{\$40{,}000}\right)\right]$$

2) The credit is also reduced if the taxpayer receives excludable adoption assistance from an employer.

d. Unused credit may be carried forward for up to 5 years and is not subject to the AGI phaseout.

Residential Mortgage Interest Credit

9. The Residential Mortgage Interest Credit is nonrefundable.

a. State and local governments can elect to issue qualified mortgage bonds (QMBs) in lieu of certain tax-exempt bonds.

1) The QMBs finance mortgage credit certificates (MCCs) issued to qualified individuals who use the MCCs when privately financing their first purchase of a principal residence.
2) The interest on the home mortgage is the base.
3) The MCC rate is between 10% and 50% (assumption is 25%).
4) If the rate exceeds 20%, the credit is limited to $2,000 per year.
5) MCC credit disallowed by the overall limit may be carried forward 3 years.

EXAMPLE

David and Lydia paid $4,800 of interest in 2012 on the mortgage given upon acquiring their first home. They received a mortgage credit certificate that specifies a 20% credit rate. They are entitled to a credit of $960 ($4,800 × 20%). The interest they may deduct, however, is reduced by the amount of the credit to $3,840 ($4,800 – $960).

Minimum Tax Credit (MTC)

10. The Minimum Tax Credit is partially refundable.

a. A credit is allowed for alternative minimum tax (AMT) paid in a tax year against regular tax liability in one or more subsequent tax years (Form 8801).

b. **Individuals.** The MTC amount is the AMT that would have been computed if the only adjustments made to taxable income in computing AMTI were those for (tax-favored) items that result in deferral, as opposed to exclusion, of income.

1) To compute the MTC amount, recompute the most recent year's AMT without adjustment for the following (exclusion) items, and add carryover MTC:

a) Standard deduction,
b) Personal exemptions deduction,
c) Miscellaneous itemized deductions,
d) Tax-exempt interest on private activity bonds (except ones issued in 2009 or 2010),
e) Interest expense (e.g., home mortgage interest for nonacquisition indebtedness and investment interest),
f) Medical expenses,
g) Depletion, and
h) Taxes.

c. **Corporations.** A corporation's credit for AMT is for both deferred items and exclusion items.

d. **Limits.** The MTC allowable is limited to current-year gross regular tax (reduced by certain credits) minus current-year tentative minimum tax.

	Gross regular tax
–	Credits
–	Tentative minimum tax (for current year)
=	MTC maximum allowable

1) The current-year gross regular tax amount is reduced by the amount currently allowable for each of the following:
   a) Refundable credits
   b) Nonrefundable personal credits
   c) Foreign tax, drug testing, nonconventional source fuel credits
   d) General Business Credit

e. **Carryover.** Any MTC amount beyond the current limit may be carried forward indefinitely.

f. **Refundable AMT Credit.** This allows taxpayers to take advantage of a refundable minimum tax credit with respect to certain MTCs over 3 years old.

1) The refundable MTC can offset regular and AMT taxes and is refundable to the extent it exceeds the taxpayer's tax liability for the year.
2) It is available for 6 years, from 2007 through 2012.
3) The refundable amount is the greater of
   a) 50% of unused MTC for the year or
   b) The prior year's AMT refundable credit.

EXAMPLE

A taxpayer generated a $150,000 AMT credit in 2004 when the taxpayer exercised some profitable ISOs. For 2008, the entire $150,000 amount counts as a long-term unused AMT credit, since the whole amount was generated before 2005. For 2007, the taxpayer had no refundable AMT credit because the taxpayer's credit was not yet old enough.

The taxpayer's 2008 refundable AMT credit amount figured under the annual limitation rule is $75,000 (0.50 × $150,000). The taxpayer can collect the entire $75,000 simply filing out a Form 8801 (Credit for Prior-Year Minimum Tax) and including it with the taxpayer's 2008 Form 1040. This means the taxpayer can use the $75,000 credit to reduce the taxpayer's 2008 federal income tax bill (including any AMT) to as low as zero. Any leftover credit amount will be sent to the taxpayer in cash.

For 2009, the taxpayer's long-term unused AMT credit amount is the $75,000 left over from 2008. Under the annual limitation rule, the entire $75,000 is refundable because it equals the 2008 refundable credit amount. So the taxpayer can collect the entire $75,000 simply by filing the taxpayer's 2009 Form 1040.

The taxpayer gets to collect the whole $150,000 over 2 years.

Earned Income Credit (EIC)

11. The Earned Income Credit is refundable.

a. Under Sec. 32(a), the EIC is available to individuals who have earned income and gross income below certain thresholds.

1) An individual is not eligible for the EIC if (s)he does not include his/her correct SSN on the return claiming the credit.
2) Individual taxpayer identification numbers (ITINs) disqualify the taxpayer and/or the otherwise qualifying child (QC) from the credit.
3) Married individuals who file separately are not eligible for the EIC.
4) The EIC increases for individuals having at least one QC.
5) The credit is not available for taxpayers who fraudulently claim the EIC.

b. An individual without a QC must have his/her principal residence in the U.S. for more than half of the tax year, be at least 25 but not over 64 years old, and not be a dependent of another.

c. **QC tests.** In order for a child to be a QC, three tests must be met:

   1) Relationship. The child must be related by birth or adoption or be an eligible foster child or stepchild.
   2) Residency. The taxpayer must provide the child's principal place of abode for more than half of the year.
   3) Age. The child must be under age 19 at the close of the tax year, be permanently disabled, or be a student under the age of 24.

d. **Child claimed by both parents.** In the event that two or more taxpayers claim the same child in the same calendar year, the child will be the qualifying child for the parents first and then for the taxpayer with the highest AGI.

   1) If both of a qualifying child's parents seek to claim the credit, but do not file jointly, then the parent with whom the child resides the longest period of time during the year may claim the child.
   2) The parent with the highest AGI will be able to claim the child as a qualifying child in the event the child spends an equal amount of time with each parent during the year (Publication 504).

e. **QC of another person.** A taxpayer (or spouse if filing a joint return) who is a qualifying child of another person cannot claim the EIC.

   1) This applies even if the person for whom the taxpayer is the qualifying child does not claim the EIC or meet the criteria in order to claim the EIC.

f. **Earned income** includes wages, salaries, tips, and net earnings from self-employment.

   1) It does not include nontaxable compensation (e.g., military allowances), welfare benefits (e.g., AFDC), veteran's benefits, pensions, annuities, unemployment compensation, and scholarships.
   2) Disqualified income includes interest, dividends, capital gain net income, positive passive income, nonbusiness rents or royalties.
   3) For 2012, the amount of disqualified income that causes a taxpayer to become ineligible for the EIC is $3,200.

g. **Calculation of EIC.** Multiply the individual's earned income by the applicable percentage.

   1) EIC: Maximum Amounts, 2012

Type of Taxpayer	Applicable Percentage	Earned Income Amount	Maximum EIC
0 QC	7.65%	$ 6,210	$ 475
1 QC	34.00%	$ 9,320	$3,169
2 QC	40.00%	$13,090	$5,236
3 or more QC	45.00%	$13,090	$5,891

h. **Phaseout of EIC.** Decrease the maximum EIC by any phaseout, which is determined by multiplying the applicable phaseout percentage by the excess of the amount of the individual's AGI (or earned income, if greater) over the beginning amount.

   1) No EIC is available when AGI or earned income exceeds the completed phaseout amount.
   2) EIC: Phaseout Amounts, 2012

Type of Taxpayer	Applicable Phaseout Percentage	Beginning Phaseout Amount	Beginning Phaseout Amt. for Joint Filers	Completed Phaseout Amount	Completed Phaseout Amt. for Joint Filers
0 QC	7.65%	$ 7,770	$12,980	$13,980	$19,190
1 QC	15.98%	$17,090	$22,300	$36,920	$42,130
2 QC	21.06%	$17,090	$22,300	$41,952	$47,162
3 or more QC	21.06%	$17,090	$22,300	$45,060	$50,270

Stop and review! You have completed the outline for this subunit. Study questions 1 through 28 beginning on page 167.

6.2 OTHER TAXES

Alternative Minimum Tax (AMT)

1. The alternative minimum tax is an income tax in addition to the regular income tax (Form 6251).
   a. The **formula** for computing AMT is below.

AMT FORMULA

	Taxable Income	
+	Tax preferences	
+	Personal exemptions	
+	Standard deduction if taxpayer does not itemize	
+/–	Certain other adjustments	
	Alternative minimum taxable income (AMTI)	
–	Exemption amount	2012
	Married filing jointly	$78,750
	Single	$50,600
	Married filing separately	$39,375
	Alternative minimum tax base	
×	Rate	2012
	AMT base (married filing jointly)	
	First $175,000	26%
	Excess	28%
	Tentative minimum tax	
–	Regular income tax	
	Alternative minimum tax	

1) AMT income (AMTI) is based on taxable income (TI).
   a) AMTI is TI after amounts are added or subtracted for tax preferences, adjustments, and loss limitations.
   b) The AMT base is AMTI reduced by an exemption amount and any AMT NOL carryover.
2) Tentative AMT is determined by multiplying a rate times the AMT base after a reduction for the AMT Foreign Tax Credit.
   a) For corporations, a 20% rate applies.
   b) For individuals, a two-tiered graduated rate schedule applies.
      i) A 26% rate applies to the first $175,000 ($87,500 if married filing separately) of AMTI (net of the exemption amount).
      ii) A 28% rate applies to any excess.

3) AMT is the excess tentative AMT over regular income tax.
4) AMT must be reported and paid at the same time as regular tax liability. Estimated payments of AMT are required.
5) Sec. 53 allows a credit for the amount AMT exceeds the regular tax for a tax year. The credit carries forward indefinitely.

b. **Tax preference items.** These items generate tax savings by reducing the taxpayer's taxable income. Therefore, they must be added back to taxable income when computing AMTI.

1) **Qualified small business stock.** When computing taxable income, noncorporate taxpayers may exclude up to 100% of gain realized on the sale or exchange of qualified small business stock acquired after September 27, 2010, and held more than 5 years. The exclusion percentage drops to 75% for stock acquired after February 17, 2009, and before September 28, 2010; and to 50% for stock acquired before February 18, 2009. Generally, 7% of the exclusion is a tax preference item for AMT. However, stock sold between September 27, 2010, and January 1, 2014, is excluded from tax preference treatment.
2) **Private activity bonds.** Add any tax-exempt interest minus expenses (including interest) attributable to earning it. Bonds issued in 2009 and 2010 are excluded from tax preference treatment.
3) **Percentage depletion.** Add any excess of deduction claimed over adjusted basis.
4) **Intangible drilling costs (IDC).** Add any excess of IDC amortized over 10 years over 65% of net income from oil, gas, and geothermal properties.

c. Usually, **adjustments** eliminate "time value" tax savings from accelerated deductions or deferral of income. An adjustment is an increase or a decrease to TI in computing AMTI.

1) Adjustments Affecting **Corporate and Noncorporate Taxpayers**

a) **Installment sales.** The installment method is not allowed for a disposition of stock in trade in the ordinary course of business (e.g., inventory). Add any balance (+ or –) of current-year gain recognized disregarding the installment method, minus gain recognized under the installment method.

b) **Long-term contracts.** The percentage-of-completion method must be used to determine AMTI. Add any balance (+ or –) if the completed-contract or cash-basis method is normally used.

i) The same percentage of completion must be used for AMT and regular tax.
ii) Small construction contracts require a simplified method of allocating costs in applying the percentage-of-completion method. The contract's estimated duration must be less than 2 years.
iii) No AMT adjustment is made for home construction contracts.

c) **Pollution control facilities (certified).** For property placed in service after 1986, the 5-year amortization method for depreciation must be replaced by the alternate depreciation system [Sec. 168(g)]. Add any balance (+ or –).

d) **Mining exploration and development.** If for regular tax purposes these expenditures were expensed, the expenditures must be capitalized and amortized over a 10-year period for AMT. Add any balance (+ or –) for the difference.

i) Tax loss. If a worthless mine is abandoned, expenditures capitalized but unamortized can be deducted from AMTI.

e) **Net operating loss (NOL) adjustments.** To determine the NOL amount for AMT,

i) Subtract all amounts added to TI as tax preference amounts to the extent they increased the regular tax NOL.

ii) Tax adjustments made for the AMTI calculation (+ or –) must be made for the NOL calculation.

f) Distributions from a trust or estate.

2) **Noncorporate adjustments** affect only noncorporate taxpayers.

a) **Research and experimental expenditures.** Add any balance (+ or –) of regular tax deduction claimed for the year (normally expensed), minus expenditures capitalized and amortized over 10 years (beginning in year made).

b) **Personal exemptions and the standard deduction.** No deduction for, or in lieu of, personal exemptions may be claimed against AMTI. Furthermore, the standard deduction cannot be claimed for AMTI purposes.

c) **Certain itemized deductions.** Some itemized deductions that were claimed for regular tax purposes may not be claimed for AMTI purposes. Disallowed deductions include

i) Miscellaneous deductions subject to the 2% AGI floor.

ii) State, local, or foreign payments. Likewise, any refunds of these taxes can be excluded from AMTI.

iii) Medical expenses that do not exceed 10% of AGI (instead of 7.5% for regular tax purposes).

iv) Investment expenses that exceed the taxpayer's net investment income.

v) Tax-exempt interest on private activity bonds, which is included in investment income.

vi) Home equity refinancing (i.e., interest on loan amount qualified for regular itemized tax deduction, in excess of acquisition amount).

d) **Circulation expenditures.** Add any balance (+ or –) of regular tax deduction for the year (normally expensed), minus the expenditures capitalized and amortized over 3 years (beginning in year made).

e) **Incentive stock option (ISO).** Add any balance (+ or –) of the FMV of the stock when exercised, minus the amount paid for stock.

d. **AMT NOL.** The alternative minimum tax net operating loss (AMT NOL) is technically an adjustment to taxable income (TI).

1) After tax preferences have been computed and added to TI and all other adjustments have been computed and made, one of the two AMT NOL adjustment steps is performed.

2) **NOL year.** Compute the AMT NOL. It is carried back or forward to another tax year.

a) The AMT NOL is modified for each of the tax preferences and other adjustments for the current tax year.

3) **Profit year.** An AMT NOL is a final adjustment to TI in computing AMTI in a tax year in which (before reduction by part or all of unused AMT NOLs) there is AMTI.

a) Limit: 90% of AMTI. Alternative NOL may not offset more than 90% of the AMT base (computed without the alternative NOL deduction).

e. **AMT exemption.** An exemption is allowed that reduces AMTI to produce the AMT base. The basic exemption is phased out at $.25 for each dollar of AMTI above a threshold. All members of a controlled group must share the exemption amount.

AMT EXEMPTION AMOUNT (Tax year 2012)

Entity/Filing Status	Basic Amount	Threshold	Cap
Corporation	$40,000	$150,000	$310,000
Married filing jointly	78,750	150,000	465,000
Surviving spouse	78,750	150,000	465,000
Head of household	50,600	112,500	314,900
Unmarried and not the above two	50,600	112,500	314,900
Married filing separately	39,375	75,000	232,500

f. **AMT FTC.** Only one credit is allowed in computing AMT: the AMT Foreign Tax Credit (FTC). The AMT FTC is the lower of the FTC or 90% of gross tentative AMT computed before any AMT NOL deduction and FTC.

g. **Minimum Tax Credit (MTC).** A credit is allowed for AMT paid in a tax year against regular tax liability in one or more subsequent tax years.

1) **Individuals.** The MTC amount is the AMT that would have been computed if the only adjustments made to TI in computing AMTI were those for (tax-favored) items that result in deferral, as opposed to exclusion, of income.

a) To compute the MTC amount, recompute the most recent year's AMT without adjustment for the following (exclusion) items, and add carryover MTC:

i) Standard deduction
ii) Personal exemptions deduction
iii) Miscellaneous itemized deductions
iv) Tax-exempt interest on private activity bonds
v) Personal interest expense
vi) Charitable contributions of appreciated property
vii) Medical expenses
viii) Depletion
ix) Taxes

Employment Taxes and Withholding

2. **Social Security (FICA) tax.** Employers are required to pay tax based on their employee's pay. An employee's wages include all remuneration for employment, including the cash value of all wages paid in a medium other than cash.

a. The employer must

1) Pay 6.20% of the first $110,100 (2012) of wages paid for old-age, survivors, and disability insurance (OASDI), plus

2) Pay 1.45% of all wages for the hospital insurance (Medicare) portion. This tax has no cap.

b. For 2012, the employer must withhold 4.20% for OASDI and 1.45% for Medicare from the employee's wages.

1) The employee's contribution (tax) must be withheld upon each payment of wages computed at the same rate up to the same maximum base.

2) Any overwithholding is taken as a credit against the income tax if the overwithholding resulted from multiple-employer withholding.

c. Contributions made by the employee are not tax deductible by the employee, while those made by the employer are deductible by the employer.

d. An employer must pay FICA taxes for all household employees, e.g., baby-sitters and maids, who are paid more than $1,800 during the year.

1) Household employees are exempt from withholdings on noncash payments (e.g., goods, lodging, food, or services) made in exchange for household work.

2) Schedule H is a simplified form that may be used by employers of household workers in private homes. The form is filed, and the employment taxes can be paid with the employer's annual Form 1040.

3. **Self-employment tax.** The FICA tax liability is imposed on net earnings from self-employment at twice the rate that applies to an employer minus 2%, that is, at the rate of 13.3% [6.20% + 4.20% + (2 × 1.45%)].

a. In order to figure self-employment tax liability, a self-employed person is entitled to deduct an amount equal to the employer's portion of the tax. This reduced amount of self-employment net income is net earnings from self-employment and is multiplied by the self-employment tax rate to arrive at the amount of self-employment tax.

1) Net earnings from self-employment = NI from self-employment – (.0765 × NI from self-employment).

b. Instead of reducing net income from self-employment by 7.65%, the reduced amount (i.e., net earnings from SE) may be computed by multiplying net income from self-employment by 92.35%.

c. Self-employment income is equal to the net earnings an individual derives from self-employment during any tax year.

d. Net income from self-employment does not include rents, gain (or loss) from disposition of business property, capital gain (or loss), nonbusiness interest, or dividends.

e. An individual who has less than $400 in net earnings from self-employment during the year has no self-employment income.

f. For 2012, the self-employed person is allowed a deduction for the employer portion of the FICA tax paid to arrive at his/her AGI. The deduction is 50% of the FICA tax paid plus $1,100 if FICA taxes from self-employment are more than $14,643.30. If FICA taxes from self-employment are $14,643.30 or less, then the deduction percentage is 57.51%.

g. The income inclusion for self-employment taxes differs from gross income inclusion in the case of ministers and/or clergymen.

1) A minister may exclude the rental value of his/her home or parsonage if it is connected with the performance of religious duties.

2) The rental value is not excluded from the income used to compute self-employment taxes.

3) Any wages received by ministers and/or clergymen on a W-2 is not subject to Social Security but is included in self-employment income, unless one of the following applies:

a) The minister and/or clergyman is a member of a religious order who has taken a vow of poverty.

b) The minister and/or clergyman asks the Internal Revenue Service (IRS) for an exemption from SE tax for his/her services and the IRS approves his/her request.

c) The minister and/or clergyman is subject only to the Social Security laws of a foreign country under the provisions of a Social Security agreement between the United States and that country.

4. **Unemployment (FUTA) tax.** This tax is imposed on employers. The tax is 6.0% (6.2% before July 1, 2011) of the first $7,000 of wages paid to each employee. The employee does not pay any portion of FUTA.
   a. Employers are required to pay unemployment taxes for 2012 if they pay wages of $1,500 or more for any quarter in 2011 or 2012.
   b. Up to 5.4% of the 6.0% is allowable as a credit, based on state unemployment taxes paid.
5. **Household employee tax.** The employer is subject to tax if (s)he
   a. Paid one household employee cash wages of $1,800 or more during the year,
   b. Withheld federal income tax at the request of the employee, or
   c. Paid total cash wages of $1,000 or more in any calendar quarter to household employees.
      1) These amounts are subject to FUTA taxes.
6. With regard to income tax withholding and Social Security, Medicare, and federal unemployment, no differences are recognized among full-time employees, part-time employees, and temporary employees.
7. If an individual is required to report employment taxes or give tax statements to employees, (s)he must have an employer identification number (EIN).
   a. The EIN is a nine-digit number the IRS issues to identify the tax accounts of employers.
8. Penalties are applied when an employer fails to make a required deposit on time.
   a. The penalties do not apply if any failure to make a proper and timely deposit was due to reasonable cause and not to willful neglect.
   b. For amounts not properly or timely deposited, the penalty rates are
      1) 2% for deposits made 1 to 5 days late,
      2) 5% for deposits made 6 to 15 days late, and
      3) 10% for deposits made 16 or more days late.

Stop and review! You have completed the outline for this subunit. Study questions 29 through 33 beginning on page 175.

6.3 PAYMENTS

Estimated Tax Payments

1. The IRC is structured to obtain at least 90% of the final income tax through withholding and estimated tax payments. Individuals who earn income not subject to withholding must pay estimated tax on that income in quarterly installments.
   a. **Calendar-year due dates.** For a calendar-year taxpayer, the installments are due by
      1) April 15 (January through March),
      2) June 15 (April and May),
      3) September 15 (June - August), and
      4) January 15 (September - December) of the following year.

      NOTE: Dates are adjusted for weekends and holidays.
   b. Underpayment of the fourth installment does not result in penalty if on or before January 31 of the following tax year, an individual both files a return and pays the amount computed payable on that return.
      1) Any underpayment penalties from the first three quarterly installments will not increase any further.

c. Each of the following is treated as payment of estimated tax:
   1) The election to apply an overpayment of tax in a prior tax year, which has not been refunded, to the following year's tax return
      a) It is applied to the first required installment due.
   2) Amount of federal income tax (FIT) withheld (by an employer) from wages
      a) The aggregate amount is treated as if an equal part was paid on each due date, unless the individual establishes the actual payment dates.
   3) Direct payment by the individual (or another on his/her behalf)
      a) It is applied to the first estimated tax payment due.
   4) Excess FICA withheld when an employee has two or more employers during a tax year who withheld (in the aggregate) more than the ceiling on FICA taxes
d. **Installment percentage.** Each installment must be 25% of the least of the following amounts:
   1) 100% of the prior year's tax (if a return was filed)
   2) 90% of the current year's tax
   3) 90% of the annualized current year's tax (applies when income is uneven)
e. **Safe harbor rule.** Taxpayers whose 2011 tax returns showed AGI in excess of $150,000 ($75,000 for married filing separately) must apply the safe harbor rule. This rule requires the taxpayer to make estimated payments of the lesser of 110% of the 2011 tax liability or 90% of the 2012 tax liability.
f. A taxpayer is not required to make a payment until the first period in which there is income (Publication 505).
g. Tax refers to the sum of the regular tax, AMT, self-employment tax, and household employee tax.
h. **Penalty.** A penalty is imposed if, by the quarterly payment date, the total of estimated tax payments and income tax withheld is less than 25% of the required minimum payment for the year.
   1) The penalty is determined each quarter.
   2) The penalty is the federal short-term rate plus 3% times the underpayment.
   3) The penalty is not allowed as an interest deduction.
i. The penalty will not be imposed if any of the following apply:
   1) Actual tax liability shown on the return for the tax year (after reduction for amounts withheld by employers) is less than $1,000.
   2) No tax liability was incurred in the prior tax year.
   3) The IRS waives it for reasonable cause shown.
j. **Farmers or fishermen** who expect to receive at least two-thirds of their gross income from farming or fishing activities (or did in the prior tax year) may pay estimated tax in one installment.
   1) For 2012, the installment can be made as late as January 15, 2013, without penalty. The installment must be for the entire amount of estimated tax.
   2) Alternatively, the farmer or fisherman does not need to make an installment payment if (s)he files his/her tax return for 2012 and pays the entire amount due by March 1, 2013.
   3) Wages received as a farm employee are not farm income.
   4) S corporation distributions from farming are farm income to the shareholder.

Excess Social Security Credit

2. An employer must deduct and withhold Social Security tax on an employee's first $110,100 of wages. For 2012, the withholding rate is 4.2%.
   a. When the maximum withholding is exceeded due to the correct withholding of two or more employers, a special refund of the excess amount may be obtained only by claiming a credit for the amount.
      1) The credit must be claimed in the same manner as if such special refund were an amount deducted and withheld as income tax at the source.
      2) The credit is computed separately for each spouse on a joint return.
   b. When an employer incorrectly withholds Social Security taxes on more than the maximum amount, a credit may not be claimed for the excess.
      1) The employer should refund the overcollection to the employee.

Claims for Refund

3. Taxpayers have a limited amount of time in which to file a claim for a credit or refund. Taxpayers encountering trouble obtaining a refund or other tax issues may request assistance from the Taxpayer Advocate Service by submitting Form 911.
   a. **Form 1040X.** Taxpayers file a claim for refund on Form 1040X with the Internal Revenue Service Center where the original return was filed.
      1) A separate form for each year or period involved is filed.
      2) An explanation of each item of income, deduction, or credit on which the refund claim is based is included.
   b. **Statute of limitations.** Generally, taxpayers must file a claim for credit or refund within 3 years from the date the original return was filed or 2 years from the date the tax was paid, whichever is later.
      1) The Tax Court can consider taxes paid during the 3-year period preceding the date of a notice of deficiency for determining any refund due to a nonfiler.
      2) If a claim is made within 3 years after the filing of the return, the credit or refund cannot be more than the part of the tax paid within the 3 years (plus the length of any extension of time granted for filing the return) before the claim was filed.
         a) If a claim is filed after the 3-year period but within the 2 years from the time a tax was paid, the credit for refund cannot be more than the tax paid within the 2 years immediately before the filed claim.
      3) The period of limitations on credits and refunds can be suspended for individuals during periods they are unable to manage their financial affairs because of physical or mental impairment that is medically determinable and either
         a) Has lasted or can be expected to last continuously for at least 12 months or
         b) Can be expected to result in death.

Stop and review! You have completed the outline for this subunit. Study questions 34 through 39 beginning on page 176.

QUESTIONS

6.1 Tax Credits

1. For the current year, Gannon Corporation has U.S. taxable income of $500,000, which includes $100,000 from a foreign division. Gannon paid $45,000 of foreign income taxes on the income of the foreign division. Assuming Gannon's U.S. income tax for the current year before credits is $170,000, its maximum Foreign Tax Credit for the current year is

A. $9,000

B. $45,000

C. $34,000

D. $136,000

Answer (C) is correct.

REQUIRED: The Foreign Tax Credit that can be claimed in the current year.

DISCUSSION: The Foreign Tax Credit is allowed under Sec. 27 and Sec. 901 for foreign income taxes paid or accrued during the year and is limited by Sec. 904(a). The limitation is the proportion of the taxpayer's tentative U.S. income tax (before the Foreign Tax Credit) that the taxpayer's foreign source taxable income bears to his/her worldwide taxable income for the year. (See Publication 514.) The following calculation should be made:

$$\frac{\text{Foreign source taxable income}}{\text{Worldwide taxable income}} \times \text{U.S. income tax} = \text{Foreign tax credit limitation}$$

The unused credit of $11,000 ($45,000 – $34,000) may be carried back 1 year and then forward to the following 10 taxable years [Sec. 904(c)].

Answer (A) is incorrect. The credit is limited to 20% of the U.S. tax, not 20% of the foreign tax. Answer (B) is incorrect. The maximum Foreign Tax Credit for the current year is limited and does not equal foreign income taxes paid. Answer (D) is incorrect. This amount is Gannon's liability after subtracting the Foreign Tax Credit.

2. Carol, an individual taxpayer, received a Form 1099-Div from her global mutual fund that showed dividend income of $500 and foreign taxes withheld of $70. This is the only foreign source income she received for the year. Her income tax before any credits is $4,320. On which of the following forms may Carol elect to claim a credit for the foreign tax paid?

A. Form 1040, Line 63, "2012 estimated tax payments ...," with a disclosure statement.

B. Form 1040, "Tax and Credits," Foreign Tax Credit.

C. Form 1040, Schedule A, *Itemized Deductions*, line 8, "Other taxes."

D. Form 1040, Schedule B, by electing to reduce the dividend income by $140 ($70 × 2).

Answer (B) is correct.

REQUIRED: The correct form to claim a credit for the foreign tax paid.

DISCUSSION: Line 47 of Form 1040 is located under the heading "Tax and Credits" and is labeled "Foreign Tax Credit." This is where a taxpayer would claim a credit on foreign tax paid.

Answer (A) is incorrect. A taxpayer claims a Foreign Tax Credit on line 47 of Form 1040, under the heading "Tax and Credits." Answer (C) is incorrect. Form 1040, Schedule A, *Itemized Deductions*, line 8, "Other taxes," is the line used to deduct a foreign tax paid, not receive a credit. Answer (D) is incorrect. A taxpayer claims a Foreign Tax Credit on line 47 of Form 1040, under the heading "Tax and Credits."

3. Ginger is a United States citizen who paid the following 2012 foreign income taxes:

- $10,000 tax paid to England on consulting fee income
- $5,000 tax paid to Spain on earned income for which she claimed the foreign earned income exclusion
- $1,000 tax paid to France, which she deducted as an itemized deduction

These were Ginger's only sources of income during 2012. Her U.S. tax liability was $23,000. What amount of Foreign Tax Credit can she claim on her 2012 return?

A. $16,000

B. $0

C. $10,000

D. $7,000

Answer (B) is correct.

REQUIRED: The amount of Foreign Tax Credit that can be claimed.

DISCUSSION: A taxpayer may elect either a credit or deduction for income taxes paid to other countries or U.S. possessions. (S)he may not elect to do both a credit and a deduction. (See Publication 514.) Since Ginger already claimed the foreign earned income exclusion for the $5,000 tax paid to Spain and she has already deducted the $1,000 tax paid to France, she can only take a deduction for the tax paid to England. Thus, Ginger may not claim a credit.

Answer (A) is incorrect. The taxes paid to France and Spain have already been excluded or deducted from income. Answer (C) is incorrect. Ginger already claimed a deduction for the taxes paid to France. Answer (D) is incorrect. This amount is the difference between the total tax paid to foreign countries and the amount owed to the U.S.

4. Virginia's earned income for 2012 was $24,000. She paid $3,000 to a qualifying child care center for the care of her 2-year-old son while she worked. She received $2,000 from Social Services to assist with her child care expenses. Compute Virginia's Child Care Credit for 2012 from the following excerpt from the child and dependent care table:

IF your adjusted gross income is:		THEN the percentage is:
Over	But not over	
$ 0	$15,000	35%
$15,000	$17,000	34%
$17,000	$19,000	33%
$19,000	$21,000	32%
$21,000	$23,000	31%
$23,000	$25,000	30%
$25,000	$27,000	29%

A. $300

B. $900

C. $930

D. $310

Answer (A) is correct.

REQUIRED: The amount of the Child Care Credit.

DISCUSSION: The Child Care Credit is limited to $3,000 for one qualifying child. Virginia received $2,000 from Social Services to assist with her child care expenses; however, she must deduct this amount from the expenses that she paid for child care. The amount of expense that she must use for calculating her credit is $1,000 ($3,000 – $2,000). You must find the income bracket that Virginia is in (over $23,000, but not over $25,000) and multiply the expenses that she paid during the year for child care by the applicable percentage (30%). Thus, the credit for Virginia for 2012 is $300 ($1,000 × 30%). (See Publication 503.)

Answer (B) is incorrect. You must reduce the expenses paid by Virginia by the amount she received from Social Services to assist with her child-care expenses. Answer (C) is incorrect. You must reduce the expenses paid by Virginia by the amount she received from Social Services to assist with her child-care expenses. In addition, Virginia's income is over $23,000, but not over $25,000. Answer (D) is incorrect. Virginia's income is over $23,000, but not over $25,000.

5. All of the following child and dependent care expenses may qualify as work-related for purposes of the Child and Dependent Care Credit except

A. The cost of care provided to a qualifying person outside the home.

B. The cost of getting a qualifying person from the home to the care location and back.

C. The cost of household services that are partly for the well-being of a qualifying person.

D. The cost of sending a child to school if the child is in a grade below kindergarten and the cost is incident to and cannot be separated from the cost of care.

Answer (B) is correct.

REQUIRED: The child or dependent care expense that does not qualify as employment-related.

DISCUSSION: Employment-related expenses are paid for household services and for the care of a qualifying individual [Sec. 21(b)(2)]. Expenses are only classified as work-related if they are incurred to enable the taxpayer to be gainfully employed. The cost of transporting a qualifying individual to a place where care is provided is not considered to be incurred for the individual's care [Publication 17 and Reg. 1.44A-1(c)(3)].

Answer (A) is incorrect. The cost of care provided outside the home qualifies as long as the dependent regularly spends at least 8 hours a day in the taxpayer's home. Answer (C) is incorrect. The cost of household services for the care of a qualifying individual is included as qualified expenses. Answer (D) is incorrect. Expenses incurred in sending a child to school before (s)he enters kindergarten are included as qualified expenses.

6. Carmella is divorced and has two children, ages 3 and 9. For 2012, her adjusted gross income is $30,000, all of which is earned income. Carmella's younger child stays at her employer's on-site child care center while she works. The benefits from this child care center qualify to be excluded from her income. Carmella's employer reports the value of this service as $3,000 for the year. This amount is shown in box 10 of Carmella's Form W-2, but is not included in taxable wages in box 1. A neighbor cares for Carmella's older child after school, on holidays, and during the summer. Carmella pays her neighbor $3,000 for this care. What is Carmella's Child Care Credit for 2012?

A. $900

B. $810

C. $480

D. $600

Answer (B) is correct.

REQUIRED: The taxpayer's maximum allowable credit for child care.

DISCUSSION: Sec. 21(a) allows a credit equal to the applicable percentage of employment-related expenses. The applicable percentage is 35%, reduced (but not below 20%) by one percentage point for each $2,000 (or fraction thereof) by which adjusted gross income exceeds $15,000 (Publication 17). Carmella's adjusted gross income exceeded $15,000 by $15,000, so the applicable percentage is 35% – 8% = 27%.

Because Carmella has two qualifying children, she may apply the credit up to $6,000 of her child care expenses less the excludable employer dependent-related expenses of $3,000. Therefore, Carmella's maximum credit is $810 [($6,000 – $3,000) × 27%].

7. Ruth had wages of $34,000, and her husband John's wages were $27,000. They have three children ages 3, 6, and 9. They paid a total of $7,200 to Creative Child Care School, Inc. Assuming a 20% credit rate, what will be their Child Care Credit?

A. $1,440

B. $1,200

C. $6,000

D. $7,200

Answer (B) is correct.

REQUIRED: The amount of the Child Care Credit.

DISCUSSION: Beginning in 2005, the maximum amount of employment-related expenses to which the credit may be applied is $3,000 if one qualifying child or dependent is involved, or $6,000 if two or more are involved. The maximum credit that can be claimed in this situation is $1,200 (20% of $6,000 limit). (See Publication 17.)

8. Which one of the following could prevent an individual from qualifying for the Child and Dependent Care Credit?

A. Unearned income of more than $400.

B. Paying for care for more than one qualifying person.

C. Not identifying the care provider on the tax return.

D. Paying for child care while looking for work.

Answer (C) is correct.

REQUIRED: The event that could cause an individual to be disqualified for the Child and Dependent Care Credit.

DISCUSSION: Taxpayers must provide each dependent's taxpayer identification number in order to claim the credit, as well as the identifying number of the service provider [Publication 17, Secs. 21(e)(9) and 21(e)(10), and Notice 89-71].

9. Jerry has two dependent children, Greg and Mandy, who are attending an accredited college in 2012. Greg is a fifth-year senior who spent $7,000 for tuition and fees. Mandy, a freshman with no prior post-secondary education, had tuition expenses of $4,000. Jerry meets all the income and filing status requirements for the education credits. There is no tax-free assistance to pay these expenses. Jerry's tax liability before credits equals $14,000. What is the maximum credit that Jerry may claim on his 2012 tax return?

A. $2,200 Lifetime Learning Credit.

B. $5,000 AOC.

C. $2,500 AOC and $1,000 Lifetime Learning Credit.

D. $2,500 AOC and $1,400 Lifetime Learning Credit.

Answer (D) is correct.

REQUIRED: The maximum credit that Jerry may claim on his 2012 tax return.

DISCUSSION: There are two education-related credits: the AOC and the Lifetime Learning Credit. These credits may be claimed by the individuals for tuition, fee, and book expenses incurred by students pursuing college or graduate degrees or vocational training. In 2012, the AOC provides a maximum allowable credit of $2,500 per student for each of the first 4 years of post-secondary education. The calculation is the sum of 100% of the first $2,000 and 25% of the second $2,000 paid. The Lifetime Learning Credit allows a credit of 20% of the amount of tuition paid by the taxpayer and is available for the first $10,000 of tuition (Publication 17).

Answer (A) is incorrect. Jerry is entitled to the Lifetime Learning Credit as well as the AOC. Answer (B) is incorrect. In 2012, the AOC is only available for individuals who are in their first 4 years of post-secondary education. Answer (C) is incorrect. Twenty percent of the first $10,000 of tuition is eligible for the Lifetime Learning Credit.

10. In 2012, Jonathan Smith paid his educational expenses at a community college where he completed his freshman year and began his sophomore year. His father, John Smith, provides more than half of the support for Jonathan and claims an exemption for him on his tax return. Which of the following is true?

A. Jonathan is eligible to take the AOC on his 2012 tax return.

B. John is eligible to take the AOC on his 2012 tax return.

C. Jonathan and John may split the AOC between their 2012 tax returns.

D. Neither may take the AOC.

Answer (B) is correct.

REQUIRED: The true answer regarding the AOC.

DISCUSSION: The AOC may be taken by a taxpayer who claims a dependent exemption for an eligible student on his tax return. The student claimed as a dependent is not eligible to take the credit (Publication 17).

11. Which of the following is not a qualifying student for purposes of the Lifetime Learning Credit?

A. A student in a graduate program.

B. A part-time student (less than half-time).

C. A student in a vocational program.

D. All are qualifying students for the Lifetime Learning Credit.

Answer (D) is correct.

REQUIRED: The individual who is not eligible for the Lifetime Learning Credit.

DISCUSSION: Generally, students who qualify for the AOC also qualify for the Lifetime Learning Credit. Additionally, graduate students, students enrolled part-time, and students enrolled in a vocational program qualify for the Lifetime Learning Credit (Publication 17 and Sec. 25A).

12. Which of the following statements is not true regarding tax benefits for education?

A. The AOC may be claimed for tuition expenses incurred in the first 4 years of post-secondary education.

B. The dollar limitations for the AOC are calculated on a per-student basis.

C. The Lifetime Learning Credit is allowed for tuition paid for graduate program studies.

D. Room and board are qualifying expenses for the AOC.

Answer (D) is correct.

REQUIRED: The incorrect statement regarding tax benefits for education.

DISCUSSION: The AOC provides a maximum nonrefundable tax credit of $2,500 per student for each of the first 4 years of post-secondary education. The $2,500 per year is the sum of 100% of the first $2,000 of qualified expenses and 25% of the next $2,000 of qualified expenses. The Lifetime Learning Credit provides a credit of 20% of qualified tuition expenses paid by the taxpayer for any year the AOC is not claimed. The maximum credit allowed per year is $10,000 of qualified tuition and fees paid for the taxpayer, the taxpayer's spouse, and/or the taxpayer's dependents. Eligible expenses for both of these credits include tuition and fees required for enrollment. Books and required course materials are allowed for the AOC but not the Lifetime Learning Credit. However, the credits may not be used for room and board, activity fees, athletic fees, insurance expense, or transportation. (See Publication 970.)

Answer (A) is incorrect. The AOC can be claimed for tuition expenses incurred in the first 4 years of post-secondary education. Answer (B) is incorrect. The dollar limitations for the AOC are calculated on a per-student basis. Answer (C) is incorrect. The Lifetime Learning Credit is allowed for tuition paid for graduate program studies.

13. For purposes of claiming the Child Tax Credit, which of the following is not true for a qualifying child?

A. Child must be under age 16 at the end of the year.

B. Child must be a citizen or resident of the United States.

C. Child must be claimed as your dependent.

D. Child may be an eligible foster child.

Answer (A) is correct.

REQUIRED: The false statement regarding requirements for a qualifying child for the Child Tax Credit.

DISCUSSION: A qualifying child for the purposes of the Child Tax Credit is defined as a child, descendant, stepchild, eligible foster child, sibling, or descendant of siblings (1) who is a U.S. citizen, (2) for whom the taxpayer may claim a dependency exemption, and (3) who is less than 17 years old at the close of the tax year. Accordingly, a child is not required to be under the age of 16 at the end of the year to receive the Child Tax Credit; (s)he must be under the age of 17 (Publication 17 or 972).

Answer (B) is incorrect. The child is required to be a citizen or resident of the U.S. in order to be a qualifying child for the purposes of the Child Tax Credit. Answer (C) is incorrect. The child is required to be the taxpayer's dependent in order to be a qualifying child for the purposes of the Child Tax Credit. Answer (D) is incorrect. The child is required to be a child, descendant, stepchild, eligible foster child, siblings, or descendant of siblings in order to be a qualifying child for the purposes of the Child Tax Credit.

14. For which of the following dependent children will a parent not be allowed a Child Tax Credit?

A. 15-year-old daughter.

B. 12-year-old foster child.

C. 19-year-old stepchild.

D. 16-year-old grandchild.

Answer (C) is correct.

REQUIRED: The child who does not qualify for the Child Tax Credit.

DISCUSSION: A "qualifying child" is a child, descendant, stepchild, eligible foster child, sibling, or descendant of siblings. The child must also be under 17 years of age and be claimed as a dependent by the taxpayer (Publication 17 or 972).

15. Which of the following statements is not true regarding the Child Tax Credit for 2012?

A. A qualifying child must be under age 13 at the end of 2012.

B. The Child Tax Credit is refundable up to 15% of earned income in excess of $3,000.

C. The Child Tax Credit may be limited depending on modified adjusted gross income.

D. The maximum Child Tax Credit for each qualifying child is $1,000 in 2012.

Answer (A) is correct.

REQUIRED: The false statement regarding the Child Tax Credit for 2011.

DISCUSSION: For purposes of eligibility for the Child Tax Credit, a qualifying child is a child, descendant, stepchild, eligible foster child, sibling, or descendant of siblings. The child must also be under the age of 17 and be claimed as a dependent by the taxpayer. The credit is for $1,000 per qualifying child (Publication 17 or 972).

16. In 2012, Ralph spent $6,000 on qualified residential energy property costs for his vacation home in Palm Beach. What is his maximum Nonbusiness Energy Property Credit for 2012?

A. $0

B. $500

C. $1,800

D. $6,000

Answer (A) is correct.

REQUIRED: The maximum amount for the Residential Energy Credit.

DISCUSSION: There is a tax credit of up to $500 for qualified residential energy property. However, the credit only applies to the taxpayer's principal residence within the U.S. Ralph's home in Palm Beach is a vacation home and therefore not his principal residence. The calculation of the credit amount allowed is irrelevant.

Answer (B) is incorrect. This amount is the lifetime limit that would apply if the home qualified. The home is a vacation home and not Ralph's principal residence. Therefore, the credit is disallowed. Answer (C) is incorrect. The home is a vacation home and not Ralph's principal residence; therefore, the credit is disallowed. Even if the home qualified, the lifetime credit is limited to $500. A credit percentage of 30 only applied in 2009 and 2010. Answer (D) is incorrect. The home is a vacation home and not Ralph's principal residence. Therefore, the credit is disallowed. Even if the home qualified, the lifetime credit is limited to $500.

17. Mr. and Mrs. Robinson are both over age 65 and file a joint return. During the current year, they received $4,000 in nontaxable benefits from Social Security. This was their only nontaxable income. Their adjusted gross income was $12,000. How much can they claim as tentative credit for the elderly?

A. $0

B. $225

C. $375

D. $525

Answer (C) is correct.

REQUIRED: The amount the taxpayers may claim as a credit for the elderly.

DISCUSSION: In the case of an individual who has attained age 65 before the close of the taxable year, Sec. 22(a) allows a credit equal to 15% of the individual's Sec. 22 amount. On a joint return when both spouses are eligible for the credit, the Sec. 22 amount is equal to an initial amount of $7,500 reduced by any amounts received as Social Security benefits or otherwise excluded from gross income [Sec. 22(c)(3)]. The Sec. 22 amount is also reduced by one-half of the excess of adjusted gross income over $10,000 (in the case of a joint return), which is $1,000 [($12,000 – $10,000) × 50%] for the Robinsons. (See Publication 524.)

Initial Sec. 22 amount	$ 7,500
Less Social Security	(4,000)
Less AGI limitation	(1,000)
Sec. 22 amount	$ 2,500
	× .15
Robinsons' tentative credit for the elderly	$ 375

Authors' Note: The actual credit received would be $0 because there would be no taxable income after subtracting the basic standard deduction, the additional standard deduction, and the personal exemptions.

Answer (A) is incorrect. A credit is available to qualified elderly people. Answer (B) is incorrect. The AGI limitation is only 50% of the excess of AGI over $10,000. Answer (D) is incorrect. The initial Sec. 22 amount must be reduced by an AGI limitation.

18. Mr. and Mrs. Greg adopted a child in the current year. During the year, the Gregs' qualified adoption expenses were $19,000, and they had an AGI of $232,000. What is the Gregs' Adoption Credit for 2012?

A. $0

B. $6,325

C. $12,650

D. $19,000

Answer (A) is correct.

REQUIRED: The amount of Adoption Credit allowed for 2012.

DISCUSSION: Taxpayers may claim a credit of up to $12,650 for 2012 (Sec. 23). However, the credit is fully phased out when a taxpayer's AGI exceeds $229,710. Therefore, the Gregs cannot take any of the Adoption Credit.

19. Liz incurred qualified adoption expenses of $14,000 in 2012. Liz's AGI for 2012 was $60,000. What is the amount of the credit Liz can take in 2012 for the adoption expenses she incurred?

A. $0

B. $7,000

C. $12,650

D. $14,000

Answer (C) is correct.

REQUIRED: The amount of the credit for adoption expenses.

DISCUSSION: A credit is allowed for qualified adoption expenses incurred after 1996 (Sec. 23). The maximum credit for 2012 is $12,650 per child (Publication 17). Liz's AGI is well below the threshold.

Answer (A) is incorrect. A credit is allowed for qualified adoption expenses incurred after 1996 (Sec. 23), and it is not fully eliminated until the taxpayer's AGI reaches $229,710 (Publication 17). Answer (B) is incorrect. The maximum credit is $12,650 for a child. Answer (D) is incorrect. The maximum credit is $12,650 for a child.

20. A taxpayer paid $7,000 of interest in 2012 on the mortgage given upon acquiring her first home. The taxpayer received a MCC, which specifies a 30% credit rate. How much of a credit is the taxpayer entitled to?

A. $2,000

B. $2,100

C. $5,000

D. $7,000

Answer (A) is correct.

REQUIRED: The calculation of Residential Mortgage Interest Credit and applicable limits.

DISCUSSION: Under Sec. 25, MCCs are issued to qualified individuals when privately financing their first purchase of a principal residence (see Publication 530). If the specified rate exceeds 20%, the credit is limited to $2,000.

Answer (B) is incorrect. This amount ignores the $2,000 limit when the rate exceeds 20%. Answer (C) is incorrect. This amount is the maximum interest deduction allowed when the credit is taken. Answer (D) is incorrect. The credit is the applicable percentage of the interest paid, subject to a limit when the rate exceeds 20%.

21. The Minimum Tax Credit (MTC) allocable for the current year is limited to

A. Current-year gross regular tax (reduced by certain credits) minus current-year tentative minimum tax.

B. Current-year gross regular tax (without regard to any credits) minus current-year tentative minimum tax.

C. Current-year gross regular tax (reduced by certain credits) plus current-year tentative minimum tax.

D. Current-year gross regular tax (reduced by certain credits) minus previous-year tentative minimum tax.

Answer (A) is correct.

REQUIRED: The true statement regarding the Minimum Tax Credit.

DISCUSSION: The MTC allowable is limited to current-year gross regular tax (reduced by certain credits) minus current-year tentative minimum tax.

Answer (B) is incorrect. The current-year gross regular tax is reduced by certain credits. Answer (C) is incorrect. Current-year tentative minimum tax is subtracted from current-year gross regular tax. Answer (D) is incorrect. Current-year, not previous-year, tentative minimum tax is subtracted from current-year gross regular tax.

22. Michael had to pay $4,000 alternative minimum tax last year. This year, his regular income tax is $60,000 and alternative minimum tax on his income is $57,000, so he will pay only regular income tax. How much credit for prior year minimum tax can he take this year?

A. $0

B. $4,000

C. $2,000

D. $3,000

Answer (D) is correct.

REQUIRED: The allowable credit for prior-year minimum tax payment.

DISCUSSION: A credit is allowed for the amount of adjusted net minimum tax for all tax years reduced by the Minimum Tax Credit for all prior tax years (Sec. 53). The credit may be carried forward indefinitely as a credit against regular tax liability. The credit is limited to the extent that the regular tax liability reduced by other nonrefundable credits exceeds the tentative minimum tax for the year. Therefore, his credit is $3,000.

Answer (A) is incorrect. A credit is available equal to the prior alternative minimum tax paid in the prior year. The credit is subject to a limitation. Answer (B) is incorrect. The credit is limited to the extent that the regular tax liability exceeds the tentative minimum tax for the year. Answer (C) is incorrect. A credit is available equal to the prior alternative minimum tax paid in the prior year. The credit is subject to a limitation.

23. In Year 1, Ron and Cindy had an alternative minimum tax (AMT) liability of $19,000. This was the first tax year in which they had ever paid the AMT. They recomputed the AMT amount using only exclusion preferences and adjustments; the recomputation resulted in a $8,500 AMT liability. In Year 2, Ron and Cindy had a regular tax liability of $45,000. Their tentative minimum tax liability was $42,000. What is the amount of Ron and Cindy's Minimum Tax Credit (MTC) carryover to Year 2? What is the amount of the carryover that can be used in Year 2?

	Carryover to Year 2	Carryover Used
A.	$19,000	$3,000
B.	$19,000	$8,500
C.	$10,500	$3,000
D.	$8,500	$8,500

Answer (C) is correct.

REQUIRED: The taxpayer's MTC carryover for Year 1 and the amount that can be used in Year 2.

DISCUSSION: For the first tax year that the AMT is owed, the MTC is the portion of the AMT attributable to deferral preferences or adjustments. Exclusion preferences or adjustments are disallowed itemized deductions or standard deduction, personal exemptions, excess percentage depletion, tax-exempt interest from private activity bonds (not issued in 2009 or 2010), and excluded gain from the sale of small business stock (excluding gains between September 27, 2010, and December 31, 2011). In Year 1, the deferral preferences and adjustments resulted in a $10,500 MTC ($19,000 – $8,500). This credit can be carried over to Year 2 and used to the extent that the regular tax liability exceeds the tentative minimum tax. This amount is $3,000 ($45,000 – $42,000).

24. Which of the following is not a test to determine if a child is a qualifying child for the Earned Income Credit (EIC)?

A. Relationship.

B. Age.

C. Residency.

D. Support.

Answer (D) is correct.

REQUIRED: The item that is not a test to determine if a child qualifies under the EIC.

DISCUSSION: In order for a child to be a qualifying child, three tests must be met: (1) The child must be related by birth or adoption or be an eligible foster child or stepchild; (2) the taxpayer must provide the child's principal place of abode for more than half of the year; and (3) the child must be under age 19 at the close of the tax year, be permanently disabled, or be a student under the age of 24.

25. The Earned Income Credit is available to

A. Persons with a qualifying child.

B. Persons without a qualifying child.

C. Persons who are age 40.

D. All of the answers are correct.

Answer (D) is correct.

REQUIRED: The individuals who qualify for the Earned Income Credit.

DISCUSSION: A taxpayer can be eligible for the Earned Income Credit by having a qualifying child or meeting three qualifications: (1) The individual must have his/her principal place of abode in the United States for more than one-half of the taxable year, (2) the individual must be at least 25 years old and not more than 64 years old at the end of the taxable year, and (3) the individual cannot be claimed as a dependent of another taxpayer for any tax year beginning in the year the credit is being claimed.

26. For the current year, for purposes of the Earned Income Credit, which of the following amounts qualifies as earned income?

A. Earnings from self-employment.

B. Excluded combat-zone pay.

C. Unemployment compensation.

D. Value of meals or lodging provided by an employer for the convenience of the employer.

Answer (A) is correct.

REQUIRED: The item that qualifies as earned income.

DISCUSSION: Earned income includes all wages, salaries, tips, and other employee compensation (including union strike benefits), plus the amount of the taxpayer's net earnings from self-employment. For purposes of the Earned Income Credit, earned income does not include nontaxable compensation such as the basic quarters and subsistence allowances for the military, parsonage allowances, the value of meals and lodging furnished for the convenience of the employer, and excludable employer-provided dependent care benefits. Earned income does not include interest and dividends, welfare benefits, veterans' benefits, pensions or annuities, alimony, Social Security benefits, workers' compensation, unemployment compensation, and taxable scholarships or fellowships.

27. Which of the following is earned income for Earned Income Credit purposes?

A. Unemployment compensation.

B. Alimony.

C. The wages of a minister who has an exemption from self-employment tax.

D. The wages of an inmate working in the prison laundry.

Answer (C) is correct.

REQUIRED: The qualifications for earned income.

DISCUSSION: The Earned Income Credit is based on all earned income, which includes wages, salaries, tips, other employee compensation, and net earnings from self employment. Earned income does not include interest and dividends, welfare benefits, veteran's benefits, pensions or annuities, alimony, Social Security benefits, workers' compensation, unemployment compensation, taxable scholarships or fellowships that are not reported on the taxpayer's W-2 form, amounts received for services performed by prison inmates while in prison, amounts that are subject to Code Sec. 871(a), or payments received from work activities if sufficient private sector employment is not available and from community service programs.

28. Rose, a single parent, has two children ages 10 and 13. She earned $25,000 in 2012, and her investments earned $2,000 interest income. Taxable income on her 2012 return was $18,000. After applying her withholding, Rose's tax due was $700. Using the following Earned Income Credit information, determine Rose's balance due/overpayment for 2012:

- Credit figured using $27,000 adjusted gross income = $3,149
- Credit figured using $25,000 earned income = $3,570
- Credit figured using $18,000 taxable income = $5,044

A. $2,449 overpayment (refund).

B. $4,434 overpayment (refund).

C. $2,870 overpayment (refund).

D. $0, carryover $3,185 credit to next year.

Answer (A) is correct.

REQUIRED: The amount of Earned Income Credit to be reported.

DISCUSSION: The initial Earned Income Credit for a taxpayer with two children is determined by multiplying the earned income by 40% with a maximum credit of $5,236. The Earned Income Credit is reduced by any adjusted gross income exceeding $17,090. Thus, the $27,000 adjusted gross income will be used to compute the credit. Since tax before the credit is $700, Rose would receive a refund of $2,449 ($3,149 – $700).

Answer (B) is incorrect. The $18,000 taxable income is not to be used to figure the Earned Income Credit. Answer (C) is incorrect. The $25,000 earned income is not to be used to figure the Earned Income Credit. Answer (D) is incorrect. If a credit is available, it is to be taken/refunded in the current year.

6.2 Other Taxes

29. In 2011, Ted and Alice had an alternative minimum tax liability of $19,000. This is the first tax year in which they ever paid the alternative minimum tax. They recomputed the alternative minimum tax using only exclusion preferences and adjustments. This resulted in an $8,500 alternative minimum tax liability. In 2012, Ted and Alice have a regular tax liability of $45,000. Their tentative minimum tax liability is $42,000. What is the Minimum Tax Credit carryover to 2013?

A. $19,000

B. $16,000

C. $7,500

D. $0

Answer (C) is correct.

REQUIRED: The taxpayer's MTC carryover.

DISCUSSION: For the first tax year that the AMT is owed, the MTC is the portion of the AMT attributable to deferral preferences or adjustments. Exclusion preferences or adjustments are disallowed itemized deductions or standard deduction, personal exemptions, excess percentage depletion, tax-exempt interest from private activity bonds not issued in 2009 or 2010, and excluded gain from the sale of small business stock except for gains between September 27, 2010, and December 31, 2013. In 2011, the deferral preferences and adjustments result in a $10,500 MTC ($19,000 – $8,500). This credit can be carried over to 2012 and used to the extent that the regular tax liability exceeds the tentative minimum tax. This amount is $3,000 ($45,000 – $42,000). Therefore, the $10,500 MTC offsets the $3,000 excess, and a $7,500 MTC is carried forward to 2013 (Publication 17).

Answer (A) is incorrect. This amount is the AMT liability before recomputation. Answer (B) is incorrect. Only $7,500 is carried forward to 2013. Answer (D) is incorrect. There is a carryforward to 2013.

30. Alternative minimum tax for individuals requires certain adjustments and preferences. Which of the following is a preference or adjustment item for noncorporate taxpayers?

A. Personal exemptions.

B. Incentive stock options.

C. Tax-exempt interest on certain private activity bonds (not issued in 2009 or 2010).

D. All of the answers are correct.

Answer (D) is correct.

REQUIRED: The item that is a preference or adjustment item for noncorporate taxpayers.

DISCUSSION: Several adjustments affect only noncorporate taxpayers. Personal exemptions, tax-exempt interest on private activity bonds (not issued in 2009 or 2010), which is included in investment income, and incentive stock options are examples of these adjustments (Publication 17).

Answer (A) is incorrect. Incentive stock options and tax-exempt interest on certain private activity bonds (not issued in 2009 or 2010) are also preference or adjustment items for noncorporate taxpayers when determining the alternative minimum tax. Answer (B) is incorrect. Personal exemptions and tax-exempt interest on certain private activity bonds (not issued in 2009 or 2010) are also preference or adjustment items for noncorporate taxpayers when determining the alternative minimum tax. Answer (C) is incorrect. Personal exemptions and incentive stock options are also preference or adjustment items for noncorporate taxpayers when determining the alternative minimum tax.

31. In computing the alternative minimum tax for individuals, which one of the following is not an adjustment or tax preference for alternative minimum tax purposes?

A. Personal exemptions.

B. Tax-exempt interest on certain private activity bonds (not issued in 2009 or 2010).

C. Standard deduction.

D. Contributions to an Individual Retirement Arrangement (IRA).

Answer (D) is correct.

REQUIRED: The item that is not an adjustment or a tax preference for arriving at alternative minimum taxable income.

DISCUSSION: Taxable income must be adjusted to arrive at alternative minimum taxable income (AMTI). The adjustments are described in Secs. 56 and 58, with tax preferences in Sec. 57. The adjustments with respect to itemized deductions of an individual are contained in Sec. 56(b)(1). Contributions to an IRA have no effect on AMTI (Publication 17).

Answer (A) is incorrect. Personal exemptions are not allowed as deductions in arriving at alternative minimum taxable income under Sec. 56(b) and, therefore, must be added back as adjustments to taxable income for arriving at alternative minimum taxable income. Answer (B) is incorrect. It is a tax preference item. Answer (C) is incorrect. The standard deduction is not allowed as a deduction in arriving at alternative minimum taxable income under Sec. 56(b) and therefore must be added back as adjustments to taxable income for arriving at alternative minimum taxable income.

32. When determining his alternative minimum tax, Leslie had the following adjustments and preference items:

Personal exemption	$3,800
Itemized deduction for state taxes	2,800
Refund of prior-year state income tax	300
Cash contributions	2,250
Capital gain	700
Depletion in excess of adjusted basis	400

What are the amounts of tax preference items and adjustments to taxable income for alternative minimum tax purposes on Leslie's 2012 tax return?

	Preference	Adjustments
A.	$400	$6,300
B.	$1,000	$300
C.	$1,700	$6,600
D.	$2,250	$7,000

Answer (A) is correct.

REQUIRED: The amounts of tax preference items and adjustments.

DISCUSSION: The depletion is a tax preference item that must be added back for alternative minimum tax purposes. The adjustments, on the other hand, include the personal exemption and itemized deduction. The refund of prior-year state income tax must be subtracted from the adjustment total. Thus, the tax preference items total $400, and the adjustments equal $6,300.

33. Rev. Janice Burton is a full-time minister at the Downtown Missionary Church. The church allows her to use the parsonage that has an annual fair rental value of $4,800. The church pays an annual salary of $13,200, of which $1,200 is designated for utility costs. Her utility costs during the year were $1,000. What is Rev. Burton's income for self-employment tax purposes?

A. $18,000

B. $13,200

C. $12,200

D. $13,400

Answer (A) is correct.

REQUIRED: The computation of a minister's income for self-employment tax purposes.

DISCUSSION: In the case of a minister, net earnings from self-employment in connection with the performance of religious duties are computed without regard to Sec. 107 (exclusion of rental value of home or parsonage) (Publication 517). Therefore, the $13,200 annual salary plus the $4,800 rental value is used to determine Rev. Burton's self-employment taxes.

Answer (B) is incorrect. The annual salary and rental value of the parsonage are combined to determine the self-employment tax. Answer (C) is incorrect. The rental value of the parsonage is included in income for self-employment tax purposes. Answer (D) is incorrect. The rental value of the parsonage and the utility costs are included in income for self-employment tax purposes.

6.3 Payments

34. Violet made no estimated tax payments for 2012 because she thought she had enough tax withheld from her wages. In January 2013, she realized that her withholding was $2,000 less than the amount needed to avoid a penalty for the underpayment of estimated tax so she made an estimated tax payment of $2,500 on January 10. Violet filed her 2012 return on March 1, 2013, showing a refund due her of $100. Which of the following statements is not true regarding the estimated tax penalty?

A. Violet will not owe a penalty for the quarter ending December 31, 2012, because she made sufficient payment before January 15, 2013.

B. Violet will not owe a penalty for any quarter because her total payments exceed her tax liability.

C. Violet could owe a penalty for one or all of the first three quarters even though she is due a refund for the year.

D. If Violet owes a penalty for any quarter, the underpayment will be computed from the date the amount was due to the date the payment is made.

Answer (B) is correct.

REQUIRED: The false statement regarding the estimated tax penalty.

DISCUSSION: A penalty may be imposed if, by the quarterly payment date, the total of estimated tax payments and income tax withheld is less than 25% of the required minimum payment for the year. The penalty is determined each quarter. In addition, it is calculated by adding 3 percentage points to the federal short-term rate and multiplying this percent by the amount of the underpayment. Finally, the penalty is not allowed as an interest deduction. Although Violet paid her tax liability by the due date for the last quarter, she may still be assessed a penalty for not making estimated tax payments in the first three quarters of the year. (See Publication 505.)

Answer (A) is incorrect. Violet will not owe a penalty on the last quarter because she paid the balance of her estimated tax liability by the due date of the last quarter. Answer (C) is incorrect. Violet could owe a penalty on one or all of the first three quarters of the year because she did not make quarterly payments of estimated tax. Answer (D) is incorrect. The penalties on estimated tax are computed as of the due date for the quarter in which the estimated tax was due and will be assessed for the period between that due date and the date in which the payment was made.

35. Marge Godfrey sold her investment property March 30, 2012, at a gain of $50,000. Marge expects to owe $10,000 in additional income taxes on this sale. She had a tax liability of $900 for 2011 and will have no withholding for 2012. Marge's first estimated tax payment is due on what date?

A. April 30, 2012.

B. April 15, 2012.

C. January 31, 2013.

D. June 15, 2012.

Answer (B) is correct.

REQUIRED: The date the first payment of estimated tax is due.

DISCUSSION: Marge must make estimated payments because she had a tax liability in the previous year. Estimated tax payments are not required until the first period in which there is income (IRS Pub. 505). If income subject to estimated tax occurs in the first payment period, then the first payment is due by the due date of the first payment period, April 15, 2012. Marge has estimated income in the first period.

Answer (A) is incorrect. Estimated tax is due on April 15 for income made in the first payment period. Answer (C) is incorrect. Estimated tax is due on April 15 for income made in the first payment period. Answer (D) is incorrect. Marge had income in the first payment period.

36. All of the following individuals file their income tax returns as single. Which one is required to make estimated tax payments for 2012?

A. Ms. Kirkland, who had no tax liability for 2011, expects to owe $2,500 self-employment tax for 2012 (she has no withholding tax or credits).

B. Mr. Brady, who had a $2,000 tax liability for 2011, expects a $2,100 tax liability for 2012 and withholding of $1,900.

C. Ms. Evans, who had no tax liability for 2011, expects a tax liability of $4,900 for 2012, with $3,500 withholding.

D. Mr. Jones, who had a 2011 tax liability of $9,500, expects a tax liability of $12,400 for 2012, with $8,500 withholding.

Answer (D) is correct.

REQUIRED: The individual who must make estimated tax payments.

DISCUSSION: In general, individuals must make estimated tax payments or be subject to a penalty (Sec. 6654). Amounts withheld from wages are treated as estimated tax payments. The annual estimated payment that must be made is equal to the lesser of (1) 90% of the tax for the current year or (2) 100% of the tax for the prior year (Publication 17). Also, no penalty will apply to an individual whose tax for the year, after credit for withheld tax, is less than $1,000. Mr. Jones does not meet either the 90% or the 100% test, and his tax after credit for withholding is not less than $1,000. Therefore, he will have to make estimated tax payments.

Answer (A) is incorrect. Ms. Kirkland had no tax liability in the prior year. Answer (B) is incorrect. The difference between Mr. Brady's withholding and his tax liability is less than $1,000. Answer (C) is incorrect. Ms. Evans had no tax liability in the prior year.

37. For 2012, Mike and Denise, calendar-year taxpayers, had gross income comprised of the following:

Wages received as a farm employee	$26,000
Gross income from Schedule F dairy operations	40,000
Distributable share of an S corporation's gross income from farming	12,000
Long-term capital gains from stock sales	18,000
Short-term capital losses from stock sales	(21,000)

They have made no estimated tax payments as of December 31, 2012, and the withholding from wages is not sufficient to relieve them from the estimated tax penalty. Which of the following statements is true if they make an estimated tax payment by January 15, 2013?

A. They will avoid the estimated tax penalty since they are qualified farmers.

B. They will avoid the estimated tax penalty since all of their earned income is from farming activities.

C. They will not avoid the estimated tax penalty since their farm income does not comprise two-thirds of their gross income.

D. They can avoid the estimated tax penalty only by filing their return by March 1, 2013, and paying all the tax due.

Answer (C) is correct.

REQUIRED: The true statement regarding estimated tax payments.

DISCUSSION: Sec. 6654(i) allows farmers or fishermen who expect to receive at least two-thirds of their gross income from farming or fishing activities, or who received at least two-thirds of their gross income for the prior tax year from farming or fishing, to pay estimated tax for the year in one installment. If Mike and Denise had received two-thirds of their gross income from farming, they could have waited until 1/15/13 to make their 2012 estimated tax payment without penalty. They would have been required to pay the entire estimated tax for the year at that time. Mike and Denise's gross income for the year was $96,000 ($26,000 + $40,000 + $12,000 + $18,000). Losses are not included in the calculation of gross income. Their gross income from farming was $52,000 ($40,000 Schedule F + $12,000 S corp.). Wages received as a farm employee or capital gains are not included in farm income. Therefore, 54% of their gross income came from farming. At least 67% of their gross income must come from farming activities in order to avoid the penalty. (See Publication 505.)

Answer (A) is incorrect. Two-thirds of their gross income must come from farming for them to qualify as farmers. Answer (B) is incorrect. Wages, distributive share of an S corporation, and capital gains are not included as farm income. Answer (D) is incorrect. They cannot avoid the estimated tax penalty.

38. An employee who has had Social Security tax withheld in an amount greater than the maximum for a particular year may claim

A. Such excess as either a credit or an itemized deduction, at the election of the employee, if that excess resulted from correct withholding by two or more employers.

B. Reimbursement of such excess from his/her employers if that excess resulted from correct withholding by two or more employers.

C. The excess as a credit against income tax, if that excess resulted from correct withholding by two or more employers.

D. The excess as a credit against income tax, if that excess was withheld by one employer.

Answer (C) is correct.

REQUIRED: The proper treatment when a taxpayer overpays the Social Security tax.

DISCUSSION: When an employee overpays the Social Security tax, proper adjustments must be made. If the overpayment cannot be adjusted, the amount must be refunded. If the overpayment resulted from correct withholding by two or more employers, the extra Social Security tax may be used to reduce income taxes.

Answer (A) is incorrect. The overpayment is not available as a deduction. Answer (B) is incorrect. It is not the employer's responsibility to refund the tax (the employer turned it over to the government). Answer (D) is incorrect. The extra Social Security tax may be used to reduce income taxes only when an employee has worked for two or more employers.

39. Ms. B filed her Year 1 Form 1040 on April 15, Year 2, but did not pay her tax liability of $3,000. On June 15, Year 3, she paid the tax in full. In Year 4, Ms. B discovered additional deductions for Year 1 that will result in a refund of $1,000. To receive her refund, Ms. B must file an amended income tax return by (assuming no relevant days are Saturdays, Sundays, or holidays)

A. April 15, Year 5.

B. June 15, Year 5.

C. April 15, Year 6.

D. June 15, Year 6.

Answer (B) is correct.

REQUIRED: The date for filing a refund claim for taxes paid after the related return was filed.

DISCUSSION: Sec. 6511(b) states that a claim for a refund must be filed within the time limits established in the statute of limitations on refunds. Sec. 6511(a) provides that refunds may be made 3 years from the time the return was filed or 2 years from the time the tax was paid, whichever is later (Publication 17). Here, 2 years from the time the tax was paid is the later date, so Ms. B must file a claim before June 15, Year 5.

STUDY UNIT SEVEN
BASIS

(5 pages of outline)

The concept of basis is important in federal income taxation. Generally, basis is the measurement of a taxpayer's investment in property, which the taxpayer is entitled to have returned without tax consequences. The property basis is generally used in determining the gain or loss associated with the property.

7.1 COST BASIS

When a taxpayer acquires property, his/her basis in the property is initially cost, substituted, transferred, exchanged, or converted basis.

1. **Cost basis** is the sum of capitalized acquisition costs.
2. **Substituted basis** is computed by reference to basis in other property.
3. **Transferred basis** is computed by reference to basis in the same property in the hands of another.
4. **Exchanged basis** is computed by reference to basis in other property previously held by the person.
5. **Converted basis** is when personal-use property is converted to business use; the basis of the property is the lower of its basis or the FMV on the date of conversion.

Capitalized Acquisition Costs

6. Initial basis in purchased property is the cost of acquiring it. Only capital costs are included, i.e., those for acquisition, title acquisition, and major improvements.

Common Capitalized Costs (for Sec. 1012)

Purchase Price (Stated)

Note: Not unstated interest

Closing Costs

Brokerage commissions
Prepurchase taxes
Sales tax on purchase
Title transfer taxes
Title insurance
Recording fees
Attorney fees
Document review, preparation

Miscellaneous Costs

Appraisal fees
Freight
Installation
Testing

Major Improvements

New roof
New gutters
Extending water line to property
Demolition costs and losses

Expenses Not Properly Chargeable to a Capital Account

a. Costs of maintaining and operating property are not added to basis, e.g., interest on credit related to the property, insurance (e.g., casualty), ordinary maintenance or repairs (e.g., painting).

Uniform Capitalization Rules

7. Costs for construction of real or tangible personal property to be used in trade or business are capitalized.
   a. All costs necessary to prepare the property for its intended use are capitalized, including both direct and most allocable indirect costs, e.g., for permits, materials, equipment rent, compensation for services (minus any work opportunity credit), and architect fees.
   b. Construction period interest and taxes must be capitalized as part of building cost.
8. Cost basis includes the FMV of property given up. If it is not determinable with reasonable certainty, use FMV of property received.
   a. Capital acquisition expenditures may be made by cash, by cash equivalent, in property, with liability, or by services.
   b. A rebate to the purchaser is treated as a reduction of the purchase price. It is not included in basis or in gross income.

Liabilities

9. Acquisition basis is
   a. Increased for notes to the seller (minus unstated interest)
   b. Increased for liabilities to which the acquired property is subject
10. The FMV of property received in exchange for services is income (compensation) to the provider when it is not subject to a substantial risk of forfeiture and not restricted as to transfer. The property acquired has a tax cost basis equal to the FMV of the property.
    a. Sale of restricted stock to an employee is treated as gross income (bonus compensation) to the extent any price paid is less than the stock's FMV.
       1) While restricted, the basis is any price paid other than by services.
       2) Upon lapse of the restriction, the recipient has ordinary gross income of the spread between FMV on that date and any amounts otherwise paid.
       3) Basis is increased by that same amount.
       4) The transferee may elect to include the FMV minus the cost spread in gross income when the stock is purchased.
          a) Basis includes tax cost, but no subsequent deduction (recovery of tax cost) is allowed if the stock is forfeited by operation of the restriction.

Lump Sum Purchase

11. When more than one asset is purchased for a lump sum, the basis of each is computed by apportioning the total cost based on the relative FMV of each asset.

$$\text{Allocable cost (basis)} = \frac{\text{FMV of asset}}{\text{FMV of all assets purchased}} \times \text{Lump sum purchase price}$$

    a. Alternatively, the transferor and transferee may agree in writing as to the allocation of consideration or the FMV of any assets.
       1) The agreement is binding on the parties unless the IRS deems it improper.
          a) If improper, the residual method may be applied.

b. The residual method, particularly relevant to goodwill and going concern value when a transferor/transferee agreement is not applicable, allocates purchase price for both transferor and transferee to asset categories up to FMV in the following order:

1) Cash and cash equivalents
2) Near-cash items, such as CDs, U.S. government securities, foreign currency, and other marketable securities
3) Accounts receivable and other debt instruments, as well as other assets marked to market at least annually
   a) Note Reg. 1.338-6(b)(2)(iii) created exceptions applicable to certain specific debt instruments.
4) Property held primarily for sale to customers in the ordinary course of a trade or business or stocks that are part of dealer inventory
5) All other assets, excluding Sec. 197 intangibles
6) Sec. 197 intangibles, such as patents and covenants not to compete except goodwill and going concern value
7) Goodwill and going-concern value

NOTE: When the purchase price is lower than the aggregate FMV of the assets other than goodwill/going-concern value, the price is allocated first to the face amount of cash and then to assets listed in 2) through 6) according to relative FMVs.

Sale of Stock

12. To compute gain realized on the sale of stock, specific identification of the stock sold is used if possible. Otherwise, FIFO is assumed.

Demolition

13. Costs and losses associated with demolishing a structure are allocated to the land. The costs include the remaining basis (not FMV) of the structure and demolition costs.

Stop and review! You have completed the outline for this subunit. Study questions 1 through 10 beginning on page 184.

7.2 PROPERTY RECEIVED BY GIFT

The donee's basis in property acquired by gift is the donor's basis, increased for any gift tax paid attributable to appreciation. The donor's basis is increased by

$$\text{Gift tax paid} \times \left[\frac{\text{FMV (at time of gift)} - \text{Donor's basis}}{\text{FMV (at time of gift)} - \text{Annual exclusion}}\right]$$

NOTE: The 2012 annual exclusion for gift tax is $13,000.

1. If the FMV on the date of the gift is less than the donor's basis, the donee has a dual basis for the property.
   a. Loss basis. The FMV at the date of the gift is used if the property is later transferred at a loss.
   b. Gain basis. The donor's basis is used if the property is later transferred at a gain.
   c. If the property is later transferred for more than FMV at the date of the gift but for less than the donor's basis at the date of the gift, no gain/loss is recognized.

Depreciable Basis

2. If gift property is immediately used as business property, the basis for depreciation is the donor's AB.

3. If gift property is later converted from personal to business use, the AB is the lower of the AB or the FMV on the date of conversion.

Stop and review! You have completed the outline for this subunit. Study questions 11 through 23 beginning on page 187.

7.3 PROPERTY RECEIVED FOR SERVICES

All compensation for personal services is gross income. The form of payment is irrelevant. If property is received for services, gross income is the fair market value of the property received minus any cash or other property given.

1. Basis in property received is the amount included in income plus any cash or other property given.
2. Gross income of an employee includes any amount paid by an employer for a liability (including taxes) or an expense of the employee.

Stop and review! You have completed the outline for this subunit. Study questions 24 through 26 on page 191.

7.4 INHERITED PROPERTY

Basis is the FMV on the date of death.

1. If the executor elects the alternate valuation date, the basis of the assets is the FMV 6 months after the decedent's death.
   a. If the assets are sold or distributed within the first 6 months after death, basis equals FMV on the sale or distribution date.
2. The FMV basis rule also applies to the following property:
   a. One-half of community property interests
   b. Property acquired by form of ownership, e.g., right of survivorship, except if consideration was paid to acquire the property from a nonspouse
   c. Property received prior to death without full and adequate consideration (if a life estate was retained in it) or subject to a right of revocation
      1) Reduce basis by depreciation deductions allowed the donee.

   NOTE: The FMV rule does not apply to (1) income in respect of a decedent or (2) appreciated property given to the decedent within 1 year of death (use adjusted basis in the property immediately prior to death).

   A shareholder must report his/her ratable share of any income that is income in respect to a decedent as if (s)he had received it directly from the decedent.

EXAMPLE

The shareholder's basis in the inherited S corporation stock is its FMV on the date of death minus the ratable share of any S corporation income attributable to those shares.

3. The estate of individuals dying in 2010 can elect not to have the estate tax apply. If that election is made, the estate must use the lower of carryover basis or FMV as the basis of each asset. If the estate chooses to be subject to the estate tax, then the regular rules discussed above apply.

Stop and review! You have completed the outline for this subunit. Study questions 27 through 32 beginning on page 192.

7.5 STOCK DIVIDENDS

A corporation recognizes no gain or loss on transactions involving its own stock.

1. A proportionate distribution of stock issued by the corporation is generally not gross income to the shareholders.
   a. A shareholder allocates the aggregate adjusted basis (AB) in the old stock to the old and new stock in proportion to the FMV of the old and new stock.
      1) Basis is apportioned by relative FMV to different classes of stock if applicable.
   b. The holding period of the distributed stock includes that of the old stock.
   c. E&P are not altered for a tax-free stock dividend.

Stock Rights

2. A distribution of stock rights is treated as a distribution of the stock.
   a. Basis is allocated based on the FMV of the rights.
      1) Basis in the stock rights is zero if their aggregate FMV is less than 15% of the FMV of the stock on which they were distributed, unless the shareholder elects to allocate.
   b. Basis in the stock, if the right is exercised, is any basis allocated to the right plus the exercise price.
   c. Holding period of the stock begins on the exercise date.
   d. No deduction is allowed for basis allocated to stock rights that lapse.
      1) Basis otherwise allocated remains in the underlying stock.

Taxable Stock Distribution

3. Distributions of stock, described in a. through i. below, are subject to tax. The amount of a distribution subject to tax is the FMV of distributed stock or stock rights.
   a. If a shareholder has an option to choose between a distribution of stock or a distribution of other property, the amount of the distribution is the greater of the FMV of stock or the cash or FMV of other property.
   b. Some shareholders receive property and other shareholders receive an increase in their proportionate interests.
   c. Some common shareholders receive common stock; others receive preferred.
   d. Distribution of preferred stock is made with respect to preferred stock.
      1) Limited change in conversion ratios, by itself, does not trigger taxability.
   e. Convertible preferred stock is distributed, and the effect is to change the shareholder's proportionate stock ownership.
   f. Constructive stock distributions change proportionate interests, resulting from a transaction such as a change in conversion ratio or redemption price.
   g. E&P are reduced by the FMV of stock and stock rights distributed.
   h. Basis in the underlying stock does not change. Basis in the new stock or stock rights is their FMV.
   i. Holding period for the new stock begins on the day after the distribution date.

Stock Split

4. A stock split is not a taxable distribution.
   a. The original basis in the stock is allocated between the old stock and the new stock based on their relative fair market values.
   b. Holding period of the new stock includes that of the old stock.

Stop and review! You have completed the outline for this subunit. Study questions 33 through 40 beginning on page 194.

QUESTIONS

7.1 Cost Basis

1. Mr. Rabbitt purchased a home for $200,000. He incurred the following additional expenses:

- $200 fire insurance premiums
- $500 mortgage insurance premiums
- $400 recording fees
- $250 owner's title insurance

Compute his basis in the property.

A. $201,350

B. $200,000

C. $200,650

D. $201,150

Answer (C) is correct.

REQUIRED: The costs included in the basis of the property.

DISCUSSION: When a taxpayer purchases property, his/her basis in the property is initially cost. Cost basis is the sum of capitalized acquisition costs. Initial basis in purchased property is the cost of acquiring it. Only capital costs are included. One component of capital costs is closing costs, which includes brokerage commissions, prepurchase taxes, sales tax on purchase, title transfer taxes, title insurance, recording fees, attorney fees, and document review preparation. Expenses not properly chargeable to a capital account include costs of maintaining and operating the property (e.g., interest on credit related to the property), insurance (e.g., casualty), ordinary maintenance or repairs (e.g., painting). Mr. Rabbitt should include the cost of the home ($200,000), the recording fees ($400), and the cost of the owner's title insurance ($250) in the basis of his new home. Thus, his basis in his new home is $200,650.

Answer (A) is incorrect. Insurance is not chargeable to the basis of the property. Answer (B) is incorrect. The basis should also include the recording fees ($400) and the cost of the owner's title insurance ($250). Answer (D) is incorrect. The mortgage insurance premiums are not chargeable to the basis of the property.

2. Ed purchased a house on an acre of land from Ruth on June 30, 2012. Prior to the purchase, Ed had been renting the house from Ruth for $500 per month. Ed paid the following amounts:

- $100,000 in loan proceeds to Ruth
- $2,000 in points to the bank
- $1,000 in real estate taxes Ruth owed to the town
- $1,000 in past-due rent to Ruth
- $1,000 in closing costs to the bank for legal, recording, title insurance, and survey fees
- $1,000 in escrowed real estate taxes to the bank

What is Ed's basis in the house and land purchased from Ruth?

A. $100,000

B. $102,000

C. $104,000

D. $106,000

Answer (B) is correct.

REQUIRED: The amount of capitalized acquisition costs.

DISCUSSION: Initial basis in purchased property is the cost of acquiring it. Only capital costs are included, i.e., those for acquisition, title acquisition, and major improvements. Ed would include the loan proceeds to Ruth; the amount paid for real estate taxes Ruth owed to the town; and closing costs to the bank for legal, recording, title insurance, and survey fees. Thus, Ed's basis in the house would equal $102,000 ($100,000 loan proceeds + $1,000 real estate taxes owed by Ruth + $1,000 closing costs).

Answer (A) is incorrect. Ed may capitalize more than just the loan proceeds to Ruth. Answer (C) is incorrect. Ed may not capitalize points paid to the bank. This is prepaid interest and is not capitalized. Rather, it is amortized over the life of the loan and can be deducted as mortgage interest expense. Answer (D) is incorrect. The points paid to the bank are not capitalized. The amounts paid for past-due rent and real estate taxes are not capitalized.

3. Mr. Ng, sole proprietor of Wu Company, purchased a machine for use in his business. Mr. Ng's costs in connection with its purchase were as follows:

Cash paid to seller	$ 4,000
Note to seller	48,000
State sales tax	2,600
Machine repairs	800
Wage expense to install machine	3,200

What is the amount of Mr. Ng's basis in the machine?

A. $54,600

B. $55,200

C. $58,600

D. $57,800

Answer (D) is correct.

REQUIRED: The basis in equipment acquired by purchase.

DISCUSSION: Under Sec. 1012, the basis of property is the cost of the property. Sales tax paid in connection with the acquisition of property is treated as a cost of the property [Sec. 164(a)]. Installation and testing charges are also included as part of the cost of the property. However, the ordinary maintenance and repair costs are expensed instead of capitalized to basis. Basis is computed as follows:

Purchase price	$52,000
Sales tax	2,600
Installation and testing charges	3,200
Basis in equipment	$57,800

Answer (A) is incorrect. Wages to install the machine are included in the cost. Answer (B) is incorrect. State sales tax is included in the cost of the machine. Answer (C) is incorrect. Ordinary repairs are expensed instead of capitalized.

4. Jeff bought land with a building on it that he planned to use in his business. His costs in connection with this purchase were as follows:

Cash down payment	$ 30,000
Mortgage on property	125,000
Survey costs	2,500
Transfer taxes	1,200
Charges for installation of gas lines	3,000
Back taxes owed by seller and paid by Jeff	1,600

What is Jeff's basis in this property?

A. $163,300

B. $162,100

C. $160,300

D. $157,800

Answer (A) is correct.

REQUIRED: The amount of basis in the purchased property.

DISCUSSION: The basis of property is its original cost (Sec. 1012), plus certain fees and expenditures. These fees and expenditures include survey costs, transfer fees, and charges for the installation of utility services. The cost of property includes debt to which the property is subject (*Crane*, 331 U.S. 1, 1947). Consequently, the basis of the property includes the cash paid, any notes to the seller, and the liability to which the property was subject. Taxes paid by a buyer that were not the legal responsibility of the buyer are also allocated to the purchase price (they are not deductible under Sec. 164). Jeff's basis in the property is

Cash	$ 30,000
Mortgage	125,000
Survey costs	2,500
Transfer taxes	1,200
Charges for installation of gas lines	3,000
Seller's taxes	1,600
	$163,300

Answer (B) is incorrect. Transfer taxes are included in basis. Answer (C) is incorrect. Charges for the installation of gas lines are included in basis. Answer (D) is incorrect. Survey costs and charges for the installation of gas lines are included in basis.

5. A taxpayer purchases rental property for $160,000. She uses $25,000 cash and obtains a mortgage for $135,000. She pays closing costs of $10,000, which includes $5,000 in points on the mortgage and $5,000 for bank fees and title costs. Her initial basis in the property is

A. $35,000

B. $170,000

C. $165,000

D. $160,000

Answer (C) is correct.

REQUIRED: The acquisition costs that must be included in the basis of the property.

DISCUSSION: When a taxpayer purchases property, his/her basis in the property is initially cost. Cost basis is the sum of capitalized acquisition costs. Initial basis in purchased property is the cost of acquiring it. Only capital costs are included, i.e., those for acquisition, title acquisition, and major improvements. Expenses not properly chargeable to a capital account include costs of maintaining and operating the property (e.g., interest on credit related to the property), insurance (e.g., casualty), ordinary maintenance or repairs (e.g., painting). Thus, the cost of the property and the bank fees and title costs should be included in the basis of the property, resulting in a basis of $165,000 ($160,000 + $5,000).

Answer (A) is incorrect. The mortgage points should not be included in the basis, while the whole purchase cost should be included. Answer (B) is incorrect. The $5,000 paid for mortgage points should not be included in the basis of the rental property. Answer (D) is incorrect. The basis should also include the $5,000 that was paid for bank fees and title costs.

6. In March 2012, Jesse traded in a 2009 van for a new 2012 model. He used both the old van and the new van 75% for business. Jesse has claimed actual expenses for the business use of the old van since 2009. He did not claim a Sec. 179 deduction of the old or new van. Jesse paid $12,800 for the old van in June 2009. Depreciation claimed on the 2009 van was $7,388, which included 6 months for 2012. Jesse paid $9,800 cash in addition to a trade-in allowance of $2,200 to acquire the new van. What is Jesse's depreciable basis in the new van?

A. $11,409

B. $9,562

C. $9,009

D. $9,000

Answer (B) is correct.

REQUIRED: The depreciable basis of property acquired in an exchange.

DISCUSSION: The basis of property is generally its cost (Sec. 1012). In the case of a taxable exchange of property, the cost is the value of the property given up plus any additional cash paid. The basis for figuring depreciation for the new van is the adjusted basis of the old van, $5,412 ($12,800 – $7,388), plus any additional cash paid, $9,800, minus the excess of the total amount of depreciation that would have been allowable before the trade if the old van had been used 100% for business. The depreciation under 100% business assumption, $9,850 ($7,388 ÷ .75), is reduced by the actual depreciation, $7,388, to obtain the excess total of $2,462. The total depreciable basis for the new van is $12,750 ($5,412 + $9,800 – $2,462). This total must be reduced by the amount of personal use (25%) to determine the new depreciable basis of $9,562.

7. A taxpayer purchases real estate rental property for $150,000. She pays $25,000 cash and obtains a mortgage for $125,000. She pays closing costs of $8,000, which includes $4,000 in points on the mortgage and $4,000 for bank fees and title costs. The basis in the property is

A. $33,000 depreciation, $125,000 amortization.

B. $158,000, depreciation only.

C. $154,000 depreciation, $4,000 amortization.

D. $150,000 depreciation, $8,000 amortization.

Answer (C) is correct.

REQUIRED: The basis of the property for the purpose of depreciation and amortization.

DISCUSSION: A taxpayer may include the costs from settlement at closing when buying real property. The following may be included in the basis:

1. Abstract fees
2. Charges for installing utility services
3. Legal fees
4. Recording fees
5. Surveys
6. Transfer fees
7. Owner's title insurance
8. Any amounts the seller owes that the taxpayer agrees to pay

However, the following are not included in settlement costs; thus, they are not a part of the depreciable basis:

1. Fire insurance premiums
2. Rent for occupancy of property before closing
3. Any bills incurred for utilities or other services related to occupancy of property before closing
4. Charges connected with getting the loan
   a. Points
   b. Mortgage insurance premiums
   c. Loan assumption fees
   d. Cost of a credit report
   e. Fees for an appraisal required by a lender
5. Fees for refinancing a mortgage

When these costs are incurred in a trade or business, 1.-3. from the list above are classified as business expenses and 4.-5. from the list above must be capitalized as a cost of obtaining the loan and be amortized over the life of the loan. (See Pub. 551.) Thus, the depreciable basis is $154,000 ($25,000 cash + $125,000 mortgage + $4,000 bank fees and title costs), and the $4,000 for points is the basis for amortization over the life of the mortgage.

Answer (A) is incorrect. The amount of $154,000 is the depreciable basis, and $4,000 should be capitalized and amortized over the life of the loan. Answer (B) is incorrect. The $4,000 for points is not part of the depreciable basis; rather, it is separated as a cost of obtaining the loan and is amortized over the life of the loan. Answer (D) is incorrect. The $4,000 for bank fees and title costs should be included in the depreciable basis; it should not be capitalized and amortized.

8. Mr. Pine purchased a small office building during the year. Included in his costs were the following:

Cash down payment	$ 50,000
Mortgage on property assumed	300,000
Title insurance	2,000
Fire insurance premiums	2,000
Attorney fees	1,000
Rent to former owner to allow Mr. Pine to occupy the office building prior to closing	4,000

What is Mr. Pine's basis in the property?

A. $359,000

B. $355,000

C. $353,000

D. $350,000

Answer (C) is correct.

REQUIRED: The basis of purchased property subject to a mortgage.

DISCUSSION: The basis of property is its original cost (Sec. 1012). The cost of property includes debt to which the property is subject (Crane, 331 U.S. 1, 1947). Further, the cost of property includes necessary expenses paid in connection with the acquisition of the property. The attorney fees and title insurance are included in the cost of the property. The fire insurance premiums and rent expense, however, are not paid in connection with the acquisition of the property. Thus, the basis is $353,000 ($50,000 cash payment + $300,000 mortgage assumed + $2,000 title insurance + $1,000 attorney fees).

Answer (A) is incorrect. The fire insurance premiums and the rent are not paid in connection with the acquisition of the property. Answer (B) is incorrect. The fire insurance premiums are not paid in connection with the acquisition of the property. Answer (D) is incorrect. Necessary expenses paid in connection with the acquisition of the property are included in basis.

9. Charles, the landlord, made several repairs and improvements to his rental house. He spent $1,500 to add carpeting in the hallway, $550 for a stove, $750 for a refrigerator, $170 to replace the broken faucet in the bathroom, and $590 to replace damaged shingles on the roof. How much of these costs must he depreciate?

A. $3,560

B. $2,800

C. $1,300

D. $3,390

Answer (B) is correct.

REQUIRED: The expenditures that require capitalization.

DISCUSSION: Generally, expenses that add to the value of, substantially prolong the useful life of, or adapt the property to a new or different use are considered capital expenditures and are not currently deductible. Thus, capital expenditures include the cost of acquiring or constructing buildings, machinery, equipment, furniture, and any similar property that has a useful life that extends substantially beyond the end of the tax year. Maintenance and repair expenditures that only keep an asset in a normal operating condition are deductible if they do not increase the value or prolong the useful life of the asset. Distinguishing between a currently deductible expenditure and a capital expenditure can be difficult because expenditures for normal maintenance and repair can cost more than a capital improvement. Normal maintenance and repair may also increase the value of an asset.

Answer (A) is incorrect. The $170 bathroom repair and $590 roof repair are not capital expenditures. Answer (C) is incorrect. The $1,500 expense of adding carpet in the hallway is considered a capital expenditure. Answer (D) is incorrect. The $590 roof repair is not a capital expenditure.

10. You incurred the following expenditures in connection with your rental property. Which of them should be capitalized?

A. New roof.

B. Install new cabinets.

C. Pave driveway.

D. All of the answers are correct.

Answer (D) is correct.

REQUIRED: The rental property expenses that should be capitalized.

DISCUSSION: Generally, expenses that add to the value of, substantially prolong the useful life of, or adapt the property to a new or different use are considered capital expenditures and are not currently deductible. Thus, capital expenditures include the cost of acquiring or constructing buildings, machinery, equipment, furniture, and any similar property that has a useful life that extends substantially beyond the end of the tax year. Maintenance and repair expenditures that only keep an asset in a normal operating condition are deductible if they do not increase the value or prolong the useful life of the asset. Installing a new roof, installing new cabinets, and paving a driveway are all major improvements that add to the value of the property.

7.2 Property Received by Gift

11. Which of the following is the depreciable basis in rental property that is placed in service immediately upon receiving it as a gift if the donor's basis was more than the fair market value of the property?

A. The fair market value on the date of the gift plus or minus any required adjustments to basis.

B. The fair market value of the property on the date of conversion to rental property.

C. The donor's basis of the property plus or minus any required adjustments to basis.

D. All of the answers are correct.

Answer (C) is correct.

REQUIRED: The basis of property that is placed in service immediately upon receiving it as a gift.

DISCUSSION: If converted from personal to business use, the depreciable basis is AB on the date of conversion (plus or minus any required adjustments to basis) if FMV is less than AB.

Answer (A) is incorrect. The adjustments are made to the donor's basis, not FMV. Answer (B) is incorrect. The property FMV is less than AB. Answer (D) is incorrect. Adjustments are made to the donor's basis, not FMV.

12. Jerry received 2 acres of land valued at $10,000 as a gift. The donor's adjusted basis was $12,000. Jerry subsequently sold the land for $20,000. For purposes of computing his gain, what is Jerry's basis in the land?

A. $12,000

B. $10,000

C. $8,000

D. $2,000

Answer (A) is correct.

REQUIRED: The basis of a gift that was sold at a gain.

DISCUSSION: If the FMV on the date of the gift is less than the donor's basis, the donee has a dual basis for the property. The FMV at the date of the gift is used if the property is later transferred at a loss. The donor's basis is used if the property is later transferred at a gain. Since the land was sold at a gain, Jerry's basis in the land is the same as the donor's basis, or $12,000.

Answer (B) is incorrect. This amount would have been Jerry's basis if the land had been sold at a loss. Answer (C) is incorrect. This amount is the gain realized on the sale of the land, not Jerry's basis in the land. Answer (D) is incorrect. This amount is the difference between the FMV on the date of the gift and the donor's basis in the land.

13. Juan received a gift of property from his uncle. When the gift was made in 2012, the property had a fair market value of $100,000 and an adjusted basis to his uncle of $40,000. Gift tax on the transfer, completely paid by Juan's uncle, was $14,500. What is Juan's basis in the property?

A. $40,000

B. $50,000

C. $60,000

D. $110,000

Answer (B) is correct.

REQUIRED: The donee's basis in property on which gift tax was paid.

DISCUSSION: The basis of property acquired by gift is generally the donor's adjusted basis [Sec. 1015(a)], increased by a gift tax paid applicable to appreciation [Sec. 1015(d)]. The gift tax applicable to appreciation is the appreciation divided by the taxable gift times the gift tax.

Donor's adjusted basis	$40,000
Gift tax*	10,000
Donee's basis	$50,000

$$*\frac{\$100{,}000 - \$40{,}000}{\$100{,}000 - \$13{,}000} \times \$14{,}500 = \$10{,}000$$

Answer (A) is incorrect. The basis must be increased by a portion of the gift tax. Answer (C) is incorrect. The basis is determined by adding the applicable gift tax to the donor's adjusted basis. Answer (D) is incorrect. The basis is determined by adding the applicable gift tax to the donor's adjusted basis.

14. Charles gave his daughter, Jane, a residential house. He had purchased the house for $250,000 in 1997. The fair market value on the date of the gift was $300,000. Charles had added a $25,000 roof the year before he gave it to Jane. Jane converts the house to a residential rental property within 1 year of the gift when the FMV was $320,000. Jane's basis in the property is

A. $300,000

B. $250,000

C. $225,000

D. $275,000

Answer (D) is correct.

REQUIRED: The basis of real property converted to residential rental property.

DISCUSSION: Real property that is converted to residential rental property has a basis that is the adjusted basis of the donor, plus the cost for any improvements or additions, minus any deductions for casualty or loss (Publication 551). The adjusted basis of the property is $275,000 ($250,000 + $25,000).

Answer (A) is incorrect. The basis of personal property converted to rental property is the lesser of the adjusted basis or the FMV on the date of the conversion. Answer (B) is incorrect. The adjusted basis is the original cost ($250,000) plus any additions or improvements that are permanent ($25,000), making the adjusted basis $275,000. Answer (C) is incorrect. The $25,000 for the roof should be added to the original cost, not subtracted, to arrive at the adjusted basis.

15. Jane acquired an acre of land as a gift. At the time of the gift, the acre had a fair market value (FMV) of $20,000. The donor's adjusted basis in the land was $15,000. No gift tax was paid on the gift. No events occurred to increase or decrease her basis in the property. Jane later sold the acre for $10,000. What is Jane's gain or loss on the sale?

A. $5,000 loss.

B. $10,000 loss.

C. $0 no gain or loss.

D. $10,000 gain.

Answer (A) is correct.

REQUIRED: The gain/loss recognized on the sale of property received by gift.

DISCUSSION: The basis of property acquired by gift is generally the donor's adjusted basis [Sec. 1015(a)]. When computing a loss, the donee assumes the lesser of the FMV at the date of transfer or the donor's adjusted basis. Therefore, Jane assumes the lesser adjusted basis of $15,000 and subtracts her $10,000 amount realized to yield a $5,000 loss.

Answer (B) is incorrect. The loss is limited by the adjusted basis of the property at the time of transfer. Answer (C) is incorrect. A loss is realized. Answer (D) is incorrect. No gain is realized on the sale.

16. In 2012, your father gave you a gift of property with a fair market value (FMV) of $75,000. His adjusted basis was $50,000. The gift tax paid was $7,440. What is your basis in the property?

A. $57,440

B. $75,000

C. $50,000

D. $53,000

Answer (D) is correct.

REQUIRED: The basis of property acquired by gift.

DISCUSSION: The basis of property acquired by gift is generally the donor's adjusted basis [Sec. 1015(a)], increased by a gift tax paid applicable to appreciation [Sec. 1015(d)]. The gift tax applicable to appreciation is the appreciation divided by the taxable gift times the gift tax.

Donor's adjusted basis	$50,000
Gift tax*	3,000
Donee's basis	$53,000

$$*\frac{\$75,000 - \$50,000}{\$75,000 - \$13,000} \times \$7,440 = \$3,000$$

Answer (A) is incorrect. Only a percentage of gift tax paid is added to adjusted basis. Answer (B) is incorrect. The FMV does not become the donee's basis. Answer (C) is incorrect. A percentage of gift tax paid is added to adjusted basis.

17. In 2012, Christian received a gift of property from his mother that had a fair market value of $50,000. Her adjusted basis was $20,000. She paid a gift tax of $6,660. What is Christian's basis in the property?

A. $50,000

B. $56,660

C. $26,660

D. $25,400

Answer (D) is correct.

REQUIRED: A taxpayer's basis in property received by gift after the donor paid gift tax.

DISCUSSION: The basis of property acquired by gift is generally the donor's adjusted basis [Sec. 1015(a)], increased by a gift tax paid applicable to appreciation [Sec. 1015(d)]. The gift tax applicable to appreciation is the appreciation divided by the taxable gift times the gift tax.

Donor's adjusted basis	$20,000
Gift tax*	5,400
Donee's basis	$25,400

$$*\frac{\$50,000 - \$20,000}{\$50,000 - \$13,000} \times \$6,660 = \$5,400$$

Answer (A) is incorrect. The donee's basis is the donor's adjusted basis plus a portion of the gift tax paid. Answer (B) is incorrect. Only a portion of the gift tax paid is added to the donor's basis to determine the donee's adjusted basis. In addition, the donor's basis is based on the donor's adjusted basis. Answer (C) is incorrect. Only a portion of the gift tax paid is added to the donor's basis to determine the donee's adjusted basis.

18. Darryl received several acres of land from his mother as a gift. At the time of the gift, the land had a fair market value of $95,000. The mother's adjusted basis in the land was $105,000. Two years later, Darryl sold the land for $90,000. No events occurred that increased or decreased Darryl's basis in the land. What was Darryl's gain or loss on the sale of the land?

A. $(15,000)

B. $(5,000)

C. $5,000

D. $10,000

Answer (B) is correct.

REQUIRED: The amount of gain or loss to be reported upon the sale of property acquired by gift.

DISCUSSION: For determining gain on the sale of property acquired by gift, the basis is the donor's adjusted basis. Darryl's sale results in no gain ($90,000 sales price – $105,000 basis). For determining loss on the sale of property acquired by gift, the basis may not exceed the fair market value of the property at the date of the gift. Hence, there is a $5,000 loss ($90,000 sales price – $95,000 basis).

Answer (A) is incorrect. The FMV at the date of the gift is used as basis for determining the amount of loss. Answer (C) is incorrect. The donor's adjusted basis is used for determining the amount of gain. Answer (D) is incorrect. The sales price over either the FMV or the donor's adjusted basis is used to determine the amount of gain or loss.

19. Donna received land as a gift from her grandfather. At the time of the gift, the land had a fair market value of $80,000 and an adjusted basis of $100,000 to Donna's grandfather. One year later, Donna sold the land for $105,000. What was her gain or loss on this transaction?

A. $5,000

B. $15,000

C. $20,000

D. No gain or loss.

Answer (A) is correct.

REQUIRED: The gain (loss) on the sale of property acquired by gift.

DISCUSSION: The FMV of the land was less than the donor's basis in the land ($100,000) at the date of transfer. Therefore, Donna (the donee) has a dual basis in the land. The grandfather's (donor's) basis is used since the property is subsequently sold at a gain. Donna's sale results in a $5,000 gain ($105,000 sales price – $100,000 basis = $5,000 gain).

Answer (B) is incorrect. The amount of gain is determined by subtracting the donor's adjusted basis from the sales price. Answer (C) is incorrect. The amount of gain is determined by subtracting the donor's adjusted basis from the sales price. Answer (D) is incorrect. The sales price exceeds Donna's basis in the land.

20. On June 1, 2012, Kirk received a gift of income-producing real estate having a donor's adjusted basis of $50,000 at the date of the gift. The fair market value of the property at the date of the gift was $40,000. Kirk sold the property for $46,000 on August 1, 2012. How much gain or loss should Kirk report for 2012?

A. No gain or loss.

B. $4,000 short-term capital loss.

C. $4,000 ordinary loss.

D. $6,000 short-term capital gain.

Answer (A) is correct.

REQUIRED: The amount of gain or loss to be reported upon the sale of property acquired by gift.

DISCUSSION: Normally, when a gift is received, the donee takes the donor's basis in the property. However, if the property's FMV on the date of transfer is less than the donor's basis in the property, the donee has a dual basis in the property. Since the property is resold at more than the FMV on the date of the gift but less than the donor's basis on the date of the gift, no gain or loss is recognized.

Answer (B) is incorrect. The FMV at the date of the gift is used to determine the amount of loss. Answer (C) is incorrect. The FMV at the date of the gift is used to determine the amount of loss. Answer (D) is incorrect. The donor's adjusted basis is used to determine the amount of gain.

21. Mr. Lemon had purchased 300 shares of ABC stock in 1993 for $7 a share. In 2003, he gave 200 shares to his son Robert. At the time of this gift, the stock had a fair market value of $5 a share. In 2012, Robert sold 100 shares for $4 a share. What is Robert's basis in the stock sold in 2012?

A. $700

B. $600

C. $500

D. $400

Answer (C) is correct.

REQUIRED: The basis of stock sold for a loss after being received by gift.

DISCUSSION: Normally, when a gift is received, the donee takes the donor's basis in the property. However, if the property's FMV on the date of transfer is less than the donor's basis in the property, the donee has a dual basis in the property. Since the property is resold at less than the FMV on the date of the gift, a loss results. Therefore, the donee uses the FMV at the date of the gift as his/her basis.

Answer (A) is incorrect. A loss, not a gain, is calculated. Answer (B) is incorrect. The basis for loss is the lower of the donor's basis or FMV on the date of gift. Answer (D) is incorrect. The selling price is $400.

22. In 2010, Paul received a boat as a gift from his father. At the time of the gift, the boat had a fair market value of $60,000 and an adjusted basis of $80,000 to Paul's father. After Paul received the boat, nothing occurred affecting Paul's basis in the boat. In 2012, Paul sold the boat for $75,000. What is the amount and character of Paul's gain?

A. Ordinary income of $15,000.

B. Long-term capital gain of $15,000.

C. Long-term capital loss of $5,000.

D. Neither a gain nor a loss.

Answer (D) is correct.

REQUIRED: The amount and character of a gain to be reported upon the sale of property acquired by gift.

DISCUSSION: For determining gain on the sale of property acquired by gift, the basis is the donor's adjusted basis. Paul's sale results in no gain ($75,000 sales price – $80,000 basis). For determining loss on the sale of property acquired by gift, the basis may not exceed the fair market value of the property at the date of the gift. Hence, there is no loss ($75,000 sales price – $60,000 basis).

Answer (A) is incorrect. None of the proceeds will be characterized as ordinary income. Answer (B) is incorrect. In determining gain on the sale of property acquired by gift, the basis is the donor's adjusted basis. For determining loss on the sale of property acquired by gift, the basis may not exceed the fair market value of the property at the date of the gift. Paul has neither a gain nor a loss. Answer (C) is incorrect. In determining gain on the sale of property acquired by gift, the basis is the donor's adjusted basis. For determining loss on the sale of property acquired by gift, the basis may not exceed the fair market value of the property at the date of the gift. Paul has neither a gain nor a loss.

23. In 2011, Tony received a gift of 200 shares of mutual funds stock. The stock was worth $20,000 when Tony received it. The donor had originally paid $10,000 for the stock when he bought it in 2007. Tony sold the stock for $15,000 in 2012. What is Tony's basis in the stock, disregarding gift tax?

A. $0

B. $20,000

C. $10,000

D. $15,000

Answer (C) is correct.

REQUIRED: The donee's basis in mutual funds stock received by gift.

DISCUSSION: The basis of the gift Tony received equals $10,000. The FMV at the date of the gift equals $20,000. Since the FMV exceeds the donor's basis in the stock, Tony must use the basis of the donor, $10,000.

Answer (A) is incorrect. The donee must use either the donor's basis or the FMV on the date of transfer. Answer (B) is incorrect. The FMV is greater than the donor's basis in the stock. Thus, Tony must use the donor's basis. Answer (D) is incorrect. The FMV is greater than the donor's basis in the stock. Thus, Tony must use the donor's basis.

7.3 Property Received for Services

24. All of the following statements concerning the basis of property received for services are true except

A. If you receive property for services, your basis is equal to the fair market value of the property received.

B. If your employer allows you to purchase property at less than fair market value, include the fair market value of the property in income.

C. If you receive property for services and the property is subject to restrictions, your basis in the property is its fair market value when it becomes substantially vested.

D. If your employer allows you to purchase property at less than fair market value, your basis in the property is its fair market value.

Answer (B) is correct.

REQUIRED: The false statement regarding the basis of property received for services.

DISCUSSION: In general, the basis for property received for services is its fair market value. However, the basis used by an employee who received property from an employer at less than its fair market value is the purchase price plus the amount included in the employee's income. The amount included in the employee's income is the difference between the fair market value and the price paid. Thus, even in such a case, the basis is the property's fair market value.

Answer (A) is incorrect. The basis of property received for services is its FMV. Answer (C) is incorrect. The basis of property that is received for services and is subject to restrictions is not included in income until the restrictions are lifted, and then the basis is its FMV. Answer (D) is incorrect. The basis of property purchased from an employer is the purchase price plus the income recognized, which, in effect, is the FMV.

25. Ms. G performed interior decorating services for Mr. K and accepted property as payment in lieu of cash. Ms. G and Mr. K originally agreed upon a price of $4,500 for Ms. G's services. At the time of the exchange, the property had an estimated fair market value of $5,000, based on sales of similar property and an adjusted basis to Mr. K of $2,000. What is the amount Ms. G must include in her income, and what is her basis in the property received?

	Income	Basis
A.	$5,000	$2,000
B.	$5,000	$5,000
C.	$4,500	$4,500
D.	$4,500	$2,000

Answer (B) is correct.

REQUIRED: The amount to be included in gross income and the basis to be taken in property exchanged for services performed.

DISCUSSION: Sec. 83 provides that the receipt of property for services provided is a taxable transaction. Reg. 1.61-2(d)(1) provides that if property or services are paid for with property, the fair market value of the property must be included in gross income as compensation. Accordingly, Ms. G would include $5,000 in gross income and take an adjusted basis in the property equal to its fair market value of $5,000.

Answer (A) is incorrect. The adjusted basis of the property is equal to its fair market value of $5,000. Answer (C) is incorrect. The income and basis are valued as the FMV of the property, and not the agreed upon price. Answer (D) is incorrect. The income and the basis are equal to the FMV of the property.

26. In 2010, Mary purchased 10 shares of Acorn Corporation common stock for $100 per share. In 2011, Mary purchased an additional 10 shares of Acorn Corporation common stock for $200 per share. At the end of 2012, Acorn Corporation declared a 2-for-1 common stock split. What is Mary's total basis in her Acorn Corporation common stock?

A. $3,000

B. $4,000

C. $5,000

D. $6,000

Answer (A) is correct.

REQUIRED: The total basis of common stock after a 2-for-1 split.

DISCUSSION: A stock split results in an increase in the number of shares held by the taxpayer but no change in the total basis. The basis can therefore be calculated as follows: (10 shares × $100) + (10 shares × $200) = $3,000.

7.4 Inherited Property

27. John and Fred owned, as joint tenants with right of survivorship, business property that they purchased for $40,000. John furnished one fourth of the purchase price, and Fred furnished three-fourths of the purchase price. Depreciation deductions allowed before Fred's death were $8,000. Under local law, each had a one-half interest in the income from the property. At the time of Fred's death, the fair market value of the property was $80,000, three-fourths of which is includible in Fred's estate. What is John's basis in the property at the date of Fred's death?

A. $80,000

B. $60,000

C. $66,000

D. $56,000

Answer (C) is correct.

REQUIRED: The basis of property received as a result of being a joint tenant with right of survivorship.

DISCUSSION: John's basis immediately after the property was purchased was $10,000 (1/4 of $40,000). He was permitted half of the depreciation, which decreased his basis to $6,000. After Fred's death, when John acquires the property in its entirety, the FMV (due to the step-up in basis) of the portion owned by Fred is included to have a final basis to John of $66,000 ($6,000 + $60,000). (See Publication 551.)

Answer (A) is incorrect. John's basis in the property is not equal to the property's FMV. Answer (B) is incorrect. John's basis in one-fourth of the property (prior to death) is added to the FMV of Fred's portion of the property. Answer (D) is incorrect. John and Fred's basis in the property prior to Fred's death was not equal.

28. Mr. King inherited 100 shares of Corporation LX stock from his father, who died on March 4, 2012. His father paid $17 per share for the stock on May 3, 1987. The fair market value of the stock on the date of death was $63 per share. On September 4, 2012, the fair market value of the stock was $55 per share. Mr. King sold the stock for $68 per share on December 3, 2012. The executor of the estate did not elect the alternate valuation date for valuing the father's estate. An estate tax return was filed. What was Mr. King's basis in the stock on the date of the sale?

A. $1,700

B. $4,600

C. $5,500

D. $6,300

Answer (D) is correct.

REQUIRED: The basis of inherited property when the alternate valuation date is not elected.

DISCUSSION: The basis of property received from a decedent is generally the fair market value of the property on the date of the decedent's death [Sec. 1014(a)]. If the alternate valuation date for the estate tax return is elected by the executor, the basis of the assets is their fair market value 6 months after death. Mr. King's basis in the stock is the $6,300 fair market value on March 4 (the date of his father's death).

Answer (A) is incorrect. The original basis does not carry over when property is inherited. Answer (B) is incorrect. The difference between the fair market value on date of death and the original basis does not determine the new basis. Answer (C) is incorrect. The alternate valuation date was not elected.

29. In Year 1, Mr. Green received a gift of rental property from Mr. Blue. Mr. Blue retained the power to transfer this property to his son in his will. At the time of the gift, Mr. Blue's adjusted basis in the property was $18,000, and the property's fair market value was $24,000. No gift tax was paid. In Year 1 and Year 2, Mr. Green deducted a total of $2,000 of depreciation. In Year 3, Mr. Blue died but did not exercise his power to transfer the property. The rental property given to Mr. Green was included in the gross estate as a revocable transfer. The value of the rental property for estate tax purposes was the fair market value at Mr. Blue's death, $28,000. What is Mr. Green's basis in the property after Mr. Blue's death?

A. $18,000

B. $22,000

C. $26,000

D. $28,000

Answer (C) is correct.

REQUIRED: The basis of property received as a revocable gift before the transferor dies.

DISCUSSION: The basis of property acquired from a decedent is the fair market value of the property at the date of the decedent's death [Sec. 1014(a)]. If the property is acquired before the death of the decedent, the basis is reduced by the depreciation deduction allowed the donee. Mr. Green's basis in the property is

Fair market value at Mr. Blue's death	$28,000
Less depreciation deducted by donee	(2,000)
Basis in the property	$26,000

The property was included in Mr. Blue's taxable estate under Sec. 2038 because he retained the right to revoke the transfer to Mr. Green.

Answer (A) is incorrect. Mr. Blue's adjusted basis in the property was $18,000. Answer (B) is incorrect. Mr. Green's basis in the property is its fair market value at Mr. Blue's death, not its fair market value while Mr. Blue held the property. Answer (D) is incorrect. FMV must be reduced by the depreciation taken by Green.

30. Mr. More inherited 2,000 shares of Corporation Zero stock from his father, who died on March 4, 2012. His father paid $10 per share for the stock on September 4, 1986. The fair market value of the stock on the date of death was $50 per share. On September 4, 2012, the fair market value of the stock was $60 per share. Mr. More sold the stock for $75 per share on July 3, 2012. The estate qualified for, and the executor elected, the alternate valuation date. An estate tax return was filed. What was Mr. More's basis in the stock on the date of the sale?

A. $100,000

B. $120,000

C. $130,000

D. $150,000

Answer (D) is correct.

REQUIRED: The basis of inherited property when the alternate valuation date is elected.

DISCUSSION: The basis of property received from a decedent is generally the fair market value of the property on the date of the decedent's death [Sec. 1014(a)]. If the executor elects the alternate valuation date for the estate tax return, the basis of the assets is their fair market value 6 months after death or the date of sale or distribution if earlier. Mr. More's basis in the stock is $150,000, the fair market value on the date of sale (2,000 shares × $75 per share).

Answer (A) is incorrect. This amount was the value on the date of death, not on the date of sale. Answer (B) is incorrect. The 6-month alternate valuation date is not used if the property is sold after the decedent's death but within the 6 months after the decedent's death. Answer (C) is incorrect. The correct per-share value of the stock is $75, not $65.

31. Mr. Apple and Ms. Melon purchased a small apartment house at the beginning of 2005 for $400,000, which they held for investment. Each furnished one-half of the purchase price, and each had a half interest in the income from the property. They held the apartment in joint tenancy with the right of survivorship (i.e., a tenancy in which the interest of the first tenant to die passes to the survivor on the death of the first tenant to die). They depreciated the apartment house at the rate of $10,000 per year. On December 31, 2012, Mr. Apple died. At the date of Mr. Apple's death, the apartment house had an adjusted basis (cost minus depreciation) of $320,000 and a fair market value of $550,000. What is Ms. Melon's basis as of the date of Mr. Apple's death?

A. $500,000

B. $435,000

C. $400,000

D. $320,000

Answer (B) is correct.

REQUIRED: The basis of jointly held property that is inherited.

DISCUSSION: The basis of property received from a decedent is generally the fair market value of the property on the date of the decedent's death [Sec. 1014(a)]. Under Sec. 2040, the general rule is that the gross estate of a decedent includes the entire value of property held jointly at the time of death except that portion of the property that was acquired by the other joint owner for adequate and full consideration. In this question, each investor contributed one-half of the purchase price. Therefore, when Mr. Apple died, his gross estate included only one-half of the apartment house. Accordingly, Ms. Melon will receive only a step-up in basis for that one-half of property included in Mr. Apple's estate. Ms. Melon's basis in the apartment house is $435,000 [$275,000 (1/2 of $550,000 FMV that represents Mr. Apple's portion) + $160,000 (Ms. Melon's original one-half basis in the property of $200,000 minus her share of depreciation of $40,000)].

Answer (A) is incorrect. The amount of $500,000 cannot be the basis. Answer (C) is incorrect. The amount of $400,000 is the total original basis for both investors. Answer (D) is incorrect. The amount of $320,000 is the total original basis reduced by depreciation.

32. Richard collected baseball cards as a hobby. Richard had shared his interest in this hobby with his niece Susan, who was also an avid card collector. At the time of his death in 2012, Richard's collection had a fair market value of $10,000 and an adjusted basis of $2,000, while Susan's collection had a fair market value of $5,000 and an adjusted basis of $1,000. Upon his death, Richard's entire card collection went to Susan. With the death of her uncle, Susan lost interest in the hobby and sold all of the cards for $20,000. What is Susan's gain on the sale of these baseball cards?

A. $5,000

B. $9,000

C. $13,000

D. $17,000

Answer (B) is correct.

REQUIRED: The gain realized from sale of property received by gift.

DISCUSSION: The basis of inherited property is FMV at date of death. Susan's basis in the cards she inherited from Richard is $10,000. Susan cannot adjust her basis in the cards she owns to FMV. Her basis in the cards she owns remains at $1,000. Susan must realize a gain of $9,000 [$20,000 – ($10,000 + $1,000)].

Answer (A) is incorrect. The gain is calculated by subtracting the basis in the property from the amount realized. Susan cannot adjust her basis in the cards she owns to the FMV. She must use her adjusted basis when calculating gains and losses. Answer (C) is incorrect. Susan's basis in the cards she owns prior to transfer is $1,000, not $5,000. Also, the basis in the cards given to her equals $10,000, not $2,000. Therefore, total basis should equal $11,000, not $7,000. Answer (D) is incorrect. The basis in the cards would equal the FMV of the cards received from Richard plus the basis of the cards that Susan already owns.

7.5 Stock Dividends

33. Alex bought four shares of common stock for $200. Later the corporation distributed a share of preferred stock for every two shares of common. At the date of distribution, the common stock had a FMV of $60 and preferred stock had a FMV of $40. What is Alex's basis in the common stock and the preferred stock after the nontaxable stock dividend?

A. $200 common; $80 preferred.

B. $150 common; $50 preferred.

C. $60 common; $40 preferred.

D. $240 common; $80 preferred.

Answer (B) is correct.

REQUIRED: The basis in common stock and preferred stock after a nontaxable stock dividend.

DISCUSSION: Since the preferred stock dividend was nontaxable, the original basis of the common stock would be allocated between the common stock and the preferred stock based on the relative fair market values of each on the date of the stock dividend (Reg. 1.307-1). The market values of Alex's common and preferred stock on the date of the dividend were $240 and $80, respectively. Alex's tax basis in the common stock after the receipt of the dividend is $150 [($240 ÷ $320) × $200]. Alex's tax basis in the preferred stock is $50 [($80 ÷ $320) × $200].

34. Nature Corporation declared and distributed a stock dividend of one share for each 10 shares held by shareholders. Donna had 100 shares ($5.50 per share basis) and received 10 additional shares with a fair market value of $6.00 per share. Which of the following is most applicable to the stock dividend?

A. 100 shares at $5.50 per share basis and 10 shares at zero basis per share.

B. 110 shares at $5 per share basis and $55 taxable income.

C. 110 shares at $5 per share.

D. 100 shares at $5 per share basis and 10 shares at $6 per share basis.

Answer (C) is correct.

REQUIRED: The statement most applicable to stock dividends.

DISCUSSION: The amount of money invested in the stock remains the total basis for all stock. A stock dividend means that the same basis is split between more shares of stock. In addition, stock dividends are not generally taxed (unless specified otherwise in a specific code section). The total basis in the stock is $550 (100 shares × $5.50/share). With the addition of 10 more shares of stock, the per share basis is $5 ($550 ÷ 110 shares).

Answer (A) is incorrect. The per share basis is recalculated with the stock received as a dividend. Answer (B) is incorrect. Stock dividends are not typically taxed. Answer (D) is incorrect. The per share basis is recalculated with the stock received as a dividend.

35. In 2010, Sam bought 200 shares of stock at $9 per share for a total cost of $1,800. In 2011, he bought 300 shares at $12 per share for a total of $3,600. In 2012, the stock split 3-for-1. What is the basis per share in the stock after the split?

A. 200 shares at $9 and 300 shares at $12.

B. 600 shares at $3 and 900 shares at $4.

C. 200 shares at $3 and 300 shares at $4.

D. 600 shares at $9 and 900 shares at $12.

Answer (B) is correct.

REQUIRED: The basis per share in stock after a split.

DISCUSSION: A distribution of common stock as a stock split is generally a tax-free distribution. The basis of the original stock is allocated between it and the new stock based on their relative fair market values. Here, all the stock has the same fair market value, so the basis per share should be calculated as total basis divided by total number of shares. The 200 shares purchased in 2010 have a basis of $1,800 (200 shares × $9 per share), which must be allocated to the additional 400 shares from the stock split. The basis for the 2010 stocks will be $3 per share ($1,800 ÷ 600). The 300 shares purchased in 2011 have a basis of $3,600 (300 shares × $12), which must be allocated to the additional 600 shares from the stock split. The basis for the 2011 stocks will be $4 per share ($3,600 ÷ 900).

Answer (A) is incorrect. In a stock split, the number of shares, not the basis per share, increases. Answer (C) is incorrect. In a stock split, the number of shares increases and the original basis must be allocated to the new shares. Answer (D) is incorrect. The original basis must be allocated to the new shares.

36. On January 3, 2012, Irene purchased 300 shares of common stock in Corporation Y for $120 per share. Four months later, she purchased 100 additional shares at $180 per share. On December 10, 2012, Irene received a 20% nontaxable stock dividend. The new and the old stock are identical. What is the amount of Irene's basis in each share of stock after the stock dividend?

A. 480 shares at $112.50 per share.

B. 360 shares at $120 per share and 120 shares at $180 per share.

C. 360 shares at $120 per share and 120 shares at $150 per share.

D. 360 shares at $100 per share and 120 shares at $150 per share.

Answer (D) is correct.

REQUIRED: The shareholder's basis in stock after a stock dividend.

DISCUSSION: A distribution of common stock as a stock dividend on common stock is generally a tax-free distribution. The basis of the original stock is allocated between it and the distributed stock based on their relative fair market values. Here, all the stock has the same fair market value, so the basis per share should be calculated as total basis divided by total number of shares. Because there are two sets of identical stocks with different bases, the basis calculation is done on a pro rata basis. The stock dividend is equal to 80 shares (400 × 20%). Thus, 360 shares [300 + .75(80)] will have a basis equal to $100 per share ($36,000 ÷ 360), and 120 shares [$100 + .25(80)] will have a basis equal to $150 per share ($18,000 ÷ 120).

Answer (A) is incorrect. Basis must be calculated on a pro rata basis. Answer (B) is incorrect. The basis per share is calculated by dividing the original basis in the stock by the new amount of stock allocated to it after the stock dividend. Answer (C) is incorrect. The basis per share is calculated by dividing the original basis in the stock by the new amount of stock allocated to it after the stock dividend.

37. In Year 1, Corey bought 200 shares of ABC stock at $10 a share. In Year 2, Corey bought an additional 100 shares of ABC stock at $20 a share. In Year 3, ABC declared a 2-for-1 stock split. How many shares of ABC stock does Corey own, and what is the basis of the stock?

A. 400 shares at $5 a share and 200 shares at $10 a share.

B. 400 shares at $10 a share and 200 shares at $20 a share.

C. 200 shares at $20 a share and 100 shares at $40 a share.

D. 600 shares at $6.67 a share.

Answer (A) is correct.

REQUIRED: The shareholder's basis in stock after a stock split.

DISCUSSION: A distribution of common stock as a stock split is generally a tax-free distribution. The basis of the original stock is allocated between it and the new stock based on their relative fair market values. Here, all the stock has the same fair market value, so the basis per share should be calculated as total basis divided by total number of shares. The 200 shares purchased in Year 1 have a basis of $2,000 (200 shares × $10 per share), which must be allocated to the additional 200 shares from the stock split. The basis for the Year 1 stocks will be $5 per share ($2,000 ÷ 400). The 100 shares purchased in Year 2 have a basis of $2,000 (100 shares × $20), which must be allocated to the additional 100 shares from the stock split. The basis for the Year 2 stocks will be $10 per share ($2,000 ÷ 200).

Answer (B) is incorrect. The original basis must be allocated to the new shares. Answer (C) is incorrect. In a stock split, the number of shares, not the basis per share, increases. Answer (D) is incorrect. Stocks with different bases must be separately identified.

38. During 1996, John purchased 50 shares of common stock in Corporation D for $4,500. In 2007, D declared a stock dividend of 20%. The new stock received by John in the stock dividend was identical to the old stock. In 2012, D's stock split 3-for-1 at a time when the fair market value was $120 per share. What is John's basis in each of his shares of D's stock if both distributions were nontaxable?

A. $120 per share.

B. $90 for 50 shares and $0 for all additional shares.

C. $75 for 60 shares and $142.50 for 120 shares.

D. $25 per share.

Answer (D) is correct.

REQUIRED: The shareholder's basis in stock after a stock dividend and a stock split.

DISCUSSION: A distribution of common stock as a stock dividend on common stock is generally a tax-free distribution. The same is true for a stock split. Under Sec. 307(a), the basis of the original stock is allocated between it and the distributed stock based on their relative fair market values. Here, all the stock has the same fair market value, so the basis per share is calculated as total basis divided by total number of shares. John's total number of shares is 180 [(50 + 10) × 3]. His basis per share is $25 ($4,500 ÷ 180 shares).

Answer (A) is incorrect. The basis in each share is not equal to the FMV at the time of the stock split. Answer (B) is incorrect. The basis per share is equal to the total basis divided by the total number of shares. There is no allocation to different blocks of stock. Answer (C) is incorrect. The basis per share is equal to the total basis divided by the total number of shares. There is no allocation to different blocks of stock.

39. In 2007, Mr. Chang purchased 50 shares of common stock in Corporation D for $1,000. In 2009, Corporation D declared a stock dividend of two shares of its common stock for each 10 shares held. In 2012, D's common stock split 2-for-1 at a time when the fair market value was $20 a share. What is Mr. Chang's basis in each of his shares of D's stock (rounded to the nearest dollar) if both distributions were tax-free and all the stock received was identical to the stock purchased?

A. $8 per share.

B. $20 for 100 shares and $0 for all additional shares.

C. $17 for 60 shares and $20 for 60 shares.

D. $20 per share.

Answer (A) is correct.

REQUIRED: The shareholder's basis in stock after a stock dividend and a stock split.

DISCUSSION: A distribution of common stock as a stock dividend on common stock is generally a tax-free distribution. The same is true for a stock split. Under Sec. 307(a), the basis of the original stock is allocated between it and the distributed stock based on their relative fair market values. Here, all the stock has the same fair market value, so the basis per share is calculated as total basis divided by total number of shares. Mr. Chang's total number of shares is 120 [(50 + 10) × 2]. His basis per share (rounded to the nearest dollar) is $8 ($1,000 ÷ 120 shares = $8.333).

Answer (B) is incorrect. The basis per share is equal to the total basis divided by the total number of shares. There is no allocation to different blocks of stock. Answer (C) is incorrect. The basis per share is equal to the total basis divided by the total number of shares. There is no allocation to different blocks of stock. Answer (D) is incorrect. The basis in each share is not equal to the FMV at the time of the stock split.

40. In 2010, Melanie Tyson bought 100 shares of XYZ stock for $1,000, or $10 a share. In 2011, she bought 100 shares of XYZ stock for $1,600, or $16 a share. In 2012, XYZ declared a 2-for-1 stock split. Which of the following is true?

A. Melanie now has 200 shares with a basis of $5 per share.

B. Melanie now has 200 shares with a basis of $8 per share.

C. Melanie now has 400 shares with a basis of $6.50 per share.

D. Melanie now has 200 shares with a basis of $5 per share and 200 shares with a basis of $8 per share.

Answer (D) is correct.

REQUIRED: The taxpayer's basis and number of shares after a stock split.

DISCUSSION: A distribution of common stock as a stock split is generally a tax-free distribution. The basis of the original stock is allocated between it and the new stock based on their relative fair market values. The 100 shares purchased in 2010 have a basis of $1,000 (100 shares × $10 per share), which must be allocated to the additional 100 shares from the stock split. The basis for the 2010 stocks will be $5 per share ($1,000 ÷ 200). The 100 shares purchased in 2011 have a basis of $1,600 (100 shares × $16), which must be allocated to the additional 100 shares from the stock split. The basis for the 2011 stocks will be $8 per share ($1,600 ÷ 200).

Answer (A) is incorrect. The stock split also applies to the second purchase of XYZ stock. Answer (B) is incorrect. The stock split also applies to the first purchase of XYZ stock. Answer (C) is incorrect. Since the stock purchases attribute a different basis to each purchase of the stock, the stock should be separately maintained, and the stock split will not cause an average of basis.

STUDY UNIT EIGHT
ADJUSTMENTS TO ASSET BASIS AND CAPITAL GAINS AND LOSSES

(9 pages of outline)

The basis of an asset is generally its cost, but it may be adjusted over the course of time due to various events. The basis of property must be increased by capital expenditures and decreased by capital returns. Increases in basis have the effect of reducing the amount of gain realized or increasing the amount of realized loss. Decreases in basis have the effect of increasing the amount of realized gain or decreasing the amount of loss.

8.1 ADJUSTMENTS TO ASSET BASIS

Initial basis is adjusted consistent with tax-relevant events. Adjustments include the following:

Subsequent to Requisition

1. Certain expenditures subsequent to acquisition are property costs, and they increase basis, e.g., legal fees to defend title or title insurance premiums.

Prolong Life

2. Basis must be increased for expenditures that substantially prolong the life of the property or materially increase its value.
   a. Examples include major improvements (e.g., new roof, addition to building) and zoning changes.
   b. Maintenance, repair, and operating costs are not capitalized.
3. An increase to basis may result from a liability to the extent it is secured by real property and applied to extend its life.

Depreciation

4. Depreciation taken on business property will decrease the basis.
   a. The base for MACRS depreciation is the cost.
   b. All assets depreciated under the General Depreciation System (GDS) under MACRS must be included in a class of depreciation, such as 5-, 7-, or 20-year property.
   c. A few of the depreciation classes follow.
      1) Five-year property includes automobiles; computers and peripheral equipment; office machinery (such as typewriters, calculators, and copiers); any property used in research and experimentation; and appliances, carpets, furniture, etc., used in a residential real estate activity.
      2) Seven-year property includes office furniture and fixtures (such as desks, files, and safes), agricultural machinery and equipment, and any property that does not have a class life and has not been designated by law as being in any other class.
      3) Residential real property is any property from which 80% or more of its gross rental income comes from dwelling units. This property has a recovery period of 27 1/2 years.

4) Nonresidential real property is Sec. 1250 property.

a) It includes office buildings, stores, or warehouses that are not classified as residential real property and are not otherwise specified to have a life less than 27 1/2 years.

b) The recovery period of this property is 39 years.

5. Basis must be reduced by the larger of the amount of depreciation allowed or allowable (even if not claimed). Unimproved land is not depreciated.

a. Sec. 179 expense is treated as a depreciation deduction. (The Sec. 179 amount is $500,000 for 2012.)

Contributed Property

6. A shareholder does not recognize gain on the voluntary contribution of capital to a corporation.

a. The shareholder's stock basis is increased by the basis in the contributed property.
b. The corporation has a transferred basis in the property.

Dividends

7. Distributions out of earnings and profits (E&P) are taxable as dividends.

a. Dividends are taxable and therefore do not reduce basis.

Return of Capital

8. When a corporation makes a distribution that is not out of E&P, it is a nontaxable return of capital (until basis is reduced to zero).

a. Distributions in excess of basis are treated as capital gain.
b. When a shareholder has purchased several stocks, the distribution is applied on a specific identification method, if applicable.

1) The FIFO method is used when specific identification is impossible.
2) If a shareholder purchases stock in different lots and at different times, and it is impossible to definitely identify the shares subject to a return of capital, the basis of the earliest shares purchased is reduced first [Reg. 1.1012-1(c)].

Stock Rights

9. The basis of stock acquired in a nontaxable distribution (e.g., stock rights) is allocated a portion of the basis of the stock upon which the distribution was made.

a. The basis is allocated in proportion to the FMV of the original stock and the distribution as of the date of distribution.

b. If the FMV of the stock rights is less than 15% of the FMV of the stock upon which it was issued, the rights have a zero basis (unless an election is made to allocate basis).

Tax Benefits

10. Basis adjustment is required for certain specific items that represent a tax benefit. Three examples follow:

Casualty Losses

a. Basis is reduced by the amount of the casualty loss, by any amounts recovered by insurance, and by any amounts for which no tax benefit was received, e.g., $100 floor for each casualty occurrence for individuals.

Debt Discharge

b. Specific exclusion from gross income is allowed to certain insolvent persons for debt discharged. Reduction in basis is required for certain amounts excluded.

Credit on Asset Purchases

c. Credits are allowed on certain asset purchases, such as building rehabilitation, energy equipment, and low-income housing.

1) A partial or full amount of the credit must be deducted from the basis.

Partial Disposition of Property

11. The basis of the whole property must be equitably apportioned among the parts; relative FMV is generally used.

Personal Use Converted to Business Use

12. Basis for depreciation is the lesser of the FMV of the property at the conversion date or the adjusted basis at conversion.

Leasehold Improvements

13. Generally, lessors do not report income when a lessee makes leasehold improvements or when the leasehold improvements revert to the lessor at the termination of the lease.

a. Thus, the lessor has a zero basis in the leasehold improvements.

Stop and review! You have completed the outline for this subunit. Study questions 1 through 6 beginning on page 205.

8.2 HOLDING PERIOD (HP)

1. The holding period of an asset is measured in calendar months, beginning on the date after acquisition and including the disposal date.

a. The holding period may include that of the transferor.
b. If the property is held for 1 year or less, it is considered short-term.
c. If it is held for more than 1 year, it is long-term.

Acquisition by or of	Holding Period - Starts or by reference to
Sale or exchange	Acquisition*
Gift: for gain	Donor's acquisition
for loss	Acquisition
Inheritance	Automatic LT
Nontaxable exchanges	
Like-kind (Sec. 1031)	Include HP of exchanged asset**
Corporate stock (Sec. 351)	Include HP of contributed asset**
Property in entity	Include transferor's HP
Stock dividend (307)	Include HP of "old stock"
Partnership interest (Sec. 721)	Include HP of contributed asset**
Property in entity	Include transferor's HP**
Ordinary income property	Exchange
Involuntary conversion (Sec. 1033)	Include HP of converted asset
Residence	Acquisition
Use conversion (T/B & personal)	Include period of prior use
Optioned property	Exclude option period
Securities	Trading date
Short sales (Ss)	Earlier of Ss closing or property sale date
Commodity futures	LT after 6-month HP
Capital gain dividend	Automatic LT

* Always start computation using day after date of applicable acquisition.

** If capital asset or Sec. 1231 property; otherwise, the holding period starts the day after date of exchange.

Stop and review! You have completed the outline for this subunit. Study questions 7 through 11 beginning on page 207.

8.3 CAPITAL GAINS AND LOSSES

A capital gain or loss is realized on the sale or exchange of a capital asset.

Capital Assets

1. All property is characterized as a capital asset, unless expressly excluded.
   a. The following types of property are not capital assets:
      1) Inventory (or stock in trade)
      2) Property held primarily for sale to customers in the ordinary course of a trade or business (e.g., homes held by builder)
      3) Real or depreciable property used in a trade or business
      4) Accounts or notes receivable acquired in the ordinary course of trade or business for services rendered or for 1) or 2) above
      5) Copyrights and artistic compositions held by the person who composed them, including letters
      6) Certain U.S. government publications acquired at reduced cost
   b. Property held either for personal use or for the production of income is a capital asset, but dealer property is not. Personal-use gain is capital gain. Losses from personal-use property are not deductible unless they are from a casualty or theft. Personal-use property losses not being deductible includes not even being recognized and offsetting capital gains.
   c. Examples of capital assets are personal homes, furnishings, automobiles, stocks, bonds, commodities, partnership interests, land, internally generated goodwill, contract rights, patents, and trade secrets.

Goodwill

   d. Goodwill is a capital asset when generated within the business.
      1) Goodwill acquired with the purchase of a trade or business is an amortizable intangible asset under Sec. 197.
      2) This ability to amortize characterizes acquired goodwill as a Sec. 1231 asset rather than as a capital asset.

Option

   e. An option is treated the same as the underlying property.

Stocks, Bonds, Commodities

   f. Stocks, bonds, commodities, and the like are capital assets unless they are dealer property.
      1) A dealer holds an asset primarily for sale to customers in the ordinary course of his/her trade or business.
      2) A dealer may identify particular assets as held for investment by the close of business day of acquisition.
         a) Such assets are capital.
         b) A trader buys and sells assets for his/her own account. They are capital assets in that they are not considered held for sale to customers.

Land Investment

g. Land held primarily for investment (capital asset) that is then subdivided may be treated as converted to property held for sale in a trade or business.

1) Mere subdivision for sale of land held by other than a C corporation does not establish that it is held for sale in a trade or business.

2) The subdivided land is treated as a capital asset if particular conditions are satisfied, e.g., if no substantial improvements have been made to the land while held by the person.

Sale or Exchange

2. Generally, under Sec. 1001, all gains are realized on the "sale or other disposition of property." This includes sales or exchanges that are required in characterizing a realized gain or loss as capital.

a. A sale is a transfer of property in exchange for money or a promise to pay money while an exchange is a transfer of property in return for other properties or services.

b. For real property, a sale or exchange occurs on the earlier of the date of conveyance or the date that the burdens of ownership pass to the buyer.

c. Also, liquidating distributions and losses on worthless securities are treated as sales or exchanges.

Gain (Loss) Recognized

3. All realized gains must be recognized unless the IRC expressly provides otherwise. Conversely, no deduction is allowed for a realized loss unless the IRC expressly provides for it. The following formula shows computation of gain or loss realized:

	Money received (or to be received)		
+	FMV of other property received[1]		
+	Liability relief[2]		
–	Money or other property given up		
–	Selling expenses[3]		Amount realized
–	Liabilities assumed[2]	–	Adjusted basis
=	Amount realized	=	Gain (loss) realized

1. *If the FMV of other property received is not determinable with reasonable certainty, FMV of the property given up is used.*
2. *Whether recourse or nonrecourse.*
3. *Selling expenses are subtracted from gross receivables to yield the amount realized.*

a. Long-term capital gain or loss (LTCG or LTCL) is realized from a capital asset held for more than 1 year. Short-term capital gain or loss (STCG or STCL) is realized if the asset was held 1 year or less.

b. For individuals, net capital gain (NCG) is the excess of net LTCG over net STCL. Net STCG is not included in NCG [Sec. 1222(11)].

c. Net STCG is treated as ordinary income for individuals. NCG rates do not apply to net STCG.

1) Net STCG = STCG – STCL.
2) But net STCG may be offset by net LTCL.

Capital Gains Rates

d. For individuals, capital transactions involving long-term holding periods are grouped by tax rates. The maximum capital gains rates are 15% (0% for taxpayers in the 10% and 15% income tax brackets), 25%, or 28%.

   1) The "28% basket" includes gains or losses from the sale of collectibles and gains from Sec. 1202 (certain small business) stock.

   2) The "25% basket" includes long-term capital gains from the sale or exchange of depreciable real property that would be treated as ordinary income if the property were depreciable personal property (i.e., Sec. 1245 property), unless already treated as ordinary income under another provision.

      a) The effect of this provision is that any unrecaptured Sec. 1250 gains will be taxed at a rate of 25%.

   3) The "15% basket" includes long-term capital gains and losses on assets held for over 12 months.

e. After gains and losses are classified in the appropriate baskets, losses for each long-term basket are first used to offset any gains within that basket.

f. If a long-term basket has a net loss, the loss will be used first to offset net gain for the highest long-term rate basket, then to offset the next highest rate basket, and so on.

EXAMPLE

A taxpayer realizes a $10,000 net loss in the 15% basket, a $5,000 net gain in the 25% basket, and an $8,000 net gain in the 28% basket. The taxpayer will first apply the net loss against the gain in the 28% basket, reducing the gain in this basket to zero. Then, the remaining $2,000 loss is applied against the gain in the 25% basket, leaving a $3,000 net capital gain in the 25% basket.

Carryover of NLTCL

g. A carryover of a net long-term capital loss from a prior year is used first to offset any net gain in the 28% basket, then to offset any net gain in the 25% basket, and finally to offset any net gain in the 15% basket. Likewise, net STCL is also used first to offset net gain for the highest long-term basket and so on.

EXAMPLE

A taxpayer has a $1,000 long-term capital loss carryover, a net short-term capital loss of $2,000, a $1,000 net gain in the 28% basket, and a $5,000 net gain in the 15% basket. Both losses are first applied to offset the 28% rate gain, using the $1,000 loss carryover first until completely exhausted. Since no gain exists in the 28% basket after applying the carryover, the net STCL is then applied against the next highest gain in the 15% basket. As a result, only a $3,000 net capital gain remains in the 15% basket.

Corporations

h. For corporations, all capital gain (ST or LT) is taxed at the corporation's regular tax rate.

Loss Limits

i. An individual may offset a net capital loss with net capital gains. If the individual does not have net capital gains, (s)he recognizes a net capital loss in the current year up to the lesser of $3,000 ($1,500 for married filing separately) or ordinary income. An individual may carry forward any excess CLs indefinitely.

   1) The carryforward is treated as a CL incurred in the subsequent year.

   2) Net STCL is treated as having been deductible in the preceding year before net LTCL.

   3) There can be no carryover from a decedent to his/her estate.

j. A corporation may use CLs only to offset CGs each year. A corporation must carry the excess CL back 3 years and forward 5 years and characterize all carryovers as STCLs (regardless of character).

Schedule D

k. Schedule D (Form 1040) is used to compute and summarize total capital gains and/or losses on the sale or disposition of capital assets listed on Form 8949, and the summary combines the long-term gains/losses with the short-term gains/losses. Form 8949 basically replaces the former Schedule D-1, but it includes all transactions. The previous form (Schedule D-1) was just a continuation of Schedule D.

1) When these capital gains and losses all net to a gain, it is called "capital gain net income" [Sec. 1222(a)].

2) If a taxpayer has capital gain distributions and no other capital gains or losses, the capital gains distributions may be reported directly on Form 1040 or Form 1040A.

l. Liabilities discharged in bankruptcy are treated as a short-term capital loss on Schedule D to a creditor who is an individual.

1) The loss is short-term capital loss regardless of how long the debt was in the hands of the creditor.

m. Individuals may be able to report capital gain distributions on their Form 1040 if the following conditions are met:

1) They only have capital gains from box 2a from Form 1099-DIV to report.

2) No amounts appear in box 2b (unrecaptured section 1250 gain), box 2c (section 1202 gain), or box 2d [collectibles (28%) gain].

3) They are not filing Form 4952, *Investment Interest Expense Deduction*, or, if the amount on line 4g of that form includes any qualified dividends, it also includes all net capital gain from the disposition of property held for investment.

Stop and review! You have completed the outline for this subunit. Study questions 12 through 23 beginning on page 209.

8.4 CAPITAL GAINS ON SALES OF STOCK

Gains and Losses

1. Gains and losses from the disposition of securities are generally determined and taxed like gains and losses from the disposition of other property.

   a. Securities held by investors are capital assets.

Return of Capital

2. A return of capital distribution reduces basis and becomes a capital gain when the shareholder's basis in the stock reaches zero.

Undistributed Gains

3. Undistributed capital gains earned in a mutual fund are taxed as capital gains in the current period.

   a. A credit is allowed for any tax paid by the mutual fund on behalf of the taxpayer.

60/40 Rule

4. Generally, positions in regulated futures contracts, foreign currency contracts, nonequity options, and dealer equity options in an exchange using the mark-to-market system are treated as if they were sold on the last day of the year.

   a. Any capital gains or losses arising under this rule are treated as if they were 60% long-term and 40% short-term without regard to the holding period.

Stop and review! You have completed the outline for this subunit. Study questions 24 through 37 beginning on page 213.

8.5 SECTIONS 1202 AND 1244 STOCK

50% Exclusion

1. Taxpayers may exclude 50% of the gain from the sale or exchange of qualified small business stock (QSB stock).
   a. The stock must have been issued after August 10, 1993, and held for more than 5 years.
   b. For Section 1202 stock acquired after February 17, 2009, and before September 28, 2010, the exclusion increases to 75%.
   c. For Section 1202 stock acquired after September 27, 2010, and before January 1, 2014, the exclusion increases to 100%.

Asset Limits

2. Qualified small business stock must be that of a domestic C corporation with aggregate gross assets not exceeding $50 million.
3. The corporation must have at least 80%, by value, of its assets used in the active conduct of a qualified business.
   a. A qualified business is any business other than
      1) The performance of personal services (e.g., banking, financing, and leasing),
      2) Any farming business,
      3) Any extractive industry, and
      4) Hospitality businesses (e.g., hotels and restaurants).

Annual Gain Limit

4. The aggregate annual gain for which a taxpayer may qualify under Sec. 1202 is limited to the greater of $10 million or 10 times the adjusted tax basis of qualified stock disposed of by the taxpayer during the year.

Rate

5. Sec. 1202 stock qualifying for the 50% or 75% exclusions are taxed at the 28% rate.

AMT Preference

6. An alternative minimum tax (AMT) preference is equal to 7% of the excluded gain. Since this is an exclusion preference, there is no minimum tax credit allowed.

Gain Rollover

7. Individuals are allowed to roll over capital gains from the sale of Sec. 1202 stock if other small business stock is purchased within 60 days after the date of sale.
   a. The small business stock being sold must have been held for more than 6 months, and the sale must have taken place after August 5, 1997.
   b. The normal rules of nontaxable exchange apply to the gain being deferred, the basis of the small business stock acquired, and the holding period for the acquired stock.
   c. Qualified small business (QSB) stock held through pass-through entities qualifies for the rollover rules (Rev. Proc. 98-48, 1998-38 IRB 7).
      1) A pass-through entity may make the election if the entity sells QSB stock held more than 6 months and purchases replacement QSB stock during the 60-day period beginning on the date of sale.
         a) The benefit of deferral will flow through to the taxpayers (other than C corporations) that held interests in the entity during the entire period in which the entity held the QSB stock.

2) If a pass-through entity sells QSB stock held for more than 6 months, an individual who has held an interest in the entity and who purchases replacement QSB stock may make the rollover election with respect to the individual's share of any gain on the sale that the entity does not defer under Sec. 1045.
   a) The individual's interest in the entity must be held during the entire period in which the entity held the QSB stock.
   b) The purchase of replacement QSB stock must take place during the 60-day period beginning on the date of the sale of the QSB stock.

d. If a person has more than one sale of QSB stock in a tax year that qualifies for the rollover election, the person may make the rollover election for any one or more of those sales.

Sec. 1244

8. An individual may deduct, as an ordinary loss, a loss from the sale or exchange or from worthlessness of "small business stock" (Sec. 1244 stock) issued by a qualifying small business corporation.
   a. A corporation qualifies if the amount of money and other property it receives as a contribution to capital does not exceed $1 million.
      1) This determination is to be made at the time the stock is issued.
   b. The shareholder must be the original owner of the stock.
   c. The maximum amount deductible as an ordinary loss in any one year is $50,000 ($100,000 on a joint return).
   d. If a taxpayer makes capital investments in the corporation without receiving stock, the loss must be allocated between the investments where stock was received and investments where stock was not received.
      1) Losses from investments without receiving stock are not eligible for Sec. 1244.
   e. The loss is shown on Form 4797.

Stop and review! You have completed the outline for this subunit. Study questions 38 and 39 beginning on page 217.

QUESTIONS

8.1 Adjustments to Asset Basis

1. Which of the following will decrease the basis of property?

A. Depreciation.

B. Return of capital.

C. Recognized losses on involuntary conversions.

D. All of the answers are correct.

Answer (D) is correct.

REQUIRED: The item that will decrease the basis of property.

DISCUSSION: Basis must be reduced by the larger of the amount of depreciation allowed or allowable (even if not claimed). A return of capital is a tax-free distribution that reduces a stock's basis by the amount of the distribution. If a shareholder's basis has been reduced to zero because of a tax-free return of capital, any excess amounts received are treated as a capital gain. Under Sec. 1033(b), the basis of the replacement property from an involuntary conversion is reduced by any gain not recognized.

Answer (A) is incorrect. Return of capital and recognized losses on involuntary conversions will also reduce the basis of property. Answer (B) is incorrect. Depreciation and recognized losses on involuntary conversions will also reduce the basis of property. Answer (C) is incorrect. Depreciation and return of capital will also reduce the basis of property.

2. In January of the current year, Mrs. Black purchased an office building and used office furnishings. The used office furnishings consisted of chairs, desks, and file cabinets. Of the purchase price, $900,000 was allocated to the office building and $50,000 was allocated to the used office furnishings. According to the General Depreciation System (GDS) under MACRS for depreciation, what recovery period must she use for the purchased items?

A. 27 1/2 years for the entire asset, building and furnishings.

B. 39 years for the building and 5 years for the used office furnishings.

C. 27 1/2 years for the building and 7 years for the used office furnishings.

D. 39 years for the building and 7 years for the used office furnishings.

Answer (D) is correct.

REQUIRED: Classifying depreciable property for the General Depreciation System (GDS) under MACRS.

DISCUSSION: Depreciation may be taken on property that is depreciable under MACRS. Such property must be appropriately classified and depreciation taken over the recovery period prescribed by the IRC. Nonresidential real property is Sec. 1250 property. It includes office buildings, stores, or warehouses that are not classified as residential real property and are not otherwise specified to have a life less than 27 1/2 years. The recovery period of this property is 39 years. Seven-year property includes office furniture and fixtures (such as desks, files, and safes), agricultural machinery and equipment, and any property that does not have a class life and has not been designated by law as being in any other class. Thus, the building will have a recovery life of 39 years and the office furniture a recovery life of 7 years.

Answer (A) is incorrect. The real property is 39-year property, and the office equipment is 7-year property. Answer (B) is incorrect. Office machinery, not office equipment, is depreciable over a 5-year depreciable period. Answer (C) is incorrect. The office building is not residential rental property.

3. All of the following statements regarding a return of capital distribution based on your stock are true except

A. A return of capital reduces the basis of your stock.

B. When the basis of your stock has been reduced to zero, you should report any additional return of capital as a capital loss.

C. Any liquidating distribution you receive is not taxable to you until you have recovered the basis of your stock.

D. If the total liquidating distributions you receive are less than the basis of your stock, you may have a capital loss.

Answer (B) is correct.

REQUIRED: The false statement regarding a return of capital distribution based on stock.

DISCUSSION: A return of capital is a tax-free distribution that reduces a stock's basis by the amount of the distribution. If a shareholder's basis has been reduced to zero because of a tax-free return of capital, any excess amounts received are treated as a capital gain.

4. Mrs. Yee purchased stock in Jones Corporation in 2007 for $500. In 2010, she received a distribution of $800 when Jones had no current or accumulated earnings and profits. In 2012, Mrs. Yee received a $200 dividend when Jones had earnings and profits in excess of its dividend distribution. There has been no other activity on this stock. What is Mrs. Yee's basis in her Jones Corporation stock as of December 31, 2012?

A. $(500)

B. $(300)

C. $0

D. $500

Answer (C) is correct.

REQUIRED: The basis in stock after the distributions in excess of basis.

DISCUSSION: Sec. 316 provides specific rules to determine whether a distribution is taxable as a dividend or is a tax-free return of capital. If a corporation has a distribution that is deemed to be made out of earnings and profits, then the distribution would be taxable as a dividend. If a corporation has no earnings and profits, the distribution is deemed a return of capital and is tax-free until basis is reduced to zero. A return of capital reduces the stock basis while distributions in excess of basis are treated as capital gains and do not reduce basis. Likewise, a taxable dividend has no effect on basis.

Answer (A) is incorrect. A shareholder's stock basis cannot be reduced below zero. Distributions in excess of basis and nontaxable dividends do not reduce basis. Answer (B) is incorrect. A shareholder's stock basis cannot be reduced below zero. Distributions in excess of basis and nontaxable dividends do not reduce basis. Answer (D) is incorrect. A tax-free return of capital reduces basis until the basis reaches zero.

5. During 2012, Julia received a dividend payment from Corporation X in the amount of $500 and a distribution (return of capital payment) on the Block B shares in the amount of $800. Julia had originally purchased Corporation X stock for $2,000 in 2003 (Block A) and purchased additional Corporation X stock for $1,000 (Block B) in 2004. Julia's basis in each of the two blocks of stock at the end of 2012, assuming no other transactions, is

	Block A	Block B
A.	$700	$200
B.	$2,000	$200
C.	$1,466	$734
D.	$1,200	$1,000

Answer (B) is correct.

REQUIRED: The basis in each of two blocks of stock when specific identification is possible.

DISCUSSION: If a shareholder purchases stock in different lots and at different times and it is possible to definitely identify the shares subject to a return of capital, the specific identification method should be used. Therefore, the $800 return of capital is applied entirely against Block B, the stock purchased in 2004. The dividend represents a return on capital and does not reduce the stock basis.

Answer (A) is incorrect. The dividend does not reduce the stock basis. Answer (C) is incorrect. The return of capital is not allocated between the two blocks of stock. Answer (D) is incorrect. The return of capital is applied on a FIFO basis only if the specific identification method is impossible.

6. Ms. Cross owns a house that she rents to non-related parties. She incurred the following costs during the current year:

- $400 to resurface a tub in the master bathroom
- $500 to paint the kitchen after installing new cabinets
- $2,000 to replace cabinets in the kitchen
- $600 to replace the built-in dishwasher

How should these costs be characterized and in what amounts?

A. $3,100 as improvements to be capitalized and $400 as repairs.

B. $400 as improvements to be capitalized and $3,100 as repairs.

C. $3,500 as improvements to be capitalized.

D. $2,000 as improvements to be capitalized and $1,500 as repairs.

Answer (A) is correct.

REQUIRED: Distinguishing improvements that are capitalized from repairs.

DISCUSSION: Basis must be increased for expenditures that substantially prolong the life of the property or materially increase its value. Examples include major improvements (e.g., new roof, addition to building) and zoning changes. Maintenance, repair, and operating costs are not capitalized; $3,100 ($2,000 + $500 + $600) is capitalized. The $400 incurred to resurface the tub is considered repairs and is expensed when incurred. The amount incurred to replace the cabinets is not expensed because it is part of a project that materially appreciates the value of the property.

Answer (B) is incorrect. The $3,100 incurred increases the value of the property and cannot be expensed. The $400 incurred, however, is considered a repair and should not be capitalized. Answer (C) is incorrect. The $400 incurred to resurface the tub in the master bathroom is not an improvement to be capitalized. Answer (D) is incorrect. The $500 incurred to paint the kitchen is part of a project that materially enhances the value of the property. The $600 incurred to replace the built-in dishwasher is capitalized, not expensed. This is not a maintenance or repair cost.

8.2 Holding Period (HP)

7. The holding period for determining short-term and long-term gains and losses includes which of the following?

A. The day you acquired the property.

B. In the case of a bank that repossessed real property, the time between the original sale and the date of repossession.

C. The donor's holding period in the case of a gift if your basis is the donor's adjusted basis.

D. All of the answers are correct.

Answer (C) is correct.

REQUIRED: The true statement regarding holding periods.

DISCUSSION: In the case of property received as a gift, the basis of the property is generally the same as the donor's basis. The basis may be increased by a portion or all of the gift tax paid on the transfers. When this occurs, the holding period is carried over from the donor.

Answer (A) is incorrect. The holding period generally begins the day following the acquisition date. Answer (B) is incorrect. The holding period does not include the time between the original sale and the date of repossession. Answer (D) is incorrect. Not all of the statements are correct.

8. Emma's brother purchased 100 shares of Clockwork, Inc., stock for $10 per share on December 30, 2010. Emma inherited the shares of Clockwork stock from her brother on September 15, 2011, when it had a fair market value of $15 per share. On December 20, 2012, she sold the stock for $20 per share. What is the amount and character of her gain?

A. The gain of $1,000 is short-term capital gain.

B. The gain of $1,000 is long-term capital gain.

C. The gain of $500 is long-term capital gain.

D. The gain of $500 is short-term capital gain.

Answer (C) is correct.

REQUIRED: The amount and character of a gain.

DISCUSSION: The basis for inherited property is the fair market value (FMV) on the date of the death or at some alternate date (as specified in the tax code). In addition, all inherited property has a long term holding period. A gain is determined by subtracting the adjusted basis from the amount realized.

Amount realized	$2,000	(100 shares × $20/share)
– Adjusted basis	(1,500)	(100 shares × $15/share)
Gain	$ 500	

Thus, Emma has a long-term gain of $500.

Answer (A) is incorrect. The holding period of an inheritance is always long-term, and the basis of the stock is $15 per share. Answer (B) is incorrect. The basis of the stock is $15 per share. Answer (D) is incorrect. The holding period of an inheritance is always long-term.

9. Albina purchased 1,000 shares of Global Tech Growth mutual fund on February 15, 2011, for $15 per share. On January 31, 2012, she sold the 1,000 shares of Global Tech Growth mutual fund for $4.50 per share. Albina had no other capital transactions in 2012. Which of the following is true?

A. Albina has a short-term capital loss of $10,500 on her 2012 tax return, and she will be allowed to offset $10,500 of her earnings.

B. Albina has a short-term capital loss of $3,000 on her 2012 tax return and no carryover.

C. Albina has a short-term capital loss of $10,500 in 2012 and can deduct $3,000 on her tax return. She can carry forward a short-term loss of $7,500 to 2013.

D. Albina has a short-term capital loss of $10,500 in 2012 and can deduct $3,000 on her tax return. She can carry forward a long-term loss of $7,500 to 2013.

Answer (C) is correct.

REQUIRED: The true statement about the capital transaction.

DISCUSSION: A short-term capital loss is defined as a loss on a capital asset that has a holding period of less than a year. In addition, the maximum amount of capital loss that can be deducted per year is $3,000. Any additional capital loss may be carried forward to subsequent years. For individuals, if you hold investment property more than one year, any capital gain or loss is a long-term capital gain or loss. If you hold the property 1 year or less as Albina did, any capital gain or loss is a short-term capital gain or loss. However, in the case of corporations, all losses that are carried forward, whether they are long term or short term, become short-term capital losses for the subsequent year.

Albina's short-term capital loss is

Amount realized	$ 4,500	(1,000 shares × $4.50/share)
+ Adjusted basis	(15,000)	(1,000 shares × $15/share)
Loss	$(10,500)	

She can deduct $3,000 on the 2012 tax return and carry forward $7,500 ($10,500 – $3,000) to 2013.

Answer (A) is incorrect. A capital loss deduction is limited to $3,000. The remaining $7,500 should be carried forward. Answer (B) is incorrect. The short-term capital loss was $10,500 ($15,000 – $4,500). The remaining $7,500 should be carried forward. Answer (D) is incorrect. The $7,500 loss that is carried forward is a short-term capital loss.

10. If 100 shares of stock are purchased on February 14, 2012, what is the earliest date on which the stock can be sold and the gain or loss can qualify for the long-term holding period?

A. August 14, 2013.

B. February 15, 2013.

C. February 14, 2013.

D. August 15, 2013.

Answer (B) is correct.

REQUIRED: The earliest date in which the stock can be sold and the gain/loss qualify for the long-term holding period.

DISCUSSION: The holding period of an asset for purposes of long-term gain treatment is more than 1 year from the date of acquisition, not including the day of acquisition but including the day of disposition.

Answer (A) is incorrect. An asset must only be held for greater than 1 year to qualify for long-term treatment. Answer (C) is incorrect. The holding period of an asset does not include the day of acquisition but does include the day of disposition. Answer (D) is incorrect. An asset must only be held for greater than 1 year to qualify for long-term treatment.

11. On June 1, 2010, Mr. Smart purchased investment land. On January 31, 2011, Mr. Smart traded the land plus cash for some other investment land in a nontaxable exchange. On August 15, 2012, he sold the land received in the nontaxable exchange for a gain. What is the character of Mr. Smart's gain for 2012?

A. Short-term capital gain.

B. Long-term capital gain.

C. Part short-term capital gain and part long-term capital gain.

D. Ordinary income.

Answer (B) is correct.

REQUIRED: The character of gain from the sale of land received in a nontaxable exchange.

DISCUSSION: If property received in an exchange has the same basis in whole or in part as that of the property given (and if the property given is a capital asset or a Sec. 1231 asset), the holding period of the property received includes the period for which the property given was held [Sec. 1223(1)]. Thus, when the property is sold, the holding period includes the holding period of the property exchanged. And, under Sec. 1222, capital assets held more than 1 year are treated as long-term.

Answer (A) is incorrect. The gain is long-term. Nontaxable transactions normally give rise to a carryover of basis; thus, Mr. Smart held the land for more than 1 year. Answer (C) is incorrect. All of the gain is long-term. Answer (D) is incorrect. The asset is a capital asset. Thus, the gain is characterized as a capital gain.

8.3 Capital Gains and Losses

12. Mark sold a building for $100,000 cash plus property with a fair market value (FMV) of $10,000. He had purchased the building 5 years ago for $85,000. He made $30,000 worth of improvements and deducted $25,000 for depreciation. The buyer assumed Mark's real estate taxes of $12,000 and mortgage of $20,000 on the building. What is the amount realized on the sale of the building?

A. $110,000

B. $142,000

C. $130,000

D. $145,500

Answer (B) is correct.

REQUIRED: The amount realized on the sale of real property.

DISCUSSION: The amount realized under Sec. 1001 includes money received, fair market value of other property received, and any liabilities of which the seller is relieved. Mark's amount realized is $142,000 ($100,000 cash + $10,000 fair market value property + $32,000 liabilities relieved).

Answer (A) is incorrect. Any liabilities of which the seller is relieved is included in their amount realized. Answer (C) is incorrect. The $12,000 of real estate taxes assumed by the buyer count as a liability of which the seller is relieved. Answer (D) is incorrect. The amount realized under Sec. 1001 includes money received, FMV of other property received, and any liabilities of which the seller is relieved.

13. All of the following statements are true except

A. The totals for short-term capital gains and losses and the totals for long-term capital gains and losses must be figured separately.

B. When you carry over any capital loss, its character will be long-term.

C. If the total of your capital gains is more than the total of your capital losses, the excess is taxable.

D. The yearly limit on the amount of the capital loss you can deduct in excess of capital gains is $3,000 ($1,500 if you are married filing separately).

Answer (B) is correct.

REQUIRED: The false statement regarding capital gains and losses.

DISCUSSION: Excess capital losses retain their identity as either long-term or short-term losses in the year to which they are carried. This is true for individuals only, not for corporations.

14. Milton spent $70,000 for a building that he used in his business. He made improvements at a cost of $20,000 and deducted a depreciation of $10,000. He sold the building for $100,000 cash and received property having a fair market value of $20,000. The buyer assumed Milton's real estate taxes of $3,000 and a mortgage of $17,000 on the building. Selling expenses were $4,000. The gain on the sale is

A. $10,000

B. $56,000

C. $40,000

D. $52,000

Answer (B) is correct.

REQUIRED: The gain on sale of property in return for various assets and assumption of liabilities.

DISCUSSION: Publication 544 calculates the gain on sale as follows:

Amount realized:		
Cash	$100,000	
FMV of property received	20,000	
Real estate taxes assumed by buyer	3,000	
Mortgage assumed by buyer	17,000	$140,000
Adjusted basis:		
Cost of building	$ 70,000	
Improvements	20,000	
Total	$ 90,000	
Minus: Depreciation	(10,000)	
Adjusted basis	$ 80,000	
Plus: Selling expenses	4,000	84,000
Gain on sale		$ 56,000

Answer (A) is incorrect. The gain is equal to the excess of the amount realized over the adjusted basis of the property plus selling expenses. Answer (C) is incorrect. The real estate taxes and mortgage assumed by the buyer are added to the total amount realized. Answer (D) is incorrect. The selling expenses are added to adjusted basis.

15. Mr. Nehru had the following capital transactions during the current year:

Short-term capital gain	$1,000
Short-term capital loss	2,700
Long-term capital gain	6,500
Long-term capital loss	1,800

What is the amount of Mr. Nehru's capital gain net income (or loss) on his current year Schedule D?

A. $7,500

B. $3,000

C. $4,700

D. $(3,000)

Answer (B) is correct.

REQUIRED: The amount of capital gain net income in the Schedule D summary.

DISCUSSION: Schedule D is used to report capital gains and losses, and the summary combines the long-term gains/losses with the short-term gains/losses. When these capital gains and losses all net to a gain, it is called "capital gain net income" [Sec. 1222(9)]. This has occurred in the question and is computed below.

Net long-term capital gain ($6,500 – $1,800)	$4,700
Net short-term capital gain ($1,000 – $2,700)	(1,700)
Capital gain net income	$3,000

Do not confuse the term "capital gain net income" with the term "net capital gain." A "net capital gain" is the excess of net long-term capital gains over net short-term capital losses. It does not include net short-term capital gains. The difference is important because the "net capital gain" term is used in applying the 15% maximum tax rate (0% for taxpayers in the 15% tax bracket) on capital gains. The 15% maximum tax rate for individuals does not apply to net short-term capital gains.

Answer (A) is incorrect. Gains are netted with losses in order to determine net capital gain net income. Answer (C) is incorrect. Short-term losses are netted with long-term gains to determine capital gain net income. Answer (D) is incorrect. The gains exceed the losses.

16. A married couple has a $40,000 short-term capital loss, a $20,000 collectible long-term capital gain, and a $25,000 long-term capital gain subject to the 15% rate. What are the amount and the character of their capital gain/(loss) after netting the gains and losses?

A. $5,000 long-term gain taxed at 28%.

B. $5,000 long-term gain taxed at 15%.

C. $(20,000) short-term loss and $25,000 long-term gain taxed at 15%.

D. $0

Answer (B) is correct.

REQUIRED: The netting process of capital gains and losses.

DISCUSSION: The short-term capital loss is first used to offset the $20,000 collectible long-term capital gain that would be taxed at 28%. The remaining $20,000 of the short-term capital loss is then offset against the $25,000 long-term capital gain taxed at 15%. The $5,000 remaining long-term capital gain taxed at 15% is reported on the return and is subject to tax.

Answer (A) is incorrect. The loss is first netted against the 28% gain, not the 15% gain. Answer (C) is incorrect. The remaining $20,000 short-term loss is then applied against the $25,000 gain taxed at 15%. Answer (D) is incorrect. The short-term capital loss does not completely eliminate the gain.

17. How should an individual report the following transactions on the tax return?

Total short-term capital losses	$ 6,000
Total short-term capital gains	15,000
Total long-term capital losses	10,000
Total long-term capital gains	10,000

A. $25,000 net capital gain.

B. $0 net capital gain.

C. $9,000 net capital gain.

D. $22,000 net capital gain.

Answer (B) is correct.

REQUIRED: The amount of net capital gain.

DISCUSSION: For individuals, net capital gain (NCG) is the excess of net LTCG over net STCL. Net STCG is not included in NCG. Under Sec. 1222(11) the term "net capital gain" means the excess of the net long-term capital gain for the taxable year over the net short-term capital loss for such year.

Net LTCG/L = $0 ($10,000 – $10,000)
Net STCG/L = $9,000 gain ($15,000 – $6,000)

Thus, NCG = $0 – $0 = $0

Net STCG is treated as ordinary income for individuals. Net capital gain rates do not apply to net STCG. The net STCG = $9,000.

Answer (A) is incorrect. LTCG are not added to STCG. They are reduced by LTCL producing an LTCG/L. Answer (C) is incorrect. There is a net STCG of $9,000, not an NCG. Answer (D) is incorrect. There is no way to combine STCG/L or LTCG/L to produce a $22,000 NCG.

18. Elton declared bankruptcy in the current year. Included in the liabilities discharged in the bankruptcy was a $15,000 personal loan Elton had received from his friend, Edward, 2 years ago. How would Edward treat this for tax purposes?

A. Ordinary loss on Form 4797.

B. Long-term capital loss on Schedule D.

C. Short-term capital loss on Schedule D.

D. Investment expense subject to 2% miscellaneous itemized deduction limitation.

Answer (C) is correct.

REQUIRED: Tax treatment of a $15,000 bad debt from a loan to a friend.

DISCUSSION: If a nonbusiness bad debt becomes totally worthless within the tax year, it is treated as a short-term capital loss. Short-term capital losses are reported on Schedule D of Form 1040.

Answer (A) is incorrect. This bad debt is not related to a business and is a short-term capital loss. Thus, it would not be reported on Form 4797, *Sales of Business Property*. Answer (B) is incorrect. Bad debt acquired through nonbusiness activities is always a short-term loss, regardless of the length of the loan. Answer (D) is incorrect. Bad debt from a loan is not an investment expense, it is a short-term capital loss. Thus, it is not subject to a 2% miscellaneous itemized deduction limitation.

19. A married couple has $150,000 of taxable income made up of $100,000 of ordinary income; a $200,000 long-term loss subject to the 15% rate; and $350,000 received in the sale of a residential building in 2012 that they had purchased in 1985 for $300,000. The building had a basis of $100,000. Assume that depreciation recapture at ordinary income rates is $10,000. What are the amount and the character of their capital gain/(loss) after netting the gains and losses?

A. $0

B. $200,000 long-term capital gain taxed at 15%.

C. $40,000 long-term capital gain taxed at 15%.

D. $40,000 long-term capital gain taxed at 25%.

Answer (D) is correct.

REQUIRED: The proper netting process of capital gains and losses with Sec. 1231 assets.

DISCUSSION: A residential building purchased in 1985 is a Sec. 1250 asset. Only the excess depreciation of $10,000 is recaptured as ordinary income. The unrecaptured Sec. 1250 gain is the amount of depreciation that would be recaptured if the asset were a Sec. 1245 asset or $200,000 ($300,000 purchase price minus $100,000 basis) less the $10,000 that has already been recognized as ordinary income. Thus, the unrecaptured Sec. 1250 gain is $190,000. The remaining $50,000 gain from the sale of the building is a long-term capital gain taxed at 15% ($250,000 gain minus $10,000 ordinary income minus $190,000 unrecaptured Sec. 1250 gain). The $200,000 long-term capital loss subject to the 15% tax rate is combined with the $50,000 gain taxed at 15% from the sale of the building, leaving a $150,000 loss. The net $150,000 loss in the 15% category is then offset against the $190,000 gain in the 25% category, leaving a $40,000 gain taxed at the 25% rate.

Answer (A) is incorrect. There is a capital gain on the sale of the asset. Answer (B) is incorrect. The long-term capital loss is subject to the 15% rate. Answer (C) is incorrect. The gain is taxed at 25%, not 15%.

20. Sharon sold two collections during 2012. These were her only sales. Determine the amount and character of her gains/(losses) on these sales.

- Coin collection she began as a child with a basis of $1,000, sold for $5,000
- Collection of original short stories she wrote in 2009, sold for $20,000

A. $20,000 long-term capital gain.

B. $24,000 long-term capital gain.

C. $4,000 long-term capital gain and $20,000 ordinary income.

D. $24,000 ordinary income.

Answer (C) is correct.

REQUIRED: The amount and character of various sales of assets.

DISCUSSION: A copyright; a literary, musical, or artistic composition; a letter or memorandum; or similar property created by one's personal efforts is an ordinary income asset. Coin collections are listed as capital assets. Thus, it must be recognized as a capital gain or loss at its sale.

Answer (A) is incorrect. Literary property created through personal efforts is an ordinary income asset. Also, coin collections are to be classified as capital assets. Answer (B) is incorrect. Literary property created through personal efforts is an ordinary income asset. Answer (D) is incorrect. Coin collections are to be classified as capital assets.

21. During 2012, Nicholas made the following dispositions of property:

- Sold publicly traded stock, which cost $2,000 and had been held for 2 years, for $3,000
- Sold land, which cost $20,000 and had been held for 9 months, to his brother for $16,000

How should Nicholas report these dispositions on his 2012 return?

A. $1,000 long-term capital gain.

B. $3,000 long-term capital loss.

C. $3,000 short-term capital loss.

D. $3,000 ordinary loss.

Answer (A) is correct.

REQUIRED: The amount and character of gains and losses from the disposition of capital assets.

DISCUSSION: A capital gain or loss on the sale of property held more than 1 year is a long-term capital gain or loss. Both stock and land are classified as capital assets. However, under Sec. 267, losses are not allowed on sales or exchanges of property between related parties.

Answer (B) is incorrect. Losses are not allowed on sales or exchanges of property between related parties. Answer (C) is incorrect. Losses are not allowed on sales or exchanges of property between related parties. Answer (D) is incorrect. Both stock and land are classified as capital assets. However, losses are not allowed on sales or exchanges of property between related parties.

22. In computing the gain or loss from a sale or trade of property, which statement below best describes the amount you realize?

A. The money you actually receive.

B. The fair market value of the property on the transaction date.

C. Everything you receive for the property.

D. The value of any services you received.

Answer (C) is correct.

REQUIRED: Amount realized from a transaction.

DISCUSSION: When computing the gain or loss from a transaction, the taxpayer must compute the amount realized from the transaction. The amount realized equals the sum of money received, the FMV of property received, and liability relief, less selling expenses and liabilities assumed.

Answer (A) is incorrect. The amount realized is more than actual cash money received. Answer (B) is incorrect. The amount realized does not necessarily equal the FMV of the property on the transaction date. Answer (D) is incorrect. The value of services received does not necessarily equal the amount realized.

23. John is a furniture maker and carpenter. John makes half of his income as an employee of Concept Designs, Inc., a fine furniture manufacturing corporation. He makes the other half of his income from a personal business where he purchases, renovates, and then resells houses. In January of 2012, John purchases a house that is not his residence for $50,000. He spends $10,000 in materials renovating the house, which he sells in November of 2012 for $90,000. What is the amount and character of John's gain from this transaction?

A. $20,000 ordinary gain.

B. $30,000 short-term capital gain.

C. $30,000 ordinary gain.

D. $20,000 short-term capital gain.

Answer (C) is correct.

REQUIRED: Gain realized from sale of house when taxpayer engages in business of buying houses, renovating them, and selling them.

DISCUSSION: When a taxpayer holds property for sale to customers in the ordinary course of a trade or business, such property cannot be considered a capital asset. John's gain from the sale equals the amount realized less his adjusted basis in the property. The amount realized equals the selling price, $90,000. The adjusted basis in the property equals the purchase price, $50,000, plus the renovations made to the property, $10,000. Thus, John's gain equals $30,000 [$90,000 – ($50,000 + $10,000)] and is ordinary.

Answer (A) is incorrect. The gain equals $30,000, not $20,000. Answer (B) is incorrect. The gain is an ordinary gain, not a short-term capital gain. Answer (D) is incorrect. The amount of the gain is $30,000, not $20,000. The gain is an ordinary gain, not a short-term capital gain.

8.4 Capital Gains on Sales of Stock

24. Rose had the following transactions during 2012:

Sale of ACB stock (basis $400)	$800
Commission paid on sale of ACB stock	$ 50
Received 200 extra shares of DEF in stock split (fair market value)	$800
Decrease in value of GHI mutual fund	$600
JKL stock declared worthless (basis $700) -- no stock value	$ 0

What is the net gain or loss Rose will claim on her Schedule D?

A. $350 loss.

B. $1,000 gain.

C. $300 gain.

D. $650 loss.

Answer (A) is correct.

REQUIRED: The gain or loss to be claimed on Schedule D.

DISCUSSION: A gain or loss is determined by subtracting the adjusted basis of the property from the amount realized. To calculate adjusted basis you begin with the unadjusted basis of the property, which is usually its cost. The unadjusted basis is then adjusted for any expenditure, receipt, loss, or other item that is chargeable to the capital account. The amount realized is the money received on the sale or exchange of property plus the fair market value of any property or services received in the exchange. The 200 shares of DEF received in a stock split are not taxable. These additional shares get added in with Rose's other DEF shares and then her basis is reallocated to her new share total. The decrease in the value of Rose's GHI mutual fund is also not a taxable event. A gain or loss is not recognized until sale or exchange has occurred (securities that become worthless during the year are deemed sold on the last day of the year). Rose's net loss claimed on Schedule D is computed as follows:

Rose's Gain or Loss

	ACB Stock	JKL Stock
Amount Realized	$ 800	$ 0
– Adjusted Basis (400 + 50)	450	(700)
Gain (Loss)	$ 350	$(700)
Net Loss	$(350)	

Answer (B) is incorrect. Rose has a net loss of $350. Answer (C) is incorrect. The amount of $300 includes a gain of $800 for the DEF stock and a loss of $600 for the GHI mutual fund, neither of which has been realized. In addition, this gain fails to subtract the adjusted basis for the ACB stock. Answer (D) is incorrect. Rose has a net loss of $350.

25. Herb files single and had the following capital gains and losses in 2012:

- $500 loss on the sale of stock he purchased on January 14, 2012, and sold on August 10, 2012
- $5,000 loss on the sale of stock purchased October 1, 2011, and sold November 1, 2012
- $1,000 gain on the sale of a vacant lot held for 5 years

How should Herb's capital gains and losses be initially reported on Schedule D?

A. $4,500 long-term loss.

B. $4,000 long-term loss and $500 short-term loss.

C. $4,500 long-term loss and $1,000 short-term loss.

D. $5,500 long-term loss and $1,000 short-term gain.

Answer (B) is correct.

REQUIRED: The amount and character of the gains and losses to be reported on Schedule D.

DISCUSSION: A long-term capital gain or loss is realized from a capital asset held for more than 1 year. A short-term capital gain or loss is realized if the asset was held 1 year or less. Since the $500 loss on the sale of stock was held for less than 1 year, it is considered a short-term capital loss. The $5,000 loss on the sale of stock and the $1,000 gain on the sale of a vacant lot were held for more than 1 year; thus, they are classified as long-term, resulting in a long-term capital loss of $4,000 ($5,000 – $1,000). Therefore, Herb will initially report a $4,000 long-term capital loss and a $500 short-term capital loss on his Schedule D.

Answer (A) is incorrect. The $500 loss on the sale of stock should be classified as a short-term capital loss. Answer (C) is incorrect. Herb can only claim a $4,000 long-term capital loss and a $500 short-term capital loss. Answer (D) is incorrect. Herb can only claim a $4,000 long-term capital loss and a $500 short-term capital loss.

26. Sam purchased 100 shares of stock in 2003 for $2,500. The company had no earnings or profits in 2011 or 2012. In 2011, Sam received a return of capital distribution on that stock of $2,000, and in 2012, he received a second return of capital distribution on that stock of $2,000. What amount should he report on his 2012 tax return?

A. Nothing until the shares are sold.

B. $1,500 as ordinary dividend income.

C. $1,500 as long-term capital gain income.

D. $2,000 as return of capital income.

Answer (C) is correct.

REQUIRED: The amount and type of income to be reported on the taxpayer's return.

DISCUSSION: A return of capital is a tax-free distribution that reduces a stock's basis by the amount of the distribution. If a shareholder's basis is reduced to zero because of a tax-free return of capital, any excess amounts received are treated as a capital gain.

Answer (A) is incorrect. A capital gain must be recognized on a distribution of capital after the basis in the stock is zero. Answer (B) is incorrect. A capital gain is recognized. Answer (D) is incorrect. A capital gain is recognized.

27. Larry purchased stock in 2007 for $100. During 2010, he received a return of capital of $80 on this stock. During 2012, he received another return of capital of $30. Larry had no other stock transactions in 2012. What amount should he report on his 2012 income tax return, and what is his basis in the stock at the end of 2012?

A. $30 capital gain, $100 stock basis.

B. $30 dividend income, $100 stock basis.

C. $10 capital gain, zero stock basis.

D. $10 dividend income, zero stock basis.

Answer (C) is correct.

REQUIRED: The amount and type of gain and the basis in the stock.

DISCUSSION: A return of capital is a tax-free distribution that reduces a stock's basis by the amount of the distribution. If a shareholder's basis is reduced to zero because of a tax-free return of capital, any excess amounts received are treated as a capital gain.

Answer (A) is incorrect. A return of capital reduces basis, and a capital gain is not recognized until basis is reduced to zero. Answer (B) is incorrect. A return of capital reduces basis, and any gain, after basis is reduced to zero, is a capital gain. Answer (D) is incorrect. A capital gain is recognized when a return of capital distribution exceeds the stock's remaining basis.

28. Maggie trades stock in ABC Company with an adjusted basis of $7,000 for DEF Company stock with a fair market value of $10,000. She had no other transactions during the year. What is the amount realized and what is her gain or loss on this transaction?

A. The amount realized is $10,000, and the amount of gain is $3,000.

B. The amount realized is $10,000, and the amount of loss is $3,000.

C. The amount realized is $7,000, and the amount of gain is $4,000.

D. The amount realized is $17,000, and the amount of gain is $3,000.

Answer (A) is correct.

REQUIRED: The amount realized and gain recognized in the exchange of stock.

DISCUSSION: All realized gains must be recognized unless the IRC expressly provides otherwise. Conversely, no deduction is allowed for a realized loss unless the IRC expressly provides for it. The amount realized in most cases is the money received, plus the FMV of other property received, and liability relief, minus money or other property given up, selling expenses, and liabilities assumed. The gain (loss) realized is the amount realized less the adjusted basis. Thus, Maggie has realized $10,000 on this exchange, of which her gain is $3,000 ($10,000 – $7,000).

Answer (B) is incorrect. Maggie realized a gain on the exchange of stock. Answer (C) is incorrect. The amount realized is equal to the FMV of the property she received, and the gain is only $3,000 ($10,000 – $7,000). Answer (D) is incorrect. The amount realized is equal to the FMV of the property she received.

29. Billy Luker made several stock sales during 2012. Determine the net capital gain or loss for the following transactions:

Date Purchased	Cost	Date Sold	Sales Price
1-1-12	$ 4,000	6-2-12	$ 6,000
7-6-11	10,000	7-7-12	14,000
7-6-11	20,000	7-6-12	17,000
4-3-11	5,000	6-2-12	4,000

A. $2,000 net short-term capital gain.

B. $3,000 net long-term capital gain and $1,000 net short-term capital loss.

C. $2,000 net capital gain.

D. $4,000 net long-term capital gain and $2,000 net short-term capital loss.

Answer (C) is correct.

REQUIRED: The net capital gain/loss resulting from several stock sales.

DISCUSSION: The term "net long-term capital gain" means the excess of long-term capital gains for the taxable year over the long-term capital losses for such year (IRC Sec. 1222). Sec. 1222 states that gains and losses resulting from the sale or exchange of capital assets held 1 year or less are characterized as short-term. All other gains are characterized as long-term. The first and third stock sales are short-term and equal a net $1,000 loss. The second and fourth stock sales are long-term and equal a net $3,000 gain. The NCG is $2,000 ($3,000 net LTCG – $1,000 net STCL).

30. Yang and May Ling (husband and wife) owned a fashionable handbag store in New York, which they report as a sole proprietorship on their individual return. They had the following types of transactions during the 2012 year:

- $600,000 gain from the sale of a rare coin collection May Ling inherited in February of 2011. The sale occurred in the month of July.
- $100,000 received in accounts receivable from sales of 500 bags in November of 2012.
- $50,000 gain from sale of stocks held in their personal account that were purchased in 2010.
- $5,000 for the purchase of supplies, such as computer paper, invoices, etc., used in the business.

From the information provided, what is the proper gross amount and characterization of capital transactions that Yang and May Ling should report for the year 2012?

A. $650,000 as long-term capital gain.

B. $695,000 as ordinary income.

C. $50,000 as long-term capital gain.

D. $95,000 as short-term capital gain.

Answer (A) is correct.

REQUIRED: Proper gross amount and characterization of capital transactions that Yang and May Ling should report.

DISCUSSION: A capital gain or loss is realized on the sale or exchange of a capital asset, unless expressly excluded. Property held either for personal use or for the production of income is a capital asset, but dealer property is not. Inherited assets are considered held long-term. Yang and May Ling realize a long-term capital gain on the sale of their rare coin collection. The Lings must also recognize a long-term capital gain on the sale of their stock that was purchased in 2010. In total, the Lings must recognize a $650,000 long-term capital gain.

Answer (B) is incorrect. The $100,000 collected from accounts receivable is ordinary income, not a capital gain. Moreover, the $5,000 spent for supplies is not deductible from the capital gains. Answer (C) is incorrect. The sale of the rare coin collection should be included in the long-term capital gains. Answer (D) is incorrect. The collections from receivables is not a capital gain. Moreover, the $5,000 spent for supplies is not deductible from the capital gains.

31. Paula received notice that her mutual fund had allocated a long-term capital gain to her account in 2012 in the amount of $3,500 and had paid federal tax on her behalf in the amount of $1,225 on the gain. No amount was to be paid to Paula on the gain, but it would be credited to her account. All of the following statements are true except

A. Paula is allowed a credit for the federal tax paid on her behalf of $1,225.

B. Paula will report a long-term capital gain of $3,500.

C. Paula will increase her basis in the stock by $2,275.

D. Paula will not report any gain because nothing was paid to her.

Answer (D) is correct.

REQUIRED: The false statement about the taxation of mutual funds.

DISCUSSION: A mutual fund is a regulated investment company, the taxation of which is determined by Sec. 852. Dividends paid by the mutual fund to shareholders are taxed. Undistributed capital gains must be included in income by shareholders, but a credit is allowed for their proportionate share of any tax on the capital gain paid by the mutual fund. Therefore, Paula must report the full $3,500 as a long-term capital gain.

Answer (A) is incorrect. A credit is allowed for taxes paid by a mutual fund. Answer (B) is incorrect. A long-term capital gain must still be recognized if earned even if it is not distributed. Answer (C) is incorrect. Basis is increased by the amount of recognized gain.

32. Karen Smith bought Coca-Cola stock for $475 on March 31, 2012. On November 15, 2012, Karen received a non-taxable distribution of $155 on the 50 shares of stock she owned. She sold the stock for $300 on December 22, 2012. What is her gain or loss on the sale?

A. $175 gain.

B. $175 loss.

C. $20 gain.

D. $20 loss.

Answer (D) is correct.

REQUIRED: The amount of loss on the sale of stock following a nontaxable stock distribution.

DISCUSSION: Since the distribution is nontaxable, it is considered a return of capital that reduces the basis of the stock. The basis of the stock cannot be decreased below zero. Karen's basis in the stock is reduced because of the distribution from $475 to $320 ($475 – $155 distribution). When it is sold for $300, the recognition of a $20 loss occurs ($300 realized – $320 adjusted basis).

33. Vanessa inherited 100 shares of stock from her grandmother when her grandmother died on December 10, 2011. At that time, the fair market value of the stock was $50 per share. Vanessa's grandmother paid $40 per share when she purchased the stock July 1, 2011. If Vanessa sells all 100 shares for $60 per share on June 30, 2012, how should she report the sale on her return for 2012?

A. $1,000 short-term capital gain.

B. $2,000 short-term capital gain.

C. $1,000 long-term capital gain.

D. $2,000 long-term capital gain.

Answer (C) is correct.

REQUIRED: The correct treatment of the disposition of stock acquired from a decedent.

DISCUSSION: The basis of property received from a decedent is generally the fair market value of the property on the date of the decedent's death. Basis in the stock is the fair market value (the date of her grandmother's death). Any asset received from a decedent is considered held long-term no matter how long it is held. Thus, Vanessa has a long-term capital gain of $1,000 (100 × $60 – 100 × $50).

Answer (A) is incorrect. Assets received from a decedent are considered long-term no matter how long they are held. Answer (B) is incorrect. The basis of property received from a decedent is generally the fair market value of the property at the date of the decedent's death. Also, assets received from a decedent are considered long-term no matter how long they are held. Answer (D) is incorrect. The basis of property received from a decedent is generally the fair market value of the property at the date of the decedent's death.

34. Ms. Birch purchased the following stocks:

- 300 shares of Music Corp. on 1/18/04 for $3,000
- 200 shares of Play Corp. on 2/11/05 for $2,000
- 600 shares of Fun Corp. on 4/27/11 for $16,000
- 100 shares of Book Corp. on 12/19/11 for $8,000

On April 27, 2012, Ms. Birch sold all of the above stock for the following amounts:

Music Corp.	$ 5,000
Play Corp.	10,000
Fun Corp.	4,000
Book Corp.	14,000

What are Ms. Birch's net long-term capital gains or losses (LTCG/LTCL) and short-term capital gains or losses (STCG/STCL) on the above transactions?

A. LTCG, $10,000; STCL, $6,000.

B. LTCG, $16,000; STCL, $12,000.

C. LTCL, $2,000; STCG, $6,000.

D. None of the answers are correct.

Answer (A) is correct.

REQUIRED: The amount of net long-term and short-term capital gain or loss for 2012.

DISCUSSION: Long-term capital gain or loss is the gain or loss from the sale or exchange of a capital asset held for more than 1 year (Sec. 1222). If the capital gain or loss is not long-term, it is short-term.

A net long-term capital gain is the excess of long-term capital gains over long-term capital losses. The two long-term transactions (Music Corp. and Play Corp.) resulted in a net long-term capital gain of $10,000.

A net short-term capital gain is the excess of short-term capital gains over short-term capital losses. There were two short-term transactions (Fun Corp. and Book Corp.), resulting in a net short-term capital loss of $6,000.

35. Mr. and Mrs. Able are investors in a mutual fund that is not part of a qualified retirement plan. For 2012, the fund notified them that it had allocated a $9,500 long-term capital gain to their account. Of this total, only $4,500 was distributed in 2012. In addition, the fund paid $500 federal tax on their behalf. What is the correct amount of long-term capital gain that the Ables should report on their 2012 tax return?

A. $10,000

B. $9,500

C. $5,000

D. $4,500

Answer (B) is correct.

REQUIRED: The amount of long-term capital gain to be included in gross income.

DISCUSSION: A mutual fund is a regulated investment company, the taxation of which is determined by Sec. 852. Dividends paid by the mutual fund to shareholders are taxed. Undistributed capital gains must be included in income by shareholders, but a credit is allowed for their proportionate share of any tax on the capital gain paid by the mutual fund. Therefore, the Ables must report the full $9,500 as a long-term capital gain.

Answer (A) is incorrect. The $500 of federal income taxes paid is not reported as capital gain but is taken by the Ables as a credit. Answer (C) is incorrect. Both the distributed and the undistributed amounts of capital gain must be reported as income. Answer (D) is incorrect. The actual amount of the gain, not only the amount distributed, must be reported.

36. In Year 1, Nancy bought 100 shares of Trauna, Inc., for $5,000, or $50 a share. In Year 2, Nancy bought 100 shares of Trauna stock for $8,000, or $80 a share. In Year 3, Trauna declared a 2-for-1 stock split. Nancy sold 50 shares of the stock she received from the stock split for $2,000. She could not definitely identify the shares she sold. What is the amount of Nancy's net capital gain from this sale for Year 3?

A. $0

B. $750

C. $1,625

D. $2,000

Answer (B) is correct.

REQUIRED: The gain from the sale of stock purchased at different times.

DISCUSSION: Under Reg. 1.1012-1(c), the basis and holding period of stock acquired in several different transactions are determined by specific identification of the stock sold. If the stock sold cannot be identified to any purchase or lot, it is assumed to be the first stock purchased or acquired; i.e., the FIFO (first-in, first-out) rule is applied. The additional shares received from the stock split are distributed proportionately to the shares purchased at $50 per share and the shares purchased at $80 per share, and the original basis is allocated among the new shares. The new basis for the Year 1 shares is $25 per share ($5,000 ÷ 200). Therefore, the net capital gain is $750.

Amount realized	$2,000
Basis (50 × $25)	1,250
Net capital gain	$ 750

Answer (A) is incorrect. A gain is recognized to the extent that the amount realized exceeds the adjusted basis of the new shares. Answer (C) is incorrect. A gain is recognized to the extent that the amount realized exceeds the adjusted basis of the new shares. Answer (D) is incorrect. Stocks received in a stock split are allocated a portion of the original shares' basis.

37. Kiran bought stock in the Big Bang Corporation in 2007 for $2,000. In 2011, Kiran received a return of capital distribution of $100 as a partial return on her investment. In 2012, Kiran sold the stock for $3,000. Her basis in the stock is

A. $3,000

B. $2,100

C. $1,900

D. $2,000

Answer (C) is correct.

REQUIRED: Basis in stock after receiving a return of capital distribution.

DISCUSSION: The original basis in Kiran's stock is $2,000, the original purchase. Kiran must adjust the basis for the return of capital distribution of $100. Therefore, Kiran's basis at the time of disposition equals $1,900 ($2,000 – $100).

Answer (A) is incorrect. The basis in the stock must not necessarily equal the selling price of the stock. Answer (B) is incorrect. The $100 return of capital distribution decreases the basis of the stock. Answer (D) is incorrect. The $100 return of capital distribution decreases the basis of the stock.

8.5 Sections 1202 and 1244 Stock

38. Small business stock under Sec. 1202 is subject to special taxation. Which of the following statements is false regarding this stock?

A. There is a 50% exclusion from gain on stock held more than 5 years.

B. The gain may be deferred if reinvested in other qualified small business stock within 60 days of the sale.

C. The AMT preference on the small business stock is 50% of the excluded gain.

D. C corporation stock is eligible for the small business stock provisions.

Answer (C) is correct.

REQUIRED: The false statement regarding small business stock under Sec. 1202.

DISCUSSION: An alternative minimum tax (AMT) preference is equal to 7% of the excluded gain. Since this is an exclusion preference, there is no minimum tax credit allowed.

Answer (A) is incorrect. There is a 50% exclusion from gain on stock held more than 5 years. Answer (B) is incorrect. The gain may be deferred if reinvested on other qualified small business stock within 60 days of the sale. Answer (D) is incorrect. C corporation stock is eligible for the small business stock provisions.

39. Shannon and Dan Smith (wife and husband) purchased Section 1244 (small business) stock in 2012. Which of the following statements is true?

A. If they incurred a loss on Section 1244 stock, they can deduct the loss as a capital loss rather than as an ordinary loss.

B. If the stock becomes worthless, they can claim an ordinary loss limited to $50,000 individually or $100,000 together on a joint return, per year.

C. If the loss is $60,000 and Shannon does not have any other losses, Dan can only deduct $50,000 as ordinary loss on the joint return.

D. If they incurred a gain on Section 1244 stock, they should treat it as ordinary gain.

Answer (B) is correct.

REQUIRED: The true statement regarding Sec. 1244 stock.

DISCUSSION: Taxpayers may deduct losses on Sec. 1244 stock as ordinary up to $50,000 in any 1 year ($100,000 on a joint return).

Answer (A) is incorrect. The loss is treated as ordinary rather than as capital. Answer (C) is incorrect. Up to $100,000 may be deducted on a joint return. Answer (D) is incorrect. The gain is treated as a capital gain rather than as ordinary income.

STUDY UNIT NINE
BUSINESS PROPERTY, RELATED PARTIES, AND INSTALLMENT SALES

(8 pages of outline)

This study unit involves a discussion of related party sales, the sale of business property, and installment sales. Special rules prevent taxpayers from receiving unwarranted tax benefits. Losses on sales to related parties are disallowed, except for sales in corporate liquidation rules. Depreciation is recaptured on the sale of business property in order to prevent taxpayers from taking ordinary depreciation deductions and then receiving capital gain treatment at the time of sale of the property. When payments from the sale of property are received after the year of sale, gain recognition is deferred for each payment until the payment's corresponding tax year.

9.1 RELATED PARTY SALES

These rules limit tax avoidance between related parties.

1. Gain recognized on sale is ordinary income when an asset is transferred to a related person in whose hands the asset is depreciable (see Publication 544).
   a. For this unique situation, "related" means:
      1) A person and the person's controlled entity(ies),
      2) A taxpayer and any trust in which the taxpayer (or spouse) is a beneficiary,
      3) An executor and a beneficiary of an estate, and
      4) An employer and a welfare benefit fund controlled directly or indirectly by the employer (or related person).

Loss Nonrecognition

2. Loss realized on sale or exchange of property to a related person is not recognized.
   a. The transferee takes a cost basis.
   b. There is no adding of holding periods.
   c. Gain realized on a subsequent sale to an unrelated party is recognized only to the extent it exceeds the previously disallowed loss.
   d. Loss realized on a subsequent sale to a third party is recognized, but the previously disallowed loss is not added to it.

Related Parties

3. Related parties under Sec. 267(b) and (c), generally, for purposes of these provisions include
   a. Ancestors, lineal descendants, spouses, and siblings.
      1) Nephews and nieces are not descendants.
   b. Trusts and beneficiaries thereof.
   c. Controlled entities (50% ownership).

   NOTE: Constructive ownership rules between family members apply.

4. Loss on sale or exchange of property between a partnership and a person owning more than 50% of the capital or profit interests in the partnership is not recognized.

Employer-Employee Transactions

5. An employee is not a related party to the employer for purposes of the related-party sale rules.
   a. When an employer sells assets to an employee at less than FMV, the difference between FMV and the sales price is considered compensation to the employee.
      1) Since the employee pays tax on the compensation, his/her basis in the new property will be FMV.

Interspousal Transfer

6. No gain or loss is recognized on the transfer of property between spouses or, incident to a divorce, on transfers of property to a former spouse.
   a. The transferee takes a carryover basis in the property.
   b. These rules apply whether the transfer is a gift, a sale, or an exchange.

Stop and review! You have completed the outline for this subunit. Study questions 1 through 10 beginning on page 227.

9.2 BUSINESS PROPERTY

Secs. 1231, 1245, and 1250 recharacterize gain or loss. Secs. 1245 and 1250 also accelerate recognition of certain installment gain that would otherwise be deferred.

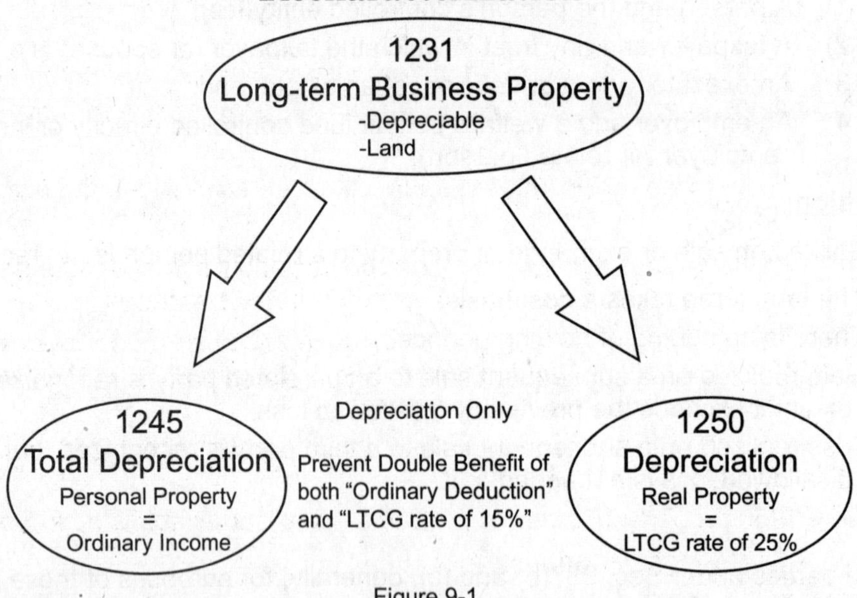

Figure 9-1

Section 1245 Property

1. A realized gain on the disposition of Sec. 1245 property is ordinary income to the extent of all depreciation or amortization taken.
   a. Amounts expensed under Sec. 179 are considered depreciation deductions. Depreciation deductions may be taken for the taxable year the business property is placed in service.

b. Property is considered placed in service when it is ready and available for a specific use.

c. The downward basis adjustment for a general business credit is considered a deduction allowed for depreciation and is subject to recapture.

d. The realized gain in excess of the depreciation taken may be treated as a gain from the sale or exchange of Sec. 1231 property.

2. Sec. 1245 property generally is depreciable personal property.

   a. It is tangible/intangible, depreciable/amortizable personal property (e.g., equipment, patent); recovery property, including specified real property; and tax benefit property (e.g., qualified Sec. 179 expense property).

   b. Other tangible property (excluding a building or its structural components) includes property used as an integral part of a trade or business, e.g., manufacturing or production equipment.

   c. Intangible, amortizable (Sec. 197) personal Sec. 1245 property examples include

      1) Leaseholds of Sec. 1245 property
      2) Professional athletic contracts, e.g., major league baseball
      3) Patents
      4) Livestock
      5) Goodwill acquired after August 10, 1993, in connection with the acquisition of a trade or business

   d. Particular types of property are treated as Sec. 1245 property due to an attributable tax benefit. An example is amortized pollution control facilities.

Section 1250 Ordinary Income

3. Sec. 1250 property is all depreciable real property that is not Sec. 1245 property, such as a building or its structural components.

   a. Sec. 1250 property is subject to its own recapture rules. For the three items listed below, the aggregate gain realized on the sale or disposition of Sec. 1250 property is ordinary income.

      1) The excess of accelerated depreciation taken over S-L depreciation is ordinary income.

         a) Partial reduction of excess depreciation is provided for under Sec. 1250 for low-income housing and rehabilitated structures.

      2) For corporations, the gain must be computed under both Sec. 1245 and 1250. If Sec. 1245 gain is larger than Sec. 1250 gain, 20% of the difference is characterized as ordinary income.

      3) For property held 1 year or less, any depreciation is recaptured as ordinary income.

   b. Sec. 1250 property includes depreciable real property not listed in Sec. 1245 acquired

      1) Prior to 1981 or after 1986 or
      2) During 1981 through 1986 and either residential property or property depreciated using the S-L method.

   c. Land is not Sec. 1250 property, but leases of land are Sec. 1250 intangible properties. Certain improvements to land may be treated as land, e.g., dams and irrigation systems.

   d. Examples of Sec. 1250 property include shopping malls, an apartment or office building, low-income housing, rented portions of residences, and escalators or elevators (placed in service after 1986).

e. Income received or accrued for more than one asset is allocated to each asset by agreement, by FMV, or by the residual method.
   1) To compute Sec. 1245 and Sec. 1250 ordinary income, an amount realized allocable to an asset must be further allocated to each use of a mixed-use asset for each tax year.
   2) Apportionment is on the basis of relative time or amount of asset usage, e.g., 5% of automobile usage for business or one-half of house used as rental property.

f. Recapture of post-1986 residential rental property and nonresidential real property is not required because they must be depreciated under the S-L method.

Section 1231 Property

4. Unlike the recapture provisions in Secs. 1245 and 1250, Sec. 1231 is beneficial to the taxpayer.
   a. When Sec. 1231 property gains exceed losses (a net Sec. 1231 gain), each gain or loss is treated as being from the sale of a long-term capital asset.
   b. If Sec. 1231 property losses exceed gains (a net Sec. 1231 loss), each gain or loss is considered ordinary.
   c. Section 1231 property is property held for more than 1 year and includes
      1) All real or depreciable property used in a trade or business, or
      2) Involuntarily converted capital assets held in connection with a trade or business or in a transaction entered into for a profit.
   d. Examples of Sec. 1231 property include apartment buildings, parking lots, manufacturing equipment, and involuntarily converted investment artwork.
   e. Examples that are not Sec. 1231 property include personal-use property and inventory.
   f. Sec. 1231 has a two-step test.
      1) Step 1: Determine net gain or loss from all casualties or thefts of Sec. 1231 property for the tax year. Gain or loss from involuntary conversions by other than casualty or theft is included in Step 2 but not Step 1.
         a) If the result is a net loss, each gain or loss is treated as ordinary income or loss.
         b) If the result is a net gain, each gain or loss is included in Step 2.
      2) Step 2: Determine net gain or loss from all dispositions of Sec. 1231 property for the year, including the property included in Step 1 only if Step 1 resulted in a net gain.
         a) If the result is a net loss, each gain or loss is treated as ordinary income or loss.
         b) If the result is a net gain, each gain or loss is treated as a long-term capital gain or loss, subject to the recapture rules under i. on the next page.

Allocation

   g. Allocation is required when Sec. 1245 or Sec. 1250 property is also Sec. 1231 property and only a portion of gain recognized is Sec. 1245 or Sec. 1250 OI.

EXAMPLE

The taxpayer sold a second residence for $800,000. The land had a cost of $100,000, and the house had a cost of $300,000. The selling price was allocated as follows: $200,000 to the land and $600,000 to the house. The taxpayer also sold a residential rental building and land for $1,200,000. The land had a basis of $200,000, and the building had a basis of $200,000. The building cost $400,000 and had been depreciated using accelerated depreciation under ACRS. The excess of accelerated depreciation over straight line was $50,000. The selling prices of the land and building were $400,000 and $800,000, respectively. In addition, the taxpayer had a $600,000 casualty loss on a business-use aircraft.

	Personal Use		Prod. of Income/Bus.		
	Land	Improvements	Land	Depreciable	Total
Cost	$100,000	$300,000	$200,000	$ 400,000	$1,000,000
Depreciation taken	0	0	0	(200,000)	
Amount realized	200,000	600,000	400,000	800,000	2,000,000
Gain realized	100,000	300,000	200,000	600,000	1,200,000
Sec. 1250 OI				$ 50,000	
Sec. 1231 gain				550,000	
Other Sec. 1231 loss (casualty 100% business-use aircraft)				$(600,000)	
Sec. 1231 ordinary loss				(50,000)	
LTCG	$100,000	$300,000	$200,000	$ 0	$ 600,000

- The taxpayer has a $100,000 gain ($200,000 – $100,000) on the sale of the personal land.
- There is a $300,000 gain ($600,000 – $300,000) on the sale of the second residence.
- The business land has a $200,000 gain ($400,000 – $200,000).
- The residential rental building has a $600,000 gain ($800,000 – $200,000).
  - The $50,000 accelerated depreciation over the straight-line depreciation is recaptured as ordinary income.
- The remaining $550,000 gain on the rental property is offset by the business casualty loss, creating an ordinary loss of $50,000 ($550,000 – $600,000).
  - The $50,000 ordinary income from the depreciation recapture is offset by the $50,000 Sec. 1231 ordinary loss.

h. The installment method can apply to Sec. 1231 property.

i. Recapture. Net gain on Sec. 1231 property is treated as ordinary income to the extent of unrecaptured net Sec. 1231 losses from preceding tax years.

1) Unrecaptured net Sec. 1231 losses are the total of net Sec. 1231 losses for the last 5 tax years, reduced by net Sec. 1231 gains characterized as ordinary income under Sec. 1231(c).

EXAMPLE

Eric has unrecaptured Sec. 1231 losses of $4,500 from 2 years ago. This year, he has a net Sec. 1231 gain of $7,600. Of this gain, $4,500 will be recharacterized as ordinary, and the remaining $3,100 will be classified as long-term capital gain.

2) Sec. 1245 and 1250 recapture is computed before Sec. 1231 recapture, but Sec. 1231 recapture is computed before Steps 1 and 2 on the previous page.

3) Sec. 1231 merely characterizes gain or loss. Any Section 1231 gain that is recharacterized as capital gain will first consist of 28% gain, then 25% gain, and finally 15% gain.

Installment Sales

5. All gain realized from a disposal of recapture property in an installment sale is characterized as ordinary income (OI) by Sec. 1245 or Sec. 1250 and must be recognized in the period of sale. Excess gain over Sec. 1245 or Sec. 1250 OI is accounted for by the installment method.

Gift Property

6. Neither Sec. 1245 nor Sec. 1250 applies to a gift disposition.
   a. Any gain realized by the donee upon a subsequent taxable disposition is subject to Sec. 1245 and Sec. 1250 characterization up to the sum of any potential Sec. 1245 and Sec. 1250 OI at the time of the gift and any Sec. 1245 and Sec. 1250 OI potential arising between gift and subsequent disposition.

Inherited Property

7. Neither Sec. 1245 nor Sec. 1250 applies to a disposition by bequest, devise, or intestate succession. Exceptions include the following:
   a. Sec. 1245 and Sec. 1250 OI is recognized for a transfer at death to the extent of any income in respect of a decedent (IRD).
   b. Sec. 1245 OI potential also results from depreciation allowed to a decedent because the depreciation does not carry over to the transferee.

Section 351 Exchange for Stock

8. Generally, no gain is recognized upon an exchange of property for all the stock of a newly formed corporation.
   a. Sec. 1245 and Sec. 1250 OI is limited to any amount of gain recognized in a Sec. 351 transaction.

Like-Kind Exchanges

9. Sec. 1245 applies to the amount of gain recognized plus the FMV of non-Sec. 1245 property received (e.g., boot) that is not already taken into account in calculating the recognized gain.

Stop and review! You have completed the outline for this subunit. Study questions 11 through 20 beginning on page 229.

9.3 INSTALLMENT SALES

The installment method must be used to report installment sales unless election is made not to apply the method. An installment sale is a disposition of property in which at least one payment is to be received after the close of the tax year in which the disposition occurs.

1. Installment sales do not apply to the following dispositions:
   a. Inventory personal property sales
   b. Revolving credit personal property sales
   c. Dealer dispositions, including dispositions of
      1) Personal property of a type regularly sold by the person on the installment plan
      2) Real property held for sale to customers in the ordinary course of trade or business
   d. Securities, generally, if publicly traded
   e. Sales on agreement to establish an irrevocable escrow account
2. Not excluded from installment sale deferral are
   a. Certain sales of residential lots or timeshares subject to interest on the deferred tax
   b. Property used or produced in a farming business

Realized Gain

3. The amount of realized gain to be recognized in a tax year is equal to the gross profit multiplied by the ratio of payments received in the current year divided by the total contract price.

$$\text{Realized gain} = \text{Gross profit} \times \frac{\text{Payments received in the current year}}{\text{Total contract price}}$$

   a. Recognize, as income, payments received multiplied by the gross profit ratio.
      1) Excess of liability assumed over adjusted basis (AB) and selling expenses is treated as part of the down payment.
      2) A payment is considered paid in full if the balance is placed into an irrevocable escrow account (i.e., amounts that cannot revert to the purchaser) at a later date.
   b. The gross profit ratio is the ratio of the gross profit to the total contract price.
   c. The gross profit is the sales price reduced by any selling expenses (including debt forgiveness) and adjusted basis.
      1) When the selling price is reduced in a future year, the gross profit on the sale will also be reduced.
         a) The gross profit percentage must be recalculated for the remaining periods by using the reduced sales price and subtracting the gross profit already recognized.
      2) Gross profit includes the unrecognized gain on sale of a personal residence.
   d. The sales price is the sum of any cash received, liability relief, and installment notes from the buyer. It does not include imputed interest.
   e. The total contract price is the amount that will be collected.
      1) An existing mortgage assumed is not collected by the seller.
      2) Contract price includes the excess of liability assumed over AB and selling expenses.
         a) When the liability exceeds the AB and selling expenses, the gross profit percentage is 100%.

$$\text{Gross profit ratio} = \frac{\text{Gross profit}}{\text{Contract price}} = \frac{\text{Selling price} - \text{Selling exp.} - \text{Adj. basis}}{\text{Amount to be collected}}$$

Character of Gain

4. Character of gain recognized depends on the nature of the property in the transferor's hands.
5. The full amount of Sec. 1245 and Sec. 1250 ordinary gain ("depreciation recapture") must be recognized in the year of sale, even if it exceeds payments received.
   a. The gain is added to basis before further applying the installment method.

Anti-Avoidance Rule

6. An anti-avoidance rule applies to an installment sale of property to a related party. On a second disposition (by the related party transferee in the first sale), payments received must be treated as a payment received by the person who made the first (installment) sale to a related party.
   a. A second disposition by gift is included. The FMV is treated as the payment.
   b. Death of the first disposition seller or buyer does not accelerate recognition.

Repossession

7. The seller of personal property recognizes as gain or loss any difference between the FMV of repossessed property and the AB of an installment sale obligation satisfied by the repossession. If real property, recognize the lesser of
   a. Cash and other property (FMV) received in excess of gain already recognized or
   b. Gross profit in remaining installments less repossession costs.

Interest

8. Interest is imposed on deferred tax on obligations from nondealer installment sales (of more than $150,000) outstanding at the close of the tax year.
   a. This interest is applied if the taxpayer has nondealer installment receivables of over $5 million at the close of the tax year from installment sales of over $150,000 that occurred during the year.
   b. This interest is not applied to
      1) Personal-use property,
      2) Residential lots and time shares, and
      3) Property produced or used in the farming business.

Disposition of Installment Obligations

9. Excess of the FMV over the AB of an installment obligation is generally recognized as income if it is transferred.
   a. FMV is generally the amount realized.
   b. If a gift, use the face value of the obligation.
   c. The adjusted basis is generally determined by the following formula:

      `Face value × (100% − Gross profit percentage)`

   d. Characterize as if the property for which the installment obligation was received was sold.
   e. A disposition of the installment obligation is deemed to occur when the obligation is transferred by gift, is forgiven, or becomes unenforceable.
   f. Exceptions. Disposition of obligations by the following events can result in the transferee treating payments as the transferor would have:
      1) Transfers to a controlled corporation
      2) Corporate reorganizations and liquidations
      3) Contributions to capital of, or distributions from, partnerships
      4) Transfer between spouses incident to divorce
      5) Transfer upon death of the obligee

Stop and review! You have completed the outline for this subunit. Study questions 21 through 38 beginning on page 232.

QUESTIONS

9.1 Related Party Sales

1. Jim sells stock that he purchased in 1999 to his brother John for a $500 loss. He also sells a truck purchased in 2010 to ABC Corporation, his 100%-owned C corporation, for a profit of $800, including $500 of depreciation recapture. What is the effect of these transactions on Jim's 2012 tax return?

A. A loss of $500 on the stock and no gain on the truck.

B. A disallowed loss on the stock, $500 ordinary gain, and $300 long-term capital gain on the truck.

C. A loss of $500 on the stock and $800 ordinary gain on the truck.

D. A disallowed loss on the stock and $800 ordinary gain on the truck.

Answer (D) is correct.

REQUIRED: The effect of the sale of assets to related parties on a tax return.

DISCUSSION: The loss on the sale of a capital asset (such as stock) is not allowed when sold to a member of the individual's family [Sec. 267(b)]. Capital gain treatment is denied when depreciable property is sold between related taxpayers [Sec. 1239(a)]. This rule pertains to sales or exchanges between the following:

1. A person and all entities controlled by such person
2. A taxpayer and any trust of which the taxpayer is a beneficiary unless the beneficiary's interest is because of a remote possibility to a contingency
3. An executor of an estate and a beneficiary of the estate, unless the sale or exchange is in satisfaction of a monetary value bequeathed to the beneficiary (see Sec. 1293)

Answer (A) is incorrect. A loss is disallowed when property is sold to one's brother, and an ordinary gain of $800 may be recognized for the truck. Answer (B) is incorrect. A capital gain is disallowed when a taxpayer sells depreciable property to an entity that (s)he controls. Answer (C) is incorrect. A loss is disallowed on property sold to one's brother.

2. Robert sold his Lebec Corporation stock to his sister Karen for $8,000. Robert's cost basis in the stock was $15,000. Karen later sold this stock to Dana, an unrelated party, for $15,500. What is Karen's realized gain?

A. $500

B. $7,000

C. $7,500

D. $0

Answer (C) is correct.

REQUIRED: The amount of realized gain when stock is sold after acquisition from a related party in a loss transaction.

DISCUSSION: Under Sec. 267, losses are not allowed on sales or exchanges of property between related parties. Brothers and sisters are related parties. Robert realized a $7,000 ($15,000 – $8,000) loss on the sale but may not deduct it. On the subsequent sale, Karen realized a $7,500 gain ($15,500 sales price – $8,000 basis). However, she does not have to recognize the entire gain because the Sec. 267(d) disallowed loss is used to offset the subsequent gain on the sale of the property. Karen would recognize a $500 gain.

Answer (A) is incorrect. Karen's basis in the stock for computing a realized gain is $8,000, not $15,000. Answer (B) is incorrect. This amount represents Robert's nondeductible loss. Answer (D) is incorrect. This is the amount of Karen's recognized gain if sold for $15,000.

3. Geena paid $10,000 for stock in a start-up company. A few months after she bought it, she sold the stock to her brother Henry for $8,000, its current value. Later, he sold the stock to an unrelated party for $15,000. What gain or loss should Geena and Henry recognize on their tax returns in the year of sale?

A. Geena recognizes $2,000 loss; Henry recognizes $7,000 gain.

B. Geena recognizes $2,000 loss; Henry recognizes $5,000 gain.

C. Geena recognizes $0 loss; Henry recognizes $7,000 gain.

D. Geena recognizes $0 loss; Henry recognizes $5,000 gain.

Answer (D) is correct.

REQUIRED: The treatment of a loss on the sale of stock to a related party and the amount recognized on a subsequent sale to an unrelated party.

DISCUSSION: Under Sec. 267, losses are not allowed on sales or exchanges of property between related parties. Siblings are related parties for this purpose. Thus, Geena's loss of $2,000 on the sale of the stock is disallowed. On the subsequent sale, Henry realized a $7,000 gain. However, he recognizes only a $5,000 gain [Sec. 257(d)]. The disallowed loss is used to offset the subsequent gain on the sale of the property ($7,000 realized gain – $2,000 disallowed loss).

Answer (A) is incorrect. Geena's loss is disallowed under Sec. 267. Answer (B) is incorrect. Geena's loss is disallowed under Sec. 267. Answer (C) is incorrect. Geena's disallowed loss reduces her brother Henry's realized gain on the sale of the property to $5,000.

4. In April 2012, Pamela sold stock with a cost basis of $15,000 to Lisa, her sister, for $10,000. In September 2012, Lisa sold the same shares of stock to their cousin, Niki, for $8,000. What is the amount of Pamela's deductible loss for 2012?

A. $0

B. $2,000

C. $5,000

D. $7,000

Answer (A) is correct.

REQUIRED: The treatment of a loss on the sale of stock acquired from a related party in a loss transaction.

DISCUSSION: Under Sec. 267, losses are not allowed on sales or exchanges of property between related parties. Sisters are related parties for this purpose. Thus, Pamela's loss of $5,000 on the sale of stock is disallowed.

5. In May of the current year, Automatic, Inc., sold land with a basis to Automatic of $10,000 to Jack, its 60% shareholder, for $8,000. In July, Jack sold the land to an unrelated party for $11,000. What is the amount of Jack's recognized gain?

A. $0

B. $1,000

C. $2,000

D. $3,000

Answer (B) is correct.

REQUIRED: The amount of recognized gain when property is sold after acquisition from a related party in a loss transaction.

DISCUSSION: Under Sec. 267, losses are not allowed on sales or exchanges of property between related parties. Related parties include an individual and a corporation in which the individual owns more than 50% of the outstanding stock. Automatic, Inc., realized a $2,000 loss on the sale but may not deduct it. On the subsequent sale, Jack realized a $3,000 gain. However, he recognizes only a $1,000 capital gain [Sec. 267(d)]. The disallowed loss is used to offset the subsequent gain on the sale of the property ($3,000 realized gain – $2,000 disallowed loss).

Answer (A) is incorrect. Jack must recognize a $1,000 capital gain. Answer (C) is incorrect. Jack's recognized gain is only $1,000. Answer (D) is incorrect. The disallowed loss offsets the realized gain.

6. In February 2012, Auto Repair, Inc., sold a car with a basis of $12,000 to Mark, its 55% shareholder, for $10,000. In June 2012, Mark sold the car to an unrelated party for $15,000. What is the amount of Mark's recognized gain?

A. $0

B. $2,000

C. $3,000

D. $5,000

Answer (C) is correct.

REQUIRED: The amount of recognized gain when property is sold after acquisition from a related party in a loss transaction.

DISCUSSION: Under Sec. 267(a)(1), losses are not allowed on sales or exchanges of property between related parties. Related parties include an individual and a corporation in which the individual owns more than 50% of the outstanding stock. Auto Repair, Inc., realized a $2,000 loss on the sale but may not deduct it. On the subsequent sale, Mark realized a $5,000 gain. However, he recognizes only a $3,000 capital gain [Sec. 267(d)]. The disallowed loss is used to offset the subsequent gain on the sale of the property ($5,000 realized gain – $2,000 disallowed loss).

Answer (A) is incorrect. The amount realized from the sale is greater than the basis, so a gain must be recognized. Answer (B) is incorrect. The disallowed loss is not a limit on the amount of recognized gain. Answer (D) is incorrect. The disallowed loss may be used to offset the realized gain.

7. Mr. Smith decided to retire from his business in 2012. Included in his assets was a large delivery truck for which he had paid $35,000 in 2008. Mr. Smith had offers to buy his truck for $25,000 from two local truck dealers. He decided instead to sell his truck for $15,000 to his long-time employee, John Pine, as partial compensation for John's helping Mr. Smith wind up his business. What is John's basis in the truck?

A. $35,000

B. $25,000

C. $15,000

D. None of the answers are correct.

Answer (B) is correct.

REQUIRED: The amount of basis in an employee bargain purchase.

DISCUSSION: If an employer transfers property to an employee at less than its fair market value, whether or not the transfer is in the form of a sale or exchange, the difference may be income to the purchaser as compensation for personal services (Reg. Sec. 1.61-2). The basis of the property will be the amount paid increased by the amount previously included in income. John will recognize $10,000 ($25,000 FMV – $15,000 paid) of income on the employee bargain purchase. His basis will be $25,000 ($15,000 cash paid + $10,000 income recognized).

Answer (A) is incorrect. The original basis of the truck is not carried over in an employee bargain purchase. Answer (C) is incorrect. The basis is the amount paid plus the amount of previously recognized income on the purchase. Answer (D) is incorrect. John's basis in the truck is $25,000.

8. Larry sold stock with a cost basis of $10,500 to his son for $8,500. Larry cannot deduct the $2,000 loss. His son sold the same stock to an unrelated party for $15,000, realizing a gain. What is his son's reportable gain?

A. $6,500

B. $4,500

C. $2,000

D. No gain.

Answer (B) is correct.

REQUIRED: The amount of gain recognized when property is sold after acquisition from a related party in a loss transaction.

DISCUSSION: Under Sec. 267(a)(1), losses are not allowed on sales or exchanges of property between related parties. Related parties include a father and a son. Larry realized a $2,000 loss on the sale but may not deduct it. On the subsequent sale, his son realized a $6,500 gain. However, he recognizes only a $4,500 reportable gain. The disallowed loss is used to offset the subsequent gain on the sale of the property ($6,500 realized gain – $2,000 disallowed loss).

Answer (A) is incorrect. The gain must be offset by the disallowed loss. Answer (C) is incorrect. This is the amount by which the gain will be offset. Answer (D) is incorrect. A gain must be reported.

9. Mark owned 100% of the stock in Gathers Corporation. In 2012, Gathers Corporation sold a computer with an adjusted basis of $5,000 and a fair market value of $8,000 to Mark's Uncle Seth for $4,000. What is the amount of Gathers Corporation's deductible loss on the sale of this computer in 2012?

A. $(4,000)

B. $(3,000)

C. $(1,000)

D. $0

Answer (C) is correct.

REQUIRED: Realization of losses from sales with related parties.

DISCUSSION: Tax laws limit tax avoidance between related parties. Losses realized on sale or exchange of property to a related person is not recognized. The transferee takes a cost basis. Uncles, however, are not considered related parties for federal income tax purposes. Gathers may recognize a loss on the sale of $1,000 ($4,000 selling price – $5,000 basis).

Answer (A) is incorrect. Gathers cannot subtract the selling price from the FMV to arrive at the recognizable loss. Answer (B) is incorrect. Gathers cannot subtract the adjusted basis from the FMV to arrive at the recognizable loss. Answer (D) is incorrect. Mark's Uncle Seth is not a related party for federal income tax purposes. Therefore, Gathers is allowed to recognize a loss on this transaction.

10. Alf owns all of the shares of Waxman Corporation, a manufacturer of finished leather products. Alf also owns a 60% partnership interest and his friend Richard owns a 40% partnership interest in York Real Estate Rentals, LLC. York owns and leases warehouse space to numerous businesses. In 2012, York sold a building with an adjusted basis of $100,000 to Waxman for $80,000. What is the amount of York's deductible loss in 2012 from this transaction?

A. $(20,000)

B. $(12,000)

C. $(8,000)

D. $0

Answer (D) is correct.

REQUIRED: Deductible loss when selling to a related party.

DISCUSSION: Loss realized on sale or exchange of property to a related person is not recognized. The transferee takes a cost basis. There is no adding of holding period. Controlled entities (50% ownership) are considered controlled entities for tax purposes. Because Alf owns more than 50% of the corporation and the partnership, York is not able to recognize any loss from the transaction.

Answer (A) is incorrect. None of the loss may be recognized. Answer (B) is incorrect. None of the loss is recognized. The code provides for no proration of the loss. Answer (C) is incorrect. The partnership cannot recognize 40% of the loss. None of the loss may be recognized because the parties are considered related.

9.2 Business Property

11. Allen purchased a trademark on January 1 of last year for $150,000. On January 1 of this year, Allen sold the trademark for $200,000. How much of Allen's gain on the sale of the trademark is Sec. 1245 gain?

A. $5,000

B. $10,000

C. $50,000

D. $60,000

Answer (B) is correct.

REQUIRED: The amount of Sec. 1245 gain.

DISCUSSION: Under Sec. 197, a trademark is an intangible asset that is amortizable over a 15-year period, beginning in the month of acquisition. Total amortization for the period January 1 of last year through January 1 of this year equals $10,000 ($150,000 ÷ 15). Allen's realized gain is $60,000 [$200,000 sales price – ($150,000 cost – $10,000 amortization)]. Sec. 1245 requires the gain to be recognized as ordinary income to the extent of the amortization taken. Therefore, $10,000 of the $60,000 gain is Sec. 1245 gain [Sec. 1245(a)(3)].

Answer (A) is incorrect. A trademark is amortized on a straight-line method over a 15-year period. Answer (C) is incorrect. Sec. 1245 gain is recognized only to the extent of the amortization taken. Answer (D) is incorrect. Sec. 1245 gain is recognized only to the extent of the amortization taken.

12. In January 2010, Ms. Doering purchased a $10,000 car to use 100% in her real estate business. Her MACRS deductions for the car were $2,000 in 2010 and $3,200 in 2011. She did not elect the Sec. 179 deduction. In 2012, she took a $960 (1/2-year) MACRS depreciation and sold the car in May for $7,000. What is the amount and character of her gain on the sale of her business auto?

A. $2,200 capital gain.

B. $3,160 capital gain.

C. $3,160 ordinary income.

D. $6,160 ordinary income.

Answer (C) is correct.

REQUIRED: The amount and character of gain on the sale of depreciable business property.

DISCUSSION: Under Sec. 1001, the gain realized and recognized on the sale of property is the excess of the amount realized over the adjusted basis. Ms. Doering's adjusted basis is $3,840 ($10,000 cost – $6,160 depreciation taken). The gain realized on the sale is $3,160 ($7,000 – $3,840). Sec. 1245 requires the recapture of ordinary income up to the amount of depreciation taken. Because the amount of depreciation taken exceeds the realized gain, the entire gain is recaptured and is ordinary income.

Answer (A) is incorrect. The realized gain is the sale price less adjusted basis. Any gain up to the amount of depreciation taken is ordinary income under Sec. 1245. Answer (B) is incorrect. The realized gain is subject to the Sec. 1245 recapture provisions and is ordinary income. Answer (D) is incorrect. The amount of $6,160 is the depreciation taken on the car.

13. The Quick Torch Insurance Agency owns the land and building in which its offices are located. The agency also owns its office furniture, company cars, office equipment, and client files. Which of the following is not Sec. 1245 property?

A. The office equipment.

B. The office furniture.

C. The company cars.

D. The client files.

Answer (D) is correct.

REQUIRED: The asset that is not Sec. 1245 property.

DISCUSSION: Sec. 1245 property includes property depreciable under Sec. 167, which is either personal property or specified real property, and most recovery property under Sec. 168. Client files are not Sec. 1245 property because they are neither depreciable nor recovery property.

Answer (A) is incorrect. Office equipment used in a trade or business is Sec. 1245 property. Answer (B) is incorrect. Office furniture used in a trade or business is Sec. 1245 property. Answer (C) is incorrect. Company cars used in a trade or business are Sec. 1245 property.

14. If the fair market value of Sec. 1245 property is greater than its basis, which of the following transactions will give rise to Sec. 1245 income?

A. Disposition at death.

B. Disposition by gift.

C. A like-kind exchange in which boot is received.

D. A Sec. 351 exchange with a newly formed corporation for all of its stock.

Answer (C) is correct.

REQUIRED: The transaction to which Sec. 1245 applies.

DISCUSSION: The general rule of Sec. 1245(a) is that it applies notwithstanding any other section of the Code. However, Sec. 1245(b) provides certain exceptions and limitations for its application. In a like-kind exchange, Sec. 1245 applies to the amount of gain recognized plus the fair market value of non-Sec. 1245 property received that is not already taken into account in calculating the recognized gain. Under Sec. 1031, the amount of gain recognized is the smaller of the gain realized or boot received.

Answer (A) is incorrect. Sec. 1245(b) provides that it will not apply to dispositions by death. Answer (B) is incorrect. Sec. 1245(b) provides that it will not apply to dispositions by gift. Answer (D) is incorrect. Sec. 1245(b) provides that depreciation will be recaptured on a Sec. 351 exchange only to the extent that gain is recognized under Sec. 351. Generally, no gain is recognized upon the transfer of assets to a new corporation solely for stock.

15. You purchased a heating, ventilating, and air conditioning (HVAC) unit for your rental property on December 15. It was delivered on December 28 and was installed and ready for use on January 2. When should the HVAC unit be considered placed in service?

A. December 15.

B. December 28.

C. December 31.

D. January 2.

Answer (D) is correct.

REQUIRED: The date a depreciable business asset is placed in service.

DISCUSSION: Publication 946 states, "You place property in service when it is ready and available for a specific use, whether in a business activity, an income-producing activity, a tax-exempt activity, or a personal activity."

16. Which of the following assets will not qualify for gain or loss treatment under Sec. 1231?

A. Factory machine acquired March 1, 2011; sold August 1, 2012.

B. Land used as a parking lot acquired August 1, 2011; sold September 1, 2012.

C. Sculpture acquired August 1, 2011, by an investor for the purpose of making a profit on it; destroyed in a fire on September 1, 2012.

D. Personal automobile acquired August 1, 2011; destroyed in a collision on September 1, 2012.

Answer (D) is correct.

REQUIRED: The asset that is not Sec. 1231 property.

DISCUSSION: Sec. 1231 property is depreciable or real property used in a trade or business and held for more than 1 year or an involuntarily converted nonpersonal capital asset (i.e., held in connection with a trade or business or a transaction entered into for profit) held for more than 1 year. The personal automobile is a personal-use capital asset and does not qualify for treatment under Sec. 1231.

17. In July, Tommy Tromboni sold a printing press used in his business that originally cost him $10,000 for $10,000. His adjusted basis at the time of the sale was $1,000, and Tommy paid $1,000 in selling expenses. What is the amount of the gain that would be ordinary income under Sec. 1245?

A. $0

B. $8,000

C. $9,000

D. $10,000

Answer (B) is correct.

REQUIRED: The amount of gain classified as ordinary income under Sec. 1245.

DISCUSSION: Under Sec. 1001, the gain realized and recognized on the sale of property is the excess of the amount realized over its adjusted basis. Selling expenses also reduce the gain recognized. Thus, Tommy recognizes

Money received	$10,000
Less: Adjusted basis of printing press	(1,000)
Selling expenses	(1,000)
Realized and recognized gain	$ 8,000

Sec. 1245 requires the recapture of ordinary income up to the amount of depreciation taken. Thus, the full $8,000 recognized gain must be recaptured as ordinary income since $9,000 of depreciation expense was incurred ($10,000 original basis – $1,000 ending basis).

Answer (A) is incorrect. A portion of the recognized gain is classified as ordinary income. Answer (C) is incorrect. Selling expenses and the adjusted basis both reduce the amount realized. Answer (D) is incorrect. Selling expenses and the adjusted basis both reduce the amount realized.

18. Keith, a business taxpayer, sold the following business assets during 2012:

Machinery:	
Sales price	$45,000
Original cost	40,000
Accumulated depreciation	15,000
Computer equipment:	
Sales price	34,000
Original cost	28,000
Accumulated depreciation	16,000

Keith had net Sec. 1231 losses in 2011 of $8,000. What is the amount and character of Keith's gain for 2012?

A. $39,000 ordinary income; $3,000 Sec. 1231 gain.

B. $31,000 ordinary income; $11,000 Sec. 1231 gain.

C. $16,000 ordinary income; $26,000 Sec. 1231 gain.

D. $0 ordinary income; $42,000 Sec. 1231 gain.

Answer (A) is correct.

REQUIRED: The amount and character of a gain on the disposition of Sec. 1231 and Sec. 1245 property.

DISCUSSION: Sec. 1231 property is depreciable or real property used in a trade or business and held for more than 1 year or an involuntarily converted nonpersonal capital asset (i.e., held in connection with a trade or business or a transaction entered into for profit) held for more than 1 year. A taxpayer who has a net Sec. 1231 gain (i.e., excess of Sec. 1231 gains over Sec. 1231 losses) for the tax year must review the 5 most recent preceding tax years for possible recapture of net Sec. 1231 losses for such years. If there were any net Sec. 1231 losses during this period, the taxpayer must treat the current year's net Sec. 1231 gain as ordinary income to the extent of the amount of unrecaptured net Sec. 1231 losses for that past period [Code Sec. 1231(c)]. The losses are to be recaptured on a first-in, first-out (FIFO) basis. Keith realizes a total gain of $42,000. Since the assets also qualify as Sec. 1245 property, this Sec. 1231 gain is recharacterized as ordinary income to the extent of depreciation recaptured ($31,000) and to the extent of any unaccounted for Sec. 1231 loss ($8,000). The remaining $3,000 is recognized as a Sec. 1231 gain.

Answer (B) is incorrect. Gains on the sale of Sec. 1231 assets can be recharacterized as ordinary to the extent of any unaccounted for prior Sec. 1231 losses. Answer (C) is incorrect. Depreciation recapture and Sec. 1231 losses may recharacterize gains as ordinary. Answer (D) is incorrect. Depreciation recapture and Sec. 1231 losses may recharacterize gains as ordinary.

19. A gain on the disposition of Sec. 1245 property is treated as ordinary income to the extent of

A. Depreciation allowed or allowable.

B. Excess of the accelerated depreciation allowed or allowable over the depreciation figured for the same period using the straight-line method.

C. Excess of the appreciated value over depreciation allowed or allowable using the straight-line method.

D. The difference between the amount realized over the cost of the property.

Answer (A) is correct.

REQUIRED: The maximum amount of gain on the disposition of Sec. 1245 property that can be characterized as ordinary income.

DISCUSSION: A gain on the disposition of Sec. 1245 property is treated as ordinary income to the extent of the total amount of depreciation allowed or allowable. The recaptured gain cannot exceed the amount of the realized gain.

Answer (B) is incorrect. The method of depreciation used makes no difference in the calculation of ordinary income. Answer (C) is incorrect. The excess of the appreciated value over depreciation allowed under any method receives Sec. 1231 treatment. Answer (D) is incorrect. The amount realized in excess of the asset's original cost is Sec. 1231 gain.

20. Mary Brown purchased an apartment building on January 1, 1986, for $200,000. The building was depreciated using the straight-line method. On December 31 of the current year, the building was sold for $210,000 when the asset basis net of accumulated depreciation was $140,000. On her current-year tax return, Brown should report

A. Sec. 1231 gain of $70,000.

B. Ordinary income of $70,000.

C. Sec. 1231 gain of $60,000 and ordinary income of $10,000.

D. Sec. 1231 gain of $10,000 and ordinary income of $60,000.

Answer (A) is correct.

REQUIRED: The amount and character of gain that must be recognized.

DISCUSSION: When depreciable property used in a trade or business is sold by a noncorporate owner at a gain, first Sec. 1245 and Sec. 1250 are applied; then the balance of the gain not recaptured as ordinary income is Sec. 1231 gain. In this case, Sec. 1245 does not apply (the building is residential rental property acquired before 1987), and Sec. 1250 recapture is limited to the excess of accelerated depreciation taken by the taxpayer over straight-line depreciation. Since the building was depreciated on the straight-line method, the entire $70,000 gain ($210,000 – $140,000) is Sec. 1231 gain.

9.3 Installment Sales

21. Mildred and John purchased 40 acres of undeveloped land 40 years ago for $120,000. They paid personal real estate taxes of $50,000, which they elected to add to the property's basis. They sold the property for $600,000, having total settlement costs of $70,000. The settlement costs are allowable as an expense of sale. Mildred and John received a down payment of $100,000 with the balance to be paid over 15 years. What is their gross profit percentage?

A. 60%

B. 72%

C. 68.33%

D. 82%

Answer (A) is correct.

REQUIRED: The gross profit percentage.

DISCUSSION: The gross profit percentage is the ratio of the gross profit to the total contract price. The gross profit is the sales price reduced by any selling expenses and adjusted basis ($600,000 sales price – $70,000 selling expenses – $170,000 adjusted basis = $360,000 gross profit). The total contract price is the amount that will be collected, $600,000. The gross profit percentage is then calculated as follows:

$$\frac{\$360{,}000 \text{ gross profit}}{\$600{,}000 \text{ contract price}} = .60 \text{ or } 60\%$$

Answer (B) is incorrect. The $100,000 down payment is not taken into consideration when calculating the gross profit percentage. Answer (C) is incorrect. The $50,000 of real estate taxes must be added back to the basis of the property. Answer (D) is incorrect. The real estate taxes must be added back to the basis of the property, and the $70,000 settlement costs should be subtracted from the selling price when calculating the gross profit percentage.

22. During 2012, Marcus sold real property that had an adjusted basis to him of $120,000 to Andrew for $250,000. On the sale, Marcus had depreciation recapture of $20,000, which he correctly reported as ordinary income. Andrew paid $50,000 as a down payment and agreed to pay $25,000 per year plus interest for the next 8 years beginning January 9, 2013. Marcus incurred selling expenses of $15,000. For 2012, what is the amount of capital gain from this transaction to be included by Marcus in his gross income?

A. $11,000

B. $19,000

C. $22,000

D. $23,000

Answer (B) is correct.

REQUIRED: The amount of gain in the year of an installment sale.

DISCUSSION: The amount of gain under Sec. 453 is the proportion of the payments received in the year that the gross profit bears to the total contract price. The contract price is the total amount the seller will ultimately collect from the buyer. Sec. 453(i) requires full recognition of depreciation recapture and an addition of the amount treated as ordinary income to the basis of the property for determining gain or loss. Marcus's gross profit is $95,000 [$250,000 sales price – ($120,000 adjusted basis + $20,000 depreciation recapture) – $15,000 selling expenses]. Since $50,000 was received in the year of the sale, the gain is $19,000.

$$\frac{\$95,000 \text{ gross profit}}{\$250,000 \text{ contract price}} \times \$50,000 = \$19,000$$

Answer (A) is incorrect. Depreciation recapture must be added back to the basis. Answer (C) is incorrect. Selling expenses are deducted from the sales price in order to determine gross profit. Answer (D) is incorrect. Depreciation recapture must be added back to the basis.

23. During 2012, Judy sold a pleasure boat that had an adjusted basis to her of $60,000 to Terry for $100,000. Terry paid $20,000 as a down payment and agreed to pay $20,000 per year plus interest for the next 4 years. What is the amount of gain to be included in Judy's gross income for 2012?

A. $8,000

B. $16,000

C. $20,000

D. $24,000

Answer (A) is correct.

REQUIRED: The amount of gain in the year of an installment sale.

DISCUSSION: The amount of gain under Sec. 453 is the proportion of the payments received in the year that the gross profit bears to the total amount the seller will ultimately collect from the buyer. Judy's gross profit is $40,000 ($100,000 sales price – $60,000 adjusted basis). Since $20,000 was received in the year of sale, the gain is $8,000.

$$\frac{\$40,000 \text{ gross profit}}{\$100,000 \text{ contract price}} \times \$20,000 = \$8,000$$

Answer (B) is incorrect. The gross profit is not $80,000. Answer (C) is incorrect. The gain is limited to the gross profit percentage. Answer (D) is incorrect. The gross profit percentage must be used to determine the amount of gain.

24. In 2012, Ray sold land with a basis of $40,000 for $100,000. He received a $20,000 down payment and the buyer's note for $80,000. In 2013, he received the first of four annual payments of $20,000 each, plus 12% interest. What is the gain to be reported in 2012?

A. None.

B. $8,000

C. $12,000

D. $20,000

Answer (C) is correct.

REQUIRED: The amount of gain reported on an installment sale.

DISCUSSION: The transaction qualifies for treatment as an installment sale. The amount of gain under Sec. 453 is the proportion of the payments received in the year that the gross profit bears to the total contract price. The contract price is the total amount the seller will ultimately collect from the buyer. Ray's gross profit is $60,000 ($100,000 sales price – $40,000 adjusted basis). Since $20,000 was received in 2012 (the year sold), the gain is $12,000.

$$\frac{\$60,000 \text{ gross profit}}{\$100,000 \text{ contract price}} \times \$20,000 = \$12,000$$

Answer (A) is incorrect. A gain must be reported on the sale. Answer (B) is incorrect. It is the amount of the payment that is considered a return of capital. Answer (D) is incorrect. Only the portion that is not a return of capital must be reported as a gain. This portion is determined by calculating the gross profit percentage.

25. Arlene sold property with an adjusted basis of $35,000 to Sandy for $50,000. Sandy paid cash of $5,000 and assumed an existing mortgage of $20,000. Sandy signed an installment note for the $25,000 balance at 8% interest. Payments on the note were to be made at the rate of $5,000 a year plus interest beginning 1 year after the date of the contract. Arlene did not elect out of the installment method. What is the amount of gain that Arlene should include in the first year after the date of the contract?

A. $5,000

B. $2,500

C. $1,500

D. $4,500

Answer (B) is correct.

REQUIRED: The amount of gain a taxpayer should include in the first year of an installment sales contract.

DISCUSSION: The installment method is a special method of reporting gains (not losses) from sales of property for which at least one payment is received in a tax year after the year of sale. Under the installment method, gain from an installment sale is prorated and recognized over the years in which payments are received. The amount of gain from an installment sale that is taxable in a given year is calculated by multiplying the payments received in that year by the gross profit ratio for the sale. The gross profit ratio is equal to the anticipated gross profit divided by the total contract price. The gross profit is equal to the selling price of the property minus its adjusted basis. The total contract price is equal to the selling price minus that portion of qualifying indebtedness assumed by, or taken subject to, the buyer that does not exceed the seller's basis in the property (adjusted to reflect commissions and other selling expenses). Arlene realized a $15,000 gain on the sale, and this amount serves as the anticipated gross profit in the gross profit ratio. The total contract price is $30,000 ($50,000 selling price – $20,000 mortgage assumed by buyer). Accordingly, the gross profit ratio is 50% ($15,000 ÷ $30,000), and a $2,500 gain is recognized ($5,000 payment × 50%).

Answer (A) is incorrect. A portion of the payment constitutes a return of capital. Answer (C) is incorrect. The gross profit ratio is not 30%. Answer (D) is incorrect. Interest on the outstanding debt is not added to the amount of gain recognized.

26. Mr. Pickle purchased property from Mr. Apple by assuming an existing mortgage of $12,000 and agreeing to pay an additional $6,000, plus interest, over the next 3 years. Mr. Apple had an adjusted basis of $8,800 in the building and paid selling expenses totaling $1,200. What were the sales price and the contract price in this transaction?

	Sales Price	Contract Price
A.	$6,000	$12,000
B.	$18,000	$9,200
C.	$18,000	$8,000
D.	$18,000	$6,000

Answer (C) is correct.

REQUIRED: The sales price and contract price in an installment sale transaction.

DISCUSSION: The sales price includes any cash paid, relief of seller's liability by buyer, and any installment note given by the buyer. Here, the sales price is $18,000 ($12,000 relief of liability + $6,000 installment note). The contract price is the total amount the seller will ultimately collect from the buyer. However, if an existing mortgage assumed by the buyer exceeds the adjusted basis of the property, such excess (reduced by selling expenses) is treated as a payment and must be included both in the contract price and in the first year's payment received. The contract price is $8,000 ($6,000 note + $3,200 mortgage in excess of basis – $1,200 selling expenses).

Answer (A) is incorrect. The sales price includes the $12,000 relief of liabilities, and the contract price is not the value of the existing mortgage. Answer (B) is incorrect. The contract price is reduced by the selling expenses. Answer (D) is incorrect. The contract price is increased by the $3,200 mortgage in excess of basis and reduced by the selling expenses.

27. Ethel and George sold an investment property they purchased 10 years ago for $300,000. The property was sold for $700,000 with a down payment of $140,000. What is the gross profit percentage?

A. 57.14%

B. 22.86%

C. 28.57%

D. None of the answers are correct.

Answer (A) is correct.

REQUIRED: The amount of gross profit percentage.

DISCUSSION: The amount of gain under Sec. 453 is the proportion of the payments received in the year that the gross profit bears to the total contract price. The contract price is the total amount the seller will ultimately collect from the buyer. (See Publication 537.) Ethel and George's gross profit is $400,000 ($700,000 sales price – $300,000 adjusted basis). Therefore, their gross profit percentage is 57.14% ($400,000 ÷ $700,000).

Answer (B) is incorrect. A 22.86% gross profit is found by dividing $160,000 by $700,000. Answer (C) is incorrect. A 28.57% gross profit is found by dividing $200,000 by $700,000. Answer (D) is incorrect. The correct gross profit percentage is 57.14%.

28. During 2010, Joshua sold land with an adjusted basis to him of $120,000 to Caleb for $200,000. In 2010, Caleb made a down payment of $80,000 and agreed to pay $30,000 per year plus interest for the next 4 years beginning January 2011. After Caleb made the payment in 2011, Joshua and Caleb agreed to reduce the overall sales price to $185,000 and the yearly payments to $25,000. What is the amount that Joshua should include in income for 2012?

A. $7,000

B. $8,400

C. $10,000

D. $12,000

Answer (A) is correct.
REQUIRED: The amount of gain recognized in an installment sale when the contract price is reduced.
DISCUSSION: Under Sec. 453, income recognized on an installment sale is the proportion of payments received in the year that the gross profit bears to the total contract price. The gross profit is generally the selling price less the basis in the property and less selling expenses. However, when a gain is deferred or excluded, the gross profit must be subtracted by this nonrecognized portion of gain to calculate the gross profit percentage properly. The contract price is the selling price reduced by any indebtedness the buyer assumed or took.
If the selling price is reduced at a later date, the gross profit on the sale will also change. The gross profit percentage must be recalculated for the remaining periods by using the reduced sales price and subtracting the gross profit already recognized. The amount includible in 2012 is determined as follows:

Gross profit ($185,000 sales price – $120,000 basis)	$65,000
Less: Gain recognized to date [$110,000 payments × ($80,000 original gross profit ÷ $200,000 original sales price)]	(44,000)
Remaining gain	$21,000
Adjusted gross profit ratio ($21,000 remaining gain ÷ $75,000 remaining payments)	28%
Multiplied by: Payment received in 2012	25,000
Gain recognized in 2012	$ 7,000

29. Dennis and Martha sell their lake house (which they have owned for 10 years and spend each summer in) for $250,000. Their original cost was $175,000, and they had improvements of $25,000. They have never used the house as a business or rental property. They agreed to take $50,000 down and finance the balance. Monthly payments are to begin next year. How much capital gain must they report in the year of sale?

A. $10,000

B. $50,000

C. $15,000

D. $0

Answer (A) is correct.
REQUIRED: The amount of capital gain to be reported.
DISCUSSION: The amount of gain under Sec. 453 is the proportion of the payments received in the year that the gross profit bears the total amount to the seller. Gross profit, $50,000, is found by subtracting the adjusted basis, $200,000 ($175,000 + $25,000) from the sales price, $250,000. Next, the gross profit percentage, 20%, is found by dividing the gross profit, $50,000, by the sales price ($250,000). The capital gain is found by multiplying the gross profit percentage, 20%, by the down payment, $50,000. The capital gain is $10,000.
Answer (B) is incorrect. This amount is the gross profit, not the reported capital gain. Answer (C) is incorrect. The capital gain is the gross profit percentage multiplied by the gross profit. Answer (D) is incorrect. There is a capital gain which must be reported when the gross profit can be foreseen by the seller.

30. Jim and Jean purchased a vacation home in 2005 for $100,000. They sold the property for $500,000 in 2012 and received a down payment of $200,000. They took a mortgage from the purchaser for the remaining $300,000. What is Jim and Jean's gross profit percentage on this sale?

A. 40%

B. 60%

C. 80%

D. None of the answers are correct.

Answer (C) is correct.
REQUIRED: The calculation of the gross profit percentage.
DISCUSSION: The gross profit percent is the difference between the price the property was sold for and the price the property was purchased at, divided by the price for which the property was sold, multiplied by 100. The gross profit percent for Jim and Jean is calculated below.

$$\frac{\$500{,}000 - \$100{,}000}{\$500{,}000} \times 100 = 80\%$$

31. In an installment sale, if the buyer assumes a mortgage that is greater than the installment sale basis of the property sold,

A. There is never a profit or a loss.

B. The transaction is disqualified as an installment sale.

C. The gross profit percentage is always 100%.

D. The gain is treated as short-term capital gain.

Answer (C) is correct.

REQUIRED: The statement that applies when a buyer assumes a mortgage greater than the installment sale basis of the property sold.

DISCUSSION: In an installment sale when the buyer assumes a mortgage that is greater than the basis of the asset, the seller is required to recognize the excess mortgage as a payment in year of sale and also increase the contract price by the amount of the excess. If the contract price were not increased, the gross profit percentage would be greater than 100%. The amount of increase in the contract price will make the contract price equal to the gross profit, thus giving a gross profit percentage of 100%.

Answer (A) is incorrect. The installment sale may give rise to a profit or loss. Answer (B) is incorrect. The presented circumstance does not prevent the sale from qualifying as an installment sale. Answer (D) is incorrect. Any gain realized from a disposal of recaptured property in an installment sale is characterized as ordinary income by Secs. 1245 and 1250.

32. Cheryl sold a boat, which had cost her $3,600, for $6,000. The boat was not used in a trade or business or held for rent. Cheryl accepted a $1,800 down payment and an installment obligation calling for 30 monthly payments of $140, plus interest. After receiving 8 months' payments, Cheryl sold the installment obligation for $2,500. What was Cheryl's gain or loss on the disposition of the installment obligation?

A. $820

B. $(420)

C. $2,192

D. $652

Answer (D) is correct.

REQUIRED: The income recognized on the disposition of an installment obligation.

DISCUSSION: Sec. 453B provides that, when an installment obligation is disposed of, gain or loss is recognized to the extent of the difference between the basis of the obligation and the amount realized (or the fair market value of the obligation if disposed of other than by sale or exchange). The adjusted basis of the obligation is equal to the face amount of the obligation reduced by the gross profit that would be realized if the holder collected the face amount [Sec. 453B(b)]. The face amount is $3,080 [($140 × 30) – ($140 × 8)]. The basis is $1,848 [$3,080 face amount × (100% – 40% gross profit percentage)].

Since Cheryl sold the installment obligation, the excess of the amount realized over Cheryl's basis in the obligation is recognized as income on the transfer. This amount of income is $652 ($2,500 amount realized – $1,848 basis). The gain is treated as resulting from the sale or exchange of the property in respect of which the installment obligation was originally held.

33. In December of 2010, Bob sold land to Natalie for $80,000. He reported the sale using the installment method. At the time of the sale, the land had an adjusted basis of $20,000. Natalie made a down payment of $25,000 in 2010 and agreed to pay $11,000 per year plus interest for the next 5 years. The payments were to be made May 1 of each year. Before the 2012 payment was made, Bob sold the installment obligation for $30,000. What is Bob's gain (or loss) for 2012 on the sale of the installment obligation?

A. $(14,000)

B. $(10,500)

C. $19,000

D. $22,500

Answer (C) is correct.

REQUIRED: The income recognized on the disposition of an installment obligation.

DISCUSSION: Sec. 453B provides that, when an installment obligation is disposed of, gain or loss is recognized to the extent of the difference between the basis of the obligation and the amount realized (or the fair market value of the obligation if disposed of other than by sale or exchange). The adjusted basis of the obligation is equal to the face amount of the obligation reduced by the gross profit that would be realized if the holder collected the face amount [Sec. 453B(b)]. The basis is $11,000 [$44,000 face amount × (100% – 75% gross profit percentage)].

Since Bob sold the installment obligation, the excess of the amount realized over Bob's basis in the obligation is recognized as income on the transfer. This amount of income is $19,000 ($30,000 amount realized – $11,000 basis). The gain is treated as resulting from the sale or exchange of the property in respect of which the installment obligation was originally held.

Answer (A) is incorrect. The face value of the note is not its basis. Answer (B) is incorrect. The basis of the obligation is determined by multiplying the face value times (100% gross profit percentage). Answer (D) is incorrect. The basis of the obligation is determined by multiplying the face value times (100% gross profit percentage).

34. With respect to the disposition of an installment obligation, which of the following is false?

A. No gain or loss is recognized on the transfer of an installment obligation between a husband and wife if incident to a divorce.

B. If the obligation is sold, the gain or loss is the difference between the basis in the obligation and the amount realized.

C. A gift of an installment obligation is considered a disposition.

D. If an installment obligation is canceled, it is not treated as a disposition.

Answer (D) is correct.

REQUIRED: The false statement with respect to the disposition of an installment obligation.

DISCUSSION: Sec. 453B provides that, when an installment obligation is disposed of, gain or loss is recognized to the extent of the difference between the basis of the obligation and the amount realized (or the fair market value of the obligation if disposed of other than by sale or exchange). The main purpose of Sec. 453B is to prevent the shifting of income between taxpayers. Sec. 453B(a) expressly requires recognition whether the obligation is sold or otherwise disposed of. Cancelation of an installment obligation is a disposition of the obligation.

Answer (A) is incorrect. Sec. 453B(g) excludes from the definition of a disposition a transfer between husband and wife incident to a divorce. The same tax treatment with respect to the obligation that would have applied to the transferor then applies to the transferee. Answer (B) is incorrect. The gain or loss on sale of an installment obligation is the difference between the amount realized and the basis in the obligation. Answer (C) is incorrect. A gift is a disposition for purposes of Sec. 453B.

35. Each of the following situations would be considered a disposition of an installment obligation except

A. An installment obligation that you give as a gift.

B. An installment obligation for which you accept part payment on the balance of the buyer's installment debt to you and forgive the rest of the debt.

C. An installment obligation assumed by a new buyer at a rate of interest higher than the rate paid by the original buyer.

D. An installment obligation that has become unenforceable.

Answer (C) is correct.

REQUIRED: The situation that is not considered a disposition of an installment obligation.

DISCUSSION: Sec. 453B provides that, when an installment obligation is disposed of, gain or loss is recognized to the extent of the difference between the basis of the obligation and the amount realized (or the fair market value of the obligation if disposed of other than by sale or exchange). The main purpose of Sec. 453B is to prevent the shifting of income between taxpayers. Sec. 453B(a) expressly requires recognition whether the obligation is sold or otherwise disposed of. An installment obligation assumed by a new buyer does not cause a shift in income and is therefore not a disposition of an installment obligation.

Answer (A) is incorrect. The transfer of an installment obligation by gift is treated as a disposition. Answer (B) is incorrect. The cancelation of an installment obligation is treated as a disposition. Answer (D) is incorrect. An unenforceable installment obligation is treated as a disposition.

36. You sold a residential lot 2 years ago and reported the $20,000 capital gain on the installment method. In the third year of payments, the buyer defaulted and you had to repossess the lot. In the first year you reported $5,000 ($10,000 × 50%) and $3,000 ($6,000 × 50%) in the second year. No payments were received in the third year, and you spent $2,500 in legal fees to repossess the property. What is the taxable gain you must report on the repossession?

A. $0

B. $9,500

C. $8,000

D. $4,000

Answer (C) is correct.

REQUIRED: The amount of taxable gain to be reported for a repossession.

DISCUSSION: If you repossess your property after making an installment sale, you must figure the following amounts: (1) Your gain (or loss) on the repossession and (2) your basis in the repossessed property. The rules for figuring these amounts depend on the kind of property you repossess. The rules for repossessions of personal property differ from those for real property. The taxable gain for the repossession of real property is figured using the following schedule.

1) Payments received before repossession		$16,000
2) Minus: Gain reported		8,000
3) Gain on repossession		$ 8,000
4) Gross profit on sale		$20,000
5) Gain reported (line 2)	$8,000	
6) Plus: Repossession costs	2,500	10,500
7) Subtract line 6 from line 4		$ 9,500
8) Taxable gain (lesser of line 3 or 7)		$ 8,000

Answer (A) is incorrect. A gain exists on the repossession of this property. Answer (B) is incorrect. The lesser of the two methods of computing the capital gain must be chosen. Answer (D) is incorrect. This property is real property, and the gain must be computed using the schedule for real property.

37. In 2003, Sally sold a personal residence on the installment method. She needed cash in 2012, so she sold the note for $7,500 when the balance due her was $9,000. Her gross profit percentage was 47.5%. How much profit must Sally report on the disposition of the obligation?

A. $2,775

B. $7,500

C. $0

D. $3,225

Answer (A) is correct.

REQUIRED: The amount of profit recognized on the disposition of an installment obligation.

DISCUSSION: The balance due to Sally was $9,000. The basis of the receivable is $4,725 [$9,000 × (1 – 47.5%)]. The amount realized is $7,500, and therefore Sally recognizes a profit of $2,775 ($7,500 – $4,725).

Answer (B) is incorrect. The receivable has a basis of $4,725. Answer (C) is incorrect. The amount realized exceeds the basis of the receivable by $2,775. Answer (D) is incorrect. The basis of the receivable is 52.5% of $9,000, not 47.5%.

38. The owner of unimproved land with a basis of $40,000 sold the property for $100,000 in 2007. The seller accepted a note for the entire $100,000 sales price. In 2012, when the buyer still owed $10,000, the note was sold for $9,000 cash. How should the disposition of the note be reported on the seller's 2012 return?

A. $5,000 capital gain.

B. $5,000 ordinary income.

C. $2,000 capital gain.

D. $1,000 capital loss.

Answer (A) is correct.

REQUIRED: The amount and character of income to be reported from the disposition of a note.

DISCUSSION: Sec. 453B provides that, when an installment obligation is disposed of, gain or loss is recognized to the extent of the difference between the basis of the obligation and the amount realized (or the fair market value of the obligation if disposed of other than by sale or exchange). The adjusted basis of the obligation is equal to the face amount of the obligation reduced by the gross profit that would be realized if the holder collected the face amount [Sec. 453B(b)]. The basis is $4,000 [$10,000 face amount × (100% – 60% gross profit percentage)]. Since the seller sold the installment obligation, the excess of the amount realized over the seller's basis in the obligation is recognized as income on the transfer. This amount of income is $5,000 ($9,000 amount realized – $4,000 basis). The gain is treated as resulting from the sale or exchange of the property in respect of which the installment obligation was originally held. If the original sale resulted in a capital gain or loss, the disposition of the obligation will result in a capital gain or loss.

Answer (B) is incorrect. If the original sale resulted in a capital gain or loss, the disposition of the obligation will result in a capital gain or loss. The original sale of land resulted in a capital gain. Answer (C) is incorrect. Sec. 453B provides that, when an installment obligation is disposed of, gain or loss is recognized to the extent of the difference between the basis of the obligation and the amount realized (or the fair market value of the obligation if disposed of other than by sale or exchange). The adjusted basis of the obligation is equal to the face amount of the obligation reduced by the gross profit that would be realized if the holder collected the face amount [Sec. 453B(b)]. Answer (D) is incorrect. Sec. 453B provides that, when an installment obligation is disposed of, gain or loss is recognized to the extent of the difference between the basis of the obligation and the amount realized (or the fair market value of the obligation if disposed of other than by sale or exchange). The adjusted basis of the obligation is equal to the face amount of the obligation reduced by the gross profit that would be realized if the holder collected the face amount [Sec. 453B(b)].

STUDY UNIT TEN
NONRECOGNITION PROPERTY TRANSACTIONS

(5 pages of outline)

Generally, a taxpayer recognizes a gain when the fair market value of the property received is greater than the adjusted basis of the property given up. This study unit deals with situations in which there may be nonrecognition of the gain or loss. This nonrecognition can be temporary, as in the deferral of gain on a like-kind exchange, or it can be permanent, as in the exclusion of the gain on a sale of a principal residence.

10.1 SALE OF A PRINCIPAL RESIDENCE

Sec. 121 provides an exclusion upon the sale of a principal residence. No loss may be recognized on the sale of a personal residence.

Ownership and Occupancy

1. The exclusion is available if the individual owned and occupied the residence for an aggregate of at least 2 of the 5 years before the sale.
2. The exclusion may be used only once every 2 years.

Exclusion Amount

3. A taxpayer may exclude up to $250,000 ($500,000 for married taxpayers filing jointly) of realized gain on the sale of a principal residence.
   a. The exclusion is increased to $500,000 for married individuals filing jointly if
      1) Either spouse meets the ownership test,
      2) Both spouses meet the use test, and
      3) Neither spouse is ineligible for the exclusion by virtue of a sale or an exchange of a residence within the last 2 years.
   b. A surviving spouse can qualify for the $500,000 exclusion if the residence is sold within 2 years of the other spouse's death.
4. The exclusion is determined on an individual basis. Therefore, for married couples who do not share a principal residence but file joint returns, a $250,000 exclusion is available for a qualifying sale or exchange of each spouse's principal residence.
5. If a single individual eligible for the exclusion marries a person who used the exclusion within 2 years before marriage, the individual is entitled to a $250,000 exclusion. Even though the individual's spouse used the exclusion within the past 2 years, an individual may not be prevented from claiming the $250,000 exclusion.

Divorce Transfer

6. If a residence is transferred to a taxpayer incident to a divorce, the time during which the taxpayer's spouse or former spouse owned the residence is added to the taxpayer's period of ownership.
   a. A taxpayer who owns a residence is deemed to use it as a principal residence while the taxpayer's spouse or former spouse is given use of the residence under the terms of a divorce or separation.

Widowed Taxpayer

7. A widowed taxpayer's period of ownership of residence includes the period during which the taxpayer's deceased spouse owned the residence.

Physically or Mentally Incapable Individuals

8. If an individual becomes physically or mentally incapable of self-care, the individual is deemed to use a residence as a principal residence during the time in which the individual owns the residence and resides in a licensed care facility.
   a. The individual must have owned and used the residence as a principal residence for an aggregate period of at least 1 year during the 5 years preceding the sale or exchange.

Prorating

9. The exclusion amount may be prorated if the use, ownership, or prior sale tests are not met.
   a. The exclusion is based on the ratio of months used to 24 months and is a proportion of the total exclusion.
   b. The pro rata exclusion is allowed only if the sale is due to a change in place of employment, health, or unforeseen circumstances.

Nonqualified Use

10. The gain on the sale of the residence must be prorated between qualified and nonqualified use.
    a. Nonqualified use includes periods that the residence was not used as the principal residence of the taxpayer, prior to the last day the homeowner lived in the house.

EXAMPLE

During the 5 years prior to the sale of the house, the taxpayer lived in the house for Years 1, 2, and 4. The absence during the third year is nonqualified use, causing a reduction (prorated based on 1 year of nonqualified use) in the allowed exclusion. The absence during the fifth year does not affect the allowed exclusion since the taxpayer did not return to live in the house prior to the sale.

    b. Nonqualified use does not include use before 2009.

Principal Residence Requirement

11. Sec. 121 excludes realized gain on the sale of a principal residence only. Therefore, gain would need to be recognized on the portion of the property that is not considered a personal residence (e.g., use of a guest facility as rental property).
    a. The portion of the principal residence that is business-use property (e.g., a home office) may not qualify for gain exclusion.
    b. Realized gain may qualify for exclusion even though the entire property is used as rental property or business-use property at the time of sale.
       1) For example, the entire property is subject to gain exclusion as long as the individual owned and occupied the entire residence (as a principal residence) for an aggregate of at least 2 of the 5 years before the sale (see item 1. on the previous page).
    c. Deductions (other than depreciation) that relate solely to the rental or business-use portion of the property do not reduce the basis of the principal residence portion.
    d. Any selling expenses incurred in selling the personal residence reduce the amount realized by the seller.
    e. Any capital improvements made to the personal residence are added to the adjusted basis of the house.
    f. Any amount of gain not excludable is reported on Schedule D, *Capital Gains*.

Basis

12. Basis in a new home is its cost.

Like-Kind Exchange

13. If the residence was acquired in a Sec. 1031 like-kind exchange in which any gain was not recognized in the prior 5 years, then the Sec. 121 exclusion for gain on sale or exchange of a principal residence does not apply.

Reporting

14. If the amount of the realized gain is less than the maximum exclusion amount, the gain need not be reported on the individual's income tax return.

Stop and review! You have completed the outline for this subunit. Study questions 1 through 20 beginning on page 244.

10.2 LIKE-KIND EXCHANGES AND INVOLUNTARY CONVERSIONS

Like-Kind Exchanges

1. Sec. 1031 defers recognizing gain or loss to the extent that property productively used in a trade or business or held for the production of income (investment) is exchanged for property of like-kind.
   a. Like-kind property is alike in nature or character but not necessarily in grade or quality.
      1) Properties are like-kind if each is within a class of like nature or character, without regard to differences in use (e.g., business or investment), improvements (e.g., bare land or house), location (e.g., city or rural), or proximity.
      2) Real property is of like-kind to other real property, except foreign property.
      3) Personal property and real property are not like-kind.
      4) Examples of like-kind exchanges are car for truck, unimproved farm property for office building, store building for parking lot, and investment for business real property.
      5) A lease of real property for 30 or more years is treated as real property.
      6) Exchanges of nondepreciable tangible personal property held for investment may also qualify for like-kind treatment.
         a) Exchanges of these types of properties qualify for nonrecognition treatment only if they are of a like kind.
         b) Nondepreciable property held for investment generally includes such items as artworks, antiques, gems, stamps, precious metals, coins, and historical objects.
      7) Exchanges of intangible personal property, such as patents or copyrights, may qualify as like-kind exchanges, depending on the nature of the underlying property.
         a) Exchanges of goodwill and the going-concern value of businesses are never treated as like-kind exchanges.
   b. Liabilities are not qualified property, whether incurred or relieved of.
      1) They are treated as money paid or received (boot).
      2) If each party assumes a liability of the other, only the net liability given or received is treated as boot.
      3) Liabilities include mortgages on property.

c. The following property types do not qualify for Sec. 1031 nonrecognition:

1) Money
2) Accounts receivable
3) Liabilities
4) Inventory
5) Partnership interest
6) Securities and debt instruments, e.g., stocks, bonds

Boot

d. Boot is all nonqualified property transferred in an exchange transaction.

1) Gain recognized is equal to the lesser of gain realized or boot received.
2) Boot received includes cash, net liability relief, and other nonqualified property (at its FMV).

Loss

e. If some qualified property is exchanged, loss realized with respect to qualified or other property is not recognized.

Basis

f. Qualified property received in a like-kind exchange has an exchanged basis adjusted for boot and gain recognized.

AB of property given
\+ Gain recognized
\+ Boot given (cash, liability incurred, other property)
– Boot received (cash, liability relief, other property)
= Basis in acquired property

Deadlines

g. An exchange of like-kind properties must be completed within the earlier of

1) 180 days after the transfer of the exchanged property or
2) The due date (including extensions) for the transferor's tax return for the taxable year in which the exchange took place.

h. The taxpayer has 45 days from the date of the transfer to identify the like-kind property received in the exchange.

1) The replacement property must be clearly described in a signed, written document. The document then must be delivered to the other person involved in the exchange.

a) The identification of multiple replacement properties is permitted.

Related Parties

i. Sec. 1031(f) outlines special rules for like-kind exchanges between related parties. The taxpayer cannot dispose of the property within 2 years after the date of the last transfer that was part of the exchange in order to avoid recognizing any gain on the initial exchange.

Multiple Parties

j. There is no exception in Sec. 1031 that prohibits multiple-party transactions from qualifying as like-kind exchanges.

k. The trade of like-kind property is reported on IRS Form 8824.

Reporting Involuntary Conversions

2. A taxpayer may elect to defer recognition of gain if property is involuntarily converted into money or property that is not similar or related in service or use.
   a. Nonrecognition of gain is contingent on the involuntarily converted property being reinvested in qualified replacement property.
   b. Losses on involuntary conversions are not deferred.
   c. An involuntary conversion of property results from destruction, theft, seizure, requisition, condemnation, or the threat of imminent requisition or condemnation.
   d. When property is converted involuntarily into nonqualified proceeds and qualified property is purchased within the replacement period, an election may be made to defer realized gain to the extent that the amount realized on the conversion is reinvested in qualified replacement property.
      1) The replacement period begins on the earlier of the date of disposition or the threat of condemnation and ends 2 years after the close of the first tax year in which any part of the gain is realized.
      2) The basis in qualified replacement property is decreased by any unrecognized gain.
   e. Similar or related in service or use means that the property has,
      1) For an owner-user, functional similarity, i.e., meets a functional use test that requires that the property
         a) Have similar physical characteristics
         b) Be used for the same purpose

EXAMPLE

For an owner-user, a warehouse used to store parts for a bicycle manufacturer is not similar or related in service to a warehouse rented out for storage of household goods.

      2) For an owner-investor, a close relationship to the service or a use the previous property had to the investor, such that the owner-investor's
         a) Risks, management activities, services performed, etc., continue without substantial change

EXAMPLE

For an owner-investor, the following types of investment are not similar or related in service or use: passive leasing investment, investment in actively managed rental apartments, and speculative investment in a silver mine.

      3) For owners generally, if property held for investment or for productive use in a trade or business is involuntarily converted due to a federally declared disaster, the tangible replacement property will be deemed similar or related in service or use.
         a) Any tangible property acquired and held for productive use in a trade or business is treated as similar or related in service or use to property that was
            i) Held for investment or for productive use in a trade or business and
            ii) Involuntarily converted as a result of a federally declared disaster.

Stop and review! You have completed the outline for this subunit. Study questions 21 through 40 beginning on page 250.

QUESTIONS

10.1 Sale of a Principal Residence

1. Which of the following does not qualify for exclusion from income of all or part of the gain from the sale of their main home in 2012?

A. You sold a personal residence January 1, 2011, and excluded all the gain. You sold another personal residence December 30, 2012. You did not sell because of health problems or a change in employment.

B. You owned and lived in your house from January 1, 2008, until February 15, 2009, when you moved out and lived with your friend. You moved back into your house July 12, 2010, and then sold it October 20, 2012. The sale was not due to health problems or a change of employment.

C. Betty sells her house (that she had owned and lived in since 2002) in February 2012 and gets married 1 month later. Her husband had excluded the gain on the sale of his residence on his 2011 return.

D. You and your wife are divorced in 2007, and your spouse is allowed to live in the house until sold. The house sells on July 15, 2012.

Answer (A) is correct.

REQUIRED: The false statement regarding the exclusion of gain recognized on the sale of a principal residence.

DISCUSSION: The exclusion of gain provided by Sec. 121 may be used only once every 2 years.

Answer (B) is incorrect. The exclusion is available if the individual owned and occupied the residence for an aggregate of at least 2 of the 5 years before the sale. Answer (C) is incorrect. If a single individual eligible for the exclusion marries a person who used the exclusion within 2 years before marriage, the individual is entitled to a $250,000 exclusion. Even though the individual's spouse used the exclusion within the past 2 years, an individual may not be prevented from claiming the $250,000 exclusion. Answer (D) is incorrect. If a residence is transferred to a taxpayer incident to a divorce, the time during which the taxpayer's spouse or former spouse owned the residence is added to the taxpayer's period of ownership. Also, a taxpayer who owns a residence is deemed to use it as a principal residence while the taxpayer's spouse or former spouse is given use of the residence under the terms of a divorce or separation.

2. Leon sold his home that he had owned and occupied for 7 years. Based on the following facts, compute his recognized gain:

Signed a contract on 1/4/12 to sell his home	
Sold 6/3/12 for	$550,000
Selling expenses	9,000
Replaced and paid for a broken window 1/2/12	100
Replaced and paid for a water heater 1/2/12	350
Paid to have house painted 5/15/12	3,000
Basis of old home before repairs and improvements	110,000

A. $430,650

B. $250,000

C. $180,650

D. $0

Answer (C) is correct.

REQUIRED: The recognized gain on the sale of a principal residence.

DISCUSSION: Selling expenses reduce the proceeds received when calculating realized gain. Capital improvements to property increase the basis in the asset sold. Normal repairs, such as replacing a broken window and painting, do not constitute capital improvements. Thus, the realized gain is $430,650 [($550,000 price – $9,000 selling expenses) – ($110,000 basis + $350 heater)]. An individual may exclude $250,000 ($500,000 for married individuals filing jointly) on the sale of a principal residence provided (s)he lived there for at least 2 years. Thus, Leon will recognize $180,650 ($430,650 realized gain – $250,000 exclusion).

Answer (A) is incorrect. The realized gain is $430,650. Answer (B) is incorrect. The maximum exclusion available for an individual is $250,000. Answer (D) is incorrect. A portion of the gain must be recognized because it exceeds $250,000.

3. Husband and Wife purchased a new residence May 1, 2010. They sold their prior home on July 1, 2011, and realized a gain of $250,000, all of which they excluded. They sold the new home on August 1, 2012, because they wanted to live in a condo. What is the maximum amount of the gain they may exclude in 2012?

A. $0

B. $135,417

C. $270,833

D. $500,000

Answer (A) is correct.

REQUIRED: The maximum amount of gain that may be excluded when a personal residence is sold within 2 years.

DISCUSSION: Since the taxpayer had sold another residence within 2 years of the 2012 sale, the exclusion is not allowed.

4. Bill purchased a home for his principal residence in 2004. However, from December 31, 2009, to December 31, 2011, another location served as Bill's principal residence. Bill's basis in the home was $300,000, and he sold the home for $600,000 on December 31, 2012. What is Bill's recognized gain on the sale of the home?

A. $120,000

B. $250,000

C. $300,000

D. $50,000

Answer (A) is correct.

REQUIRED: The recognized gain on the sale of a principal residence not used for 2 consecutive years.

DISCUSSION: The $250,000 exclusion is available to an individual if (s)he owned and occupied the residence as a principal residence for an aggregate of at least 2 of the 5 years before the sale. The gain on the sale of the principal residence must be prorated between qualified and nonqualified use. Nonqualified use includes periods of time that the residence was not used as the principal residence. The period when Bill uses another location for his principal residence is nonqualified use. Bill's nonqualified use is thus 2 years (January 1, 2010 – December 31, 2011). The percentage of gain that can be excluded is 60% (3 years ÷ 5 years). Therefore, Bill can exclude gain of $180,000, and his recognized gain is $120,000 ($300,000 gain – $180,000).

Answer (B) is incorrect. The amount of $250,000 is the maximum exclusion, not the recognized gain. Answer (C) is incorrect. The amount of $300,000 is the realized gain. Answer (D) is incorrect. The amount of $50,000 does not prorate the gain for nonqualified use.

5. Which of the following statements is not a requirement that must be met before married taxpayers filing jointly can elect to exclude up to $500,000 of the gain on the sale of a personal residence?

A. Either taxpayer must be age 55 or over at the date of the sale.

B. Either spouse must have owned the home as a principal residence for 2 of the 5 previous years.

C. Both spouses must have used the home as a principal residence for 2 of the 5 previous years.

D. Neither spouse is ineligible for the exclusion by virtue of a sale or exchange of a residence within the last 2 years.

Answer (A) is correct.

REQUIRED: The statement that is not required for the exclusion of a gain on the sale of a personal residence.

DISCUSSION: Certain married individuals filing jointly may exclude up to $500,000 on the sale of a principal residence. Married individuals are eligible for a $500,000 exclusion if (1) either spouse owned the home as a principal residence for 2 of the 5 previous years, (2) both spouses used the home as a principal residence for 2 of the 5 previous years, and (3) neither spouse is ineligible for the exclusion by virtue of a sale or an exchange of a residence within the last 2 years. But even if one spouse does not meet the use test, a $250,000 exclusion may still be available for the sale. The age limitation of 55, however, is no longer applicable to the exclusion.

6. A married couple who are both self-employed and work out of their home purchased a new home in July 2010 for $420,000. In September 2010, they converted two bedrooms into office space where they meet clients in their home. In April 2012, they sold their home on which they had taken $40,000 depreciation. Their home sold for $600,000. What amount of the gain is includible in their income on their joint return?

A. $0

B. $40,000

C. $180,000

D. $220,000

Answer (D) is correct.

REQUIRED: The portion of the gain on the sale of a personal residence that must be included in income.

DISCUSSION: The taxpayer may exclude $250,000 ($500,000 for married taxpayers filing jointly) of a realized gain on the sale of a principal residence. The exclusion is available if the individual owned and occupied the residence for an aggregate of at least 2 of the 5 years before the sale. The exclusion may be used only once every 2 years. Since the couple sold their home just 21 months after they purchased it, they are not eligible for the exclusion of the gain. Accordingly, the gain that must be recognized is $220,000 [$600,000 – ($420,000 – $40,000)].

Answer (A) is incorrect. The couple is not eligible for the exclusion and must recognize the gain on the sale of the residence. Answer (B) is incorrect. This amount is the depreciation that should be deducted from the purchase price of the house to arrive at the adjusted basis, not the gain on the sale of the residence. Answer (C) is incorrect. The depreciation must be deducted from the original cost of the house to arrive at the adjusted basis, which is deducted from the amount that the house was sold for to arrive at the gain.

7. Joe and Jean, a married couple, purchased their primary residence in 1986 for $100,000. While they lived there, they made renovations at a cost of $125,000. They lived there until July 1, 2009. On June 15, 2012, the residence was sold for $800,000. From July 1, 2009, until June 15, 2012, the home was unoccupied. Joe and Jean file a joint return, and they have never excluded a gain from the sale of another home. What is their taxable gain?

A. $575,000

B. $0

C. $75,000

D. $200,000

Answer (C) is correct.

REQUIRED: The maximum taxable gain on sale of a primary residence.

DISCUSSION: Publication 523 states, "You can exclude the entire gain on the sale of your main home up to:

1. $250,000 or
2. $500,000 if all of the following are true.
   a. You are married and file a joint return for the year.
   b. Either you or your spouse meets the ownership test.
   c. Both you and your spouse meet the use test.
   d. During the 2-year period ending on the date of the sale, neither you nor your spouse excluded gain from the sale of another home."

In addition, Publication 523 states, "To claim the exclusion, you must meet the ownership and use tests. This means that during the 5-year period ending on the date of the sale, you must have:

1. Owned the home for at least 2 years (the ownership test) and

2. Lived in the home as your main home for at least 2 years (the use test).

The required 2 years of ownership and use during the 5-year period ending on the date of the sale do not have to be continuous.

You meet the tests if you can show that you owned and lived in the property as your main home for either 24 full months or 730 days (365 × 2) during the 5-year period ending on the date of sale."

The taxpayers have a gain of $575,000, of which $75,000 is taxable after the $500,000 exclusion.

Answer (A) is incorrect. The couple meet the requirements to take the $500,000 exclusion. Answer (B) is incorrect. Even after taking the $500,000 exclusion, Joe and Jean have a $75,000 taxable gain. Answer (D) is incorrect. The renovations cost of $125,000 should be added to the adjusted basis.

8. When Amelia bought her first home in 2009, she paid $100,000 plus $1,000 closing costs. In 2010, she added a deck that cost $5,000. Then, in July of 2012, a real estate dealer accepted her house as a trade-in and allowed her $125,000 toward a new house priced at $200,000. How should Amelia report this transaction on her 2012 return?

A. $19,000 long-term capital gain.

B. No reporting because the trade is not a sale.

C. $0 taxable gain and reduce her basis in her new house by $19,000.

D. No reporting required.

Answer (D) is correct.

REQUIRED: The amount and character of the disposition of a principal residence.

DISCUSSION: Amelia has a $19,000 [($125,000 – ($100,000 + $1,000 + $5,000)] long-term capital gain on the disposition of her house. However, after May 6, 1997, a taxpayer may exclude up to $250,000 of gain on the sale of a principal residence. The exclusion is available if the individual owned and occupied the residence as a principal residence for an aggregate of at least 2 of the 5 years before the sale.

Answer (A) is incorrect. Capital gains on the sale of a qualifying principal residence is excludable up to $250,000. Answer (B) is incorrect. This transaction is classified as a sale. Answer (C) is incorrect. There is no effect on her basis from the sale of her principal residence.

9. Roy and Joyce were single, and each owned a home as a separate principal residence for a number of years. In August 2011, Roy sold his home and had a gain of $130,000, which he entirely excluded. Roy and Joyce were married in October 2012. Joyce then decided to sell her principal residence for a $350,000 realized gain. They plan on filing a joint return for 2012. How much of the gain from the sale of Joyce's home can be excluded on their joint tax return for 2012?

A. $0

B. $100,000

C. $250,000

D. $350,000

Answer (C) is correct.

REQUIRED: The amount of the exclusion when one spouse does not qualify for the exclusion.

DISCUSSION: An individual may be able to exclude up to $250,000 of gain on the sale of a personal residence. This exclusion amount is $500,000 for married taxpayers filing jointly if the use and ownership requirements are met and if neither spouse has used the exclusion in the previous 2 years. But even if a single individual marries someone who has used the exclusion within 2 years before marriage, the qualifying individual is not precluded from claiming the $250,000 exclusion to which (s)he is entitled. Thus, Joyce may still claim the exclusion of $250,000 on the joint return and must recognize only $100,000.

Answer (A) is incorrect. A portion of the gain may be excluded. Answer (B) is incorrect. The amount of the gain that may be recognized is $100,000. Answer (D) is incorrect. The entire gain may not be excluded.

10. Myrtle moved in with Eddie in 2009. They then were married in 2011. Eddie had lived in this home for the past 13 years. In early 2012, Eddie and Myrtle decided that marriage was not for them; consequently, they were divorced. Eddie's home was transferred to Myrtle incident to the divorce. Myrtle then sold the house for $250,000. The basis in the home was $80,000. What is Myrtle's recognized gain on the sale of the home in 2012?

A. $0

B. $45,000

C. $170,000

D. $250,000

Answer (A) is correct.

REQUIRED: The recognized gain on the sale of a principal residence transferred to a taxpayer incident to a divorce.

DISCUSSION: Although Myrtle does not meet the ownership test because she owned the property for less than an aggregate of 2 years in the last 5 years before the sale, a special rule applies to divorced taxpayers. If a residence is transferred to a taxpayer incident to a divorce, the time during which the taxpayer's spouse or former spouse owned the residence is added to the taxpayer's period of ownership. Also, a taxpayer who owns a residence is deemed to use it as a principal residence while the taxpayer's spouse or former spouse is given use of the residence under the terms of a divorce or separation; however, Myrtle meets the use test since she lived with Eddie starting in 2009. Myrtle's ownership period includes Eddie's. Myrtle is entitled to exclude a maximum realized gain of $250,000.

Answer (B) is incorrect. The exclusion is not prorated. Answer (C) is incorrect. The realized gain is $170,000. Answer (D) is incorrect. The maximum realized gain that may be excluded by an individual is $250,000.

11. Anne, who is single, owned and used her house as her main home from January 2006 until January 2011. She then moved away and rented her home from February 2011 until she sold it in August 2012. Her home sold for $240,000, which included $20,000 of depreciation and $12,000 of selling expenses. Using a zero basis, compute the amount that is excludable from income.

A. $208,000

B. $220,000

C. $228,000

D. $240,000

Answer (A) is correct.

REQUIRED: The portion of the gain that may be excluded on the sale of a personal residence that was used as rental property before the sale.

DISCUSSION: The taxpayer may exclude $250,000 ($500,000 for married taxpayers filing jointly) of a realized gain on the sale of a principal residence. The exclusion is available if the individual owned and occupied the residence for an aggregate of at least 2 of the 5 years before the sale. The exclusion may be used only once every 2 years. The exclusion does not apply, and gain is recognized, to the extent of any depreciation with respect to the rental or business use of a principal residence after May 6, 1997. Therefore, the depreciation must be subtracted from the amount of gain to determine the amount that may be excluded. In addition, the selling costs must be subtracted from the selling price. The amount of gain realized on the sale of the house is $228,000 ($240,000 – $12,000). However, the depreciation that is attributable to the rental use of the property must be deducted from the gain to arrive at the excludable portion of the gain, which is $208,000 ($228,000 – $20,000).

Answer (B) is incorrect. The selling expenses must also be deducted to arrive at the amount of the gain that may be excluded from income. Answer (C) is incorrect. The depreciation attributable to renting the property must be deducted from the gain to arrive at the excludable portion of the gain. Answer (D) is incorrect. The selling expenses and the depreciation attributable to renting the property must be deducted from the gain to arrive at the excludable portion of the gain.

12. Karen, who is single, paid $150,000 for her residence in January 2008 and lived in it until January 2010. She then moved away and rented her home from February 2010 until she moved back in February 2011. She sold it in August 2012 for $240,000. What amount of gain on the sale of her residence is excludable from income?

A. $250,000

B. $70,380

C. $90,000

D. $240,000

Answer (B) is correct.

REQUIRED: The portion of the gain that may be excluded on the sale of a personal residence.

DISCUSSION: The taxpayer may exclude $250,000 ($500,000 for married taxpayers filing jointly) of a realized gain on the sale of a principal residence. The exclusion is available if the individual owned and occupied the residence for an aggregate of at least 2 of the 5 years before the sale. The exclusion may be used only once every 2 years. The gain on the sale of the residence must be prorated between qualified and nonqualified use. Nonqualified use includes periods that the residence was not used as the principal residence of the taxpayer. The period when Karen is renting her home is nonqualified use. Karen owns the property for 55 months (January 2008 – July 2012), but 12 months is nonqualified use. Thus, the percentage of gain that can be excluded is 78.2% (43 qualified use months ÷ 55 total months). Karen's gain is $90,000 and she can exclude $70,380.

Answer (A) is incorrect. This is the maximum amount that may be excluded from the gain on a principal residence by a single individual. Answer (C) is incorrect. This amount does not prorate the gain for nonqualified use. Answer (D) is incorrect. This is the amount the principal residence was sold for, not the gain on the principal residence.

13. Pete purchased his home on June 1, 2003. On June 1, 2008, Pete became physically incapable of self-care and entered a licensed care facility. Pete sold the residence on April 15, 2012. Pete was residing in the facility at the time of sale. Pete had purchased the home for $150,000, and he sold the home for $300,000. What is Pete's recognized gain for 2012?

A. $300,000

B. $250,000

C. $150,000

D. $0

Answer (D) is correct.

REQUIRED: The recognized gain on the sale of a personal residence when the resident enters a licensed care facility.

DISCUSSION: If an individual becomes physically or mentally incapable of self-care, the individual is deemed to use a residence as a principal residence during the time when the individual owns the residence and resides in a licensed care facility. To apply, the individual must have owned and used the residence as a principal residence for an aggregate period of at least 1 year during the 5 years preceding the sale or exchange. Pete met these requirements, so the gain is excluded.

Answer (A) is incorrect. This amount is the proceeds from the sale. Answer (B) is incorrect. This amount is the maximum amount excluded. Answer (C) is incorrect. This amount is the realized gain.

14. Patrick and Maureen are married. They purchased their residence on August 10, 1999, for $100,000. On September 20, 2012, they had a loan outstanding on the home in the amount of $95,000 when the bank foreclosed. The net proceeds from the foreclosure sale were $105,000, of which Patrick and Maureen received $10,000. What is the exclusion used by Patrick and Maureen to offset any gain?

A. $0

B. $5,000

C. $10,000

D. $250,000

Answer (B) is correct.

REQUIRED: The excluded amount on the foreclosure sale of a principal residence.

DISCUSSION: An individual may exclude $250,000 ($500,000 for married individuals filing jointly) on the sale of a principal residence provided (s)he lived there for at least 2 years. Additionally, a pro rata exclusion is available if the sale occurred prior to 2 years if the sale was as a result of a change in job locations or other unforeseen circumstances. Here, the realized gain is $5,000, and this amount is excluded because the exclusion also applies to foreclosure sales.

Answer (A) is incorrect. They are entitled to exclude the realized gain. Answer (C) is incorrect. The realized gain is $5,000, not $10,000. Answer (D) is incorrect. Only the realized gain is excluded. Also, $250,000 is the maximum amount available to an individual, not married taxpayers.

15. John bought his principal residence for $250,000 on May 3, 2011. He sold it on May 3, 2012, for $400,000. What is the amount and character of his gain?

A. Long-term, ordinary gain of $650,000.

B. Long-term, capital gain of $150,000.

C. Short-term, ordinary gain of $650,000.

D. Short-term, capital gain of $150,000.

Answer (D) is correct.

REQUIRED: The amount and character of a gain on the sale of principal residence.

DISCUSSION: Real property not used in trade or business is a capital asset (e.g., principal residence). Short-term capital is any capital held for 12 months or less starting with the day after acquisition and ending on the day of the sale. Because this sale took place within the prescribed 12-month period, it is classified as a sale of short-term capital property.

Answer (A) is incorrect. The gain on the sale of a residence owned for 1 year is a short-term capital gain, and the gain cannot exceed the selling price. Answer (B) is incorrect. The gain on the sale of a residence owned for 1 year is a short-term capital gain. Answer (C) is incorrect. The gain on the sale of a residence owned for 1 year is a short-term capital gain, and the gain cannot exceed the selling price.

16. Martha, filing single, purchased her home on July 7, 2010, and lived in it continuously until its sale on January 7, 2012. The sale is due to a change in place of employment. Her gain on the sale of the home is $300,000. She did not exclude any gain on any other home sale during this time. What is the maximum amount of gain she may exclude on this sale?

A. $125,000

B. $250,000

C. $300,000

D. $187,500

Answer (D) is correct.

REQUIRED: The maximum amount of gain a taxpayer may exclude on the sale of a principal residence.

DISCUSSION: An individual may exclude $250,000 ($500,000 for married individuals filing jointly) on the sale of a principal residence provided (s)he lived there for at least 2 years. Additionally, a pro rata exclusion is available if the sale occurred prior to 2 years if the sale was as a result of a change in job locations, health reasons, or other unforeseen circumstances. Therefore, Martha may exclude $187,500 [$250,000 × (18 ÷ 24)].

Answer (A) is incorrect. Martha resided in her home for 18, not 12, months. Answer (B) is incorrect. Martha cannot exclude the full $250,000 exemption because she did not reside at the house for at least 2 years. Answer (C) is incorrect. Martha cannot exclude the full amount of the realized gain.

17. Ms. Orchard purchased a duplex in 1998. She lived in one unit as her principal residence and rented out the other unit until she sold the duplex in February 2012. In April 2012, she bought and lived in a small single home. She did not replace the rental property. Her records showed the following:

Duplex	
Original cost	$100,000
Capital improvements	30,000
Depreciation until date of sale (rental unit only)	40,000
Selling price	250,000
Selling expenses	20,000

What is the amount of gain that Ms. Orchard may exclude in 2012?

A. $150,000

B. $140,000

C. $50,000

D. $0

Answer (C) is correct.

REQUIRED: The amount of gain excluded from the sale of a duplex used as a personal residence.

DISCUSSION: Since there are two units to the duplex, the calculations must be divided in half between the personal residence and the rental property. Accordingly, the realized gain is $50,000 [($125,000 sales price – $10,000 selling expenses) – ($50,000 cost of residence + $15,000 capital improvements)]. The depreciation does not reduce the basis of the residence portion because it is attributed to the rental unit only. The $50,000 realized gain is excluded because Ms. Orchard owned and occupied the residence for at least 2 years.

Answer (A) is incorrect. The selling price less the original cost is $150,000. Answer (B) is incorrect. The proceeds and cost must be split between the rental unit and the personal residence. Answer (D) is incorrect. The gain may be excluded.

18. Clyde, a single person, sold his principal residence for $700,000. He purchased his home 10 years ago for $150,000 and lived there until he sold it. He paid for capital improvements of $75,000, real estate commissions of $36,000, and other settlement costs of $4,000. How much taxable gain must Clyde report?

A. $0

B. $185,000

C. $435,000

D. $225,000

Answer (B) is correct.

REQUIRED: The gain that must be reported on the sale of a principal residence.

DISCUSSION: A taxpayer may exclude up to $250,000 ($500,000 for a joint return) of a gain on the sale of a principal residence if (s)he primarily resided in this home for 2 years of a 5-year period before the sale of the home. The gain is determined by subtracting the amount realized, $660,000, ($700,000 – $36,000 –$4,000) from the adjusted basis, $225,000 ($150,000 + $75,000). This yields a gain of $435,000. Clyde only has to claim $185,000 ($435,000 – $250,000) as a gain. (See Sec. 121.)

Answer (A) is incorrect. Clyde must report a $185,000 gain. Answer (C) is incorrect. This amount is the gain before deducting the $250,000 exclusion. Answer (D) is incorrect. This amount is the sum of the purchase price ($150,000) and the capital improvements ($75,000). This is the adjusted basis of the residence.

19. Robert purchased his home for $150,000 in 2002. He sold it for $350,000 (including $100,000 for the land) in 2012. This was his primary residence until it was sold. However, Robert claimed one-fifth of his home as an office for his self-employed business. He claimed a total of $6,000 depreciation over the years. The $150,000 purchase was assessed at $90,000 building and $60,000 land. What is Robert's taxable income as a result of the sale of this primary residence?

A. $6,000

B. $38,000

C. $200,000

D. $0

Answer (A) is correct.

REQUIRED: Taxable income from sale of principal residence.

DISCUSSION: Under Reg. 1.121-1(e)(i), no allocation of gain is required if both the residential and nonresidential portions of the property are within the same dwelling unit. However, Sec. 121 will not apply to the gain to the extent of any post-May 6, 1997, depreciation adjustments. Thus, the $6,000 depreciation taken must be reported as income and is taxed at a maximum rate of 25%.

Answer (B) is incorrect. The office is within the same dwelling unit. Answer (C) is incorrect. The entire gain is not taxed. Answer (D) is incorrect. The depreciation must be included in income.

20. Joe had a taxable gain on the sale of his main home, which could not be excluded on his 2012 tax return. He had no business use of the home. Which schedule does he need to submit to report the gain?

A. Schedule C, for sole proprietors.

B. Schedule A, for itemized deductions.

C. Schedule D, for capital gains.

D. Schedule SE, for self-employment income.

Answer (C) is correct.

REQUIRED: Where to report the gain on sale of principal residence that cannot be excluded.

DISCUSSION: A personal residence is a capital asset. When the taxpayer cannot exclude a portion or all of the gain from the sale of principal residence, the gain is reported on Schedule D.

10.2 Like-Kind Exchanges and Involuntary Conversions

21. A nontaxable exchange is an exchange in which any gain is not taxed and any loss cannot be deducted. To be nontaxable, the exchange must meet all of the following conditions except

A. The property must be business or investment property.

B. The property must be "like-kind" or "like-class" property.

C. The property must be tangible property.

D. The property must not be property held for sale.

Answer (C) is correct.

REQUIRED: The item that is not a requirement for a transaction to qualify as a tax-free like-kind exchange.

DISCUSSION: Sec. 1031(a)(1) requires that property qualifying for tax-free treatment must be held for productive use in a trade or business or investment. Sec. 1031(a)(2) exempts intangible property, such as stocks, bonds, and partnership interests from tax-free exchange treatment. Sec. 1031(a) requires that property exchanged tax-free must be of like-kind. Reg. 1.1031(a)-1(b) states that "like-kind" refers to the nature or character of the property, i.e., a class of property, such as real or personal property. Hence, personal property exchanged for similar personal property would qualify for tax-free treatment.

22. Which of the following statements is false with respect to the identification requirement of like-kind property?

A. You can identify more than one replacement property.

B. Money or unlike property received in full payment for property transferred will still qualify as a nontaxable exchange as long as you receive replacement property within 180 days.

C. The property to be received must be identified on or before the day that is 45 days after the date you transfer the property given up in the exchange.

D. You must clearly describe the replacement property in a signed written document and deliver it to the other person involved in the exchange.

Answer (B) is correct.

REQUIRED: The false statement regarding like-kind property.

DISCUSSION: For purposes of Sec. 1031, a deferred exchange is defined as an exchange in which, pursuant to an agreement, the taxpayer transfers property held for productive use in a trade or business or for investment (the relinquished property) and subsequently receives property to be held either for productive use in a trade or business or for investment (the replacement property). Failure to satisfy one or more of the requirements for a deferred exchange results in part or all of the replacement property received being treated as property that is not of a like kind to the property relinquished [Reg. 1.1031(k)-1(a)]. In a like-kind exchange, any unlike property or money received in full amount of consideration results in part or all of the realized gain being recognized. This result does not change merely because a deferred exchange is taking place since money and unlike property are not qualifying replacement properties [Reg. 1.1031(k)-1(f)]. Thus, money or unlike property received in full payment for property transferred will not qualify as a nontaxable exchange even though you receive replacement property within 180 days.

Answer (A) is incorrect. Reg. 1.1031(k)-1(c)(4) permits the identification of multiple replacement properties. Answer (C) is incorrect. This is one of the requirements of a deferred exchange under Sec. 1031(a)(3)(A). Answer (D) is incorrect. Reg. 1.1031(k)-1(c) requires the replacement to be unambiguously described in a written document or agreement that is delivered to the other party.

23. Which of the following examples of property may qualify for a like-kind exchange?

A. Inventories.

B. Rental house.

C. Accounts receivable.

D. Raw materials.

Answer (B) is correct.

REQUIRED: The type of property that qualifies for a like-kind exchange.

DISCUSSION: Reg. 1.1031(a)-1 indicates that the term "like-kind" refers to the nature or character of property, i.e., a class of property, such as real or personal property. For purposes of determining whether the like-kind requirement is met, property can be divided into (1) depreciable tangible personal property; (2) other personal property, such as patents, works of art, and stamp collections; and (3) real property. Therefore, the rental house qualifies for like-kind treatment because it is real property.

Answer (A) is incorrect. Inventories are not depreciable or held for investment purposes. Answer (C) is incorrect. Accounts receivable do not fall within the definition of personal property for like-kind purposes. Answer (D) is incorrect. Raw materials are the components of inventory.

24. Joe exchanged his pick-up truck with an adjusted basis of $8,000 for a new truck with a fair market value (FMV) of $7,000 and $2,000 cash. Both trucks are used in his business. What gain, if any, must Joe recognize and what is his basis in the new truck?

A. $0 gain; basis $7,000.

B. $1,000 gain; basis $8,000.

C. $1,000 gain; basis $9,000.

D. $1,000 gain; basis $7,000.

Answer (D) is correct.

REQUIRED: The gain and basis on the exchange of like-kind property.

DISCUSSION: Under Sec. 1031(a), neither gain nor loss is recognized on the exchange of like-kind property held for productive use in a trade or business. However, Sec. 1031(b) provides that if boot is received in addition to the like-kind property, gain is recognized to the extent of the fair market value of the boot. The $2,000 received is boot. Joe's realized gain is $1,000 ($7,000 FMV of truck received + $2,000 cash – $8,000 basis). Since the realized gain of $1,000 is less than the boot of $2,000, the entire $1,000 gain is recognized.

The basis of property received in a like-kind exchange is the basis of the property given up, increased by any gain recognized, and decreased by any boot received. Thus, Joe's basis is $7,000 ($8,000 substituted basis + $1,000 gain recognized – $2,000 boot received).

Answer (A) is incorrect. A $1,000 gain is recognized. Answer (B) is incorrect. The basis in the new truck is $7,000. Answer (C) is incorrect. The basis of the new truck is decreased by boot received.

25. Mr. Almond farmed a total of 200 acres of land, comprised of two parcels of land located about one-half mile apart. One parcel was 120 acres, and the second parcel was 80 acres. Mr. Almond found moving his workers and equipment between the two parcels to be very expensive. He approached the ABC farming partnership, which owned 80 acres next to Mr. Almond's 120-acre parcel, about entering into a nontaxable exchange of his 80 acres for the 80 acres owned by the partnership. Mr. Almond has a cost basis of $100,000 in his 80 acres. The fair market value of his 80 acres at the time of the proposed exchange was $400,000, and the fair market value of the ABC partnership's 80 acres was $350,000. The ABC partnership agreed to an exchange. In 2012, Mr. Almond transferred his 80 acres to the ABC partnership in exchange for ABC's 80 acres and $50,000 cash. What was the amount of Mr. Almond's recognized gain in 2012?

A. $400,000

B. $300,000

C. $50,000

D. No gain.

Answer (C) is correct.

REQUIRED: The amount of recognized gain in an exchange in which boot is received.

DISCUSSION: The transfer qualifies for nonrecognition under Sec. 1031. Mr. Almond must recognize a gain equal to the lesser of gain realized or boot received. Therefore, he must recognize a $50,000 gain, which is less than his realized gain.

Answer (A) is incorrect. This amount is the total value of the property received. Answer (B) is incorrect. This amount is the gain realized. Answer (D) is incorrect. A gain is recognized.

26. Matt Carlsen owned an office building for investment purposes on the south side of Chicago. Matt's adjusted basis in the building was $75,000 and the fair market value (FMV) was $90,000. He exchanged his investment for other real estate held for investment with a FMV of $80,000. What is Matt's basis in the new building?

A. $80,000

B. $90,000

C. $95,000

D. $75,000

Answer (D) is correct.

REQUIRED: The basis of newly acquired property following a like-kind exchange.

DISCUSSION: Sec. 1031(a) provides for the nonrecognition of gain or loss on the exchange of like-kind property held for productive use in a trade or business for investment. Like-kind refers to the nature or character of property (here, real property) and not to its grade or quality [Reg. 1.1031(a)-1(b)]. The parcels of real property are like-kind property regardless of whether they are improved, unimproved, or used for different purposes. The basis in the new building is the adjusted basis the taxpayer had in the old building, since no gain is recognized.

27. Ted and William agreed to trade apartment buildings, with Ted agreeing to pay William $10,000 cash. Ted's basis in his apartment building is $40,000. William's basis in his apartment building is $50,000. What is Ted's basis in his new apartment building?

A. $50,000

B. $40,000

C. $10,000

D. None of the answers are correct.

Answer (A) is correct.

REQUIRED: The basis of property received in a like-kind exchange.

DISCUSSION: Sec. 1031 defers recognizing gain or loss to the extent that property productively used in a trade or business or held for the production of income (investment) is exchanged for property of like-kind. Like-kind property is alike in nature or character so real property is of like-kind to other real property, except foreign property. Qualified property received in a like-kind exchange has an exchanged basis adjusted for boot and gain recognized.

	Adjusted basis of property given	$40,000
+	Gain recognized	0
+	Boot given (cash, liability incurred, other property)	10,000
–	Boot received (cash, liability relief, other property)	0
=	Basis in acquired property	$50,000

Answer (B) is incorrect. This amount does not include the $10,000 in boot given. Answer (C) is incorrect. This amount does not include the adjusted basis of the property given up. Answer (D) is incorrect. The basis is the sum of the adjusted basis of property given and boot given.

28. Mr. McCarthy exchanged real estate that he held for investment purposes for other real estate that he will hold for investment purposes. The real estate that he gave up had an adjusted basis of $8,000. The real estate that he received in the exchange had a fair market value of $10,000, and he also received cash of $1,000. Mr. McCarthy paid $500 in exchange expenses. What is the amount of gain recognized by Mr. McCarthy?

A. $1,000

B. $2,500

C. $500

D. None of the answers are correct.

Answer (C) is correct.

REQUIRED: The gain recognized on the like-kind exchange when boot is also received.

DISCUSSION: The basis of property acquired in a like-kind exchange is equal to the adjusted basis of property surrendered, decreased by any boot received and increased by any gain recognized or boot given [Sec. 1031(d)]. The gain recognized equals the lesser of the realized gain ($10,000 FMV of land + $1,000 boot received – $8,000 basis – $500 boot given) or the boot received ($1,000). The IRS has ruled that exchange expenses may be deducted in computing the amount of gain or loss realized, offset against cash payments received in determining gain to be recognized, or included in the basis of the property received (Rev. Ruling 72-456). The best action would be to offset the cash received. Therefore, Mr. McCarthy will recognize a $500 gain ($1,000 – $500).

Answer (A) is incorrect. The $1,000 boot received has not been reduced by the $500 of expenses. Answer (B) is incorrect. The $2,500 equals the realized gain. Answer (D) is incorrect. A gain of $500 is recognized.

29. Jarel transferred an apartment building held for investment to Ron, an unrelated party, in exchange for an office building. At the time of the exchange, the apartment building had a fair market value of $60,000 and an adjusted basis to Jarel of $50,000. The apartment building was subject to a liability of $15,000, which Ron assumed for legitimate business purposes. The office building had an adjusted basis to Ron of $30,000 and a fair market value of $40,000. In addition, Jarel received $5,000 cash in exchange. What is Jarel's recognized gain on this exchange?

A. $5,000

B. $15,000

C. $20,000

D. $10,000

Answer (D) is correct.

REQUIRED: The recognized gain on a like-kind exchange of property.

DISCUSSION: Since the transaction qualifies as a like-kind exchange, Sec. 1031(b) requires the realized gain to be recognized only to the extent of boot received. Reg. 1.1031(d)-2 provides that liabilities assumed by the other party are to be treated as money received by the taxpayer. Jarel's realized gain equals $10,000 ($40,000 FMV of property received + $15,000 liabilities assumed + $5,000 cash received – $50,000 adjusted basis of property given up). Jarel received boot equaling $20,000 ($5,000 cash + $15,000 liabilities). Therefore, the $20,000 of boot received is recognized only to the extent of realized gain (or $10,000).

Answer (A) is incorrect. The liabilities assumed by the other party are also treated as boot. Answer (B) is incorrect. The cash received is boot. Answer (C) is incorrect. This amount is the total boot received, and the realized gain is only $10,000.

30. In 2005, Ms. Nugget, a farmer, inherited a large parcel of land that had a fair market value of $150,000 at that time. She used the large parcel in her farming operations. In 2012, Ms. Nugget decided she no longer wanted the large parcel in her farm operations, so she offered it for sale for $250,000. Mr. Oak approached Ms. Nugget with an offer to exchange a small parcel (which Ms. Nugget wanted for her farming operations) and some farm equipment for the large parcel. The small parcel had a fair market value of $200,000, and the equipment had a fair market value of $50,000. Ms. Nugget accepted Mr. Oak's offer and entered into a partially nontaxable exchange in which she exchanged her land for Mr. Oak's land and equipment. What is Ms. Nugget's basis in the small parcel?

A. $150,000

B. $200,000

C. $250,000

D. None of the answers are correct.

Answer (A) is correct.

REQUIRED: The basis of property acquired in a like-kind exchange when boot is also received.

DISCUSSION: The basis of property acquired in a like-kind exchange is equal to the adjusted basis of property surrendered, decreased by any boot received and increased by any gain recognized or boot given [Sec. 1031(d)]. Thus, the small parcel is equal to the adjusted basis of the large parcel ($150,000), less the boot received of the equipment ($50,000), plus the gain recognized on the boot received ($50,000), or $150,000.

Answer (B) is incorrect. The fair market value of the small parcel is $200,000. Answer (C) is incorrect. The amount Ms. Nugget offered for the large parcel is $250,000. Answer (D) is incorrect. The basis is $150,000.

31. Rochelle transferred an apartment building she held for investment to Mona in exchange for land moving equipment. The apartment building was subject to a liability of $20,000, which Mona assumed for legitimate business purposes. The land moving equipment had an adjusted basis of $40,000 and a fair market value of $70,000. The apartment building had a fair market value of $100,000 and an adjusted basis of $60,000. Rochelle received $8,000 cash in addition to receiving the land moving equipment. What is Rochelle's recognized gain on this exchange?

A. $0

B. $8,000

C. $28,000

D. $38,000

Answer (D) is correct.

REQUIRED: The recognized gain on an exchange of property that is not a like-kind exchange.

DISCUSSION: Since the transaction does not qualify as a like-kind exchange, the entire realized gain must be recognized. The realized gain equals $38,000 ($70,000 FMV of property received + $8,000 cash + $20,000 liabilities assumed – $60,000 adjusted basis of property sold).

32. Ernie had an adjusted basis of $15,000 in real estate he held for investment. Ernie exchanged it for other real estate to be held for investment with a fair market value of $12,500, a truck with a fair market value of $3,000, and $1,000 cash. What is the total basis of the real estate and the truck?

A. $15,500

B. $14,000

C. $15,000

D. $16,500

Answer (A) is correct.

REQUIRED: The total basis of property after a like-kind exchange.

DISCUSSION: The basis of property acquired in a like-kind exchange is equal to the adjusted basis of property surrendered, decreased by any boot received and increased by any gain recognized or boot given [Sec. 1031(d)]. Thus, the basis of the real estate received is equal to the adjusted basis of the real estate transferred ($15,000), less the boot received of the cash ($1,000) and the truck ($3,000), plus the gain recognized on the transaction. Sec. 1031(b) requires that gain be recognized only to the extent of the lesser of boot received or gain realized. The truck and cash are boot, so the boot received is $4,000. However, the gain realized is $1,500 ($12,500 + $3,000 + $1,000 – $15,000), so only a $1,500 gain is recognized. Therefore, the adjusted basis of the real estate received is $12,500 ($15,000 adjusted basis of real estate – $4,000 boot received + $1,500 gain recognized). The total basis of the real estate and the truck is $15,500.

Answer (B) is incorrect. The basis of the properties will include the $1,500 of gain that must be recognized. Answer (C) is incorrect. The basis of property that qualifies for a like-kind exchange must be adjusted when boot property is involved. Answer (D) is incorrect. The transaction qualifies as an exchange of like-kind property.

33. Clark uses a truck in his landscaping business. Clark's sister Lois is a home decorator who uses a station wagon in her business. On December 27, 2011, Clark and Lois exchanged vehicles. The fair market value of Clark's truck was $7,000 with an adjusted basis of $6,000. The fair market value of Lois's station wagon was $7,200 with an adjusted basis of $1,000. On December 28, 2012, Clark sold the station wagon to a third party for $7,200. What is the amount of gain, if any, that Clark has to report on his 2012 return?

A. $6,200

B. $1,200

C. $0

D. $1,000

Answer (B) is correct.

REQUIRED: The amount of gain recognized when like-kind properties are exchanged between related parties.

DISCUSSION: Since the like-kind exchange is between related parties, and a subsequent sale to a third party occurred within 2 years of the exchange, then the gains deferred at the original exchange must be recognized at the date of the subsequent sale. The gain recognized is the amount realized (at the original exchange date) less the adjusted basis (at the original exchange date). In Clark's case, the amount realized is the fair market value of the station wagon ($7,200). Since boot was neither given nor received, Clark's adjusted basis in the station wagon equals his adjusted basis in the truck ($6,000). Therefore, when Clark sells the vehicle, he must report a gain of $1,200 ($7,200 FMV – $6,000 basis).

Answer (A) is incorrect. This amount is the gain if the basis is $1,000. Answer (C) is incorrect. A gain is recognized. Answer (D) is incorrect. The recognized gain is $1,200.

34. During the current year, James exchanged a computer he used in his business for a printer his sister Donna used in her legal practice. For this to be treated as a nontaxable exchange, how long must James and Donna each hold the property exchanged?

A. 6 months.

B. 1 year.

C. 2 years.

D. May be sold at any time.

Answer (C) is correct.

REQUIRED: The waiting period to dispose of the property in a like-kind exchange between related parties.

DISCUSSION: Sec. 1031(f) outlines special rules for like-kind exchanges between related parties. The taxpayer cannot dispose of the property within 2 years after the date of the last transfer that was part of the exchange in order to avoid recognizing any gain on the initial exchange.

35. Mr. Monty owned an office building that he had purchased at a cost of $600,000 and that later had an adjusted basis of $400,000. This year, he traded it to a person who was not related to him for an apartment house having a fair market value of $500,000. The apartment house has 50 units and rents to individuals. The office building has 25 units and rents to Monty's businesses. What is Mr. Monty's recognized gain or loss on this exchange?

A. $100,000 long-term capital gain.

B. $100,000 long-term capital loss.

C. $100,000 ordinary gain.

D. $0

Answer (D) is correct.

REQUIRED: The recognized gain or loss on the exchange of an office building for an apartment building.

DISCUSSION: Sec. 1031(a) provides for the nonrecognition of gain or loss on the exchange of like-kind property held for productive use in a trade or business for investment. Like-kind refers to the nature or character of property (here, real property) and not to its grade or quality [Reg. 1.1031(a)-1(b)]. The parcels of real property are like-kind property regardless of whether they are improved, unimproved, or used for different purposes.

Mr. Monty has a realized gain of $100,000 ($500,000 amount realized – $400,000 adjusted basis). However, none of this gain is recognized under Sec. 1031 since no boot property was received.

36. Mr. Cline exchanged a 30-ton press used in his business for the assets listed below. The press had an adjusted basis to Cline of $78,000.

One used 20-ton press for use in his business, fair market value	$40,000
An automobile for his personal use, fair market value	9,500
Cash	10,000

What is the amount of Mr. Cline's basis in the 20-ton press he received?

A. $40,000

B. $49,500

C. $58,500

D. $78,000

Answer (C) is correct.

REQUIRED: The basis of property acquired in a like-kind exchange when boot is received.

DISCUSSION: The exchange qualifies for like-kind treatment under Sec. 1031 since personal property used in Mr. Cline's business is exchanged for other personal property to be used in the business. The realized loss is $18,500 [($40,000 press + $10,000 cash + $9,500 fair market value of automobile) – $78,000 basis], which cannot be recognized under Sec. 1031(c). The basis of the property received is $58,500 ($78,000 adjusted basis of the property surrendered – $10,000 cash received – $9,500 fair market value of automobile).

Answer (A) is incorrect. This amount is the value of the press received. Answer (B) is incorrect. This amount is the value of the press received plus the automobile. Answer (D) is incorrect. The adjusted basis of press transferred must be reduced by the boot received.

37. Emmett transferred an apartment building he held for investment to Ray, an unrelated party, in exchange for an office building. At the time of the exchange, the apartment building had a fair market value of $90,000 and an adjusted basis to Emmett of $70,000. The apartment building was subject to a liability of $30,000, which Ray assumed for legitimate business purposes. The office building had an adjusted basis to Ray of $30,000 and a fair market value of $80,000. In addition, Emmett received $10,000 cash in exchange. What is Emmett's recognized gain on this exchange?

A. $10,000

B. $30,000

C. $40,000

D. $50,000

Answer (C) is correct.

REQUIRED: The recognized gain on a like-kind exchange of property.

DISCUSSION: Since the transaction qualifies as a like-kind exchange, Sec. 1031(b) requires the realized gain to be recognized only to the extent of boot received. Reg. 1.1031(d)-2 provides that liabilities assumed by the other party are to be treated as money received by the taxpayer. The amount realized equals $120,000 [$80,000 FMV of property received + $30,000 relief of mortgage + $10,000 cash received]. The adjusted basis of the property is $70,000. The realized gain is $50,000 ($120,000 amount realized – $70,000 adjusted basis). However, boot received is less than the gain realized. Since boot received equals $40,000, only $40,000 is recognized.

Answer (A) is incorrect. The liabilities assumed by the other part are also treated as boot. Answer (B) is incorrect. The cash received is boot. Answer (D) is incorrect. The $50,000 is the realized gain.

38. If an involuntary conversion occurs when your property is destroyed, stolen, condemned, or disposed of under the threat of condemnation and you receive other property or money in payment, such as insurance or a condemnation award, which of the following statements is true?

A. Gain or loss from an involuntary conversion of your property is usually recognized for tax purposes unless the property is your main home.

B. You may not have to report a gain on an involuntary conversion if you receive property that is similar or related in service or use to the converted property.

C. If you receive money or property that is not similar or related in service or use to the involuntarily converted property and you buy qualifying replacement property within a certain period of time, you can choose to postpone reporting the gain.

D. All of the answers are correct.

Answer (D) is correct.

REQUIRED: The amount of gain or loss recognized from an involuntary conversion.

DISCUSSION: Publication 544 states, "Gain or loss from an involuntary conversion of your property is usually recognized for tax purposes unless the property is your main home. However, depending on the type of property you receive, you may not have to report a gain on an involuntary conversion. You do not report the gain if you receive property that is similar or related in service or use to the converted property. If you receive money or property that is not similar or related in service or use to the involuntary converted property and you buy qualifying replacement property within a certain period of time, you can choose to postpone reporting the gain."

39. Joe exchanged a building for another like-kind building. Joe had a basis of $16,000, plus he had made $10,000 in improvements prior to the exchange. He exchanged it for a building worth $36,000. Joe did not recognize any gain from the exchange on his 2012 individual tax return. What is Joe's basis in the new property?

A. $26,000

B. $36,000

C. $10,000

D. $16,000

Answer (A) is correct.

REQUIRED: Basis in property received in a like-kind exchange transaction.

DISCUSSION: Joe's basis in his building is $16,000. Prior to exchanging it, Joe made $10,000 in improvements. His total basis is $26,000. Because no money exchanged hands and no gain was recognized, Joe's basis in the new property is the same as his basis in the old property.

Answer (B) is incorrect. Joe's basis equals the basis in the property given up, not the FMV of the property received. Answer (C) is incorrect. His basis does not equal the difference between the FMV of the new property and the basis of the property given up. Answer (D) is incorrect. Joe's basis is increased by $10,000 for the improvements made on the property.

40. The state condemned Joe's property. Joe did not hold the property for use in a trade or business or for investment. The adjusted basis of the property was $26,000. The state paid Joe $36,000 in 2012. Joe realized a gain of $10,000. Joe bought like-kind property for $35,000 in 2012 for the purpose of replacing the condemned property. Joe also made a proper Internal Revenue Code Sec. 1033 election to defer gain from the condemnation on his 2012 tax return. In 2012, what is the net taxable gain and where must Joe report it?

A. $36,000 on the return Schedule D.

B. $10,000 on line 21 of Form 1040.

C. $1,000 on Schedule D.

D. $26,000 on Form 4797 – *Sale of Business Property*.

Answer (C) is correct.

REQUIRED: Gain recognized from an involuntary conversion.

DISCUSSION: When property is converted involuntarily into nonqualified proceeds and qualified property is purchased within the replacement period, an election may be made to defer realized gain to the extent that the amount realized on the conversion is reinvested in qualified replacement property. Any gain is reported on Schedule D. Thus, Joe should report a gain of $1,000 ($36,000 – $35,000) on Schedule D.

Answer (A) is incorrect. Joe qualified for a Sec. 1033 deferral. Answer (B) is incorrect. Joe is not required to recognize a gain on an involuntary conversion to the extent he reinvests the proceeds in qualified replacement property. Answer (D) is incorrect. This transaction qualified under Sec. 1033 and Joe does not have to report any gain if he reinvests in the proceeds in qualified replacement property.

STUDY UNIT ELEVEN
INDIVIDUAL RETIREMENT ACCOUNTS

(10 pages of outline)

An individual retirement account (IRA) is a personal savings plan that offers tax advantages to individuals who set aside money for retirement. Two advantages include the deductibility of contributions and the tax exemption of IRA earnings until they are distributed. An IRA can be set up with most banks and similar savings institutions, mutual funds, stock brokerage firms, and insurance companies.

11.1 IRAs DEFINED

Age Limit

1. Any individual who receives taxable compensation during the year and is not age 70 1/2 by the end of the year may set up an IRA.
   a. An individual may set up a spousal IRA for a spouse, provided a joint return is filed.

Compensation

2. Compensation is defined as earned income. It includes
   a. Wages and salaries
   b. Commissions
   c. Self-employment income
   d. Alimony and separate maintenance payments
3. Compensation does not include earnings and profits from property such as rental income, interest income, dividend income or pension and annuity income, and the share of S corporation income.

Types of IRAs

4. There are five kinds of individual retirement accounts:
   a. Individual retirement account
   b. Individual retirement annuity
   c. Employer and employee association trust accounts
   d. Simplified employee pension (SEP)
   e. Savings incentive match plans for employees (SIMPLE)
5. Publication 590 also lists individual retirement bonds, but not individual savings bonds, as a permitted individual retirement account.

Fully Vested

6. Under Secs. 219(d) and 408, an IRA must be fully vested at all times, the assets of the trust cannot be commingled with other property except in a common trust fund or common investment fund, and no part of the trust funds can be used to purchase life insurance contracts.

Shareholder Status

7. Generally, IRAs and Roth IRAs are not permitted as S corporation shareholders. However, if the IRA or Roth IRA held bank stock on or after October 22, 2004, the IRA or Roth IRA is permitted to hold this stock, and the owner of the plan is considered the shareholder.
   a. Prohibited transaction rules do not apply to the sale of stock by an IRA or Roth IRA to the individual beneficiary of the trust if the following are true (American Jobs Creation Act of 2004):
      1) The stock is stock in a bank.
      2) The stock is held by the IRA or Roth IRA on or after October 22, 2004.
      3) The sale is pursuant to an S election by the bank.
      4) The sale is for FMV at the time of the sale, and the terms of the sale are otherwise at least as favorable to the IRA or Roth IRA as the terms that would apply for a sale to an unrelated party.
      5) The IRA or Roth IRA does not pay any commissions, costs, or other expenses in connection with the sale.
      6) The stock is sold in a single transaction for cash not later than 120 days after the S election is made.

Stop and review! You have completed the outline for this subunit. Study questions 1 through 5 beginning on page 266.

11.2 CONTRIBUTIONS

1. Once an IRA is set up, a taxpayer may make contributions each year in which (s)he is qualified.
   a. To qualify to make contributions, a taxpayer must not have reached age 70 1/2 during the year and must have received compensation.
   b. However, contributions are not required to be made each year.
   c. Contributions must be made by the due date of the return (not including extensions).

Contribution Limits

2. The maximum contribution that can be made during any year is the lesser of
   a. The compensation received or
   b. $5,000.
      1) Individuals age 50 and older at the end of the year can contribute an additional $1,000 (i.e., total contribution limit is $6,000).

   NOTE: For 401(k) plans, the limit is $17,000 ($22,500 if 50 or older). For 403(b) plans, the limit is $50,000 or 100% of includible compensation if less (an additional $5,500 is allowed for those 50 or older).

Inherited IRAs

3. A person may deduct contributions made to an inherited IRA only if the IRA was inherited from a spouse. Contributions or rollovers cannot be made to an IRA inherited from someone who died after December 31, 1983, and who was not a spouse. An IRA is included in the estate of the decedent who owned it.
   a. When an IRA is inherited from a person other than a spouse, the IRA cannot be treated as though it was owned by the taxpayer who inherited the IRA.

Spousal IRA Limit

4. If a joint return is filed and a taxpayer makes less than his/her spouse, the taxpayer may still contribute the lesser of
   a. The sum of his/her compensation and the taxable compensation of the spouse, reduced by the amount of the spouse's IRA contribution and contributions to a Roth IRA, or
   b. $5,000 ($6,000 if over age 50).

   NOTE: Thus, the total combined contributions to an IRA and a spouse's IRA can be as much as $10,000 for the year (plus an additional $1,000 for each spouse age 50 and older).
5. If a taxpayer has more than one IRA, the limit applies to the total contributions made to the IRAs for the year.

Deductible Contributions

6. Generally, a deduction is allowed for contributions that are made to an IRA.
   a. If neither spouse was covered for any part of the year by an employer retirement plan, the entire contribution may be deducted.
   b. If a taxpayer is not covered by an employer plan but the taxpayer's spouse is, the taxpayer may still deduct the full amount of the contribution. However, the deduction is reduced if the adjusted gross income on the joint return is greater than $173,000 but less than $183,000. The deduction is eliminated if the income is greater than $183,000.
   c. If a taxpayer is covered by a retirement plan at work, the IRA deduction will be phased out or eliminated if the taxpayer's modified AGI is between
      1) $58,000 and $68,000 for a single individual
      2) $92,000 and $112,000 for a married couple filing a joint return
      3) $0 and $10,000 for a married individual filing a separate return
   d. Deductible contributions to an IRA have to be made in cash and not any other property.
7. For an individual whose modified AGI falls within one of the phaseout ranges above, the amount that must be reduced from the IRA deduction is determined by the following equation:

$$\frac{\text{Modified AGI} - \text{Applicable minimum phaseout amount}}{\text{Maximum phaseout amount} - \text{Minimum phaseout amount}} \times \$5{,}000$$

   a. This amount is subtracted from the maximum allowable deduction to arrive at the allowable deductible amount.
   b. Round it up to the next highest multiple of $10 to find the allowable deduction.
      1) If a deduction is allowed, $200 or more is allowed.
      2) However, the deduction may not exceed the contributions made.

Rollovers

8. Generally, a rollover is a tax-free distribution of cash or other assets from one retirement plan to another retirement plan. There are two types of rollovers: direct and indirect.
   a. A direct rollover is a direct transfer of assets from one qualified plan to another qualified plan.
   b. An indirect rollover is a rollover in which the taxpayer takes physical possession of the assets (e.g., a check).
      1) The taxpayer must deposit the assets into another qualified plan within 60 days of the withdrawal to avoid taxes and penalties.

c. A rollover cannot be deducted.

d. Distributions that are not qualified distributions include the following:

   1) Required minimum distributions
   2) Hardship distributions
   3) Any series of substantially periodic distributions
   4) Corrective distributions due to excess contributions
   5) A loan treated as a distribution
   6) Dividends on employee securities
   7) The cost of life insurance coverage
   8) A distribution to the plan participant's beneficiary

e. If a taxpayer withdraws assets from an IRA, rolls over part of it tax-free, and keeps the rest, a gain must be recognized, and (s)he may be subject to the 10% tax on premature distributions.

f. The same property that was received from an old IRA may be rolled over into a new IRA.

g. If an individual inherits a traditional IRA from anyone other than a deceased spouse, the person is not permitted to treat the inherited IRA as his/her own, making direct contributions. The inherited IRA will generally not have tax assessed on the IRA assets until distributions are received.

h. The basis of a traditional IRA because of nondeductible contributions remains with the IRA.

i. Distributions from an inherited IRA must either begin by the end of the year following the death or the IRA must be completely distributed by the end of the fifth year following death.

j. When transferring an IRA account to a spouse (or an ex-spouse pursuant to a domestic relations order), taxes and penalties may be avoided by

   1) Changing the name on the IRA account or
   2) Transferring the IRA assets into another qualified plan.

Collectibles

9. Generally, an IRA is prohibited from investing in collectibles. However, an IRA may hold platinum coins as well as gold, silver, or platinum bullion.

Prohibited Transactions

10. A taxpayer may not engage in the following transactions with a traditional IRA: sell property to it, use it as security for a loan, or buy property with it for the taxpayer's personal use.

Basis in a Traditional IRA (Form 8606)

11. A taxpayer will have a cost basis in a traditional IRA if any nondeductible contributions were made.

   a. Cost basis is the sum of the nondeductible contributions to the IRA minus any withdrawals or distributions of nondeductible contributions.

   b. The difference between the taxpayer's total permitted contributions and the taxpayer's IRA deduction, if any, is the nondeductible contribution.

      1) To designate contributions as nondeductible, Form 8606 must be filed.
      2) A taxpayer must file Form 8606 to report nondeductible contributions even if (s)he does not have to file a tax return for the year [Publication 590, IRC 408 (o)(2)(B)].

Stop and review! You have completed the outline for this subunit. Study questions 6 through 26 beginning on page 268.

11.3 PENALTIES

Excess Contributions

1. Generally, an excess contribution is the amount contributed to an IRA that is more than the lesser of
   a. Its compensation received or
   b. $5,000 ($6,000 for a taxpayer age 50 and older).
2. An excess contribution could be the result of a taxpayer's contribution, a spouse's contribution, an employer's contribution, or an improper rollover contribution.
3. A 6% excise tax is imposed each year on excess contribution amounts that remain in an IRA at the end of each tax year. Distribution of excess contributions is reported on Form 1099-R in box 2a and coded in box 7.
4. The tax can be avoided if the excess contribution and the interest earned on it are withdrawn by the due date (including extensions) of the tax return.
   a. The interest earned on the excess contribution qualifies as a premature distribution and is subject to an additional tax of 10% on that distribution.
5. Under Sec. 219(f)(6), the taxpayer may treat the unused (excess) contributions from a previous year as having been made in the current year to the extent that the allowable contribution limit exceeds the actual contributions for the current year.

Premature Distributions

6. Premature distributions are amounts withdrawn from an IRA or annuity before a taxpayer reaches age 59 1/2.
   a. The additional tax on premature distributions is equal to 10% of the amount of the premature distribution that must be included in gross income. This tax is in addition to any regular income tax that is due.
   b. In certain circumstances, the additional tax does not apply to distributions from an IRA, even if they are made before a taxpayer reaches age 59 1/2 [Sec. 72(f)]. There are exceptions for
      1) Death
      2) Disability
      3) Annuity payments based on life expectancy
      4) Medical expenses exceeding 7.5% of AGI
      5) Qualified higher education expenses
      6) A qualified first-time homebuyer distribution
      7) Unemployed health insurance premium
      8) Levy under Sec. 6331
      9) Payments made under a Qualified Domestic Relations Order
      10) U.S. military reservists called to active duty
   c. If a taxpayer borrows money against an IRA, the fair market value of the IRA as of the first day of the tax year must be included in gross income. The taxpayer may also be subject to the 10% penalty tax. An individual may withdraw all or part of the assets of a traditional IRA and exclude the withdrawal from income if the individual transfers it to another traditional IRA or returns it to the same IRA within 60 days after the withdrawal.

Excess Accumulations

7. Generally, a taxpayer must begin receiving distributions by April 1 of the year following the year in which (s)he reaches age 70 1/2.
   a. If distributions are less than the required minimum distribution for the year, a 50% excise tax will be imposed on the amount not distributed.
   b. The tax may be excused if the excess accumulation is due to reasonable error and if the taxpayer is taking steps to remedy the insufficient distribution.
      1) To make a waiver request, a taxpayer must file Form 5329, pay excise tax owed, and attach a written explanation showing when excess accumulation was removed or what the taxpayer has done to have it withdrawn.
      2) Any tax paid will be refunded if the waiver is granted.
   c. The RMD amount for a year is generally equal to the participant's accrued benefit or account balance as of the end of the prior year, divided by the appropriate distribution period.
      1) Before death distributions
      2) After death distributions
      3) Death before RMDs begin
         a) Death on or after RMDs begin
   d. Required beginning dates
      1) Generally, April 1 of the calendar year following the later of the employee attaining age 70 1/2 or retiring.
      2) For a traditional IRA, April 1 of the calendar year following the employee attaining age 70 1/2.
      3) The required distribution date each year following the initial beginning date is December 31.

EXAMPLE

Lurlene is an unmarried participant in a qualified defined contribution plan. Her account balances for 5 years are as follows:

Date	Account Balance
December 31, Year 1	$275,000
December 31, Year 2	$295,000
December 31, Year 3	$320,000
December 31, Year 4	$350,000
December 31, Year 5	$340,000

Lurlene retired January 1, Year 1, and reached age 70 on May 1, Year 2. The initial RMD is based on the year in which she reached 70 1/2 (Year 2), since it is later than her retirement date. The deadlines and amounts associated with the first four RMDs are shown below:

Distribution				Calculation	
No.	RMD Date	Relevant Balance Date (Dec. 31)	Relevant Age (Dec. 31)	Balance ÷ Life Expectancy	RMD Amount
1st	April 1, Yr 3	Year 1	Yr 2: 70	$275,000 ÷ 27.4	$10,037
2nd	Dec 31, Yr 3	Year 2	Yr 3: 71	[$295,000 – $10,037] ÷ 26.5	$10,753
3rd	Dec 31, Yr 4	Year 3	Yr 4: 72	$320,000 ÷ 25.6	$12,500
4th	Dec 31, Yr 5	Year 4	Yr 5: 73	$350,000 ÷ 24.7	$14,170

Borrowing from the Plan

8. The terms of a qualified plan may permit the plan to lend money to participants without adverse income or excise tax results, if certain requirements are met.
   a. Code Sec. 73(p) basically treats loans as distributions.
      1) A loan will not be treated as a distribution to the extent loans to the employee do not exceed the lesser of
         a) $50,000 or
         b) The greater of one-half of the present value of the employee's vested accrued benefit under such plans or $10,000.
      2) The $50,000 maximum sum is reduced by the participant's highest outstanding balance during the preceding 12-month period.
   b. Plan loans generally have to be repaid within 5 years unless the funds are to acquire a principal residence for the participant.
   c. Plan loans must be amortized in level payments, made no less frequently than quarterly over the term of the loan.
   d. A pledge of the participant's interest under the plan or an agreement to pledge such interest as security for a loan by a third party, as well as a direct or indirect loan from the plan itself, is treated as a loan.

Stop and review! You have completed the outline for this subunit. Study questions 27 through 34 beginning on page 274.

11.4 ROTH IRAs

Exempt Distributions

1. A tax-free IRA (referred to as a Roth IRA) has been available since the beginning of 1998.
   a. Contributions to the Roth IRA are nondeductible, but income can be accumulated tax-free.
   b. To be treated as a Roth IRA, the account must be designated as such when it is established.

Income Limits

   c. Roth IRAs are subject to income limits. The maximum yearly contribution that can be made to a Roth IRA is phased out for single taxpayers with a modified AGI between $110,000 and $125,000, for joint filers with a modified AGI between $173,000 and $183,000, and for a married taxpayer filing separately with a modified AGI between $0 and $10,000.
   d. Modified AGI is determined by subtracting any income resulting from a conversion of a traditional IRA to a Roth IRA and any minimum required distributions from a qualified retirement plan, including an IRA, from adjusted gross income. The following items are added to adjusted gross income:
      1) Traditional IRA deduction
      2) Student loan interest deduction
      3) Tuition and fees deduction
      4) Foreign earned income and/or housing exclusion
      5) Foreign housing deduction
      6) Exclusion of bond interest
      7) Exclusion of employer-provided adoption benefits
      8) Domestic production activities deduction

Contribution Limit

2. The contribution amount is the same as the amount for a deductible IRA, and the total contribution to both deductible and nondeductible IRAs cannot exceed $5,000 per taxpayer ($6,000 for individuals who will be at least 50 years old by the end of the year).

No Age Limit

3. Unlike deductible IRAs, individuals are allowed to make contributions to the Roth IRA after reaching age 70 1/2.

Qualified Distribution

4. Qualified distributions from a Roth IRA are not included in the taxpayer's gross income and are not subject to the additional 10% early withdrawal tax.
   a. To be a qualified distribution, the distribution must satisfy a 5-year holding period and must meet one of four additional requirements.
      1) To satisfy the 5-year holding period, the Roth IRA distribution may not be made before the end of the 5-tax-year period beginning with the first tax year for which the individual made a contribution to the Roth IRA.
         a) The 5-year holding period begins to run with the tax year to which the contribution relates, not the year in which the contribution is actually made; thus, a contribution made in April 2008, designated as a 2007 contribution, may be withdrawn tax free in 2012, if it is otherwise a qualified distribution.
      2) Taxpayers must meet one of four other requirements for a tax-free distribution. The distribution must be
         a) Made on or after the date on which the individual attains age 59 1/2,
         b) Made to a beneficiary (or the individual's estate) on or after the individual's death,
         c) Attributed to the individual's being disabled, or
         d) Distributed to pay for "qualified first-time homebuyer expenses."
5. Distributions are treated as made from contributions first; thus, no portion of a distribution is treated as attributable to earnings or includible in gross income until the total of all distributions from the Roth IRA exceeds the amount of contributions. Nonqualified distributions are included in income after recovery of contribution, and they are subject to the 10% early withdrawal penalty.

Rollover

6. Distributions from one Roth IRA can be rolled over or "converted" tax-free to another Roth IRA.
7. Amounts in an ordinary IRA can be rolled into a Roth IRA.
   a. If a taxpayer has both deductible and nondeductible IRAs and only a portion of the IRAs are converted into a Roth IRA, any amount rolled into a Roth IRA will be considered to have been drawn proportionately from both the deductible and nondeductible IRAs and will be taxed accordingly.
   b. A taxpayer can rescind a transfer from a traditional IRA to a Roth IRA until (s)he files his/her tax return, including extensions.
   c. Once a taxpayer has begun periodic distributions of a traditional IRA, (s)he is able to convert his/her traditional IRA into a Roth IRA and resume the periodic payments. In addition, the 10% penalty on early distributions will not apply to unqualified distributions.

Required Distribution

8. Distributions from Roth IRAs are required only upon death.

Stop and review! You have completed the outline for this subunit. Study questions 35 through 37 on page 277.

11.5 COVERDELL EDUCATION SAVINGS ACCOUNTS (CESAs)

1. A CESA is a tax-favored education individual retirement account to help taxpayers save for a designated beneficiary's education expenses.
   a. A designated beneficiary includes anyone under the age of 18 or who is a special-needs beneficiary.

Income Limits

2. Taxpayers may contribute up to $2,000 per beneficiary per year.
   a. The phaseout range for an individual is between $95,000 and $110,000. The phaseout range for joint filers is between $190,000 and $220,000.
   b. The total contribution to all accounts on behalf of a beneficiary in any year cannot exceed $2,000.

Contributions and Earnings

3. Contributions to CESAs are nondeductible. However, earnings on contributions will be distributed tax-free provided they are used to pay the beneficiary's qualified education expenses.

Distributions

4. Distributions of income from CESAs are included in gross income and are subject to a 10% penalty to the extent they exceed qualified education expenses.

Requirements

5. Several requirements must be met for CESAs:
   a. No contribution may be accepted by the CESAs after the beneficiary attains age 18, unless the beneficiary is a special-needs individual.
   b. Contributions must be in cash.
   c. The trustee must be a bank or other qualified person.
   d. No portion of the trust's asset may be invested in life insurance contracts.
   e. Trust assets must not be commingled with other property, except in a common trust or investment fund.

Qualified Expenses

6. Qualified higher education expenses include tuition, books, fees, supplies, equipment, and special-needs services required for the enrollment at an eligible institution. Additionally, room and board may be qualified expenses if they do not exceed the minimum amounts as determined for federal financial aid programs.

7. Qualified elementary and secondary education expenses include tuition, fees, books, supplies, equipment, academic tutoring, and special-needs services required for enrollment at an eligible institution. If required or provided by an eligible institution, room, board, uniforms, transportation, and supplementary items/services (including extended day programs) are also qualified expenses. Additionally, computer-related equipment/service is a qualified expense.

8. Earnings not used for educational purposes are subject to tax when the beneficiary reaches age 30.
   a. The balance remaining in a CESA must be distributed within 30 days after the beneficiary reaches age 30 or the death of the beneficiary.
      1) A CESA may be rolled over tax-free to another beneficiary.
      2) This rule does not apply if the person receiving the distribution is a special-needs beneficiary.
   b. CESA balances must be distributed within 30 days after the death of a beneficiary.
      1) The earnings portion of the distribution is includible in the beneficiary's gross income.
      2) The CESA should designate another child as a beneficiary in case of death.
9. No income exclusion is allowed for the same expenses used for the American Opportunity Credit or the Lifetime Learning Credit.

Stop and review! You have completed the outline for this subunit. Study questions 38 through 41 on page 278.

QUESTIONS

11.1 IRAs Defined

1. Which of the following is compensation for the purpose of contributions to individual retirement accounts?

A. Deferred compensation received.

B. Foreign earned income excluded from income.

C. Pension or annuity income.

D. Taxable alimony and separate maintenance.

Answer (D) is correct.

REQUIRED: The item that is compensation for the purpose of contributions to IRAs.

DISCUSSION: Publication 590 states that compensation is defined as earned income. It includes wages and salaries, commissions, self-employment income, and alimony and separate maintenance payments. Compensation does not include earnings and profits from property such as rental income, interest income, and dividend income or pension and annuity income.

Answer (A) is incorrect. Deferred compensation received is not considered compensation but is includible in modified adjusted gross income for the purpose of contributions to IRAs. Answer (B) is incorrect. Foreign earned income excluded from income is not considered compensation but is includible in modified adjusted gross income for the purpose of contributions to IRAs. Answer (C) is incorrect. Pension or annuity income is not considered compensation but is includible in modified adjusted gross income for the purpose of contributions to IRAs.

2. Generally, an IRA contribution is limited to the lesser of $5,000 in 2012 or the taxpayer's compensation. However, which of the following items is not treated as compensation for this limitation?

A. Wages earned by an individual under the age of 18.

B. Taxable alimony.

C. Self-employment loss.

D. Commissions.

Answer (C) is correct.

REQUIRED: The item that is not considered to be earned compensation for IRA contribution purposes.

DISCUSSION: Compensation is defined as earned income. It includes

1) Wages and salaries,
2) Commissions,
3) Self-employment income, and
4) Alimony and separate maintenance payments.

Self-employment loss is not considered income for the purposes of contributing to an IRA.

Answer (A) is incorrect. Wages earned are considered income even if the individual is under the age of 18. Answer (B) is incorrect. Taxable alimony is treated as earned income and is treated as compensation for the IRA limit. Answer (D) is incorrect. Commissions are earned income and treated as compensation for the IRA limit.

3. Which one of the following types of individual retirement accounts (IRAs) cannot be established?

A. An individual retirement annuity that is purchased from a life insurance company.

B. An individual retirement account with a trustee who invests one's money in 1-ounce U.S. gold coins.

C. A simplified employee pension account.

D. An individual retirement account with a trustee who invests one's money in life insurance contracts.

Answer (D) is correct.

REQUIRED: The type of IRA that cannot be established.

DISCUSSION: An individual retirement account must be either a trust or a custodial account established in the United States for the exclusive benefit of the owner and the owner's beneficiaries. It must be established by a written document and meet the requirements of Sec. 408(a). Sec. 408(a)(4) states that no part of the amount in the account may be used to buy life insurance.

4. An individual retirement account (IRA) is a trust or custodial account created by a written document that must meet all of the following requirements, except

A. The amount in your account must be fully vested.

B. Money in your account can be used to buy a life insurance policy.

C. Assets in your account cannot be combined with other property, except in a common trust fund or common investment fund.

D. You must start receiving distributions from your account by April 1 of the year following the year in which you reach age 70 1/2.

Answer (B) is correct.

REQUIRED: The item that is not a requirement for setting up an individual retirement account.

DISCUSSION: Under Sec. 219(d) and Sec. 408, an IRA account must be fully vested at all times, the assets of the trust cannot be commingled with other property except in a common trust fund or common investment fund, and plan distributions must begin by April 1 of the calendar year following the later of the calendar year in which the employee (1) attains age 70 1/2 or (2) retires. No part of the trust funds can be used to purchase life insurance contracts.

Answer (A) is incorrect. The amount in your account must be fully vested. Answer (C) is incorrect. Assets in your account cannot be combined with other property, except in a common trust fund or common investment fund. Answer (D) is incorrect. You must start receiving distributions from your account by April 1 of the year following the year in which you reach age 70 1/2.

5. When figuring compensation for purposes of determining the amount of an allowable contribution to a traditional IRA, which of the following is an incorrect statement?

A. Pension or annuity income is not considered compensation for an IRA plan.

B. Earnings and profits from property, such as rental income, are considered compensation.

C. Interest and dividends are not considered compensation for an IRA plan.

D. Generally, amounts excluded from income are not considered compensation for an IRA plan.

Answer (B) is correct.

REQUIRED: Figuring compensation for purposes of determining the amount of an allowable contribution to a traditional IRA.

DISCUSSION: Compensation is defined as earned income. It includes

1) Wages and salaries,
2) Commissions,
3) Self-employment income, and
4) Alimony and separate maintenance payments.

Compensation does not include earnings and profits from property such as rental income, interest income, dividend income, or pension and annuity income, and the share of S corporation income.

Answer (A) is incorrect. Pension and annuity income is not considered compensation for purposes of determining the amount of an allowable contribution to a traditional IRA. Answer (C) is incorrect. Interest and dividends are not considered compensation for an IRA plan. Answer (D) is incorrect. Generally, amounts excluded from income are not considered compensation for any IRA plan.

11.2 Contributions

6. Gary and Mabel have been married for many years and file jointly. Gary was born February 21, 1940. Mabel was born April 10, 1944. They each received Social Security benefit payments throughout 2012. Gary earned $6,700 as a part-time security guard in 2012; he was not covered by any type of retirement plan. Mabel has been retired for many years. Gary and Mabel expect their 2012 adjusted gross income to exceed $92,000. What is the amount of Gary and Mabel's largest allowable spousal IRA deduction for 2012 (assume the proper amount claimed as a deduction was paid timely)?

A. $10,000

B. $6,000

C. $5,000

D. $0

Answer (B) is correct.

REQUIRED: The maximum allowable spousal IRA deduction.

DISCUSSION: An individual may not make contributions to an IRA for the year (s)he reaches age 70 1/2 or any later year. However, if the individual has received compensation, a spouse who has not reached age 70 1/2 may still deduct up to $5,000 of contributions, plus $1,000 if age 50 or older.

Answer (A) is incorrect. Gary has reached the age of 70 1/2. Mabel is over 50 and therefore eligible for the $1,000 catch-up contribution. Answer (C) is incorrect. They are allowed an extra $1,000, since Mabel is over 50 years old. Answer (D) is incorrect. Mabel may continue to deduct contributions, provided her spouse has received compensation and she has not turned age 70 1/2.

7. A contribution to a traditional individual retirement plan (IRA) is deductible for tax year 2012 in which of the following situations?

A. The individual's employer does not have a retirement plan at any time during 2012.

B. The contribution is made on August 15, 2013, under a properly filed and accepted extension.

C. The individual is covered by a retirement plan but does not have any compensation in 2012.

D. All of the answers are correct.

Answer (A) is correct.

REQUIRED: The situation that permits a contribution to a traditional IRA to be deductible for the tax year.

DISCUSSION: All IRA contributions for a particular year must be made no later than the due date for filing that year's tax return without regard to any filing extensions that may have been granted [Sec. 219(f)(3)]. Several other restrictions apply. Individuals may only make deductible contributions equal to the lesser of $5,000 ($6,000 if you are 50 or older) or 100% of compensation. Also, the amount of the deduction is phased out, based on modified AGI, if the individual is an active participant in an employer-sponsored retirement plan. Only traditional IRAs qualify for the deduction.

Answer (B) is incorrect. Contributions must be made prior to the due date of the return, regardless of extensions. Answer (C) is incorrect. Individuals may only make deductible contributions equal to the lesser of $5,000 ($6,000 if you are 50 or older) or 100% of compensation. Answer (D) is incorrect. Contributions must be made prior to the due date of the return, regardless of extensions, and individuals may only make deductible contributions equal to the lesser of $5,000 ($6,000 if you are 50 or older) or 100% of compensation.

8. Minnie's tax return for 2012 shows the following income:

- $800 wages
- $6,490 unemployment compensation
- $1,000 alimony
- $8,000 rental income from apartment buildings she owns

What is Minnie's earned income for the purpose of determining how much she can contribute to an IRA?

A. $800

B. $7,290

C. $1,800

D. $16,290

Answer (C) is correct.

REQUIRED: The amount of earned income for determining the allowable IRA contribution.

DISCUSSION: Income considered for determining contribution amounts to an IRA include wages, salaries, commissions, self-employment income (loss), and alimony and separate maintenance payments. Unemployment compensation and earnings and profits from property such as rental income is not to be included in income computations for IRA purposes. Therefore, her earned income is $1,800 ($1,000 + $800). (See Publication 590.)

Answer (A) is incorrect. Alimony is included in earned income. Answer (B) is incorrect. Unemployment compensation is not part of earned income, while alimony is. Answer (D) is incorrect. The unemployment compensation as well as the rental income are not earned income.

9. Morris, a single taxpayer, is not covered by a qualified plan at his place of employment. He wishes to establish an IRA and contribute $5,000 for 2012. An IRA may be invested in all of the following accounts except

A. Bank CD.

B. Mutual fund.

C. Annuity.

D. Artwork.

Answer (D) is correct.

REQUIRED: The item an IRA may not be invested in.

DISCUSSION: Generally, an IRA is prohibited from investing in collectibles. Artwork would be considered a collectible. However, an IRA may hold platinum coins as well as gold, silver, or platinum bullion.

Answer (A) is incorrect. An IRA may invest in bank CDs. Answer (B) is incorrect. An IRA may invest in mutual funds. Answer (C) is incorrect. An IRA may invest in annuities.

10. Which of the following would be an allowable investment for a traditional IRA?

A. Stamps that have been issued by the United States Postal Service.

B. An oil painting certified by an art expert as being an authentic original by a Dutch master artist.

C. One-ounce silver coins minted by the U.S. Treasury Department.

D. All of the answers are correct.

Answer (C) is correct.

REQUIRED: The allowed contributions to a traditional IRA.

DISCUSSION: Generally, an IRA is prohibited from investing in collectibles. However, an IRA may hold platinum coins as well as gold, silver, or platinum bullion. Thus, 1-ounce silver coins minted by the U.S. Treasury Department are considered an allowable investment for a traditional IRA.

Answer (A) is incorrect. Stamps are considered a collectible item, which are not an allowable investment. Answer (B) is incorrect. An oil painting certified by an art expert as being an authentic original by a Dutch master artist is considered a collectible item, which is not an allowable investment. Answer (D) is incorrect. Neither the stamps nor the oil painting are allowable contributions because they are collectibles.

11. Alice and Mike file a joint return for 2012 on April 15, 2013. Alice, who is a nonworking spouse, is 49. Both Alice and Mike contributed $2,000 each to a traditional IRA, although they qualified to contribute the maximum amount. They filed their return timely. On June 1, 2013, Mike's mother gave each of them $1,000. What additional amount of the gift may Alice and Mike contribute to each of their IRAs for the year 2012?

A. 0

B. $1,000

C. $500

D. $4,000

Answer (A) is correct.

REQUIRED: The maximum amount of money that can be contributed to a traditional IRA for 2012.

DISCUSSION: Contributions to Alice and Mike's IRA must be made during the 2012 tax year or made before the filing deadline in 2013. Therefore, Alice and Mike's 2012 tax year deadline for an IRA contribution for the 2012 tax year was April 15, 2013. Any contributions made after April 15, 2013, are treated as contributed in the 2013 tax year [Sec. 219 (f)(3)].

12. Celeste, who is single, worked recently for a telephone company in France and earned $1,500 for which she claimed the foreign earned income exclusion. In addition to that, she earned $1,200 as an employee of an answering service while she was in the U.S. She also received alimony of $400 for the year. What is her maximum amount of allowable contribution to a traditional IRA for the year 2012?

A. $1,600

B. $3,000

C. $1,200

D. $1,900

Answer (A) is correct.

REQUIRED: The maximum amount allowable as a contribution to a traditional IRA.

DISCUSSION: Generally, the permissible contribution to a traditional IRA for a given year is the lesser of $5,000 ($6,000 if you are 50 or older) or taxable compensation. Amounts excluded from gross income, including foreign earned income, are not compensation. Therefore, Celeste may contribute $1,600. (See Publication 590.)

Answer (B) is incorrect. The $1,500 of foreign earned income is not compensation. Answer (C) is incorrect. The alimony is treated as compensation. Answer (D) is incorrect. The U.S. wages, not the French wages, are considered compensation for the IRA calculation.

13. Sam received a total distribution of $40,000 from his employer's 401(k) plan consisting of $25,000 in cash and land with a fair market value of $15,000. If Sam decides to keep the land, what is the total amount that he can roll over to his IRA?

A. Sam may substitute $15,000 of his own funds for the property and consider his rollover to be $40,000 in cash.

B. Sam can roll over only $15,000, the value of the land he received.

C. Sam can roll over the $25,000 cash received into his IRA.

D. Sam is required to sell the land before any part of the distribution can be rolled over.

Answer (C) is correct.

REQUIRED: The amount of a retirement distribution that can be rolled over to an IRA.

DISCUSSION: Generally, a rollover is a tax-free distribution of cash or other assets from one retirement plan to another retirement plan. If the taxpayer does not make a direct transfer of assets from one retirement plan to another but instead withdraws assets from the plan, the taxpayer must deposit the assets into another qualified plan within 60 days of the withdrawal in order to avoid taxes and penalties. A rollover cannot be deducted. The taxpayer may not substitute assets in the transfer between retirement plans. (See Publication 590.)

Answer (A) is incorrect. Sam is not allowed to substitute his own funds for keeping the land. Answer (B) is incorrect. Sam is not allowed to roll over the $15,000 value of the land he received if he is keeping the land. Answer (D) is incorrect. Sam can still roll over the $25,000 in cash regardless of whether he sells the land.

14. After many years as a bachelor, Buddy, age 50, married Penny, age 63. Penny's only income was $10,800 of Social Security. They filed a joint return for year 2012 with a modified adjusted gross income of $150,000. Buddy is covered by a retirement plan at work, where he receives compensation of $112,000. He wishes to contribute to an IRA for himself and for Penny. Which of the following will provide them the greatest allowable tax benefit?

A. He may contribute $6,000 to each IRA but only take a deduction for the $6,000 to his IRA.

B. He may contribute $6,000 to each IRA but take no deduction for either IRA.

C. He may contribute $6,000 to each IRA and take a deduction of $6,000 for each IRA.

D. He may contribute $6,000 to each IRA but only take a deduction for the $6,000 to Penny's IRA.

Answer (D) is correct.

REQUIRED: The contribution(s) to an individual and spousal IRA that provide the greatest tax benefit.

DISCUSSION: If covered for any part of the year by an employer retirement plan and no social security payments were received by the individual, the IRA contribution deduction is completely eliminated if the AGI is greater than $112,000 (married filing jointly). However, since Penny received no taxable compensation, the contribution to her IRA is completely deductible. The deduction is $5,000 plus an additional $1,000 for taxpayers age 50 or older. (See Publication 590.)

Answer (A) is incorrect. The $6,000 deduction may be taken only for Penny's IRA contribution. Answer (B) is incorrect. Penny's IRA contribution is deductible. Answer (C) is incorrect. Buddy's IRA contribution is not deductible.

15. In 2012, MaryAnn, a nonworking spouse, files a joint return with Jack, who is not covered by a pension plan at work. Their AGI is $50,000, and Jack plans to contribute $5,000 to a traditional IRA. MaryAnn, who is 51, wishes to contribute to an IRA. What is the maximum amount she can contribute?

A. $5,000

B. $4,000

C. $6,000

D. $0

Answer (C) is correct.

REQUIRED: The maximum amount of contributions to an IRA.

DISCUSSION: Under Sec. 408(a)(1), the maximum contribution to an IRA that can be made every year is the lesser of the compensation received or $5,000. Individuals age 50 and older at the end of the year can contribute an additional $1,000. If Jack and MaryAnn file a joint return, they are eligible to contribute the $5,000 on MaryAnn's behalf and the additional $1,000 for being over 50 years of age.

Answer (A) is incorrect. The $5,000 limit does not take into account the extra $1,000 MaryAnn is allowed to contribute for being over 50 years of age. Answer (B) is incorrect. The $4,000 limit was the 2007 limit on IRA contributions and does not take into account the $1,000 contribution for being over 50 years of age. Answer (D) is incorrect. MaryAnn is allowed to contribute to an IRA.

16. In December 2009, Gail worked for ABC Co. and participated in its retirement plan. On February 1, 2012, Gail was employed by XYZ Corp., which has a qualified retirement plan. On March 1, 2012, the ABC Co. plan administrator distributed to Gail her vested share of the plan. Gail was 42 years old at the time of distribution. Which of the following will allow Gail to avoid paying taxes and penalties on her withdrawal?

A. Deposit the plan funds in a local bank.

B. Contribute the distribution to the XYZ Corp. plan within 60 days.

C. Donate the plan funds to a charity.

D. None of the answers are correct.

Answer (B) is correct.

REQUIRED: The qualifying distribution rollover.

DISCUSSION: A taxpayer can avoid taxes and penalties on a distribution of assets from a qualified retirement plan if the assets are deposited into another qualified plan within 60 days. (See Publication 575.) Sec. 408(d)(3)(A) allows an eligible rollover distribution from an individual retirement account to be rolled over into a qualified employer plan, a 403(b) tax-sheltered annuity, or a Sec. 457 deferred compensation plan. This is true regardless of whether the distribution IRA qualifies as a conduit IRA.

Answer (A) is incorrect. The only way for Gail to avoid taxes and penalties is to transfer the retirement plan assets into another qualified plan within 60 days of the withdrawal. Answer (C) is incorrect. The only way for Gail to avoid taxes and penalties is to transfer the retirement plan assets into another qualified plan within 60 days of the withdrawal. Answer (D) is incorrect. A correct answer choice is provided.

17. Which of the following statements is false with respect to setting up an individual retirement account (IRA)?

A. An IRA cannot be set up with joint ownership of husband and wife.

B. A taxpayer cannot roll over assets from his IRA to his spouse's IRA.

C. A taxpayer may be eligible to set up an IRA for a spouse regardless of whether the spouse received compensation.

D. An individual who files a joint return and is not covered by an employer retirement plan can deduct the entire contribution to an IRA, regardless of the amount of his/her adjusted gross income, even if the spouse is covered by an employer's plan.

Answer (D) is correct.

REQUIRED: The false statement regarding setting up an IRA.

DISCUSSION: Beginning in 1998, an individual may deduct the contributions to an IRA even if his/her spouse is covered by an employer plan. However, the deduction is phased out if the couple's AGI is more than $173,000 but less than $183,000. The deduction is eliminated if the AGI on the joint return is $183,000 or more.

18. George, single and age 40, is covered by a pension plan at work. For 2011, George could have contributed and deducted $5,000 to his individual retirement account but could only afford to contribute $2,000, which he did on April 14, 2012. After April 15, 2012, George contributed $5,000. Since his modified AGI for 2012 was over $58,000, George computed that his reduced IRA deduction for 2012 was $600. Which of the following is not an option available for George?

A. He can deduct $3,600 in 2012 since he had a carryover from the immediately preceding tax year.

B. He can withdraw the nondeductible $4,400 contribution by April 15, 2013.

C. He can leave the entire contribution in the IRA and elect to treat the entire $5,000 as a nondeductible contribution.

D. He can leave the entire contribution in the IRA as a $600 deductible contribution and a $4,400 nondeductible contribution.

Answer (A) is correct.

REQUIRED: The options a taxpayer has regarding an IRA when the taxpayer is only allowed a reduced reduction but has made the full contribution.

DISCUSSION: The maximum contribution that may be made to an IRA during the year is the lesser of compensation received or $5,000 ($6,000 for taxpayers age 50 and older). However, the deductible contribution is limited when the taxpayer's income reaches $58,000 ($92,000 for married filing jointly) and is completely phased out when the taxpayer's income reaches $68,000 ($112,000 for married filing jointly). Thus, the taxpayer is allowed to make a contribution of up to $5,000 without a penalty but can only deduct an amount that is determined by his/her income. A taxpayer who has made a contribution in excess of the deductible amount can take out the amount of the contribution that is in excess of the deductible contribution [as long as (s)he does so before his/her tax return is due] and treat the entire contribution as nondeductible, or (s)he may leave the entire contribution in the IRA and deduct the allowable deduction. George could not deduct an extra $3,000 ($5,000 – $2,000) due to carryover from a previous year because the maximum deduction is still only $600, regardless of whether there is a carryover.

Answer (B) is incorrect. George has the option of withdrawing the nondeductible $4,400 contribution by April 15, 2013. Answer (C) is incorrect. George has the option of treating his entire contribution as nondeductible. Answer (D) is incorrect. George has the option of leaving the entire contribution in the IRA and only treating the $600 as deductible and the other $4,400 as nondeductible.

19. Margaret is fully vested. She will receive Social Security benefits at retirement but has no other retirement plan coverage. Her present and past employers have not had retirement plans available. In 2012, she files as single, and her earnings are $61,000. Also in 2012, she contributes $5,000 to a traditional IRA. How much of the $5,000 contribution may she deduct?

A. $0

B. $3,500

C. $5,000

D. $1,500

Answer (C) is correct.

REQUIRED: The deduction a taxpayer may take for his/her traditional IRA contribution.

DISCUSSION: Margaret is able to take a full $5,000 deduction for her contribution to an IRA. She is not a member of a retirement plan; thus, her deduction is not reduced.

Answer (A) is incorrect. Margaret is entitled to a deduction. Answer (B) is incorrect. The amount of $3,500 ($5,000 – $1,500) would be the allowed deduction if Margaret was a member of a retirement plan. Answer (D) is incorrect. The amount of $1,500 [($61,000 – $58,000) ÷ ($68,000 – $58,000) × $5,000] is the reduction Margaret would be required to make if she were a member of a retirement plan.

20. Kimberly, age 30, a full-time student with no taxable compensation, married Michael, age 30, during 2012. For the year, Michael had taxable compensation of $35,000. He plans to contribute and deduct $5,000 to his traditional IRA. If he and Kimberly file a joint return, how much may each deduct in 2012 for contributions to their individual traditional IRAs and what is the compensation Kimberly uses to figure her contribution limit?

	IRA Deduction	Compensation for Kimberly to Figure IRA Contribution Limit
A.	$5,000	$30,000
B.	$5,000	$35,000
C.	$4,000	$35,000
D.	$2,000	$32,500

Answer (A) is correct.

REQUIRED: The maximum deductible amount that can be contributed to a traditional IRA and the amount of compensation that should be used to figure an IRA contribution limit.

DISCUSSION: Under Sec. 219(c), if a joint return is filed and a taxpayer makes less than his/her spouse, the taxpayer may still contribute the lesser of

1) The sum of his/her compensation and the taxable compensation of the spouse, reduced by the amount of the spouse's IRA contribution and contributions to a Roth IRA, or
2) $5,000 ($6,000 if over age 50).

Kimberly is still eligible to deduct the full $5,000 for her IRA contribution. However, the income is based upon Michael's $35,000 income reduced by his $5,000 IRA contribution.

Answer (B) is incorrect. The $35,000 of compensation is reduced by Michael's IRA contribution. Answer (C) is incorrect. The limit on IRA deductions is $5,000. Answer (D) is incorrect. The limit on IRA deductions is $5,000, and Michael's compensation limit is reduced by his $5,000 contribution for a total compensation limit of $30,000.

21. Peter and Jill are married and file a joint return. In 2012, Jill was a media relations manager for a large firm and earned $98,000; Peter owns a graphic design business that showed a net profit of $500 for 2012. In 2012, Jill was covered by an employer's plan and Peter was not. Their modified annual gross income was $178,000. What is the maximum deductible amount that Peter can contribute to a traditional IRA?

A. $0

B. $500

C. $2,500

D. $5,000

Answer (C) is correct.

REQUIRED: The maximum deductible amount that can be contributed to a traditional IRA.

DISCUSSION: In general, the maximum deduction for a contribution to a traditional IRA is the lesser of taxable compensation for the year or $5,000 ($6,000 for taxpayers age 50 and older). However, if a joint return is filed and one spouse is covered, phaseouts may be applied based on the couple's AGI. In this instance, a partial deduction is permitted. With the couple's modified AGI of $178,000, Peter is allowed a $2,500 [($178,000 – $173,000) ÷ 10,000 × $5,000] deductible contribution. (See Pub. 590, pp. 8, 9, & 12.)

Answer (A) is incorrect. The phaseout is only $2,500, not $5,000, therefore leaving a $2,500 deductible contribution, not $0. Answer (B) is incorrect. With the joint return filed, AGI thresholds dictate Peter's deductible contribution, which in this case is in excess of his taxable compensation. Answer (D) is incorrect. The IRA deduction is phased out by $2,500 because the couple's AGI is too large to permit full deduction.

22. Rena is a single, 72-year-old chemical engineer. She works part-time for a pharmaceutical company and earned $22,000 in 2012. Her modified adjusted gross income is $36,000. She participates in her employer's pension plan and profit sharing plan. In 2012, she contributed $5,000 to a traditional IRA. How much of her contribution can Rena deduct in 2012?

A. $0

B. $1,400

C. $1,600

D. $5,000

Answer (A) is correct.

REQUIRED: The deductible contribution to a traditional IRA.

DISCUSSION: The normal contribution permitted to a traditional IRA is the lesser of $5,000 ($6,000 if you are 50 or older) or taxable compensation. Generally, the deduction is limited to the contribution or a general limit dependent upon possible employee retirement coverage. However, no contribution (or deduction) is permitted to a traditional IRA account after an individual attains the age of 70 1/2. Therefore, the deduction is $0. (See Publication 590.) In general, if the excess contributions for a year are not withdrawn by the date on which your return for the year is due (including extensions), you are subject to a 6% tax. You must pay the 6% tax each year on excess amounts that remain in your traditional IRA at the end of your tax year. The tax cannot be more than 6% of the value of your IRA as of the end of your tax year.

23. Edwin and Donna were married. Edwin had established a traditional IRA to which he made contributions and had taken no distributions. The total value of the IRA was $50,000, of which $20,000 was nondeductible contributions. As the spousal beneficiary, which of the following applies to Donna?

A. Edwin's $20,000 basis in the IRA may be treated as basis to Donna.

B. When Donna receives the distribution, she may not roll it over to her own traditional IRA.

C. Donna must begin receiving periodic distributions by December 31 of the fifth year following Edwin's death.

D. Donna must pay a 10% penalty on the funds in the IRA if she receives an immediate distribution after Edwin's death.

Answer (A) is correct.

REQUIRED: The statement applicable to a spousal beneficiary of an inherited traditional IRA.

DISCUSSION: The basis attached to a traditional IRA because of non-deductible contributions remains with the IRA. If it is inherited to a spouse, the basis received is considered to belong to the spousal beneficiary. (See Publication 590.)

Answer (B) is incorrect. Donna is permitted to roll the distribution over to her own traditional IRA. Answer (C) is incorrect. Donna may roll the distribution into her IRA. Answer (D) is incorrect. The 10% penalty is not assessed if immediate distribution occurs after the spouse's death.

24. Lenny and Norma file a joint return for tax year 2012. Lenny is covered by a retirement plan but Norma is not. Norma wishes to make a contribution to a traditional IRA, and her earnings alone are $1,500. The combined earnings on the joint return are $173,000 (the same as the modified AGI). Which of the following is true?

A. Norma may make a nondeductible contribution of $1,500.

B. Norma may make a deductible contribution of $5,000.

C. Norma may not make any contribution.

D. Norma may make a deductible contribution of $1,500 and a nondeductible contribution of $3,500.

Answer (B) is correct.

REQUIRED: The contribution that can be made to a traditional IRA for a taxpayer that files a joint return.

DISCUSSION: Sec. 219(c) provides rules for deducting contributions to a spousal IRA. If one spouse is eligible to make deductible IRA contributions, the other spouse may contribute up to $5,000 if a joint return is filed. The additional $5,000 spousal IRA deduction is available even if the other spouse has no compensation for the year. The phaseout begins with AGI more than $173,000, so Norma may contribute $5,000.

Answer (A) is incorrect. The contribution is not limited to Norma's earnings. Answer (C) is incorrect. Norma is entitled to a deductible contribution. Answer (D) is incorrect. Norma is entitled to a $5,000 deductible contribution.

25. Joe Smith never married and had no children. When he died, he left all of his assets, including his traditional IRA, to his nephew, David. What is David allowed to do with the inherited IRA?

A. He could make additional direct contributions to the IRA, treating it as his own.

B. He could roll over amounts out of the inherited IRA to another IRA tax-free.

C. He could make additional contributions, which were rollovers from Roth IRAs.

D. None of the answers are correct.

Answer (D) is correct.

REQUIRED: The allowable treatment of an inherited IRA.

DISCUSSION: If an individual inherits a traditional IRA from anyone other than a deceased spouse, the person is not permitted to treat the inherited IRA as his/her own, making direct contributions. The inherited IRA will generally not have tax assessed on the IRA assets until distributions are received. (See Publication 590.)

Answer (A) is incorrect. The inherited IRA cannot have additional direct contributions made as if it were the heir's own. Answer (B) is incorrect. Rolling over amounts to another IRA tax-free are only permitted if inherited from a spouse. Answer (C) is incorrect. Additional contributions that were rollovers from Roth IRAs are not permitted.

26. Dave, age 40, had a traditional IRA with a $40,000 balance at the beginning of 2012. All of Dave's contributions have been tax deductible. On July 1, 2012, Dave borrowed $20,000 from the IRA account. Which of the following would be a correct statement regarding the effects of this transaction?

A. This would not be a prohibited transaction, provided that the loan called for periodic payments and an interest rate at least equal to the applicable federal rate (AFR).

B. Dave would be required to include $20,000 in income as a distribution in 2012.

C. Dave would be required to include $40,000 in income as a distribution in 2012.

D. Dave would not have to include the $20,000 in income if it were used for qualified higher education expenses.

Answer (C) is correct.

REQUIRED: Income effect from an IRA early withdrawal.

DISCUSSION: Publication 590 states, "Generally, a prohibited transaction is any improper use of your traditional IRA account ... by any disqualified person." Examples of prohibited transactions include

- Borrowing money from it
- Selling property to it
- Receiving unreasonable compensation for managing it
- Using it as security for a loan
- Buying property for personal use (present or future) with IRA funds

These transactions stop the account from being an IRA. "If you borrow money against your traditional IRA annuity contract, you must include in your gross income the fair market value of the annuity contract as of the first day of your tax year."

Answer (A) is incorrect. Borrowing money from a traditional IRA is a prohibited transaction regardless of payment plan. Answer (B) is incorrect. The FMV of the IRA at the beginning of the year is included in gross income. Answer (D) is incorrect. If an individual withdraws funds from an IRA prematurely for higher education expenses, the individual is not subject to the 10% early withdrawal penalty; however, the withdrawn amount must be included in gross income as long as the IRA contributions were tax deductible.

11.3 Penalties

27. With regard to excess contributions to an IRA, which of the following statements is false?

A. A taxpayer may deduct from gross income, in the first year available, the amount of the excess contribution in the IRA, from the preceding years up to the difference between the maximum amount that is deductible in the year and the amount actually contributed during the year.

B. If a taxpayer has an excess contribution in his/her IRA as a result of a rollover, and the excess occurred because the taxpayer had incorrect information required to be supplied by the plan, the taxpayer can withdraw the excess contribution.

C. If the excess contribution for a year is not withdrawn by the date a taxpayer's return is due, the taxpayer is subject to an 8% tax.

D. Generally, an excess contribution is the amount contributed to an IRA that is more than the smaller of the following amounts: (1) a taxpayer's taxable compensation or (2) $5,000 ($6,000 if age 50 or older).

Answer (C) is correct.

REQUIRED: The false statement regarding excess contributions to an IRA.

DISCUSSION: In general, if the excess contribution for a year and any earnings on it are not withdrawn by the due date of the return, the taxpayer is subject to a 6% tax.

28. Sunnie is single and does not actively participate in her employer's pension plan. She received taxable compensation of $3,500 in Year 1 and $4,000 in Year 2. Her modified adjusted gross income was $26,000 in both years. For Year 1, she contributed $5,000 to her IRA but deducted only $3,500 on her income tax return. For Year 2, she contributed $2,500 but deducted $4,000 on her income tax return. Based on this information, which of the following statements is true?

A. Sunnie must pay an excise tax on the excess contribution for Year 1 and also for Year 2 since she did not withdraw the excess.

B. Sunnie must pay an excise tax for Year 1 on the $1,500 excess contribution made in Year 1, but since she properly treated the Year 1 excess contribution as part of her Year 2 deduction, she does not owe the excise tax for Year 2.

C. Sunnie will be assessed a 10% tax for early withdrawals when she withdraws the excess contribution.

D. Sunnie should claim an IRA deduction of only $1,500 for Year 2.

Answer (B) is correct.

REQUIRED: The true statement regarding deductions and contributions to an IRA.

DISCUSSION: Sec. 408 limits contributions to an IRA to the lesser of $5,000 ($6,000 if you are 50 or older) or the amount of compensation includible in the taxpayer's gross income. Sunnie's Year 1 contributions should have been limited to $3,500. She therefore had $1,500 of excess contributions in Year 1 ($5,000 – $3,500). Under Sec. 4973, a nondeductible 6% excise tax is imposed on excess contributions to an IRA. Under Sec. 219(b), the deduction for contributions to an IRA is limited to the lesser of $5,000 or the amount of compensation that must be included in gross income. Sunnie's $3,500 deduction in Year 1 was correct. In Year 2, Sunnie contributed only $2,500 but deducted $4,000. Under Sec. 219(f)(6), Sunnie may treat the $1,500 unused contributions from Year 1 as having been made in Year 2. Therefore, her allowable deduction for IRA contributions in Year 2 is $4,000.

Answer (A) is incorrect. Sunnie did not make excess contributions in Year 2. Answer (C) is incorrect. A 6% excise tax is assessed when the excess contributions are made. Answer (D) is incorrect. Sunnie can claim an IRA deduction of $4,000 for Year 2.

29. Martin, age 35, made an excess contribution to his traditional IRA in 2012 of $1,000, which he withdrew by April 15, 2013. At the same time, he withdrew the $50 income that was earned on the $1,000. Which of the following statements is true?

A. Martin must include the $50 in his gross income in 2012.

B. Martin would have to pay the 6% excise tax on the $1,050.

C. Martin would have to pay the 10% additional tax on the $50 as an early distribution.

D. Martin would have to pay the 10% additional tax on the $50 as an early distribution and also include the $50 in gross income in 2012.

Answer (D) is correct.

REQUIRED: The true statement regarding an excess contribution and the tax that will be assessed.

DISCUSSION: If a taxpayer makes an excess contribution during the year, (s)he can avoid tax on the excess contribution and the interest earned on it if they are withdrawn before the due date (including extensions) of the tax return. However, the interest will qualify as a premature distribution, since it would have been distributed before Martin was age 59 1/2. The additional tax on premature distributions is equal to 10% of the amount of the premature distribution that must be included in gross income. This tax is in addition to any regular income tax that is due. Thus, the $50 of interest that was withdrawn from the IRA must be included in income and is subject to an additional tax of 10%.

Answer (A) is incorrect. Martin would also have to pay the 10% additional tax on the $50 as an early distribution. Answer (B) is incorrect. Since Martin withdrew the excess contribution and the interest earned on this contribution, he is not liable for a 6% excise tax. Answer (C) is incorrect. Martin must also include the $50 in his gross income in 2012.

30. In which situation must a taxpayer pay the additional 10% tax on a premature distribution from his/her IRA?

A. Taxpayer, age 45, became totally disabled.

B. Taxpayer, age 50, died, and the IRA was distributed to his beneficiaries.

C. Taxpayer, age 30, withdrew his entire balance in an IRA and invested it in another IRA at another bank 45 days after the withdrawal from the first bank.

D. Taxpayer, age 40, used the distribution to pay emergency medical bills for his wife. The medical bills equal 5% of the couple's AGI.

Answer (D) is correct.

REQUIRED: The situation in which the taxpayer must pay the additional 10% tax.

DISCUSSION: Distributions from an IRA to a participant before (s)he reaches age 59 1/2 are subject to a 10% penalty tax. Taxpayers are exempted from this penalty tax if the distribution is attributable to the taxpayer becoming disabled or is made on or after the taxpayer's death. Certain other exceptions apply, but payment of medical expenses is not one of them, unless the medical expenses exceed the Sec. 213 nondeductible floor. Since the medical expenses are only 5% of the couple's AGI, they are below the 7.5%-of-AGI nondeductible floor, and the 10% penalty applies to the entire distribution.

Answer (A) is incorrect. The distribution is attributable to the taxpayer's becoming disabled. Answer (B) is incorrect. The distribution was made after the taxpayer's death. Answer (C) is incorrect. Reinvesting the proceeds of one IRA into another IRA within 60 days qualifies as a tax-free rollover.

31. Generally, which of the following is a prohibited transaction concerning your traditional IRA?

A. Withdraw funds for qualified higher education expenses.

B. Pledge your IRA account as security for your mortgage.

C. Withdraw funds for qualified medical expenses.

D. Withdraw funds to purchase your first home.

Answer (B) is correct.

REQUIRED: The transaction concerning a traditional IRA that is prohibited.

DISCUSSION: In certain circumstances, the additional tax does not apply to distributions from an IRA, even if they are made before a taxpayer reaches age 59 1/2. There are exceptions from the penalty for

1) Death
2) Disability
3) Annuity payments based on life expectancy
4) Medical expenses exceeding 7.5% of AGI
5) Qualified higher education expenses
6) A qualified first-time homebuyer distribution
7) Unemployed health insurance premium
8) Levy under Sec. 6331
9) Payments made under a Qualified Domestic Relations Order
10) U.S. military reserves called to active duty

32. In 2012, Ivan was over age 70 1/2. The balance at the beginning of 2012 of his traditional IRA was $41,000. All of his IRA contributions had been tax deductible. The required minimum distribution for 2012 was $3,000. If Ivan only took a distribution of $1,000, what is the amount of excise tax that Ivan would have to pay on the excess accumulation?

A. $120

B. $200

C. $1,000

D. $2,400

Answer (C) is correct.

REQUIRED: The excise tax that must be paid when the required distribution is not made.

DISCUSSION: Generally, a taxpayer must begin receiving distributions by April 1 of the year following the year in which (s)he reaches age 70 1/2. If distributions are less than the required minimum distribution for the year, a 50% excise tax will be imposed on the amount not distributed. Since Ivan was required to receive a distribution of $3,000 and he only received a distribution of $1,000, he is required to pay a tax of $1,000 [($3,000 – $1,000) × 50%].

Answer (A) is incorrect. A 6% excise tax is imposed on excess contributions, not excess accumulations. Answer (B) is incorrect. A 10% excise tax is imposed on premature distributions, not excess accumulations. Answer (D) is incorrect. Ivan is only required to pay a tax on 50% of the amount that he was required to withdraw during the year.

33. John failed to take required minimum distributions from his traditional IRA. The excess accumulation is subject to a penalty of

A. 6%

B. 10%

C. 15%

D. 50%

Answer (D) is correct.

REQUIRED: The amount of excise tax that will be imposed on excess accumulation in a traditional IRA.

DISCUSSION: Generally, under Sec. 4974, a taxpayer must begin receiving distributions by April 1 of the year following the year in which (s)he reaches age 70 1/2. If distributions are less than the required minimum distribution for the year, a 50% excise tax will be imposed on the amount not distributed. The tax may be excused if the excess accumulation is due to reasonable error and the taxpayer is taking steps to remedy the insufficient distribution.

Answer (A) is incorrect. A 6% excise tax is imposed each year on excess contribution amounts that remain in an IRA at the end of each tax year. Answer (B) is incorrect. A 10% tax is imposed on premature distributions. Answer (C) is incorrect. Excise tax is 50% for excess accumulation.

34. Gina, who is single, received taxable compensation of $1,700 in 2011 and $2,500 in 2012. She did not actively participate in a pension plan. She contributed $2,000 in 2011 and $2,000 in 2012 to her IRA. On March 18, 2012, she withdrew $300 of her 2011 contribution plus the interest accumulated on it from her IRA and did not deduct that amount on her 2011 tax return. Based on this information, what is the amount of her excess contributions subject to the 6% tax?

A. $0

B. $300

C. $500

D. $800

Answer (A) is correct.

REQUIRED: The amount of excess contributions subject to the 6% tax.

DISCUSSION: In general, an individual who withdraws an excess contribution made during a tax year and the interest earned on it before the return due date will not be subject to the excess contributions tax. This rule is available only for individuals who did not take a deduction for the amount of the excess contribution.

11.4 Roth IRAs

35. What is the maximum amount that Darlene, who is single, may contribute to a Roth IRA in 2012? She has AGI of $113,000 and is under 50 years of age.

A. $5,000

B. $4,000

C. $1,000

D. $0

Answer (B) is correct.

REQUIRED: The maximum Roth IRA contribution for a single taxpayer in 2012.

DISCUSSION: Roth IRAs are subject to income limits. The maximum yearly contribution that can be made to a Roth IRA is phased out for single taxpayers with adjusted gross income (AGI) between $110,000 and $125,000. Since Darlene's AGI is between the income limits, her allowable contribution is reduced. The amount of the reduction is calculated as follows:

$$\frac{\$113{,}000 - \$110{,}000}{\$125{,}000 - \$110{,}000} \times \$5{,}000 = \$1{,}000$$

Therefore, Darlene's maximum contribution is $4,000 ($5,000 – $1,000).

Answer (A) is incorrect. Darlene's AGI is within the phaseout range and must be reduced. Answer (C) is incorrect. This figure is the amount of the reduction. Answer (D) is incorrect. Darlene's AGI is not larger than $125,000; thus, a reduced contribution is still allowed.

36. Which of the following is true regarding contributions to a Roth IRA?

A. Contributions may be made regardless of age, provided other requirements are met.

B. Contributions may be deducted if you are within certain income limits.

C. Contributions may be deducted if you are not covered under a retirement plan.

D. Contributions may not be deducted, but earnings are taxable when distributed.

Answer (A) is correct.

REQUIRED: The true statement regarding contributions to a Roth IRA.

DISCUSSION: Publication 590 states that, unlike deductible IRAs, individuals are allowed to make contributions to the Roth IRA after reaching age 70 1/2. Also, amounts can be left in the Roth IRA as long as the taxpayer lives.

Answer (B) is incorrect. Contributions to a Roth IRA cannot be deducted. Answer (C) is incorrect. Contributions to a Roth IRA cannot be deducted. Answer (D) is incorrect. Qualified distributions from a Roth IRA are not included in the taxpayer's gross income.

37. Which of the following amounts may be converted directly to a Roth IRA, provided all requirements are met?

A. Amounts in a SIMPLE IRA, and the 2-year participation period has been met.

B. Amounts in a traditional IRA inherited from a person other than a spouse.

C. Hardship distribution from a 401(k) plan.

D. Required minimum distributions from a traditional IRA.

Answer (A) is correct.

REQUIRED: The amount permitted to be converted to a Roth IRA, provided all requirements are met.

DISCUSSION: Amounts carried in a SIMPLE IRA may be converted assuming the required 2-year participation period has been met. (See Publication 590.)

Answer (B) is incorrect. A traditional IRA inherited from a person other than a spouse is not convertible. Answer (C) is incorrect. Hardship distributions are not directly convertible. Answer (D) is incorrect. Required minimum distributions from a traditional IRA are not permissible conversions.

11.5 Coverdell Education Savings Accounts (CESAs)

38. Jim and Carolyn, who are married, established a CESA to pay for the future college expenses of their infant son. They file jointly and have a modified AGI of $80,000. What is the maximum contribution they can make to an education IRA in the current year?

A. $8,000

B. $4,000

C. $500

D. $2,000

Answer (D) is correct.

REQUIRED: The maximum contribution available for an education savings account.

DISCUSSION: Joint filers with modified AGI below $190,000 ($95,000 for singles) may contribute up to $2,000 per beneficiary (child) per year. The amount a taxpayer is able to contribute to an education savings account is limited if modified AGI exceeds certain threshold amounts. The limit is phased out for joint filers with modified AGI at or greater than $190,000 and less than $220,000 and for single filers with modified AGI at or greater than $95,000 and less than $110,000.

39. Which of the following is not an account requirement for a CESA?

A. Contributions must be made before the trust beneficiary reaches age 18.

B. All contributions must be in cash.

C. Upon the death of the beneficiary, any balance in the fund must not be distributed to the beneficiary's estate.

D. The trustee must be a bank or other qualified individual.

Answer (C) is correct.

REQUIRED: The statement that is not a requirement of a CESA.

DISCUSSION: A CESA is a tax-exempt trust. Seven requirements must be met for a CESA:

1. No contribution may be accepted by the CESA after the beneficiary attains age 18.
2. Except in the case of rollover contributions, annual contributions may not exceed $2,000.
3. Contributions must be in cash.
4. The trustee must be a bank or other qualified person.
5. No portion of the trust's assets may be invested in life insurance contracts.
6. Trust assets must not be commingled with other property, except in a common trust or investment fund.
7. Upon death of the beneficiary, any balance in the fund must be distributed to the beneficiary's estate within 30 days of death.

40. Which of the following statements is false regarding a CESA?

A. Any CESA balance must be distributed when the beneficiary turns 30.

B. The income portion of distributions not used for education is included in taxable income and is subject to a 10% penalty.

C. Contributions cannot be made after the beneficiary turns 18.

D. Stock may be contributed to the CESA.

Answer (D) is correct.

REQUIRED: The false statement regarding a CESA.

DISCUSSION: A CESA is a tax-exempt trust. In order to qualify as a CESA, contributions must be made in cash.

41. Which of the following expenses are qualified higher education expenses for purposes of a CESA?

A. Tuition and fees.

B. Books and supplies.

C. Room and board.

D. All of the answers are correct.

Answer (D) is correct.

REQUIRED: The expenses that are qualified higher education expenses for a CESA.

DISCUSSION: Qualified higher education expenses include tuition, fees, books, supplies, and equipment required for the enrollment at an eligible institution. Additionally, room and board may be qualified expenses if they do not exceed the minimum amounts as determined for federal financial aid programs.

STUDY UNIT TWELVE
GIFT TAX

(5 pages of outline)

The gift tax is a wealth transfer tax that applies if a property transfer occurs during a person's lifetime. The property transferred may be real, personal, tangible, or intangible. Both the gift tax and the estate tax are part of a unified transfer tax system under which gratuitous transfers of property between persons are subject to taxation.

12.1 GIFT TAX RETURN

A donor is required to file a gift tax return, Form 709, for any gift(s), unless all gifts are excluded under the annual $13,000 exclusion, the deduction for qualified charitable gifts, or the deduction for qualified transfers to the donor's spouse. These exclusions apply for gifts of present interests only. Any gift of a future interest requires the filing of Form 709. Gift splitting does not excuse the donor from the requirement to file.

Due Date

1. A gift tax return is due on the 15th of April following the calendar year in which a gift was made. But a gift tax return for a year of death is due no later than the estate tax return due date.
   a. A calendar-year taxpayer who receives an extension of time for filing his/her income tax return automatically receives an extension to that same extended due date for filing his/her gift tax return for that same year.

Marital Exclusion

2. A taxpayer does not have to file a gift tax return to report gifts to his/her spouse. This rule does not apply if either
   a. The spouse is not a U.S. citizen and the total gifts exceed $139,000 or
   b. The taxpayer makes any gift of a terminable interest that does not meet the power of appointment exception.

Charitable Gifts

3. If the only gifts a taxpayer makes during the year are deductible as gifts to charities, the taxpayer is not required to file a return.
   a. The entire interest in the property must be transferred to the qualified charity.
   b. If only a partial interest was transferred, a return must be filed.
   c. If a taxpayer made both charitable and noncharitable gifts, all gifts must be included on the return.

Filing Requirement

4. If the total value of gifts of present interests to any donee is $13,000 or less, the taxpayer need not report on Form 709, Schedule A, any gifts (except gifts of future interests) that were made to that donee.
5. If the total value of the gifts of present interests to any donee is more than $13,000, the taxpayer must report all such gifts that were made during the year to or on behalf of that donee.
   a. This includes those gifts that will be excluded under the annual exclusion.

Form 709

6. Publication 950 excludes the following from taxable gifts:

   a. The annual exclusion ($13,000 for 2012)
   b. Gifts to a spouse
   c. Charitable gifts
   d. Political contributions
   e. Qualified tuition payments
   f. Medical costs

7. See Subunit 12.2 for definitions of qualified tuition and medical costs.

Stop and review! You have completed the outline for this subunit. Study questions 1 through 15 beginning on page 283.

12.2 GIFT TAX

Gift tax is a tax of the transfer, imposed on the donor. The table below presents the basic tax formula, modified for the gift tax.

	Gift Amount FMV on date of gift, for all gifts in the calendar year
–	Exclusions Annual exclusion $13,000 per donee Gift splitting between spouses
–	Deductions Marital Charitable
=	Taxable Gifts for Current Year
+	Taxable Gifts for Prior Years
=	Taxable Gifts to Date
×	Tax Rate
=	Tentative Gift Tax
–	[Prior year's gifts × Current tax rates]
–	Unified Credit – Unified Credit of Prior Periods
=	Gift Tax Liability

Amount of Gift

1. Any excess of FMV of transferred property over the FMV of consideration for it is a gift.

	FMV of transferred property: given
–	FMV of consideration (property, money, etc.): received
	Gift amount

   a. A gift is complete when the giver has given over dominion and control such that (s)he is without legal power to change its disposition.

EXAMPLE

R opens a joint bank account with A, I, and H, with R as the only depositor to the account. R, A, I, and H may each withdraw money. A gift is complete only when A, I, or H withdraws money.

b. Gifts completed when the donor is alive (inter vivos gifts) are the only ones subject to gift tax. Transfers made in trust are included.

   1) Property passing by will or inheritance is not included.

c. To the extent credit is extended with less than sufficient stated interest, the Code imputes that interest is charged. If the parties are related, the lender is treated as having made a gift of the imputed interest to the borrower.

   1) Gift loans are excluded if the aggregate outstanding principal is not more than $10,000.

d. Basis in a gift is basis in the hands of the donor plus gift tax attributable to appreciation.

EXAMPLE

Thomas made a gift to his daughter of a piece of land with a FMV of $93,000. The land had a basis to Thomas of $60,000. He made a taxable gift of $80,000 and paid a gift tax of $36,000. The basis of the land to the daughter is carryover basis of $60,000 plus the gift tax attributable to the appreciation.

$$\$60{,}000 + \left(\frac{\$33{,}000 \text{ increase in value}}{\$80{,}000 \text{ taxable gift}} \times \$36{,}000\right) = \$74{,}850$$

Annual Exclusion

2. The first $13,000 of gifts of present interest to each donee is excluded from taxable gift amounts. The annual exclusion is indexed to reflect inflation.

   a. The $13,000 exclusion applies only to gifts of present interests.

   b. A present interest in property includes an unrestricted right to the immediate possession or enjoyment of property or to the income from property (such as a life estate or a term for years). Gifts of future interest in property (such as remainders or reversions) do not qualify for the annual exclusion.

EXAMPLE

Edward sets up a trust with the income going to his daughter for her life and the remainder to his granddaughter. Edward has made a gift of a present interest to his daughter and a future interest to his granddaughter.

Medical or Tuition Costs

3. Excluded from taxable gifts are amounts paid on behalf of another individual as tuition to an educational organization or for medical care.

   a. The payment must be made directly to the third party, i.e., the medical provider or the educational organization.

   b. Amounts paid for room, board, and books are not excluded.

Support

4. Transfers that represent support of a former spouse or a child are not gifts. Generally, child support payments end at age 18.

Political Contributions

5. Political contributions are not subject to gift tax and are not reported on the return.

Marital Deduction

6. The amount of a gift transfer to a spouse is deducted in computing taxable gifts. Donor and donee must be married at the time of the gift, and the donee must be a U.S. citizen.
   a. The deduction may not exceed the amount includible as taxable gifts.
   b. Otherwise, the amount of the deduction is not limited.

EXAMPLE

Sid Smith gave his wife, Mary, a diamond ring valued at $20,000 and cash gifts of $30,000 during 2012. Sid is entitled to a $13,000 exclusion with respect to the gifts to Mary. His marital deduction is $37,000, i.e., the portion that would have constituted taxable gifts.

Charitable Deduction

7. The FMV of property donated to a qualified charitable organization is deductible. Like the marital deduction, the amount of the deduction is the amount of the gift reduced by the $13,000 exclusion with respect to the donee.

Qualified Tuition Program

8. Payments to a qualified tuition program (QTP), also known as a 529 plan, are not to be confused with qualified tuition costs (explained on the previous page).
   a. A taxpayer may elect to treat up to $65,000 of a contribution to a QTP as if made ratably over a 5-year period.
   b. By making the election, the contribution will be excluded each year under the $13,000 annual limit.
   c. Any contribution in excess of the $65,000 limit is reported for the year of contribution (as opposed to being apportioned over the 5 years).
   d. Contributions to QTPs do not qualify for the education exclusion.

Computing the Gift Tax

9. Tentative tax is the sum of taxable gifts to each person for the current year and for each preceding year times the gift tax rate. Taxable gifts to a person is the total of gift amounts (FMV) in excess of exclusions and the marital and charitable deductions for a calendar year.
   a. The unified transfer tax rates are used.
      1) Current-year applicable rates are applied to both current and preceding years' taxable gifts.
      2) The rate is 18% for taxable gifts up to $10,000.
      3) The rates increase in small steps (e.g., 2%, 3%) over numerous brackets.
      4) The maximum rate is 35% on cumulative gifts in excess of $500,000 in 2012.
   b. The tentative gift tax is reduced by the product of prior years' taxable gifts and the current-year rates.
   c. Tentative tax may also be reduced by any unified credit, also called the applicable credit amount (ACA). The ACA is a base amount ($1,772,800) reduced by amounts allowable as credits for all preceding tax years. This excludes the first $5.12 million of taxable gifts.
   d. *Gift tax liability for a current year = Tentative tax − (Prior-year gifts × Current rates) − ACA.*

Stop and review! You have completed the outline for this subunit. Study questions 16 through 31 beginning on page 287.

12.3 GIFT SPLITTING

If both spouses consent, married couples may consider a gift made by one spouse to any person other than the other spouse as made one-half by each spouse.

1. A married couple is not allowed gift splitting if
   a. The couple is not married at the time of the gift.
   b. The couple divorces after the gift, and the spouse who made the gift remarries before the end of the calendar year.
   c. One of the spouses is a nonresident alien.
2. A joint gift tax return does not exist.
   a. Each spouse must file his/her own gift return.
   b. A spouse may simply give his/her consent to gift splitting by signing the donor spouse's return if all the requirements of one of the following exceptions are met:
      1) Only one spouse made any gifts, and the total value of these gifts did not exceed $26,000.
      2) One spouse made gifts of more than $13,000 but less than $26,000, and the only gifts made by the other spouse were gifts of not more than $13,000.
3. If taxpayers elect to split gifts, all gifts made by both spouses to third-party donees must be split. The only exception is if the taxpayer gives the spouse a general power of appointment over a gift the taxpayer made.
4. If spouses elect to split gifts, both spouses are jointly and severally liable.

Stop and review! You have completed the outline for this subunit. Study questions 32 through 38 beginning on page 292.

QUESTIONS

12.1 Gift Tax Return

1. Generally, in which of the following scenarios must a gift tax return be filed?

A. You gave gifts to an individual (other than your spouse) totaling more than $13,000.

B. You gave a gift of a future interest that was less than $13,000.

C. You wish to split gifts with your spouse.

D. All of the answers are correct.

Answer (D) is correct.

REQUIRED: The situation(s) in which a gift tax return must be filed.

DISCUSSION: A donor is required to file a gift tax return, Form 709, for any gift(s), unless all gifts are excluded under the annual $13,000 exclusion, the exclusion for qualified charitable gifts, or the deduction for qualified transfers to the donor's spouse. These exclusions apply for gifts of present interest only. Any gift of a future interest requires the filing of Form 709 since the exclusion does not apply. Gift splitting does not excuse the donor from the requirement to file.

2. Form 709, *United States Gift (and Generation-Skipping Transfer) Tax Return*, is required to be filed for

A. A transfer of a present interest that is not more than the annual exclusion ($13,000).

B. A qualified transfer for educational or medical expenses.

C. A transfer of a future interest that is not more than the annual exclusion ($13,000).

D. A transfer to your spouse that qualifies for the unlimited marital deduction.

Answer (C) is correct.

REQUIRED: The transfer that requires the filing of Form 709.

DISCUSSION: In general, Form 709, *United States Gift (and Generation-Skipping Transfer) Tax Return*, is required for any gift of a future interest.

Answer (A) is incorrect. Present interest gifts are excluded from gift taxation if they are less than the annual exclusion. Answer (B) is incorrect. Transfers for qualified educational or medical needs of the recipient are not gifts. Answer (D) is incorrect. Transfers to a spouse that qualify for the marital deduction do not require the filing of a return.

3. Nancy's books and records reflect the following for the year. Which transaction would require filing Form 709, *United States Gift (and Generation-Skipping Transfer) Tax Return*?

A. Gratuitously transferred a vehicle with a fair market value of $22,000 to her fiance a month before they were married.

B. Donated $14,000 to a qualified political organization.

C. Paid $22,000 to St. Francis Hospital for her aunt's unreimbursed medical expenses.

D. Paid $14,000 to State University for her brother's tuition.

Answer (A) is correct.

REQUIRED: The transaction that requires the filing of a gift tax return.

DISCUSSION: Sec. 6019 provides that a gift tax return must be filed unless all gifts may be excluded under the $13,000 exclusion of Sec. 2503(b), or the charitable gifts provision of Sec. 6019(3), or unless they may be deducted under the marital deduction rules of Sec. 2523(a). The gift to the fiance must be reported since he does not qualify for the marital deduction at the time of the gift.

Answer (B) is incorrect. Donations to political organizations do not require a gift tax return to be filed. They are not "gifts." Answer (C) is incorrect. The expenses qualify for the medical payment exclusion of 2503(e). They are not "gifts." Answer (D) is incorrect. The expense qualifies for the educational payment exclusion of 2503(e). It is not a "gift."

4. The annual gift tax exclusion amount is allowed on which of the following gifts?

A. $30,000 cash to Friend A.

B. $30,000 car to Friend B.

C. $30,000 remainder interest to Friend C.

D. Both $30,000 cash to Friend A and a $30,000 car to Friend B.

Answer (D) is correct.

REQUIRED: The transaction that requires a gift tax return.

DISCUSSION: The annual gift exclusion is available on gifts of present interest to each donee. A present interest in property includes an unrestricted right to the immediate use, possession, or enjoyment of property or to the income from property (such as a life estate or term for years but not remainders or reversions).

5. Which of the following situations would require the filing of Form 709?

A. You and your spouse agree to split your gifts, which total $18,000.

B. You gave more than $13,000 during the year to any one donee.

C. Any of the gifts you made were of a future interest.

D. All of the answers are correct.

Answer (D) is correct.

REQUIRED: The situation(s) requiring the filing of Form 709.

DISCUSSION: A gift tax return must be filed for gifts that exceed $13,000 and were split with a spouse. Additionally, a return is required to be filed if more than $13,000 is gifted to any one donee or if any of the gifts were of a future interest.

Answer (A) is incorrect. Along with the requirement to file split gifts, Form 709 is required when $13,000 is given to any one donee or for any gifts of a future interest. Answer (B) is incorrect. Along with the requirement to file for gifts exceeding $13,000 to any one donee, Form 709 is required for gift splitting or gifts of a future interest. Answer (C) is incorrect. Along with the requirement to file if the gift is of a future interest, Form 709 is required for gift splitting or gifts that exceed $13,000 to any one donee.

6. John made the following transfers during tax year 2012:

- To his neighbor in the amount of $17,000
- To his nephew in the amount of $14,000
- To his uncle in the amount of $15,000

All of the transfers are gifts that qualify for the annual exclusion. John files one Form 709 for tax year end December 31, 2012. What is the total annual exclusion amount for gifts listed on John's 2012 Form 709 filing?

A. $46,000

B. $39,000

C. $13,000

D. $12,000

Answer (B) is correct.

REQUIRED: The annual exclusion amount.

DISCUSSION: Sec. 2503(b) authorizes a $13,000 exclusion from gross income for income tax purposes and is available to an unlimited number of donees.

Answer (A) is incorrect. The amount of $46,000 is the total value of the gifts. Answer (C) is incorrect. John is allowed three $13,000 exclusions, one exclusion for each donee. Answer (D) is incorrect. The exclusion amount for tax year 2008 is $12,000.

7. Tom, who is married, gave a vase worth $40,000 to his sister, Julie. Tom's basis in the vase is $10,000. What amount will Tom report as the value of the gift on Form 709?

A. $10,000

B. $20,000

C. $30,000

D. $40,000

Answer (D) is correct.

REQUIRED: The value of the gift.

DISCUSSION: The amount of a gift is the fair market value of what was given. In this situation, the fair market value is $40,000, which is what Tom will report as the value of the gift on Form 709.

Answer (A) is incorrect. The basis of the vase is $10,000. Answer (B) is incorrect. The value of the gift is $40,000. Answer (C) is incorrect. The difference between the fair market value of the vase and the basis of the vase is $30,000.

8. Mary Smith made only the following transfers of interest in personal property during the tax year:

- $40,000 cash to the Democratic Party, a political organization [as defined in Sec. 527(e)(1)]
- $25,000 cash to Good Care Health, Inc., for medical care [as defined in Sec. 213(d)] of her ailing resident father
- 100 shares of common stock of ABC, Inc., with a basis to Mary of $5,000 and a fair market value (FMV) of $10,000 to Save the Walnut Foundation, a Sec. 501(c)(3) organization

What is the total amount of gifts that must be reported on Mary's gift tax return?

A. $75,000

B. $70,000

C. $10,000

D. Mary does not need to file Form 709 for the tax year.

Answer (D) is correct.

REQUIRED: The requirement for filing a gift tax return.

DISCUSSION: "Taxable gifts" means the total amount of gifts made during the calendar year reduced by the charitable and marital deductions [Sec. 2503(a)]. Three types of transfers are not subject to the gift tax: (1) transfers to political organizations, (2) payments that qualify for the educational exclusion, and (3) payments that qualify for the medical exclusion. These transfers are not "gifts" and are not listed on a gift tax return. If the only gifts made during the year are deductible as gifts to charities, a gift tax return is not required as long as the entire interest in the property was transferred. Thus, Mary is not required to file a tax return because the first two items are not considered gifts, and a gift tax return is not required for the third item.

Answer (A) is incorrect. Cash to a political organization and cash for medical care are not considered gifts. A gift tax return is not required if the only gift made was to a charity. Answer (B) is incorrect. Cash to a political organization and cash for medical care are not considered gifts. A gift tax return is not required if the only gift made was to a charity. In addition, a gift is equal to the FMV of transferred property, not the basis. Answer (C) is incorrect. A gift tax return is not required if the only gift made was of an entire interest to a charity.

9. The following transfers were made by Ed during 2012. What is the gross amount of gifts to be included on Ed's 2012 Form 709 filing?

- $16,000 to the United Way
- $13,000 to a political organization
- $21,000 paid directly to his nephew's college for tuition
- $14,000 paid directly to his niece for her college tuition

A. $35,000

B. $14,000

C. $30,000

D. $51,000

Answer (C) is correct.

REQUIRED: The gross amount of gifts required on Form 709.

DISCUSSION: If you are required to file a return to report noncharitable gifts and you made gifts to charities, you must include all of your gifts to charities on the return. The $21,000 and the $13,000 are not considered gifts and are not included in total gifts. Therefore, Ed must only include the $16,000 contribution to the United Way and the $14,000 paid directly to his niece.

Answer (A) is incorrect. The $21,000 is exempted as a gift, and the contribution to the United Way is included as a charitable contribution. Answer (B) is incorrect. Ed was required to file a return to report his noncharitable gifts, and this fact requires him to include all gifts to charities (the United Way) on the return. Thus, he also must include the $16,000 contribution to the United Way. Answer (D) is incorrect. The $21,000 is exempted as a gift and is not included on the gift tax return.

10. For calendar year 2012, if a gift tax return is required to be filed and the donor is not deceased, what is the due date of the return excluding extensions?

A. Within 75 days of making the gift.

B. On or before December 31, 2012.

C. No earlier than January 1, 2013, and no later than April 15, 2013.

D. Within 180 days of making the gift.

Answer (C) is correct.

REQUIRED: The due date of a gift tax return if the donor is not deceased.

DISCUSSION: Form 709 must generally be filed for the year 2012 after January 1, but not later than April 15, 2013.

Answer (A) is incorrect. The return is to be filed between January 1 and April 15, 2013. Answer (B) is incorrect. The filing does not occur before the end of the year 2012. Answer (D) is incorrect. The filing date is not dependent on the gift date, but rather the calendar year.

11. In which of the following circumstances would a gift tax return be due?

A. Check for $25,000 to son.

B. Transfer of stock valued at $30,000 to spouse.

C. Payment of a friend's $16,000 tuition expense.

D. None of the answers are correct.

Answer (A) is correct.

REQUIRED: Filing requirements of a gift tax return.

DISCUSSION: A donor is required to file a gift tax return, Form 709, for any gift(s), unless all gifts are excluded under the annual $13,000 exclusion and the deduction for qualified transfers to the donor's spouse. These exclusions apply for gifts of present interests only. Any gift of a future interest requires the filing of Form 709. The tuition expense is not a "gift." Gift splitting does not excuse the donor from the requirement to file. A check for $25,000 to a son exceeds the amount of the exclusion.

Answer (B) is incorrect. The deduction for qualified transfers to the donor's spouse is permitted. Answer (C) is incorrect. An exclusion exists for payment of tuition. It is not considered a "gift." Answer (D) is incorrect. A check for $25,000 to a son does not qualify for an exclusion.

12. On June 15, 2012, Marlo made a transfer by gift in an amount sufficient to require the filing of a gift tax return. If Marlo did not request an extension of time for filing the 2012 gift tax return, the due date for filing was

A. December 31, 2012.

B. March 15, 2013.

C. April 15, 2013.

D. June 17, 2013.

Answer (C) is correct.

REQUIRED: The date that a gift tax return is due.

DISCUSSION: Under Sec. 6075, gift tax returns are due on or before the 15th day of April following the close of the calendar year in which a gift was made. Since Marlo made a gift in 2012, Form 709 is due by April 15, 2013.

Answer (A) is incorrect. The return may be filed anytime before April 15 of the close of the following year. Answer (B) is incorrect. The return may be filed anytime before April 15 of the close of the following year. Answer (D) is incorrect. The return must be filed on or before April 15 of the following year.

13. Which of the following entities are required to file Form 709, *United States Gift Tax Return*?

A. An individual.

B. An estate or trust.

C. A corporation.

D. An individual, an estate or trust, and a corporation.

Answer (A) is correct.

REQUIRED: Entity required to file Form 709, *United States Gift Tax Return*.

DISCUSSION: The only entity required to file Form 709 is an individual taxpayer.

Answer (B) is incorrect. An estate or trust is not required to file Form 709. Answer (C) is incorrect. A corporation is not required to file Form 709. Answer (D) is incorrect. Both an estate or trust and a corporation are not required to file Form 709.

14. Cassy, a single individual, has not been required to file a gift tax return in any prior year. In 2012, Cassy paid $14,000 tuition directly to State University for her sister, Andrea. She gave her brother $10,000 to pay medical bills for his daughter. She also donated $20,000 to the United Way. Must Cassy file a gift tax return?

A. No.

B. Yes, because the gift to her sister exceeded $13,000.

C. Yes, because the United Way donation exceeded $13,000.

D. Yes, because the total gifts she gave during the year exceeded $13,000.

Answer (A) is correct.

REQUIRED: The requirements for filing a gift tax return.

DISCUSSION: Publication 950 states, "The general rule is that any gift is a taxable gift. However, there are many exceptions to this rule. Generally, the following gifts are not taxable gifts.

- Gifts that are not more than the annual exclusion for the calendar year.
- Tuition or medical expenses you pay for someone . . .
- Gifts to charities."

According to the instructions to Form 709, a gift tax return is not required if all the gifts are fully excluded under the $13,000 annual exclusion. A gift tax return is not required for a gift to charity if it is fully deductible and the entire interest in the property is transferred to the qualified charity. Qualified tuition/medical costs and political contributions are not "gifts."

Answer (B) is incorrect. The gift to Cassy's sister was for tuition, and it was paid directly to the university. Answer (C) is incorrect. The donation was to a charity and is fully deductible. Answer (D) is incorrect. Cassy did not make any taxable gifts that exceeded the annual exclusion.

15. On February 4, Year 1, Mr. Smith made a gift in an amount sufficient to require the filing of a federal gift tax return. On October 5, Year 1, Mr. Smith died. No estate tax return will need to be filed for Mr. Smith. Assuming extensions have not been obtained, the gift tax return, Form 709, must be filed by (assuming none of the dates are Saturdays, Sundays, or holidays)

A. April 15, Year 1.

B. March 15, Year 2.

C. April 15, Year 2.

D. July 5, Year 2.

Answer (C) is correct.

REQUIRED: The date that Form 709, *United States Gift Tax Return*, is due.

DISCUSSION: Under Sec. 6075, gift tax returns are due on or before the 15th day of April following the close of the calendar year in which a gift was made. Since Mr. Smith made a gift in Year 1, Form 709 is generally due by April 15, Year 2. If the date falls on a weekend or holiday, the return is due the next business day.

If an estate tax return were required of Mr. Smith's estate, this return would be due no later than 9 months after the date of death unless an extension was obtained [Sec. 6075(a)]. The due date for the gift tax return for the year of death is no later than the estate tax return due date [Sec. 6075(b)(3)]. Since an estate tax return is not being filed, the due date does not change.

Answer (A) is incorrect. The return is due on April 15 following the calendar year in which the gift is made. Answer (B) is incorrect. The return is due on April 15 following the calendar year in which the gift is made. Answer (D) is incorrect. An estate return was not required to be filed.

12.2 Gift Tax

16. During 2012, Barbara gave her daughter the following gifts:

	Fair Market Value	Basis
Cash	$10,000	$10,000
100 shares of ABC Corp.	25,000	5,000
Vacant land	50,000	60,000

What is the gross amount of gifts given by Barbara in 2012?

A. $75,000

B. $85,000

C. $95,000

D. None of the answers are correct.

Answer (B) is correct.

REQUIRED: The gross amount of gifts given when the FMV and basis differ.

DISCUSSION: The amount of a gift made in property is the fair market value of the property at the date of the gift (Reg. 25.2512-1). The fair market value is that which would occur in an arm's-length transaction between a willing buyer and a willing seller in the normal market. Therefore, Barbara must include $85,000 of gifts on her 2012 tax return ($10,000 + $25,000 + $50,000).

Answer (A) is incorrect. The gross amount of gifts is the FMV of the distributed properties before any exclusion. Answer (C) is incorrect. The greater of the FMV or adjusted basis is not used to determine the gross amount of gifts. Answer (D) is incorrect. The amount of $85,000 is the gross amount of gifts given by Barbara in 2012.

17. During 2012, Sadie made the following transfers:

- She deeded her personal residence to her daughter and herself to be held in joint tenancy. The fair market value of the residence at the time of transfer was $150,000.
- She placed a $30,000 bank account in joint tenancy with her daughter. Neither she nor her daughter made any withdrawals in 2012.
- She placed a $20,000 bank account in joint tenancy with her daughter. During 2012, Sadie withdrew $2,000, and her daughter withdrew $5,000 from the account.
- She bought $10,000 in U.S. savings bonds registered as payable to herself or her daughter. Neither she nor her daughter cashed any of the bonds during 2012.

What is the gross amount of gifts given by Sadie in 2012?

A. $105,000

B. $90,000

C. $80,000

D. $5,000

Answer (C) is correct.

REQUIRED: The gross amount of gifts given during the year.

DISCUSSION: If a donor buys property with his/her own funds and the title to such property is held by the donor and the donee as joint tenants with right of survivorship and, if either the donor or the donee may give up those rights by severing his/her interest, the donor has made a gift to the donee in the amount of half the value of the property.

If the donor creates a joint bank account for him/herself and the donee [or a similar kind of ownership by which (s)he can get back the entire fund without the donee's consent], the donor has made a gift to the donee when the donee draws on the account for his/her own benefit. The amount of the gift is the amount that the donee took out without any obligation to repay the donor. If the donor buys a U.S. savings bond registered as payable to him/herself or the donee, there is a gift to the donee when (s)he cashes the bond without any obligation to account to the donor. Therefore, Sadie's gross amount of gifts given is $80,000 ($75,000 for the house + $5,000 for the amount withdrawn).

Answer (A) is incorrect. One-half of all the gifts is not the proper treatment of bank accounts in joint tenancy or savings bonds. Answer (B) is incorrect. The savings bonds are not considered a gift until they are cashed. Answer (D) is incorrect. One-half the value of the personal residence is treated as a gift.

18. Ralph gave his aunt an antique clock during tax year 2012. He had purchased the clock for $15,000 in 2008. The fair market value at the date of the transfer was $21,000. What amount should be recorded on Form 709 as the value of this gift?

A. $15,000

B. $8,000

C. $21,000

D. $2,000

Answer (C) is correct.

REQUIRED: The amount of gifts given when the FMV and basis differ.

DISCUSSION: Reg. 25.2512-1 states that the amount of a gift made in property is the fair market value of the property at the date of the gift. Therefore, the value of the gift is $21,000.

Answer (A) is incorrect. The adjusted basis of the gift is $15,000. Answer (B) is incorrect. The annual exclusion reduces the taxable gift, not the value. Answer (D) is incorrect. The annual exclusion is not deducted from the adjusted basis.

19. During the current year, Mr. and Mrs. X made joint gifts to their son of the following items:

- A painting with an adjusted basis of $15,000 and a fair market value of $45,000.
- Stock with an adjusted basis of $27,000 and a fair market value of $30,000.
- An auto with an adjusted basis of $15,000 and a fair market value of $17,000.
- An interest-free loan of $8,000 for a boat (for the son's personal use) on January 1 of the current year, which was repaid by their son on December 31 of the current year. Assume the applicable federal rate was 11% per annum.

What is the gross amount of gifts includible in Mr. and Mrs. X's gift tax return?

A. $92,880

B. $92,000

C. $57,880

D. $57,000

Answer (B) is correct.

REQUIRED: The gross amount of gifts including an interest-free loan.

DISCUSSION: The amount of a gift made in property is the fair market value of the property on the date of the gift [Sec. 2512(a)]. The auto, painting, and stock have a combined fair market value of $92,000.

In general, an interest-free loan results in deemed transfers of interest between the borrower and lender. When the two parties are related, the lender is deemed to have made a gift of the interest amount to the borrower [Sec. 7872(a)(1)]. However, Sec. 7872(c)(2) excludes gift loans between individuals from this provision if the aggregate outstanding principal does not exceed $10,000. Accordingly, the $8,000 interest-free loan does not result in a gift.

Answer (A) is incorrect. The amount of $92,880 includes $880 worth of interest from the loan. Loans under $10,000 are excluded from gift taxation. Answer (C) is incorrect. The amount of $57,880 includes $880 worth of interest, and the other properties are valued at their adjusted-basis amounts. Loans under $10,000 are excluded from gift taxation. Answer (D) is incorrect. The amount of $57,000 values the properties at their adjusted-basis amounts.

20. During 2012, Dave gave his daughter Joan the following items: stock with a fair market value of $42,000 and an adjusted basis of $45,000, a boat with a fair market value of $5,000 and an adjusted basis of $3,000, and a print with a fair market value of $12,000 and an adjusted basis of $5,000. What is the gross amount of gifts includible in Dave's gift tax return for 2012?

A. $50,000

B. $53,000

C. $59,000

D. $62,000

Answer (C) is correct.

REQUIRED: The gross amount of includible gifts.

DISCUSSION: The amount of a gift made in property is the fair market value of the property at the date of the gift (Reg. 25.2512-1). The fair market value is that which would occur in an arm's-length transaction between a willing buyer and a willing seller in the normal market. Therefore, Dave must include $59,000 of gifts on his 2012 tax return ($42,000 + $5,000 + $12,000).

Answer (A) is incorrect. The lesser of the FMV or adjusted basis is not used to determine the gross amount of gifts. Answer (B) is incorrect. The gross amount of gifts is not the total of the adjusted bases of the distributed properties. Answer (D) is incorrect. The greater of the FMV or adjusted basis is not used to determine the gross amount of gifts.

21. All of the following are deductions allowed in determining the gift tax except

A. A gift to the state of Pennsylvania for exclusively public purposes.

B. The value of any gift made to one's spouse, who is not a United States citizen.

C. A gift made to one's spouse, a United States citizen, in excess of $139,000.

D. A gift of a copyrightable work of art to a qualified organization if the copyright is not transferred to the charity.

Answer (B) is correct.

REQUIRED: The deduction that is not allowed in determining the gift tax.

DISCUSSION: Although a full marital deduction is available for a gift to a spouse who is a U.S. citizen, regardless of the citizenship or residence of the donor, the marital deduction for a gift made to a spouse who is not a U.S. citizen is limited to $139,000 for 2012.

22. Jack, a single individual, made the following gifts in 2012:

Payment directly to sister's qualifying college for tuition	$20,000
Payment directly to sister's qualifying college for room and board	$25,000
Cash to nephew	$10,000
Cash to brother	$30,000

What is the gross amount of gifts that Jack must include on his 2012 Form 709, *United States Gift Tax Return*?

A. $85,000

B. $40,000

C. $65,000

D. $55,000

Answer (D) is correct.

REQUIRED: The gross amount of gifts that Jack must include on Form 709, *United States Gift (and Generation-Skipping Transfer) Tax Return.*

DISCUSSION: Sec. 6019 provides that a gift tax return must be filed for almost all taxable gifts. Specifically excluded from the requirement for filing are transfers that qualify for and do not exceed the $13,000 annual exclusion of Sec. 2503(b). The payment to Jack's sister's college for tuition is not included (this is not considered a "gift"). The amount given for room and board is included, however. The cash payment made to the nephew is excluded due to the $13,000 annual exclusion. The total amount included is $55,000 ($25,000 room and board + $30,000 cash to brother).

Answer (A) is incorrect. The $20,000 payment for tuition is excluded for education expenses (this is not considered a "gift"), and the cash payment to the nephew is excluded because of the annual exclusion. Answer (B) is incorrect. The amount reported equals the amount given for room and board and the amount given to the brother. Answer (C) is incorrect. The cash given to Jack's nephew is below the $13,000 threshold and is not included.

23. Listed below are gifts Joan made during 2012.

- $25,000 gift to a nonprofit home for the underprivileged
- $13,000 gift to her daughter
- $13,000 in contributions to an historical museum
- $40,000 gift to her spouse

What is the amount of taxable gifts to be reported on Form 709 for 2012?

A. $0

B. $38,000

C. $51,000

D. $78,000

Answer (A) is correct.

REQUIRED: The donor's taxable gifts for the current year.

DISCUSSION: "Taxable gifts" means the total amount of gifts made during the calendar year reduced by the charitable and marital deductions [Sec. 2503(a)]. The first $13,000 of gifts of present interests made to each donee during the year is excluded [Sec. 2503(b)]. All of Joan's transfers qualify for exclusion from gift taxation.

24. Lanny won $10 million at a casino in 2010 and invested in mutual funds. When he married Judy in 2011, they signed prenuptial agreements. Then, in 2012, Lanny decided to give away some of his money. He made the following gifts:

- $100,000 cash to Judy
- $50,000 to each of his three adult children
- $50,000 to the Republican Party

What are the total taxable gifts that Lanny made in 2012? (Assume no gift splitting was elected.)

A. $200,000

B. $300,000

C. $111,000

D. $150,000

Answer (C) is correct.

REQUIRED: The total amount of taxable gifts assuming no gift splitting was elected.

DISCUSSION: The total of the taxable gifts is the total gift amount of $250,000 minus exclusions for each gift and the marital deduction. The $50,000 transfer to the Republican Party is not subject to gift tax, and it is not included in the total taxable gifts.

	Total Gifts	Exclusions and Deductions	Taxable Gifts
Judy	$100,000	$(100,000)	$ 0
Child 1	50,000	(13,000)	37,000
Child 2	50,000	(13,000)	37,000
Child 3	50,000	(13,000)	37,000
Total	$250,000	$(139,000)	$111,000

Answer (A) is incorrect. The $50,000 transfer to the Republican Party is not subject to gift tax. Answer (B) is incorrect. The total amount of money Lanny gave away is $300,000. Answer (D) is incorrect. The total amount of gifts is reduced by the $13,000 exclusion for each child.

25. During the calendar year, John made the following payments:

- $15,000 to a qualified political party
- $20,000 to a local hospital for his mother's recent operation
- $25,000 to the state university for his nephew's tuition expense
- $15,000 to his favorite qualified charity

What is the gross amount that John must report on his gift tax return (Form 709)?

A. John does not have to file a gift tax return for the calendar year.

B. $75,000

C. $60,000

D. $15,000

Answer (A) is correct.

REQUIRED: The gross amount to be reported on the gift tax return (Form 709).

DISCUSSION: Not all transfers of money are subject to gift tax. Included in those excluded transfers are those to political organizations [defined in Sec. 527(e)(1)], amounts paid for qualified education expenses, and amounts paid for providing medical care. Additionally, the $15,000 transfer to the charity qualifies for exclusion when no other items are taxable.

Answer (B) is incorrect. The amounts paid to the political organization, the hospital, the qualified charity, and the university for tuition are excluded transfers. Answer (C) is incorrect. No gift return must be filed for the political, educational, and medical payments. Answer (D) is incorrect. The charitable contribution qualifies for exclusion when no other items are taxable.

26. During the calendar year, Mary gave several gifts to relatives. Which of the following gifts must be reported in an annual gift tax return?

1. $25,000 to her mother to help pay for medical expenses
2. A $20,000 federal tax-exempt municipal bond to her sister
3. 100 shares of stock to her daughter (Mary's basis in the stock was $10,000 and the fair market value at the date of gift was $20,000)
4. $20,000 to a qualified university for her son's dormitory fees

A. 2 and 4.

B. 2, 3, and 4.

C. 3 only.

D. 1, 2, 3, and 4.

Answer (D) is correct.

REQUIRED: Reportable gifts on the gift tax return.

DISCUSSION: All gifts must be included on the gift tax return. Because the payment was not made directly to the medical institution, it is a gift to her mother. The federal tax-exempt bond may be exempt for income tax, but not gift tax purposes. The stock is also subject to the gift tax. Finally, because the expenses for Mary's son were for dormitory and not tuition, they must be included in the gift return as well.

27. Donald is a tax return preparer. His client, Jody Black, told him that she had made several gifts during 2012. She asked whether she should file a gift tax return and, if so, how much tax she would owe. Jody has never given a taxable gift before. Donald reviewed Jody's gift transactions as follows:

1. Paid her parents' medical bills, $13,000 for her father and $9,000 for her mother
2. Bought a sports car for her son at a cost of $38,000
3. Gave $16,000 cash to her church
4. Prepared her will, leaving her vacation cabin, valued at $75,000, to her sister
5. Sent a wedding gift of $1,000 to her niece

What is Donald's best answer to Jody's questions?

A. No return is due because gifts to family are excluded.

B. Jody must file a gift tax return and will owe tax on $26,000.

C. Jody must file a gift tax return, but she will not owe tax because of the unified credit.

D. None of the answers are correct.

Answer (C) is correct.

REQUIRED: The determination for filing a gift tax return and the amount of gift tax due.

DISCUSSION: A tax return must be filed if there are any taxable gifts. After the $13,000 exclusion, Jody will have a taxable gift of $25,000 to her son. For gifts made in 2012, the applicable credit amount is $1,772,800, reduced by the amount allowable as an applicable credit amount for all preceding calendar years [Sec. 2505(a)].

Answer (A) is incorrect. A return must be filed if there are any taxable gifts. Only gifts to spouses are allowed with no limit. The gift to her son is taxable in excess of the annual exclusion. Answer (B) is incorrect. Due to the applicable credit, no tax will be owed. Answer (D) is incorrect. A gift tax return must be filed, but no tax will be owed because of the applicable credit amount (unified credit).

28. In 2012, Linda gave her daughter a gift of land that had a fair market value of $5,131,000. She made no gifts from 1991 through 2012. In 1991, she used $1,506,800 of her applicable credit amount to offset gift tax otherwise due. What amount of applicable credit amount can Linda use to offset gift tax due on the 2012 gift?

A. $1,772,800

B. $266,000

C. $13,000

D. $0

Answer (B) is correct.

REQUIRED: The calculation of allowable applicable credit.

DISCUSSION: For gifts made in 2012, the applicable credit amount is $1,772,800 reduced by the amount allowable as an applicable credit amount for all preceding calendar years [Sec. 2505(a)]. Since Linda used $1,506,800 of applicable credit amount in previous years, the amount of applicable credit amount she may use in 2012 is $266,000 ($1,772,800 – $1,506,800).

Answer (A) is incorrect. The full amount of the applicable credit amount may not be taken when the credit was used in a prior year. Answer (C) is incorrect. This amount is the annual exclusion. Answer (D) is incorrect. The applicable credit amount has increased since 1991, and the excess may be used to offset current gift tax.

29. Margaret's 2012 Form 709, page 1, has the following entries:

- $1,785,000 tax of current-year gifts
- $1,772,800 maximum unified credit
- $1,530,800 credit used in prior years

Based on this information, what is the balance due on Margaret's Form 709 Gift Tax Return this year?

A. $0

B. $12,200

C. $1,543,000

D. $254,200

Answer (C) is correct.

REQUIRED: The deductible amount of unified credit.

DISCUSSION: The applicable credit amount available to offset tax due on the current year's gifts is equal to the statutory credit for the current year reduced by the sum of the amounts allowable as a credit to the individual for all preceding calendar years [Sec. 2505(a)]. The credit may not exceed the tax for the calendar year. For 2012, the statutory credit is $1,772,800. Therefore, Margaret's balance on Form 709 is $1,543,000 [$1,785,000 – ($1,772,800 – $1,530,800)].

Answer (A) is incorrect. Margaret's tax on current year gifts exceed her available unified credit. Answer (B) is incorrect. Margaret cannot use any part of her unified credit used in prior years. Answer (D) is incorrect. Margaret should deduct her maximum unified credit reduced by any credit used in prior years.

30. Which of the following statements is true in respect to determining the amount of net gift tax?

A. There is a one-time marital deduction of $600,000.

B. The annual exclusion is limited to a total of $13,000 per year per donor.

C. The applicable credit amount may be used to reduce up to $1,772,800 of gift tax liability per year.

D. The applicable credit amount claimed may not exceed the tax for the calendar year.

Answer (D) is correct.

REQUIRED: The true statement regarding net gift tax.

DISCUSSION: The applicable credit amount available to offset tax due on the current year's gifts is equal to the statutory credit for the current year reduced by the sum of the amounts allowable as a credit to the individual for all preceding calendar years [Sec. 2505(a)]. The credit may not exceed the tax for the calendar year. For 2012, the statutory credit is $1,772,800.

Answer (A) is incorrect. There is an unlimited marital deduction. Answer (B) is incorrect. The annual exclusion is available to each individual recipient. Answer (C) is incorrect. The applicable credit amount of $1,772,800 is a one-time credit and is eliminated when it is used up.

31. Which of the following statements regarding the annual exclusion for gift taxes is true?

A. The gift of a present interest to more than one donee as joint tenants qualifies for only one annual exclusion.

B. A gift of a future interest cannot be excluded under the annual exclusion.

C. The annual exclusion amount for 2012 is $14,000.

D. None of the answers are correct.

Answer (B) is correct.

REQUIRED: True statement regarding the annual exclusion for gift taxes.

DISCUSSION: The first $13,000 of gifts of present interest to each donee is excluded from taxable gift amounts. The $13,000 exclusion applies only to gifts of present interests.

Answer (A) is incorrect. The gift would qualify for two annual exclusions. Answer (C) is incorrect. The annual exclusion for 2012 is $13,000. Answer (D) is incorrect. A correct answer is given.

12.3 Gift Splitting

32. Which of the following statements concerning gift splitting is false?

A. To qualify for gift splitting, a couple must be married at the time the gift is made to a third party.

B. Both spouses must consent to the use of gift splitting.

C. For gift tax purposes, a husband and wife must file a joint income tax return to qualify for the gift splitting benefits.

D. The annual gift tax exclusion allows spouses who consent to split their gifts to transfer up to $26,000 to any one person during any calendar year without gift tax liability, if the gift qualifies as a present interest.

Answer (C) is correct.

REQUIRED: The false statement concerning gift splitting.

DISCUSSION: Sec. 2513 allows a gift to be treated as made one-half by the donor and one-half by the donor's spouse. The spouses are not required to file a joint income tax return.

Answer (A) is incorrect. The donor must be married at the time of the gift to qualify for gift splitting. Answer (B) is incorrect. Both spouses must consent to the use of gift splitting. Answer (D) is incorrect. Gift splitting allows spouses who consent to split their gifts to exclude the first $26,000 of each gift of a present interest.

33. George and Helen are husband and wife. During 2012, George gave $34,000 to his brother and Helen gave $26,000 to her niece. George and Helen both agree to split the gifts they made during the year. What is the taxable amount of gifts, after the annual exclusion, each must report on Form 709?

A. George and Helen each have taxable gifts of $17,000.

B. George has a taxable gift of $21,000 and Helen has a taxable gift of $13,000.

C. George and Helen each have taxable gifts of $4,000.

D. George has a taxable gift of $8,000 and Helen has a taxable gift of zero.

Answer (C) is correct.

REQUIRED: The total amount of taxable gifts to be reported by a spouse who elects gift splitting.

DISCUSSION: Gift splitting allows spouses to treat each gift as made one-half by each. This allows each spouse to exclude the first $13,000 of each gift of a present interest to a third person in a calendar year, for a total exclusion of $26,000 per donee. The $34,000 gift to George's brother is treated as half given by George, the other half given by Helen. The same rule applies for the gift to Helen's niece. Since half of the gift to Helen's niece is $13,000, the annual exclusion applies and neither George nor Helen must report the gift to the niece. George and Helen, for tax purposes, are considered to have given $17,000 each to George's brother. This amount is reduced by the $13,000 annual exclusion. Thus, George and Helen each have taxable gifts of $4,000.

Answer (A) is incorrect. This answer disregards the $13,000 annual exclusion for each donee. Answer (B) is incorrect. Helen and George have elected to split gifts. Moreover, the $13,000 annual exclusion applies to both the gift to George's brother and the gift to Helen's niece. Answer (D) is incorrect. The couple has agreed to gift splitting. Therefore, Helen and George would split the gift and each would report $4,000 of taxable gifts.

34. During 2012, Wellington made the following gifts:

- $40,000 cash to son Willis
- Land worth $100,000 to wife Paula
- A $16,000 painting to niece Marlene

Wellington and Paula elect gift splitting. Paula's only gift in 2012 was a $50,000 cash gift to her mother. What is the amount of the taxable gifts to be reported by Wellington in 2012?

A. $19,000

B. $53,000

C. $153,000

D. $206,000

Answer (A) is correct.

REQUIRED: The total amount of taxable gifts to be reported by a spouse who elects gift splitting.

DISCUSSION: Gift splitting allows spouses to treat each gift as made one-half by each. This allows each spouse to exclude the first $13,000 of each gift of a present interest to a third person in a calendar year, for a total exclusion of $26,000 per donee. The land that Wellington gave to his wife qualifies for the unlimited marital deduction and is not included as a taxable gift. Thus, Wellington's taxable gift amount is $19,000.

	Gift Amount	Exclusion	Taxable Gift
Son	$ 20,000	$ (13,000)	$ 7,000
Wife	100,000	(100,000)	0
Niece	8,000	(8,000)	0
Paula's mother	25,000	(13,000)	12,000
Total	$153,000	$(132,000)	$19,000

Answer (B) is incorrect. The answer ignores the effect of annual exclusions. Answer (C) is incorrect. The answer ignores the effect of the annual exclusions, unlimited marital deductions, and gift splitting. Answer (D) is incorrect. The answer ignores the effect of the annual exclusions, unlimited marital deductions, and gift splitting.

35. Mr. Fred Wall bought a house that cost $50,000 for an unrelated friend, Gloria Wilson, in 2012. Mrs. Wall made no gifts in 2012. In filing their gift tax returns for 2012, Mr. and Mrs. Wall should file Form 709, *United States Gift Tax Return*, as follows:

A. Mr. Wall should file a gift tax return reporting the $50,000 gift and taking a $13,000 annual exclusion.

B. File one joint gift tax return reporting the $50,000 gift and taking a $13,000 annual exclusion for each spouse, or a $26,000 exclusion.

C. File two gift tax returns, one for Mr. Wall and one for Mrs. Wall, with each spouse signing the consent section of the other's gift tax return signifying that the spouse agrees to treat all gifts as made one-half by each spouse. A $13,000 annual exclusion may be taken on each return.

D. Either Mr. Wall should file a gift tax return reporting the $50,000 gift and taking a $13,000 annual exclusion or Mr. and Mrs. Wall should file two gift tax returns, one for Mr. Wall and one for Mrs. Wall, with each spouse signing the consent section of the other's gift tax return signifying that the spouse agrees to treat all gifts as made one-half by each spouse. A $13,000 annual exclusion may be taken on each return.

Answer (D) is correct.

REQUIRED: The proper methods of gift splitting.

DISCUSSION: A gift tax return must be filed for a transfer that exceeds the annual exclusion. Fred may either report the entire gift on his gift tax return and take the $13,000 exclusion or elect to split the gift between his wife and himself. Gift splitting allows spouses to treat each gift as made one-half by each. This allows each spouse to exclude the first $13,000 of each gift of a present interest to a third person in a calendar year, for a total exclusion of $26,000 per donee. Gift splitting is not available to a couple if they legally divorce after the gift and one of the spouses remarries before the end of the calendar year.

Answer (A) is incorrect. Fred may also choose to split the gift between his wife and himself. Answer (B) is incorrect. There is no such thing as a joint gift tax return. Answer (C) is incorrect. Fred may also choose to include the entire gift on his gift tax return.

36. Which of the following statements regarding gift splitting is true?

A. The couple must have been married at the time the gift was given, but either or both spouses may be remarried during the year.

B. The couple must have been married at the time the gift was given, and the spouse who gave the gift may not be remarried during the year.

C. The couple need not be married at the time of the gift, but must be married by the end of the year.

D. The couple must be married at all times during the year.

Answer (B) is correct.

REQUIRED: The true statement regarding gift splitting.

DISCUSSION: Publication 950 states, "If you or your spouse make a gift to a third party, the gift can be considered as made one-half by you and one-half by your spouse." Furthermore, Instructions for Form 709 state that if a taxpayer is divorced or widowed after the gift, you [can]not remarry during the rest of the calendar year to qualify for gift splitting.

Answer (A) is incorrect. A married couple is not allowed gift splitting if the couple divorces after the gift, and one of the spouses remarries before the end of the calendar year. Answer (C) is incorrect. A married couple is not allowed gift splitting if the couple is not married at the time of the gift. Answer (D) is incorrect. The couple can divorce after the gift, but neither spouse can remarry before the end of the calendar year.

37. Valerie and Dino, who were married in 2005, made a gift to their son Michael on January 2, 2012. In July 2012, Valerie and Dino were legally divorced. Valerie married Scott on December 20, 2012. Which answer below best describes this situation?

A. The gift splitting benefits are available to Valerie and Dino if Valerie consents.

B. The gift splitting benefits are not available to Valerie and Dino because they were divorced in 2012.

C. The gift splitting benefits are not available to Valerie and Dino because Valerie remarried in 2012.

D. The gift splitting benefits are available to Valerie and Dino because they were married at the time the gift was made.

Answer (C) is correct.

REQUIRED: The proper gift splitting treatment when a couple divorces and one of the spouses remarries.

DISCUSSION: Gift splitting allows spouses to treat each gift as made one-half by each. This allows each spouse to exclude the first $13,000 of each gift of a present interest to a third person in a calendar year, for a total exclusion of $26,000 per donee. Gift splitting is not available to a couple if they legally divorce after the gift and one of the spouses remarries before the end of the calendar year.

Answer (A) is incorrect. Valerie and Dino were divorced and Valerie remarried. Answer (B) is incorrect. Valerie remarried before the end of the year. Answer (D) is incorrect. Valerie and Dino were divorced and Valerie remarried.

38. John and Mary were married on July 1, 2012. During 2012, John gave the following gifts:

- 2/21/12 - $10,000 worth of ABC Corp. stock to John's son David
- 4/20/12 - $30,000 worth of vacant land to John's daughter Susan
- 10/31/12 - $100,000 cash to Mary
- 11/18/12 - $20,000 worth of XYZ Corp. stock to John's son David

Mary did not make any gifts during 2012. John and Mary agreed to split gifts for 2012. What is the amount of gifts that can be split between John and Mary in 2012?

A. $160,000

B. $60,000

C. $20,000

D. None of the answers are correct.

Answer (C) is correct.

REQUIRED: The total amount of gifts that may be split when a couple is married during the year.

DISCUSSION: If both spouses consent, a gift made by one spouse to any person other than the other spouse is considered as made one-half by each spouse (Sec. 2513). However, only gifts that were made while the couple were actually married at the time of the gift qualify for gift splitting. Because John and Mary were not married until July 1 and the transfer to Mary qualifies as an unlimited marital deduction, only the $20,000 gift to David may be split.

Answer (A) is incorrect. Only gifts made while a couple is married may be split. Answer (B) is incorrect. The gifts made before July 1 may not be split. Answer (D) is incorrect. A correct answer is given.

STUDY UNIT THIRTEEN
ESTATE TAX

(8 pages of outline)

Estate taxes are wealth transfer taxes that apply to dispositions of property that occur as a result of the transferor's death. The tax base for the federal estate tax is the total of the decedent's taxable estate and adjusted taxable gifts. The taxable estate is the gross estate minus allowable deductions. Current-year applicable rates are applied to both current and preceding years' taxable gifts. The rate is 18% for taxable gifts up to $10,000. The rates increase in small steps (e.g., 2%, 3%) over numerous brackets. The maximum rate is 35% on cumulative taxable gifts and estates in excess of $5.12 million in 2012.

13.1 THE GROSS ESTATE (GE)

A decedent's gross estate includes the FMV of all property, real or personal, tangible or intangible, wherever situated, to the extent the decedent owned a beneficial interest at the time of death.

1. Included in the GE are such items as cash, personal residence and effects, securities, other investments (e.g., real estate, collector items), and other personal assets, such as notes and claims (e.g., dividends declared prior to death if the record date had passed) and business interests (e.g., interest in a sole proprietorship, partnership interest).
   a. Special tax-avoidance rules are established for U.S. citizens or residents who surrender their U.S. citizenship or long-term U.S. residency.

Decedent's Liabilities

2. Liabilities of the decedent generally do not affect the amount of the GE unless the estate actually pays them.

Dower/Curtesy

3. The GE includes the value of the surviving spouse's interest in property as dower or curtesy.
   a. Dower and curtesy are common-law rights recognized in some states, usually in modified form.
      1) Dower entitles a surviving wife to a portion of lands her husband owned and possessed during their marriage.
      2) Curtesy entitles a surviving husband to a life estate in all of his wife's land if they had children.

Joint Tenants with the Right of Survivorship

4. The GE includes the full value of property held as joint tenants with the right of survivorship, except to the extent of any part that is shown to have originally belonged to the other person and for which adequate and full consideration was not provided by the decedent (i.e., the other tenant provided consideration).
   a. The GE includes 50% of property held as joint tenants by spouses or as tenants by the entirety regardless of the amount of consideration provided by each spouse.

Power of Appointment

5. The value of property interests over which the decedent had a general power of appointment (POA) is included in the GE. A POA is a power exercisable in favor of the decedent, his/her estate, his/her creditors, or the creditors of his/her estate.

Government Obligations

6. Bonds, notes, bills, and certificates of indebtedness of the federal, state, and local governments are included in the GE, even if interest on them is exempt from income tax.

Insurance Proceeds

7. The GE includes insurance proceeds on the decedent's life in certain situations.
   a. The insurance proceeds are payable to or for the estate (including if payable to the executor).
   b. The decedent had any incident of ownership in the policy at death, e.g.,
      1) Right to change beneficiaries
      2) Right to terminate the policy
   c. The proceeds of insurance policies given to others by the decedent within 3 years of death are included in the estate. This is an exception to the "gifts within 3 years of death rules."
   d. The proceeds included under c. above are allocated proportionately if the premiums are partially paid by the insured and partially paid by someone else.

EXAMPLE

Twenty years before her death, Joanna bought a $200,000 term life insurance policy. One year before her death, she irrevocably transferred the policy and all incidents of ownership to a trust that paid the last year's premiums. Joanna's GE included $190,000 of proceeds since Joanna paid 95% of the premiums.

Annuities and Survivor Benefits

8. The GE includes the value of any annuity receivable by a beneficiary by reason of surviving the decedent if either of the following statements applies:
   a. The annuity was payable to the decedent
   b. The decedent had the right to receive the annuity or payment
      1) Either alone or in conjunction with another
      2) For his/her life or for any period not ascertainable without reference to his/her death or for any period that does not end before his/her death

Medical Insurance

9. Medical insurance reimbursements due the decedent at death are treated as property in which the decedent had an interest.

Gifts within 3 Years of Death

10. Gifts made within 3 years of death are not included in the GE of a decedent except for certain transfers, such as transfers of life insurance and property in which a life estate was retained.
    a. The GE does include gift taxes paid on gifts within 3 years before death.

Inter Vivos Transfer

11. The GE includes assets transferred during life in which the decedent retained, at death, any of the following interests:
    a. A life estate, an income interest, possession or enjoyment of assets, or the right to designate who will enjoy the property
    b. A 5% or greater reversionary interest if possession was conditioned on surviving the decedent
    c. The power to alter, amend, revoke, or terminate the transfer
    d. An interest in a qualified terminable interest property (QTIP) trust

Valuing the Gross Estate

12. Value is the FMV of the property unless a special valuation rule is used.
    a. Real property is usually valued at its highest and best use.
    b. A transfer of interests in a corporation or partnership to a family member is subject to estate tax-freeze rules.
        1) Generally, the retained interest is valued at zero.
    c. Valuing property at FMV is referred to as stepped-up basis. Of course, if an asset declined in value, it would be a stepped-down basis.
13. The executor may elect to value the estate at either the date of death or the alternate valuation date. An alternate valuation date election is irrevocable.
    a. The election can be made only if it results in a reduction in both the value of the gross estate and the sum of the federal estate tax and the generation-skipping transfer tax (reduced by allowable credits).
    b. The alternate valuation date is 6 months after the decedent's death.
        1) Assets sold or distributed before then are valued on the date of sale or distribution.
        2) Assets, the value of which is affected by mere lapse of time, are valued as of the date of the decedent's death, but adjustment is made for value change from other than mere lapse of time.
            a) Examples of such assets are patents, life estates, reversions, and remainders.
            b) The value of such assets is based on years.
            c) Changes due to time value of money are treated as from more than mere lapse of time.

Stop and review! You have completed the outline for this subunit. Study questions 1 through 14 beginning on page 302.

13.2 DEDUCTIONS AND CREDITS

Deductions from the Gross Estate

1. Deductions from the GE in computing the taxable estate (TE) include ones with respect to expenses, claims, and taxes.

NOTE: A deductible amount is allowed against gross income on the decedent's final income tax return only if the right to deduct them from the GE is waived.

    a. Expenses for selling property of an estate are deductible if the sale is necessary to
        1) Pay the decedent's debts
        2) Pay expenses of administration
        3) Pay taxes
        4) Preserve the estate
        5) Effect distribution
    b. Administration and funeral expenses are deductible.
    c. Claims against the estate (including debts of the decedent) are deductible.
        1) Medical expenses paid within 1 year of death may be deducted on either the estate tax return or the final income tax return (not both).
    d. Unpaid mortgages on property are deductible if the value of the decedent's interest is included in the GE.

e. State inheritance taxes are deductible from the gross estate. Federal estate taxes and income tax paid on income earned and received after the decedent's death are not deductible.

f. Casualty or theft losses incurred during the settlement of the estate are deductible if they were not deducted on the estate's income tax return.

Charitable Contributions

g. Bequests to qualified charitable organizations are deductible.

1) The entire interest of the decedent in the underlying property must generally be donated.
2) Trust interests may enable deductible transfer of partial interests in underlying property.
3) An inter vivos contribution (vs. a bequest) may result in exclusion from the GE and a current deduction for regular taxable income.

Marital Transfers

h. Outright transfers to a surviving spouse are deductible from the GE to the extent the interest is included in the gross estate.

1) The surviving spouse must be a U.S. citizen when the estate tax return is filed.
2) A marital deduction is allowed for transfers of QTIP. These transfers allow a marital deduction where the recipient spouse is not entitled to designate which parties will eventually receive the property.
3) QTIP is defined as property that passes from the decedent in which the surviving spouse has a qualifying income interest for life and to which an election applies.
4) A spouse has a qualifying income interest for life if (s)he is entitled to all the income from the property that is paid at least annually, and no person has a power to appoint any portion of the property to anyone other than the surviving spouse unless the power cannot be exercised during the spouse's lifetime.

Credits

2. Four credits are available to offset federal estate tax liability:

a. Applicable credit amount (ACA). The ACA is a base amount ($1,772,800 in 2012) not reduced by amounts allowable as credits for gift tax for all preceding tax years.

1) The ACA offsets the estate tax liability that would be imposed on a taxable estate of up to $5.12 million computed at current rates (2012).
2) The ACA was formerly called the unified credit.
3) Any unused amount by a deceased spouse may be used by the surviving spouse in addition to the surviving spouse's own exclusion amount. Under this portability election, the surviving spouse could potentially have an available exclusion amount of $10.24 million.

EXAMPLE

The deceased spouse only used $3.12 million of the allowed exclusion. The surviving spouse is allowed a $7.12 million exclusion ($5.12 million surviving spouse original amount + $2 million unused by the deceased spouse).

b. A credit is allowable for death taxes paid to foreign governments.

c. A credit is allowable on gift tax paid on gifts included in the gross estate.

d. Prior transfers. A credit is allowed for taxes paid on transfers by or from a person who died within 10 years before or 2 years after the decedent's death.

1) Amounts creditable are the lesser of the following:

a) Estate tax paid by the (prior) transferor
b) Amount by which the assets increase the estate tax

2) Adjustment is made to the credit for transfers more than 2 years prior to the decedent's death.

Income in Respect of a Decedent

3. Beneficiaries may take a deduction for the estate tax paid on income earned before death but received after the decedent's death (income in respect of a decedent).

a. The deduction is taken by individuals on Schedule A.

Stop and review! You have completed the outline for this subunit. Study questions 15 through 24 beginning on page 306.

13.3 ESTATE TAX PAYMENT AND RETURN

The executor is required to file Form 706, *United States Estate Tax Return*, if the gross estate at the decedent's death exceeds $5.12 million. Adjusted taxable gifts made by the decedent during his/her lifetime reduce the threshold.

Return Due Date

1. The estate tax return is due within 9 months after the date of the decedent's death. An extension of up to 6 months may be granted.

Payment Due Date

2. Time for payment may be extended for a period of 1 year past the due date. For reasonable cause, the time for payment may be extended for up to 10 years.

Assessment Period

3. The general period for assessment of estate tax is 3 years after the due date for a timely filed Form 706.

a. The assessment period is extended an additional (fourth) year for transfers from an estate.

Tax Charged to Property

4. Estate tax is charged to estate property.

a. If the tax on part of the estate distributed is paid out of other estate property, equitable contribution from the distributee beneficiary is recoverable.

b. The executor is ultimately liable for payment of the taxes.

Closely Held Business

5. An estate that includes a substantial interest in a closely held business may be allowed to delay payment of part of the estate tax if that interest exceeds 35% of the gross estate.

a. A closely held business includes the following if carrying on a trade or business:

1) A corporation, if it has 45 or fewer shareholders or if 20% or more in value of the voting stock is included in the gross estate

2) A partnership, if it has 45 or fewer partners or if 20% or more of the capital interests in the partnership is included in the gross estate

Stop and review! You have completed the outline for this subunit. Study questions 25 through 29 beginning on page 309.

13.4 GENERATION-SKIPPING TRANSFERS

1. The Generation-Skipping Transfer Tax (GSTT) is imposed separately and in addition to gift and estate taxes on transfers directly to or in trust for the sole benefit of a person at least two generations younger than the transferor.
   a. GSTT is generally imposed on each generation-skipping transfer (GST).

Transfer Types

   b. There are three types of GSTs:
      1) Direct skips
      2) Taxable distributions
      3) Taxable terminations

Direct Skip

2. A direct skip is a transfer of an interest in property, subject to estate tax or gift tax, to a skip person. The transferor is liable for the tax.
3. A **skip person** is either a natural person assigned to a generation that is two or more generations below the transferor or a trust, all interests of which are held by skip persons.
4. In the case of related persons, a skip person is identified by reference to the family tree.
   a. For example, a grandchild is two generations below the grandparent.
5. In the case of nonrelated persons, a skip person is identified by reference to age differences.
   a. For example, an individual born between 37 1/2 years and 62 1/2 years after the transferor is two generations below the transferor.

Taxable Distribution

6. A taxable distribution is a distribution from a trust to a skip person of income or principal, other than a distribution that is a direct skip or taxable termination. The transferee is liable for the tax.

Taxable Termination

7. A taxable termination is a termination of an interest in property held in trust. A taxable termination has not occurred if, immediately after the termination, a nonskip person has an interest in the property or if distributions are not permitted to be made to a skip person at any time following the termination.
   a. Termination may be by lapse of time, release of power, death, or otherwise.
   b. The trustee is liable to pay the tax.
8. The GSTT approximates the maximum federal estate tax that would have applied to the transfer on the date of the transfer.

Exemption

9. Each individual is allowed a $5.12 million exemption in 2012 that (s)he, or his/her executor, may allocate to GST property. The exemption is indexed for inflation.
   a. Gift splitting applies to GSTTs; $10.24 million is allocable.

EXAMPLE

Parent dies, leaving $3.5 million in trust to a child and the remainder to grandchildren. The entire $3.5 million is allocated to property held in trust. The child dies 25 years later, and the property held in trust is now worth $10 million. No GSTT is imposed.

10. Inter vivos gifts are exempt from the GSTT if they are not subject to gift tax due to the $13,000 annual exclusion or the medical/tuition exclusion.

Computation

11. The GSTT is computed by multiplying the taxable amount by the applicable rate.
    a. The applicable rate is the maximum federal rate multiplied by the inclusion ratio.
        1) The maximum federal rate is 35% (for 2012).
        2) The inclusion ratio is

$$1 - \left(\frac{\text{Transferor's Exemption Allocable to Property Transferred}}{\text{FMV Property Transferred} - (\text{Estate Tax} + \text{Charitable Deduction})}\right)$$

12. The GSTT does not apply when neither the federal estate tax nor the federal gift tax applies.
    a. General power of appointment includes the trust in the estate; thus, it is not subject to GSTT.

Termination Tax

13. Generation-Skipping Termination Tax
    a. The interest of a non-skip person terminates by reason of death, expiration of time, or another reason, and a skip person becomes the recipient of the trust property.

EXAMPLE

Under a parent's will, a trust is created with income to a child for life and corpus to grandchild. The child's death is an event that terminates the child's interest in the trust, causing a taxable termination.

The grandchild is a skip person, two generations below the parents.

    b. The trustee files and pays the tax.

Distribution Tax

14. Generation-Skipping Distribution Tax (GSDT)
    a. GSDT applies to trust distributions out of income or corpus to a beneficiary at least two generations below the grantor, while an older generation beneficiary has an interest in the trust.

EXAMPLE

A trust is created by a parent for a child. The trust allows for distributions to the grandchild during the child's lifetime. A taxable distribution occurs when a distribution is made from the trust to the grandchild.

    b. The distributee is entitled to a federal income tax deduction for GSDT imposed on current distributions of trust income.
    c. The basis of property received is increased by the proportion of GSDT imposed.
    d. The distributee reports and pays GSDT.
        1) A trustee's payment of GSDT is deemed an additional distribution to a beneficiary.

Direct Skips

15. A direct skip occurs when one or more generations are bypassed altogether, and property is transferred directly to or in trust for a skip person.
    a. Direct Skip Gift Tax (DSGT)
        1) The tax is imposed on gifts by an individual to a third generation or below beneficiary.
        2) The tax applies only to the FMV of the property given.
        3) Only the gift tax annual exclusion and the generation-skipping tax exemption apply.

4) The donor is liable for both the gift tax and the DSGT.
   a) The donor trustor is liable if the transfer is in trust.
   b) The donee can add a proportion of the DSGT to his/her income tax basis in property received.
   c) The DSGT is added to federal taxable gifts, and it increases the federal gift tax.

b. Direct Skip Estate Tax (DSET)
   1) The DSET applies when there is a bequest by an individual to a third generation or below beneficiary.
   2) The donor estate is liable for the estate tax and the DSET.
   3) Any unallocated $5.12 million generation-skipping tax exemptions are used to reduce taxable direct skip bequests.
   4) The basis is FMV at date of death.
      a) It is not increased by DSET.

Stop and review! You have completed the outline for this subunit. Study questions 30 through 40 beginning on page 310.

QUESTIONS

13.1 The Gross Estate (GE)

1. Chester is preparing the estate tax return, Form 706, for his deceased brother John. John died December 15 of the current year. Which of the following will not be included in John's gross estate?

A. Real estate that will be passed to John when his parents die.

B. Stocks and bonds owned by John at his death.

C. Land that John had signed a contract to sell, but the sale of which was not completed.

D. Property jointly owned by John and his spouse.

Answer (A) is correct.

REQUIRED: The item not included in a decedent's GE.

DISCUSSION: A decedent's gross estate includes the FMV of all property, real or personal, tangible or intangible, wherever situated, to the extent the decedent owned a beneficial interest at the time of death. Special tax-avoidance rules are established for U.S. citizens or residents who surrender their U.S. citizenship or long-term U.S. residency. Included in the GE are such items as cash, personal residence and effects, securities, other investments (e.g., real estate, collector items), and other personal assets, such as notes and claims (e.g., dividends declared prior to death if the record date had passed) and business interests (e.g., partnership interest). The GE includes the value of the surviving spouse's interest in property as dower or curtesy. John does not include the real estate in his gross estate since he does not own the real estate. However, the discounted value of his remainder interest in the real estate would be included in his gross estate. John is still the owner of the land that is under contract.

2. Laura's gross estate equals $6,000,000. Given the following information, determine Laura's taxable estate:

Charitable contribution specified in Laura's will	$100,000
Funeral expenses	10,000
Medical expenses claimed on Laura's Form 1040	20,000

A. $5,870,000

B. $5,880,000

C. $5,890,000

D. $6,000,000

Answer (C) is correct.

REQUIRED: Laura's taxable estate.

DISCUSSION: The estate is allowed to take a deduction for the charitable contribution and the funeral expenses. The medical expenses are not allowed to be deducted on Laura's gross estate because the expenses were already claimed on Laura's Form 1040. Medical expenses paid within 1 year of death may be deducted on either the estate tax return or the final income tax return, but not both. Therefore, the taxable estate is $5,890,000 ($6,000,000 – $100,000 – $10,000).

Answer (A) is incorrect. The estate is not allowed to take a deduction for the medical expenses because the expenses were already deducted on Laura's final Form 1040. Answer (B) is incorrect. The estate is entitled to a deduction for the charitable contribution and the funeral expenses. No deduction is allowed for the medical expenses because the expenses were already deducted on Laura's final Form 1040. Answer (D) is incorrect. The estate is entitled to a deduction for the charitable contribution and the funeral expenses.

3. Which of the following items are included in a decedent's gross estate?

- The decedent's IRA, where the decedent's spouse is the named beneficiary.
- A checking account with the decedent's daughter as a joint tenant. The daughter's funds were used to set up the account.
- Assets held in the decedent's revocable grantor trust.

A. All of the assets are included in the decedent's estate.

B. The IRA and checking account are included in the decedent's estate.

C. The IRA and the assets in the revocable grantor trust are included in the decedent's estate.

D. None of the assets are included in the decedent's estate.

Answer (C) is correct.

REQUIRED: The items included in a decedent's gross estate.

DISCUSSION: Instructions for Form 706 state, "The gross estate includes all property in which the decedent had an interest. . . . It also includes: . . . Annuities; the includible portion of joint estates with right of survivorship . . . Property over which the decedents possessed a general power of appointment; . . ." Schedule E states, "Generally, you must include the full value of the jointly owned property in the gross estate. However, the full value should not be included if you can show . . . that any part of the property was acquired with consideration originally belonging to the surviving joint tenant or tenants. In this case, you may exclude from the value of the property any amount proportionate to the consideration furnished by the other tenant or tenants."

Answer (A) is incorrect. The checking account is not included in the decedent's estate. Answer (B) is incorrect. The checking account is not included in the decedent's estate. Answer (D) is incorrect. The IRA and the assets in the revocable grantor trust are included in the decedent's estate.

4. Sam is single. Given the following information, determine the value of Sam's gross estate:

	FMV at Date of Death
Cash	$ 15,000
Life insurance on Sam's life (payable to his estate)	200,000
Jointly owned property (percentage includible-100%)	100,000

A. $315,000

B. $115,000

C. $265,000

D. $65,000

Answer (A) is correct.

REQUIRED: The value of a decedent's gross estate.

DISCUSSION: A decedent's gross estate includes the FMV of all property (real or personal, tangible or intangible, wherever situated) to the extent the decedent owned a beneficial interest at the time of death. Included in the gross estate are such items as cash; personal residence and effects; securities; other investments; and other personal assets, such as notes and claims and business interests. The gross estate also includes other items, such as the full value of property held as joint tenants with the right of survivorship, except to the extent of any part that is shown to have originally belonged to the other person and for which adequate and full consideration was not provided by the decedent and insurance proceeds on the decedent's life if either the insurance proceeds are payable to or for the estate or if the decedent had any incident of ownership in the policy at death. Therefore, $315,000 is the value of Sam's gross estate ($15,000 cash + $200,000 life insurance + $100,000 jointly owned property).

Answer (B) is incorrect. It does not include the life insurance payable to the estate. Answer (C) is incorrect. It only includes half of the jointly owned property. Answer (D) is incorrect. It only includes half of the jointly owned property and does not include the life insurance payable to the estate.

5. Following are the fair market values of Wald's assets at the date of death:

Personal effects and jewelry	$150,000
Land bought by Wald with Wald's funds 5 years prior to death and held with Wald's sister as joint tenants with right of survivorship	800,000

The executor of Wald's estate did not elect the alternate valuation date. The amount includible as Wald's gross estate in the federal estate tax return is

A. $150,000

B. $550,000

C. $800,000

D. $950,000

Answer (D) is correct.

REQUIRED: The amount includible on the estate tax return.

DISCUSSION: Under Sec. 2033, the value of the gross estate includes the value of all property in which the decedent had an interest at the time of death. Therefore, the value of the personal effects and jewelry is included in the gross estate.

Sec. 2040 states that a decedent's gross estate includes the value of property held jointly at the time of the decedent's death by the decedent and another person with right of survivorship. The value to be included depends upon how much of the purchase price or other consideration was supplied by the decedent. If the decedent furnished only a part of the purchase price, only a corresponding portion of the property is so included. If, as in this case, the decedent furnished the entire purchase price of the jointly held property, the value of the entire property is included in the gross estate. Therefore, Wald must include the entire value of the jointly held property in his gross estate.

Answer (A) is incorrect. The amount of $150,000 excludes the value of the land. Answer (B) is incorrect. The amount of $550,000 includes only one-half of the value of the land. Answer (C) is incorrect. The amount of $800,000 excludes the value of the personal effects and jewelry.

6. When Lisa's husband died in 2009, he set up a qualified terminable interest property (QTIP) trust, naming Lisa as the beneficiary for her life. Lisa died in 2012. Given the following information, determine the value of Lisa's gross estate:

	FMV at Date of Death
Lisa's revocable grantor trust	$ 750,000
QTIP trust	1,000,000

A. $0

B. $750,000

C. $1,000,000

D. $1,750,000

Answer (D) is correct.

REQUIRED: Items included in decedent's gross estate.

DISCUSSION: Lisa must include the value of both the trusts in her gross estate. Lisa is the owner at her death of a revocable grantor trust. The QTIP trust allowed her husband to take a marital deduction at his death and must be included in Lisa's estate.

Answer (A) is incorrect. Lisa must include both trusts when valuing the gross estate. Answer (B) is incorrect. The amount of $750,000 does not include the value of the QTIP trust. Answer (C) is incorrect. The $1,000,000 does not include the value of the revocable grantor trust.

7. After Mary died on June 30 of the current year, her executor identified the following items belonging to her estate:

- Personal residence with a fair market value of $400,000 and an existing mortgage of $100,000
- Certificate of deposit in the amount of $150,000 of which $10,000 was accrued interest payable at maturity on August 1
- Stock portfolio with a value at date of death of $2,000,000 and a basis of $500,000
- Life insurance policy, with her daughter named as an irrevocable beneficiary, in the amount of $150,000

Assuming that no alternate valuation date is elected, what is the gross value of Mary's estate?

A. $2,700,000

B. $2,090,000

C. $2,550,000

D. $2,450,000

Answer (C) is correct.

REQUIRED: The gross value of decedent's estate.

DISCUSSION: The gross value of Mary's estate includes items valued at their gross amount. The $100,000 mortgage is deducted after the gross valuation of the estate. Therefore, the gross value is $2,550,000 ($400,000 + $150,000 + $2,000,000). The life insurance is excluded under Sec. 2042 because there is no incidence of ownership of the decedent.

Answer (A) is incorrect. The life insurance proceeds are excluded. Answer (B) is incorrect. The portfolio is valued at its FMV at the date of death, not her basis, and the CD's accrued interest is not deducted. Answer (D) is incorrect. The mortgage is not subtracted from the gross value of the estate.

8. Mr. Park died on December 1 of the current year. The alternate valuation method was not elected. The assets in his estate were valued as of the date of death as follows:

Home	$ 400,000
Car	30,000
Stocks, bonds, and savings	350,000
Jewelry	25,000
Dividends declared November 15, not paid as of December 1	5,000
Accrued interest on savings as of December 1	2,500
Life insurance (proceeds receivable by the estate)	1,300,000

What is the amount of Mr. Park's gross estate?

A. $2,112,500

B. $2,110,000

C. $2,105,000

D. $1,812,500

Answer (A) is correct.

REQUIRED: The amount of the gross estate.

DISCUSSION: Under Sec. 2033, the value of the gross estate includes the value of all property in which the decedent had an interest at the time of death. Therefore, the value of the home, stocks, car, accrued interest, and jewelry is included in the gross estate. Section 2042 requires the inclusion of proceeds from life insurance policies when the proceeds are receivable by, or for the benefit of, the estate. A dividend is includible in the decedent's gross estate only if the decedent died after the record date of the dividend; the record date is the date when the shareholder of record becomes entitled to receive the dividend, in this case, the declaration date. Therefore, all of the items are included in the gross estate.

Answer (B) is incorrect. The accrued interest is included in the gross estate. Answer (C) is incorrect. The accrued interest and dividends declared are included in the gross estate. Answer (D) is incorrect. The life insurance proceeds are included in the gross estate.

9. Harry, a single person, died in 2012. The executor does not elect the alternate valuation date. Given the following information, determine the value of Harry's gross estate.

Assets of the Estate	FMV at Date of Death
Certificates of deposit	$ 100,000
Mortgage receivable on sale of property	2,000,000
Paintings and collectibles	500,000
Income tax refund due from 2011 individual tax return	30,000
Household goods and personal effects	20,000

A. $2,600,000

B. $2,650,000

C. $2,620,000

D. $2,120,000

Answer (B) is correct.

REQUIRED: The value of the decedent's gross estate.

DISCUSSION: A decedent's gross estate includes the FMV of all property, real or personal, tangible or intangible, wherever situated, to the extent the decedent owned a beneficial interest at the time of death. Included in the gross estate are such items as cash, personal residence and effects, securities, other investments, and other personal assets, such as notes and claims and business interests. The gross estate also includes other items, such as the full value of property held as joint tenants with the right of survivorship, except to the extent of any part that is shown to have originally belonged to the other person and for which adequate and full consideration was not provided by the decedent and insurance proceeds on the decedent's life if either the insurance proceeds are payable to or for the estate or if the decedent had any incident of ownership in the policy at death. Therefore, $2,650,000 is the value of Harry's estate ($100,000 certificates + $2,000,000 mortgage receivable + $500,000 paintings and collectibles + $30,000 income tax refund + $20,000 household goods and effects).

Answer (A) is incorrect. The value of the gross estate includes the value of the income tax refund due and the household goods and personal effects. Answer (C) is incorrect. The value of the gross estate includes the value of the income tax refund due. Answer (D) is incorrect. The value of the gross estate includes the value of the paintings and collectibles.

10. Candace died on January 20, 2012. The assets included in her estate were valued as follows:

	1/20/12	7/20/12	10/20/12
House	$ 900,000	$ 800,000	$ 700,000
Stocks	1,850,000	1,600,000	2,000,000

The executor sold the house on October 20, 2012, for $700,000. The alternate valuation date was properly elected. What is the value of Candace's estate?

A. $2,750,000

B. $2,700,000

C. $2,400,000

D. $2,300,000

Answer (C) is correct.

REQUIRED: The true value of the decedent's estate if the alternate valuation date is elected.

DISCUSSION: Under Sec. 2032, if the executor elects to use the alternate valuation date, the estate's assets are valued as of the date 6 months after the decedent's death. Assets that are sold or distributed within that 6-month period are valued as of the date of sale or distribution. Any asset sold after the 6-month period is valued at the alternate valuation date.

Because the home was sold after the 6-month period following the decedent's death, it is valued as of the alternate valuation date. Its value for estate tax purposes is therefore $800,000. The stocks are included in the estate at their alternate-valuation-date value. Thus, the value of Candace's estate is $2,400,000 ($800,000 + $1,600,000).

Answer (A) is incorrect. The alternate valuation date allows the property to be valued 6 months from the date of death. Answer (B) is incorrect. The alternate valuation date allows the property to be valued 6 months from the date of death. Answer (D) is incorrect. The property was sold after the 6-month period.

11. John, who was not married, died on October 12, 2012. He did not leave any of his assets to charity. Given the following information, may the executor of the estate make the alternate valuation election and, if so, what is the value of the gross estate on the alternate valuation date?

	FMV Date of Death	FMV Alternate Valuation
Residence	$2,000,000	$2,010,000
Installment note	5,000	500
Stock	600,000	350,000
Expenses	(450,000)	(300,000)

A. No, the election cannot be made.

B. Yes, the election can be made. The alternate value of the gross estate is $2,350,500.

C. Yes, the election can be made. The alternate value of the gross estate is $2,360,500.

D. Yes, the election can be made. The alternate value of the gross estate is $2,365,000.

Answer (C) is correct.

REQUIRED: Determine the value of the gross estate under the alternate valuation election.

DISCUSSION: The election can be made only if it results in a reduction in the value of the gross estate. The assets are valued on the date 6 months after the date of the decedent's death. Expenses are not included in the gross estate. Therefore, the gross estate includes the value of the residence, the stock, and the value of the installment note on the alternate valuation date. (See Instructions for Form 706.) It is assumed that the installment note declined in value. Any payments made on the installment note between the date of death and the alternative date are added to the estate value on the alternative date.

Answer (A) is incorrect. The election can be made since it reduces the value of the gross estate. Answer (B) is incorrect. The residence is valued on the alternate valuation date. The installment note is valued on the alternative date. Answer (D) is incorrect. The installment note is valued on the alternative date.

12. Ms. Pub died on February 28, 2012. The assets that comprised her estate were valued as follows:

	2/28/12	6/28/12	8/28/12
House	$1,000,000	$ 900,000	$ 800,000
Stocks	1,950,000	1,975,000	1,875,000
Bonds	500,000	500,000	540,000

The executor sold the home on June 28, 2012, for $900,000. The executor properly elected the alternate-valuation-date method. What is the value of Ms. Pub's estate?

A. $3,215,000

B. $3,315,000

C. $3,375,000

D. $3,450,000

Answer (B) is correct.

REQUIRED: The value of the decedent's estate if the alternate valuation date is elected.

DISCUSSION: Under Sec. 2032, if the executor elects to use the alternate valuation date, the estate's assets are valued as of the date 6 months after the decedent's death. Assets that are sold or distributed within that 6-month period are valued as of the date of sale or distribution. Because the home was sold within the 6-month period after the decedent's death, it is valued as of the date of sale. Its value for estate tax purposes is therefore $900,000. The stocks and the bonds are included in the estate at their alternate-valuation-date value. Therefore, the value of the estate is $3,315,000 ($900,000 + $1,875,000 + $540,000).

Answer (A) is incorrect. The house was sold within the 6-month period. Answer (C) is incorrect. The stocks and bonds are not valued at the date the home was sold. Answer (D) is incorrect. The property is not valued at the date of death.

13. Carl died on June 1, 2012. After determining that an estate tax return will be required, his executor decided to use the alternate valuation date for valuing the gross estate. Which of the following dates will be the alternate valuation date?

A. April 15, 2013.

B. December 31, 2012.

C. December 1, 2012.

D. On or before the due date of the *United States Estate Tax Return*.

Answer (C) is correct.

REQUIRED: The date if the alternate valuation date is selected to value the gross estate.

DISCUSSION: Under Sec. 2032, if the executor elects to use the alternate valuation date, the estate's assets are valued as of the date 6 months after the decedent's death.

14. Mrs. Flame passed away on March 15, 2012. The assets included in her estate were properly valued as follows:

	3/15/12	7/15/12	9/15/12
Personal residence	$1,500,000	$1,600,000	$1,700,000
Stocks held	1,000,000	700,000	750,000

The executor sold the home on July 15, 2012, for $1,600,000. The alternate valuation date was properly elected. What is the value of the estate reported for estate tax purposes?

A. $2,450,000

B. $2,500,000

C. $2,350,000

D. $2,300,000

Answer (C) is correct.

REQUIRED: The true value of the decedent's estate if the alternate valuation date is elected.

DISCUSSION: Under Sec. 2032, if the executor elects to use the alternate valuation date, the estate's assets are valued as of the date 6 months after the decedent's death. Assets that are sold or distributed within that 6-month period are valued as of the date of sale or distribution. Because the home was sold within the 6-month period after the decedent's death, it is valued as of the date of sale. Its value for estate tax purposes is therefore $1,600,000. The stocks are included in the estate at their alternate-valuation-date value. Therefore, the value of the estate is $2,350,000 ($1,600,000 + $750,000).

Answer (A) is incorrect. The house was sold within the 6-month period. Answer (B) is incorrect. The property is not valued at the date of death. Answer (D) is incorrect. The stocks are not valued at the date the home was sold.

13.2 Deductions and Credits

15. Which of the following amounts paid may be claimed as a credit on the estate tax return?

A. Charitable contributions.

B. Generation-skipping transfer tax.

C. State death taxes paid.

D. None of the above.

Answer (D) is correct.

REQUIRED: Credit on estate tax return.

DISCUSSION: None of the credits may be taken on the estate tax return.

Answer (A) is incorrect. Charitable contributions are a deduction from the gross estate, not a credit against the estate tax liability. Answer (B) is incorrect. The generation-skipping transfer tax is imposed as a separate tax, in addition to the gift and estate taxes, on generation-skipping transfers that are taxable distributions or terminations with respect to a generation-skipping trust or direct skips. Answer (C) is incorrect. The credit for state death taxes paid was repealed in 2005 and replaced with a deduction.

16. Which of the following tax credits are allowed on an estate tax return (Form 706)?

A. Credit for foreign death taxes.

B. Credit for federal gift taxes (pre-1977).

C. Credit for tax on prior transfers.

D. All of the answers are correct.

Answer (D) is correct.

REQUIRED: The allowed tax credits on an estate tax return.

DISCUSSION: Sec. 2013 allows a credit for taxes paid on prior transfers. The credit applies to a transfer of property by or from a person who died within 10 years before, or within 2 years after, the decedent's death. Sec. 2014 allows a credit for death taxes paid to foreign governments, and Sec. 2012 allows for a credit for gift taxes paid on federal gift taxes (pre-1977).

17. What amount of a decedent's taxable estate is effectively tax-free if the maximum applicable credit amount is taken?

A. $3,500,000

B. $1,455,800

C. $1,730,800

D. $5,120,000

Answer (D) is correct.

REQUIRED: The amount of a decedent's taxable estate that is effectively tax-free.

DISCUSSION: In the case of decedents dying in 2012, the applicable credit amount (ACA) allowed under Sec. 2010 is $1,772,800 [Sec. 2011(a)]. The ACA against the estate tax is not reduced by the amount of ACA used against the gift tax during life. However, there is not a double benefit. Instead, the ACA used for lifetime gifts is taken into account in the initial computation of the estate tax, i.e., tax on the sum of the taxable estate plus prior gifts, less gift taxes imposed at current rates. The $1,772,800 ACA offsets the estate tax liability that would be imposed on a taxable estate of up to $5.12 million computed at the rates in Sec. 2001(c). The ACA was formerly called the unified credit.

Answer (A) is incorrect. The tax-free amount in 2009 was $3.5 million. Answer (B) is incorrect. The $1,455,800 ACA offsets the estate tax liability that would be imposed on a taxable estate of up to $3,500,000 computed at the rates in Sec. 2001(c) in 2009. Answer (C) is incorrect. The $1,772,800 ACA offsets estate tax liability that would be imposed on a taxable estate of up to $5.12 million.

18. Mr. Rich died in the current year. The following expenses and credit relate to the estate:

Administrative expenses	$ 12,500
Funeral expenses	8,500
State inheritance tax	33,000
Applicable credit amount	1,772,800

What amount can the executrix of Mr. Rich's estate deduct from the gross estate in figuring the taxable estate?

A. $21,000

B. $54,000

C. $1,793,800

D. $1,826,800

Answer (B) is correct.

REQUIRED: The amount of allowable deductions from the gross estate.

DISCUSSION: Under Sec. 2053, deductions from the gross estate are allowed for funeral expenses, administration expenses, state inheritance taxes, and claims against the estate for unpaid mortgages on property in which the value of the decedent's interest is included in the value of the gross estate. The applicable credit amount is a credit that reduces the tentative estate tax.

Answer (A) is incorrect. This amount does not include the state inheritance tax. Answer (C) is incorrect. The ACA is not a deduction from the gross estate. In addition, state inheritance tax is deductible. Answer (D) is incorrect. The ACA is not a deduction from the gross estate.

19. Which of the following statements is true regarding allowable deductions on Form 706, *United States Estate Tax Return*?

A. Penalties incurred as the result of a federal estate tax deficiency are deductible administrative expenses.

B. Attorney fees paid incidental to litigation incurred by the beneficiaries are a deductible administrative expense.

C. Executor's commissions may be deducted if they have actually been paid or if it is expected that they will be paid.

D. Funeral expenses are not an allowable expense.

Answer (C) is correct.

REQUIRED: True statement regarding allowable deductions on Form 706.

DISCUSSION: Executor's commissions may be deducted if they have actually been paid or if it is expected that they will be paid.

Answer (A) is incorrect. Penalties imposed by the IRS for deficiencies are not deductible on Form 706. Answer (B) is incorrect. Attorney fees paid incidental to litigation incurred by the beneficiaries are not deductible on Form 706. They may be deductible on the beneficiaries' Form 1040. Answer (D) is incorrect. Funeral expenses are deductible on Form 706.

20. Which of the following items is not an allowable deduction on a decedent's estate tax return?

A. Bequest to a surviving ex-spouse.

B. Property taxes accrued before death but not paid until after death.

C. Executor's fees for administering the estate.

D. None of the items is allowed as a deduction against the decedent's estate.

Answer (A) is correct.

REQUIRED: The item that is not an allowable deduction on a decedent's estate tax return.

DISCUSSION: Publication 559 states that accrued taxes "are allowable as a deduction for estate tax purposes as claims against the estate and also are allowable as deductions in respect of a decedent for income tax purposes."

In addition, Publication 559 states, "Expenses of administering an estate can be deducted either from the gross estate in figuring the federal estate tax on Form 706 or from the estate's gross income in figuring the estate's income tax on Form 1041."

Publication 559 excludes a deduction for a bequest when: "It is required by the terms of the will, . . . it is a gift or bequest of a *specific sum of money or property* . . . [and] it is paid out in three or fewer installments under the terms of the will." A bequest to a spouse qualifies for a deduction.

Answer (B) is incorrect. Accrued taxes are allowable as a deduction for estate tax purposes. Answer (C) is incorrect. Expenses of administering an estate can be deducted for estate tax purposes. Answer (D) is incorrect. A deduction is not allowed for a bequest when it is required by the terms of the will, it is a bequest of a specific sum of money or property, and it is paid out in three or fewer installments under the terms of the will.

21. B died in the current year. The state of residence was not a community property state. From the items listed below, what are the allowable deductions from the gross estate?

Funeral expenses	$ 3,500
Executor and administrative fees	5,000
Mortgage on jointly held property, one-half purchase price paid by B	70,000
Transfers of cash to B's spouse	60,000
Expense of filing estate's income tax return	500

A. $68,500

B. $73,500

C. $103,500

D. $135,000

Answer (C) is correct.

REQUIRED: The amount of allowable deductions from the gross estate.

DISCUSSION: Under Sec. 2053, deductions from the gross estate are allowed for funeral expenses, administration expenses, and claims against the estate for unpaid mortgages on property in which the decedent has an interest that is included in the value of the gross estate. Only one-half of the mortgage may be deducted because only one-half the value of the property is included in B's estate. Sec. 2056 allows a marital deduction from the gross estate for most transfers to a surviving spouse. No provision allows the expense of filing the estate's income tax return to be deducted against the gross estate. Such amount can be deducted on the estate's income tax return (Form 1041). The allowable deductions are computed as follows:

Funeral expenses	$ 3,500
Executor and administrative fees	5,000
Mortgage ($70,000 × 1/2)	35,000
Cash to spouse	60,000
Allowable deductions	$103,500

Answer (A) is incorrect. The amount of $68,500 excludes B's half of the mortgage. Answer (B) is incorrect. The amount of $73,500 excludes executor and administrative fees and transfers of cash to B's spouse and includes the full amount of the mortgage. Answer (D) is incorrect. The amount of $135,000 excludes the funeral expenses and includes the full amount of the mortgage.

22. Form 706, *United States Estate (and Generation-Skipping Transfer) Tax Return*, was filed for the estate of John Doe in 2012. The gross estate tax was $250,000. Which of the following items is not credited against the gross estate tax to determine the net estate tax payable?

A. Applicable credit amount.

B. Credit for gift taxes.

C. Marital deduction.

D. Credit for foreign death taxes.

Answer (C) is correct.

REQUIRED: The credit that is not deductible in the determination of the estate tax payable.

DISCUSSION: There is no credit for a marital deduction. Instead the marital deduction is deductible in arriving at the taxable estate. The estate tax is then computed on the taxable estate.

Answer (A) is incorrect. Sec. 2010 allows an applicable credit amount of $1,772,800 against the estate tax. Answer (B) is incorrect. Indirectly, there is a credit for gift taxes. This reduction occurs because the gross estate tax is computed on the taxable estate and all prior transfers. Subtracted from that is the amount of tax paid on prior transfers (gifts) based on current rates to arrive at the net estate tax. Answer (D) is incorrect. There is a credit for death taxes paid to foreign governments.

23. All of the following items can be claimed as deductions against a decedent's estate except

A. Specific bequest to son.

B. Executor's fees.

C. Legal fees to settle estate.

D. Charitable bequests.

Answer (A) is correct.

REQUIRED: Deductions against a decedent's estate.

DISCUSSION: Publication 559 states, "Expenses of administering an estate can be deducted either from the gross estate in figuring the federal estate tax on Form 706 or from the estate's gross income in figuring the estate's income tax on Form 1041." Bequests to qualified charitable organizations are deductible. Publication 559 excludes a deduction for a bequest when: "It is required by the terms of the will, . . . it is a gift or bequest of a specific sum of money or property . . . [and] it is paid out in three or fewer installments under the terms of the will."

24. Charlie Jones is preparing Form 706, *United States Estate Tax Return*, for his brother John, who died June 30, 2012. Charlie has identified gross estate items totaling $1,000,000. Considering the following potential deductions and other information, what will be John's estate?

Funeral expenses paid out of the estate	$ 10,000
Value of the residence owned jointly with John's spouse that will pass to the spouse (this property is included in the gross estate)	240,000
Mortgage on residence	20,000
Value of property given to charitable organizations per John's will	50,000

A. $730,000

B. $740,000

C. $720,000

D. None of the answers are correct.

Answer (C) is correct.

REQUIRED: The taxable estate after deductions.

DISCUSSION: Deductions from the GE in computing the taxable estate (TE) include ones with respect to the following:

1. Administration and funeral expenses are deductible.
2. Unpaid mortgages on property are deductible if the value of the decedent's interest is included in the GE.
3. Bequests to qualified charitable organizations are deductible.
4. Outright transfers to a surviving spouse are deductible from the GE, to the extent the interest is included in the gross estate.

John's estate is computed as follows:

GE items	$1,000,000
Funeral expenses	(10,000)
Marital transfer ($240,000 – $20,000 mortgage on residence)	(220,000)
Charitable contribution	(50,000)
Total estate	$ 720,000

Answer (A) is incorrect. The $10,000 of funeral expenses is deductible. Answer (B) is incorrect. The $20,000 unpaid mortgage is deductible. Answer (D) is incorrect. John's estate is $720,000.

13.3 Estate Tax Payment and Return

25. If a person died in 2012, an estate tax return must be filed if the value of the gross estate at the date of death was more than

A. $5,120,000

B. $3,500,000

C. $2,000,000

D. $1,500,000

Answer (A) is correct.

REQUIRED: The amount of the gross estate that requires filing an estate tax return.

DISCUSSION: In 2012, Sec. 6018 provides that, when the gross estate of a decedent exceeds $5,120,000, the personal representative must file an estate tax return.

Answer (B) is incorrect. The exemption amount in 2009 was $3,500,000. Answer (C) is incorrect. The exemption amount in 2008 was $2,000,000. Answer (D) is incorrect. The exemption amount in 2005 was $1,500,000.

26. Mr. Brown died on September 30, 2012. His gross estate was valued at $1,480,000. Unless an extension is granted, a *United States Estate Tax Return* (Form 706) must be filed on or before

A. April 15, 2013.

B. January 15, 2013.

C. June 30, 2013.

D. A *United States Estate Tax Return* does not have to be filed.

Answer (D) is correct.

REQUIRED: Filing date of the *United States Estate Tax Return* (Form 706).

DISCUSSION: Normally, Form 706 must be filed within 9 months after the decedent's death unless an extension is filed with Form 4768. However, no *United States Estate Tax Return* has to be filed because the value of $1,480,000 of the gross estate is below the $5,120,000 exemption amount for 2012.

27. Anna died January 20, 2012. John, the executor, filed Form 706, *United States Estate (and Generation-Skipping Transfer) Tax Return*, on June 30, 2012. John paid the tax due and distributed the assets on September 30, 2012. The assets were properly valued at $5.2 million on the date of death. The alternate valuation method was not elected. Generally, what is the last day that estate tax may be assessed upon recipients of property?

A. September 30, 2015.

B. October 20, 2015.

C. June 30, 2016.

D. October 20, 2016.

Answer (D) is correct.

REQUIRED: The period for assessment of estate tax when transfers from an estate are made.

DISCUSSION: Although the general period for assessment of estate tax is 3 years after the due date for a timely filed Form 706, the assessment period is extended an additional (fourth) year for transfers from an estate.

28. Unless an extension is received, Form 706, *United States Estate Tax Return*, must be filed

A. By the 15th day of the 4th month following the month of death.

B. Within 9 months of the date of death.

C. Within 6 months of the date of death.

D. No later than the due date of the estate income tax return.

Answer (B) is correct.

REQUIRED: The due date of an estate tax return.

DISCUSSION: The estate tax return is due within 9 months after the date of the decedent's death. An extension of up to 6 months may be granted.

29. On June 30, 2012, Rita died with a taxable estate of $5,650,000 and estate taxes payable of $67,500. Victor, the executor, filed the estate tax return on December 31, 2012. He distributed all the assets of the estate without paying the estate tax liability. Dustin, one of several beneficiaries, received $35,000. What are the tax assessments against Victor and Dustin?

	Victor	Dustin
A.	$67,500	$0
B.	$32,500	$35,000
C.	$67,500	$35,000
D.	$67,500	$67,500

Answer (C) is correct.

REQUIRED: The liability of an executor and a beneficiary for estate tax due.

DISCUSSION: An executor is personally liable for unpaid estate taxes. An estate beneficiary is also personally liable but only to the extent of the value of assets (s)he received from the estate.

13.4 Generation-Skipping Transfers

30. Edwin gave his grandson Todd $30,000. Todd is 15 years old and lives with his parents. Which of the following statements regarding the generation-skipping transfer tax is true?

A. Because the gift is subject to the generation-skipping transfer tax, it is not subject to the regular gift tax.

B. The gift is subject to both the regular gift tax and the generation-skipping transfer tax.

C. The gift is not subject to the generation-skipping transfer tax because Todd's parents are still alive.

D. If Edwin had transferred the funds into a trust solely for his grandson's benefit, the gift would not be subject to the generation-skipping transfer tax.

Answer (B) is correct.

REQUIRED: The true statement regarding generation-skipping transfer tax.

DISCUSSION: The generation-skipping transfer tax (GSTT) is imposed, separately and in addition to gift and estate taxes, on transfers directly or in trust for the sole benefit of a person at least two generations younger than the transferor. Instructions for Form 709 specify requirements for gifts that are subject to both regular gift tax and the GSTT.

Answer (A) is incorrect. The gift is subject to gift tax in addition to the GSTT. Answer (C) is incorrect. The gift is subject to both gift tax and GSTT. Answer (D) is incorrect. Direct transfers as well as transfers in trust are subject to GSTT.

31. The generation-skipping transfer tax is imposed

A. Instead of the gift tax.

B. Instead of the estate tax.

C. As a separate tax in addition to the gift and estate taxes.

D. On transfers of future interest to beneficiaries who are more than one generation above the donor's generation.

Answer (C) is correct.

REQUIRED: The applicability of the GSTT.

DISCUSSION: The generation-skipping transfer tax (GSTT) is imposed, as a separate tax in addition to the gift and estate taxes, on generation-skipping transfers that are any taxable distributions or terminations with respect to a generation-skipping trust or direct skips [Sec. 2611(a)]. A taxable termination means the termination of an interest held in trust unless (1) immediately after the termination a non-skip person has an interest in the trust, or (2) at no time after the termination may a distribution be made to a skip person [Sec. 2612(a)(1)]. A skip person is a natural person assigned to a generation that is two or more generations below the transferor or a trust, all interests of which are held by skip persons.

Answer (A) is incorrect. The GSTT is a separate tax in addition to the gift tax. Answer (B) is incorrect. The GSTT is a separate tax in addition to the estate tax. Answer (D) is incorrect. The GSTT prevents tax avoidance by transferring property directly to a person more than one generation below the donee.

32. Which of the following is not a characteristic of a skip person as it pertains to the GSTT tax?

A. A natural person.

B. A person only one generation below the generation of the donor.

C. A person two or more generations below the generation of the donor.

D. A donee of a gift.

Answer (B) is correct.

REQUIRED: The definition of a skip person.

DISCUSSION: A skip person is defined in Sec 2613(a) as a natural person assigned to a generation that is two or more generations below the generation assignment of the transferor.

33. Which of the following is a correct statement of the events that may trigger a generation-skipping transfer tax?

A. A taxable termination only.

B. A taxable distribution only.

C. A taxable termination or a taxable distribution but not a direct skip.

D. A taxable termination, a taxable distribution, or a direct skip.

Answer (D) is correct.

REQUIRED: The event which may trigger a generation-skipping transfer tax.

DISCUSSION: A generation-skipping transfer is defined as a taxable termination, a taxable distribution, or a direct skip [Sec. 2611(a)]. A taxable termination is a termination (by death, lapse of time, release of power, or otherwise) of an interest in property held in trust, unless immediately after the termination, a non-skip person has an interest in the property or if at no time after the termination may a distribution be made to a skip person [Sec. 2612(a)]. A taxable distribution is any distribution from a trust to a skip person if it is not a taxable termination or a direct skip [Sec. 2612(b)]. A direct skip is a transfer subject to the estate tax or the gift tax of an interest in property to a skip person. A skip person is a natural person assigned to a generation that is two or more generations below the generation assignment of the transferor or a trust where all interests are held by skip persons [Sec. 2613(a)].

Answer (A) is incorrect. It is not the only event that may trigger a generation-skipping transfer tax. Answer (B) is incorrect. It is not the only event that may trigger a generation-skipping transfer tax. Answer (C) is incorrect. A direct skip may trigger a generation-skipping transfer tax.

34. Kramer (age 63) established a trust and named his second wife, Theresa (age 50), as income beneficiary for 20 years. After 20 years, Kramer's son Trevor (age 40) and nephew Bob (age 25) are to receive lifetime income interests. After the death of both Trevor and Bob, the remainder passes equally to Kramer's granddaughter Sara (age 20) and great-granddaughter Hope (age 1). How many younger generations are there in this trust arrangement?

A. 4

B. 3

C. 2

D. 1

Answer (B) is correct.

REQUIRED: The number of younger generations in the trust arrangement.

DISCUSSION: Younger generations refer to generations younger than the transferor's generation. An individual who is a lineal descendant of a grandparent of the grantor is assigned to the generation that results from comparing the number of generations between the grandparent and such individual with the number of generations between the grandparent and the transferor [Sec. 2651(b)(1)]. An individual who has been married to the transferor is assigned to the transferor's generation [Sec. 2651(c)(1)].

Since Theresa is married to the transferor, she is assigned to the same generation as Kramer. Trevor and Bob are assigned to one generation below the transferor's generation. Sara is assigned to two generations below the transferor's generation. Hope is assigned to three generations below the transferor's generation.

Answer (A) is incorrect. Theresa is assigned to the same generation as Kramer. Answer (C) is incorrect. Sara is assigned the second generation younger than Kramer. Answer (D) is incorrect. Hope is assigned the third generation younger than Kramer.

35. Kramer (age 63) established a trust and named his second wife, Theresa (age 50), as income beneficiary for 20 years. After 20 years, Kramer's son Trevor (age 40) and nephew Bob (age 25) are to receive lifetime income interests. Trevor died 22 years after the trust was established, and Bob died 34 years after the trust was established. After the death of both Trevor and Bob, the remainder passes equally to Kramer's granddaughter Sara (age 20) and great-granddaughter Hope (age 1). Assuming both Sara and Hope were alive when Bob died, how many times is the generation-skipping transfer tax levied?

A. Never.

B. Once.

C. Twice.

D. Three times.

Answer (B) is correct.

REQUIRED: The number of times the generation-skipping transfer tax is levied.

DISCUSSION: The generation-skipping transfer tax (GSTT) is imposed on generation-skipping transfers, which are any taxable distributions or terminations with respect to a generation-skipping trust or direct skips [Sec. 2611(a)]. A taxable termination means the termination of an interest held in trust unless (1) immediately after the termination a non-skip person has an interest in the trust, or (2) at no time after the termination may a distribution be made to a skip person [Sec. 2612(a)(1)]. A skip person is a natural person assigned to a generation that is two or more generations below the transferor or a trust, all interests of which are held by skip persons. A non-skip person is any person who is not a skip person [Sec. 2613(b)].

Trevor and Bob are one generation below the transferor and are non-skip persons. There is no taxable termination on Trevor's death since Bob, a non-skip person, has an interest in the trust. Both Sara and Hope are skip persons, so there is a taxable termination on Bob's death.

Answer (A) is incorrect. The generation-skipping transfer tax must be levied after Bob's death. Answer (C) is incorrect. The generation-skipping transfer tax must be levied only once after Bob's death. Answer (D) is incorrect. The generation-skipping transfer tax must be levied only once after Bob's death.

36. Which of the following is a true statement about the taxable amount of a generation-skipping transfer?

A. The taxable amount for a direct skip and a taxable termination are the same.

B. The taxable amount for a taxable termination is the value of the property received by the transferee reduced by expenses incurred by the transferee in connection with the determination, collection, or refund of the GSTT.

C. The taxable amount for a taxable distribution is the value of all property distributed less allowable expenses, debt, and taxes.

D. If a generation-skipping transfer tax on a taxable distribution is paid by the generation-skipping trust, an amount equal to the taxes paid by the trust will be treated as a taxable distribution.

Answer (D) is correct.

REQUIRED: The true statement about the taxable amount of a generation-skipping transfer.

DISCUSSION: Under Sec. 2603, the transferee is liable for the GSTT on a taxable distribution. Therefore, if the GSTT on a taxable distribution is paid by the trust, the transferee is deemed to have received an additional taxable distribution equal to the amount of taxes paid by the trust [Sec. 2621(b)].

Answer (A) is incorrect. The taxable amount of a direct skip is the amount received by the transferee before taxes, (Sec. 2623) but the taxable amount of a taxable termination (Sec. 2622) is the value of all property, with respect to which the termination occurred, reduced by deductions similar to those deductible against a gross estate under Sec. 2053 (taxes, debt, certain expenses). Answer (B) is incorrect. It describes the taxable amount of a taxable distribution (Sec. 2621) but not a taxable termination. Answer (C) is incorrect. The taxable amount of a taxable distribution is the value of property received by the transferee less any expense incurred by the transferee in connection with the determination, collection, or refund of the GSTT.

37. In 2012, which of the following statements about the generation-skipping transfer exemption is false?

A. An individual (or his/her executor) can allocate a $5.12 million exemption to property with respect to which (s)he is the transferor.

B. All appreciation that occurs to property covered by the allocation of the $5.12 million exemption is also covered by the exemption up to a limit of $8 million.

C. If a married couple elects gift-splitting for a transfer, the transferred property may be allocated a GSTT exemption of up to $10.24 million.

D. The GST exemption may be allocated to an inter vivos transfer on a timely filed gift tax return or later statement of allocation filed with the IRS.

Answer (B) is correct.

REQUIRED: The false statement about the generation-skipping transfer exemption of $5.12 million in 2012.

DISCUSSION: If all or part of the $5.12 million exemption is allocated to trust property, all appreciation that occurs after the allocation to the property covered by the exemption is also exempt from the GSTT. There is no $8 million limit.

38. Pearl gave $5.12 million in securities to her granddaughter Ruby in 2012. Pearl, a widow, had never made any gift to Ruby prior to the 2012 transfer. Pearl allocated $512,000 of her GST exemption to this direct skip. What is the generation-skipping transfer tax amount and who must pay it?

	Tax	Payor
A.	$1,612,800	Pearl
B.	$1,612,800	Ruby
C.	$1,792,000	Pearl
D.	$1,792,000	Ruby

Answer (A) is correct.

REQUIRED: The calculation of the generation-skipping transfer tax on a direct skip in 2012.

DISCUSSION: The GSTT is the product of the taxable amount of the transfer times the applicable rate (Sec. 2602). The applicable rate is the maximum federal estate tax rate for the date of the direct skip (35% for 2012) times the inclusion ratio (Sec. 2641). The taxable amount of the transfer is $5.12 million. The inclusion ratio is one minus the fraction whose numerator is the GST exemption allocated to the property transferred, and whose denominator is the value of the transfer involved in the direct skip reduced by federal estate tax, state death taxes, and charitable deductions related to the property. The inclusion ratio in this case is

$$1 - \frac{\$512{,}000}{\$5{,}120{,}000} = .90$$

The generation-skipping transfer tax is the product of the taxable amount (i.e., amount transferred times the inclusion ratio) times the applicable rate (Sec. 2602). The applicable rate is the maximum federal estate tax rate for decedents dying on the date of the direct skip (35% for 2012). The tax on this transfer is $1,612,800 ($5,120,000 × 35% × .90). The transferor, Pearl, is liable for the tax on the direct skip [Sec. 2603(a)(3)].

Answer (B) is incorrect. Sec. 2603 states that the transferor (Pearl), not the transferee (Ruby), is responsible for the GSTT. Answer (C) is incorrect. The amount transferred multiplied by the maximum federal estate tax rate is $1,792,000. It should also be multiplied by the 0.90 inclusion ratio. Answer (D) is incorrect. The amount transferred multiplied by the maximum federal estate tax rate is $1,792,000. It should also be multiplied by the 0.90 inclusion ratio, and Ruby is not responsible for the GSTT.

39. In 2012, Jim's will established a trust for his son, Kevin, and his grandsons. In 2013, a taxable termination occurred when Kevin died, and trust assets were distributed to grandsons Mark and John. Jim's executor allocated $1,500,000 of his exemption to the trust, which had a value of $6,500,000 at that time. When the taxable termination occurred in 2013, trust assets had a value of $9,000,000. State death taxes attributable to trust property were $500,000. What is the generation-skipping transfer tax due on the taxable termination?

A. $1,575,000

B. $1,706,250

C. $2,231,250

D. $2,362,500

Answer (D) is correct.

REQUIRED: The calculation of the generation-skipping transfer tax on a taxable termination.

DISCUSSION: The generation-skipping transfer tax is the product of the taxable amount times the applicable rate (Sec. 2602). The applicable rate is the maximum federal estate tax rate for the date of the taxable termination, taxable distribution, or direct skip (35%) times the inclusion ratio, which is 3/4 {1 – [$1,500,000 ÷ ($6,500,000 – $500,000)]} (Sec. 2641). The inclusion ratio is 1 minus a fraction whose numerator is the GST exemption allocated to the trust and whose denominator is generally the value of the property transferred into the trust reduced by the sum of federal estate taxes or state death taxes attributable to the property and paid by the trust and charitable deductions with respect to the trust property [Sec. 2642(a)]. The taxable amount of a taxable termination is the value of all property with respect to which the taxable termination has occurred ($9,000,000) reduced by expenses, deductions, and taxes that would be allowable under Sec. 2053 if this were an estate. State death taxes are not allowable deductions under Sec. 2053(c)(1)(B), so the taxable amount is $9,000,000. The generation-skipping transfer tax is $2,362,500 ($9,000,000 × 35% × 3/4), and the tax will be paid by the trustee from trust assets.

Answer (A) is incorrect. It uses the initial value of the trust reduced by the state death taxes as the tax base. Answer (B) is incorrect. It uses the initial value of the trust ($6,500,000) as the tax base. Answer (C) is incorrect. It deducts the state death taxes from the 2013 value of the trust property as the tax base.

40. In 2012, Jim's will established a trust for his son, Kevin, and his grandsons. In 2013, a taxable termination occurred when Kevin died, and trust assets were distributed to grandsons, Mark and John. Jim's executor allocated $1,500,000 of his exemption to the trust, which had a value of $6,500,000 at that time. When the taxable termination occurred in 2013, trust assets had a value of $12,500,000. State death taxes attributable to trust property were $500,000. What is the inclusion ratio used to calculate the GSTT?

A. 1/8

B. 1/4

C. 3/4

D. 7/8

Answer (C) is correct.

REQUIRED: The inclusion ratio for a generation-skipping transfer with an exemption and death taxes.

DISCUSSION: The inclusion ratio multiplied by the maximum federal estate tax rate determines the tax rate for a generation-skipping transfer. The inclusion ratio is 1 minus a fraction whose numerator is the GST exemption allocated to the trust and whose denominator is generally the value of the property transferred into the trust reduced by the sum of (1) federal estate taxes or state death taxes attributable to the property and paid by the trust and (2) charitable deductions with respect to the trust property [Sec. 2642(a)]. The inclusion ratio in this case is

$$1 - \frac{\$1{,}500{,}000}{\$6{,}500{,}000 - \$500{,}000} = 3/4$$

Answer (A) is incorrect. Using the trust assets' value in 2013 and not subtracting it from 1 resulted in 1/8. Answer (B) is incorrect. When determining the inclusion ratio, 1/4 should be subtracted from 1. Answer (D) is incorrect. The trust assets were incorrectly valued at $12,500,000 for the inclusion ratio.

APPENDIX A
CALCULATING PHASEOUTS

The EA exam topics include several items (exclusions, deductions, credits, exemptions, etc.) that are phased out based on the amount of the taxpayer's income. In this appendix, we present the general formulas required for calculating the appropriate amounts subject to a phaseout. The details specific to each exam topic are presented in the related Knowledge Transfer Outline material.

The income limits are most often based on adjusted gross income or a modification of such. A taxpayer with income at or below the minimum amount of the phaseout range (i.e., lower threshold) will not have any reduction to the maximum amount of the exclusion, deduction, etc. (i.e., 100% is allowed). A taxpayer with income at or above the maximum amount of the phaseout range (i.e., upper threshold) will not be allowed any of the exclusion, deduction, etc. (i.e., 100% is disallowed).

The most common method/formula simply multiplies the maximum amount of the exclusion, deduction, etc., by the difference of the taxpayer's AGI and the lower threshold over the difference of the upper threshold and the lower threshold. This is referred to as a **proportionate** reduction.

$$\text{Amount (exclusion, deduction, etc.)} \times \frac{\text{AGI} - \text{Applicable minimum phaseout amount}}{\text{Maximum phaseout amount} - \text{Minimum phaseout amount}}$$

EXAMPLE

A $2,500 deduction of interest paid on qualified education loans begins to be phased out for joint filers when AGI exceeds $125,000 and is completely phased out when AGI reaches $155,000. Assume for this example that the couple's AGI is $135,000. The $2,500 deduction would be reduced by $833 for a total allowed deduction of $1,667.

$$\$2{,}500 \times \frac{\$135{,}000 - \$125{,}000}{\$155{,}000 - \$125{,}000} = \$833$$

Alternative calculation: $\$2{,}500 \times \left[1 - \left(\frac{\$135{,}000 - \$125{,}000}{\$155{,}000 - \$125{,}000}\right)\right]$

Other phaseouts are based on a percentage and are calculated as follows:

$$(\text{AGI} - \text{Applicable minimum phaseout amount}) \times \text{Applicable percentage}$$

EXAMPLE

A single taxpayer who otherwise qualifies for a $475 Earned Income Credit with no qualifying child has AGI of $10,750. The taxpayer's allowed credit would be reduced by $228 for a total credit allowed of $247. The applicable phaseout percentage for a single taxpayer with no qualifying child is 7.65%.

($10,750 – $7,770) × 7.65% = $228

Alternative calculation: $475 – [($10,750 – $7,770) × 7.65%]

Finally, other phaseouts are performed in steps (i.e., not proportionate over the applicable income range).

1. (AGI - Applicable minimum phaseout amount) / Step amount = Step designator (always round up)
2. Step designator × Designated amount = Reduction amount
3. Maximum credit - Reduction amount = Allowable credit

EXAMPLE

Taxpayers filing jointly with a $3,000 Child Tax Credit and AGI of $114,400 are allowed a credit of only $2,750.

1) ($114,400 – $110,000) / $1,000 = 4.4, which rounds up to 5
2) 5 × $50 = $250
3) $3,000 – $250 = $2,750

INDEX

Success Stories

I just passed Parts One, Two, and Three of the Special Enrollment Exam! I have such a sense of relief and accomplishment. The Gleim materials were paramount to my success. The Gleim resources made the material organized and manageable. It would be easy to become overwhelmed with the scope of material the SEE covers, but Gleim allows candidates to take it one step at a time. I passed all parts on the first attempt, so I can't argue with these amazing results. Thanks so much; Gleim was well worth it!

- Adam Waters

Fantastic study program. I passed all 3 parts of the EA exam in 90 days thanks to the program! Everyone from Gleim that I had contact with during that time was professional and very helpful. Thanks again!

- Randy Smith

Thank you for your support, interest, and counseling during the last four and a half months as I prepared for and succeeded in passing each of the 3 parts of the EA examination on my first attempt. The materials and resources provided really do prepare individuals for success. I intend on completing the evaluation on the website and to tell anyone who will listen how well your team does in preparing candidates for this difficult task.

- Lawrence Rosenberg, EA

The GLEIM Review gave me a systematic and comprehensive flow for learning the required knowledge. The Practice Exams and Study Sessions in the Test Prep were great in drilling the information into my understanding and retention capacity. I could not have done it without the GLEIM Review. Most certainly I will continue to use GLEIM in my professional career as an enrolled agent.

- Thomas Porter

CPA CMA CIA EA RTRP EQE CPE

GLEIM CPA REVIEW SYSTEM

Includes: Gleim Online, Review Books, Test Prep Online, Simulation Wizard, Audio Review, Practice Exam, CPA Review: A System for Success booklet, plus bonus Book Bag. $989.95 x ____ = $________

Also available by exam section (does not include Book Bag).

GLEIM CMA REVIEW SYSTEM

Includes: Gleim Online, Review Books, Test Prep Software Download, Essay Wizard, Audio Review, Practice Exam, CMA Review: A System for Success booklet, plus bonus Book Bag. $739.95 x ____ = $________

Also available by exam part (does not include Book Bag).

GLEIM CIA REVIEW SYSTEM

Includes: Gleim Online, Review Books, Test Prep Software Download, Audio Review, Practice Exam, CIA Review: A System for Success booklet, plus bonus Book Bag. $824.95 x ____ = $________

Also available by exam part (does not include Book Bag).

GLEIM EA REVIEW SYSTEM

Includes: Gleim Online, Review Books, Test Prep Online, Audio Review, Exam Rehearsal, EA Review: A System for Success booklet, plus bonus Book Bag. $629.95 x ____ = $________

Also available by exam part (does not include Book Bag).

GLEIM RTRP REVIEW SYSTEM

Includes: Gleim Online, Question Bank Online, Exam Rehearsal, 15 hours of CE. $189.95 x ____ = $________

"THE GLEIM EQE SERIES" EXAM QUESTIONS AND EXPLANATIONS

Includes: 5 Books and *Test Prep Software Download.* $112.25 x ____ = $________

Also available by part.

GLEIM ONLINE CPE

Try a FREE 4-hour course at gleim.com/cpe

- Easy-to-Complete
- Informative
- Effective

Contact **GLEIM® PUBLICATIONS** for further assistance:

gleim.com
800.874.5346
sales@gleim.com

SUBTOTAL $________

Complete your order on the next page

Subject to change without notice.

GLEIM® PUBLICATIONS, INC.

P. O. Box 12848 Gainesville, FL 32604

TOLL FREE:	800.874.5346	Customer service is available (Eastern Time):
LOCAL:	352.375.0772	8:00 a.m. - 7:00 p.m., Mon. - Fri.
FAX:	352.375.6940	9:00 a.m. - 2:00 p.m., Saturday
INTERNET:	gleim.com	Please have your credit card ready,
EMAIL:	sales@gleim.com	or save time by ordering online!

SUBTOTAL (from previous page) $________

Add applicable sales tax for shipments within Florida. ________

Shipping (nonrefundable) 14.00

TOTAL $________

Email us for prices/instructions on shipments outside the 48 contiguous states, or simply order online.

NAME (please print) ________________________________

ADDRESS ________________________ Apt. ________
(street address required for UPS/Federal Express)

CITY __________________ STATE ______ ZIP ________

____ MC/VISA/DISC/AMEX ____ Check/M.O. Daytime Telephone (____) __________

Credit Card No. ________ - ________ - ________ - ________

Exp. ____ / ____ Signature ________________________
Month / Year

Email address ________________________________

1. We process and ship orders daily, within one business day over 98.8% of the time. Call by 3:00 pm for same day service.
2. Gleim Publications, Inc. guarantees the immediate refund of all resalable texts, unopened and un-downloaded Test Prep Software, and unopened and un-downloaded audios returned within 30 days of purchase. Accounting and Academic Test Prep online courses may be canceled within 30 days of purchase if no more than the first study unit or lesson has been accessed. In addition, Online CPE courses may be canceled within 30 days of adding the course to your Personal Transcript if the outline has not yet been accessed. Accounting Exam Rehearsals and Practice Exams may be canceled within 30 days of purchase if they have not been started. Aviation online courses may be canceled within 30 days of purchase if no more than two study units have been accessed. This policy applies only to products that are purchased directly from Gleim Publications, Inc. No refunds will be provided on opened or downloaded Test Prep Software or audios, partial returns of package sets, or shipping and handling charges. Any freight charges incurred for returned or refused packages will be the purchaser's responsibility.
3. Please PHOTOCOPY this order form for others.
4. No CODs. Orders from individuals must be prepaid.

Subject to change without notice. 02/13

For updates and other important information, visit our website.

GLEIM KNOWLEDGE TRANSFER SYSTEMS®

gleim.com